# 1st Workshop on Multilingual Representation Learning (MRL 2021)



Punta Cana, Dominican Republic
11 November 2021

ISBN: 978-1-7138-9185-7

**Printed from e-media with permission by:**

Curran Associates, Inc.
57 Morehouse Lane
Red Hook, NY 12571

proceedings.com

**Some format issues inherent in the e-media version may also appear in this print version.**



Printed with permission by Curran Associates, Inc. (2024)

For permission requests, please contact the Association for Computational Linguistics at the address below.

Association for Computational Linguistics
209 N. Eighth Street
Stroudsburg, Pennsylvania 18360

Phone: 1-570-476-8006
Fax: 1-570-476-0860

acl@aclweb.org

**Additional copies of this publication are available from:**

Curran Associates, Inc.
57 Morehouse Lane
Red Hook, NY 12571 USA
Phone: 845-758-0400
Fax: 845-758-2633
Email: curran@proceedings.com
Web: www.proceedings.com

MRL 2021

# The 1st Workshop on Multilingual Representation Learning

## Proceedings of the Conference

November 11, 2021

# Message from the General Chair

Multilingual representation learning methods have recently been found to be extremely efficient in learning features useful for transfer learning between languages and demonstrating potential in achieving successful adaptation of natural language processing (NLP) models into languages or tasks with little to no training resources. On the other hand, there are many aspects of such models which have the potential for further development and analysis in order to prove their applicability in various context. These contexts include different NLP tasks and also understudied language families, which face important obstacle in achieving practical advances that could improve the state-of-the-art in NLP of various low-resource or underrepresented languages.

The aim of this workshop is to form the first research community in multilingual representation learning providing the rapidly growing number of researchers working on the topic with a means of communication and an opportunity to present their work and exchange ideas. The main objectives of the workshop are constructing and presenting a wide array of multilingual representation learning methods, including their theoretical formulation and analysis, practical aspects such as the application of current state-of-the-art approaches in transfer learning to different tasks or studies on adaptation into previously under-studied context; providing a better understanding on how the language typology may impact the applicability of these methods and motivate the development of novel methods that are more generic or competitive in different languages; and promoting collaborations in developing novel software libraries or benchmarks in implementing or evaluating multilingual models that would accelerate progress in the field.

The proceedings presents the collection of original research contributions submitted by various and greatly diverse parts of the community which advance the conventional approaches to understanding and implementing multi-lingual representation learning methods, immediately extending their applicability as well as proposing previously unexplored ideas. As the organizing committee we are deeply grateful to the engagement and response from the community and hope to continue to foster the collaborative environment the workshop achieves at its first organization.

## Message from the Program Chairs

Having been organized for the first time in an emerging area of cutting-edge research, the Workshop on Multilingual Representation Learning has received a large amount of interest from the community, with 56 submissions to the program. 50 of these submissions were long papers describing original research and 6 presented ongoing or previously published work in the form of extended abstracts. Our program committee consisted of 55 experts in the area from all over the world, conducting research in the industry as well as academia. The committee worked throughly on every submission and selected 19 research papers and 5 extended abstracts to be presented at the workshop. We are glad to present our proceedings gathering the products of a great collaborative effort which we hope will inspire many new ideas to be presented at future events of our workshop with increasing capacity in the years to come.

## Organizing Committee

Duygu Ataman, New York University
Alexandra Birch, University of Edinburgh
Alexis Conneau, Google
Orhan Firat, Google
Sebastian Ruder, Deepmind
Gozde Gul Sahin, TU Darmstadt

## Program Committee

Badr Abdullah, University of Saarland
David Ifeoluwa Adelani, Saarland University
Gustavo Aguliar, Amazon
Roee Aharoni, Google
Orevaoghene Ahia, InstaDeep
Chantal Amrhein, University of Zurich
Timothy Baldwin, University of Melbourne
Ankur Bapna, Google
Chistos Baziotis, University of Edinburgh
Eleftheria Briakou, University of Maryland
Marcel Bollman, Jonkoping University
Iacer Calixto, University of Amsterdam
Mona Diab, Facebook
Sumanth Doddapaneni, IIT Madras
Steffen Eger, TU Darmstadt
Akiko Eriguchi, Microsoft
Xavier Garcia, Google
Ankush Garg, Google
Goran Glavas, University of Mannheim
Hila Gonen, Facebook
Naman Goyal, Facebook
Melvin Johnson, Google
Yova Kementchedjhieva, University of Copenhagen
Simran Khanuja, Google
Christopher Klamm, TU Darmstadt
Sneha Kudugunta, Google
Surafel Melaku Lakew, Amazon
Kaushal Kumar Maurya, Indian Institute of Techonlogy Hyderabad
Stephen Mayhew, Duolingo
Todor Mihaylov, Facebook
Jamshidbek Mirzakhalov, University of South Florida
Ji-Ung Lee, TU Darmstadt
Graham Neubig, Carnegie Mellon University
Dmitry Nikolaev, Stockholm University
Yusuke Oda, LegalForce
Atul Kr. Ojha, National University of Ireland Galway
Arturo Oncevay, University of Edinburgh
Kelechi Ogueji, InstaDeep
Rajaswa Patil, TCS Research
Jonas Pfeiffer, TU Darmstadt
Leonardo Ribeiro, TU Darmstadt
Phillip Rust, University of Copenhagen

Rico Sennrich, University of Zurich
Aditya Siddhant, Google
Jorg Tiedemann, University of Helsinki
Ahmet Ustun, University of Groningen
Jannis Vamvas, University of Zurich
Clara Vania, Amazon
Ivan Vulic, University of Cambridge
Andreas Waldis, TU Darmstadt
Kexin Wang, TU Darmstadt
Taro Watanabe, NAIST
Genta Indra Winata, Bloomberg
Luke Zettlemoyer, Facebook
Biao Zhang, University of Edinburgh

# Table of Contents

# Conference Program

**Thursday November 11, 2021**

**10:00–10:30**

*Language Models are Few-shot Multilingual Learners*
Genta Indra Winata, Andrea Madotto, Zhaojiang Lin, Rosanne Liu, Jason Yosinski and Pascale Fung

**10:30–11:00**

*Learning Contextualised Cross-lingual Word Embeddings and Alignments for Extremely Low-Resource Languages Using Parallel Corpora*
Takashi Wada, Tomoharu Iwata, Yuji Matsumoto, Timothy Baldwin and Jey Han Lau

**11:00–12:00**

*Clustering Monolingual Vocabularies to Improve Cross-Lingual Generalization*
Riccardo Bassani, Anders Søgaard and Tejaswini Deoskar

*Do not neglect related languages: The case of low-resource Occitan cross-lingual word embeddings*
Lisa Woller, Viktor Hangya and Alexander Fraser

*Specializing Multilingual Language Models: An Empirical Study*
Ethan C. Chau and Noah A. Smith

*Learning Cross-lingual Representations for Event Coreference Resolution with Multi-view Alignment and Optimal Transport*
Duy Phung, Hieu Minh Tran, Minh Van Nguyen and Thien Huu Nguyen

*Multilingual and Multilabel Emotion Recognition using Virtual Adversarial Training*
Vikram Gupta

*Analyzing the Effects of Reasoning Types on Cross-Lingual Transfer Performance*
Karthikeyan K, Aalok Sathe, Somak Aditya and Monojit Choudhury

*Identifying the Importance of Content Overlap for Better Cross-lingual Embedding Mappings*
Réka Cserháti and Gábor Berend

*On the Cross-lingual Transferability of Contextualized Sense Embeddings*
Kiamehr Rezaee, Daniel Loureiro, Jose Camacho-Collados and Mohammad Taher Pilehvar

*Small Data? No Problem! Exploring the Viability of Pretrained Multilingual Language Models for Low-resourced Languages*
Kelechi Ogueji, Yuxin Zhu and Jimmy Lin

**13:45–14:15**

*Mr. TyDi: A Multi-lingual Benchmark for Dense Retrieval*
Xinyu Zhang, Xueguang Ma, Peng Shi and Jimmy Lin

**14:15–14:45**

*VisualSem: a high-quality knowledge graph for vision and language*
Houda Alberts, Ningyuan Huang, Yash Deshpande, Yibo Liu, Kyunghyun Cho, Clara Vania and Iacer Calixto

**14:45–15:45**

*Vyākarana: A Colorless Green Benchmark for Syntactic Evaluation in Indic Languages*
Rajaswa Patil, Jasleen Dhillon, Siddhant Mahurkar, Saumitra Kulkarni, Manav Malhotra and Veeky Baths

*Improving the Diversity of Unsupervised Paraphrasing with Embedding Outputs*
Monisha Jegadeesan, Sachin Kumar, John Wieting and Yulia Tsvetkov

*The Effectiveness of Intermediate-Task Training for Code-Switched Natural Language Understanding*
Archiki Prasad, Mohammad Ali Rehan, Shreya Pathak and Preethi Jyothi

*Shaking Syntactic Trees on the Sesame Street: Multilingual Probing with Controllable Perturbations*
Ekaterina Taktasheva, Vladislav Mikhailov and Ekaterina Artemova

*Multilingual Code-Switching for Zero-Shot Cross-Lingual Intent Prediction and Slot Filling*
Jitin Krishnan, Antonios Anastasopoulos, Hemant Purohit and Huzefa Rangwala

# Language Models are Few-shot Multilingual Learners

**Genta Indra Winata[1*], Andrea Madotto[1,3*], Zhaojiang Lin[1], Rosanne Liu[2,3], Jason Yosinski[3], Pascale Fung[1]**

[1]The Hong Kong University of Science and Technology

[2]Google Brain [3]ML Collective

{giwinata, amadotto, zlinao}@connect.ust.hk

## Abstract

General-purpose language models have demonstrated impressive capabilities, performing on par with state-of-the-art approaches on a range of downstream natural language processing (NLP) tasks and benchmarks when inferring instructions from very few examples. Here, we evaluate the multilingual skills of the GPT and T5 models in conducting multi-class classification on non-English languages without any parameter updates. We show that, given a few English examples as context, pre-trained language models can predict not only English test samples but also non-English ones. Finally, we find the in-context few-shot cross-lingual prediction results of language models are significantly better than random prediction, and they are competitive compared to the existing state-of-the-art cross-lingual models and translation models.

## 1 Introduction

The progress in language model (LM) pre-training (Peters et al., 2018; Devlin et al., 2019; Radford et al., 2019; Yang et al., 2019; Liu et al., 2019a; Brown et al., 2020; Liu et al., 2020a; Lewis et al., 2020; Raffel et al., 2020; Gao et al., 2020a) has led to the possibility of conducting few-shot learning, that is, learning a new task using a small number of examples without any further training or gradient computation. Few-shot learning alleviates the cost for extensive labeled data, which is beneficial since collecting high-quality labeled data is resource-intensive and expensive. It also reduces the cost for model fine-tuning, which requires tremendous GPU or TPU resources. Few-shot learning can be seen as a *one-for-all plug-and-play* computational model that can be applied to various natural language tasks, from sentiment analysis for text classification to story generation, provided only a small context (Brown et al., 2020).

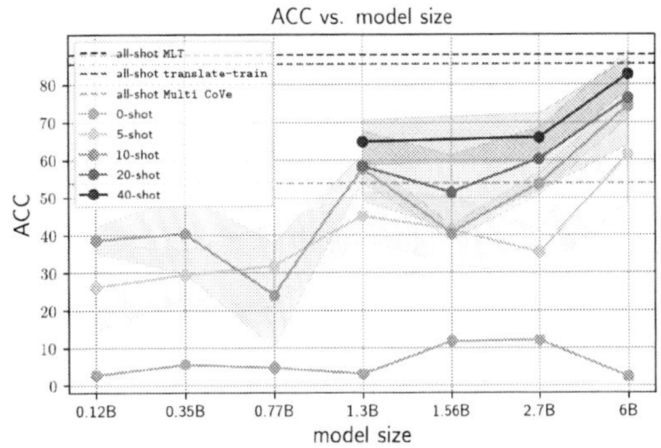


Figure 1: Accuracy vs. model size on English-Spanish MNLU dataset. Cross-lingual in-context learning with LMs (i.e., context with few English examples tested on Spanish sentences) performs as well as models trained in cross-lingual setting (Liu et al., 2020b) and translation baselines.

The idea of few-shot learning is also relevant to address the low-resource issue in non-English languages. Few-shot learning has been applied to NLP tasks (Brown et al., 2020; Madotto et al., 2020b; Lu et al., 2021; Perez et al., 2021; Liu et al., 2021a,b; Cahyawijaya et al., 2021a). Common approaches to solve the low-resource issue are to pre-train models with self-supervised learning using unlabelled monolingual text data collected from various resources available online (Wilie et al., 2020; Le et al., 2020; Martin et al., 2020; Eddine et al., 2020; Nguyen and Nguyen, 2020; Scheible et al., 2020; Bhattacharjee et al., 2021; Lee et al., 2020; Cahyawijaya et al., 2021b; Park et al., 2021) and then apply pre-training on the source language and fine-tune on the target languages (Schuster et al., 2019; Lin et al., 2019; Winata et al., 2019, 2021; Pfeiffer et al., 2020; Zheng et al., 2021; Lin et al., 2021b). Conversely, the few-shot learning does not need any training from the source and target languages. Figure 1 shows how it is possible to utilize pre-trained models on non-English languages, such as Spanish, as the performance is not random,

* Equal contribution



*Proceedings of the 1st Workshop on Multilingual Representation Learning*, pages 1–15
November 11, 2021. ©2021 Association for Computational Linguistics

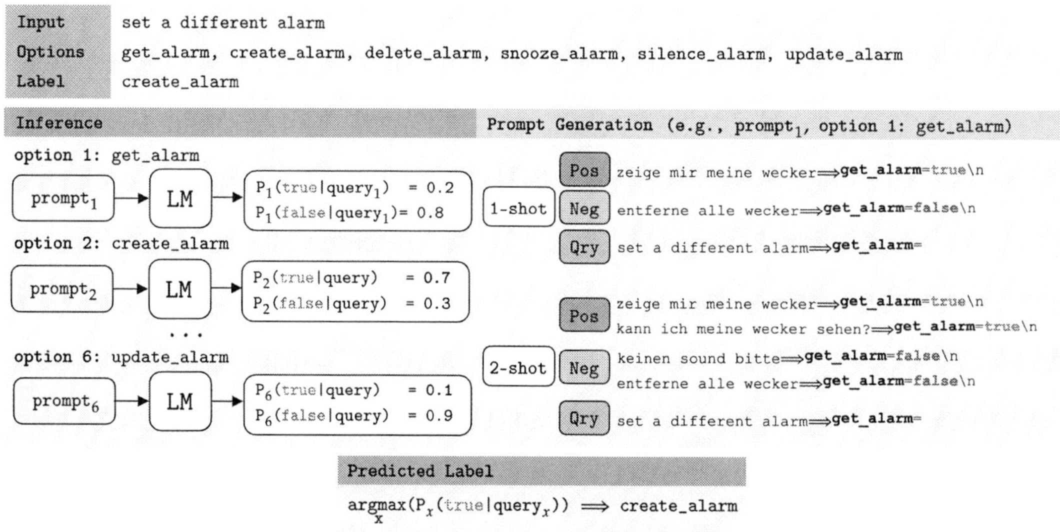


Figure 2: Example of the inference and query generation on the few-shot learning, where the source language and target language are German and English, respectively.

and the performance increases as the models are given more samples. We conjecture that pre-trained models may be able to adapt to languages that are similar to English. However, for many language tasks, it is difficult to collect a large supervised training dataset as language experts (e.g., linguists or native speakers) are required to annotate the data.

Another line of work is to apply cross-lingual transfer on English with the same task as the target languages (Ponti et al., 2018; Artetxe and Schwenk, 2019; Liu et al., 2019b; Lauscher et al., 2020; Liu et al., 2020b, 2021c; Chen et al., 2021). However, such methods still need to apply a fine-tuning step to update the model for fast adaptation, which can be challenging for large pre-trained models – some models require substantial memory capacity – since the models have to be trained on high-performing machines. Different from the aforementioned method, in-context learning using an LM does not allow any parameter updates. Thus, the process does not need to compute and store the gradients for backward propagation.

In this work, we investigate the practicality of applying few-shot learning in the multilingual setting for four languages, English, French, German, and Spanish, on natural language understanding intent prediction tasks using publicly available LMs that are mainly trained on English data. We show that, given a few English examples as context, pre-trained LMs can predict not only English test samples, but also non-English ones (Figure 2). To the best of our knowledge, no existing works have studied these tasks in multilingual settings. We conjecture that the English LMs can still produce good results on languages that are closely related to English. We construct the inference for the multi-class prediction setup by extending the idea from Madotto et al. (2020b) of applying multiple binary predictions on each class. Instead of guiding the model to generate *true* or *false* like in their work, which is not consistent and sometimes generates other words –, we introduce *maximum confidence prediction*. This method considers the confidence of predicting a certain label to provide a prediction. We design this as a multiple-choice task in which the confidence of the prediction for all possible classes is compared. Each class's confidence score is computed by normalizing the logits of generating the *next boolean token* given the prompt as the context. This method is considered to be more scalable than the simple $k$-way few-shot learning, where we need to put all data in a single prompt, since we only have a fixed maximum sequence length and, in the deployment, each forward step can be run in parallel to speed up the process. To increase the difficulty of the challenge, we also propose a cross-lingual task, where the context and query are in different languages.

Overall, we find that conditional generative LMs, such as the GPT-2 (Radford et al., 2019), $\text{GPT}_{\text{NEO}}$ models (Gao et al., 2020a), and T5 models (Raffel et al., 2020) have the capability to predict non-English languages, and adding more shots and using larger models achieves a substantial increment in performance, making it significantly better than random, which indicates the models are able to understand the prompt. We only focus on GPT and T5 models. T5 models do not perform as well as GPT models, which might be caused by the pre-training strategy. Experimental results in the cross-lingual setting demonstrate that pre-trained LMs make correct predictions. To summarize, our contributions are as follows:

- We study few-shot learning in the multilingual setting on four languages without any gradient updates. We use the publicly available GPT and T5 LMs, and compare the results to those from the zero-shot and fine-tuning approaches.

- We propose a simple and straightforward approach to perform few-shot learning on multi-class classification by applying binary prediction and considering the confidence of predicting the boolean tokens.

- We display the zero-shot, one-shot, and many-shot proficiency of the LMs in the cross-lingual setting when the language of the prompt is different from the target language.

## 2 Few-shot Multilingual Learners

First, we briefly define the notation of the input and output of the task, and then we introduce our method to design prompts for few-shot in-context learning. [1]

### 2.1 Notation and Tasks

Let us define $D$ as the distribution over the dataset and $P$ as the prompt that we use as the input of the LM $\theta$. The prompt $P = [D_{pos}, D_{neg}, Q]$ is a concatenation of few-shot samples: positive samples $D_{pos}$, negative samples $D_{neg}$, and the query $Q$, where $D_{pos}, D_{neg} \sim D$. $D_{pos}$ is a sample with a label that is the same as the query, and $D_{neg}$ is a sample that is taken from the dataset $D$ with a label other than the query. $\theta$ takes $P$ as the input of the model, and the LM generates a word $y$. We define the task $T_{s \rightarrow t}$, where $s$ is the source language and $t$ is the target language.

In this paper, we focus on the intent detection task in the monolingual and cross-lingual settings. In the monolingual setting, the source language is the same as the target language, and in the cross-lingual setting, we take the source language as different from the target language ($s \neq t$). We design our task as a multiple-choice problem, in which each sample has a label $l \in L$, where $L$ is the set of possible labels. We predict the boolean (true or false) for each sample and take the highest prediction confidence.

### 2.2 Prompt Generation

We define the task by designing prompts to perform few-shot learning. We design our task as a binary classification for multi-class prediction by following Madotto et al. (2020b). The idea is to guide the model to predict the boolean tokens, *true* and *false*. We examine the usage of two types of LMs, GPT and T5 models, and we construct prompts specific to each model. We use a specific way to probe the LMs to perform the few-shot prediction since they are trained with different learning objectives. Table 1 shows the format of the prefix we use for the GPT and T5 models. $X_i$ is one of the few-shot samples, and $X_i^*$ is the sample from other classes. For the GPT models, we only input the prefix by concatenating positive and negative samples with the query. Specifically for the T5 models, we add an additional token after the query and let the model predict that particular token during the generation step.

| Model | Prompt |
|---|---|
| GPT | `[SAMPLES]` $Q \rightarrow$ |
| T5 | `[SAMPLES]` $Q \rightarrow$ `[MASK]` |
| **`[SAMPLES]` Format** | **Example** |
| $X_1 \rightarrow$ `true\n` | zeige mir meine wecker=>get_alarm=true\n |
| $X_1^* \rightarrow$ `false\n` | entferne alle wecker=>get_alarm=false\n |
| ... | ... |
| $X_k \rightarrow$ `true\n` | kann ich meine wecker sehen?=>get_alarm=true\n |
| $X_k^* \rightarrow$ `false\n` | keinen sound bitte=>get_alarm=false\n |

Table 1: Prompt format given a few German examples as context.

Figure 2 shows an example of how we generate the prompt in $k$-shot settings. We create $L$ prompts and apply $L$ forward steps for each sample. For each prompt, $k$ positive and negative samples are randomly drawn from the dataset. It is worthwhile to note that the sampling method is similar to $k$-way few-shot learning, but the samples are not merged

[1]The code is released at `https://github.com/gentaiscool/few-shot-lm`.

into a single prompt. We do this because we want to give more shots as the prompt to the LMs as they have a limitation on the number of tokens they can accept as input (1,024 tokens in GPT-$2_{\text{XL}}$ and 2,048 tokens in $\text{GPT}_{\text{NEO}}$). We add a special token `\n` as a separator between each sample, as shown in Table 1.

### 2.3 Maximum Confidence Prediction

To get the final prediction of each sample, first, we compute the score of predicting the next boolean (true or false [2]) given the prompt $X_i$ for label $i$: $P_\theta(y = \texttt{true}|X_i)$ and $P_\theta(y = \texttt{false}|X_i)$ from the prediction distribution. Then, we normalize the score to get the probability of generating the *true* token to measure how much confidence the LM has to predict label $i$. We collect all the confidence scores over all label options and choose the highest confidence score among them, as follows:

$$\text{MC}(X, L) = \underset{i \in L}{\text{argmax}} \frac{P_\theta(y = \texttt{true}|X_i)}{\sum_b P_\theta(y = b|X_i)}, \quad (1)$$

where $b \in \{\texttt{true}, \texttt{false}\}$. We take the label with the highest confidence score as $\text{MC}(X, L)$.

### 2.4 Choices of Samples

For in-context learning, choosing the order of samples is essential (Lu et al., 2021). Here, we examine the impact of the order of the samples. We construct the probing set in two ways: (1) shuffle the few-shot samples and measure the variance in performance after changing their order, and (2) arrange the positive samples before the negative samples. We find that the latter works well, specifically on the T5 models.

## 3 Baselines

In this work, we compare the few-shot learning performance with other common approaches: zero-shot, zero-shot cross-task, and fine-tuning.

### 3.1 Zero-shot Cross-Task

One way to solve zero-shot prediction is by using entailment models to calculate the entailment score between sequences and labels. Given a pre-trained LM $\psi$ with an entailment head, a set of hypotheses $H$, and possible labels $L$, the model accepts two inputs, the hypothesis $h \in H$ and label $l \in L$, and generates the entailment score given any combinations of the hypothesis and label $P_\psi(y = \texttt{entail}|h, l)$:

$$\text{ES}(H, L) = \underset{h,l \in \{H,L\}}{\text{argmax}} P_\psi(y = \texttt{entail}|h, l). \quad (2)$$

### 3.2 Zero-shot In-Context Learning

This approach is very similar to our few-shot approach. It does not need any samples, and the model is only given natural language instruction. However, instead of using the prompt like in the few-shot setting, we can set up the prompt in a question-and-answer (Q&A) format as follows:

`Q:` Is `'<INTENT>'` the intent of `'<TEXT>'`? `A:`. (3)

### 3.3 Fine-tuning

Fine-tuning is the most common approach to updating a pre-trained model's weights when training with a labeled dataset. The advantage of this approach is strong performance since we give supervised signals with the correct labels to the model. For fine-tuning, we use the same sets of few-shot samples as in the in-context learning. In Section 4.2, we provide the hyper-parameters used in the experiments.

## 4 Experiments

### 4.1 Datasets and Metrics

We use an English natural language understanding (NLU) dataset, SNIPS (Coucke et al., 2018), and two multilingual NLU datasets, MTOP (Li et al., 2021) and Multilingual NLU (MultiNLU) (Schuster et al., 2019). MTOP includes four languages, English (`en`), French (`fr`), German (`de`), and Spanish (`es`), and Multilingual NLU includes two languages, English (`en`) and Spanish (`es`). We measure the model performance by calculating the average and standard deviation of the accuracy with three runs.

### 4.2 Experiment Settings

We set up the experiment in two settings: monolingual and cross-lingual. In the monolingual setting, we test the ability of the model to conduct few-shot in-context learning on four languages: English (`en`), French (`fr`), German (`de`), and Spanish (`es`). In the cross-lingual setting, we test its ability to predict a query from a non-English language

[2]Notice that some tokenizers (e.g., T5) splits "true" in two sub-tokens. We compute the score of the first sub-token only since it is significantly different for the two label (i.e. "tr" and "fal").

| Models | SNIPS | MTOP | | | | MultiNLU | |
|---|---|---|---|---|---|---|---|
| | en | de | en | es | fr | en | es |
| Random | 14.29 | 15.07 | 15.25 | 15.55 | 14.36 | 8.33 | 8.33 |
| Full-training SOTA | 99.00‡ | 88.80† | 94.00† | 90.10† | 89.60† | 99.11* | 98.90* |
| *Zero-shot Cross-Task Prediction* | | | | | | | |
| BART$_{\text{LARGE}}$ 0.4B | 74.43 | 24.80 | 43.41 | 36.06 | 24.77 | 65.60 | 34.77 |
| XLM-R$_{\text{LARGE}}$ 0.6B | 68.00 | 54.30 | 53.37 | 51.67 | 51.99 | 77.79 | 66.35 |
| *Few-shot Learning (K-shot)* | | | | | | | |
| GPT-2 0.1B | 39.33 ± 8.58 | 40.03 ± 6.34 | 35.46 ± 0.92 | 36.18 ± 2.12 | 41.16 ± 5.65 | 51.59 ± 12.83 | 37.56 ± 7.14 |
| GPT-2$_{\text{MEDIUM}}$ 0.3B | 65.71 ± 2.80 | 52.94 ± 5.12 | 63.35 ± 3.01 | 54.33 ± 4.75 | 50.6 ± 2.44 | 72.21 ± 14.88 | 50.25 ± 4.99 |
| GPT-2$_{\text{LARGE}}$ 0.8B | 71.43 ± 10.27 | 50.94 ± 6.63 | 59.70 ± 4.50 | 52.38 ± 2.65 | 44.75 ± 1.11 | 62.36 ± 13.82 | 58.04 ± 5.28 |
| GPT-2$_{\text{XL}}$ 1.6B | 78.43 ± 3.16 | 78.43 ± 3.16 | 73.93 ± 1.21 | 56.61 ± 2.02 | 45.21 ± 2.54 | 79.04 ± 5.05 | 64.74 ± 7.64 |
| GPT$_{\text{NEO}}$ 1.3B | 84.19 ± 2.78 | 67.17 ± 2.50 | 82.40 ± 1.90 | 73.51 ± 0.95 | 66.3 ± 1.29 | 89.70 ± 1.28 | 85.77 ± 2.53 |
| GPT$_{\text{NEO}}$ 2.7B | 91.24 ± 0.68 | 71.57 ± 5.94 | 81.51 ± 0.39 | 76.94 ± 0.83 | 70.31 ± 1.99 | 83.76 ± 3.14 | 87.82 ± 1.55 |
| GPT$_{\text{NEO-J}}$ 6B | **93.38 ± 0.76** | **80.97 ± 3.21** | **89.66 ± 0.50** | **84.18 ± 0.32** | **85.04 ± 1.18** | **94.32 ± 1.14** | **88.54 ± 6.18** |
| T5$_{\text{LARGE}}$ 0.8B | 23.57 ± 8.93 | 41.84 ± 7.63 | 36.02 ± 5.26 | 49.49 ± 6.32 | 40.41 ± 5.97 | 37.57 ± 15.23 | 21.20 ± 6.51 |
| T5$_{\text{3B}}$ 3B | 46.52 ± 6.69 | 50.81 ± 6.45 | 46.17 ± 4.06 | 46.45 ± 4.39 | 44.38 ± 0.22 | 31.46 ± 18.18 | 31.60 ± 14.90 |
| GPT$_{\text{NEO}}$ 2.7B (ordered) | 86.71 ± 1.62 | 55.69 ± 3.45 | 55.12 ± 4.01 | 50.77 ± 4.41 | 50.70 ± 2.47 | 63.33 ± 7.14 | 61.51 ± 1.63 |
| T5$_{\text{LARGE}}$ 0.8B (ordered) | 25.90 ± 18.51 | 63.06 ± 4.56 | 51.92 ± 3.90 | 62.71 ± 6.30 | 55.91 ± 3.82 | 38.97 ± 14.80 | 63.10 ± 4.46 |
| T5$_{\text{3B}}$ 3B (ordered) | **93.00 ± 3.00** | **74.11 ± 2.69** | **65.03 ± 1.87** | **66.97 ± 1.35** | **68.89 ± 2.51** | **80.12 ± 3.95** | **86.60 ± 2.40** |
| *Fine-tuning (40-shot)* | | | | | | | |
| mBERT 0.2B | 88.57 ± 3.14 | 25.21 ± 2.31 | 41.44 ± 5.59 | 33.82 ± 10.08 | 16.54 ± 5.54 | 84.88 ± 1.59 | 87.87 ± 3.29 |
| XLM-R$_{\text{BASE}}$ 0.3B | 87.95 ± 1.39 | 27.47 ± 11.90 | 37.03 ± 5.11 | 27.16 ± 5.51 | 13.8 ± 6.50 | 77.06 ± 3.16 | 74.85 ± 1.53 |

Table 2: Zero-shot and few-shot results in the monolingual setting. The SOTA results are taken from †Li et al. (2021), ‡Qin et al. (2019), and *Schuster et al. (2019).

with the English context (en→XX). In the few-shot in-context learning, we use $k$-way-few-shot classification, taking $k$ samples. For each model, we take $k \in [0, 5, K]$, where $K \leq 40$ is the largest number of few-shot samples that can be passed to the model as input and is divisible by 10 without exceeding the maximum input token limit. We utilize an NVIDIA Tesla V100 16GB GPU to run the inference so that the model is ensured to fit in a single GPU, and we use 16-bit precision.

**Model details** We run experiments on a variety of publicly available models:[3] four sizes of GPT-2 models (0.1B, 0.3B, 0.8B and 1.6B), three sizes of GPT$_{\text{NEO}}$ models (1.3B, 2.7B, and 6B), and two sizes of T5 models (0.8B and 3B). Table 3 shows the details of each pre-trained model.

**Baselines** We use the same sets of few-shot samples for the baselines. We run fine-tuning on the pre-trained models mBERT (Devlin et al., 2019) and XLM-R (Conneau et al., 2020), and also compare our models with the zero-shot cross-task models using pre-trained models XLM-R, fine-tuned on XNLI (Conneau et al., 2018), and BART, fine-tuned on MNLI (Williams et al., 2018);[4] a random baseline; and state-of-the-art results reported on each dataset. For the finetuning, we use a learning rate of 5e-5 with a decay of 0.9 for every epoch, and a batch size of 32. We apply an early stopping after 5 epochs without any improvement on the validation set.

| Model Name | $n_{\text{params}}$ | $n_{\text{layers}}$ | $n_{\text{hidden}}$ | $n_{\text{ffn}}$ |
|---|---|---|---|---|
| GPT-2 | 0.1B | 12 | 768 | |
| GPT-2$_{\text{MEDIUM}}$ | 0.3B | 24 | 768 | - |
| GPT-2$_{\text{LARGE}}$ | 0.8B | 36 | 1,280 | - |
| GPT-2$_{\text{XL}}$ | 1.6B | 48 | 1,600 | - |
| GPT$_{\text{NEO}}$ | 1.3B | 24 | 2,048 | - |
| GPT$_{\text{NEO}}$ | 2.7B | 32 | 2,560 | - |
| GPT$_{\text{NEO-J}}$ | 6B | 28 | 4096 | 16,384 |
| T5$_{\text{LARGE}}$ | 0.8B | 24 | 1,024 | 4,096 |
| T5$_{\text{3B}}$ | 3B | 24 | 1,024 | 16,384 |

Table 3: Model architecture.

[3] The models except GPT$_{\text{NEO-J}}$ are taken from https://huggingface.co/. The GPT$_{\text{NEO-J}}$ model is taken from https://github.com/kingoflolz/mesh-transformer-jax/

[4] The XLM-R model fine-tuned with XNLI data can be accessed at https://huggingface.co/joeddav/xlm-roberta-large-xnli. The BART model fine-tuned with MNLI data can be accessed at https://huggingface.co/facebook/bart-large-mnli

| Models | MTOP | | | MultiNLU |
|---|---|---|---|---|
| | en→de | en→es | en→fr | en→es |
| *Fine-tuning (all-shot on source language, zero-shot on target language)* | | | | |
| Seq2Seq w/ CRISS (Li et al., 2021) | 36.10 | 48.60 | 46.60 | - |
| Seq2Seq w/ XLM-R (Li et al., 2021) | 42.30 | 50.30 | 43.90 | - |
| NLM (Liu et al., 2021d) | 54.91 | 59.99 | 58.16 | - |
| X2Parser (Liu et al., 2021d) | **56.16** | **60.30** | **58.34** | - |
| Multi CoVe (Schuster et al., 2019) | - | - | - | 53.89 |
| Translate-Train (Liu et al., 2020b) | - | - | - | 85.39 |
| MTL (Liu et al., 2020b) | - | - | - | **87.88** |
| *Few-shot Learning (K-shot)* | | | | |
| GPT-2 `0.1B` | 23.89 ± 1.52 | 27.10 ± 3.19 | 26.14 ± 0.54 | 38.60 ± 3.54 |
| GPT-$2_{\text{MEDIUM}}$ `0.3B` | 39.61 ± 5.42 | 41.81 ± 4.66 | 42.40 ± 3.84 | 40.40 ± 10.48 |
| GPT-$2_{\text{LARGE}}$ `0.8B` | 30.94 ± 4.45 | 34.69 ± 6.50 | 33.04 ± 4.56 | 23.99 ± 14.02 |
| GPT-$2_{\text{XL}}$ `1.6B` | 42.88 ± 4.94 | 48.43 ± 4.42 | 50.67 ± 4.50 | 51.31 ± 9.87 |
| $\text{GPT}_{\text{NEO}}$ `1.3B` | 56.14 ± 2.75 | 63.14 ± 2.52 | 60.25 ± 3.32 | 64.82 ± 5.94 |
| $\text{GPT}_{\text{NEO}}$ `2.7B` | 58.27 ± 1.28 | 64.79 ± 1.69 | 62.30 ± 1.60 | 65.91 ± 6.42 |
| $\text{GPT}_{\text{NEO-J}}$ `6B` | **79.41 ± 1.18** | **81.57 ± 0.83** | **77.85 ± 1.63** | **82.66 ± 4.19** |
| $\text{T5}_{\text{LARGE}}$ `0.8B` | 37.14 ± 5.44 | 38.14 ± 3.20 | 33.53 ± 4.85 | 14.95 ± 16.34 |
| $\text{T5}_{\text{3B}}$ `3B` | 35.35 ± 7.07 | 34.64 ± 6.21 | 37.26 ± 8.68 | 14.11 ± 14.01 |
| $\text{GPT}_{\text{NEO}}$ `2.7B` (ordered) `0.8B` | 42.23 ± 3.24 | 48.62 ± 2.60 | 46.30 ± 3.02 | 47.83 ± 5.73 |
| $\text{T5}_{\text{3B}}$ (ordered) `3B` | **52.23 ± 4.29** | **52.74 ± 3.20** | **49.72 ± 5.37** | **50.42 ± 6.01** |

Table 4: Few-shot results in the cross-lingual setting on MTOP and MultiNLU datasets.

## 5 Results and Analysis

### 5.1 Model Performance

Tables 2 and 4 show the results in the monolingual and cross-lingual settings, respectively. The tables show that the performance improvement is highly related to the size of the pre-trained model, and the performance gap between the fully trained state-of-the-art model and the few-shot learning models decreases when we use larger models, indicating the usefulness of utilizing models of bigger sizes. The performance of the models with few-shot learning is considered promising as they are not trained at all, and the best model's performance gap with the fine-tuned model is less than 10%.

**Few-shot vs. Fine-tuning.** Comparing the performance of generative models to fine-tuning, it is clear that we can achieve higher accuracy without any training. However, in this experiment, we acknowledge GPT and T5 models we use for in-context learning are larger than the models we fine-tune, and few-shot learning is much more efficient since the models are not required to store the intermediate memory. In terms of inference speed, the few-shot models require more time to run an inference step, which may cause a bottleneck when the number of few-shot samples is relatively large. This is the limitation of this method, and reducing the inference time is an open research area to improve the efficiency of in-context learning.

**Zero-shot cross-task baselines.** Surprisingly, the zero-shot cross-task models are able to predict the samples much better than the random baseline, particularly on English tasks. Overall, the XLM-$\text{R}_{\text{LARGE}}$ model performs better than the $\text{BART}_{\text{LARGE}}$ models in all tasks except SNIPS.

**GPT vs. T5 models.** In general, the GPT models outperform the T5 models in all language pairs and datasets in a head-to-head comparison: Both GPT-$2_{\text{LARGE}}$ and $\text{T5}_{\text{LARGE}}$ have a similar number of parameters (`0.8B`), but they have a significant performance difference. A similar pattern can also be observed on larger models, such as $\text{GPT}_{\text{NEO}}$ `2.7B` and $\text{T5}_{\text{3B}}$ `3B`. Although the T5 models perform worse than the GPT models, they do not have a maximum token size for the input, as the GPT models do, which is one of the advantages of using them. On the other hand, we find that changing the sample order tremendously affects the performance of the T5 models. As shown in Tables 2 and 4, the performance increases substantially when we sort the few-shot samples based on their label (i.e., first all positive and then all negative examples). Conversely, the GPT models suffer loss in performance. Thus, we can make the conclusion that changing the sample order may produce high variance in the results, as also shown in (Lu et al., 2021).

**Effectiveness on non-English languages.** Based on the results, the performance of the models is lower in the non-English languages than in English. These results are expected since the pre-trained models are mostly trained on English data. However, the differences in performance are marginal. This finding may indicate that our few-shot learning method can be effectively utilized for languages that are in the same language family as English, such as French, German, and Spanish, but this will require further investigation in the future.

**Cross-lingual results.** Based on the results in Table 4, we can see that the generative models are able to use the context from English to predict the sample in non-English languages. The cross-lingual setting is considered harder than the monolingual one since the models need to contextualize and understand the source and target languages to predict the test samples correctly. In general, the trend of the results in the cross-lingual setting is similar to the monolingual setting. In the MTOP dataset, we find that the models generally achieve higher performance for **en**$\rightarrow$**es** than for the other two target languages (**de** and **fr**). In MultiNLU, our $GPT_{NEO\text{-}J}$ closes the gap with the existing state-of-the-art baseline with fine-tuning from Liu et al. (2020b) underperforming it only by a close margin of around 4.2%, and the $GPT_{NEO\text{-}J}$ performance is only less than 3% worse than that of the Translate-Train model. These results show a promising new direction in the zero-shot cross-lingual research that can be applied to other datasets and language pairs.

### 5.2 Ablation Study

To further understand how much data we need for the in context learning, we conduct experiments with different numbers of few-shot samples, including zero-shot experiments on the MTOP and MultiNLU datasets.

**MTOP dataset.** Figures 3, 4, 5, and 6 illustrate the results with different numbers of samples on the MTOP dataset in the monolingual setting. We show a different set of k-shot results for each model according to the maximum samples that can be used in the model as input. The results consistently improved as the number of shots increases. Interestingly, the QA style's zero-shot strategy can outperform random prediction only on two or three models in each language, and the others are worse. The fine-tuning results on MTOP are thus far worse than those of few-shot learning.

**MultiNLU dataset.** Figures 7 and 8 illustrate the results with different numbers of samples on the MultiNLU dataset in the monolingual setting. The results on MultiNLU for the models with fine-tuning are closer to those of few-shot learning than those on the MTOP dataset. The reason may be the number of labels that the MTOP dataset has compared to MultiNLU. As a result, the zero-shot performance on the GPT models is sometimes worse than that of the random baseline.

## 6 Related Work

### 6.1 Few-shot In-Context Learning

Recent work on few-shot in-context learning uses LMs to solve NLP tasks (Petroni et al., 2019; Brown et al., 2020; Gao et al., 2020b; Madotto et al., 2020b; Zhao et al., 2021; Schick and Schütze, 2021; Lin et al., 2021a). In this approach, we select the appropriate prompts to trigger the LMs to behave so that they can predict the desired output (Liu et al., 2021b). However, the prompts have to be engineered to allow the LM to generate a text appropriate to solve the task. Learning to calibrate the few-shot results is also essential to reduce the model's performance variance (Zhao et al., 2021), and the selection criteria in choosing the prompts are also important (Perez et al., 2021). In another stream of work, Shin et al. (2020); Li and Liang (2021) proposed an automated method to create prompts for a diverse set of tasks by gradient-based tuning instead of manually searching for a good prompt. Using such a method, may allow us to find an optimal prompt easier, it is very difficult to discover the optimal prompts for complicated natural language processing tasks, such as semantic parsing (Liu et al., 2021b).

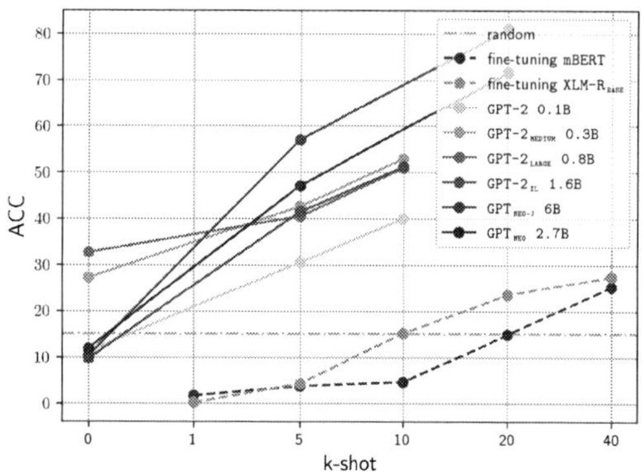


Figure 3: The results on German (de) MTOP dataset with GPT models.

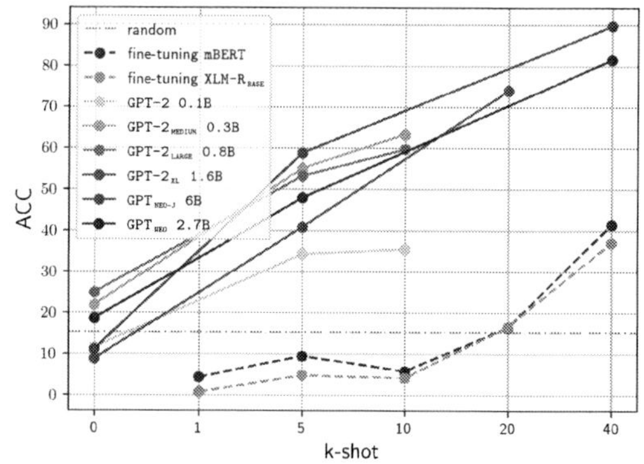


Figure 4: The results on English (en) MTOP dataset with GPT models.

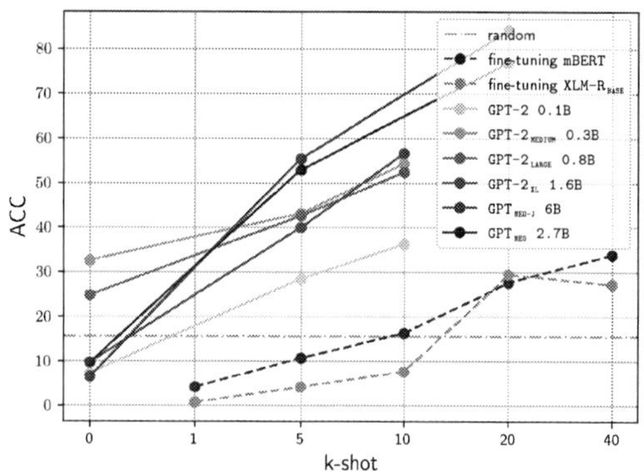


Figure 5: The results on Spanish (es) MTOP dataset with GPT models.

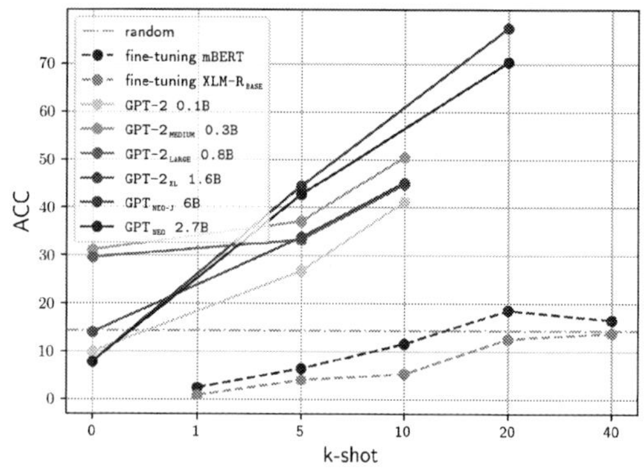


Figure 6: The results on French (fr) MTOP dataset with GPT models.

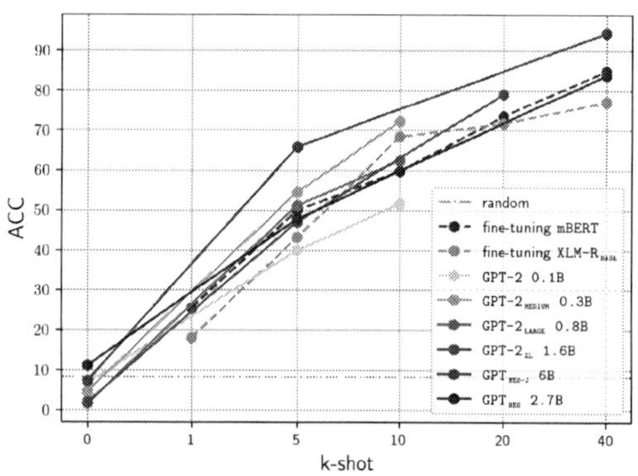


Figure 7: The results on English (en) multilingual NLU dataset with GPT models.

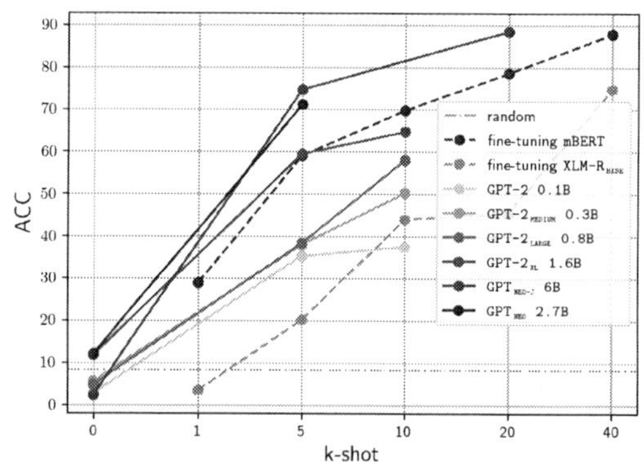


Figure 8: The results on Spanish (es) multilingual NLU dataset with GPT models.

## 6.2 Pre-trained Language Models

Recent advances in pre-trained LMs have been focused on building pre-trained encoders, such as BERT (Devlin et al., 2019), RoBERTa (Liu et al., 2019a), ELMO (Peters et al., 2018), ULM-FiT (Howard and Ruder, 2018), ELECTRA (Clark et al., 2019), XLM (Conneau and Lample, 2019), and XLM-R (Conneau et al., 2020; Goyal et al., 2021), decoder-only models, such as GPT models (Radford et al., 2019; Brown et al., 2020) and encoder-decoder models, such as T5 (Raffel et al., 2020), BART (Lewis et al., 2020), and their multilingual versions, mT5 (Xue et al., 2021) and mBART (Liu et al., 2020a).

Pre-trained encoders have been used to improve the contextualized representations of multilingual systems in various NLP tasks, for example, dialogue systems (Liu et al., 2020b, 2021d; Li et al., 2021), code-switching sequence labeling (Aguilar et al., 2020; Winata et al., 2021; Winata, 2021), and multilingual speech recognition (Datta et al., 2020; Winata et al., 2020). Meanwhile, the pre-trained encoder-decoder models, have been used for various sequence generation tasks, such as summarization (Raffel et al., 2020), conversational agents (Lin et al., 2020b,a; Madotto et al., 2020a; Wu and Xiong, 2020; Hosseini-Asl et al., 2020; Lin et al., 2021b), and knowledge grounding (Chen et al., 2020; Zhao et al., 2020).

## 7 Limitation and Future Work

**More Languages** In this paper, we explored only cross-lingual transfer learning from and to Latin-based language (e.g., English to Spanish / French / German). Extending our approach to non-Latin languages (e.g., Thai, Chinese, etc.) is challenging for two reasons: 1) we are currently using English tokenizers which are known to fails, or they assign UNK tokens when prompt with non-Latin characters, and 2) a possible little, or absent, the named entity overlap between the source and target language, which could make the English prompt completely irrelevant. The latter suggests an interesting future work, where we could study the correlation between performance and word (or token) overlapping of the source (`en`) and the target language samples.

**More Datasets and Models** Intent recognition is an important task, especially in multiple language scenarios. In future work, we plan to include the missing languages of MTOP and MultiNLU, and to add more languages from the MultiATIS++ (Xu et al., 2020) which consists of a total of 9 languages, that is, English, Spanish, German, French, Portuguese, Chinese, Japanese, Hindi, and Turkish. Moreover, to cope with the tokenization issues, we would like to explore multilingual LMs such as MT5 (Xue et al., 2021).

## 8 Conclusion

This paper demonstrates the multilingual skills of pre-trained LMs, GPT and T5, in conducting in-context learning without parameter updates. This work is our initial attempt to show the effectiveness of in-context learning in the multilingual and cross-lingual setting. It covers four different languages and explores the possibility of conducting efficient inference on low-resource tasks. We find that LMs can predict samples correctly, significantly better than the random prediction, in cross-lingual tasks with no training examples of the target languages. We would like to investigate further the applicability of this method to other tasks and languages in future work.

## Acknowledgment

We want to thank Bryan Wilie and Samuel Cahyawijaya for their support in accessing the cloud service. We also sincerely thank Zihan Liu and ML Collective members for helping with the discussion about this project. Finally, we want to thanks the reviewer of the paper for their meaningful comments and suggestions. Given the short time for the camera-ready, we tried our best to improve the final version of the paper.

## References

Gustavo Aguilar, Bryan McCann, Tong Niu, Nazneen Rajani, N. Keskar, and T. Solorio. 2020. Char2subword: Extending the subword embedding space from pre-trained models using robust character compositionality. *ArXiv*, abs/2010.12730.

Mikel Artetxe and Holger Schwenk. 2019. Massively multilingual sentence embeddings for zero-shot cross-lingual transfer and beyond. *Transactions of the Association for Computational Linguistics*, 7:597–610.

Abhik Bhattacharjee, Tahmid Hasan, Kazi Samin, M Sohel Rahman, Anindya Iqbal, and Rifat Shahriyar. 2021. Banglabert: Combating embedding barrier for low-resource language understanding. *arXiv preprint arXiv:2101.00204*.

Tom B Brown, Benjamin Mann, Nick Ryder, Melanie Subbiah, Jared Kaplan, Prafulla Dhariwal, Arvind Neelakantan, Pranav Shyam, Girish Sastry, Amanda Askell, et al. 2020. Language models are few-shot learners. *arXiv preprint arXiv:2005.14165*.

Samuel Cahyawijaya, Genta Indra Winata, Holy Lovenia, Bryan Wilie, Wenliang Dai, Etsuko Ishii, and Pascale Fung. 2021a. Greenformer: Factorization toolkit for efficient deep neural networks.

Samuel Cahyawijaya, Genta Indra Winata, Bryan Wilie, Karissa Vincentio, Xiaohong Li, Adhiguna Kuncoro, Sebastian Ruder, Zhi Yuan Lim, Syafri Bahar, Masayu Leylia Khodra, et al. 2021b. Indonlg:

Benchmark and resources for evaluating indonesian natural language generation. *arXiv preprint arXiv:2104.08200*.

Guanhua Chen, Shuming Ma, Yun Chen, Li Dong, Dongdong Zhang, Jia Pan, Wenping Wang, and Furu Wei. 2021. Zero-shot cross-lingual transfer of neural machine translation with multilingual pretrained encoders. *arXiv preprint arXiv:2104.08757*.

Wenhu Chen, Yu Su, Xifeng Yan, and William Yang Wang. 2020. KGPT: Knowledge-grounded pretraining for data-to-text generation. In *Proceedings of the 2020 Conference on Empirical Methods in Natural Language Processing (EMNLP)*, pages 8635–8648, Online. Association for Computational Linguistics.

Kevin Clark, Minh-Thang Luong, Quoc V Le, and Christopher D Manning. 2019. Electra: Pre-training text encoders as discriminators rather than generators. In *International Conference on Learning Representations*.

Alexis Conneau, Kartikay Khandelwal, Naman Goyal, Vishrav Chaudhary, Guillaume Wenzek, Francisco Guzmán, Édouard Grave, Myle Ott, Luke Zettlemoyer, and Veselin Stoyanov. 2020. Unsupervised cross-lingual representation learning at scale. In *Proceedings of the 58th Annual Meeting of the Association for Computational Linguistics*, pages 8440–8451.

Alexis Conneau and Guillaume Lample. 2019. Cross-lingual language model pretraining. *Advances in Neural Information Processing Systems*, 32:7059–7069.

Alexis Conneau, Ruty Rinott, Guillaume Lample, Adina Williams, Samuel Bowman, Holger Schwenk, and Veselin Stoyanov. 2018. Xnli: Evaluating cross-lingual sentence representations. In *Proceedings of the 2018 Conference on Empirical Methods in Natural Language Processing*, pages 2475–2485.

Alice Coucke, Alaa Saade, Adrien Ball, Théodore Bluche, Alexandre Caulier, David Leroy, Clément Doumouro, Thibault Gisselbrecht, Francesco Caltagirone, Thibaut Lavril, et al. 2018. Snips voice platform: an embedded spoken language understanding system for private-by-design voice interfaces. *arXiv preprint arXiv:1805.10190*.

Arindrima Datta, Bhuvana Ramabhadran, Jesse Emond, Anjuli Kannan, and Brian Roark. 2020. Language-agnostic multilingual modeling. In *ICASSP 2020-2020 IEEE International Conference on Acoustics, Speech and Signal Processing (ICASSP)*, pages 8239–8243. IEEE.

Jacob Devlin, Ming-Wei Chang, Kenton Lee, and Kristina Toutanova. 2019. Bert: Pre-training of deep bidirectional transformers for language understanding. In *Proceedings of the 2019 Conference of the North American Chapter of the Association for Computational Linguistics: Human Language Technologies, Volume 1 (Long and Short Papers)*, pages 4171–4186.

Moussa Kamal Eddine, Antoine J-P Tixier, and Michalis Vazirgiannis. 2020. Barthez: a skilled pretrained french sequence-to-sequence model. *arXiv preprint arXiv:2010.12321*.

Leo Gao, Stella Biderman, Sid Black, Laurence Golding, Travis Hoppe, Charles Foster, Jason Phang, Horace He, Anish Thite, Noa Nabeshima, et al. 2020a. The pile: An 800gb dataset of diverse text for language modeling. *arXiv preprint arXiv:2101.00027*.

Tianyu Gao, Adam Fisch, and Danqi Chen. 2020b. Making pre-trained language models better few-shot learners. *arXiv preprint arXiv:2012.15723*.

Naman Goyal, Jingfei Du, Myle Ott, Giri Anantharaman, and Alexis Conneau. 2021. Larger-scale transformers for multilingual masked language modeling. *arXiv preprint arXiv:2105.00572*.

Ehsan Hosseini-Asl, Bryan McCann, Chien-Sheng Wu, Semih Yavuz, and Richard Socher. 2020. A simple language model for task-oriented dialogue. *arXiv preprint arXiv:2005.00796*.

Jeremy Howard and Sebastian Ruder. 2018. Universal language model fine-tuning for text classification. In *Proceedings of the 56th Annual Meeting of the Association for Computational Linguistics (Volume 1: Long Papers)*, pages 328–339, Melbourne, Australia. Association for Computational Linguistics.

Anne Lauscher, Vinit Ravishankar, Ivan Vulić, and Goran Glavaš. 2020. From zero to hero: On the limitations of zero-shot language transfer with multilingual transformers. In *Proceedings of the 2020 Conference on Empirical Methods in Natural Language Processing (EMNLP)*, pages 4483–4499.

Hang Le, Loïc Vial, Jibril Frej, Vincent Segonne, Maximin Coavoux, Benjamin Lecouteux, Alexandre Allauzen, Benoit Crabbé, Laurent Besacier, and Didier Schwab. 2020. Flaubert: Unsupervised language model pre-training for french. In *Proceedings of the 12th Language Resources and Evaluation Conference*, pages 2479–2490.

Sangah Lee, Hansol Jang, Yunmee Baik, Suzi Park, and Hyopil Shin. 2020. Kr-bert: A small-scale korean-specific language model. *arXiv preprint arXiv:2008.03979*.

Mike Lewis, Yinhan Liu, Naman Goyal, Marjan Ghazvininejad, Abdelrahman Mohamed, Omer Levy, Veselin Stoyanov, and Luke Zettlemoyer. 2020. Bart: Denoising sequence-to-sequence pre-training for natural language generation, translation, and comprehension. In *Proceedings of the 58th Annual Meeting of the Association for Computational Linguistics*, pages 7871–7880.

Haoran Li, Abhinav Arora, Shuohui Chen, Anchit Gupta, Sonal Gupta, and Yashar Mehdad. 2021. Mtop: A comprehensive multilingual task-oriented semantic parsing benchmark. In *Proceedings of the 16th Conference of the European Chapter of the Association for Computational Linguistics: Main Volume*, pages 2950–2962.

Xiang Lisa Li and Percy Liang. 2021. Prefix-tuning: Optimizing continuous prompts for generation. *arXiv preprint arXiv:2101.00190*.

Yu-Hsiang Lin, Chian-Yu Chen, Jean Lee, Zirui Li, Yuyan Zhang, Mengzhou Xia, Shruti Rijhwani, Junxian He, Zhisong Zhang, Xuezhe Ma, et al. 2019. Choosing transfer languages for cross-lingual learning. In *Proceedings of the 57th Annual Meeting of the Association for Computational Linguistics*, pages 3125–3135.

Zhaojiang Lin, Bing Liu, Seungwhan Moon, Paul A Crook, Zhenpeng Zhou, Zhiguang Wang, Zhou Yu, Andrea Madotto, Eunjoon Cho, and Rajen Subba. 2021a. Leveraging slot descriptions for zero-shot cross-domain dialogue statetracking. In *Proceedings of the 2021 Conference of the North American Chapter of the Association for Computational Linguistics: Human Language Technologies*, pages 5640–5648.

Zhaojiang Lin, Zihan Liu, Genta Indra Winata, Samuel Cahyawijaya, Andrea Madotto, Yejin Bang, Etsuko Ishii, and Pascale Fung. 2020a. Xpersona: Evaluating multilingual personalized chatbot. *arXiv preprint arXiv:2003.07568*.

Zhaojiang Lin, Andrea Madotto, Genta Indra Winata, Peng Xu, Feijun Jiang, Yuxiang Hu, Chen Shi, and Pascale Fung. 2021b. Bitod: A bilingual multi-domain dataset for task-oriented dialogue modeling. *arXiv e-prints*, pages arXiv–2106.

Zhaojiang Lin, Andrea Madotto, Genta Indra Winata, and Pascale Fung. 2020b. Mintl: Minimalist transfer learning for task-oriented dialogue systems. In *Proceedings of the 2020 Conference on Empirical Methods in Natural Language Processing (EMNLP)*, pages 3391–3405.

Jiachang Liu, Dinghan Shen, Yizhe Zhang, Bill Dolan, Lawrence Carin, and Weizhu Chen. 2021a. What makes good in-context examples for gpt-3? *arXiv preprint arXiv:2101.06804*.

Pengfei Liu, Weizhe Yuan, Jinlan Fu, Zhengbao Jiang, Hiroaki Hayashi, and Graham Neubig. 2021b. Pre-train, prompt, and predict: A systematic survey of prompting methods in natural language processing. *arXiv preprint arXiv:2107.13586*.

Yinhan Liu, Jiatao Gu, Naman Goyal, Xian Li, Sergey Edunov, Marjan Ghazvininejad, Mike Lewis, and Luke Zettlemoyer. 2020a. Multilingual denoising pre-training for neural machine translation. *Transactions of the Association for Computational Linguistics*, 8:726–742.

Yinhan Liu, Myle Ott, Naman Goyal, Jingfei Du, Mandar Joshi, Danqi Chen, Omer Levy, Mike Lewis, Luke Zettlemoyer, and Veselin Stoyanov. 2019a. Roberta: A robustly optimized bert pretraining approach. *arXiv preprint arXiv:1907.11692*.

Zihan Liu, Jamin Shin, Yan Xu, Genta Indra Winata, Peng Xu, Andrea Madotto, and Pascale Fung. 2019b. Zero-shot cross-lingual dialogue systems with transferable latent variables. In *Proceedings of the 2019 Conference on Empirical Methods in Natural Language Processing and the 9th International Joint Conference on Natural Language Processing (EMNLP-IJCNLP)*, pages 1297–1303.

Zihan Liu, Genta Indra Winata, Zhaojiang Lin, Peng Xu, and Pascale Fung. 2020b. Attention-informed mixed-language training for zero-shot cross-lingual task-oriented dialogue systems. In *Proceedings of the AAAI Conference on Artificial Intelligence*, volume 34, pages 8433–8440.

Zihan Liu, Genta Indra Winata, Peng Xu, and Pascale Fung. 2021c. X2parser: Cross-lingual and cross-domain framework for task-oriented compositional semantic parsing. *arXiv preprint arXiv:2106.03777*.

Zihan Liu, Genta Indra Winata, Peng Xu, and Pascale Fung. 2021d. X2Parser: Cross-lingual and cross-domain framework for task-oriented compositional semantic parsing. In *Proceedings of the 6th Workshop on Representation Learning for NLP (RepL4NLP-2021)*, pages 112–127, Online. Association for Computational Linguistics.

Yao Lu, Max Bartolo, Alastair Moore, Sebastian Riedel, and Pontus Stenetorp. 2021. Fantastically ordered prompts and where to find them: Overcoming few-shot prompt order sensitivity. *arXiv preprint arXiv:2104.08786*.

Andrea Madotto, Samuel Cahyawijaya, Genta Indra Winata, Yan Xu, Zihan Liu, Zhaojiang Lin, and Pascale Fung. 2020a. Learning knowledge bases with parameters for task-oriented dialogue systems. In *Proceedings of the 2020 Conference on Empirical Methods in Natural Language Processing: Findings*, pages 2372–2394.

Andrea Madotto, Zihan Liu, Zhaojiang Lin, and Pascale Fung. 2020b. Language models as few-shot learner for task-oriented dialogue systems. *arXiv preprint arXiv:2008.06239*.

Louis Martin, Benjamin Muller, Pedro Javier Ortiz Suárez, Yoann Dupont, Laurent Romary, Éric Villemonte de la Clergerie, Djamé Seddah, and Benoît Sagot. 2020. Camembert: a tasty french language model. In *Proceedings of the 58th Annual Meeting of the Association for Computational Linguistics*, pages 7203–7219.

Dat Quoc Nguyen and Anh Tuan Nguyen. 2020. Phobert: Pre-trained language models for vietnamese. In *Proceedings of the 2020 Conference on*

*Empirical Methods in Natural Language Processing: Findings*, pages 1037–1042.

Sungjoon Park, Jihyung Moon, Sungdong Kim, Won Ik Cho, Jiyoon Han, Jangwon Park, Chisung Song, Junseong Kim, Yongsook Song, Taehwan Oh, et al. 2021. Klue: Korean language understanding evaluation. *arXiv preprint arXiv:2105.09680*.

Ethan Perez, Douwe Kiela, and Kyunghyun Cho. 2021. True few-shot learning with language models. *arXiv preprint arXiv:2105.11447*.

Matthew Peters, Mark Neumann, Mohit Iyyer, Matt Gardner, Christopher Clark, Kenton Lee, and Luke Zettlemoyer. 2018. Deep contextualized word representations. In *Proceedings of the 2018 Conference of the North American Chapter of the Association for Computational Linguistics: Human Language Technologies, Volume 1 (Long Papers)*, pages 2227–2237.

Fabio Petroni, Tim Rocktäschel, Sebastian Riedel, Patrick Lewis, Anton Bakhtin, Yuxiang Wu, and Alexander Miller. 2019. Language models as knowledge bases? In *Proceedings of the 2019 Conference on Empirical Methods in Natural Language Processing and the 9th International Joint Conference on Natural Language Processing (EMNLP-IJCNLP)*, pages 2463–2473.

Jonas Pfeiffer, Ivan Vulić, Iryna Gurevych, and Sebastian Ruder. 2020. Mad-x: An adapter-based framework for multi-task cross-lingual transfer. *arXiv preprint arXiv:2005.00052*.

Edoardo Maria Ponti, Ivan Vulić, Goran Glavaš, Nikola Mrkšić, and Anna Korhonen. 2018. Adversarial propagation and zero-shot cross-lingual transfer of word vector specialization. In *Proceedings of the 2018 Conference on Empirical Methods in Natural Language Processing*, pages 282–293.

Libo Qin, Wanxiang Che, Yangming Li, Haoyang Wen, and Ting Liu. 2019. A stack-propagation framework with token-level intent detection for spoken language understanding. In *Proceedings of the 2019 Conference on Empirical Methods in Natural Language Processing and the 9th International Joint Conference on Natural Language Processing (EMNLP-IJCNLP)*, pages 2078–2087.

Alec Radford, Jeffrey Wu, Rewon Child, David Luan, Dario Amodei, and Ilya Sutskever. 2019. Language models are unsupervised multitask learners. *OpenAI blog*, 1(8):9.

Colin Raffel, Noam Shazeer, Adam Roberts, Katherine Lee, Sharan Narang, Michael Matena, Yanqi Zhou, Wei Li, and Peter J Liu. 2020. Exploring the limits of transfer learning with a unified text-to-text transformer. *Journal of Machine Learning Research*, 21:1–67.

Raphael Scheible, Fabian Thomczyk, Patric Tippmann, Victor Jaravine, and Martin Boeker. 2020. Gottbert: a pure german language model. *arXiv preprint arXiv:2012.02110*.

Timo Schick and Hinrich Schütze. 2021. It's not just size that matters: Small language models are also few-shot learners. In *Proceedings of the 2021 Conference of the North American Chapter of the Association for Computational Linguistics: Human Language Technologies*, pages 2339–2352.

Sebastian Schuster, Sonal Gupta, Rushin Shah, and Mike Lewis. 2019. Cross-lingual transfer learning for multilingual task oriented dialog. In *Proceedings of the 2019 Conference of the North American Chapter of the Association for Computational Linguistics: Human Language Technologies, Volume 1 (Long and Short Papers)*, pages 3795–3805.

Taylor Shin, Yasaman Razeghi, Robert L Logan IV, Eric Wallace, and Sameer Singh. 2020. Eliciting knowledge from language models using automatically generated prompts. In *Proceedings of the 2020 Conference on Empirical Methods in Natural Language Processing (EMNLP)*, pages 4222–4235.

Bryan Wilie, Karissa Vincentio, Genta Indra Winata, Samuel Cahyawijaya, Xiaohong Li, Zhi Yuan Lim, Sidik Soleman, Rahmad Mahendra, Pascale Fung, Syafri Bahar, et al. 2020. Indonlu: Benchmark and resources for evaluating indonesian natural language understanding. In *Proceedings of the 1st Conference of the Asia-Pacific Chapter of the Association for Computational Linguistics and the 10th International Joint Conference on Natural Language Processing*, pages 843–857.

Adina Williams, Nikita Nangia, and Samuel Bowman. 2018. A broad-coverage challenge corpus for sentence understanding through inference. In *Proceedings of the 2018 Conference of the North American Chapter of the Association for Computational Linguistics: Human Language Technologies, Volume 1 (Long Papers)*, pages 1112–1122.

Genta Indra Winata. 2021. Multilingual transfer learning for code-switched language and speech neural modeling. *arXiv preprint arXiv:2104.06268*.

Genta Indra Winata, Samuel Cahyawijaya, Zihan Liu, Zhaojiang Lin, Andrea Madotto, and Pascale Fung. 2021. Are multilingual models effective in code-switching? In *Proceedings of the Fifth Workshop on Computational Approaches to Linguistic Code-Switching*, pages 142–153.

Genta Indra Winata, Andrea Madotto, Chien-Sheng Wu, and Pascale Fung. 2019. Code-switched language models using neural based synthetic data from parallel sentences. In *Proceedings of the 23rd Conference on Computational Natural Language Learning (CoNLL)*, pages 271–280.

Genta Indra Winata, Guangsen Wang, Caiming Xiong, and Steven Hoi. 2020. Adapt-and-adjust: Overcoming the long-tail problem of multilingual speech recognition. *arXiv preprint arXiv:2012.01687*.

Chien-Sheng Wu and Caiming Xiong. 2020. Probing task-oriented dialogue representation from language models. In *Proceedings of the 2020 Conference on Empirical Methods in Natural Language Processing (EMNLP)*, pages 5036–5051.

Weijia Xu, Batool Haider, and Saab Mansour. 2020. End-to-end slot alignment and recognition for cross-lingual nlu. In *Proceedings of the 2020 Conference on Empirical Methods in Natural Language Processing (EMNLP)*, pages 5052–5063.

Linting Xue, Noah Constant, Adam Roberts, Mihir Kale, Rami Al-Rfou, Aditya Siddhant, Aditya Barua, and Colin Raffel. 2021. mt5: A massively multilingual pre-trained text-to-text transformer. In *Proceedings of the 2021 Conference of the North American Chapter of the Association for Computational Linguistics: Human Language Technologies*, pages 483–498.

Zhilin Yang, Zihang Dai, Yiming Yang, Jaime Carbonell, Russ R Salakhutdinov, and Quoc V Le. 2019. Xlnet: Generalized autoregressive pretraining for language understanding. *Advances in Neural Information Processing Systems*, 32:5753–5763.

Tony Z Zhao, Eric Wallace, Shi Feng, Dan Klein, and Sameer Singh. 2021. Calibrate before use: Improving few-shot performance of language models. *arXiv preprint arXiv:2102.09690*.

Xueliang Zhao, Wei Wu, Can Xu, Chongyang Tao, Dongyan Zhao, and Rui Yan. 2020. Knowledge-grounded dialogue generation with pre-trained language models. In *Proceedings of the 2020 Conference on Empirical Methods in Natural Language Processing (EMNLP)*, pages 3377–3390, Online. Association for Computational Linguistics.

Bo Zheng, Li Dong, Shaohan Huang, Wenhui Wang, Zewen Chi, Saksham Singhal, Wanxiang Che, Ting Liu, Xia Song, and Furu Wei. 2021. Consistency regularization for cross-lingual fine-tuning. *arXiv preprint arXiv:2106.08226*.

## A Full k-shot Results

This appendix shows the results on few-shot monolingual and cross-lingual settings on SNIPS, MTOP, and multilingual NLU datasets over a different number of samples.

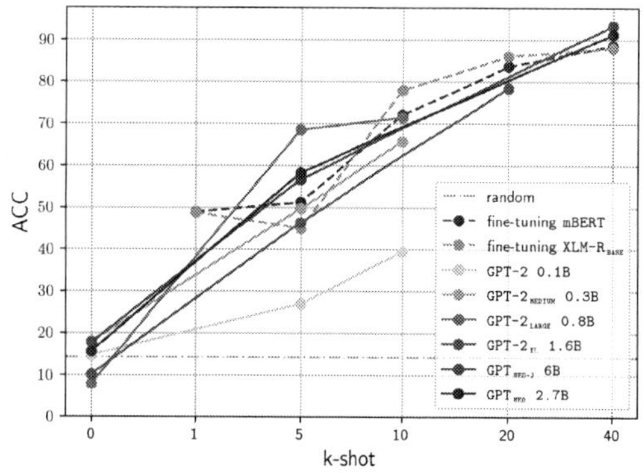


Figure 9: The acc results on English (en) SNIPS with GPT models.

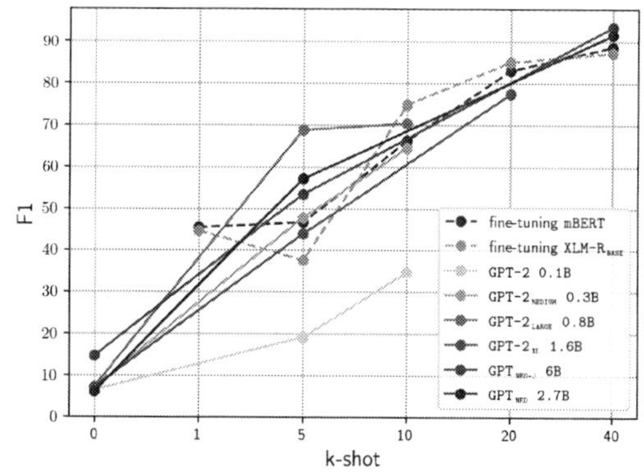


Figure 10: The f1 results on English (en) SNIPS with GPT models.

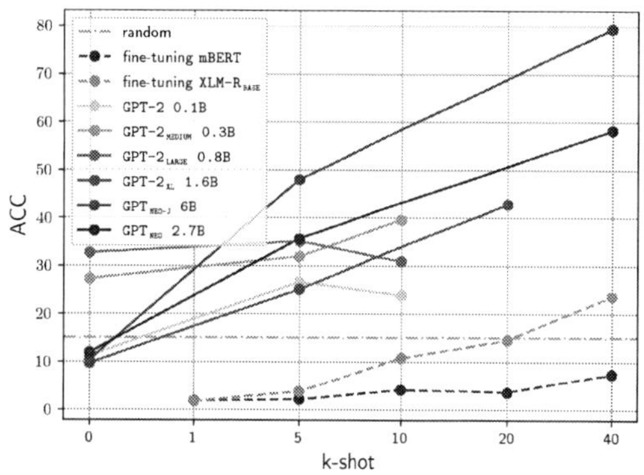


Figure 11: The acc results on the cross-lingual setting, English-German (de) MTOP dataset with GPT models.

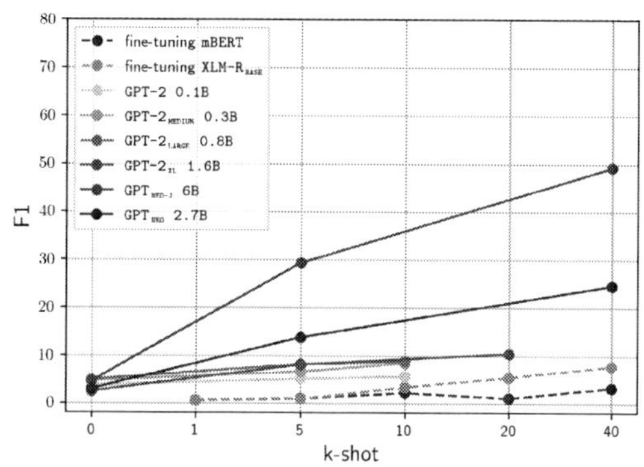


Figure 12: The f1 results on the cross-lingual setting, English-German (de) MTOP dataset with GPT models.

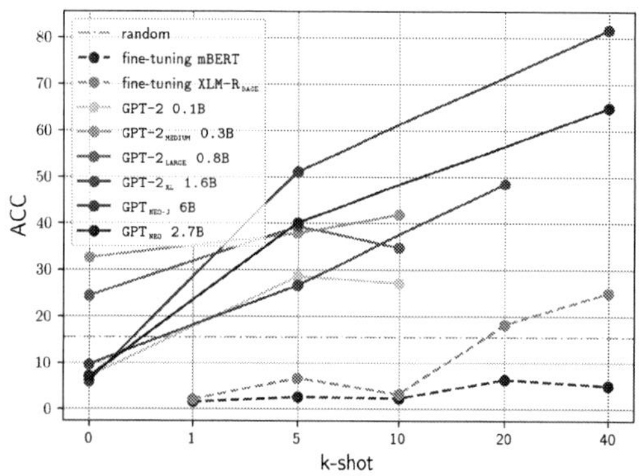


Figure 13: The acc results on the cross-lingual setting, English-Spanish (es) MTOP dataset with GPT models.

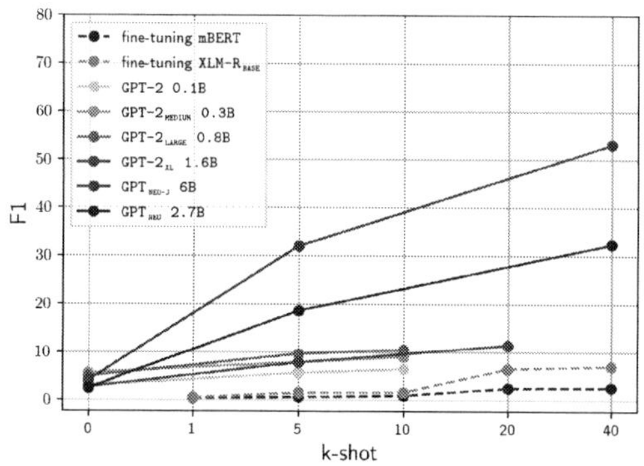


Figure 14: The f1 results on the cross-lingual setting, English-Spanish (es) MTOP dataset with GPT models.

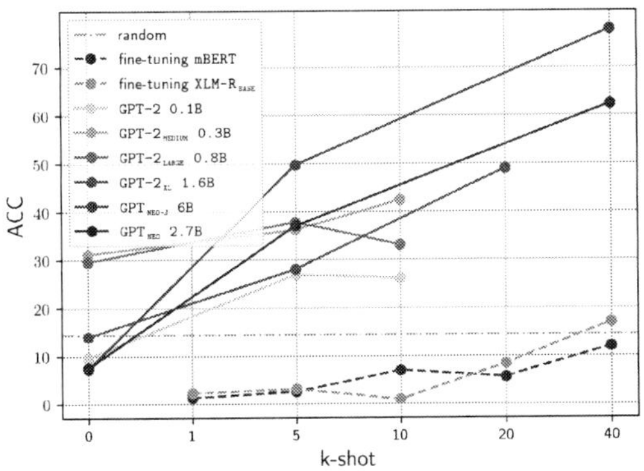


Figure 15: The acc results on the cross-lingual setting, English-French (fr) MTOP dataset with GPT models.

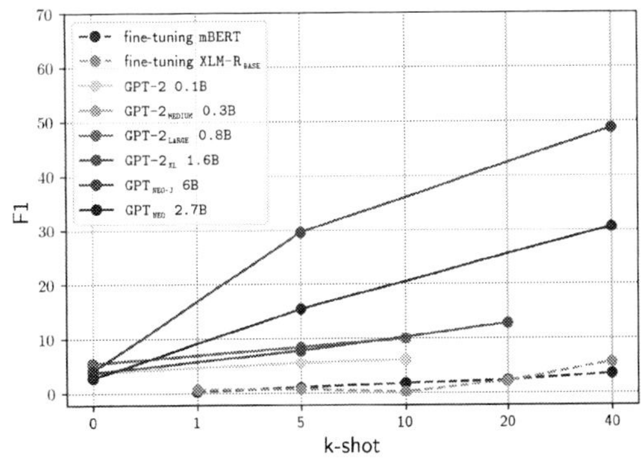


Figure 16: The f1 results on the cross-lingual setting, English-French (fr) MTOP dataset with GPT models.

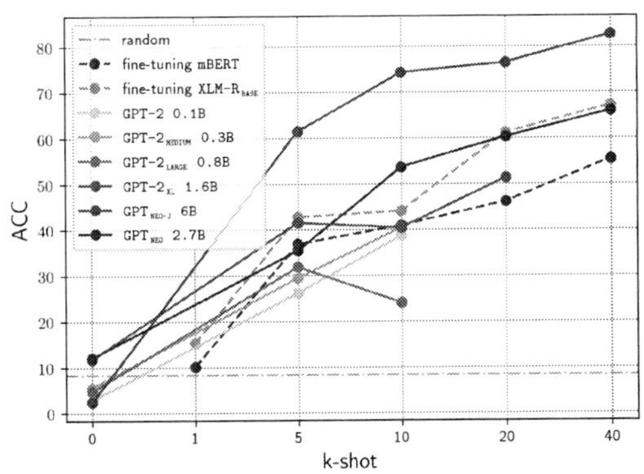


Figure 17: The acc results on the cross-lingual setting, English-Spanish (es) multilingual NLU dataset with GPT models.

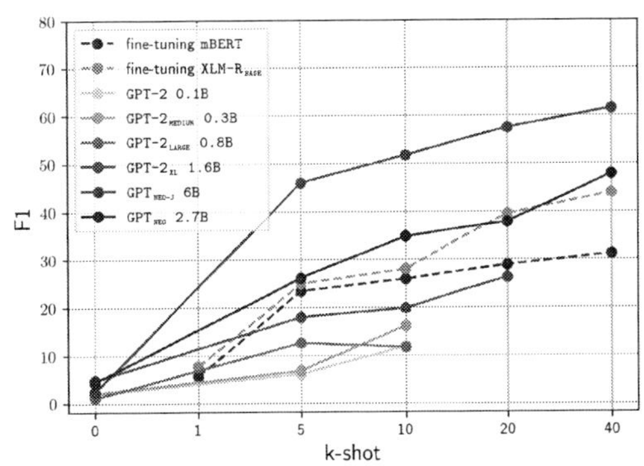


Figure 18: The f1 results on the cross-lingual setting, English-Spanish (es) multilingual NLU dataset with GPT models.

# Learning Contextualised Cross-lingual Word Embeddings and Alignments for Extremely Low-Resource Languages Using Parallel Corpora

**Takashi Wada**[1*] **Tomoharu Iwata**[2,3] **Yuji Matsumoto**[3*] **Timothy Baldwin**[1] **Jey Han Lau**[1]

[1] School of Computing and Information Systems, The University of Melbourne
[2] NTT Communication Science Laboratories
[3] RIKEN Center for Advanced Intelligence Project (AIP)
twada@student.unimelb.edu.au,
tomoharu.iwata.gy@hco.ntt.co.jp, yuji.matsumoto@riken.jp,
{tbaldwin, jeyhan.lau}@unimelb.edu.au

## Abstract

We propose a new approach for learning contextualised cross-lingual word embeddings based on a small parallel corpus (e.g. a few hundred sentence pairs). Our method obtains word embeddings via an LSTM encoder-decoder model that simultaneously translates and reconstructs an input sentence. Through sharing model parameters among different languages, our model jointly trains the word embeddings in a common cross-lingual space. We also propose to combine word and subword embeddings to make use of orthographic similarities across different languages. We base our experiments on real-world data from endangered languages, namely Yongning Na, Shipibo-Konibo, and Griko. Our experiments on bilingual lexicon induction and word alignment tasks show that our model outperforms existing methods by a large margin for most language pairs. These results demonstrate that, contrary to common belief, an encoder-decoder translation model is beneficial for learning cross-lingual representations even in extremely low-resource conditions. Furthermore, our model also works well on high-resource conditions, achieving state-of-the-art performance on a German-English word-alignment task.[1]

## 1 Introduction

Cross-lingual word embedding learning has the goal of learning representations for words of different languages in a common space (Mikolov et al., 2013b; Conneau et al., 2018; Levy et al., 2017). Cross-lingual representations are beneficial for finding correspondences between languages, and are utilised in many downstream tasks such as machine translation (Lample et al., 2018; Artetxe et al., 2018b) and cross-lingual named entity recognition (Xie et al., 2018).

The recent trend in cross-lingual embedding models is to leverage an enormous amount of monolingual data for each of the target languages, e.g. by training word embeddings monolingually and mapping them into a common space. Another approach is to jointly train cross-lingual word embeddings in the same space. Recently, cross-lingual masked language models such as mBERT (Devlin et al., 2019) have succeeded in learning cross-lingual representations using large-scale monolingual data for multiple languages.

However, when dealing with endangered languages, there is generally no such large-scale corpus of monolingual data, and when trained under low-resource settings, modern pretraining methods do not perform well (Hu et al., 2020). In this paper, we propose a joint-training method that learns contextualised cross-lingual word embeddings using a small parallel corpus, of the scale and form constructed by field linguists for language documentation purposes. Compared to previous models based on parallel corpora, our model has two strengths: (1) while previous models extend bag-of-words models such as Skip-Gram (Mikolov et al., 2013a) and capture only rudimentary word order information, our model encodes sentences with LSTMs (Hochreiter and Schmidhuber, 1997) and generates contextualised word embeddings; and (2) our model trains subword-aware word embeddings and captures orthographic similarities among the languages.

We perform evaluation over bilingual lexicon induction and word alignment. Both tasks are extremely important to facilitate language documentation, revitalisation, and education of endangered languages. We run experiments targeting three endangered languages — Yongning Na, Shipibo-Konibo, and Griko (Section 3.1) — as well as four high-resource language pairs, and show that our model substantially outperforms strong baselines for most language pairs.

*This work was partially done at Nara Institute of Science and Technology.

[1]Our code is available at https://github.com/twadada/multilingual-nlm



*Proceedings of the 1st Workshop on Multilingual Representation Learning*, pages 16–31
November 11, 2021. ©2021 Association for Computational Linguistics

## 2 Methodology

### 2.1 Model Architecture

Our proposed model is based an LSTM[2] encoder-decoder model with attention (Luong et al., 2015b), trained with translation and reconstruction objectives (Figure 1). Suppose our model encodes a sentence $\langle x_1^s ..., x_N^s \rangle$ in the source language $s$ and decodes a sentence $\langle y_1^t ..., y_M^t \rangle$ in the target language $t$. The encoder employs bi-directional LSTMs $f$, which are shared among all languages:

$$r_i^s = E^s x_i^s, \quad (1)$$

$$u_1^s ..., u_N^s = f(r_1^s ..., r_N^s), \quad (2)$$

where $x_i^s$ denotes a one-hot vector. In cross-lingual tasks, we employ $r_i^s$ and $u_i^s$ as the static and contextualised word embeddings of $x_i^s$. Given the encoder states $u^s$, the decoders $\overrightarrow{g}^t$ and $\overleftarrow{g}^t$ translate (when $s \neq t$) or reconstruct (when $s = t$) the input sentence left-to-right and right-to-left. We train separate decoders for each language and direction to allow for the differences of word order.[3] Similar to ELMo (Peters et al., 2018), the decoding is performed independently in both directions:

$$r_i^t = E^t y_i^t, \quad (3)$$

$$p(y_1^t ..., y_M^t, \text{EOS}) = \prod_{i=1}^{M+1} p(y_i^t | \overrightarrow{h}_i, u^s),$$

$$\overrightarrow{h}_i = \overrightarrow{g}^t(\overrightarrow{h}_{i-1}, r_{i-1}^t),$$

$$p(\text{BOS}, y_1^t ..., y_M^t) = \prod_{i=0}^{M} p(y_{M-i}^t | \overleftarrow{h}_{M-i}, u^s),$$

$$\overleftarrow{h}_i = \overleftarrow{g}^t(\overleftarrow{h}_{i+1}, r_{i+1}^t).$$

The output layer and attention mechanism are shared across the two directions:

$$p(y_i^t | h_i, u^s, r^s) = \text{softmax}({E^t}^\top h_i'), \quad (4)$$

$$h_i' = W(\bar{u}_i^s + \bar{r}_i^s + h_i), \quad (5)$$

$$\bar{u}_i^s = \sum_{j=1}^{N} \alpha_{i,j}^t u_j^s, \quad \bar{r}_i^s = \sum_{j=1}^{N} \alpha_{i,j}^t r_j^s, \quad (6)$$

$$\alpha_{i,j}^t = \frac{\exp(h_i u_j^s)}{\sum_{k=1}^{N} \exp(h_i u_k^s)}, \quad (7)$$

[2]We use LSTM rather than Transformer (Vaswani et al., 2017) because LSTM is less sensitive to hyper-parameters and performs better at translation under extremely low resource conditions (Zhang et al., 2020).

[3]In our preliminary experiments, we have found that learning language-specific decoders improves cross-lingual embeddings for distant languages, e.g. SOV and SVO languages.

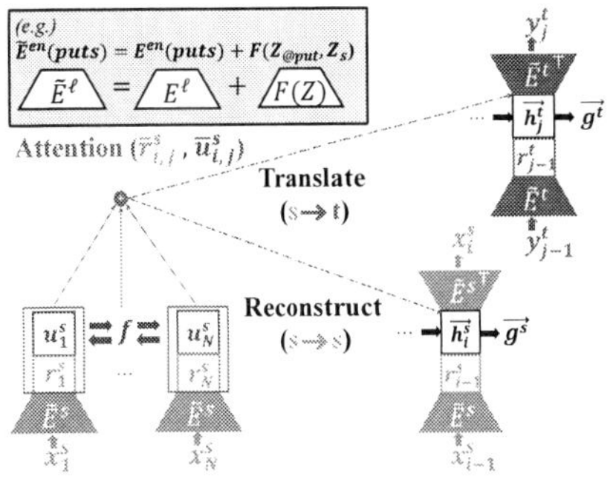


Figure 1: Our proposed model.

where $h_i$ denotes either $\overrightarrow{h_i}$ or $\overleftarrow{h_i}$, and $N$ is the number of words in the source sentence $x^s$. In Eqn. (4), we use the word embedding parameters $E^t$ for the output layer (weight tying: Inan et al. (2017); Press and Wolf (2017)). This technique can reduce the number of the language-specific parameters substantially, encouraging the model to use the same space across languages. When calculating attention weight in Eqn. (7), the model uses dot products of the encoder and decoder hidden states to encourage them to be in the same embedding space. In Eqn. (6), our model attends to the word embeddings as well as the hidden states to consider more direct relations between source and target word embeddings, i.e. ${r_i^t}^\top W \bar{r}_i^s$ directly contributes to the probability $p(y_i^t)$.[4] Furthermore, we employ very aggressive dropout (Srivastava et al., 2014), which is applied to all the input and output word embeddings $E^\ell$ in Eqns. (1), (3), and (4), as well as to $\bar{u}_i^s + \bar{r}_i^s + h_i$ in Eqn. (5) before the linear transformation, with the dropout rate all set to 0.5. We show that this strong regularisation leads to better cross-lingual representations.

### 2.2 Shared Subword Embeddings

To incorporate orthographic information into word embeddings, we propose a simple yet effective method to combine word and subword embeddings, inspired by FastText (Bojanowski et al., 2017). For each word $w_i^\ell$, we calculate its subword-aware word embedding $\tilde{E}_{w_i}^\ell$ as follows:

$$\tilde{E}_{w_i}^\ell = E_{w_i}^\ell + \text{F}(Z_{k \in \text{Q}(w_i)}), \quad (8)$$

[4]This simplifies the lexical model proposed by Nguyen and Chiang (2018). While they apply separate output layers to the weighted average of word embeddings and hidden states, we have found that sharing the same output layer ($E^t$) performed the best, suggesting that the optimal model architecture is different between word and sentence translations.

where F(·) denotes the subword encoding function; $Z_k$ denotes the $k$-th subword embedding and Q($w_i$) denotes the indices of the subwords included in $w_i$. The subword embeddings $Z$ are shared among all languages, capturing orthographic similarities across languages. For the encoding function F(·), we experiment with two methods:[5] (1) average pooling ("$\mathbf{SW_{ave}}$"); and (2) applying a convolutional neural network (CNN) function which is shared among all languages, followed by average pooling ("$\mathbf{SW_{cnn}}$"). For instance, the embedding of the English word *puts* is represented by its language-specific word embedding $E^{en}_{puts}$ and shared subword embeddings $Z_{@put}$ and $Z_s$, where @ in *@put* denotes the beginning of a word. To segment words into subwords, we apply SentencePiece (Kudo and Richardson, 2018).[6]

Distinct from a standard NMT model, we use the subword-aware embeddings $\tilde{E}^{\ell}$ not only as the input layers in Eqns. (1) and (3), but also as the output layer in Eqn. (4) (Figure 1). In this way, we encourage the model to learn subword correspondences between the source and target languages through attention, i.e. Eqns. (4) and (5). In monolingual language modelling, Assylbekov and Takhanov (2018) have previously shown the effectiveness of sharing morpheme-aware embeddings between the input and output layers.

### 2.3 Training

Given a parallel corpus aligned between languages $s$ and $t$, our model is trained to minimise the following training loss $J = J_{s,t} + J_{t,s}$, where $J_{s,t} = \sum_{j=1}^{C_{s,t}} \Delta(x_j, p(x^s_j|x^s_j)) + \Delta(y_j, p(y^t_j|x^s_j))$. Here, $C_{s,t}$ is the number of aligned sentences between languages $s$ and $t$, and $\Delta$ denotes the cross entropy loss. The first and second terms represent the reconstruction and translation loss, respectively. Our model can also take multiple parallel corpora as input and generate multilingual word embeddings. In this case, we sum the loss calculated on each parallel corpus. For instance, we train our multilingual model to minimise the loss $J = J_{nru,en} + J_{en,nru} + J_{nru,fr} + J_{fr,nru} + J_{nru,zh} + J_{zh,nru}$ given three parallel corpora of nru–en, nru–fr, and nru–zh,[7] where some sentences are aligned between more than two languages. To balance the corpus size, we perform oversampling to ensure that $C_{s,t}$ is the same regardless of the language pairs $s$ and $t$. Our model hyper-parameters are detailed in Appendix A.[8]

| src–tgt | #Sents | #Tokens | | #Vocab | |
|---|---|---|---|---|---|
| | | src | tgt | src | tgt |
| nru-en | 605 | 4,690 | 7,849 | 1,860 | 942 |
| nru-fr | 3,833 | 33,816 | 75,997 | 8,801 | 4,797 |
| nru-zh | 1,766 | 15,127 | 21,598 | 4,704 | 2,459 |
| shp-es | 14,276 | 198,024 | 214,127 | 20,654 | 14,781 |
| grk-it (s) | 330 | 2,374 | 2,384 | 689 | 456 |
| grk-it (l) | 9,788 | 207,294 | 178,980 | 12,697 | 9,813 |

Table 1: The statistics of the parallel corpora of endangered languages used in this paper. grk-it (s) and (l) denote the smaller and larger corpora, respectively.

## 3 Experiments

### 3.1 Data

We conduct experiments on real-world data sets for three endangered languages: Yongning Na (nru), Shipibo-Konibo (shp), and Griko (grk) (Table 1).[9] The URLs of the data are shown in Appendix B.

#### 3.1.1 Yongning Na

Yongning Na is an unwritten Sino-Tibetan language with less than 50,000 speakers (Do et al., 2014). Due to the lack of a writing system, textual data must be professionally transcribed from speech by linguists, which precludes the use of the latest pretraining methods such as BERT (Devlin et al., 2019). As a cross-lingual resource for Na, there exists a phonemically transcribed corpus that has been translated into French, Chinese, and English, which is a part of the Pangloss Collection (Michailovsky et al., 2014). However, there are two challenges in learning cross-lingual representations from this data. First, the syntax and orthography of the languages are very different: Na is an SOV language with rich tonal morphology (Michaud, 2017), while the others are SVO languages. Second, there is a lot of noise in the parallel corpora. For instance, some words or phrases in the translations are written in brackets, indicating alternative translations, subsidiary information, or words that are implicit in the original Na sentences (Table 2). To clean the data, we use the pre-

[5]Dropout is always applied to subword embeddings.

[6]We also tried using character n-grams like FastText, but observed worse results. For Chinese, we segment words into characters due to the large number of character types.

[7]"nru" is the ISO-639-3 language code for Na.

[8]They are tuned on a small subset of de-en or fr-en data.

[9]Note that Griko is not included in ISO-639-3, and "grk" is an arbitrary (non-assigned) designator used in this paper.

| | | |
|---|---|---|
| Na | raw | njɤ˧ \| ɑ˩ʁo˧ \| ə˧si˧-ɳɯ˧ ʐwɤ˩qʰv̩˩mv̩˩-hĩ˧ lɑ˩ ɲi˩ mæ˩! |
| | cln | njɤ˧ ɑ˩ʁo˧ ə˧si˧-ɳɯ˧ ʐwɤ˩qʰv˩mv˩-hĩ˧ lɑ˩ ɲi˩ mæ˩ |
| English | raw | It (i.e. this story) is only what (we've) heard our great-grandmother tell. |
| | cln | it is only what heard our great grandmother tell |

Table 2: An example Na–English parallel sentence before and after pre-processing ("raw" vs. "cln")

processing code used in Adams et al. (2017) with minor modifications.[10]

#### 3.1.2 Shipibo-Konibo

Shipibo-Konibo is an indigenous language spoken by around 35,000 native speakers in the Amazon region of Peru (Vasquez et al., 2018), and is "definitely endangered" according to the UNESCO's Atlas of the World's Languages in Danger (Moseley, 2010). There is no large monolingual corpus for the language,[11] but for cross-lingual resources there are two parallel corpora aligned with Spanish, which are extracted from the Bible and educational books (Galarreta et al., 2017). Similar to Na, Shipibo-Konibo is an SOV language with very rich morphology (Valenzuela, 1997; Vasquez et al., 2018), whereas Spanish is an SVO language.

#### 3.1.3 Griko

Griko is a Greek dialect spoken in southern Italy, and "severely endangered" according to UNESCO. There is no large-scale monolingual corpus of Griko, but there are two Griko–Italian parallel corpora (Zanon Boito et al., 2018; Anastasopoulos et al., 2018), with the smaller one including gold word alignment annotations. However, Griko has never had a consistent orthography, and hence its tokenisation and word segmentation differ across these corpora: the smaller data set is based on orthographic conventions from Italian, while the larger one follows the concept of a phonological word (Anastasopoulos et al., 2018). Unlike the Na and Shipibo-Konibo data sets, Griko and Italian are very similar in many ways: they both use the Latin script and have similar syntax. Therefore, the main challenge comes from the data paucity and inconsistent orthography in Griko, both of which are common problems for endangered languages.

### 3.2 Baselines

We compare our model against various cross-lingual models that are trained on a parallel corpus. First, we compare our model against a recently-proposed word-alignment model based on **mBERT** (Dou and Neubig, 2021).[12] It fine-tunes mBERT on parallel corpora using various cross-lingual objectives, and achieves state-of-the-art performance on word alignment tasks across many language pairs. We also include Levy et al. (2017), Luong et al. (2015a), and Sabet et al. (2020) as recent word embedding baselines, which we denote as **SENTID**, **BIVEC** and **BIS2V**, respectively. All of these baselines are very similar in terms of methodology: SENTID trains a Skip-Gram model that predicts a sentence ID (which is assigned to each set of parallel sentences) from the component words; BIVEC trains a Skip-Gram model that predicts the context cross-lingually based on the word-alignment information;[13] and BIS2V trains a Continuous Bag-of-Words (CBOW) model that predicts a target word from the rest of the sentence and its parallel sentence. Sabet et al. (2020) and Marie and Fujita (2019) show that these joint learning models perform better than mapping-based methods, which align monolingual word embeddings cross-lingually.[14] Regarding the vocabulary size and word embedding dimension, we always use the same values for all the baselines and our model, to ensure fairness.[15]

In addition to these neural baselines, we also compare our model against statistical word alignment methods, namely GIZA++ (Och and Ney, 2003) and Fast Align (Dyer et al., 2013). These are pre-neural methods based on the IBM models

[10] We use white space as the word delimiter and keep all tones in Na sentences, as removing tones increases polysemy in the bilingual dictionary we use for evaluation. For Chinese, we perform word segmentation using the Stanford Word Segmenter (Chang et al., 2008) after data cleaning.

[11] Recently, Bustamante et al. (2020) attempted to scrape monolingual data from PDF documents, but the size of the resulting data is still too small (22k sentences) to apply the latest pretraining methods.

[12] We used the bert-base-multilingual-cased model, following the original paper.

[13] We use Fast Align to generate the alignment.

[14] Besides, Wada et al. (2019) show that the mapping models perform very poorly on low-resource conditions. Based on these findings, we did not include them as our baselines.

[15] Except for the mBERT baseline, which has its pre-defined vocabulary and word embedding dimension, i.e. 768.

(Brown et al., 1993), and still serve as de facto standard models to generate word alignments (Cao et al., 2020; Aldarmaki and Diab, 2019). For all the baselines, we use the authors' implementations.[16]

### 3.3 Experimental Settings and Evaluation

In our experiments, we train cross-lingual embeddings for five low-resource language pairs: Griko–Italian, Shipibo-Konibo–Spanish and Na–{French, Chinese, English}. For the Griko–Italian pair, we evaluate models on a cross-lingual word alignment task and report alignment accuracy (1−AER). We use the gold alignments manually annotated over the 330 Griko–Italian sentences. To produce alignments using Giza++ and Fast Align, we train them on the 330 sentences with or without additional 10k sentences from a second corpus,[17] and combine forward and backward alignments using the grow-diag-final-and heuristic. For the word embedding-based methods, we train them on the same data, and align each word in a sentence to the closest word in its translation using static or contextualised word embeddings.[18] To calculate word similarity, we use cross-domain similarity local scaling (Conneau et al., 2018):

$$\mathrm{CSLS}(x,y) = 2\cos(x,y) - \frac{1}{K}\sum_{y_t \in \mathcal{N}_T(x)} \cos(x, y_t) - \frac{1}{K}\sum_{x_t \in \mathcal{N}_S(y)} \cos(x_t, y),$$

where $\cos(x, y)$ denotes cosine similarity between $x$ and $y$, and $\mathcal{N}_T(x)$ and $\mathcal{N}_S(y)$ denote the $K$ nearest words to $x$ or $y$ in a target or source sentence; we set $K$ to 3 in the word alignment task. For the mBERT baseline, we follow the authors in using the softmax function.[19]

For the Shipibo-Konibo–Spanish and Na–{French, Chinese, English} pairs, we perform bilingual lexicon induction (BLI). That is, for each source word in a bilingual dictionary, we extract the $k$ nearest words from the whole target vocabulary and see whether they are listed as translations in the dictionary. We set $k$ to 1 or 5, and report P@1 and P@5. For evaluation, we use a Shipibo-Konibo–Spanish dictionary[20] (Maguiño-Valencia et al., 2018) and Na–French–Chinese–English dictionaries (Michaud, 2018). Based on extracting words that are present in the parallel corpora, we identified 79, 262, 215 and 87 word pairs for Shipibo-Konibo–Spanish, Na–French, Na–Chinese, and Na–English.[21] To perform BLI with GIZA++ and Fast Align, we use their source-to-target probability table. We also try using the result of bidirectional word alignments, aligning each word to the most frequently aligned words to it.[22] For the neural baselines and our model, we use static word embeddings and employ CSLS to measure the word embedding similarities. To obtain static word embeddings using mBERT, we calculate the contextualised representations for each word (calculated as the average of its subword embeddings), and take the average over all word occurrences.[23] In BLI, $\mathcal{N}_T(x)$ and $\mathcal{N}_S(y)$ denote the $K$ closest words extracted from the whole vocabulary, with $K = 10$, following Conneau et al. (2018).

### 3.4 Model Selection

Since our evaluation data (i.e. bilingual dictionaries and gold word alignments) is extremely limited, we do not have access to validation data to perform model selection over. Therefore, for all methods except ours, we run the models with different configurations and **report the best scores of the baselines on the test data to show their upper-bound performance**, which clearly gives a significant advantage to the baselines.[24] For Fast Align and GIZA++, we train the models for 5 (default), 10, 15, or 20 iterations independently, and

[16] Fast Align: https://github.com/clab/fast_align, Giza++: https://github.com/moses-smt/giza-pp, SENTID: https://bitbucket.org/omerlevy/xling_embeddings/src/default, BIVEC: https://github.com/lmthang/bivec, BIS2V https://github.com/epfml/Bi-Sent2Vec, and mBERT https://github.com/neulab/awesome-align

[17] This is a standard training and evaluation setup for these unsupervised word alignment models: the main objective of word alignment is to extract equivalent words from parallel texts, not to perform translation on held-out data.

[18] We align words bidirectionally and use the grow-diag-final-and heuristic to produce the final result.

[19] We also experimented with the CSLS method and got comparable results.

[20] In this dictionary, sets of synonyms are aligned cross-lingually and we regard each member of them as translations.

[21] Since the Shipibo-Konibo–Spanish parallel corpora contain pairs of words as well as sentences, we include them in the evaluation data and remove them from training data.

[22] We use the probability tables as a backup when there are less than $k$ aligned words.

[23] We also tried taking the average of the static subword embeddings of mBERT, but observed much worse results.

[24] In addition, we tuned the hyper-parameters of BIS2V and BIVEC based on P@1 on the na–en test data, based on the observation that they were very sensitive to hyper-parameters in low-resource conditions (e.g. BIVEC ranged from 5.4 to 33.8 P@1 in the na–en BLI task). Refer to Appendix C for the hyper-parameters of the baselines we used in our experiments.

| src–tgt | P@$k$ | mBERT | SENTID | BIVEC | BIS2V | Fast Align | | GIZA++ | | OURS | | |
|---|---|---|---|---|---|---|---|---|---|---|---|---|
| | | MLM | SG | SG | CBOW | Ptable | +Align | Ptable | +Align | Word | $+SW_{ave}$ | $+SW_{cnn}$ |
| nru–en | 1 | 1.8 | 29.7 | 32.9 | 26.6 | 23.0 | 21.6 | 25.7 | 21.6 | 30.2 | 32.0 | **35.6** |
| | 5 | 4.1 | 50.9 | 50.4 | 44.6 | 48.6 | 50.0 | 43.2 | 47.3 | 50.9 | **56.3** | 51.8 |
| nru–fr | 1 | 0.2 | 22.7 | 23.6 | 19.6 | 23.6 | 20.8 | 22.2 | 15.7 | 27.3 | 29.9 | **32.1** |
| | 5 | 0.8 | 37.7 | 40.1 | 30.2 | 35.2 | 36.1 | 32.9 | 37.5 | 43.7 | **47.8** | 46.0 |
| nru–zh | 1 | 0.5 | 28.7 | 31.9 | 25.1 | 31.6 | 29.9 | 29.4 | 25.7 | 31.6 | 36.7 | **38.5** |
| | 5 | 1.2 | 44.8 | 50.6 | 46.0 | 46.0 | 44.4 | 44.4 | 46.5 | 49.6 | **56.1** | 55.4 |
| shp–es | 1 | 12.0 | 25.1 | 29.5 | 26.2 | 31.1 | 32.8 | 34.4 | 26.2 | 35.0 | 35.0 | **35.5** |
| | 5 | 18.0 | 45.9 | 43.7 | 38.8 | 47.5 | 47.5 | 42.6 | 45.9 | 54.6 | 57.9 | **59.0** |

Table 3: The performance on bilingual lexicon induction (BLI). "+Align" indicates bidirectional alignments are used with the probability table (Ptable) as backup. The scores of the neural models are averaged over three runs.

report the best score.[25] For the neural baselines, we evaluate each model-checkpoint and report the best score; we fine-tune the mBERT baseline for 40,000 steps[26] with 20 checkpoints, and train SENTID and BIS2V for 1,000 epochs with 100 checkpoints to ensure convergence. For BIVEC, we increase the training corpus size by 20 times by duplicating the sentences and train the model for 50 epochs with 50 checkpoints.[27]

For our model, on the other hand, we use a simple early-stopping criterion that doesn't require external data. First, we build a pseudo bilingual dictionary from the training data. To retrieve pseudo bilingual word pairs, we compute the Dice Coefficient (Dice, 1945; Smadja et al., 1996) and extract pairs of words that appear $\geq 3$ times in each language and whose Dice Coefficient is $\geq 0.8$ across two languages. We perform model selection based on the BLI performance on this pseudo dictionary.

### 3.5 Results

Table 3 shows the results for BLI.[28] We run the neural baselines and our model three times with different seeds and report the average score since neural models can be unstable with little data. It clearly shows that our model outperforms all the baseline models by a large margin for every language pair. It also shows that utilising shared subword embeddings (+SW$_{ave}$ and +SW$_{cnn}$) further improves

| src–tgt | Word | | +SW$_{ave}$ | | +SW$_{cnn}$ | |
|---|---|---|---|---|---|---|
| | bi | multi | bi | mult | bi | multi |
| nru–en | 30.2 | **34.2** | 32.0 | **37.8** | 35.6 | **40.5** |
| nru–fr | 27.3 | **28.7** | **29.9** | 29.8 | **32.1** | 30.7 |
| nru–zh | 31.6 | **36.9** | 36.7 | **40.1** | 38.5 | **40.8** |

Table 4: Our model performance (P@1) on BLI when the model is trained on two and four languages ("bi" vs. "multi"). All scores are averaged over three runs.

our model. Compared to the neural baselines, our model performs better even without subword information, demonstrating its efficiency. The mBERT baseline performs very poorly, likely because of its sub-optimal tokenisation for endangered languages. Table 4 compares our bilingual and multilingual models. The multilingual model is trained jointly on the three parallel corpora, sharing parameters among the four languages. The table shows that the multilingual model achieves better performance overall, especially for Na–English and Na–Chinese, where the number of the aligned sentences is much smaller than for Na–French. This result demonstrates that our model is not only able to embed multiple languages into the same space, but also benefits from extra sentences aligned between additional languages.

Table 5 shows the results for the Griko–Italian word alignment task. It shows that our model performs the best of all the models when they are trained on the 330 sentences only. This is particularly surprising given that encoder-decoder models are usually not effective when trained on small-scale data of magnitude 100s of sentence pairs. The result also shows that our model produces much better static word embeddings than SENTID, BIVEC and BIS2V, demonstrating the

[25]For GIZA++, we trained HMM and IBM models 1, 3, and 4 with the same number of iterations, following the default setting. We also tune the number of word classes chosen among {10, 20, 30, 40, 50}.

[26]This follows the original paper, and with those steps the model converged well in our experiments as well.

[27]Without this, it performed very poorly, likely because the code is optimised for reasonably-sized data. Moreover, we trained BIVEC using the word alignments produced by the best Fast Align model, and thus it's doubly optimised.

[28]We present an analysis of retrieved words in Appendix D.

| src–tgt | #Sents | mBERT | SENTID | BIVEC | BIS2V | Fast Align | GIZA++ | OURS | | | |
|---|---|---|---|---|---|---|---|---|---|---|---|
| | | MLM | SG | SG | CBOW | Align | Align | Word (static) | Word | $+SW_{\text{ave}}$ | $+SW_{\text{cnn}}$ |
| grk–it | 330 | 91.1 | 66.7 | 59.2 | 65.3 | 90.2 | 93.3 | 88.0 | 93.1 | 93.4 | **93.5** |
| | +10k | **93.1** | 61.8 | 56.1 | 58.1 | 87.1 | 81.0 | 86.6 | 92.6 | 93.0 | 93.0 |

Table 5: The performance (1−AER) on the Griko-Italian word alignment task with or without additional 10k parallel sentences. "Word (static)" is the result when our model uses static word embeddings instead of contextualised ones. The scores of the neural models are averaged over three runs.

importance of considering word order information. When we use the additional 10k sentences, the performance of the baselines drops substantially except for mBERT,[29] likely because of the differences in domains and tokenisation schemes, with the smaller Griko corpus closely following Italian norms. On the other hand, our model achieves good results under both conditions, indicating the robustness of our model to noisy real-world data.

### 3.6 Results on High-Resource Languages

To investigate how our model performs on high-resource conditions, we conduct additional word-alignment experiments on four high-resource language pairs: Japanese-English (ja-en), English-Inuktitut (en-iu), German-English (de-en), and English-French (en-fr). Regarding Inuktitut, there is no large-scale monolingual data, making it a salient test case for our model. We use benchmark word-alignment data sets for each language pair,[30] where the de-en and en-fr data sets contain about 2M and 1M parallel sentences, and the ja-en and en-iu ones about 0.3M. We apply SentencePiece to each corpus[31] and use them to train all the models except for mBERT, for which we use its pre-trained tokeniser. To perform word alignment, first we align subwords and align words if any of their subwords is aligned.[32] We use the same model selection criteria (Section 3.4) to report the upper bound of the baselines.[33]

[29]We conjecture this is because the additional data helped mBERT (esp. its positional embeddings) to learn that these two languages have very similar syntax.

[30]Kyoto Free Translation Task (Neubig, 2011) (ja-en); the Legislative Assembly of Nunavut (Martin et al., 2003) (en-iu); Europarl (Koehn, 2005) (de-en); and Canadian Hansards (Germann, 2001; Mihalcea and Pedersen, 2003) (en-fr).

[31]For the en-iu corpus, we segmented the Inuktitut sentences only, as there is a significant gap between the English and Inuktitut vocabulary size, i.e. 22k vs. 400k.

[32]GIZA++ and Fast Align also benefit from this method.

[33]We train the word embedding baselines for 100 epochs and the mBERT baseline for 40,000 steps with 20 checkpoints, and Fast Align and GIZA++ for 5, 10, 15 or 20 epochs, using 50 word classes (Moses default) for GIZA++.

| Model | en-iu | | | ja-en | | |
|---|---|---|---|---|---|---|
| | P | R | 1−A | P | R | 1−A |
| mBERT | 69.7 | 86.7 | 74.0 | 73.9 | 56.4 | 64.0 |
| SENTID | 72.9 | 86.3 | 75.3 | 57.7 | 46.8 | 51.7 |
| BIVEC | 67.4 | 84.4 | 70.3 | 56.3 | 46.1 | 50.7 |
| BIS2V | 65.2 | 82.8 | 68.4 | 52.3 | 41.3 | 46.2 |
| Fast Align | 80.5 | 96.0 | 82.8 | 61.7 | 51.7 | 56.3 |
| GIZA++ | 85.7 | 93.5 | 87.1 | 71.3 | 55.9 | 62.7 |
| OURS (static) | 73.1 | 88.6 | 75.6 | 59.4 | 48.0 | 53.1 |
| OURS | 83.5 | **99.3** | 85.6 | 62.7 | 65.5 | 64.1 |
| OURS$+SW_{\text{ave}}$ | 83.0 | 98.8 | 85.2 | 63.0 | **66.9** | 64.9 |
| OURS$+SW_{\text{ave}}$+null | **91.8** | 97.0 | **92.8** | **75.2** | 59.7 | **66.6** |

Table 6: Precision ("P"), Recall ("R") and 1−AER ("1−A") of word alignment on high-resource conditions. P and R are calculated based on possible and sure alignments, resp. "+null" denotes the result with null alignments.

Table 6 shows the results of the ja-en and en-iu word alignment experiments. It demonstrates that our model (OURS) significantly outperforms the other static word-embedding baselines. It also outperforms mBERT in en-iu and even in ja-en, which is very surprising given that mBERT is pre-trained on large-scale monolingual data for Japanese and English.[34] We also tried training our subword-aware model (OURS+$SW_{\text{ave}}$) by segmenting subwords into smaller word pieces and learning "subsubword" embeddings. The result shows that this approach improves our model for ja-en but not en-iu, probably because some Japanese characters (e.g. kanji) contain much semantic information. When compared to the word alignment tools, our model outperforms Fast Align and is comparable to GIZA++, achieving lower precision and higher recall. This is because, unlike GIZA++, our simple alignment algorithm based on CSLS cannot handle NULL alignments (untranslatable words) and generates more alignments than necessary. To handle those words, we apply the following heuristic: discard

[34]Inuktitut is not included in the training data of mBERT, accounting for its poor performance on en-iu.

| Model | Method | Training Data | de-en | en-fr |
|---|---|---|---|---|
| Jalili Sabet et al. (2020) | Masked LM | monolingual | 18.8 | 7.6 |
| Fast Align | Statistical Model | bilingual | 27.0 | 10.5 |
| eflomal | Statistical Model | bilingual | 22.6 | 8.2 |
| GIZA++ | Statistical Model | bilingual | 20.6 | 5.9 |
| Zenkel et al. (2020) | Pre-trained NMT+Aligner | bilingual | 16.0 | 5.0 |
| Chen et al. (2020) | Pre-trained NMT+Aligner | bilingual | 15.4 | 4.7 |
| Dou and Neubig (2021)+α-entmax | Fine-tuned Masked LM | monolingual+bilingual | 16.1 | **4.1** |
| Dou and Neubig (2021)+sotmax | Fine-tuned Masked LM | monolingual+bilingual | 15.6 | 4.4 |
| Dou and Neubig (2021)+α-entmax (β = 1) | Fine-tuned Masked LM | monolingual+multilingual | 15.0 | 4.5 |
| Dou and Neubig (2021)+sotmax (β = 1) | Fine-tuned Masked LM | monolingual+multilingual | 15.1 | 4.5 |
| OURS | NMT | bilingual | 16.4 | 9.1 |
| OURS +null | NMT | bilingual | **14.0** | 4.5 |

Table 7: Comparison of AER scores among various word alignment models. All the scores except for ours are cited from Dou and Neubig (2021). "+null" denotes the result with null alignments.

alignments between $x$ and $y$ if $\text{CSLS}(x, y) \leq 0$ or $\cos(x, y) \leq \min(\cos(x, \text{BOS}), \cos(\text{BOS}, y))$. This improves our model substantially ("**+null**" in Table 6) and it outperforms all the baselines.[35]

Lastly, Table 7 shows the results of the de-en and en-fr experiments. We cite the scores of the baselines from Dou and Neubig (2021), and report AER instead of 1−AER following the original table. It shows that "OURS +null" performs comparably to mBERT for en-fr (4.5 vs. 4.1), and outperforms it for de-en (14.0 vs. 15.0), establishing a new state-of-the-art with much less data and fewer parameters. The table also shows that our method is much simpler than the other NMT-based models (Zenkel et al., 2020; Chen et al., 2020), which pretrain an NMT model and then train an alignment model on top of it. Another important difference is that our model can produce cross-lingual representations while the NMT-based baselines can generate word alignments only.

### 3.7 Alignment with Pre-trained Embeddings

To employ large-scale monolingual data, we try initialising word embeddings of a high-resource language with pre-trained word embeddings, and train the word embeddings of a low-resource language in the same embedding space. During training, we freeze the pre-trained embeddings $E^{\ell}_{pre}$ and apply the element-wise operation $a \otimes E^{\ell}_{pre} + b$, where $a$ and $b$ are trainable vectors and shared among all the words in $E^{\ell}_{pre}$. For the other words, we train subword-aware embeddings ($SW_{\text{ave}}$) from scratch.

[35] For grk-it, the performance (1−AER) slightly dropped, e.g. "$+SW_{\text{cnn}}$+null" achieved 92.3/93.2 w/w.o the 10k sentences, likely because there are very few NULL alignments.

| Model | Source | Retrieved Words (Top 3) |
|---|---|---|
| BIVEC<br>OURS<br>+ Pre | ʐo˩<br>(lunch,<br>noon) | **lunch**, woman, lunchtime<br>**lunch**, lunchtime, outside<br>**lunch**, lunchtime, dinner |
| BIVEC<br>OURS<br>+ Pre | ʈʂʰɯ˧-qo˧<br>(here) | **here**, fireplace, beam<br>**here**, sat, there<br>**here**, there, where |
| BIVEC<br>OURS<br>+ Pre | kwɑ˧tsʰɑ˧<br>(coffin) | **coffin**, rush, near<br>**coffin**, rush, placed<br>**coffin**, cremated, corpse |

Table 8: Examples of retrieved words on nru-en BLI. "+ Pre" denotes the use of pre-trained embeddings.

We conduct an experiment on nru-en, where we pre-train English word embeddings using FastText on 10M sentences sampled from web-crawled data, OSCAR (Ortiz Suárez et al., 2020). The model achieves 30.6/52.3 on P@1/5, underperforming OURS$+SW_{\text{ave}}$ without pre-training (32.0/56.3), possibly because of the domain difference between the parallel and monolingual data. However, a closer look at the matched words reveals that pre-training can improve the retrieval performance in several cases, as shown in Table 8 (more examples are in Appendix D). It shows that even though all the models successfully match the correct words, our models retrieve more relevant words to the target word, especially when trained with pre-trained embeddings. This suggests that pre-training may benefit the model on other semantic tasks. Pre-training also makes it possible to measure the similarities between Na words and English words that are out-of-vocabulary in the parallel corpus.

| Model | nru | | | | ja-en |
|---|---|---|---|---|---|
| | en | fr | zh | multi | |
| OURS+$SW_{\text{ave}}$ (+null) | **32.0** | **29.9** | 36.7 | **35.9** | **66.6** |
| −(sub)subword | 30.2 | 27.3 | 31.6 | 33.3 | 65.9 |
| −$E^{\ell}_{w_i}$ in Eqn. (8) | 27.5 | 21.4 | **40.8** | 28.2 | 59.7 |
| −Bkw ($\overleftarrow{g}$) | 30.2 | 28.6 | 34.9 | 33.1 | 64.8 |
| −dropout | 27.9 | 25.1 | 29.6 | 27.0 | 60.3 |
| −weight tying | 24.3 | 23.4 | 29.0 | 32.5 | 63.9 |
| −reconstuction | 0.9 | 1.2 | 0.4 | 34.8 | 36.5 |

Table 9: Ablation results for our model (P@1 (nru) or 1−AER (ja-en)). "multi" indicates the average P@1 of our multilingual model over the three language pairs.

### 3.8 Ablation Studies

To investigate the effectiveness of our model, we perform ablation studies, targeting: shared subword embeddings, word-specific embeddings $E^{\ell}_{w_i}$ in Eqn. (8), backward decoding, dropout, weight tying, and the reconstruction objective. Table 9 shows the results. Without the reconstruction loss (i.e. the standard NMT model), the model performs very poorly in the bilingual settings. In the multilingual setting, however, the reconstruction is not essential because the model is trained to translate multiple languages into Na, which forces the source languages to be encoded in the same space. The table also shows that weight tying is very effective. We find this result intriguing, as usually it does not affect translation quality very much (Press and Wolf, 2017). In our model, however, weight tying is crucial in two ways: first, it reduces the number of parameters and prevents the model from learning word embeddings in different spaces; and second, it introduces more direct connections between source and target (sub)word embeddings through attention. Aggressive dropout is also effective in all the conditions, preventing the model from learning language-specific embeddings using different spaces. Word-specific embeddings also improve the model performance except for nru-zh.[36] Lastly, backward decoding also improves performance, incorporating right-to-left contexts into the word embeddings.

## 4 Related Work

There are two main approaches to learning cross-lingual word embeddings. One is to learn a matrix that aligns pretrained monolingual embeddings. Most such methods exploit bilingual dictionaries to learn the mapping matrix (Mikolov et al., 2013b; Xing et al., 2015; Joulin et al., 2018), but recently a number of methods have succeeded in learning the matrix without supervision (Zhang et al., 2017; Conneau et al., 2018; Artetxe et al., 2018a). However, Wada et al. (2019) show that this approach does not work well on low-resource conditions. The second approach is to jointly train cross-lingual embeddings in a common space. Most existing methods extend bag-of-words models (e.g. Skip-Gram) to incorporate cross-lingual information provided by parallel or comparable corpora (Hermann and Blunsom, 2014; Vulic and Moens, 2016; Levy et al., 2017; Dufter et al., 2018a,b; Luong et al., 2015a; Sabet et al., 2020; Sarioglu Kayi et al., 2020), or bilingual dictionaries (Gouws and Søgaard, 2015; Duong et al., 2016). Recently, masked language models such as XLM (Conneau and Lample, 2019) and mBERT (Devlin et al., 2019) have been shown to generate cross-lingual representations without parallel data, but require an enormous amount of monolingual data, which is not available for endangered languages.

Similar to our work, some papers use multilingual neural machine translation models to obtain cross-lingual representations (Eriguchi et al., 2018; Schwenk and Douze, 2017; Artetxe and Schwenk, 2019; Schwenk, 2018). However, they employ extremely large and/or multilingual data aligned among more than two languages (e.g. Europarl, United Nations). Another important difference is that their methods focus on learning cross-lingual *sentence* representations only (i.e. not at the word level), and are evaluated on cross-lingual sentence retrieval or sentence classification tasks.

## 5 Conclusion

We propose a new approach for learning contextualised cross-lingual word embeddings that can be trained with a tiny parallel corpus. We evaluate models on real-world data for three endangered languages, and also on benchmark data sets for four high-resource languages, and show that our model outperforms existing methods at bilingual lexicon induction and word alignment.

## 6 Acknowledgement

We are grateful to Oliver Adams and Alexis Michaud for providing us with the pre-processing code and detailed instructions for Na data.

[36] This is likely because Chinese words can be represented well by their component characters (Li et al., 2019). However, in "mutli", $E^{\ell}_{w_i}$ is beneficial for nru-zh as well.

## References


Oliver Adams, Adam Makarucha, Graham Neubig, Steven Bird, and Trevor Cohn. 2017. Cross-lingual word embeddings for low-resource language modeling. In *Proceedings of the 15th Conference of the European Chapter of the Association for Computational Linguistics: Volume 1, Long Papers*, pages 937–947, Valencia, Spain. Association for Computational Linguistics.

Hanan Aldarmaki and Mona Diab. 2019. Context-aware cross-lingual mapping. In *Proceedings of the 2019 Conference of the North American Chapter of the Association for Computational Linguistics: Human Language Technologies, Volume 1 (Long and Short Papers)*, pages 3906–3911, Minneapolis, Minnesota. Association for Computational Linguistics.

Antonios Anastasopoulos, Marika Lekakou, Josep Quer, Eleni Zimianiti, Justin DeBenedetto, and David Chiang. 2018. Part-of-speech tagging on an endangered language: a parallel Griko-Italian resource. In *Proceedings of the 27th International Conference on Computational Linguistics*, pages 2529–2539, Santa Fe, New Mexico, USA. Association for Computational Linguistics.

Mikel Artetxe, Gorka Labaka, and Eneko Agirre. 2018a. A robust self-learning method for fully unsupervised cross-lingual mappings of word embeddings. In *Proceedings of the 56th Annual Meeting of the Association for Computational Linguistics (Volume 1: Long Papers)*, pages 789–798, Melbourne, Australia. Association for Computational Linguistics.

Mikel Artetxe, Gorka Labaka, Eneko Agirre, and Kyunghyun Cho. 2018b. Unsupervised neural machine translation. In *Proceedings of the 6th International Conference on Learning Representations*, Vancouver, BC, Canada.

Mikel Artetxe and Holger Schwenk. 2019. Massively multilingual sentence embeddings for zero-shot cross-lingual transfer and beyond. *Transactions of the Association for Computational Linguistics*, 7:597–610.

Zhenisbek Assylbekov and Rustem Takhanov. 2018. Reusing weights in subword-aware neural language models. In *Proceedings of the 2018 Conference of the North American Chapter of the Association for Computational Linguistics: Human Language Technologies, Volume 1 (Long Papers)*, pages 1413–1423, New Orleans, Louisiana. Association for Computational Linguistics.

Piotr Bojanowski, Edouard Grave, Armand Joulin, and Tomas Mikolov. 2017. Enriching word vectors with subword information. *Transactions of the Association for Computational Linguistics*, 5:135–146.

Peter F. Brown, Stephen A. Della Pietra, Vincent J. Della Pietra, and Robert L. Mercer. 1993. The mathematics of statistical machine translation: Parameter estimation. *Computational Linguistics*, 19(2):263–311.

Gina Bustamante, Arturo Oncevay, and Roberto Zariquiey. 2020. No data to crawl? monolingual corpus creation from PDF files of truly low-resource languages in Peru. In *Proceedings of the 12th Language Resources and Evaluation Conference*, pages 2914–2923, Marseille, France. European Language Resources Association.

Steven Cao, Nikita Kitaev, and Dan Klein. 2020. Multilingual alignment of contextual word representations. In *Proceedings of the 8th International Conference on Learning Representations*, Virtual Conference, Formerly Addis Ababa, Ethiopia.

Pi-Chuan Chang, Michel Galley, and Christopher D. Manning. 2008. Optimizing Chinese word segmentation for machine translation performance. In *Proceedings of the Third Workshop on Statistical Machine Translation*, pages 224–232, Columbus, Ohio. Association for Computational Linguistics.

Yun Chen, Yang Liu, Guanhua Chen, Xin Jiang, and Qun Liu. 2020. Accurate word alignment induction from neural machine translation. In *Proceedings of the 2020 Conference on Empirical Methods in Natural Language Processing (EMNLP)*, pages 566–576, Online. Association for Computational Linguistics.

Alexis Conneau and Guillaume Lample. 2019. Cross-lingual language model pretraining. In H. Wallach, H. Larochelle, A. Beygelzimer, F. d'Alché-Buc, E. Fox, and R. Garnett, editors, *Advances in Neural Information Processing Systems 32*, pages 7059–7069. Curran Associates, Inc.

Alexis Conneau, Guillaume Lample, Marc'Aurelio Ranzato, Ludovic Denoyer, and Hervé Jégou. 2018. Word translation without parallel data. In *Proceedings of the 6th International Conference on Learning Representations*, Vancouver, BC, Canada.

Jacob Devlin, Ming-Wei Chang, Kenton Lee, and Kristina Toutanova. 2019. BERT: Pre-training of deep bidirectional transformers for language understanding. In *Proceedings of the 2019 Conference of the North American Chapter of the Association for Computational Linguistics: Human Language Technologies, Volume 1 (Long and Short Papers)*, pages 4171–4186, Minneapolis, Minnesota. Association for Computational Linguistics.

Lee R. Dice. 1945. Measures of the amount of ecologic association between species. *Ecology*, 26(3):297–302.

Thi-Ngoc-Diep Do, Alexis Michaud, and Eric Castelli. 2014. Towards the automatic processing of Yongning Na (Sino-Tibetan): developing a 'light' acoustic model of the target language and testing 'heavyweight' models from five national languages. In *4th International Workshop on Spoken Language Technologies for Under-resourced Languages (SLTU 2014)*, pages 153–160, St Petersburg, Russia.

Zi-Yi Dou and Graham Neubig. 2021. Word alignment by fine-tuning embeddings on parallel corpora. In *Proceedings of the 16th Conference of the European Chapter of the Association for Computational Linguistics: Main Volume*, pages 2112–2128, Online. Association for Computational Linguistics.

Philipp Dufter, Mengjie Zhao, Martin Schmitt, Alexander Fraser, and Hinrich Schütze. 2018a. Embedding learning through multilingual concept induction. In *Proceedings of the 56th Annual Meeting of the Association for Computational Linguistics (Volume 1: Long Papers)*, pages 1520–1530, Melbourne, Australia. Association for Computational Linguistics.

Philipp Dufter, Mengjie Zhao, and Hinrich Schütze. 2018b. Multilingual embeddings jointly induced from contexts and concepts: Simple, strong and scalable. *CoRR*, abs/1811.00586.

Long Duong, Hiroshi Kanayama, Tengfei Ma, Steven Bird, and Trevor Cohn. 2016. Learning crosslingual word embeddings without bilingual corpora. In *Proceedings of the 2016 Conference on Empirical Methods in Natural Language Processing*, pages 1285–1295, Austin, Texas. Association for Computational Linguistics.

Chris Dyer, Victor Chahuneau, and Noah A. Smith. 2013. A simple, fast, and effective reparameterization of IBM model 2. In *Proceedings of the 2013 Conference of the North American Chapter of the Association for Computational Linguistics: Human Language Technologies*, pages 644–648, Atlanta, Georgia. Association for Computational Linguistics.

Akiko Eriguchi, Melvin Johnson, Orhan Firat, Hideto Kazawa, and Wolfgang Macherey. 2018. Zero-shot cross-lingual classification using multilingual neural machine translation. *CoRR*, abs/1809.04686.

Ana-Paula Galarreta, Andrés Melgar, and Arturo Oncevay. 2017. Corpus creation and initial SMT experiments between Spanish and Shipibo-Konibo. In *Proceedings of the International Conference Recent Advances in Natural Language Processing, RANLP 2017*, pages 238–244, Varna, Bulgaria. INCOMA Ltd.

U. Germann. 2001. Aligned hansards of the 36th parliament of canada.

Stephan Gouws and Anders Søgaard. 2015. Simple task-specific bilingual word embeddings. In *Proceedings of the 2015 Conference of the North American Chapter of the Association for Computational Linguistics: Human Language Technologies*, pages 1386–1390, Denver, Colorado. Association for Computational Linguistics.

Karl Moritz Hermann and Phil Blunsom. 2014. Multilingual models for compositional distributed semantics. In *Proceedings of the 52nd Annual Meeting of the Association for Computational Linguistics (Volume 1: Long Papers)*, pages 58–68, Baltimore, Maryland. Association for Computational Linguistics.

Sepp Hochreiter and Jürgen Schmidhuber. 1997. Long short-term memory. *Neural Computation*, 9(8):1735–1780.

Junjie Hu, Sebastian Ruder, Aditya Siddhant, Graham Neubig, Orhan Firat, and Melvin Johnson. 2020. Xtreme: A massively multilingual multi-task benchmark for evaluating cross-lingual generalization. *CoRR*, abs/2003.11080.

Hakan Inan, Khashayar Khosravi, and Richard Socher. 2017. Tying word vectors and word classifiers: A loss framework for language modeling. In *Proceedings of the 5th International Conference on Learning Representations*, Toulon, France.

Masoud Jalili Sabet, Philipp Dufter, François Yvon, and Hinrich Schütze. 2020. SimAlign: High quality word alignments without parallel training data using static and contextualized embeddings. In *Findings of the Association for Computational Linguistics: EMNLP 2020*, pages 1627–1643, Online. Association for Computational Linguistics.

Armand Joulin, Piotr Bojanowski, Tomas Mikolov, Hervé Jégou, and Edouard Grave. 2018. Loss in translation: Learning bilingual word mapping with a retrieval criterion. In *Proceedings of the 2018 Conference on Empirical Methods in Natural Language Processing*, pages 2979–2984, Brussels, Belgium. Association for Computational Linguistics.

Diederik P. Kingma and Jimmy Ba. 2015. Adam: A method for stochastic optimization. In *Proceedings of the 3rd International Conference on Learning Representations*.

Philipp Koehn. 2005. Europarl: A Parallel Corpus for Statistical Machine Translation. In *Conference Proceedings: the tenth Machine Translation Summit*, Phuket, Thailand. Asia-Pacific Association for Machine Translation.

Taku Kudo and John Richardson. 2018. SentencePiece: A simple and language independent subword tokenizer and detokenizer for neural text processing. In *Proceedings of the 2018 Conference on Empirical Methods in Natural Language Processing: System Demonstrations*, pages 66–71, Brussels, Belgium. Association for Computational Linguistics.

Guillaume Lample, Alexis Conneau, Ludovic Denoyer, and Marc'Aurelio Ranzato. 2018. Unsupervised machine translation using monolingual corpora only. In *Proceedings of the 6th International Conference on Learning Representations*, Vancouver, BC, Canada.

Omer Levy, Anders Søgaard, and Yoav Goldberg. 2017. A strong baseline for learning cross-lingual word embeddings from sentence alignments. In *Proceedings of the 15th Conference of the European Chapter of the Association for Computational Linguistics: Volume 1, Long Papers*, pages 765–774, Valencia, Spain. Association for Computational Linguistics.

Xiaoya Li, Yuxian Meng, Xiaofei Sun, Qinghong Han, Arianna Yuan, and Jiwei Li. 2019. Is word segmentation necessary for deep learning of Chinese representations? In *Proceedings of the 57th Annual Meeting of the Association for Computational Linguistics*, pages 3242–3252, Florence, Italy. Association for Computational Linguistics.

Thang Luong, Hieu Pham, and Christopher D. Manning. 2015a. Bilingual word representations with monolingual quality in mind. In *Proceedings of the 1st Workshop on Vector Space Modeling for Natural Language Processing*, pages 151–159, Denver, Colorado. Association for Computational Linguistics.

Thang Luong, Hieu Pham, and Christopher D. Manning. 2015b. Effective approaches to attention-based neural machine translation. In *Proceedings of the 2015 Conference on Empirical Methods in Natural Language Processing*, pages 1412–1421, Lisbon, Portugal. Association for Computational Linguistics.

Diego Maguiño-Valencia, Arturo Oncevay-Marcos, and Marco A. Sobrevilla Cabezudo. 2018. WordNet-shp: Towards the building of a lexical database for a Peruvian minority language. In *Proceedings of the Eleventh International Conference on Language Resources and Evaluation (LREC-2018)*, Miyazaki, Japan. European Languages Resources Association (ELRA).

Benjamin Marie and Atsushi Fujita. 2019. Unsupervised joint training of bilingual word embeddings. In *Proceedings of the 57th Annual Meeting of the Association for Computational Linguistics*, pages 3224–3230, Florence, Italy. Association for Computational Linguistics.

Joel Martin, Howard Johnson, Benoit Farley, and Anna Maclachlan. 2003. Aligning and using an English-Inuktitut parallel corpus. In *Proceedings of the HLT-NAACL 2003 Workshop on Building and Using Parallel Texts: Data Driven Machine Translation and Beyond*, pages 115–118.

Boyd Michailovsky, Martine Mazaudon, Alexis Michaud, Séverine Guillaume, Alexandre François, and Evangelia Adamou. 2014. Documenting and researching endangered languages: the Pangloss Collection. In *Language Documentation & Conservation*, volume 8, pages 119–135. "University of Hawaii Press".

Alexis Michaud. 2017. *Tone in Yongning Na: lexical tones and morphotonology*, volume 13 of *Studies in Diversity Linguistics*. Language Science Press.

Alexis Michaud. 2018. Na (Mosuo)-English-Chinese dictionary. https://halshs.archives-ouvertes.fr/halshs-01204638, Version 1.2.

Rada Mihalcea and Ted Pedersen. 2003. An evaluation exercise for word alignment. In *Proceedings of the HLT-NAACL 2003 Workshop on Building and Using Parallel Texts: Data Driven Machine Translation and Beyond*, pages 1–10.

Tomas Mikolov, Kai Chen, Greg Corrado, and Jeffrey Dean. 2013a. Efficient estimation of word representations in vector space. In *Proceedings of the 1st International Conference on Learning Representations (Workshop)*, Scottsdale, Arizona, USA.

Tomas Mikolov, Quoc V. Le, and Ilya Sutskever. 2013b. Exploiting similarities among languages for machine translation. *CoRR*, abs/1309.4168.

Christopher Moseley, editor. 2010. *Atlas of the World's Languages in Danger, 3rd edn.* UNESCO Publishing, Paris. Online version: http://www.unesco.org/culture/en/endangeredlanguages/atlas.

Graham Neubig. 2011. The Kyoto free translation task. http://www.phontron.com/kftt.

Toan Nguyen and David Chiang. 2018. Improving lexical choice in neural machine translation. In *Proceedings of the 2018 Conference of the North American Chapter of the Association for Computational Linguistics: Human Language Technologies, Volume 1 (Long Papers)*, pages 334–343, New Orleans, Louisiana. Association for Computational Linguistics.

Franz Josef Och and Hermann Ney. 2003. A systematic comparison of various statistical alignment models. *Computational Linguistics*, 29(1):19–51.

Pedro Javier Ortiz Suárez, Laurent Romary, and Benoît Sagot. 2020. A monolingual approach to contextualized word embeddings for mid-resource languages. In *Proceedings of the 58th Annual Meeting of the Association for Computational Linguistics*, pages 1703–1714, Online. Association for Computational Linguistics.

Adam Paszke, Sam Gross, Francisco Massa, Adam Lerer, James Bradbury, Gregory Chanan, Trevor Killeen, Zeming Lin, Natalia Gimelshein, Luca Antiga, Alban Desmaison, Andreas Kopf, Edward Yang, Zachary DeVito, Martin Raison, Alykhan Tejani, Sasank Chilamkurthy, Benoit Steiner, Lu Fang, Junjie Bai, and Soumith Chintala. 2019. Pytorch: An imperative style, high-performance deep learning library. In H. Wallach, H. Larochelle, A. Beygelzimer, F. d'Alché-Buc, E. Fox, and R. Garnett, editors, *Advances in Neural Information Processing Systems 32*, pages 8024–8035. Curran Associates, Inc.

Matthew Peters, Mark Neumann, Mohit Iyyer, Matt Gardner, Christopher Clark, Kenton Lee, and Luke Zettlemoyer. 2018. Deep contextualized word representations. In *Proceedings of the 2018 Conference of the North American Chapter of the Association for Computational Linguistics: Human Language Technologies, Volume 1 (Long Papers)*, pages 2227–2237,

New Orleans, Louisiana. Association for Computational Linguistics.

Ofir Press and Lior Wolf. 2017. Using the output embedding to improve language models. In *Proceedings of the 15th Conference of the European Chapter of the Association for Computational Linguistics: Volume 2, Short Papers*, pages 157–163, Valencia, Spain. Association for Computational Linguistics.

Ali Sabet, Prakhar Gupta, Jean-Baptiste Cordonnier, Robert West, and Martin Jaggi. 2020. Robust cross-lingual embeddings from parallel sentences. *ArXiv 1912.12481*.

Efsun Sarioglu Kayi, Vishal Anand, and Smaranda Muresan. 2020. MultiSeg: Parallel data and subword information for learning bilingual embeddings in low resource scenarios. In *Proceedings of the 1st Joint Workshop on Spoken Language Technologies for Under-resourced languages (SLTU) and Collaboration and Computing for Under-Resourced Languages (CCURL)*, pages 97–105, Marseille, France. European Language Resources association.

Holger Schwenk. 2018. Filtering and mining parallel data in a joint multilingual space. In *Proceedings of the 56th Annual Meeting of the Association for Computational Linguistics (Volume 2: Short Papers)*, pages 228–234, Melbourne, Australia. Association for Computational Linguistics.

Holger Schwenk and Matthijs Douze. 2017. Learning joint multilingual sentence representations with neural machine translation. In *Proceedings of the 2nd Workshop on Representation Learning for NLP*, pages 157–167, Vancouver, Canada. Association for Computational Linguistics.

Frank Smadja, Kathleen R. McKeown, and Vasileios Hatzivassiloglou. 1996. Translating collocations for bilingual lexicons: A statistical approach. *Computational Linguistics*, 22(1):1–38.

Nitish Srivastava, Geoffrey Hinton, Alex Krizhevsky, Ilya Sutskever, and Ruslan Salakhutdinov. 2014. Dropout: A simple way to prevent neural networks from overfitting. *Journal of Machine Learning Research*, 15:1929–1958.

Pilar M. Valenzuela. 1997. Basic verb types and argument structures in Shipibo-Conibo. Master's thesis, University of Oregon.

Alonso Vasquez, Renzo Ego Aguirre, Candy Angulo, John Miller, Claudia Villanueva, Željko Agić, Roberto Zariquiey, and Arturo Oncevay. 2018. Toward Universal Dependencies for Shipibo-Konibo. In *Proceedings of the Second Workshop on Universal Dependencies (UDW 2018)*, pages 151–161, Brussels, Belgium. Association for Computational Linguistics.

Ashish Vaswani, Noam Shazeer, Niki Parmar, Jakob Uszkoreit, Llion Jones, Aidan N Gomez, Ł ukasz Kaiser, and Illia Polosukhin. 2017. Attention is all you need. In I. Guyon, U. V. Luxburg, S. Bengio, H. Wallach, R. Fergus, S. Vishwanathan, and R. Garnett, editors, *Advances in Neural Information Processing Systems 30*, pages 5998–6008. Curran Associates, Inc.

Ivan Vulic and Marie-Francine Moens. 2016. Bilingual distributed word representations from document-aligned comparable data. *Journal of Artificial Intelligence Research*, 55(1):953–994.

Takashi Wada, Tomoharu Iwata, and Yuji Matsumoto. 2019. Unsupervised multilingual word embedding with limited resources using neural language models. In *Proceedings of the 57th Annual Meeting of the Association for Computational Linguistics*, pages 3113–3124, Florence, Italy. Association for Computational Linguistics.

Jiateng Xie, Zhilin Yang, Graham Neubig, Noah A. Smith, and Jaime Carbonell. 2018. Neural cross-lingual named entity recognition with minimal resources. In *Proceedings of the 2018 Conference on Empirical Methods in Natural Language Processing*, pages 369–379, Brussels, Belgium. Association for Computational Linguistics.

Chao Xing, Dong Wang, Chao Liu, and Yiye Lin. 2015. Normalized word embedding and orthogonal transform for bilingual word translation. In *Proceedings of the 2015 Conference of the North American Chapter of the Association for Computational Linguistics: Human Language Technologies*, pages 1006–1011. Association for Computational Linguistics.

Marcely Zanon Boito, Antonios Anastasopoulos, Aline Villavicencio, Laurent Besacier, and Marika Lekakou. 2018. A Small Griko-Italian Speech Translation Corpus. In *Proceedings of the 6th International Workshop on Spoken Language Technologies for Under-Resourced Languages*, pages 29–31, Gurugram, India. International Speech Communication Association.

Thomas Zenkel, Joern Wuebker, and John DeNero. 2020. End-to-end neural word alignment outperforms GIZA++. In *Proceedings of the 58th Annual Meeting of the Association for Computational Linguistics*, pages 1605–1617, Online. Association for Computational Linguistics.

Meng Zhang, Yang Liu, Huanbo Luan, and Maosong Sun. 2017. Adversarial training for unsupervised bilingual lexicon induction. In *Proceedings of the 55th Annual Meeting of the Association for Computational Linguistics (Volume 1: Long Papers)*, pages 1959–1970, Vancouver, Canada. Association for Computational Linguistics.

Shiyue Zhang, Benjamin Frey, and Mohit Bansal. 2020. ChrEn: Cherokee-English machine translation for endangered language revitalization. In *Proceedings of the 2020 Conference on Empirical Methods in Natural Language Processing (EMNLP)*, pages 577–595, Online. Association for Computational Linguistics.

| Parameter | Resource Condition | | |
|---|---|---|---|
| | low | medium | high |
| Epoch | 200/100 | 10 | 10 |
| Batch Size | 16 | 80 | 80 |
| Enc LSTM Layers | 1 | 2 | 3 |
| Dec LSTM Layers | 1 | 1 | 2 |
| Dropout Rate | 0.5 | 0.5 | 0.5 |
| Gradient Clipping | 5 | 5 | 5 |
| LSTM Hidden State | 500 | 500 | 768 |
| Word Embedding | 500 | 500 | 768 |
| Subword Embedding | 500 | 500 | – |
| CNN Hidden State | 500 | – | – |
| CNN Window Size | 3 | – | – |

Table 10: Hyper-parameters of our model in low- and high-resource experiments. The first column ("low") denotes the hyper-paramertes for low-resource languages, the second ("medium") for ja-en and iu-en, the last ("high") for de-en and en-fr. CNN is used in low-resource experiments only due to its high computational cost.

| src-tgt | OURS | | |
|---|---|---|---|
| | Word | $+SW_{\text{ave}}$ | $+SW_{\text{cnn}}$ |
| nru–en | 11.2 | 11.7 | 12.5 |
| nru–zh | 13.3 | 14.2 | 15.0 |
| nru–fr | 16.6 | 17.3 | 18.0 |
| grk–it (s) | 10.3 | 10.8 | 11.5 |
| grk–it (s+l) | 21.3 | 22.2 | 23.0 |
| shp–es | 27.5 | 28.4 | 29.2 |

Table 11: The number of parameters (in millions) of our model.

| src-tgt | #Sents | OURS | | |
|---|---|---|---|---|
| | | Word | $+SW_{\text{ave}}$ | $+SW_{\text{cnn}}$ |
| nru–en | 605 | 2 | 3 | 7 |
| nru–zh | 1766 | 8 | 10 | 45 |
| nru–fr | 3833 | 21 | 31 | 212 |
| shp–es | 14276 | 96 | 160 | 1382 |
| ja–en | 331024 | 1565 | 1795 | – |

Table 12: Run-time (in seconds) of our model per one epoch on a single GPU.

# A Details of Our Model

We report the details of our model to ensure reproducibility. Our model was trained using PyTorch (Paszke et al., 2019) on a single GPU.

## A.1 Hyper Parameters

Table 10 shows the hyper-parameters of our model. We tuned the hyper-parameters on low and medium conditions using a subset of the de-en or en-fr data sets. We used the same embedding size in both low and medium resource conditions for simplicity. For very high-resource languages (i.e. de-en and en-fr), we simply increased the number of the encoder and decoder layers by one and set the embedding size to the same as that of mBERT to have a fair comparison. We use Adam (Kingma and Ba, 2015) as the optimiser with the default learning rate. In low-resource experiments, we train our model for 200 epochs in the Na and Griko bilingual experiments, and for 100 epochs for other languages. To learn our subword-aware models, we applied SentencePiece separately to each language with the vocabulary size set to 1,000 (in low-resource experiments) or 1,000 + the number of character types (for ja-en and en-iu).

## A.2 Number of Parameters

Table 11 shows the number of parameters of our model in millions. In low-resource experiments, most of the model parameters are located in LSTMs (9.5 millions) because the vocabulary sizes are very small. While our model itself is clearly more complex than the neural baselines (except for mBERT), the dimension of the word embeddings, which our model is trained for, is set to the same for all the models to ensure fairness.

## A.3 Run-time

Table 12 shows the run-time of our model in seconds. Although computationally more expensive than baseline models (except mBERT), it scales well and can be fully trained using a GPU in less than a minute for nru-zh.

# B Language Resources

Here we provide the URLs (in footnotes) from which we obtained the language resources we used in our experiments: Griko-Italian[37], Na-{English, French, Chinese}[38], Shipibo-Konibo-Spanish[39],

[37] https://bitbucket.org/antonis/grikoresource/src/master/ and https://github.com/antonisa/griko-italian-parallel-corpus

[38] https://github.com/alexis-michaud/na

[39] http://chana.inf.pucp.edu.pe/resources/parallel-corpus

| Soruce Word | Method | Retrieved Words |
|---|---|---|
| | BIVEC | **then**, well, calculates, the, counts |
| tʰi˩˥ (then, so, plane) | OURS ($+SW_{\text{ave}}$) | **then**, well, but, **so**, and |
| | + Pre | **then**, well, sikee, quickly, and |
| | BIVEC | also, **again**, place, roof, beams |
| wɤ˩˥ (again) | OURS ($+SW_{\text{ave}}$) | also, **again**, well, haenke, halves |
| | + Pre | also, haenke, **again**, and, once |
| | BIVEC | **house**, building, houses, build, built |
| ʑi˧mi˧ (house, farm) | OURS ($+SW_{\text{ave}}$) | **house**, building, main, room, build |
| | + Pre | **house**, building, home, houses, housed |
| | BIVEC | **here**, fireplace, beam, halves, hearth |
| ʈʂʰɯ˧-qo˧ (here) | OURS ($+SW_{\text{ave}}$) | **here**, sat, there, way, where |
| | + Pre | **here**, there, where, area, looking |
| | BIVEC | story, edge, strong, told, eighteen |
| mæ˩ (water) | OURS | cry, right, arrive, eat, strong |
| | + Pre | need, want, mupae, heard, terrifically |
| | BIVEC | wow, **mother**, living, so, mmm |
| ə˧mi˧ (mother, aunt) | OURS | wow, **mother**, alas, daughter, how |
| | + Pre | wow, **mother**, ggimi, truly, really |
| | BIVEC | **home**, family, lives, homes, else |
| ɑ˩ʁo˧ (home) | OURS ($+SW_{\text{ave}}$) | **home**, family, want, at, members |
| | + Pre | **home**, family, families, household, homes |

Table 13: Examples of retrieved words on nru-en BLI.

Japanese-English[40], English-Inuktitut[41], a Shipibo-Konibo-Spanish dictionary[42] and Na–French–Chinese–English dictionaries[43]. To download and pre-process the German-English and French-English data, we used the script at `https://github.com/lilt/alignment-scripts`, which is also used by Zenkel et al. (2020) and Chen et al. (2020). For other langauges, when the data is not pre-lowercased, we lowercased them. For ja-en, we applied SentencePiece to both languages independently and with the vocabulary size set to 20k. For en-iu, since there is a significant gap between the English and Inuktitut vocabulary size, i.e. 22k vs. 400k, we applied SentencePiece to Inuktitut only, with the vocabulary size set to 20k.

[40] `http://www.phontron.com/kftt/`

[41] `http://web.eecs.umich.edu/~mihalcea/wpt05/`

[42] `http://chana.inf.pucp.edu.pe/resources/wordnet-shp`

[43] `https://github.com/alexis-michaud/na/tree/master/DICTIONARY`

## C Hyper Parameters of the Baselines

In this section, we describe the hyper parameters of the baselines we used in our experiments. For SENTID, we used the default settings since they are already optimised for low-resource data (25k sentences from Bible) and works well on both small and large data. For BIS2V, we set the number of negatives sampling to 5, max length of word n-gram to 2, and the number of n-gram dropout to 1. In high-resource experiments, we changed the number of n-gram dropout to 4. For BIVEC, we set the subsampling rate to 0.001, bi-weight to 2, and the number of negative sampling to 5. In high-resource experiments, we set the sampling value to 0.01 and the negative sampling value to 10. We observed BIVEC very sensitive to the subsampling rate and bi-weight: the performance ranged from 5.4 to 33.8 (P@1) in the nru-en BLI task. We tuned these hyperparameters of BIVEC and BIS2V based on the last-checkpoint model performance on the test data of nru-en and en-iu. For the mBERT baseline, we used their default setting.

For GIZA++ and Fast Align, we used their default hyper-parameters unless mentioned otherwise. In BLI, we set the counts increment cutoff and probability cutoff thresholds to 0 in GIZA++, and remove the probability cutoff in Fast Align to avoid pruning low-probability words.

## D Examples of Retrieved Words on BLI

Table 13 shows some examples of retrieved words on the Na-English BLI task. The source words are chosen by sorting the Na words in the dictionary based on the frequency in the Na-English corpus, and selecting the seven most frequent ones. The table shows that, although P@5 and P@1 are nearly the same for all the methods, our model matches more semantically and/or grammatically related words to the target word than BIVEC, the best performing baseline.[44] For instance, given the source word tʰi˩˥, OURS ($+SW_{\text{ave}}$) retrieved its translations "then" and "so", and also other conjunctions "and" and "but", while BIVEC was able to retrieve "then" only and the other retrieved words are irrelevant to it, such as "calculates" and "counts". For the source word ʈʂʰɯ˧-qo˧, all the models successfully retrieved its translation "here". However, while our models also retrieved relevant words to it, such as "there" and "where" , BIVEC retrieved completely irrelevant words such as "beam". These results suggest that our models encode more semantic and syntactic information into the word embeddings by taking word order information into account.

[44] Note that since the Na-English parallel corpus is extremely small, the size of the English vocabulary from which the words are retrieved is also very small (i.e. 942 word types) Besides, as shown in Table 2, the corpus is also very noisy and contains some ungrammatical sentences. Therefore, it is inevitable to some extent that some of the retrieved words are irrelevant to the source word.

# Clustering Monolingual Vocabularies to Improve Cross-Lingual Generalization

**Riccardo Bassani**
Utrecht University
Netherlands
r.bassani@students.uu.nl

**Anders Søgaard**
University of Copenhagen
Denmark
soegaard@di.ku.dk

**Tejaswini Deoskar**
Utrecht University
Netherlands
t.deoskar@uu.nl

## Abstract

Multilingual language models exhibit better performance for some languages than for others (Singh et al., 2019), and many languages do not seem to benefit from multilingual sharing at all, presumably as a result of poor multilingual segmentation (Pyysalo et al., 2020). This work explores the idea of learning multilingual language models based on clustering of monolingual segments. We show significant improvements over standard multilingual segmentation across nine languages on a question answering task, both in a small model regime and for a model of the size of BERT-base.

## 1 Introduction

Since its release in 2018, multilingual BERT (mBERT) has been extensively analyzed. For instance, mBERT has been shown to facilitate zero-shot cross-lingual transfer, but transfer performance is significantly worse for typologically distant languages (Pires et al., 2019). This is because cross-lingual generalization is only partial, with some language-specific partitioning of the representational space (Libovický et al., 2019; Singh et al., 2019; Pires et al., 2019).

Moreover, mBERT relies on a single, multilingual tokenizer to create its vocabulary (WordPiece, Schuster and Nakajima (2012)), a subword tokenizer based on an algorithm similar to BPE (Gage, 1994). The multilingual tokenizer lets subwords be shared across different languages, but the approach penalizes outlier languages, whose words end up being segmented according to statistics derived from high-resource languages (Pyysalo et al., 2020; Chung et al., 2020).

In this study, we propose a novel method for building a multilingual vocabulary that is more fair to outlier languages: The core idea is *to train mBERT-like language models on multilingual clusters of monolingual tokens derived from monolingual tokenizations into vocabularies of equal size.* We argue this approach brings us the best of two worlds: monolingual (dedicated) tokenization and multilingual input representations.

**Contributions** Our main contribution is devising a novel way of learning multilingual vocabularies that are more fair to outlier languages. Our approach relies on clusters, and we analyze these clusters in depth. Next, we induce a multilingual mBERT-like language model from cluster representations of input sentences and evaluate this language model on the downstream task of cross-lingual question answering. We show that the model trained on our cluster representations improves over our baseline, trained with standard mBERT tokenization, across nine typologically diverse languages. We observe the same improvements across two different language model sizes.

**Related work** Pyysalo et al. (2020) showed how training monolingual BERT models instead of a single multilingual one can improve performance for some languages even if the amount of training data decreases. A possible cause of this phenomenon could be identified in the better quality of tokenization that can be reached when a dedicated monolingual vocabulary is used. This thesis is also supported by the findings of Conneau et al. (2020) on the importance of vocabulary size to a multilingual language model's performance.

In order to overcome the issues deriving from the use of a single multilingual vocabulary, Chung et al. (2020) propose to cluster together similar languages and to learn vocabularies for language clusters. Their methods proves to be effective, with a significant reduction of maximum description length, and significant improvements on QA, NER and XNLI tasks. This suggests that multilingual model can benefit from the use of a vocabulary that more fairly represents all languages.

In this paper, we take this approach one step further and propose a method which clusters the



*Proceedings of the 1st Workshop on Multilingual Representation Learning*, pages 32–40
November 11, 2021. 

output of monolingual tokenizations, merging dedicated vocabularies into a single vocabulary of token clusters.

## 2 Multilingual Vocabulary Induction

The key idea of our method is to build a single multilingual model from the output of dedicated, monolingual tokenizers, i.e., language-specific subword vocabularies, by clustering the obtained subwords by semantic similarity. A single model is then trained on the desired number of clusters, learning an embedding for each cluster. This allows for implicitly using a very large vocabulary without increasing model complexity, hopefully leading to better segmentation for outlier languages and better generalization across languages.

Our approach involves three steps:

(i) Creation of monolingual subword vocabularies.
(ii) Clustering monolingual subwords into multilingual subword clusters.
(iii) Training a multilingual language model on multilingual subword clusters and evaluating it on a downstream task.

These steps are described in turn below. An overview of the entire process is given in Figure 2.

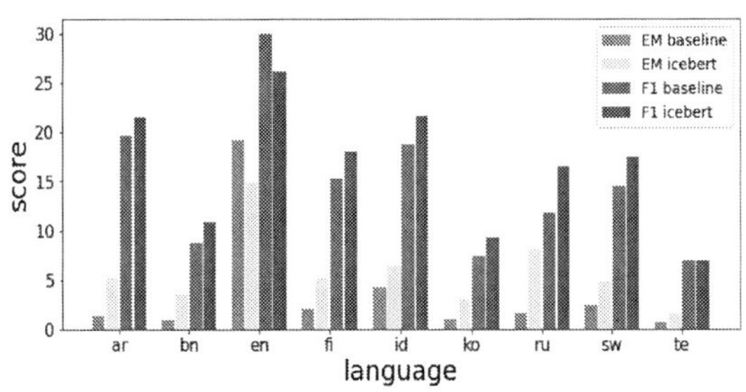


Figure 1: EM and F1 scores for the baseline and the ICEBERT model, across nine languages.

### 2.1 Vocabulary creation

First, monolingual vocabularies were created starting from the BPEmb vocabularies offered by Heinzerling and Strube (2018). BPEmb[1] is a collection of BPE-based subword embeddings in 275 languages. Monolingual vocabularies are available in different sizes. We extracted vocabularies of size 30k[2]

[1]//bpemb.h-its.org/

[2]This vocabulary size was chosen to be similar to the size of the monolingual BERT's vocabulary, leaving the 30k most frequent tokens in each language.

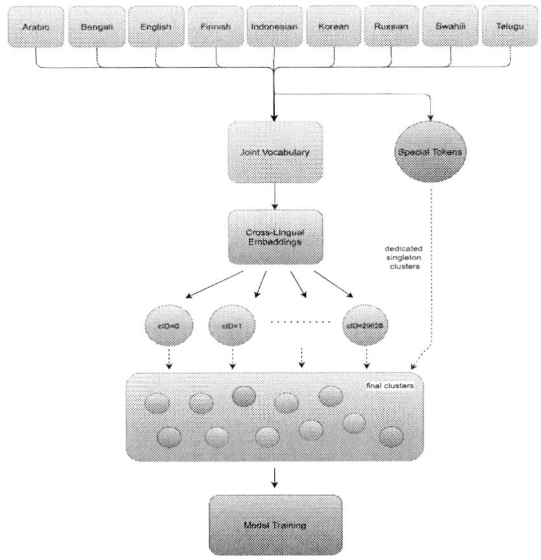


Figure 2: Overview of the three phases of the project. From top to bottom: joint vocabulary creation, subword clustering, and model training. The clusters are identified by clusters IDs (cIDs), and are represented as circles in the figure. Blue circles represent clusters obtained by partitioning the translation graph, while red circles represent singleton clusters dedicated to special tokens.

for the 9 languages present in the TyDiQA benchmark (Clark et al., 2020): Arabic, Bengali, English, Finnish, Indonesian, Korean, Russian, Swahili, and Telugu. These languages are typologically very different and as such provide for downstream evaluation of multilingual language models.

A joint vocabulary was created by concatenating the mono-lingual vocabularies and marking subwords with a language identifier. Digits, punctuation and other special symbols, which are largely language-agnostic, were not marked this way, but assigned dedicated, singleton clusters. Following Dufter and Schütze (2020), we mapped all digits to zero.

### 2.2 Subword clustering

The goal of subword clustering is to obtain clusters made of tokens from different languages that are semantically similar. The ideal clusters will therefore contain tokens which are near-translations of each other. Moreover, we want clusters to be generally small and of similar size. Large clusters are undesirable, since they tend to be semantically vague or inconsistent. Therefore, while allowing some variance in cluster size, we limit the maximum cluster size.

**Cross-lingual embeddings creation** The subwords in the joint vocabulary were clustered by semantic similarity exploiting the already available BPEmb-embeddings. We started from the monolingual BPEmb embeddings of size $d = 300$, and projected them into a shared semantic space by mapping all vectors but the English ones into the English vector space. The mapping was performed using the scripts and seed dictionaries published by Glavas et al. (2019).[3] In particular, we relied on the PROC algorithm to solve the Procrustes problem (Schönemann, 1966). Seed dictionaries were available for English-Russian and English-Finnish, containing 5000 training pairs and 2000 test pairs. Dictionaries for the remaining languages were derived from Google Translate and can be shared for resource purposes upon request.[4]

The mapping provides us with 300-dimensional multilingual embeddings, which we evaluate on a bilingual lexicon induction (BLI) task. For each source/target language pair, and for each word pair in the rtest dictionary, the top $k$ translations of the source word are extracted from the target language vocabulary as its $k$ nearest neighbours, measured by cosine similarity. Precision at $k$ (p@$k$) scores are used to quantify the fraction of times in which the gold translation (the one in the test dictionary) is present among the top $k$ extracted translations. The mean reciprocal rank (MRR) gives an idea of the average rank of the gold translation among the predicted translations, as expressed by the formula $\frac{1}{|Q|}\sum_{i=1}^{|Q|}\frac{1}{rank_i}$, where $Q$ is the set of all the tokens in the target vocabulary. The created multilingual embeddings achieve good average scores on BLI (p@1=0.193, p@5=0.384 p@10=0.454, MRR=0.283).

**Translation graph creation** Instead of simply clustering the tokens considering only the distance between embeddings, we aim to carefully create small clusters of similar sizes, ideally containing synonyms and translations.[5] To this end, we create a sparse graph containing for each subword, the top-$k$ translations in each language, i.e., the top-$k$ nearest neighbors in the projected space. We eliminate from this sparse translation graph all non-symmetric edges, so that the obtained graph contains an edge between subword_1 and subword_2 if and only if subword_1 is among the top-$k$ translations of subword_2, *and* vice versa.

To select the most adequate value for $k$, we examine the distribution of clique sizes in each graph. $k$ must be high enough to avoid having many subwords which are not in (non-single-ton) cliques. If $k$ is too high, however, cliques may contain subwords that are not reciprocal translations/synonyms.

Figure 3 shows how, as expected, the number of singletons (cliques containing only one subword) decreases as $k$ increases. We select $k = 5$, which is the smallest value that gives us a reasonably low number of isolated subwords: With $k = 5$, there are 1232 isolated subwords, requiring 1232 dedicated clusters.

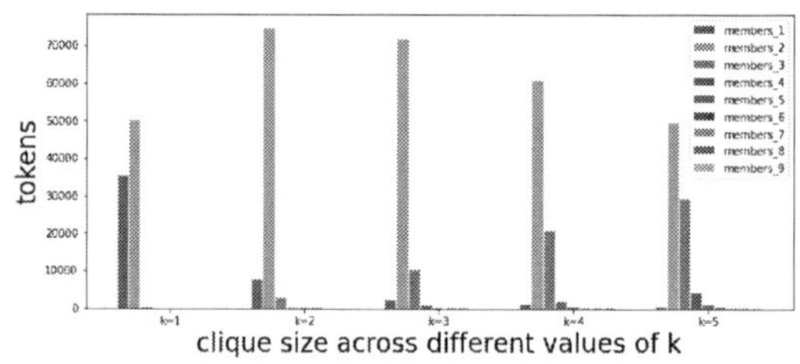


Figure 3: Number of tokens belonging to a clique of size at most $s$, for $s$ in [1,9] and for different values of $k$. The blue bar represents tokens belonging only to singletons, the orange bar tokens belonging to cliques of size at most 2, the green one tokens belonging to cliques of size at most 3, etc.

Note that cliques do not capture all translations, as shown in the example below, where $x_2$ has three translations despite not being in any clique of size higher than 2.

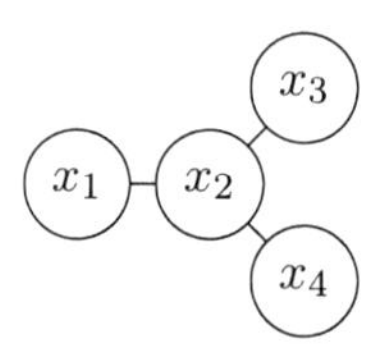


In Figure 4, we plot the average number of languages per clique, across different clique sizes. We see that most small cliques contain translation pairs, not merely synonym pairs in the same language.

**Graph Partitioning** In order to obtain final clusters of similar size, we apply the METIS algorithm on the sparse translation graph. The METIS algorithm was first introduced in 1995 (Karypis and

[3]https://github.com/codogogo/xling-eval

[4]Glavas et al. (2019) showed that by applying a bootstrapping algorithm it is possible to obtain similar performances with seed dictionaries containing only 1000 pairs. Artetxe et al. (2018) also discuss inducing dictionary seeds in a completely unsupervised manner.

[5]We ran early experiments to verify that simple $k$-means clustering performs poorly.

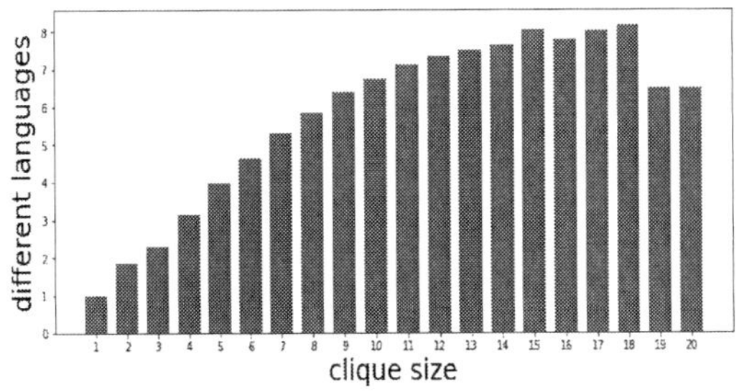


Figure 4: Average number of different languages in a clique, across different clique sizes

Kumar, 1995), and is now available both as a standalone software[6] and as a Python package.[7] It solves the multiway graph partitioning problem, which consists in finding a partition of the vertex set into a given number of balanced sets while minimizing cut weight (Hashimoto et al., 2010).

The main parameters of the METIS balanced graph partitioning algorithm are two:

1. **p**: the number of parts in which the graph must be divided. We set this value to 28500. This was done to reach a final number of clusters of approximately 30000, considering that 665 clusters are reserved for the special tokens, and the post-processing performed on the partition.

2. **v**: the load imbalance tolerance, defining that the cluster size must not be higher than $\left\lceil \frac{N}{p} * (1 + v) \right\rceil$, where **N** is the number of nodes in the graph and **p** the number of parts the graph must be split into. This value was set to 1.5, in order to allow for a moderate degree of flexibility with the clusters size.

With these parameter values, the algorithm produced a partition made of groups of size varying between 1 and 23 (the 81 empty groups were immediately removed). Figure 5 shows that the large majority of the groups have size 7, 8 or 9, which, since we are clustering subwords from 9 languages, is exactly the desired size.

The METIS partitions contain only one group of size 1. How can it be explained, if the previous graph analysis detected the presence of 1,232 isolated subwords? The answer is that the "cut" objective of the METIS algorithm simply aims to minimize the number of edges cut by the partition. Therefore, it is not necessarily penalized when grouping together disconnected nodes. This holds not only for the METIS algorithm, but for $k$-way graph partitioning in general, its goal being minimizing the number of edges whose incident vertexes belong to different subsets (Karypis and Kumar, 1995). Despite this, however, graph partitioning algorithms prefer grouping together highly connected nodes, therefore the METIS algorithm can prove to be adequate for our task. The specific problem of isolated subwords can be solved by removing from the partition the 1,232 isolated subwords detected before, and assigning them to dedicated clusters. Upon doing so, we analyzed whether the so-many groups of size 7, 8, and 9 actually reflected the graph structure, or whether they were an artifact of the METIS algorithm?

[6]http://glaros.dtc.umn.edu/gkhome/metis/metis/overview
[7]https://github.com/networkx/networkx-metis

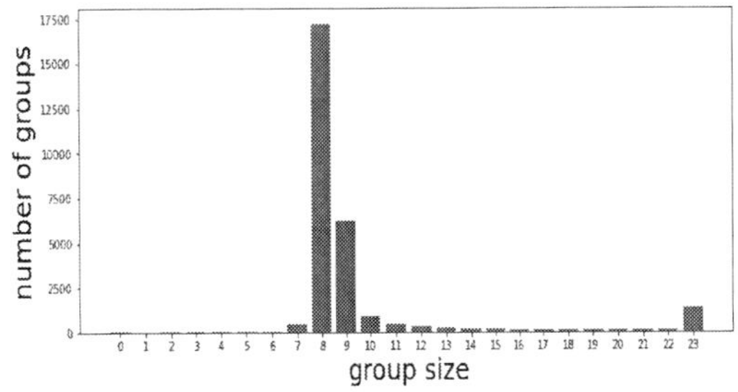


Figure 5: Distribution of the sizes of the groups in the partition obtained with the (28500, 1.5) METIS algorithm. Most groups have size 8, close to the number of languages.

To answer this question, we looked at the distribution of shortest-path lengths across all pairs of subwords belonging to the same group. Figure 6 shows that most of the subwords inhabiting the same clusters are immediate neighbours (length=1) or share a neighbour (length=2).

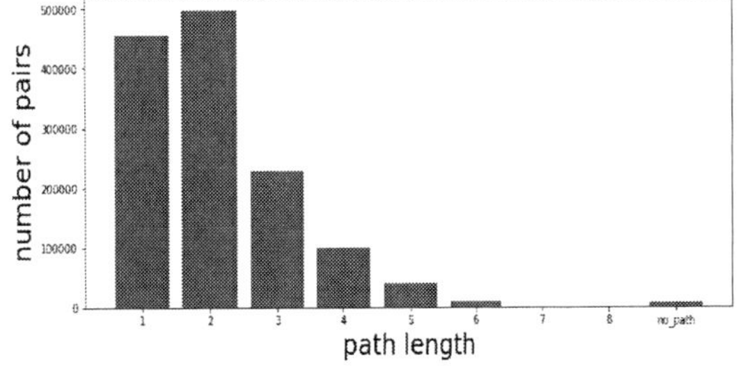


Figure 6: Distribution of shortest path lengths across intra-cluster pairs of tokens. Clusters of size 1 were not considered.

Only around 100 intra-cluster pairs are not connected. We split the 19 groups containing such pairs into 39 groups so that all their members were connected. Finally, 665 singletons were added for the multilingual special tokens. This resulted in a total of 30292 clusters containing 270314 subwords. Some randomly selected clusters are reported in Figure 7.

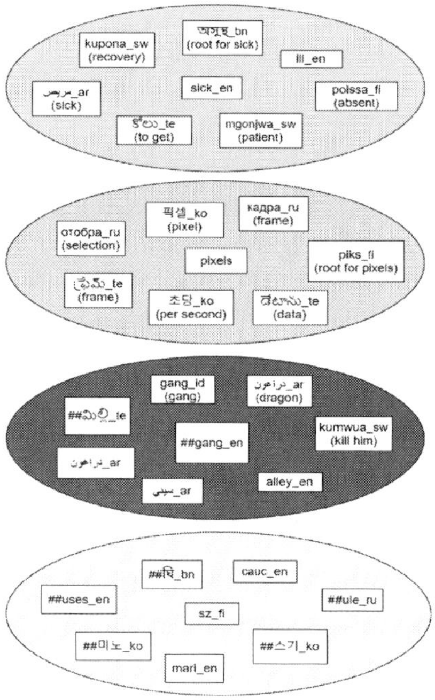


Figure 7: Examples of clusters created by the METIS algorithm. Each token is reported both in the original language and in English, except from the cases when providing an English translation is not possible. This happens for many strict subwords in the red and in the yellow clusters. For most clusters it is possible to identify an underlying concept: sick (green), pixel/data (cyan), gang/violence (red), while it is infeasible for some other clusters, especially the ones mainly made of strict subwords (yellow).

## 3 Model Training

Once the clustering was completed, a BERT vocabulary was built extending the set of cluster IDs (cIDs) with BERT special tokens, to give a vocabulary size of 30397, similar to the one of the original BERT model. We called our model ICEBERT, an acronym for Interlingual-Clusters Enhanced BERT.

| | |
|---|---|
| INPUT: | Goodmorning world! |
| TOK.: | ['good_en' '##morning_en' 'world_en' '!_en'] |
| cIDS: | 28121 5132 14568 29913 |

Table 1: Input example tokenization and rewriting

### 3.1 ICEBERT training

To train our ICEBERT model on cluster IDs instead that actual subwords, we decided to take the following approach:

At training time, the entire training corpus was mapped to cluster IDs (cIDs). Each sentence was first tokenized using a lowercase BPEmb monolingual tokenizer. Before calling the tokenizer, the sentences were lowercased and digits replaced by zeros. After the tokenization was completed, all tokens were marked with a language ID. Each token was then mapped to its cID, using the token $\rightarrow$ cID dictionary created in the clustering phase. The model was then trained with a fictitious tokenizer, whose vocabulary contained the string representations of cIDs: "0", "1", ... "30291". In this way, the model's tokenizer simply separates strings of cIDs according to white spaces, while the optimal subword tokenization is made by language-specific tokenizers. See example in Table 1.

At inference time, the same actions are performed. This means that the input to the model must be mapped to cIDs before being fed to the model. This is fairly simple and quick. For some downstream tasks, the model prediction must be modified to take into account the differences between the original input and the mapped one (e.g., span indexes in question answering). The greatest challenge would occur in generation tasks, since generated cIDs can correspond to multiple subwords. In this paper, we limit evaluation to question answering.

### 3.2 Baseline Training

As our baseline tokenizer, we trained a SentencePiece[8] model on a balanced Wikipedia corpus of 100k sentences, covering all the 9 languages in the experiment. Early experiments showed that uncasing the input data led to a drop in performance, as also reported in mBERT's documentation.[9] The baseline vocabulary size is set to be the same as the ICEBERT's one.

[8] https://github.com/google/sentencepiece

[9] https://github.com/google-research/bert/blob/master/multilingual.md

### 3.3 Small-Scale Pretraining

We first adopted the quick experimental setup[10] proposed by Dufter and Schütze (2020) to pre-train a small-BERT model using a training corpus of 180k sentences from Wikipedia (20k per language). The sentences were shuffled to avoid any bias towards a specific language. The model was pretrained for only 10 epochs (*vs.* 100 in Dufter and Schütze, 2020) to account for the larger amount of training data (around ten times more). All the remaining hyperparameters were kept as in the original small-BERT article except from the batch size, which was reduced to 128. The training required less than ninety minutes on a single Tesla T4 GPU. As a baseline, we pretrained a model of the same size, with the same hyperparameters, and on the same training corpus[11], omitting the mapping to cIDs.

The models were finetuned for 20 epochs, with an AdamW optimizer with learning rate equal to 5e-5. We trained both the baseline and the model five different times, and report average results for each language in Figure 8.

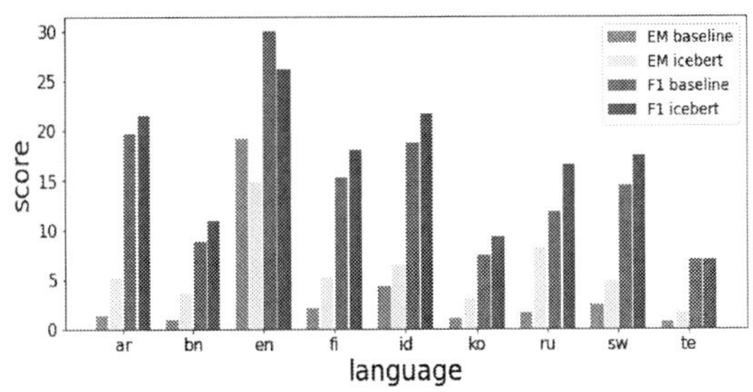


Figure 8: EM and F1 scores for the small baseline and ICEBERT model, across 9 languages.

### 3.4 Large-Scale Pre-training

The positive results obtained in the small-scale experiment motivated the training of a large ICEBERT model.

**Configuration** In the large-scale setting we trained two models of the size of the original BERT model, BERT$_{\text{BASE}}$. Our model, ICEBERT$_{\text{BASE}}$, therefore has an hidden size of 768, an intermediate size of 3072, 12 hidden layers and 12 attention heads. We mostly used the training hyperparameters reported by (Devlin et al., 2018) in the BERT paper: an AdamW optimizer (lr=1e-4 with linear decay, $\beta_1 = 0.9$, $\beta_2 = 0.999$, weight decay=0.01, epsilon=1e-6, warmup steps=10,000, dropout probability=0.1), 1,000,000 of training steps, a maximum sequence length of 512 and a batch size of 64 (8 per core).

**Training Corpus** As training corpus, we concatenated the Wikipedia corpora of all the 9 languages included in the study. To compensate for the different Wikipedia sizes across languages, we took an approach similar to the one adopted by Devlin et al. (2018). They performed exponentially smoothed weighting of the data during pretraining data creation. This means that they sampled sentences according to a multinomial distribution $q_{i i=1...N}$, where:

$$q_i = \frac{p_i^\alpha}{\sum_{j=1}^N p_j^\alpha} \quad \text{being} \quad p_i = \frac{n_i}{\sum_{j=1}^N n_j} \quad ; \tag{1}$$

The parameter $\alpha \in (0, 1)$ controls the degree to which low-resource languages are over-sampled: the closer it is to zero, the closer the number of lines across different languages. Devlin et al. (2018) chose a value of $\alpha = 0.7$ in their paper. Successive works, however, used lower values of $\alpha$ (Lample and Conneau, 2019, Conneau et al., 2020). Xue et al. (2020) recently showed how exponential sampling works best with a value of $\alpha = 0.3$. We therefore used $\alpha = 0.3$ to compute the values of the multinomial distribution $q_{i i=1...N}$. We then created an augmented corpus by keeping fixed the size of the English corpus and duplicating the other languages' data in order to achieve the desired ratios between corpora. During this process we also concatenated/split consecutive lines in the corpus so that each line was made of approximately 512 tokens. This was necessary since the Transformers library handling training on TPUs does not support automatic creation of balanced input segments, but requires the input dataset to be provided as a line by line dataset, i.e. so that each line corresponds to a sequence. If a line is longer than the maximum sequence length (512 in our case), it is truncated. If it is shorter, it is padded with [PAD] tokens. Wikipedia lines exhibit a great variance, ranging from single words to full paragraphs. To avoid waste of data, and that most of the input sequences were made predominantly by [PAD] tokens, we pre-processed the corpus as described above. The ICEBERT cIDs corpus was created after this pre-processing step, so that the two corpora

[10] hidden layers=12, hidden size=64, intermediate size=256, attention head=1. Total paramaters=2612989.

[11] shuffled using the same random indexes

contained exactly the same lines. The corpora were finally shuffled according to a shared indexes list. This resulted in a training corpus of approximately 80GB for the baseline and 70GB for ICEBERT[12].

**Pretraining Costs** It is important to notice that, despite the total number of training steps being the same as in $\text{BERT}_{\text{BASE}}$, the lower batch size implies that the model is actually trained on $\frac{1}{4}$ of the training data. A full-training was not feasible with the given resources (almost 4 weeks per model on a single v3-8 TPU), but we decided to undertrain rather than downscaling, based on the findings of Li et al. (2020), who claimed that larger models tend to achieve better performance than smaller models when trained for the same time.

The training took approximately 5 days per model on a GCP cluster made of a nd2-highmem-8 compute engine (8 vCPUs, 64 GB memory) accelerated by a v3-8 TPU node (8 cores, 128 GiB of TPU memory). The cost of the training on Google Cloud Platform amounted to little more than 60$ per model for the compute engine, while the TPUs where made available for free by Google as part of the TRC program[13]. The costs covered by this offer amount to 300$ per model if using a pre-emptible v3-8 TPUs, or to 1000$ per model if using an on-demand device.

**Fine-Tuning** The models were finetuned for 2 epochs, with an AdamW optimizer with a learning rate of $1e{-}5$, following Hu et al. (2020) approach[14]. We finetuned both the baseline and the model three different times.

### 3.5 Evaluation

We evaluate our models on TyDiQA-GoldP (Clark et al., 2020), a question answering task covering the nine (9) target languages. The model input is a question and a background passage, called *context*, which contains the answer, and the task is to predict the contiguous span of characters that human annotators have indicated, provides an answer to the question. Models are evaluated with the two metrics proposed in the SQuAD 1.1 paper (Rajpurkar et al., 2016):

1. EM: Exact match, measures the percentage of predictions exactly matching any one of the ground truth answers.
2. F1: (Macro-averaged) F1 score. Computes the F1 score between the prediction and ground truth answers, treating them as bags of tokens. For each prediction, the maximum score over all the ground truth answers is taken. The scores are then averaged over all the questions.

Our models were fine-tuned only on the English TyDiQA training dataset and applied to unseen languages at test time. This protocol is commonly referred to as unsupervised cross-lingual transfer or zero-shot cross-lingual learning.

The fine-tuning data comprises 231 batches of size 16. To train the ICEBERT model, the English dataset was mapped to cluster-IDs, following the method described in Section 3.1. The input labels, i.e., the span indexes, also had to be mapped to match the indexes of the mapped answers in the mapped contexts. The text in the test dataset was mapped to cluster IDs in the same way as for the training dataset. The span indexes output by the model were then adjusted to extract the correct text span in the original contexts, and the extracted answers were evaluated with EM and F1.

## 4 Results

Figures 9 shows the EM and the F1 scores across all nine languages, for the base architecture. Average results are reported in Table 2, which also gives the performances of the small models and of the fully trained mBERT model, as reported by Hu et al. (2020), for comparison.

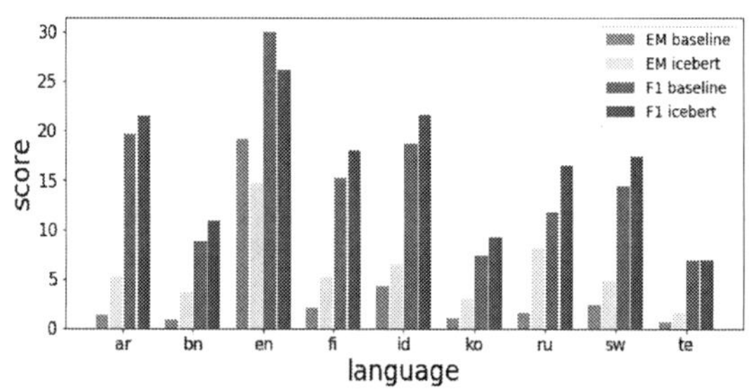


Figure 9: EM and F1 scores for the baseline and the ICEBERT model, across nine languages.

## 5 Discussion and Future Work

ICEBERT significantly improves over the baseline, across both the experimental settings and

[12]In UTF-8 encoding foreign characters often takes more than 8 bits, therefore by mapping foreign characters to digits the size of the corpus is reduced. The size of the English corpus, on the other hand, is increased, since many short tokens (e.g. punctuation) are mapped to 5-digits cluster IDs.

[13]https://sites.research.google/trc/

[14]The learning rate was adjusted to take into account the difference batch size (16 instead of 32).

| model | EM | F1 |
|---|---|---|
| Baseline$_{\text{SMALL}}$ | 1.80 | 12.89 |
| ICEBERT$_{\text{SMALL}}$ | **4.74** | **15.30** |
| Baseline$_{\text{BASE}}$ | 10.96 | 21.49 |
| ICEBERT$_{\text{BASE}}$ | **11.36** | **23.18** |
| mBERT | 41.46 | 57.74 |

Table 2: Exact Match and F1 average scores across all languages different from English. On top of the baseline's and the ICEBERT model's performance, the scores obtained by the fully-trained mBERT model are also reported.

evaluation metrics. The base architecture F1 improvements moving from baseline tokenization to ICEBERT tokenization (1.7 F1) are encouraging. ICEBERT$_{\text{BASE}}$ improves over the baseline over almost all languages. Languages which are typologically distant from English, like Arabic, Russian, and Telugu, benefit the most from the clustering, as shown by the reported increments in performance. The most significant improvements can be observed on Arabic and Telugu (the language with the lowest baseline scores among the ones included in the study). Excluding Korean, for which performance is extremely poor, the only two languages for which significant improvements were not seen, are Indonesian and Swahili, which are morphosyntactically most similar to English.

As shown in Table 2, the ICEBERT$_{\text{BASE}}$ model significantly outperforms the ICEBERT$_{\text{SMALL}}$ model, but its scores remain well below the fully trained mBERT$_{\text{BASE}}$ model, as reported by Hu et al. (2020). We hope that the performance improvements of ICEBERT tokenization scale to more competitive models as well, but the model sizes considered here were limited by the available resources. Our model is also limited in training only on nine languages. Including more languages is perfectly possible and would only affect clustering time. Finally, we only considered question answering in this study. We expect our conclusions to generalize to other tasks, but this remains an open question for now.

In the paper we have compared clustering of monolingual vocabularies to multilingual segmentation, i.e., BPE on concatenated corpora. Other alternatives have been proposed in the literature, including multilevel tokenization (Wang et al., 2021) and tokenization-free, character-based modeling (Clark et al., 2021). It is beyond the scope of this paper to systematically compare all these different approaches. The idea of using sequences of token group IDs to represent input sentences was previously explored in Wulff and Søgaard (2015), who used finite state automata instead of clusters.

## 6 Conclusion

This study aimed to improve multilingual language models by training them on clusters of monolingual segments. The proposed approach yielded good quality clusters able to group semantically similar words and subwords across languages. Our clustering strategy led to improvements over standard segmentation and training methods on the majority of the included languages, when evaluated on a question answering task.

## References

Mikel Artetxe, Gorka Labaka, and Eneko Agirre. 2018. A robust self-learning method for fully unsupervised cross-lingual mappings of word embeddings. In *Proceedings of the 56th Annual Meeting of the Association for Computational Linguistics (Volume 1: Long Papers)*, pages 789–798, Melbourne, Australia. Association for Computational Linguistics.

Hyung Won Chung, Dan Garrette, Kiat Chuan Tan, and Jason Riesa. 2020. Improving multilingual models with language-clustered vocabularies. In *Proceedings of the 2020 Conference on Empirical Methods in Natural Language Processing (EMNLP)*, pages 4536–4546, Online. Association for Computational Linguistics.

Jonathan H. Clark, Eunsol Choi, Michael Collins, Dan Garrette, Tom Kwiatkowski, Vitaly Nikolaev, and Jennimaria Palomaki. 2020. Tydi qa: A benchmark for information-seeking question answering in typologically diverse languages.

Jonathan H. Clark, Dan Garrette, Iulia Turc, and John Wieting. 2021. Canine: Pre-training an efficient tokenization-free encoder for language representation.

Alexis Conneau, Kartikay Khandelwal, Naman Goyal, Vishrav Chaudhary, Guillaume Wenzek, Francisco Guzmán, Edouard Grave, Myle Ott, Luke Zettlemoyer, and Veselin Stoyanov. 2020. Unsupervised cross-lingual representation learning at scale. In *ACL*, pages 8440–8451. Association for Computational Linguistics.

Jacob Devlin, Ming-Wei Chang, Kenton Lee, and Kristina Toutanova. 2018. BERT: pre-training of deep bidirectional transformers for language understanding. *CoRR*, abs/1810.04805.

Philipp Dufter and Hinrich Schütze. 2020. Identifying necessary elements for bert's multilinguality.

Philip Gage. 1994. A new algorithm for data compression. *C Users Journal*.

Goran Glavas, Robert Litschko, Sebastian Ruder, and Ivan Vulic. 2019. How to (properly) evaluate cross-lingual word embeddings: On strong baselines, comparative analyses, and some misconceptions. *CoRR*, abs/1902.00508.

Hideki Hashimoto, Youhei Sonobe, and Mutsunori Yagiura. 2010. A multilevel scheme with adaptive memory strategy for multiway graph partitioning. In *Learning and Intelligent Optimization*, pages 188–191, Berlin, Heidelberg. Springer Berlin Heidelberg.

Benjamin Heinzerling and Michael Strube. 2018. BPEmb: Tokenization-free Pre-trained Subword Embeddings in 275 Languages. In *Proceedings of the Eleventh International Conference on Language Resources and Evaluation (LREC 2018)*, Miyazaki, Japan. European Language Resources Association (ELRA).

Junjie Hu, Sebastian Ruder, Aditya Siddhant, Graham Neubig, Orhan Firat, and Melvin Johnson. 2020. Xtreme: A massively multilingual multi-task benchmark for evaluating cross-lingual generalization.

George Karypis and Vipin Kumar. 1995. Multilevel graph partitioning schemes. In *ICPP (3)*, pages 113–122. CRC Press.

Guillaume Lample and Alexis Conneau. 2019. Cross-lingual language model pretraining. *CoRR*, abs/1901.07291.

Zhuohan Li, Eric Wallace, Sheng Shen, Kevin Lin, Kurt Keutzer, Dan Klein, and Joseph E. Gonzalez. 2020. Train large, then compress: Rethinking model size for efficient training and inference of transformers. *CoRR*, abs/2002.11794.

Jindrich Libovický, Rudolf Rosa, and Alexander Fraser. 2019. How language-neutral is multilingual bert? *CoRR*, abs/1911.03310.

Telmo Pires, Eva Schlinger, and Dan Garrette. 2019. How multilingual is multilingual BERT? In *Proceedings of the 57th Annual Meeting of the Association for Computational Linguistics*, pages 4996–5001, Florence, Italy. Association for Computational Linguistics.

Sampo Pyysalo, Jenna Kanerva, Antti Virtanen, and Filip Ginter. 2020. Wikibert models: deep transfer learning for many languages.

Pranav Rajpurkar, Jian Zhang, Konstantin Lopyrev, and Percy Liang. 2016. Squad: 100, 000+ questions for machine comprehension of text. *CoRR*, abs/1606.05250.

Mike Schuster and Kaisuke Nakajima. 2012. Japanese and korean voice search. In *ICASSP*, pages 5149–5152. IEEE.

P.H. Schönemann. 1966. A generalized solution of the orthogonal procrustes problem. *Psychometrika*, 31:1–10.

Jasdeep Singh, Bryan McCann, Richard Socher, and Caiming Xiong. 2019. BERT is not an interlingua and the bias of tokenization. In *Proceedings of the 2nd Workshop on Deep Learning Approaches for Low-Resource NLP (DeepLo 2019)*, pages 47–55, Hong Kong, China. Association for Computational Linguistics.

Xinyi Wang, Sebastian Ruder, and Graham Neubig. 2021. Multi-view subword regularization. In *Proceedings of the 2021 Conference of the North American Chapter of the Association for Computational Linguistics: Human Language Technologies*, pages 473–482, Online. Association for Computational Linguistics.

Julie Wulff and Anders Søgaard. 2015. Learning finite state word representations for unsupervised Twitter adaptation of POS taggers. In *Proceedings of the Workshop on Noisy User-generated Text*, pages 162–166, Beijing, China. Association for Computational Linguistics.

Linting Xue, Noah Constant, Adam Roberts, Mihir Kale, Rami Al-Rfou, Aditya Siddhant, Aditya Barua, and Colin Raffel. 2020. mt5: A massively multilingual pre-trained text-to-text transformer. *CoRR*, abs/2010.11934.

# Do not neglect related languages: The case of low-resource Occitan cross-lingual word embeddings

**Lisa Woller** and **Viktor Hangya** and **Alexander Fraser**
Center for Information and Language Processing
LMU Munich
lisa_woller@web.de, {hangyav, fraser}@cis.lmu.de

## Abstract

Cross-lingual word embeddings (CLWEs) have proven indispensable for various natural language processing tasks, e.g., bilingual lexicon induction (BLI). However, the lack of data often impairs the quality of representations. Various approaches requiring only weak cross-lingual supervision were proposed, but current methods still fail to learn good CLWEs for languages with only a small monolingual corpus. We therefore claim that it is necessary to explore further datasets to improve CLWEs in low-resource setups. In this paper we propose to incorporate data of related high-resource languages. In contrast to previous approaches which leverage independently pre-trained embeddings of languages, we (i) train CLWEs for the low-resource and a related language jointly and (ii) map them to the target language to build the final multilingual space. In our experiments we focus on Occitan, a low-resource Romance language which is often neglected due to lack of resources. We leverage data from French, Spanish and Catalan for training and evaluate on the Occitan-English BLI task. By incorporating supporting languages our method outperforms previous approaches by a large margin. Furthermore, our analysis shows that the degree of relatedness between an incorporated language and the low-resource language is critically important.

## 1 Introduction

Cross-lingual word embeddings (CLWEs) are important for a wide range of NLP tasks including bilingual lexicon induction (BLI) (Vulić and Korhonen, 2016; Patra et al., 2019), Machine Translation (Lample et al., 2018), and cross-lingual transfer learning (Xiao and Guo, 2014; Schuster et al., 2019). Two main types of approaches to learn CLWEs are mapping methods, where a set of pre trained monolingual embeddings is projected into another monolingual space (Mikolov et al., 2013), and joint methods, where the monolingual and cross-lingual objectives are optimized jointly (e.g., Klementiev et al., 2012; Lample et al., 2018).

Since recent research is more and more interested in dealing with low-resource languages, learning multilingual representations for low-resource languages is important as well (Conneau et al., 2018; Kementchedjhieva et al., 2018; Vulić et al., 2019). However, a lack of parallel data impairs the performance of existing strongly supervised models, which is why a lot of recent research focuses on reducing the need for parallel data (Artetxe et al., 2017; Smith et al., 2017; Artetxe et al., 2018; Conneau et al., 2018). Mapping methods are sensitive to the approximate isomorphism of embedding spaces, which is not the case for many languages (Søgaard et al., 2018). The low isomorphism of distant language pairs was tackled by learning CLWEs jointly (Lample et al., 2018; Ormazabal et al., 2019; Devlin et al., 2019). However, they rely on large monolingual corpora which are not available for many languages. Furthermore, the lack of large data leads to low isomorphism as well, since it results in low-quality monolingual embedding spaces (Michel et al., 2020). Hence, mapping methods, which rely on the assumption of approximate isomorphism cannot be fruitfully applied in many cases.

However, as there are still only poor CLWEs for many low-resource language pairs (Vulić et al., 2019), we argue that in addition to reducing requirements for training data, methods which offer opportunities precisely for low-resource setups, like leveraging data from linguistically related high-resource languages, should be considered as well. While there exist NLP systems that make use of related languages, e.g., in Machine Translation (Nakov and Ng, 2012; Nguyen and Chiang, 2017), only few work focuses on including them directly into CLWEs. An approach considering a related language in order to improve CLWEs for low-resource language pairs, including English-



*Proceedings of the 1st Workshop on Multilingual Representation Learning*, pages 41–50
November 11, 2021. ©2021 Association for Computational Linguistics

Occitan, has been proposed by Kementchedjhieva et al. (2018). However, using pre-trained monolingual embedding spaces, they do not take into account that monolingual representations of low-resource languages might be of poor quality, which can impede mapping performance.

In this paper, we propose a method where, in contrast to previous work, we consider both addressing the issue of monolingual embedding quality and leveraging information from a supporting language. To this end, we learn multilingual representations for a low-resource source language, a related language, and a target language in two steps: First, we train CLWEs for the low-resource language and the related higher-resource language using the *joint-align* approach by Wang et al. (2020). In that manner, the internal structure of the low-resource embeddings becomes more similar to the structure of the higher-quality related language embeddings. In the second step, we map the resulting CLWE space to the target space using the supervised *MUSE* model (Conneau et al., 2018). Since the first step results in a higher-quality embedding space for the source language, a better mapping to the target space can be found due to their higher isomorphism.

In our experiments, we learn representations for Occitan together with a related language and English. Occitan is a low-resource Romance language, which is related to high-resource languages like French and Spanish, and especially closely related to Catalan. Since particularly good CLWEs exist for each of the three related languages paired with English, we make use of monolingual data from these languages in order to obtain better representations for Occitan and English.

By evaluating our final multilingual embedding space on the Occitan-English BLI task, we show that our method improves CLWEs for these languages compared to all the baseline settings. Furthermore, we find that there are significant differences in how much of an improvement is achieved with each of the supporting languages. Investigating the impact of multiple factors, such as the pairwise linguistic relatedness of the source, target and the related languages, their BLI performance and the dataset sizes of the individual languages, we found the relatedness of the low-resource and the related language to be most influential.

Figure 1: The Occitan-speaking area and its dialects.

## 2 Related work

**The Occitan language** Occitan is a Romance language which is spoken in the south of France, in the Aran Valley (a part of Catalonia, Spain), in a small region in Italy at the French border and in Monaco (see Figure 1[1], where the ensemble of all colored areas represents the Occitan-speaking territory). However, it is not used as a primary language in any of these countries and it only has an official status in Catalonia.

The language the closest related to Occitan is Catalan and they both belong to the Occitano-Romance languages (Bec, 1970). It is also closely related to other Romance languages, e.g., French and Spanish. Occitan is (like all Romance languages) an inflectional language which is morphologically richer than English: there is no case inflection, but it has a rather complex inflectional system for verbs. Occitan word order follows the subject-verb-object regularities and it is therefore syntactically very similar to English. However, like Spanish and Catalan, but unlike French and English, Occitan is a so-called *pro-drop* language, i.e., a conjugated verb can be used without a personal pronoun and hence the subject position does not necessarily have to be filled in an Occitan sentence.

The exact number of speakers of Occitan is not known for certain. Most sources report numbers between 1 and 10 millions, and there are significantly more people with passive knowledge of Occitan than active speakers (Cichon, 2002, pp. 19f). Furthermore, rather than one Occitan language, there are many different dialects (see Figure 1). However, the Languedocian variant is mostly used in written Occitan and thus in the Occitan Wikipedia, which we use for our experiments. Due to these factors

[1]The illustration is available at `http://lowlands-l.net/anniversary/images/occitania.jpg`.

the amount of available written digital resources is low.

**CLWEs for low-resource setups** A lot of research on CLWEs for low-resource languages focuses on reducing the need for cross-lingual data. Zhang et al. (2017) use adversarial training for aligning monolingual vector spaces without any bilingual signal. Conneau et al. (2018) propose an unsupervised mapping method where they combine adversarial training with a Procrustes Analysis refinement step in every iteration. Lample et al. (2018) learn CLWEs jointly for their unsupervised neural machine translation model by concatenating corpora of source and target languages and training fastText skipgram embeddings (Bojanowski et al., 2017) on this corpus. In order to combine the benefits of joint and mapping methods, Wang et al. (2020) propose an approach where they combine both methods. First, CLWEs are trained jointly on a concatenated corpus containing monolingual source and target language data. Oversharing among source and target language vocabularies is then reduced by a vocabulary reallocation step, and finally, source embeddings are mapped to the target embeddings.

However, despite the progress of unsupervised CLWE models, multiple surveys argue against focusing on fully unsupervised approaches. Firstly, giving up on every supervision signal is not necessary, since there is always a small amount of parallel data available if monolingual data is abundant (Artetxe et al., 2020). Secondly, Vulić et al. (2019) show that even the most robust unsupervised approach (Artetxe et al., 2018) cannot deal properly with multiple distant and low-resource languages.

Nevertheless, there are still a lot of languages for which even monolingual data is extremely scarce. For these languages, monolingual embeddings are usually of poor quality (Michel et al., 2020). Consequently, mapping methods are not fruitfully applicable, since they rely on high-quality monolingual embedding spaces. Adams et al. (2017) show that monolingual embedding quality of extremely low-resource languages can be improved if CLWEs for a low- and a high-resource language are trained jointly. Eder et al. (2021) propose a method for better CLWEs by using a small bilingual seed dictionary together with pre-trained monolingual embeddings of the higher-resource language for initialization. On the other hand, these approaches rely only on the source and target languages, while we show the benefits of incorporating further related languages into a multilingual space.

**Leveraging related languages** Besides reducing data requirements, it is also helpful to explore information from linguistically related high-resource languages in low-resource setups. This idea has, for example, been considered in Machine Translation (MT). Nakov and Ng (2012) propose a statistical MT model which requires only a small parallel corpus of the low-resource source and the high-resource target languages, and additionally a larger parallel corpus of a related high-resource language and the target language. Nguyen and Chiang (2017) introduce a transfer learning model for neural MT (NMT) where embeddings of shared words are kept when transferring the model from the original to a related low-resource language. Gu et al. (2018) train a NMT model where embeddings learned during training are computed from a universal embedding space which embed multiple languages. Thus, high-resource languages can provide support for related low-resource languages.

Leveraging information from related high-resource languages to build CLWEs for low-resource setups has only been considered in a few works until now. Multiple approaches were proposed to build representations involving more than two languages, but they either rely on pre-trained monolingual embeddings (Ammar et al., 2016; Heyman et al., 2019; Chen and Cardie, 2018; Alaux et al., 2018) or large training corpora (Devlin et al., 2019), and are thus not well suited for low-resource setups. Kementchedjhieva et al. (2018) proposed Multi-support Generalized Procrustes Analysis (MGPA) to directly incorporate related languages into CLWEs by learning a three-way alignment among English, a low-resource language, and a supporting language. They improve CLWE quality for multiple low-resource language pairs, including Occitan-English. However, unlike our method, MGPA does not consider the internal structure of the monolingual low-resource language space (since it relies on pre-trained monolingual embeddings).

## 3 Approach

To improve CLWEs for low-resource setups, we incorporate a related language by learning representations in two steps: First, we train CLWEs for the low-resource and a related language jointly. Subsequently, we use the resulting joint space together with a set of monolingual target language embeddings to learn the final multilingual space including the low-resource, the supporting, and the target languages. We detail the two steps below.

**Joint alignment** In the first step of our model, we train CLWEs for a low-resource and a related language jointly. This helps to make the internal structure of the low-resource embeddings more similar to the structure of the related language space. Since isomorphism of vector spaces is correlated with mapping performance (Søgaard et al., 2018; Ormazabal et al., 2019) and given that high-quality alignments among English and the supporting language exist, joint training of a low-resource and a related language allows for achieving a better mapping among the low-resource language and English as well.

Instead of simply building embeddings on the concatenated corpora of the two languages (Lample et al., 2018), we use the *joint-align* model proposed by Wang et al. (2020). In their approach, CLWEs are learned in three steps, which we outline in the following. First, unsupervised joint training is performed by running fastText skip-gram (Bojanowski et al., 2017) on the concatenated corpus consisting of monolingual data from both languages ($L_1$ and $L_2$). Since related languages share part of their vocabulary, these words act as a cross-lingual signal to automatically align the vectors of the two languages. However, this step suffers from vocabulary oversharing, i.e., the corpus of $L_1$ contains words which are only part of the vocabulary of $L_2$ due to noise and vice-versa, which leads to errors. To mitigate the issue, vocabulary reallocation is performed in the second step, where words are assigned to one of three sets: the vocabulary of only $L_1$, only $L_2$ or the so-called shared vocabulary. The reallocation is decided based on the frequency ratio of a given word in the two corpora. Using a threshold value, if a word is mainly appearing in the corpus of $L_1$ or $L_2$, it is allocated to the language specific vocabulary, otherwise it is kept in the shared vocabulary. Finally in step three, the language specific embeddings are refined by mapping word embeddings of $L_1$ to $L_2$ in order to improve the final CLWE quality. The resulting CLWE space thus consists of embeddings of shared words and aligned embeddings of non-shared words among the two languages.

| | Occitan | French | Spanish | Catalan |
|---|---|---|---|---|
| Tokens | 15.00 | 985.38 | 745.46 | 246.07 |
| Types | 0.50 | 4.89 | 4.14 | 2.35 |

Table 1: Corpora and vocabulary sizes of the extracted Wikipedia corpora (in millions).

| | Oc/Fr | Oc/Es | Oc/Ca |
|---|---|---|---|
| Types overall | 5.08 | 4.36 | 2.57 |
| Types shared | 0.31 (6.10%) | 0.28 (6.42%) | 0.28 (10.89%) |

Table 2: Vocabulary sizes of the joint corpora (in millions). 'Types shared' indicates the number of shared words among the two languages; the percentage of shared words per corpus is reported in parentheses.

**Mapping** In the second component of our approach, we use MUSE (Conneau et al., 2018) to map the embeddings resulting from joint-align training with the monolingual target language embeddings. We use the supervised version of the MUSE model, which we find to work better for our embeddings than the unsupervised version. In addition, supervised MUSE yields good results when training with identical character strings as a supervision signal (Kementchedjhieva et al., 2018). We consider this supervision method in our experiments as well to ensure that a small training dictionary is not holding back performance.

## 4 Experimental Setup

**Corpora and vocabulary** We pursue our experiments for the low-resource Occitan language and we choose French, Spanish, and Catalan as supporting languages. Like Occitan, they are all Romance languages and hence they all have a partly shared vocabulary with Occitan as well as some similarities in morphology and syntax. French and Spanish have been chosen because they are very high-resource. Catalan has been chosen because it is the language the closest related to Occitan. Furthermore, it has been shown that for all three languages, very good CLWEs together with English can be obtained (Conneau et al., 2018).

We extract Occitan, French, Spanish, and Catalan corpora from respective Wikipedia dumps.[2] Corpora and vocabulary sizes are listed in Table 1.

[2]Available at `https://dumps.wikimedia.org/`. They are preprocessed using the tools available at: `https://www.kdnuggets.com/2017/11/building-wikipedia-text-corpus-nlp.html`.

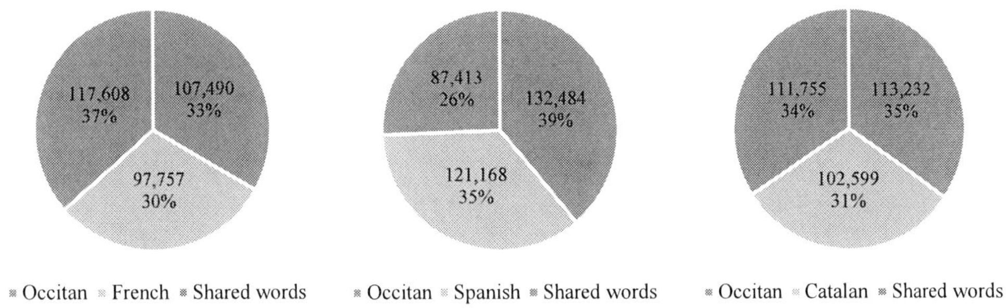


Figure 2: Number of embeddings resulting from joint-align training with Occitan and a related language.

Furthermore, in Table 2, we report vocabulary sizes of the joint corpora used for training the Occitan-related language CLWEs. We also include the number and proportion of shared words per language pair in this table.

**Embeddings** In all our experiments, we used the pre-trained English fastText wiki word vectors released by Bojanowski et al. (2017).[3] For Occitan, French, Spanish, and Catalan, we train our own monolingual embeddings using the Gensim version of fastText skipgram (Řehůřek and Sojka, 2010) with the same parameters used for the pre-trained English embeddings. This is to ensure that they are learned on the same corpora than the embeddings in our proposed model. The monolingual Occitan embedding space used for our baselines contains 111,353 word vectors. All the other monolingual spaces are restricted to the most frequent 200,000 words for training. The smaller number of Occitan embeddings is due to the small corpus and the threshold of at least five occurrences for a word to be considered when training fastText embeddings. The number of embeddings resulting from joint-align training with Occitan and each of the supporting languages is shown in Figure 2. Here, the proportion of Occitan, related language, and shared word vectors is illustrated.

**Parameters** We compare the performance of our model against multiple baselines. We use supervised MUSE (Conneau et al., 2018) and Generalized Procrustes Analysis, an extension of MUSE (GPA; Kementchedjhieva et al., 2018), as baseline models where a mapping between monolingual Occitan and monolingual English embeddings is performed. In addition, we train three baselines using Multi-support GPA (MGPA; Kementchedjhieva et al., 2018) where pre-trained monolingual embeddings from either French, Spanish or Catalan are incorporated. We use all baseline models with default parameters except the threshold for ranking candidate translation pairs, which we set to 15,000 instead of default 10,000 in all models, since it results in a better alignment.

In the first step of our proposed model, we use the joint-align model (Wang et al., 2020) for Occitan and a related language with default parameters. The only exception is that we use supervised MUSE (Conneau et al., 2018) for mapping instead of default RCSLS (Joulin et al., 2018) in order to stay consistent with the second mapping step in our model. We tested using RCSLS in both steps instead, but it did not yield a good mapping for Occitan and English. We use supervised MUSE (Conneau et al., 2018) with the same parameters as in our baseline, both within joint-align training and in the second step of our proposed model.

**Evaluation task** Our evaluation task is bilingual lexicon induction (BLI). We use it to evaluate the quality of our final multilingual embedding spaces, translating from Occitan to English. We also use it for evaluating the shared Occitan and related language spaces resulting from the first step of our model. For this purpose, we run the MUSE evaluation script (Conneau et al., 2018) and we report scores achieved with CSLS retrieval.

**Bilingual dictionaries** We extract training dictionaries for English → Occitan (En-Oc), Occitan → English (Oc-En), Occitan → French (Oc-Fr), and Occitan → Spanish (Oc-Es) from *freelang*.[4] Test dictionaries for these language pairs are ex-

[3]Available at `https://fasttext.cc/docs/en/pretrained-vectors.html`.

[4]They are based on the dictionaries available at `https://www.freelang.net/dictionary/occitan.php` (for Oc-Fr and Oc-Es see linked French and Spanish versions of freelang).

| | train | | test | |
|---|---|---|---|---|
| En → Oc | 738 | (580) | 1,225 | (1,043) |
| Oc → En | 894 | (784) | 1,225 | (1,027) |
| Oc → Es | 1,638 | (1,539) | 1,115 | (1,065) |
| Oc → Ca | 5,511 | (4,118) | 1,000 | (753) |
| Oc → Fr | 8,082 | (7,650) | 1,086 | (1,055) |

Table 3: Number of word pairs in our bilingual dictionaries (number of unique source words in parentheses).

tracted from an Occitan website.[5] For English → Occitan, we use the test dictionary that Kementchedjhieva et al. (2018) extracted from this website. We clean all the dictionaries manually in a manner that they only contain 1-to-1 pairs and that source words appearing in both the initial training and test dictionary of a certain source language → target language pair are discarded from the training dictionary. For the Occitan-Catalan (Oc-Ca) language pair, there is to our knowledge no comparable bilingual dictionary available online. We therefore create our own training and test dictionaries by extracting a Catalan → French dictionary from *freelang*[6] and using it together with our Occitan → French dictionaries for mapping Occitan and Catalan words that have the same translation into French. In addition, we check the resulting dictionaries manually to avoid improper translation pairs. Dictionary sizes are reported in Table 3. Note that especially our training dictionaries vary significantly in size, since we use all the words available from our sources for every language pair. Unfortunately, due to copyright restrictions, we are not able to release dictionaries based on *freelang*. Please follow the above instructions to recreate them.

Furthermore, we use French-English, Spanish-English, and Catalan-English training dictionaries available from MUSE (Conneau et al., 2018).

## 5 Results

We show the results for Occitan → English BLI yielded by the baselines and our model in Table 4, Settings a-f and 1-6, respectively. Note that as the mapping direction in case of MUSE and GPA, Occitan was taken as the source and English as the target language. MGPA, however, can only be trained with the low-resource and the related language on the target language side. We evaluated the resulting CLWEs for Occitan → English afterwards. For MGPA and our model, results for incorporating either French, Spanish, or Catalan are listed separately in different columns. Furthermore, Settings 1-6 of our model vary in two more dimensions. Firstly, we employ two different subsets of the shared Occitan-related language space as source embeddings: In Settings 1-4, we use the 'full space' containing vectors of words contained in the shared and language specific (Occitan and the given related language) vocabularies. In Settings 5-6, we use a 'reduced space' containing only the vectors of shared and Occitan vocabularies. Secondly, we experiment with various bilingual supervision signals: the Occitan-English training dictionary (oc-en), the dictionary of the respective incorporated related language and English (rel-en), both training dictionaries concatenated (full), or identical character string supervision (id char). In settings where the reduced source embedding space is used, we omit training with the 'rel-en' and 'full' dictionaries, since the related language words are excluded from the embedding space.

It can be seen from Table 4 that all 18 settings of our model outperform all the baseline models, i.e., regardless of which language we use for support, which subset of the shared Occitan-related language space we employ, and which initial supervision signal we use. However, there are significant differences in performance across the various settings: Relative improvements compared to the strongest baseline (MGPA ca) are between 2.78% and 15.47%. We discuss these differences in the following.

**Support from related language words** Having a closer look at the numbers in Table 4, it becomes obvious that for every incorporated language, Settings 1-4 (full space) yield better scores than Settings 5-6 (reduced). The only exception is Setting 5 in the experiments with Spanish. More precisely, if related language words are considered during training, P@1 for Occitan-English BLI is up to 4.4% higher than in settings where only Occitan and shared words are included. This shows that in terms of representing the low-resource language together with English, the multilingual embedding space containing low-resource, related language, and English words is of higher quality than the embedding space with only low-resource language

[5] http://www.occitania.online.fr/aqui.comenca.occitania/dicolist.html

[6] Available at https://www.freelang.com/dictionnaire/catalan.php.

| No. | Model | Src. emb. | Train dict. | P@1 | P@10 |
|---|---|---|---|---|---|
| a | MUSE | Oc | oc-en | 15.47 | 31.05 |
| b | | | id char | 15.91 | 30.94 |
| c | GPA | Oc | oc-en | 15.69 | 32.38 |
| d | | | id char | 15.91 | 31.71 |

| No. | Model | Src. emb. | Train dict. | French P@1 | French P@10 | Spanish P@1 | Spanish P@10 | Catalan P@1 | Catalan P@10 |
|---|---|---|---|---|---|---|---|---|---|
| e | MGPA | Oc | full | 20.77 | 35.69 | 19.01 | 34.59 | 20.66 | 36.69 |
| f | | | id char | 21.10 | 35.58 | 19.34 | 33.26 | 21.33 | 37.68 |
| 1 | Our | full space | full | 27.17 | 44.54 | 27.51 | 46.55 | 36.69 | **55.09** |
| 2 | | | oc-en | 27.17 | 42.09 | 28.29 | 46.44 | 34.83 | 53.78 |
| 3 | | | rel-en | 27.73 | 43.76 | 27.73 | 46.88 | **36.80** | 52.68 |
| 4 | | | id char | 26.73 | 41.98 | 27.95 | 45.99 | 34.39 | 52.46 |
| 5 | | reduced | oc-en | 26.05 | 43.16 | 28.63 | 46.50 | 34.06 | 53.43 |
| 6 | | | id char | 24.76 | 41.44 | 24.11 | 43.27 | 32.43 | 51.79 |

Table 4: Results for Occitan → English BLI achieved by various baselines and our model. The best P@1 and P@10 scores per incorporated language are underlined, while **bold** indicates the overall best. 'Full space' denotes using the ensemble of Occitan + related language + shared source embeddings for mapping, while the 'reduced' space only consists of Occitan + shared words. The 'full' training dictionary is a concatenation of the Occitan → English (oc-en) and the incorporated related language → English (rel-en) dictionaries.

and English words. The reason for this is that the related language does not only help to build better representations for the low-resource language in step 1 (joint-alignment) of our model, but it also helps to build a better mapping in step 2. This is due to the iterative refinement of MUSE which can update the initial training dictionary with good-quality related language-English word pairs as well in addition to the Occitan-English pairs.

**Differences across incorporated languages** Comparing performance across the different supporting languages shows that incorporating Catalan leads by far to the largest improvements (up to 15.5% P@1 compared to the strongest baseline), while French and Spanish only contribute to smaller improvements (up to 6.4% and 7.3% P@1, respectively).

We investigated multiple factors to find out where these differences come from: the quality of the Occitan-related language CLWEs, the quality of the related language-English CLWEs, and the linguistic relatedness of Occitan and an incorporated language, among others. For this purpose, we evaluate the Occitan-related language CLWEs resulting from the first step of our model as well as the embedding spaces resulting from the second step of our model on the BLI task for the respective language pairs.

| No. | Language pair | P@1 | P@10 |
|---|---|---|---|
| 1 | Occitan → French | 54.83 | 67.66 |
| 2 | Occitan → Spanish | 48.66 | 62.79 |
| 3 | Occitan → Catalan | 45.17 | 58.49 |
| 4 | French → English | 76.55 | 89.99 |
| 5 | Spanish → English | 77.23 | 90.42 |
| 6 | Catalan → English | 67.97 | 83.58 |

Table 5: Results for BLI. 1-3: Occitan-related language CLWEs resulting from the first step of our model. 4-6: Multilingual space resulting from the second step of our model.

The numbers in Table 5 show that the quality of the CLWE spaces mentioned above cannot explain that Catalan provides the best support for Occitan-English CLWEs. This is because results for French and Spanish are even better than scores for Catalan. Note, however, that Settings 1-3 in Table 5 are not completely comparable, since our test dictionaries do not contain the exact same word pairs for every language pair. Nevertheless, by evaluating the Occitan-related language CLWEs we show that the shared Occitan-Catalan space is not clearly better than the other two CLWE spaces in terms of BLI performance and thus this aspect is not responsible for the better quality of the final multilingual embeddings resulting from our model. The same holds for the evaluation of the related language-English

| Approach | | P@1 | P@10 |
|---|---|---|---|
| Baselines | MUSE | 17.74 | 31.40 |
| | GPA | 17.85 | 32.15 |
| | MGPA fr | 21.61 | 34.95 |
| | MGPA es | 19.46 | 33.44 |
| | MGPA ca | **22.47** | 36.88 |
| Our model | French | 4.76 | 32.65 |
| | Spanish | 5.84 | 31.60 |
| | Catalan | 15.34 | **43.34** |

Table 6: Results for English → Occitan BLI. (Parameters for training our model are the same as in Table 4, Setting 1.)

| Source word | MUSE | Our model |
|---|---|---|
| age | **edat** | <u>âge</u> |
| bird | **aucèl** | <u>oiseau</u> |
| bank | **banca** | bank |

Table 7: Examples of English source words and their nearest neighbors in the Occitan embeddings before and after incorporating French (**bold**: correct Occitan translation; <u>underlined</u> correct French translation).

CLWEs in Settings 4-6.

The degree of linguistic relatedness to Occitan, however, is the only factor where Catalan is clearly more favorable than French and Spanish (as described in Section 2). Consequently, we can infer that it is the decisive factor for how much support an incorporated language provides for learning better Occitan-English CLWEs.

**English → Occitan direction** In another set of experiments, we switch source and target languages to examine how our model performs when translating from English to Occitan. For completeness, we do not only reverse the evaluation direction but the mapping direction of the used CLWEs in step 2 of our approach as well, i.e., we use the pre-trained monolingual English embeddings as source and map them to the shared Occitan-related language space resulting from the first step of our model as before. We show our results for English → Occitan in Table 6, including the results of our baseline models for the same mapping direction.

We find that, contrarily to our experiments for the Occitan → English direction, our approach cannot clearly improve $P@1$ on the English → Occitan BLI task. Checking the nearest neighbors of English test source words in our shared Occitan-French space reveals that it is very French-centric. In many cases, a French word is retrieved as the nearest neighbor of an English word, as shown in Table 7. This problem does not occur in the baselines due to no shared embeddings between languages. On the other hand, the phenomenon affects other multilingual models with shared vocabularies as well, such as mBERT (Devlin et al., 2019), which are mainly used for downstream tasks, e.g., zero-shot cross-lingual transfer learning. To mitigate the issue, we experimented with excluding either French only or French only and shared words from the translation candidates, respectively. However, it did not solve the issue, since the shared vocabulary includes a large number of relevant French and Occitan words, which leads to either noise or missing Occitan words depending on their inclusion as translation candidates.

On the other hand, P@10 scores achieved by our model are comparable and even significantly higher in case of Catalan than the baseline scores. This indicates that although not being the top 1 retrieved translation, the correct Occitan translation can be found in the near neighborhood of an English source word, indicating the good quality of our CLWEs. Consequently, our embeddings are still useful for various downstream tasks in the English → Occitan direction. For instance, when using them for cross-lingual transfer learning, e.g., classifying Occitan texts using a model trained on English, noise in the Occitan target space stemming from the related language vocabulary is not an issue, since the inputs to be classified are well-formed Occitan sentences.

## 6 Conclusion

In this paper, we presented a model for improving CLWE quality in low-resource setups by learning multilingual embedding spaces with a related language. To this end, a multilingual embedding space containing the low-resource source language, a related language, and the target language words is learned in two steps: first joint training of low-resource and related language embeddings; and second mapping the resulting CLWEs to a target language space. We pursued our experiments for the low-resource language Occitan with support from French, Spanish, or Catalan in different settings. We showed that our method improves the quality of CLWEs for these languages compared to both bilingual and multilingual baselines, especially when Catalan, the closest related language to Occitan, is incorporated (up to 15.5% P@1 improvement). Investigating multiple factors, we found that the degree of linguistic relatedness of the low-resource and the incorporated language is the most decisive for how much support a language provides. Our work indicates that novel approaches should not only focus on learning better representations using small corpora but also on incorporating data from related languages.

## Acknowledgments

The work was supported by the European Research Council (ERC) under the European Union's Horizon 2020 research and innovation programme (grant agreement No. 640550) and by German Research Foundation (DFG; grant FR 2829/4-1).

## References

Oliver Adams, Adam Makarucha, Graham Neubig, Steven Bird, and Trevor Cohn. 2017. Cross-lingual word embeddings for low-resource language modeling. In *Proceedings of EACL*, pages 937–947.

Jean Alaux, Edouard Grave, Marco Cuturi, and Armand Joulin. 2018. Unsupervised Hyper-alignment for Multilingual Word Embeddings. In *Proceeding of IRLC*.

Waleed Ammar, George Mulcaire, Yulia Tsvetkov, Guillaume Lample, Chris Dyer, and Noah A. Smith. 2016. Massively multilingual word embeddings. *CoRR*, abs/1602.01925.

Mikel Artetxe, Gorka Labaka, and Eneko Agirre. 2017. Learning bilingual word embeddings with (almost) no bilingual data. In *Proceedings of ACL*, pages 451–462.

Mikel Artetxe, Gorka Labaka, and Eneko Agirre. 2018. A robust self-learning method for fully unsupervised cross-lingual mappings of word embeddings. In *Proceedings of ACL*, pages 789–798.

Mikel Artetxe, Sebastian Ruder, Dani Yogatama, Gorka Labaka, and Eneko Agirre. 2020. A call for more rigor in unsupervised cross-lingual learning. In *Proceedings of ACL*, pages 7375–7388.

Pierre Bec. 1970. *Manuel pratique de philologie romane*. Picard.

Piotr Bojanowski, Edouard Grave, Armand Joulin, and Tomas Mikolov. 2017. Enriching word vectors with subword information. *Transactions of the Association for Computational Linguistics*, 5:135–146.

Xilun Chen and Claire Cardie. 2018. Unsupervised Multilingual Word Embeddings. In *Proceedings of EMNLP*, pages 261–270.

Peter Cichon. 2002. *Einführung in die Okzitanische Sprache*. Romanistischer Verlag.

Alexis Conneau, Guillaume Lample, Marc'Aurelio Ranzato, Ludovic Denoyer, and Hervé Jégou. 2018. Word Translation Without Parallel Data. In *Proceedings of ICLR*.

Jacob Devlin, Ming-Wei Chang, Kenton Lee, and Kristina Toutanova. 2019. BERT: Pre-training of deep bidirectional transformers for language understanding. In *Proceedings of NAACL: HLT*, pages 4171–4186.

Tobias Eder, Viktor Hangya, and Alexander Fraser. 2021. Anchor-based Bilingual Word Embeddings for Low-Resource Languages. In *Proceedings of ACL-IJCNLP*, pages 227–232.

Jiatao Gu, Hany Hassan, Jacob Devlin, and Victor O.K. Li. 2018. Universal neural machine translation for extremely low resource languages. In *Proceedings of NAACL: HLT*, pages 344–354.

Geert Heyman, Bregt Verreet, Ivan Vulić, and Marie-Francine Moens. 2019. Learning Unsupervised Multilingual Word Embeddings with Incremental Multilingual Hubs. In *Proceedings of NAACL-HLT*, pages 1890–1902.

Armand Joulin, Piotr Bojanowski, Tomas Mikolov, Hervé Jégou, and Edouard Grave. 2018. Loss in translation: Learning bilingual word mapping with a retrieval criterion. In *Proceedings of EMNLP*, pages 2979–2984.

Yova Kementchedjhieva, Sebastian Ruder, Ryan Cotterell, and Anders Søgaard. 2018. Generalizing Procrustes analysis for better bilingual dictionary induction. In *Proceedings of CoNLL*, pages 211–220.

Alexandre Klementiev, Ivan Titov, and Binod Bhattarai. 2012. Inducing crosslingual distributed representations of words. In *Proceedings of COLING*, pages 1459–1474.

Guillaume Lample, Myle Ott, Alexis Conneau, Ludovic Denoyer, and Marc'Aurelio Ranzato. 2018. Phrase-based & neural unsupervised machine translation. In *Proceedings of EMNLP*, pages 5039–5049.

Leah Michel, Viktor Hangya, and Alexander Fraser. 2020. Exploring bilingual word embeddings for Hiligaynon, a low-resource language. In *Proceedings of LREC*, pages 2573–2580.

Tomás Mikolov, Quoc V. Le, and Ilya Sutskever. 2013. Exploiting similarities among languages for machine translation. *CoRR*, abs/1309.4168.

Preslav Nakov and Hwee Tou Ng. 2012. Improving statistical machine translation for a resource-poor language using related resource-rich languages. *Journal of Artificial Intelligence Research*, 44:179–222.

Toan Q. Nguyen and David Chiang. 2017. Transfer learning across low-resource, related languages for neural machine translation. In *Proceedings of IJC-NLP*, pages 296–301.

Aitor Ormazabal, Mikel Artetxe, Gorka Labaka, Aitor Soroa, and Eneko Agirre. 2019. Analyzing the limitations of cross-lingual word embedding mappings. In *Proceedings of ACL*, pages 4990–4995.

Barun Patra, Joel Ruben Antony Moniz, Sarthak Garg, Matthew R. Gormley, and Graham Neubig. 2019. Bilingual lexicon induction with semi-supervision in non-isometric embedding spaces. In *Proceedings of ACL*, pages 184–193.

Radim Řehůřek and Petr Sojka. 2010. Software framework for topic modelling with large corpora. In *Proceedings of the LREC 2010 Workshop on New Challenges for NLP Frameworks*, pages 45–50.

Tal Schuster, Ori Ram, Regina Barzilay, and Amir Globerson. 2019. Cross-lingual alignment of contextual word embeddings, with applications to zero-shot dependency parsing. In *Proceedings of NAACL: HLT*, pages 1599–1613.

Samuel L. Smith, David H. P. Turban, Steven Hamblin, and Nils Y. Hammerla. 2017. Offline bilingual word vectors, orthogonal transformations and the inverted softmax. In *Proceedings of ICLR*.

Anders Søgaard, Sebastian Ruder, and Ivan Vulić. 2018. On the limitations of unsupervised bilingual dictionary induction. In *Proceedings of ACL*, pages 778–788.

Ivan Vulić, Goran Glavaš, Roi Reichart, and Anna Korhonen. 2019. Do we really need fully unsupervised cross-lingual embeddings? In *Proceedings of EMNLP-IJCNLP*, pages 4407–4418.

Ivan Vulić and Anna Korhonen. 2016. On the role of seed lexicons in learning bilingual word embeddings. In *Proceedings of ACL*, pages 247–257.

Zirui Wang, Jiateng Xie, Ruochen Xu, Yiming Yang, Graham Neubig, and Jaime G. Carbonell. 2020. Cross-lingual alignment vs joint training: A comparative study and a simple unified framework. In *Proceedings of ICLR*.

Min Xiao and Yuhong Guo. 2014. Distributed word representation learning for cross-lingual dependency parsing. In *Proceedings of CoNLL*, pages 119–129.

Meng Zhang, Yang Liu, Huanbo Luan, and Maosong Sun. 2017. Adversarial training for unsupervised bilingual lexicon induction. In *Proceedings of ACL*, pages 1959–1970.

# Specializing Multilingual Language Models: An Empirical Study

**Ethan C. Chau**[†] **Noah A. Smith**[†⋆]
[†]Paul G. Allen School of Computer Science & Engineering, University of Washington
[⋆]Allen Institute for Artificial Intelligence
{echau18,nasmith}@cs.washington.edu

## Abstract

Pretrained multilingual language models have become a common tool in transferring NLP capabilities to low-resource languages, often with adaptations. In this work, we study the performance, extensibility, and interaction of two such adaptations: vocabulary augmentation and script transliteration. Our evaluations on part-of-speech tagging, universal dependency parsing, and named entity recognition in nine diverse low-resource languages uphold the viability of these approaches while raising new questions around how to optimally adapt multilingual models to low-resource settings.

## 1 Introduction

Research in natural language processing is increasingly carried out in languages beyond English. This includes *high-resource* languages with abundant data, as well as *low-resource* languages, for which labeled (and unlabeled) data is scarce. In fact, many of the world's languages fall into the latter category, even some with a high number of speakers. This presents unique challenges compared to high-resource languages: effectively modeling low-resource languages involves both accurately tokenizing text in such languages and maximally leveraging the limited available data.

One common approach to low-resource NLP is the *multilingual* paradigm, in which methods that have shown success in English are applied to the union of many languages' data,[1] enabling transfer between languages. For instance, multilingual contextual word representations (CWRs) from language models (Devlin et al., 2019; Huang et al., 2019; Lample and Conneau, 2019, *inter alia*) are conventionally "pretrained" on large multilingual corpora before being "finetuned" directly on supervised tasks; this pretraining-finetuning approach is derived from analogous monolingual models (Devlin et al., 2019; Liu et al., 2019; Peters et al., 2018). However, considering the diversity of the world's languages and the great data imbalance among them, it is natural to question whether the current multilingual paradigm can be improved upon for low-resource languages.

Indeed, past work has demonstrated that it can. For instance, Wu and Dredze (2020) find that multilingual models often lag behind non-contextualized baselines for the lowest-resource languages in their training data, drawing into question their utility in such settings. Conneau et al. (2020a) posit that this phenomenon is a result of limited model capacity, which proves to be a bottleneck for sufficient transfer to low-resource languages. In fact, with multilingual models only being pretrained on a limited set of languages, most of the world's languages are unseen by the model. For such languages, the performance of such models is even worse (Chau et al., 2020), due in part to the diversity of scripts across the world's languages (Muller et al., 2021; Pfeiffer et al., 2021b; Rust et al., 2021) as compared to the models' Latin-centricity (Ács, 2019).

Nonetheless, there have been multiple attempts to remedy this discrepancy by *specializing*[2] a multilingual model to a given target low-resource language, from which we take inspiration. Among them, Chau et al. (2020) augment the model's vocabulary to more effectively tokenize text, then pretrain on a small amount of data in the target language; they report significant performance improvements on a small set of low-resource languages. In a similar vein, Muller et al. (2021) propose to transliterate text in the target language

[1] Within the multilingual paradigm, a distinction is sometimes made between *massively multilingual* methods, which consider tens or hundreds of languages; and *polyglot* methods, which use only a handful. In this paper, all mentions of "multilingual" refer to the former.

[2] We use *specialization* to denote preparing a model for use on a specific target language, to the exclusion of others. This is a subset of *adaptation*, which includes all techniques that adjust a model for use on target languages, regardless of their resulting universality.

to Latin script to be better tokenized by the existing model, followed by additional pretraining; they observe mixed results and note that transliteration quality may be a confounding factor. We hypothesize that these two methods can serve as the basis for improvements in modeling a broad set of low-resource languages.

In this work, we study the effectiveness, extensibility, and interaction of these two approaches to specialization: the vocabulary augmentation technique of Chau et al. (2020) and the script transliteration method of Muller et al. (2021). We verify the performance of vocabulary augmentation on three tasks in a diverse set of nine low-resource languages across three different scripts, especially on non-Latin scripts (§2) and find that these gains are associated with improved vocabulary coverage of the target language. We further observe a negative interaction between vocabulary augmentation and transliteration in light of a broader framework for specializing multilingual models, while noting that vocabulary augmentation offers an appealing balance of performance and cost (§3). Overall, our results highlight several possible directions for future study in the low-resource setting. Our code, data, and hyperparameters are publicly available.[3]

## 2 Revisiting Vocabulary Augmentation

We begin by revisiting the Vocabulary Augmentation method of Chau et al. (2020), which we recast more generally in light of recent work (§2.1). We evaluate their claims on three different tasks, using a diverse set of languages in multiple scripts (§2.2), and find that the results hold to an even more pronounced degree in unseen low-resource languages with non-Latin scripts (§2.3).

### 2.1 Method Overview

Following Chau et al. (2020), we consider how to apply the pretrained multilingual BERT model (MBERT; Devlin et al., 2019) to a target low-resource language, for which both labeled and unlabeled data is scarce. This model has produced strong CWRs for many languages (Kondratyuk and Straka, 2019, *inter alia*) and has been the starting model for many studies on low-resource languages (Muller et al., 2021; Pfeiffer et al., 2020; Wang et al., 2020). MBERT covers the languages with the 104 largest Wikipedias, and it uses this data to construct a wordpiece vocabulary (Wu et al., 2016) and train its transformer-based architecture (Vaswani et al., 2017). Although low-resource languages are slightly oversampled, high-resource languages still dominate both the final pretraining data and the vocabulary (Ács, 2019; Devlin et al., 2019).

Chau et al. (2020) note that target low-resource languages fall into three categories with respect to MBERT's pretraining data: the lowest-resource languages in the data (Type 1), completely unseen low-resource languages (Type 2), and low-resouce languages with more representation (Type 0).[4] Due to their poor representation in the vocabulary, Type 1 and Type 2 languages achieve suboptimal tokenization and higher rates of the "unknown" wordpiece[5] when using MBERT out of the box. This hinders the model's ability to capture meaningful patterns in the data, resulting in reduced data efficiency and degraded performance.

We note that this challenge is exacerbated when modeling languages written in non-Latin scripts. MBERT's vocabulary is heavily Latin-centric (Ács, 2019; Muller et al., 2021), resulting in a significantly larger portion of non-Latin scripts being represented with "unknown" tokens (Pfeiffer et al., 2021b) and further limiting the model's ability to generalize. In effect, MBERT's low initial performance on such languages can be attributed to its inability to represent the script itself.

To alleviate the problem of poor tokenization, Chau et al. (2020) propose to specialize MBERT using Vocabulary Augmentation (VA). Given unlabeled data in the target language, they train a new wordpiece vocabulary on the data, then select the 99 most common wordpieces in the new vocabulary that replace "unknown" tokens under the original vocabulary. They then add these 99 wordpieces to the original vocabulary and continue pretraining MBERT on the unlabeled data for additional steps. They further describe a tiered variant (TVA), in which a larger learning rate is used for the embeddings of these 99 new wordpieces. VA yields strong gains over unadapted multilingual language models on dependency parsing in four low-resource languages with Latin scripts. How-

[3]https://github.com/ethch18/specializing-multilingual

[4]Muller et al. (2021) further subdivide Type 2 into Easy, Medium, and Hard languages, based on the performance of MBERT after being exposed to these languages. However, this categorization cannot be determined *a priori* for a given language.

[5]The "unknown" wordpiece is inserted when the wordpiece algorithm is unable to segment a word-level token with the current vocabulary.

ever, no evaluation has been performed on other tasks or on languages with non-Latin scripts, which raises our first research question:

**RQ1**: Do the conclusions of Chau et al. (2020) hold for other tasks and for languages with non-Latin scripts?

We can view VA and TVA as an instantation of a more general framework of vocabulary augmentation, shared by other approaches to using MBERT in low-resource settings. Given a new vocabulary $V$, number of wordpieces $n$, and learning rate multiplier $a$, the $n$ most common wordpieces in $V$ are added to the original vocabulary. Additional pretraining is then performed, with the embeddings of the $n$ wordpieces taking on a learning rate $a$ times greater than the overall learning rate. For VA, we set $n = 99$ and $a = 1$, while we treat $a$ as a hyperparameter for TVA. The related E-MBERT method of Wang et al. (2020) sets $n = |V|$ and $a = 1$. Investigating various other instantiations of this framework is an interesting research direction, though it is out of the scope of this work.

### 2.2 Experiments

We expand on the dependency parsing evaluations of Chau et al. (2020) by additionally considering named entity recognition and part-of-speech tagging. We follow Kondratyuk and Straka (2019) and compute the CWR for each token as a weighted sum of the activations at each MBERT layer. For dependency parsing, we follow the setup of Chau et al. (2020) and Muller et al. (2021) and use the CWRs as input to the graph-based dependency parser of Dozat and Manning (2017). For named entity recognition, the CWRs are used as input to a CRF layer, while part-of-speech tagging uses a linear projection atop the representations. In all cases, the underlying CWRs are finetuned during downstream task training, and we do not add an additional encoder layer above the transformer outputs. We train models on five different random seeds and report average scores and standard errors.

#### 2.2.1 Languages and Datasets

We select a set of nine typologically diverse low-resource languages for evaluation, including three of the original four used by Chau et al. (2020). These languages use three different scripts and are chosen based on the availability of labeled datasets and their exemplification of the three language types identified by Chau et al. (2020). Of the languages seen by MBERT, all selected Type 0 languages are within the 45 largest Wikipedias, while the remaining Type 1 languages are within the top 100. The Type 2 languages, which are excluded from MBERT, are all outside of the top 150.[6] Additional information about the evaluation languages is given in Tab. 1.

**Unlabeled Datasets** Following Chau et al. (2020), we use articles from Wikipedia as unlabeled data for additional pretraining in order to reflect the original pretraining data. We downsample full articles from the largest Wikipedias to be on the order of millions of tokens in order to simulate a low-resource unlabeled setting, and we remove sentences that appear in the labeled validation or test sets.

**Labeled Datasets** For dependency parsing and part-of-speech tagging, we use datasets and train/test splits from Universal Dependencies (Nivre et al., 2020), version 2.5 (Zeman et al., 2019). POS tagging uses language-specific part-of-speech tags (XPOS) to evaluate understanding of language-specific syntactic phenomena. The Belarusian treebank lacks XPOS tags for certain examples, so we use universal part-of-speech tags instead. Dependency parsers are trained with gold word segmentation and no part-of-speech features. Experiments with named entity recognition use the WikiAnn dataset (Pan et al., 2017), following past work (Muller et al., 2021; Pfeiffer et al., 2020; Wu and Dredze, 2020). Specifically, we use the balanced train/test splits of (Rahimi et al., 2019). We note that UD datasets were unavailable for Meadow Mari, and partitioned WikiAnn datasets were missing for Wolof.

#### 2.2.2 Baselines

To measure the effectiveness of VA, we benchmark it against unadapted MBERT, as well as directly pretraining MBERT on the unlabeled data without modifying the vocabulary (Chau et al., 2020; Muller et al., 2021; Pfeiffer et al., 2020). Following Chau et al. (2020), we refer to the latter approach as *language-adaptive pretraining* (LAPT). We also evaluate two monolingual baselines that are trained on our unlabeled data: fastText embeddings (FASTT; Bojanowski et al., 2017), which represent a static word vector approach; and a BERT model trained from scratch (BERT). For

[6] Based on `https://meta.wikimedia.org/wiki/List_of_Wikipedias`.

| Language | Type | Script | Family | # Sentences | # Tokens | Downsample % | # WP/Token |
|---|---|---|---|---|---|---|---|
| Bulgarian (BG) | 0 | Cyrillic | Slavic | 357k | 5.6M | 10% | 1.81 |
| Belarusian (BE) | 0 | Cyrillic | Slavic | 187k | 2.7M | 10% | 2.25 |
| Meadow Mari (MHR) | 2 | Cyrillic | Uralic | 52k | 512k | – | 2.37 |
| Vietnamese (VI) | 0 | Latin | Viet-Muong | 338k | 6.9M | 5% | 1.17 |
| Irish (GA) | 1 | Latin | Celtic | 274k | 5.8M | – | 1.83 |
| Maltese (MT) | 2 | Latin | Semitic | 75k | 1.4M | – | 2.39 |
| Wolof (WO) | 2 | Latin | Niger-Congo | 15k | 396k | – | 1.78 |
| Urdu (UR) | 0 | Perso-Arabic | Indic | 201k | 3.6M | 20% | 1.58 |
| Uyghur (UG) | 2 | Perso-Arabic | Turkic | 136k | 2.3M | – | 2.54 |

Table 1: Language overview and unlabeled dataset statistics: number of sentences, number of tokens, and average wordpieces per token under the original MBERT vocabulary.

BERT, we follow Muller et al. (2021) and train a six-layer RoBERTa model (Liu et al., 2019) with a language-specific SentencePiece tokenizer (Kudo and Richardson, 2018). For a fair comparison to VA, we use the same task-specific architectures and modify only the input representations.

#### 2.2.3 Implementation Details

To pretrain LAPT and VA models, we use the code of Chau et al. (2020), who modify the pretraining code of Devlin et al. (2019) to only use the masked language modeling (MLM) loss. To generate VA vocabularies, we train a new vocabulary of size 5000 and select the 99 wordpieces that replace the most unknown tokens. We train with a fixed linear warmup of 1000 steps. To pretrain BERT models, we use the HuggingFace Transformers library (Wolf et al., 2020). Following Muller et al. (2021), we train a half-sized RoBERTa model with six layers and 12 attention heads. We use a byte-pair vocabulary of size 52000 and a linear warmup of 1 epoch. For LAPT, VA, and BERT, we train for up to 20 epochs total, selecting the highest-performing epoch based on validation masked language modeling loss. FASTT models are trained with the skip-gram model for five epochs, with the default hyperparameters of Bojanowski et al. (2017).

Training of downstream parsers and taggers follows Chau et al. (2020) and Kondratyuk and Straka (2019), with an inverse square-root learning rate decay and linear warmup, and layer-wise gradual unfreezing and discriminative finetuning. Models are trained with AllenNLP, version 2.1.0 (Gardner et al., 2018), for up to 200 epochs with early stopping based on validation performance. We choose batch sizes to be the maximum that allows for successful training on one GPU.

### 2.3 Results

Tab. 2 presents performance of the different input representations on POS tagging, dependency parsing, and named entity recognition. VA achieves strong results across all languages and tasks and is the top performer in the majority of them, suggesting that augmenting the vocabulary addresses MBERT's limited vocabulary coverage of the target language and is beneficial during continued pretraining.

The relative gains that VA provides appear to correlate not only with language type, as in the findings of Chau et al. (2020), but also with each language's script. For instance, in Vietnamese, which is a Type 0 Latin script language, the improvements from VA are marginal at best, reflecting the Latin-dominated pretraining data of MBERT. Irish, the Type 1 Latin script language, is only slightly more receptive. However, Type 0 languages in Cyrillic and Arabic scripts, which are less represented in MBERT's pretraining data, are more receptive to VA, with VA even outperforming all other methods for Urdu. This trend is amplified in the Type 2 languages, as the improvements for Maltese and Wolof are small but significant. However, they are dwarfed in magnitude by those of Uyghur, where VA achieves up to a 57% relative error reduction over LAPT.

This result corroborates the findings of both Chau et al. (2020) and Muller et al. (2021) and answers **RQ1**. Prior to specialization, MBERT is especially poorly equipped to handle unseen low-resource languages and languages in non-Latin scripts due to its inability to model the script itself. In such cases, specialization via VA is beneficial, providing MBERT with explicit signal about the target language and script while maintaining its language-agnostic insights. On the other hand, this also motivates additional investigation into reme-

| Rep. | BE* (0) | BG (0) | GA (1) | MT (2) | UG (2) | UR (0) | VI (0) | WO (2) | Avg. |
|---|---|---|---|---|---|---|---|---|---|
| FASTT | 68.84 ± 7.16 | 88.86 ± 0.37 | 86.87 ± 2.55 | 89.68 ± 2.15 | 89.45 ± 1.37 | 90.81 ± 0.31 | 81.84 ± 1.15 | 87.48 ± 0.55 | 85.48 |
| BERT | 91.00 ± 0.30 | 94.48 ± 0.10 | 90.36 ± 0.20 | 92.61 ± 0.10 | 90.87 ± 0.13 | 89.88 ± 0.13 | 84.73 ± 0.13 | 87.71 ± 0.31 | 90.20 |
| MBERT | 94.57 ± 0.45 | 96.98 ± 0.08 | 91.91 ± 0.25 | 94.01 ± 0.17 | 78.07 ± 0.22 | 91.77 ± 0.18 | 88.97 ± 0.10 | 93.04 ± 0.20 | 91.16 |
| LAPT | **95.74 ± 0.44** | 97.15 ± 0.04 | 93.28 ± 0.19 | 95.76 ± 0.09 | 79.88 ± 0.27 | 92.18 ± 0.16 | **89.64 ± 0.20** | **94.58 ± 0.13** | 92.28 |
| VA | 95.28 ± 0.51 | **97.20 ± 0.06** | **93.33 ± 0.16** | **96.33 ± 0.09** | **91.49 ± 0.13** | **92.24 ± 0.16** | 89.49 ± 0.22 | 94.48 ± 0.20 | **93.73** |

(a) POS tagging (accuracy). *Belarusian uses universal POS tags.

| Rep. | BE (0) | BG (0) | GA (1) | MT (2) | UG (2) | UR (0) | VI (0) | WO (2) | Avg. |
|---|---|---|---|---|---|---|---|---|---|
| FASTT | 35.81 ± 2.24 | 84.03 ± 0.41 | 65.58 ± 1.21 | 68.45 ± 1.40 | 54.52 ± 1.02 | 79.33 ± 0.25 | 54.91 ± 0.79 | 70.39 ± 1.39 | 64.13 |
| BERT | 45.77 ± 1.35 | 84.61 ± 0.27 | 64.02 ± 0.49 | 65.92 ± 0.45 | 60.34 ± 0.27 | 78.07 ± 0.22 | 54.70 ± 0.27 | 60.12 ± 0.39 | 64.19 |
| MBERT | 71.83 ± 0.90 | 91.62 ± 0.23 | 71.68 ± 0.62 | 76.63 ± 0.35 | 47.70 ± 0.44 | 81.45 ± 0.26 | 64.58 ± 0.42 | 76.24 ± 0.83 | 72.72 |
| LAPT | 72.77 ± 1.12 | **92.08 ± 0.31** | **74.79 ± 0.12** | 81.53 ± 0.37 | 50.67 ± 0.34 | 81.78 ± 0.44 | **66.15 ± 0.41** | **80.34 ± 0.14** | 75.01 |
| VA | **73.22 ± 1.23** | 91.90 ± 0.20 | 74.35 ± 0.22 | **82.00 ± 0.31** | **67.55 ± 0.17** | **81.88 ± 0.25** | 65.64 ± 0.12 | 80.22 ± 0.41 | **77.09** |

(b) UD parsing (LAS).

| Rep. | BE (0) | BG (0) | GA (1) | MT (2) | UG (2) | UR (0) | VI (0) | MHR (2) | Avg. |
|---|---|---|---|---|---|---|---|---|---|
| FASTT | 84.26 ± 0.86 | 87.98 ± 0.76 | 67.21 ± 4.30 | 33.53 ± 17.89 | – | 92.85 ± 2.04 | 85.57 ± 1.98 | 35.28 ± 13.81 | 60.84 |
| BERT | 88.08 ± 0.62 | 90.31 ± 0.20 | 76.58 ± 0.98 | 54.64 ± 3.51 | 61.54 ± 3.70 | 94.04 ± 0.55 | 88.08 ± 0.15 | 54.17 ± 2.88 | 75.93 |
| MBERT | 91.13 ± 0.07 | 92.56 ± 0.09 | 82.82 ± 0.57 | 61.86 ± 2.60 | 50.76 ± 1.86 | 94.60 ± 0.34 | 92.13 ± 0.27 | 61.85 ± 3.25 | 78.46 |
| LAPT | **91.61 ± 0.74** | **92.96 ± 0.13** | 84.13 ± 0.78 | **81.53 ± 2.33** | 56.76 ± 4.91 | 95.17 ± 0.29 | 92.41 ± 0.15 | 59.17 ± 5.15 | 81.72 |
| VA | 91.38 ± 0.56 | 92.70 ± 0.11 | **84.82 ± 1.00** | 80.00 ± 2.77 | **68.93 ± 3.30** | **95.43 ± 0.22** | **92.43 ± 0.16** | **64.23 ± 3.07** | **83.74** |

(c) NER (macro F1). – indicates that a model did not converge.

Table 2: Results on POS tagging, UD parsing, and NER, with standard deviations from five random initializations. **Bolded** results are the maximum for each language, and scores in gray are not significantly worse than the best model (1-sided paired $t$-test, $p = 0.05$ with Bonferonni correction).

dies for the script imbalance at a larger scale, e.g., more diverse pretraining data.

## 2.4 Analysis

We perform further analysis to investigate VA's patterns of success. Concretely, we hypothesize that VA significantly improves the tokenizer's coverage of target languages where it is most successful. Inspired by Ács (2019), Chau et al. (2020), and Rust et al. (2021), we quantify tokenizer coverage using the percentage of tokens in the raw text that yield unknown wordpieces when tokenized with a given vocabulary ("UNK token percentage"). These are tokens whose representations contain at least partial ambiguity due to the inclusion of the unknown wordpiece.

Tab. 3 presents the UNK token percentage for each dataset using the MBERT vocabulary, averaged over each script and language type. This vocabulary is used in LAPT and represents the baseline level of vocabulary coverage. We also include the change in the UNK token percentage between the MBERT and VA vocabularies, which quantifies the coverage improvement. Both sets of values are juxtaposed against the average change in task-specific performance from LAPT to VA, representing the effect of augmenting the vocabulary on task-specific performance.

We observe that off-the-shelf MBERT already attains relatively high vocabulary coverage for Type 0 and 1 languages, as well as languages written in Latin and Cyrillic scripts. On the other hand, up to one-fifth of the tokens in Arabic languages and one-sixth of those in Type 2 languages yield an unknown wordpiece. For these languages, there is great room for increasing tokenizer coverage, and VA indeed addresses this more tangible need. This aligns with the task-specific performance improvements for each group and helps to explain our results in §2.3.

It is notable that VA does not always eliminate the issue of unknown wordpieces, even in languages for which MBERT attains high vocabulary coverage. This suggests that the remaining unknown wordpieces in these languages are more sparsely distributed (i.e., they represent low frequency sequences), while the unknown wordpieces in languages with lower vocabulary coverage represent sequences that occur more commonly. As a result, augmenting the vocabulary in such languages quickly improves coverage while associating these commonly occurring sequences with each other, which benefits the overall tokenization quality.

We further explore the association between the improvements in vocabulary coverage and task-specific performance in Fig. 1. Although we do not find that languages from the same types or scripts form clear clusters, we nonetheless observe a loose

| Lang. Group | Avg. UNK Token % (MBERT) | | | Avg. UNK Token % (Δ) | | | Avg. Task Performance (Δ) | | |
|---|---|---|---|---|---|---|---|---|---|
| (# of Langs.) | Unlabeled | UD | WikiAnn | Unlabeled | UD | WikiAnn | POS | UD | NER |
| All (9) | 5.9 % (–) | 5.2 % (–) | 6.2 % (–) | –5.3 % (–) | 4.7 % (–) | –5.8 % (–) | +1.45 (–) | +2.08 (–) | +2.02 (–) |
| Type 0 (4) | 1.0 % (↓) | 0.3 % (↓) | 1.2 % (↓) | –0.9 % (↑) | –0.3 % (↑) | –1.2 % (↑) | –0.13 (↓) | –0.04 (↓) | –0.05 (↓) |
| Type 1 (1) | 0.3 % (↓) | 0.0 % (↓) | 0.4 % (↓) | –0.3 % (↑) | –0.00 % (↑) | –0.4 % (↑) | +0.05 (↓) | –0.44 (↓) | +0.69 (↓) |
| Type 2 (4) | 12.3 % (↑) | 13.5 % (↑) | 14.8 % (↑) | –10.8 % (↓) | –12.1 % (↓) | –13.7 % (↓) | +4.03 (↑) | +5.74 (↑) | +5.23 (↑) |
| Latin (4) | 1.2 % (↓) | 0.6 % (↓) | 2.4 % (↓) | –1.2 % (↑) | –0.6 % (↑) | –2.3 % (↑) | +0.09 (↓) | –0.15 (↓) | –0.27 (↓) |
| Cyrillic (3) | 3.6 % (↓) | 0.6 % (↓) | 2.8 % (↓) | –3.6 % (↑) | –0.6 % (↑) | –2.7 % (↑) | –0.21 (↓) | +0.14 (↓) | +1.52 (↓) |
| Arabic (2) | 19.0 % (↑) | 19.2 % (↑) | 16.9 % (↑) | –16.1 % (↓) | –17.0 % (↓) | –15.5 % (↓) | +5.84 (↑) | +8.49 (↑) | +6.22 (↑) |

Table 3: Average UNK token percentage under the MBERT vocabulary (left); change in UNK token percentage from MBERT to VA vocabularies (center); and average task performance change from LAPT to VA (right). Averages are computed overall and within each script and language type, with comparisons to the overall average; all UNK token percentages are computed on the respective training sets for illustration. Note that Uyghur accounts for a large portion of the behavior of the Type 2/Arabic rows.

correlation between the two factors in question and see that VA delivers greater performance gains on Type 2 and Arabic-script languages compared to their Type 0/1 and Latin-script counterparts, respectively. To quantify the strength of this association, we also compute the language-level Spearman correlation between the change in UNK token percentage on the unlabeled dataset[7] from the MBERT to VA vocabulary and the task-specific performance improvements from LAPT to VA. The resulting $\rho$-values – 0.29 for NER, 0.56 for POS tagging, and 0.81 for UD parsing – suggest that this set of factors is meaningful for some tasks, though additional and more fine-grained analysis in future work should give a more complete explanation.

## 3 Mix-in Specialization: VA and Transliteration

We now expand on the observation made in §2.3 regarding the difficulties that MBERT encounters when faced with unseen low-resource languages in non-Latin scripts because of its inability to model the script. Having observed that VA is beneficial in such cases, we now investigate the interaction between this method and another specialization approach that targets this problem. Specifically, we consider the transliteration methods of Muller et al. (2021), in which unseen low-resource languages in non-Latin scripts are transliterated into the Latin script, often using transliteration schemes inspired by the Latin orthographies of languages related to the target language. They hypothesize that the increased similarity in the languages' writing systems, combined with MBERT's overall Latin-centricity, provides increased opportunity for crosslingual transfer.

[7]We benchmark against the unlabeled dataset instead of task-specific ones for comparability.

We can view transliteration as a inverted form of vocabulary augmentation: instead of adapting the model to the needs of the data, the data is adjusted to meet the assumptions of the model. Furthermore, the transliteration step is performed prior to pretraining MBERT on additional unlabeled data in the target language, the same stage at which VA is performed. In both cases, the ultimate goal is identical: improving tokenization and more effectively using available data. We can thus view transliteration and VA as two instantiations of a more general *mix-in* paradigm for model specialization, whereby various transformations (mix-ins) are applied to the data and/or model prior to performing additional pretraining. These mix-ins target different components of the experimental pipeline, which naturally raises our second research question:

**RQ2**: How do the VA and transliteration mix-ins for MBERT compare and interact?

### 3.1 Method and Experiments

To test this research question, we apply transliteration and VA in succession and evaluate their compatibility. Given unlabeled data in the target language, we first transliterate it into Latin script, which decreases but does not fully eliminate the issue of unseen wordpieces. We then perform VA, generating the vocabulary for augmentation based on the transliterated data.

We evaluate on Meadow Mari and Uyghur, which are Type 2 languages where transliteration was successfully applied by Muller et al. (2021). To transliterate the data, we use the same methods as Muller et al. (2021): Meadow Mari uses the `transliterate`[8] package, while Uyghur uses

[8]`https://pypi.org/project/transliterate`

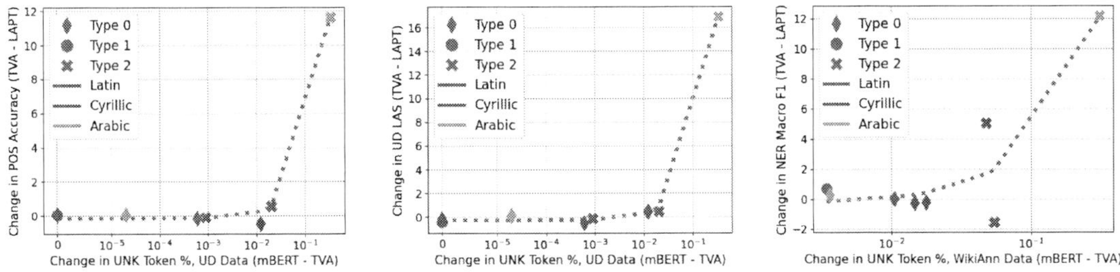


(a) POS tagging. (b) UD parsing. (c) NER.

Figure 1: Relationship between the change in UNK token percentage on task data and the change in task performance, from (MBERT/LAPT to VA), with a 1-degree line of best fit. All vocabulary values are computed on the respective training sets.

a linguistically-motivated transliteration scheme[9] aimed at associating Uyghur with Turkish. We use the same training scheme, model architectures, and baselines as in §2.2, the only difference being the use of transliterated data. This includes directly pretraining on the unlabeled data (LAPT), which is comparable to the highest-performing transliteration models of Muller et al. (2021). Although our initial investigation of VA in §2 also included non-Type 2 languages of other scripts, we omit them from our investigation based on the finding of Muller et al. (2021) that transliterating higher-resource languages into Latin scripts is not beneficial.

## 3.2 Results

Tab. 4 gives the results of our transliteration mix-in experiments. For the MBERT-based models, both VA and transliteration provide strong improvements over their respective baselines. Specifically, the improvements from LAPT to VA and LAPT to LAPT with transliteration are most pronounced. This verifies the independent results of Chau et al. (2020) and Muller et al. (2021) and suggests that in the non-Latin low-resource setting, unadapted additional pretraining is insufficient, but that the mix-in stage between initial and additional pretraining is amenable to performance-improving modifications. Unsurprisingly, transliteration provides no consistent improvement to the monolingual baselines, since the noisy transliteration process removes information without improving crosslingual alignment.

However, VA and transliteration appear to interact negatively. Although VA with transliteration improves over plain VA for Uyghur POS tagging and dependency parsing, it still slightly underperforms LAPT with transliteration for the latter. For the two NER experiments, VA with transliteration lags both methods independently. One possible explanation is that transliteration into Latin script serves as implicit vocabulary augmentation, with embeddings that have already been updated during the initial pretraining stage; as a result, the two sources of augmentation conflict. Alternatively, since the transliteration process merges certain characters that are distinct in the original script, VA may augment the vocabulary with misleading character clusters. Either way, additional vocabulary augmentation is generally not as useful when combined with transliteration, answering **RQ2**.

Nonetheless, additional investigation into the optimal amount of vocabulary augmentation might yield a configuration that is consistently complementary to transliteration and is an interesting direction for future work. Furthermore, designing linguistically-informed transliteration schemes like those devised by Muller et al. (2021) for Uyghur requires large amounts of time and domain knowledge. VA's fully data-driven nature and relatively comparable performance suggest that it achieves an appealing balance between performance gain and implementation difficulty.

# 4 Related Work

Our work follows a long line of studies investigating the performance of multilingual language models like MBERT in various settings. The exact source of such models' crosslingual ability is contested: early studies attributed MBERT's success to vocabulary overlap between languages (Cao et al., 2020; Pires et al., 2019; Wu and Dredze, 2019),

[9] https://github.com/benjamin-mlr/mbert-unseen-languages

| Rep. | MHR (NER) | | UG (NER) | | UG (POS) | | UG (UD) | |
|---|---|---|---|---|---|---|---|---|
| FASTT | 35.28 → 41.32 | (+6.04) | – | | 89.45 → 89.03 | (–0.42) | 54.52 → 54.45 | (–0.07) |
| BERT | 54.17 → 48.45 | (–5.72) | 61.54 → 63.05 | (+1.51) | 90.87 → 90.76 | (–0.09) | 60.34 → 60.08 | (–0.26) |
| MBERT | 61.85 → 63.84 | (+1.99) | 50.76 → 56.80 | (+6.04) | 78.07 → 91.34 | (+13.27) | 47.70 → 65.85 | (+18.15) |
| LAPT | 59.17 → 63.68 | (+4.51) | 56.76 → 67.57 | (+10.81) | 79.88 → 92.59 | (+12.71) | 50.67 → **69.39** | (+18.72) |
| VA | **64.23** → 63.19 | (–1.04) | **68.93** → 67.10 | (–1.83) | 91.49 → **92.64** | (+1.15) | 67.55 → 68.58 | (+1.03) |

Table 4: Comparison of model performance before and after transliteration. **Bolded** results are the maximum for each language-task pair. – indicates that a model did not converge.

but subsequent studies find typological similarity and parameter sharing to be better explanations (Conneau et al., 2020b; K et al., 2020). Nonetheless, past work has consistently highlighted the limitations of multilingual models in the context of low-resource languages. Conneau et al. (2020a) highlight the tension between crosslingual transfer and per-language model capacity, which poses a challenge for low-resource languages that require both. Indeed, Wu and Dredze (2020) find that MBERT is unable to outperform baselines in the lowest-resource seen languages. Our experiments build off these insights, which motivate the development of methods for adapting MBERT to target low-resource languages.

**Adapting Language Models** Several prior studies have proposed methods for adapting pretrained models to a downstream task. The simplest of these is to perform additional pretraining on unlabeled data in the target language (Chau et al., 2020; Muller et al., 2021; Pfeiffer et al., 2020), which in turn builds off similar approaches for domain adaptation (Gururangan et al., 2020; Han and Eisenstein, 2019). Recent work uses one or more of these additional pretraining stages to specifically train modular adapter layers for specific tasks or languages, with the goal of maintaining a language-agnostic model while improving performance on individual languages (Pfeiffer et al., 2020, 2021a; Vidoni et al., 2020). However, as Muller et al. (2021) note, the typological diversity of the world's languages ultimately limits the viability of this approach.

On the other hand, many adaptation techniques have focused on improving representation of the target language by modifying the model's vocabulary or tokenization schemes (Chung et al., 2020; Clark et al., 2021; Wang et al., 2021). This is well-motivated: Artetxe et al. (2020) emphasize representation in the vocabulary as a key factor for effective crosslingual transfer, while Rust et al. (2021) find that MBERT's tokenization scheme for many languages is subpar. Pfeiffer et al. (2021b) further observe that for languages with unseen scripts, a large proportion of the language is mapped to the generic "unknown" wordpiece, and they propose a matrix factorization-based approach to improve script representation. Wang et al. (2020) extend MBERT's vocabulary with an entire new vocabulary in the target language to facilitate zero-shot transfer to low-resource languages from English. The present study most closely derives from Chau et al. (2020), who select 99 wordpieces with the greatest amount of coverage to augment MBERT's vocabulary while preserving the remainder; and Muller et al. (2021), who transliterate target language data into Latin script to improve vocabulary coverage. We deliver new insights on the effectiveness and applicability of these methods.

## 5 Conclusion

We explore the interactions between vocabulary augmentation and script transliteration for specializing multilingual contextual word representations in low-resource settings. We confirm vocabulary augmentation's effectiveness on multiple languages, scripts, and tasks; identify the mix-in stage as amenable to specialization; and observe a negative interaction between vocabulary augmentation and script transliteration. Our findings highlight several open questions in model specialization and low-resource natural language processing at large, motivating further study in this area.

Future directions for investigation are manifold. In particular, our results in this work unify the separate findings of past works, which use MBERT as a case study; a natural continuation would extend these methods to a broader set of multilingual models, such as mT5 (Xue et al., 2021) and XLM-R (Conneau et al., 2020a), in order to obtain a clearer understanding of the factors behind specialization methods' patterns of success. While we intentionally choose a set of small unlabeled datasets to evaluate on a setting applicable to the vast majority of the world's low-resource languages, we acknowledge great variation in the amount of unlabeled data available in different languages. Continued study on the applicability of these methods to datasets of different sizes is an important future step. An interesting direction of work is to train multilingual models on data where script respresentation is more balanced, which might also allow for different output scripts for transliteration. Given that the mix-in stage is an effective opportunity to specialize models to target languages, constructing mix-ins at both the data and model level that are complementary by design has potential to be beneficial. Finally, future work might shed light on the interaction between different configurations of the adaptations studied here (e.g., the number of wordpiece types used in vocabulary augmentation).

## Acknowledgments

We thank Jungo Kasai, Phoebe Mulcaire, and members of UW NLP for their helpful comments on preliminary versions of this paper. We also thank Benjamin Muller for insightful discussions and providing details about transliteration methods and baselines. Finally, we thank the anonymous reviewers for their helpful remarks.

## References

Judit Ács. 2019. Exploring BERT's vocabulary.

Mikel Artetxe, Sebastian Ruder, and Dani Yogatama. 2020. On the cross-lingual transferability of monolingual representations. In *Proc. of ACL*.

Piotr Bojanowski, Edouard Grave, Armand Joulin, and Tomas Mikolov. 2017. Enriching word vectors with subword information. *TACL*, 5:135–146.

Steven Cao, Nikita Kitaev, and Dan Klein. 2020. Multilingual alignment of contextual word representations. In *Proc. of ICLR*.

Ethan C. Chau, Lucy H. Lin, and Noah A. Smith. 2020. Parsing with multilingual BERT, a small corpus, and a small treebank. In *Findings of ACL: EMNLP*.

Hyung Won Chung, Dan Garrette, Kiat Chuan Tan, and Jason Riesa. 2020. Improving multilingual models with language-clustered vocabularies. In *Proc. of EMNLP*.

Jonathan H. Clark, Dan Garrette, Iulia Turc, and John Wieting. 2021. Canine: Pre-training an efficient tokenization-free encoder for language representation.

Alexis Conneau, Kartikay Khandelwal, Naman Goyal, Vishrav Chaudhary, Guillaume Wenzek, Francisco Guzmán, Edouard Grave, Myle Ott, Luke Zettlemoyer, and Veselin Stoyanov. 2020a. Unsupervised cross-lingual representation learning at scale. In *Proc. of ACL*.

Alexis Conneau, Shijie Wu, Haoran Li, Luke Zettlemoyer, and Veselin Stoyanov. 2020b. Emerging cross-lingual structure in pretrained language models. In *Proc. of ACL*.

Jacob Devlin, Ming-Wei Chang, Kenton Lee, and Kristina Toutanova. 2019. BERT: Pre-training of deep bidirectional transformers for language understanding. In *Proc. of NAACL*.

Timothy Dozat and Christopher D. Manning. 2017. Deep biaffine attention for neural dependency parsing. In *Proc. of ICLR*.

Matt Gardner, Joel Grus, Mark Neumann, Oyvind Tafjord, Pradeep Dasigi, Nelson F. Liu, Matthew Peters, Michael Schmitz, and Luke Zettlemoyer. 2018. AllenNLP: A deep semantic natural language processing platform. In *Proc. of NLP-OSS*.

Suchin Gururangan, Ana Marasović, Swabha Swayamdipta, Kyle Lo, Iz Beltagy, Doug Downey, and Noah A. Smith. 2020. Don't stop pretraining: Adapt language models to domains and tasks. In *Proc. of ACL*.

Xiaochuang Han and Jacob Eisenstein. 2019. Unsupervised domain adaptation of contextualized embeddings for sequence labeling. In *Proc. of EMNLP-IJCNLP*.

Haoyang Huang, Yaobo Liang, Nan Duan, Ming Gong, Linjun Shou, Daxin Jiang, and Ming Zhou. 2019. Unicoder: A universal language encoder by pre-training with multiple cross-lingual tasks. In *Proc. of EMNLP-IJCNLP*.

Karthikeyan K, Zihan Wang, Stephen Mayhew, and Dan Roth. 2020. Cross-lingual ability of multilingual BERT: An empirical study. In *Proc. of ICLR*.

Dan Kondratyuk and Milan Straka. 2019. 75 languages, 1 model: Parsing universal dependencies universally. In *Proc. of EMNLP-IJCNLP*.

Taku Kudo and John Richardson. 2018. SentencePiece: A simple and language independent subword tokenizer and detokenizer for neural text processing. In *Proc. of EMNLP*.

Guillaume Lample and Alexis Conneau. 2019. Cross-lingual language model pretraining. In *Proc. of NeurIPS*.

Yinhan Liu, Myle Ott, Naman Goyal, Jingfei Du, Mandar Joshi, Danqi Chen, Omer Levy, Mike Lewis, Luke Zettlemoyer, and Veselin Stoyanov. 2019. Roberta: A robustly optimized bert pretraining approach.

Benjamin Muller, Antonios Anastasopoulos, Benoît Sagot, and Djamé Seddah. 2021. When being unseen from mBERT is just the beginning: Handling new languages with multilingual language models. In *Proc. of NAACL-HLT*.

Joakim Nivre, Marie-Catherine de Marneffe, Filip Ginter, Jan Hajič, Christopher D. Manning, Sampo Pyysalo, Sebastian Schuster, Francis Tyers, and Daniel Zeman. 2020. Universal Dependencies v2: An evergrowing multilingual treebank collection. In *Proc. of LREC*.

Xiaoman Pan, Boliang Zhang, Jonathan May, Joel Nothman, Kevin Knight, and Heng Ji. 2017. Cross-lingual name tagging and linking for 282 languages. In *Proc. of ACL*.

Matthew Peters, Mark Neumann, Mohit Iyyer, Matt Gardner, Christopher Clark, Kenton Lee, and Luke Zettlemoyer. 2018. Deep contextualized word representations. In *Proc. of NAACL-HLT*.

Jonas Pfeiffer, Aishwarya Kamath, Andreas Rücklé, Kyunghyun Cho, and Iryna Gurevych. 2021a. AdapterFusion: Non-destructive task composition for transfer learning. In *Proc. of EACL*.

Jonas Pfeiffer, Ivan Vulić, Iryna Gurevych, and Sebastian Ruder. 2020. MAD-X: An Adapter-Based Framework for Multi-Task Cross-Lingual Transfer. In *Proc. of EMNLP*.

Jonas Pfeiffer, Ivan Vulić, Iryna Gurevych, and Sebastian Ruder. 2021b. Unks everywhere: Adapting multilingual language models to new scripts.

Telmo Pires, Eva Schlinger, and Dan Garrette. 2019. How multilingual is multilingual BERT? In *Proc. of ACL*.

Afshin Rahimi, Yuan Li, and Trevor Cohn. 2019. Massively multilingual transfer for NER. In *Proc. of ACL*.

Phillip Rust, Jonas Pfeiffer, Ivan Vulić, Sebastian Ruder, and Iryna Gurevych. 2021. How good is your tokenizer? on the monolingual performance of multilingual language models. In *Proc. of ACL-IJCNLP*.

Ashish Vaswani, Noam Shazeer, Niki Parmar, Jakob Uszkoreit, Llion Jones, Aidan N. Gomez, Lukasz Kaiser, and Illia Polosukhin. 2017. Attention is all you need. In *Proc. of NeurIPS*.

Marko Vidoni, Ivan Vulić, and Goran Glavaš. 2020. Orthogonal language and task adapters in zero-shot cross-lingual transfer.

Xinyi Wang, Sebastian Ruder, and Graham Neubig. 2021. Multi-view subword regularization. In *Proc. of NAACL-HLT*.

Zihan Wang, Karthikeyan K, Stephen Mayhew, and Dan Roth. 2020. Extending multilingual BERT to low-resource languages. In *Findings of ACL: EMNLP*.

Thomas Wolf, Lysandre Debut, Victor Sanh, Julien Chaumond, Clement Delangue, Anthony Moi, Pierric Cistac, Tim Rault, Rémi Louf, Morgan Funtowicz, Joe Davison, Sam Shleifer, Patrick von Platen, Clara Ma, Yacine Jernite, Julien Plu, Canwen Xu, Teven Le Scao, Sylvain Gugger, Mariama Drame, Quentin Lhoest, and Alexander M. Rush. 2020. Transformers: State-of-the-art natural language processing. In *Proc. of EMNLP*.

Shijie Wu and Mark Dredze. 2019. Beto, bentz, becas: The surprising cross-lingual effectiveness of BERT. In *Proc. of EMNLP-IJCNLP*.

Shijie Wu and Mark Dredze. 2020. Are all languages created equal in multilingual BERT? In *Proc. of RepL4NLP*.

Yonghui Wu, Mike Schuster, Zhifeng Chen, Quoc V. Le, Mohammad Norouzi, Wolfgang Macherey, Maxim Krikun, Yuan Cao, Qin Gao, Klaus Macherey, Jeff Klingner, Apurva Shah, Melvin Johnson, Xiaobing Liu, Łukasz Kaiser, Stephan Gouws, Yoshikiyo Kato, Taku Kudo, Hideto Kazawa, Keith Stevens, George Kurian, Nishant Patil, Wei Wang, Cliff Young, Jason Smith, Jason Riesa, Alex Rudnick, Oriol Vinyals, Greg Corrado, Macduff Hughes, and Jeffrey Dean. 2016. Google's neural machine translation system: Bridging the gap between human and machine translation.

Linting Xue, Noah Constant, Adam Roberts, Mihir Kale, Rami Al-Rfou, Aditya Siddhant, Aditya Barua, and Colin Raffel. 2021. mT5: A massively multilingual pre-trained text-to-text transformer. In *Proc. of NAACL-HLT*.

Daniel Zeman, Joakim Nivre, Mitchell Abrams, Noëmi Aepli, Željko Agić, Lars Ahrenberg, Gabrielė Aleksandravičiūtė, Lene Antonsen, Katya Aplonova, Maria Jesus Aranzabe, Gashaw Arutie, Masayuki Asahara, Luma Ateyah, Mohammed Attia, Aitziber Atutxa, Liesbeth Augustinus, Elena Badmaeva, Miguel Ballesteros, Esha Banerjee, Sebastian Bank, Verginica Barbu Mititelu, Victoria Basmov, Colin Batchelor, John Bauer, Sandra Bellato, Kepa Bengoetxea, Yevgeni Berzak, Irshad Ahmad Bhat, Riyaz Ahmad Bhat, Erica Biagetti, Eckhard Bick, Agnė Bielinskienė, Rogier Blokland, Victoria Bobicev, Loïc Boizou, Emanuel Borges Völker, Carl Börstell, Cristina Bosco, Gosse Bouma, Sam Bowman, Adriane Boyd, Kristina Brokaitė, Aljoscha Burchardt, Marie Candito, Bernard Caron, Gauthier Caron, Tatiana Cavalcanti, Gülşen Cebiroğlu Eryiğit, Flavio Massimiliano Cecchini, Giuseppe G. A. Celano, Slavomír Čéplö, Savas Cetin, Fabricio Chalub, Jinho Choi, Yongseok Cho, Jayeol Chun, Alessandra T. Cignarella, Silvie Cinková, Aurélie Collomb, Çağrı Çöltekin, Miriam Connor, Marine Courtin, Elizabeth Davidson, Marie-Catherine de Marneffe, Valeria de Paiva, Elvis de Souza, Arantza Diaz de Ilarraza, Carly Dickerson, Bamba Dione, Peter Dirix, Kaja Dobrovoljc, Timothy Dozat, Kira Droganova, Puneet Dwivedi, Hanne Eckhoff, Marhaba Eli, Ali Elkahky, Binyam Ephrem, Olga

Erina, Tomaž Erjavec, Aline Etienne, Wograine Evelyn, Richárd Farkas, Hector Fernandez Alcalde, Jennifer Foster, Cláudia Freitas, Kazunori Fujita, Katarína Gajdošová, Daniel Galbraith, Marcos Garcia, Moa Gärdenfors, Sebastian Garza, Kim Gerdes, Filip Ginter, Iakes Goenaga, Koldo Gojenola, Memduh Gökırmak, Yoav Goldberg, Xavier Gómez Guinovart, Berta González Saavedra, Bernadeta Griciūtė, Matias Grioni, Normunds Grūzītis, Bruno Guillaume, Céline Guillot-Barbance, Nizar Habash, Jan Hajič, Jan Hajič jr., Mika Hämäläinen, Linh Hà Mỹ, Na-Rae Han, Kim Harris, Dag Haug, Johannes Heinecke, Felix Hennig, Barbora Hladká, Jaroslava Hlaváčová, Florinel Hociung, Petter Hohle, Jena Hwang, Takumi Ikeda, Radu Ion, Elena Irimia, Ọlájídé Ishola, Tomáš Jelínek, Anders Johannsen, Fredrik Jørgensen, Markus Juutinen, Hüner Kaşıkara, Andre Kaasen, Nadezhda Kabaeva, Sylvain Kahane, Hiroshi Kanayama, Jenna Kanerva, Boris Katz, Tolga Kayadelen, Jessica Kenney, Václava Kettnerová, Jesse Kirchner, Elena Klementieva, Arne Köhn, Kamil Kopacewicz, Natalia Kotsyba, Jolanta Kovalevskaitė, Simon Krek, Sookyoung Kwak, Veronika Laippala, Lorenzo Lambertino, Lucia Lam, Tatiana Lando, Septina Dian Larasati, Alexei Lavrentiev, John Lee, Phuong Lê Hồng, Alessandro Lenci, Saran Lertpradit, Herman Leung, Cheuk Ying Li, Josie Li, Keying Li, KyungTae Lim, Maria Liovina, Yuan Li, Nikola Ljubešić, Olga Loginova, Olga Lyashevskaya, Teresa Lynn, Vivien Macketanz, Aibek Makazhanov, Michael Mandl, Christopher Manning, Ruli Manurung, Cătălina Mărănduc, David Mareček, Katrin Marheinecke, Héctor Martínez Alonso, André Martins, Jan Mašek, Yuji Matsumoto, Ryan McDonald, Sarah McGuinness, Gustavo Mendonça, Niko Miekka, Margarita Misirpashayeva, Anna Missilä, Cătălin Mititelu, Maria Mitrofan, Yusuke Miyao, Simonetta Montemagni, Amir More, Laura Moreno Romero, Keiko Sophie Mori, Tomohiko Morioka, Shinsuke Mori, Shigeki Moro, Bjartur Mortensen, Bohdan Moskalevskyi, Kadri Muischnek, Robert Munro, Yugo Murawaki, Kaili Müürisep, Pinkey Nainwani, Juan Ignacio Navarro Horñiacek, Anna Nedoluzhko, Gunta Nešpore-Bērzkalne, Luong Nguyễn Thị, Huyền Nguyễn Thị Minh, Yoshihiro Nikaido, Vitaly Nikolaev, Rattima Nitisaroj, Hanna Nurmi, Stina Ojala, Atul Kr. Ojha, Adéday`ọ Olúòkun, Mai Omura, Petya Osenova, Robert Östling, Lilja Øvrelid, Niko Partanen, Elena Pascual, Marco Passarotti, Agnieszka Patejuk, Guilherme Paulino-Passos, Angelika Peljak-Łapińska, Siyao Peng, Cenel-Augusto Perez, Guy Perrier, Daria Petrova, Slav Petrov, Jason Phelan, Jussi Piitulainen, Tommi A Pirinen, Emily Pitler, Barbara Plank, Thierry Poibeau, Larisa Ponomareva, Martin Popel, Lauma Pretkalniņa, Sophie Prévost, Prokopis Prokopidis, Adam Przepiórkowski, Tiina Puolakainen, Sampo Pyysalo, Peng Qi, Andriela Rääbis, Alexandre Rademaker, Loganathan Ramasamy, Taraka Rama, Carlos Ramisch, Vinit Ravishankar, Livy Real, Siva Reddy, Georg Rehm, Ivan Riabov, Michael Rießler, Erika Rimkutė, Larissa Rinaldi, Laura Rituma, Luisa Rocha, Mykhailo Romanenko, Rudolf Rosa, Davide Rovati, Valentin Roșca, Olga Rudina, Jack Rueter, Shoval Sadde, Benoît Sagot, Shadi Saleh, Alessio Salomoni, Tanja Samardžić, Stephanie Samson, Manuela Sanguinetti, Dage Särg, Baiba Saulīte, Yanin Sawanakunanon, Nathan Schneider, Sebastian Schuster, Djamé Seddah, Wolfgang Seeker, Mojgan Seraji, Mo Shen, Atsuko Shimada, Hiroyuki Shirasu, Muh Shohibussirri, Dmitry Sichinava, Aline Silveira, Natalia Silveira, Maria Simi, Radu Simionescu, Katalin Simkó, Mária Šimková, Kiril Simov, Aaron Smith, Isabela Soares-Bastos, Carolyn Spadine, Antonio Stella, Milan Straka, Jana Strnadová, Alane Suhr, Umut Sulubacak, Shingo Suzuki, Zsolt Szántó, Dima Taji, Yuta Takahashi, Fabio Tamburini, Takaaki Tanaka, Isabelle Tellier, Guillaume Thomas, Liisi Torga, Trond Trosterud, Anna Trukhina, Reut Tsarfaty, Francis Tyers, Sumire Uematsu, Zdeňka Urešová, Larraitz Uria, Hans Uszkoreit, Andrius Utka, Sowmya Vajjala, Daniel van Niekerk, Gertjan van Noord, Viktor Varga, Eric Villemonte de la Clergerie, Veronika Vincze, Lars Wallin, Abigail Walsh, Jing Xian Wang, Jonathan North Washington, Maximilan Wendt, Seyi Williams, Mats Wirén, Christian Wittern, Tsegay Woldemariam, Tak-sum Wong, Alina Wróblewska, Mary Yako, Naoki Yamazaki, Chunxiao Yan, Koichi Yasuoka, Marat M. Yavrumyan, Zhuoran Yu, Zdeněk Žabokrtský, Amir Zeldes, Manying Zhang, and Hanzhi Zhu. 2019. Universal dependencies 2.5. LINDAT/CLARIAH-CZ digital library at the Institute of Formal and Applied Linguistics (ÚFAL), Faculty of Mathematics and Physics, Charles University.

# Learning Cross-lingual Representations for Event Coreference Resolution with Multi-view Alignment and Optimal Transport

**Duy Phung**[1], **Hieu Minh Tran**[1], **Minh Van Nguyen**[2], **and Thien Huu Nguyen**[2]
[1] VinAI Research, Vietnam
[2] Dept. of Computer and Information Science, University of Oregon, Eugene, OR, USA
{v.duypv1,v.hieutm4}@vinai.io, {minhnv,thien}@cs.uoregon.edu

## Abstract

We study a new problem of cross-lingual transfer learning for event coreference resolution (ECR) where models trained on data from a source language are adapted for evaluations in different target languages. We introduce the first baseline model for this task based on XLM-RoBERTa, a state-of-the-art multilingual pre-trained language model. We also explore language adversarial neural networks (LANN) that present language discriminators to distinguish texts from the source and target languages to improve the language generalization for ECR. In addition, we introduce two novel mechanisms to further enhance the general representation learning of LANN, featuring: (i) multi-view alignment to penalize cross coreference-label alignment of examples in the source and target languages, and (ii) optimal transport to select close examples in the source and target languages to provide better training signals for the language discriminators. Finally, we perform extensive experiments for cross-lingual ECR from English to Spanish and Chinese to demonstrate the effectiveness of the proposed methods.

## 1 Introduction

Event coreference resolution (ECR) aims to link event-trigger expressions (event mentions) in a document that refer to the same event in real world. Technically, the core problem in ECR involves predicting if two event mentions in a document corefer to each other or not (i.e., a binary classification problem). For instance, consider the following text:

*With national outrage boiling over, Bangladeshi paramilitary officers tracked down and* ***arrested*** *Sohel Rana. When loudspeakers at the rescue site announced his* ***capture****, local news reports said, the crowd broke out in cheers.*

An ECR system in information extraction (IE) should be able to recognize the coreference of the two event mentions associated with the trigger words "*arrested*" and "*capture*" in this text.

Prior work on ECR assumes the monolingual setting where training and test data are presented in the same languages. Current state-of-the-art ECR systems thus rely on large monolingual datasets to train advanced models (Nguyen et al., 2016; Choubey and Huang, 2018; Lu and Ng, 2017, 2018; Huang et al., 2019) that are only annotated for popular languages (e.g., English). As document annotation for ECR is an expensive process, porting ECR models for English to other languages is crucial and appealing to enhance the accessibility of ECR systems. To this end, this paper explores cross-lingual transfer learning for ECR where models are trained on annotated documents in English (source language) and tested on documents from other languages (target languages). To be clear, our work considers zero-resource cross-lingual learning that requires no labeled data for ECR in the target languages as well as human or machine generated parallel text. The systems in this work only have access to unlabeled text in the target languages to aid the cross-lingual learning for ECR. To our knowledge, this is the first work on cross-lingual transfer learning for event coreference resolution in the literature.

Recent advances in contextualized word embeddings have featured multilingual pre-trained language models, e.g., multilingual BERT (Devlin et al., 2019), XLM-RoBERTa (Conneau et al., 2019), that overcome the vocabulary difference of languages and produce language-universal representations for cross-lingual transfer learning in different NLP tasks (Wu and Dredze, 2019; Subburathinam et al., 2019a). In fact, such pre-trained language models have set a new standard for multilingual learning in NLP (Wu and Dredze, 2020; Nguyen et al., 2021a), serving as the baseline models for our cross-lingual transfer learning problem for ECR in this work.

How can we improve the cross-lingual performance of ECR models over multilingual language



*Proceedings of the 1st Workshop on Multilingual Representation Learning*, pages 62–73

model baselines? Treating the source and target languages as the source and target domains in domain adaptation (Chen et al., 2018a, 2019; Keung et al., 2019), one can borrow the popular technique of domain adversarial neural networks (DANN) (Ganin et al., 2016; Fu et al., 2017) to induce better language-general representations for ECR, called language adversarial neural networks (LANN) to make it consistent with our language generalization problem. As such, in addition to traditional learning objectives (e.g., cross-entropy), the key idea of LANN is to introduce a language discriminator that seeks to differentiate representation vectors for text inputs from the source and target languages. To enhance the language generalization, models will attempt to generate representation vectors so the language discriminator is fooled, i.e., its performance is minimized to align the source and target languages (Chen et al., 2018a; Keung et al., 2019). However, there are two major limitations with LANN that will be addressed to improve the cross-lingual performance for ECR models in this work.

First, taking the binary classification setting for ECR, inputs to the language discriminator in LANN involve two pairs of event mentions in the source and target languages. As coreference labels for pairs of event mentions in target languages are not available, the language discriminator will thus only aim to align marginal distributions of event mention pairs (called examples) in the source and target languages (without considering the coreference labels for the pairs). This is less optimal as the lack of coreference labels in the alignment might unexpectedly cause coreferring examples in the source language to be mapped or aligned with non-coreferring examples in the target languages and vice versa, thus impairing the discriminative nature of representation vectors for ECR. To overcome this issue, we propose to use two network architectures to obtain two complementary representation vectors for each example in both source and target languages. Representation vectors from each network will be first aligned between source and target languages using the usual LANN technique. In addition, representation vectors from the two networks will be regularized to agree with each other over same examples in target languages. As demonstrated later, this regularization helps to penalize the alignment between coreferring examples in the source language and non-coreferring examples in the target languages (and vice versa) in LANN, thus improving the representation quality.

Second, as LANN attempts to discriminate all examples in the source language from all examples in the target languages, it also employs training signals from examples whose representations are far away from each other in the source and target languages. However, it is intuitive that the most useful information for model training comes from close examples in the source and target language spaces. Including long-distance examples might even introduce noise and hurt the models' performance. Consequently, instead of using all examples for LANN, we propose to only leverage examples with close representation vectors for the language discriminator in ECR models. As such, our approach involves measuring distances between representation vectors of examples in the source and target languages to determine which examples are used for the language discriminator. To access the distance between two examples in the source and target languages, instead of only relying on the similarity of learned representations, we propose to additionally consider coreference likelihoods of examples that assign higher similarity if two examples have similar coreference likelihoods (i.e., examples with the same coreference labels are more similar to each other than others in ECR). Accordingly, our model employs Optimal Transport, a method to determine the cheapest transformation between two data distributions, as a natural solution to simultaneously incorporate both representation vectors and coreference likelihoods of examples into the distance estimation for example selection in the language discriminator of LANN. We conduct cross-lingual ECR evaluation for English, Spanish and Chinese that demonstrates the benefits of the proposed methods by significantly outperforming the baseline models. We will release experiment setups and code to push forward research on cross-lingual ECR in the future.

## 2 Related Work

Regarding coreference resolution, our work is related to studies in entity coreference resolution that aim to resolve nouns phrases/mentions for entities (Raghunathan et al., 2010; Ng, 2010; Durrett and Klein, 2013; Lee et al., 2017; Joshi et al., 2019). This work focuses on event coreference resolution that is often considered as a more challenging task than entity resolution due to the more complex structures of event mentions (Yang et al., 2015).

For event coreference resolution, although there have been works on cross-document resolution (Lee et al., 2012a; Kenyon-Dean et al., 2018; Barhom et al., 2019; Phung et al., 2021), this work is more related to prior work on within-document ECR (Lu and Ng, 2018; Tran et al., 2021). In particular, previous within-document ECR methods have applied feature-based models for pairwise classifiers (Ahn, 2006; Chen et al., 2009; Cybulska and Vossen, 2015; Peng et al., 2016), spectral graph clustering (Chen and Ji, 2009b), information propagation (Liu et al., 2014), markov logic networks (Lu et al., 2016), end-to-end modeling with event detection (Araki and Mitamura, 2015; Lu et al., 2016; Chen and Ng, 2016; Lu and Ng, 2017), and recent deep learning models (Nguyen et al., 2016; Choubey and Huang, 2018; Huang et al., 2019; Choubey et al., 2020; Tran et al., 2021). Our work is different from such prior work as we investigate a novel setting of cross-lingual transfer learning for ECR.

Cross-lingual transfer learning has been studied for other NLP and IE tasks, including sentiment analysis (Chen et al., 2018b), relation extraction (Lin et al., 2017; Zou et al., 2018; Wang et al., 2018; Nguyen and Nguyen, 2021), event extraction (Chen and Ji, 2009a; Hsi et al., 2016; Subburathinam et al., 2019b; Nguyen et al., 2021b), and entity coreference resolution (Rahman and Ng, 2012; Hardmeier et al., 2013; Martins, 2015; Kundu et al., 2018; Urbizu et al., 2019). Compared to such prior work, this paper presents two novel approaches to improve the language generalization of representation vectors based on multi-view alignment and OT. Finally, our work involves LANN that bears some similarity with DANN models in domain adaptation research of machine learning (Ganin et al., 2016; Bousmalis et al., 2016; Fu et al., 2017; Kumar et al., 2018; Naik and Rose, 2020; Ngo et al., 2021). Compared to such work, our work explores a new dimension of adversarial networks for language-invariant representation learning for texts in ECR.

## 3 Model

We formalize our ECR problem using a pairwise approach (Lu and Ng, 2018; Choubey and Huang, 2018; Barhom et al., 2019). Let $W = w_1, w_2, \dots, w_n$ be a document (with $n$ words) that contains two input event mentions with event triggers located at $w_{e_1}$ and $w_{e_2}$ in $W$ ($1 \leq e_1 < e_2 \leq n$). As such, the core problem in ECR is to perform a binary prediction to determine whether two event mentions $w_{e_1}$ and $w_{e_2}$ refer to the same event or not. An example in our ECR task thus involves an input tuple $X = (W, e_1, e_2)$ and a binary output variable $y$ to indicate the coreference of $w_{e_1}$ and $w_{e_2}$. This work focuses on cross-lingual transfer learning for ECR where training data involve input documents $W$ in English (the source language) while sentences in test data are presented in another language (the target language). To enable the zero-resource cross-lingual setting for ECR, our model takes two following inputs: $\mathcal{D}^{src} = \{(X_i = (W^i, e^i_1, e^i_2), y_i)\}_{i=1..N_{src}}$ as the training set with $N_{src}$ labeled examples in the source language (English), and $\mathcal{D}^{tar} = \{X_i = (W^i, e^i_1, e^i_2)\}_{i=N_{src}+1..N_{src}+N_{tar}}$ as the unlabeled set in the target language with $N_{tar}$ examples.

### 3.1 Baseline Model

As this is the first work on cross-lingual transfer learning for ECR, this section aims to establish a baseline method for further research. In particular, recent work has shown that multilingual pre-trained language models with deep stacks of transformer layers, e.g., multilingual BERT (Devlin et al., 2019), XLM-RoBERTa (Conneau et al., 2019), can provide strong baselines with competitive performance for zero-shot cross-lingual transfer for a variety of NLP tasks (Wu and Dredze, 2019). As such, we utilize XLM-RoBERTa[1] to obtain language-general representation vectors for a cross-lingual baseline model of ECR in this work. Given the input document and event mentions $X = (W, e_1, e_2)$ (in the source or target language), we first prepend the special token `[CLS]`, and insert two special tokens `<e>` and `</e>` right before and after the trigger words $w_{e_1}$ and $w_{e_2}$ in $W$ to mark their positions, leading to a new document $W' = \texttt{[CLS]}\, w_1 \dots w_{e_1-1}\texttt{<e>}w_{e_1}\texttt{</e>}w_{e_1+1} \dots w_{e_2-1}\texttt{<e>}w_{e_2}\texttt{</e>}\, w_{e_2+1} \dots w_n$. Afterward $W'$ is fed into the base version of XLM-RoBERTa to obtain hidden vectors for their word-pieces. Let $h_{cls}$ be the hidden vector for the special token `[CLS]`, $h^1_s$ and $h^1_e$ be the hidden vectors for the special tokens `<e>` and `</e>` surrounding $w_{e_1}$, and $h^2_s$ and $h^2_e$ be the hidden vectors for the special tokens `<e>` and `</e>` surrounding $w_{e_2}$

[1] XLM-RoBERTa is chosen due to its better performance than multilingual BERT in our experiments.

in $W$. Note that as the number of word-pieces in $W$ might exceed the maximum length of 512 in XLM-RoBERTa, we divide the word-piece sequence for $W$ into chunks of lengths equal to or smaller than 512; these chunks are then processed separately by XLM-RoBERTa. In the next step, an overall representation vector $V(X)$ for $X$, i.e., $V(X) = [h_{cls}, h_s^1, h_e^1, h_s^2, h_e^2]$, is formed and sent into an one-layer feed-forward network FF with softmax in the end to compute a distribution $P(.|X) = \texttt{FF}(V(X))$ over possible coreference labels (i.e., two possible labels) for the input $X$. Finally, the negative log-likelihood function $\mathcal{L}_{pred}$ over labeled examples in the source language $\mathcal{D}^{src}$ is employed to train the baseline model in this work: $\mathcal{L}_{pred} = -\sum_{i=1}^{N_{src}} \log P(y_i|X_i)$.

In the test time, we use the trained model to predict coreference labels for every pair of event mentions in a document. We then form a graph for each document where event mentions serve as the nodes and two event mentions are connected if their coreference label is positive. As such, connected components in this graph will be returned as event mention clusters for the document in ECR.

### 3.2 Language Adversarial Networks

To further improve the language generalization for the baseline, we explore the adaptation of domain adversarial neural networks (DANN) in domain adaptation (Ganin et al., 2016) for zero-resource cross-lingual learning (i.e., treating source and target languages as source and target domains). In language adversarial neural networks (LANN), a language discriminator $D$ is introduced to discriminate examples from the source and target languages. As such, the overall representation vector $V(X)$ for each input example $X$ is sent into the language discriminator $D$ (i.e., a two-layer feed-forward network with the sigmoid function in the end) to obtain a scalar score $D(V(X))$ to indicate whether $X$ belongs to the source language or not. The discriminator loss $\mathcal{L}_{disc}$ is then computed over both source and target language data (i.e., $\mathcal{D}^{src}$ and $\mathcal{D}^{tar}$):

$$\begin{aligned}\mathcal{L}_{disc} = \sum_{i=1}^{N_{src}+N_{tar}} & -l_i \log D(V(X_i)) \\ & - (1 - l_i) \log(1 - D(V(X_i)))\end{aligned} \tag{1}$$

where $l_i$ is the language indicator (i.e., $l_i = 1$ if $1 \leq i \leq N_{src}$; and 0 otherwise). The over all loss to train the model in this case is thus: $\mathcal{L} = \mathcal{L}_{pred} + \alpha \mathcal{L}_{disc}$ where $\alpha$ is a trade-off parameter. Note that as LANN aims to prevent the language discriminator from recognizing languages from input representation vectors, we insert the Gradient Reversal Layer (GRL) (Ganin et al., 2016) between $V(X)$ and $D$ to reverse the gradients during the backward pass from $\mathcal{L}_{disc}$. Overall, fooling the language discriminator in LANN with GRL helps eliminate language-specific features to improve generalization across languages.

### 3.3 Multi-view Alignment

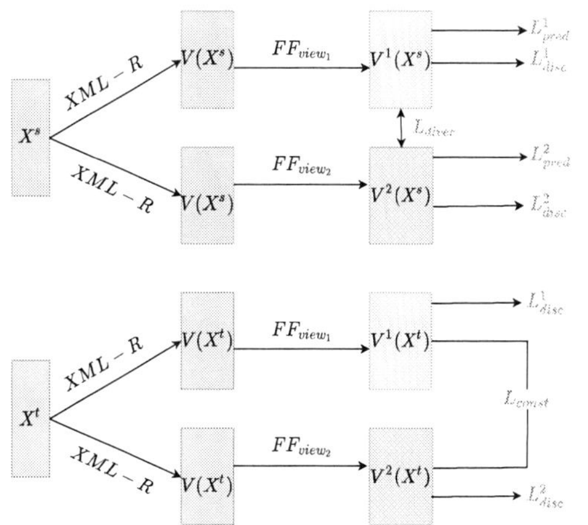


Figure 1: Multi-view alignment mechanism.

One limitation of LANN is that it only attempts to align marginal distributions of examples for ECR in the source and target languages (due to the lack of coreference labels for target examples), causing the unexpected cross-language alignment of coreferential and non-coreferential examples between two languages. To address this issue, instead of relying on one representation vector $V(X)$ for $X$, we propose to obtain two complementary representation vectors $V^1(X)$ and $V^2(X)$ for $X$ (two views) by sending $V(X)$ into two feed-forward networks with two layers $f_1$ and $f_2$: $V^1(X) = f_1(V(X))$ and $V^2(X) = f_2(V(X))$ (preserving the dimensionality of $V(X)$). Afterward, several loss and regularization terms are proposed to penalize the alignment of coreferential and non-coreferential examples across languages in LANN as follows.

First, to ensure that representation vectors $V^1(X)$ and $V^2(X)$ include discriminative information for coreference prediction, we predict the coreference label $y_i$ from both vectors using two feed-forward networks (one layer) with softmax in the end $\texttt{FF}_1$ and $\texttt{FF}_2$ to obtain distributions $P^1(.|X) = \texttt{FF}_1(V^1(X))$ and

$P^2(.|X) = \texttt{FF}_2(V^2(X))$. Negative log-likelihood loss functions $\mathcal{L}^i_{pred}$ from $P^i(.|X)$ ($i = 1, 2$) are then utilized for the loss function: $\mathcal{L}^i_{pred} = -\sum_{i=1}^{N_{src}} \log P^i(y_i|X_i)$.

Second, representation vectors of source-language examples from each view ($V^1(X)$ or $V^2(X)$) are also aligned their counterparts in the target language based on LANN with language discriminators, i.e., $D^1$ or $D^2$ respectively (two-layer feed-forward networks). As such, the discriminator loss $\mathcal{L}^k_{disc}$ for the view $V^k(X)$ ($k = 1, 2$) is:

$$\begin{aligned} \mathcal{L}^i_{disc} = & \sum_{i=1}^{N_{src}+N_{tar}} -l_i \log D(V^k(X_i)) \\ & - (1 - l_i) \log(1 - D(V^k(X_i))) \end{aligned} \quad (2)$$

Third, to encourage the diversity or complementary nature of the information captured by two views $V^1$ and $V^2$, we seek to increase the difference between representation vectors $V^1(X)$ and $V^2(X)$ over the same source-language examples $X$ in $\mathcal{D}^{src}$ by including their negative distance $\mathcal{L}_{diver}$ into the overall loss function:

$$\mathcal{L}_{diver} = -\frac{1}{N_{src}} \sum_{i=1}^{N_{src}} ||V^1(X) - V^2(X)||_2^2 \quad (3)$$

Fourth, representation vectors from two views $V^1(X)$ and $V^2(X)$ will be constrained to be consistent with each other for the same examples $X \in \mathcal{D}^{tar}$ in the target language. This is done by introducing the difference $\mathcal{L}_{const}$ between $V^1(X)$ and $V^2(X)$ over target-language examples in $\mathcal{D}^{tar}$ into the overall loss function for minimization:

$$\mathcal{L}_{const} = \frac{1}{N_{tar}} \sum_{i=N_{src}+1}^{N_{src}+N_{tar}} ||V^1(X_i) - V^2(X_i)||_2^2 \quad (4)$$

As such, consider an unexpected alignment by LANN where a set of coreferential examples $S^{src} \subset \{(X_i, y_i) \in \mathcal{D}^{src}|y_i = 1\}$ is aligned a set of non-coreferential examples $T^{tar} \subset \mathcal{D}^{tar}$ by view $V^1(X)$ ($V^1(S^{src}) \longleftrightarrow V^1(T^{tar})$). Our prediction consistency regularization $\mathcal{L}_{const}$ between two views will hep to penalize this unexpected alignment as it incorporates the difference between representation vectors from two views $V^1$ and $V^2$ over the target examples in $T^{tar}$ (i.e., $V^1(T^{tar})$ and $V^2(T^{tar})$) into the loss function. Due to the alignment $V^1(S^{src}) \longleftrightarrow V^1(T^{tar})$, this implicitly translates into injecting the difference between representation vectors in $V^1(S^{src})$ and $V^2(T^{tar})$ into the loss function. However, this difference is expected to be high to prevent the alignment between $V^1(S^{src})$ and $V^1(T^{tar})$ for two reasons: (i) $V^1$ and $V^2$ are regularized to encode different information via $\mathcal{L}_{diver}$, and (ii) $S^{src}$ and $T^{tar}$ contain examples with different coreference labels, implying the large distance between their representation vectors for ECR. Consequently, the overall loss function to train models in our two-view model is: $\mathcal{L} = \mathcal{L}_{pred} + \alpha^1_{disc}\mathcal{L}^1_{disc} + \alpha^2_{disc}\mathcal{L}^2_{disc} + \alpha_{diver}\mathcal{L}_{diver} + \alpha_{const}\mathcal{L}_{const}$ where $\alpha^1_{disc}$, $\alpha^2_{disc}$, $\alpha_{diver}$, and $\alpha_{const}$ are trade-off parameters.

### 3.4 Optimal Transport

Another limitation of LANN is that it employs all examples of the source and target language data in $\mathcal{D}^{src}$ and $\mathcal{D}^{tar}$ for the language discriminators. This is unexpected as faraway examples might not provide useful training signals for the language discriminators in general representation learning. As such, we aim to only apply the language discriminators to examples in the source and target language data that are close to each other. Given that, the major question is how to effectively estimate the distance between examples in the source and target languages in ECR for this example selection. To this end, as motivated in the introduction, our intuition is to simultaneously consider representations and coreference likelihoods of examples in $\mathcal{D}^{src}$ and $\mathcal{D}^{tar}$ to compute this distance function.

In particular, we directly use the vector $V(X)$ obtained before as the representation vector of $X$ for our example selection purpose in LANN. Afterward, to obtain a coreference likelihood score $u^X$ for an example $X$, we compute the average of the probabilities for being coreferential of $X$ from the two view's coreference distributions $P^1(y = 1|X)$ and $P^2(y = 1|X)$: $u^X = \frac{P^1(y=1|X)+P^2(y=1|X)}{2}$. Consequently, to exploit both $V(X)$ and $u^X$ of examples $X$ for distance estimation between examples, we seek to find an optimal alignment between examples in the source and target language data $\mathcal{D}^{src}$ and $\mathcal{D}^{tar}$ such that two examples with closer representation vectors and coreference likelihoods have better chance to be aligned to each other. As such, this problem can be solved naturally with optimal transport (OT) methods that facilitate the computation of the optimal mapping between two probability distributions.

Formally, given two probability distributions $p(s)$ and $q(t)$ over domains $\mathcal{S}$ and $\mathcal{T}$, and a cost function $C(s, t) : \mathcal{S} \times \mathcal{T} \rightarrow \mathbb{R}_+$ for mapping $\mathcal{S}$ to

$\mathcal{T}$, OT finds the optimal joint distribution $\pi^*(s,t)$ (over $\mathcal{S} \times \mathcal{T}$), which has marginals $p(s)$ and $q(t)$ and achieves cheapest transportation from $p(s)$ to $q(t)$, by solving the following problem:

$$\pi^*(s,t) = \min_{\pi \in \Pi(s,t)} \sum_{s \in \mathcal{S}} \sum_{t \in \mathcal{T}} \pi(s,t) C(s,t) ds dt \quad \text{s.t. } s \sim p(s) \text{ and } t \sim q(t) \tag{5}$$

where $\Pi(s,t)$ is the set of all joint distributions with marginals $p(s)$ and $q(t)$. Here, $\pi^*$ represents a matrix whose entry $(s,t)$ represents the probability of transforming the data point $s \in \mathcal{S}$ to $t \in \mathcal{T}$ to convert the distribution $p(s)$ to $q(t)$. To this end, our model defines the domains $\mathcal{S}$ and $\mathcal{T}$ in OT via representation vectors for examples in the source and target language data $\mathcal{D}^{src}$ and $\mathcal{D}^{tar}$ respectively: $\mathcal{S} = \{V(X_i) | X_i \in \mathcal{D}^{src}\}$, $\mathcal{T} = \{V(X_i) | X_i \in \mathcal{D}^{tar}\}$. As such, the cost function $C(X_i, X_j)$ ($X_i \in \mathcal{D}^{src}$, $X_j \in \mathcal{D}^{tar}$) is computed by the Euclidean distance between representation vectors of corresponding elements, i.e., $C(X_i, X_j) = ||V(X_i) - V(X_j)||_2^2$. Also, the probability distributions $p(X_i)$ and $q(X_j)$ ($X_i \in \mathcal{D}^{src}$, $X_j \in \mathcal{D}^{tar}$) are defined over the normalized likelihood scores $u^{X_i}$ and $u^{X_j}$, i.e., $p(X_i) = \mathit{softmax}(u^{X_i} | X_i \in \mathcal{D}^{src})$ and $p(X_j) = \mathit{softmax}(u^{X_j} | X_j \in \mathcal{D}^{tar})$. Based on these definitions, the element $(X_i, X_j)$ of the OT solution matrix $\pi^*$, which is obtained by solving Equation 5, can be used as the distance between the example $X_i$ and $X_j$ ($X_i \in \mathcal{D}^{src}$, $X_j \in \mathcal{D}^{tar}$), aggregating the information from both representation vectors $V(X)$ and coreference likelihoods $u^X$.

To facilitate the example selection, we leverage $\pi^*(X_i, X_j)$ to compute an overall score $v_i$ for each example $X_i \in \mathcal{D}^{src}$ to capture the closeness of $X_i$ w.r.t examples in the target language using the average distance: $v_i = \frac{\sum_{X_j \in \mathcal{D}^{tar}} \pi^*(X_i, X_j)}{|\mathcal{D}^{src}|}$. Similarly, we obtain an overall score $v_j$ for each example $X_j \in \mathcal{D}^{tar}$: $v_j = \frac{\sum_{X_i \in \mathcal{D}^{src}} \pi^*(X_i, X_j)}{|\mathcal{D}^{tar}|}$. Finally, based on the overall scores $v_i$ and $v_j$, we only select $\gamma$ percents of examples in $\mathcal{D}^{src}$ and $\gamma$ percents of examples in $\mathcal{D}^{tar}$ that have smallest scores in their corresponding sets to participate into the loss functions $\mathcal{L}^1_{disc}$ and $\mathcal{L}^2_{disc}$ of the language discriminators for representation learning (i.e., the unselected examples are not included in the discriminators' loss functions). Here, $\gamma$ is a hyper-parameter of the model. Note that as solving the OT problem in Equation 5 is intractable, we employ the entropy-based approximation of OT and solve it with the Sinkhorn algorithm (Peyre and Cuturi, 2019).

## 4 Experiments

**Datasets and Hyper-parameters**: We leverage the multilingual KBP datasets annotated by NIST (Mitamura et al., 2015, 2016, 2017) to perform cross-lingual evaluation for ECR models in this work. In particular, we use the KBP 2015 dataset (Mitamura et al., 2015) that provides annotation for 360 documents in English to train ECR models. For test and development data, we employ annotated articles for ECR in English, Spanish and Chinese of the KBP 2016 and KBP 2017 datasets. Here, KBP 2016 (Mitamura et al., 2016) involves 85 articles for each language English, Spanish and Chinese (i.e., $3 * 85 = 255$ documents in total) while the number of articles for each language in KBP 2017 (Mitamura et al., 2017) is 83 (i.e., $3 * 83 = 249$ documents). As such, for each language (English, Spanish or Chinese), when the models are tested on KBP 2016, we use a half of the KBP 2017 articles for the development data and the other half for unlabeled data in the language discriminators. Similarly for the testing on KBP 2017, articles in KBP 2016 will be used for development and unlabeled data. Finally, to focus the evaluation of cross-lingual transfer learning, we employ golden event mentions in documents in this work.

Following (Choubey and Huang, 2018; Huang et al., 2019), we employ the official KBP 2017 scorer (version 1.8) to obtain the coreference resolution performance for models. This evaluation script reports common performance metrics for ECR, including MUC (Vilain et al., 1995), $B^3$ (Bagga and Baldwin, 1998) and CEAF-e (Luo, 2005), BLANC (Lee et al., 2012b) and Average CoNLL (the average of four prior metrics).

Hyper-parameters for the models are fine-tuned by Average CoNLL scores over development data. The suggested values from the fine-tuning involve: $5e$-5 for the learning rate with the Adam optimizer (selected from [$1e$-5, $2e$-5, $3e$-5, $4e$-5, $5e$-5]); 512 for the numbers of hidden units in the middle layers of the feed-forward language discriminator $D$, $D_1$ and $D_2$ (selected from $[64, 128, 256, 512, 1024]$); $\alpha = 0.1$, $\alpha^1_{disc} = 0.1$, $\alpha^2_{disc} = 0.1$, $\alpha_{diver} = 0.01$, $\alpha_{const} = 0.01$ for the trade-off parameters in the loss functions of the models (selected from $[0.01, 0.05, 0.1, 0.5, 1]$); and $\gamma = 50\%$ for the percentage of selected examples for the language discriminators in the optimal transport (selected

| | KBP 2016 Spanish | | | | | KBP 2017 Spanish | | | | |
|---|---|---|---|---|---|---|---|---|---|---|
| Model | $B^3$ | $CEAF_e$ | MUC | BLANC | AVG-CoNLL | $B^3$ | $CEAF_e$ | MUC | BLANC | AVG-CoNLL |
| Baseline | 86.67 | 80.17 | 71.30 | 80.47 | 79.65 | 84.24 | 78.17 | 60.86 | 73.93 | 74.30 |
| LANN | 86.61 | 79.86 | 71.80 | 80.63 | 79.72 | 84.70 | 78.83 | 61.56 | 74.60 | 74.92 |
| CLMAOT | 88.65 | 82.59 | 74.72 | 82.22 | **82.05** | 85.68 | 81.10 | 63.98 | 75.69 | **76.61** |
| | **KBP 2016 Chinese** | | | | | **KBP 2017 Chinese** | | | | |
| Model | $B^3$ | $CEAF_e$ | MUC | BLANC | AVG-CoNLL | $B^3$ | $CEAF_e$ | MUC | BLANC | AVG-CoNLL |
| Baseline | 85.44 | 78.01 | 64.35 | 77.88 | 76.42 | 81.38 | 74.77 | 63.64 | 70.39 | 72.54 |
| LANN | 86.87 | 79.80 | 64.59 | 78.65 | 77.48 | 81.56 | 74.95 | 63.82 | 70.68 | 72.75 |
| CLMAOT | 89.03 | 84.17 | 66.75 | 79.02 | **79.74** | 83.01 | 77.85 | 62.97 | 69.64 | **73.37** |

Table 1: Cross-lingual performance on the test sets of KBP 2016 and 2017 for Spanish and Chinese. Models are trained on English documents of KBP 2015. The performance improvement of CLMAOT is significant with $p < 0.01$ over all datasets.

from $[10\%, 30\%, 50\%, 70\%, 90\%]$). Finally, we use the base version of XLM-RoBERTa for the models that has 768 dimensions for hidden vectors of word-pieces, leading to the dimensionality of $768*5 = 3840$ for the representation vectors $V(X)$ and determining the shape of the feed-forward networks (e.g., $\texttt{FF}$, $\texttt{FF}_1$, $\texttt{FF}_2$, $f_1$, $f_2$, $D$, $D_1$, $D_2$).

**Model Performance**: We compare the proposed model for ECR with cross-lingual multi-view alignment and optimal transport (called CLMAOT), the baseline model with XLM-RoBERTa in Section 3.1 (called Baseline), and the Baseline model introduced with LANN (called LANN) in Section 3.2. Table 1 reports the cross-lingual performance of the models on the KBP 2016 and 2017 test datasets for Spanish and Chinese (the models are trained in English documents in KBP 2015). As can be seen, LANN improves the cross-lingual performance of Baseline over different target languages and datasets (although the improvements are not significant for some datasets, i.e., KBP 2016 Spanish and KBP 2017 Chinese), thus suggesting the benefits of language discriminators for language generalization for ECR. More importantly, comparing with CLMAOT, we find that CLMAOT significantly outperforms other baseline models over different performance measures and target languages (i.e., Spanish and Chinese). In particular, for Spanish, CLMAOT is $2.33\%$ and $1.70\%$ better than LANN on the Average CoNLL scores over KBP 2016 and KBP 2017 respectively. For Chinese, the performance gaps between CLMAOT and LANN are $2.26\%$ and $0.62\%$ for KBP 2016 and KBP 2017 (with the Average CoNLL scores), thus demonstrating the effectiveness of the proposed cross-lingual model with multi-view alignment and optimal transport for representation learning in ECR.

Interestingly, we have also evaluated the ECR models (trained on English documents of KBP 2015) on the English documents of KBP 2016 and KBP 2017. The AVG-CoNLL scores of the Baseline, LANN, and CLMAOT models on KBP 2016 from our experiments are 68.64, 69.21, and 71.14 respectively while the corresponding scores for KBP 2017 involve 70.68, 71.75, and 73.48 (respectively). As such, CLMAOT is also significantly better than Baseline and LANN in English, thus highlighting the advantages of CLMAOT for ECR. Note that the worse performance of the models on English (compared to those on Spanish and Chinese) is potentially due to the larger number of event mentions in English documents in KBP 2016 and KBP 2017 (e.g., KBP 2016 has 2505, 1261, and 1390 event mentions in English, Spanish, and Chinese documents respectively).

**Ablation Study**: Two major components in the proposed model CLMAOT involve the multi-view alignment for representation vectors and the OT to select examples for LANN. This section evaluates ablated versions and variants of such components to reveal their contributions for CLMAOT. First, to highlight the importance of the proposed regularization terms in the loss function $\mathcal{L}$ for the multi-view alignment component, the following ablated models are considered: (i) **CLMAOT - LANN**: this model eliminates the language discriminators $D_1$ and $D_2$ with the loss terms $\mathcal{L}^1_{disc}$ and $\mathcal{L}^2_{disc}$ from CLMAOT; (ii) **CLMAOT - Diversity**: this model does not apply the diversity regularization over source-language examples $\mathcal{L}_{diver}$ in CLMAOT; and (iii) **CLMAOT - Consistency**: this model excludes the consistency regularization over target-language examples $\mathcal{L}_{const}$ from CLMAOT. In addition, we evaluate the variant (iv) **CLMAOT_OneView** of CLMAOT where the two-view representations $V^1(X)$ and $V^2(X)$ are not

| Model | KBP 2016 Spanish $B^3$ | $CEAF_e$ | MUC | BLANC | AVG-CoNLL | KBP 2016 Chinese $B^3$ | $CEAF_e$ | MUC | BLANC | AVG-CoNLL |
|---|---|---|---|---|---|---|---|---|---|---|
| CLMAOT | 88.65 | 82.59 | 74.72 | 82.22 | **82.05** | 89.03 | 84.17 | 66.75 | 79.02 | **79.74** |
| CLMAOT - LANN | 87.21 | 80.39 | 71.94 | 81.39 | 80.23 | 86.79 | 79.94 | 65.00 | 78.81 | 77.64 |
| CLMAOT - Diversity | 87.27 | 80.52 | 71.94 | 81.39 | 80.28 | 87.47 | 81.07 | 64.84 | 78.96 | 78.08 |
| CLMAOT - Consistency | 87.40 | 80.64 | 72.47 | 81.46 | 80.49 | 87.61 | 80.84 | 65.01 | 79.44 | 78.22 |
| CLMAOT_OneView | 86.66 | 80.29 | 71.74 | 80.75 | 79.86 | 86.65 | 79.64 | 65.53 | 79.15 | 77.74 |
| CLMAOT - OT | 87.50 | 80.84 | 72.41 | 81.65 | 80.60 | 87.22 | 80.48 | 64.95 | 78.85 | 77.88 |
| CLMAOT - $OT^{rep}$ | 87.75 | 81.03 | 73.13 | 81.84 | 80.94 | 88.26 | 82.15 | 66.02 | 79.90 | 79.08 |
| CLMAOT - $OT^{coref}$ | 87.79 | 81.45 | 73.26 | 81.75 | 81.06 | 88.29 | 82.47 | 66.09 | 79.21 | 79.02 |

Table 2: Ablation study for CLMAOT over the KBP 2016 datasets for Spanish and Chinese.

employed, thus directly using $V(X)$ for the language discriminator and avoiding the diversity and consistency regularization $\mathcal{L}_{diver}$ and $\mathcal{L}_{const}$. Note that the OT for example selection is still preserved in **CLMAOT_OneView**.

Second, for the optimal transport component, we evaluate the following variants for CLMAOT: (v) **CLMAOT - OT**: this model removes the optimal transport component and utilize all examples in the source and target languages for the language discriminators in CLMAOT ($\gamma = 100\%$); (vi) **CLMAOT - $\mathbf{OT}^{rep}$**: this variant retains the OT component; however, instead of computing the cost function $C(X_i, X_j)$ based on the representation vectors for $X_i$ and $X_j$, this version assumes a constant cost function $C_{X_i,X_j} = 1$, aiming to demonstrate the necessity of induced representation vectors for OT-based example selection for language discriminators; and (vii) **CLMAOT - $\mathbf{OT}^{coref}$**: instead of relying on coreference likelihood scores to obtain the probability distributions $p(X_i)$ and $p(X_j)$, this model assumes uniform distributions for $p(X_i)$ and $p(X_j)$ in the OT computation. The motivation for this variant is to emphasize the importance of introducing coreference likelihood scores into OT for ECR.

Table 2 presents the performance of the models on the KBP 2016 test sets for Spanish and Chinese. It is clear from the table that the proposed regularization terms in the multi-view alignment component are helpful for CLMAOT as excluding any of them would significantly hurt the performance. We attribute this to the fact that the regularization terms in multi-view alignment might prevent the alignment of examples with different coreference labels in the source and target languages for the language discriminators. In addition, Table 2 shows that the performance of CLMAOT degrades when the optimal transport component or its elements (i.e., representation vectors for cost computation

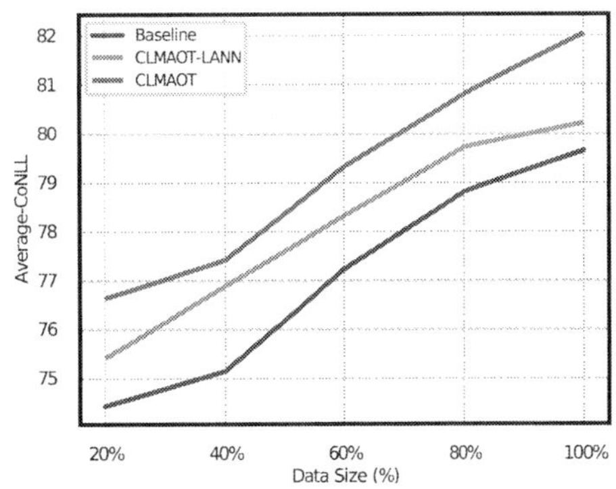


Figure 2: Learning curves over KBP 2016 for Spanish.

and coreference likelihoods for distributions) are removed. This thus proves the benefits of the designed optimal transport component in CLMAOT for cross-lingual ECR in this work.

Finally, Figures 2 and 3 show the learning curves of Baseline, **CLMAOT - LANN**, and CLMAOT over Spanish and Chinese where we vary the size of the training data in English (from KBP 2015) and test the models' performance on the KBP 2016 test data. As can be seen, CLMAOT demonstrates better cross-lingual performance than the baseline models over different sizes of the training data, thus further confirming the effectiveness of our proposed model CLMAOT for ECR.

## 5 Conclusion

This paper presents the first study on cross-lingual transfer learning for event coreference resolution. We introduce the first baseline models for this problem, leveraging a state-of-the-art pre-trained language models for multilingual NLP (i.e., XLM-RoBERTa) and LANN for language-invariant representation learning. We propose two novel techniques for cross-lingual transfer learning based multi-view alignment to avoid cross-label align-

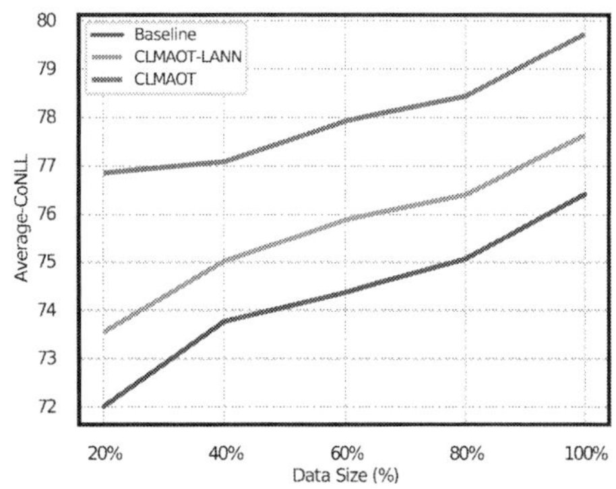


Figure 3: Learning curves over KBP 2016 for Chinese.

ment in the source and target languages and optimal transport for example selection in LANN. Our experiments provide baselines for future research and demonstrate the benefits of the proposed methods for cross-lingual transfer learning for ECR.

## Acknowledgments

This research has been supported by the Army Research Office (ARO) grant W911NF-21-1-0112 and the NSF grant CNS-1747798 to the IUCRC Center for Big Learning. This research is also based upon work supported by the Office of the Director of National Intelligence (ODNI), Intelligence Advanced Research Projects Activity (IARPA), via IARPA Contract No. 2019-19051600006 under the Better Extraction from Text Towards Enhanced Retrieval (BETTER) Program. The views and conclusions contained herein are those of the authors and should not be interpreted as necessarily representing the official policies, either expressed or implied, of ARO, ODNI, IARPA, the Department of Defense, or the U.S. Government. The U.S. Government is authorized to reproduce and distribute reprints for governmental purposes notwithstanding any copyright annotation therein. This document does not contain technology or technical data controlled under either the U.S. International Traffic in Arms Regulations or the U.S. Export Administration Regulations.

## References

David Ahn. 2006. The stages of event extraction. In *Proceedings of the Workshop on Annotating and Reasoning about Time and Events*.

Jun Araki and Teruko Mitamura. 2015. Joint event trigger identification and event coreference resolution with structured perceptron. In *Proceedings of the Conference on Empirical Methods in Natural Language Processing (EMNLP)*.

A. Bagga and B. Baldwin. 1998. Entity-based cross-document coreferencing using the vector space model. In *Proceedings of the International Conference on Computational Linguistics (COLING)*.

Shany Barhom, Vered Shwartz, Alon Eirew, Michael Bugert, Nils Reimers, and Ido Dagan. 2019. Revisiting joint modeling of cross-document entity and event coreference resolution. In *ACL*.

Konstantinos Bousmalis, George Trigeorgis, Nathan Silberman, Dilip Krishnan, and Dumitru Erhan. 2016. Domain separation networks. In *Proceedings of the Conference on Neural Information Processing Systems (NeurIPS)*.

Chen Chen and Vincent Ng. 2016. Joint inference over a lightly supervised information extraction pipeline: Towards event coreference resolution for resource-scarce languages. In *Proceedings of the Association for the Advancement of Artificial Intelligence (AAAI)*.

Xilun Chen, Ahmed Hassan Awadallah, Hany Hassan, Wei Wang, and Claire Cardie. 2019. Multi-source cross-lingual model transfer: Learning what to share. In *Proceedings of the Annual Meeting of the Association for Computational Linguistics (ACL)*.

Xilun Chen, Yu Sun, Ben Athiwaratkun, Claire Cardie, and Kilian Weinberger. 2018a. Adversarial deep averaging networks for cross-lingual sentiment classification. In *Transactions of the Association for Computational Linguistics (TACL)*.

Xilun Chen, Yu Sun, Ben Athiwaratkun, Claire Cardie, and Kilian Weinberger. 2018b. Adversarial deep averaging networks for cross-lingual sentiment classification. *Transactions of the Association for Computational Linguistics (TACL)*.

Zheng Chen and Heng Ji. 2009a. Can one language bootstrap the other: a case study on event extraction. In *Workshop on Semi-Supervised Learning for Natural Language Processing*.

Zheng Chen and Heng Ji. 2009b. Graph-based event coreference resolution. In *Proceedings of the Workshop on Graph-based Methods for Natural Language Processing*.

Zheng Chen, Heng Ji, and Robert Haralick. 2009. A pairwise event coreference model, feature impact and evaluation for event coreference resolution. In *Proceedings of the Workshop on Events in Emerging Text Types*.

Prafulla Kumar Choubey and Ruihong Huang. 2018. Improving event coreference resolution by modeling correlations between event coreference chains and document topic structures. In *Proceedings of the Annual Meeting of the Association for Computational Linguistics (ACL)*.

Prafulla Kumar Choubey, Aaron Lee, Ruihong Huang, and Lu Wang. 2020. Discourse as a function of event: Profiling discourse structure in news articles around the main event. In *Proceedings of the Annual Meeting of the Association for Computational Linguistics (ACL)*.

Alexis Conneau, Kartikay Khandelwal, Naman Goyal, Vishrav Chaudhary, Guillaume Wenzek, Francisco Guzmán, Edouard Grave, Myle Ott, Luke Zettlemoyer, and Veselin Stoyanov. 2019. Unsupervised cross-lingual representation learning at scale. *arXiv preprint arXiv:1911.02116*.

Agata Cybulska and Piek T. J. M. Vossen. 2015. "bag of events" approach to event coreference resolution. supervised classification of event templates. In *Int. J. Comput. Linguistics Appl.*

Jacob Devlin, Ming-Wei Chang, Kenton Lee, and Kristina Toutanova. 2019. BERT: Pre-training of deep bidirectional transformers for language understanding. In *Proceedings of the Conference of the North American Chapter of the Association for Computational Linguistics: Human Language Technologies (NAACL-HLT)*.

Greg Durrett and Dan Klein. 2013. Easy victories and uphill battles in coreference resolution. In *Proceedings of the Conference on Empirical Methods in Natural Language Processing (EMNLP)*.

Lisheng Fu, Thien Huu Nguyen, Bonan Min, and Ralph Grishman. 2017. Domain adaptation for relation extraction with domain adversarial neural network. In *Proceedings of the Eighth International Joint Conference on Natural Language Processing (IJCNLP)*.

Yaroslav Ganin, Evgeniya Ustinova, Hana Ajakan, Pascal Germain, Hugo Larochelle, François Laviolette, Mario March, and Victor Lempitsky. 2016. Domain-adversarial training of neural networks. In *Journal of Machine Learning Research*.

Christian Hardmeier, Jörg Tiedemann, and Joakim Nivre. 2013. Latent anaphora resolution for cross-lingual pronoun prediction. In *Proceedings of the Conference on Empirical Methods in Natural Language Processing (EMNLP)*.

Andrew Hsi, Yiming Yang, Jaime Carbonell, and Ruochen Xu. 2016. Leveraging multilingual training for limited resource event extraction. In *Proceedings of the International Conference on Computational Linguistics (COLING)*.

Yin Jou Huang, Jing Lu, Sadao Kurohashi, and Vincent Ng. 2019. Improving event coreference resolution by learning argument compatibility from unlabeled data. In *Proceedings of the Conference of the North American Chapter of the Association for Computational Linguistics: Human Language Technologies (NAACL-HLT)*.

Mandar Joshi, Danqi Chen, Y. Liu, Daniel S. Weld, Luke Zettlemoyer, and Omer Levy. 2019. Spanbert: Improving pre-training by representing and predicting spans. In *Transactions of the Association for Computational Linguistics (TACL)*.

Kian Kenyon-Dean, Jackie Chi Kit Cheung, and Doina Precup. 2018. Resolving event coreference with supervised representation learning and clustering-oriented regularization. In *Proceedings of *SEM*.

Phillip Keung, Yichao Lu, and Vikas Bhardwaj. 2019. Adversarial learning with contextual embeddings for zero-resource cross-lingual classification and NER. In *Proceedings of the Conference on Empirical Methods in Natural Language Processing (EMNLP)*.

Abhishek Kumar, Prasanna Sattigeri, Kahini Wadhawan, Leonid Karlinsky, Rogerio Feris, Bill Freeman, and Gregory Wornell. 2018. Co-regularized alignment for unsupervised domain adaptation. In *Proceedings of the Conference on Neural Information Processing Systems (NeurIPS)*.

Gourab Kundu, Avi Sil, Radu Florian, and Wael Hamza. 2018. Neural cross-lingual coreference resolution and its application to entity linking. In *Proceedings of the Annual Meeting of the Association for Computational Linguistics (ACL)*.

Heeyoung Lee, Marta Recasens, Angel Chang, Mihai Surdeanu, and Dan Jurafsky. 2012a. Joint entity and event coreference resolution across documents. In *Proceedings of the Conference on Empirical Methods in Natural Language Processing (EMNLP)*.

Heeyoung Lee, Marta Recasens, Angel Chang, Mihai Surdeanu, and Dan Jurafsky. 2012b. Joint entity and event coreference resolution across documents. In *Proceedings of the Conference on Empirical Methods in Natural Language Processing (EMNLP)*.

Kenton Lee, Luheng He, Mike Lewis, and Luke Zettlemoyer. 2017. End-to-end neural coreference resolution. In *Proceedings of the Conference on Empirical Methods in Natural Language Processing (EMNLP)*.

Yankai Lin, Zhiyuan Liu, and Maosong Sun. 2017. Neural relation extraction with multi-lingual attention. In *Proceedings of the Annual Meeting of the Association for Computational Linguistics (ACL)*.

Zhengzhong Liu, Jun Araki, Eduard Hovy, and Teruko Mitamura. 2014. Supervised within-document event coreference using information propagation. In *Proceedings of the Language Resources and Evaluation Conference (LREC)*.

Jing Lu and Vincent Ng. 2017. Joint learning for event coreference resolution. In *Proceedings of the Annual Meeting of the Association for Computational Linguistics (ACL)*.

Jing Lu and Vincent Ng. 2018. Event coreference resolution: A survey of two decades of research. In *Proceedings of the Twenty-Ninth International Joint Conference on Artificial Intelligence (IJCAI)*.

Jing Lu, Deepak Venugopal, Vibhav Gogate, and Vincent Ng. 2016. Joint inference for event coreference resolution. In *Proceedings of the International Conference on Computational Linguistics (COLING)*.

Xiaoqiang Luo. 2005. On coreference resolution performance metrics. In *Proceedings of the Conference on Empirical Methods in Natural Language Processing (EMNLP)*.

André F. T. Martins. 2015. Transferring coreference resolvers with posterior regularization. In *Proceedings of the Annual Meeting of the Association for Computational Linguistics (ACL)*.

Teruko Mitamura, Zhengzhong Liu, and Eduard H. Hovy. 2015. Overview of TAC-KBP 2015 event nugget track. In *Proceedings of the Text Analysis Conference (TAC)*.

Teruko Mitamura, Zhengzhong Liu, and Eduard H. Hovy. 2016. Overview of TAC-KBP 2016 event nugget track. In *Proceedings of the Text Analysis Conference (TAC)*.

Teruko Mitamura, Zhengzhong Liu, and Eduard H. Hovy. 2017. Events detection, coreference and sequencing: What's next? overview of the TAC KBP 2017 event track. In *Proceedings of the Text Analysis Conference (TAC)*.

Aakanksha Naik and Carolyn Rose. 2020. Towards open domain event trigger identification using adversarial domain adaptation. In *Proceedings of the Annual Meeting of the Association for Computational Linguistics (ACL)*.

Vincent Ng. 2010. Supervised noun phrase coreference research: The first fifteen years. In *Proceedings of the Annual Meeting of the Association for Computational Linguistics (ACL)*.

Nghia Trung Ngo, Duy Phung, and Thien Huu Nguyen. 2021. Unsupervised domain adaptation for event detection using domain-specific adapters. In *Findings of the Association for Computational Linguistics (ACL-IJCNLP)*.

Minh Van Nguyen, Viet Dac Lai, Amir Pouran Ben Veyseh, and Thien Huu Nguyen. 2021a. Trankit: A light-weight transformer-based toolkit for multilingual natural language processing. In *Proceedings of the 16th Conference of the European Chapter of the Association for Computational Linguistics: System Demonstrations (EACL)*.

Minh Van Nguyen and Thien Huu Nguyen. 2021. Improving cross-lingual transfer for event argument extraction with language-universal sentence structures. In *Proceedings of the Sixth Arabic Natural Language Processing Workshop*.

Minh Van Nguyen, Tuan Ngo Nguyen, Bonan Min, and Thien Huu Nguyen. 2021b. Crosslingual transfer learning for relation and event extraction via word category and class alignments. In *Proceedings of the 2021 Conference on Empirical Methods in Natural Language Processing (EMNLP)*.

Thien Huu Nguyen, , Adam Meyers, and Ralph Grishman. 2016. New york university 2016 system for kbp event nugget: A deep learning approach. In *Proceedings of the Text Analysis Conference (TAC)*.

Haoruo Peng, Yangqiu Song, and Dan Roth. 2016. Event detection and co-reference with minimal supervision. In *Proceedings of the Conference on Empirical Methods in Natural Language Processing: Findings (EMNLP)*.

Gabriel Peyre and Marco Cuturi. 2019. Computational optimal transport: With applications to data science. In *Foundations and Trends in Machine Learning*.

Duy Phung, Tuan Ngo Nguyen, and Thien Huu Nguyen. 2021. Hierarchical graph convolutional networks for jointly resolving cross-document coreference of entity and event mentions. In *Proceedings of the Fifteenth Workshop on Graph-Based Methods for Natural Language Processing (TextGraphs-15)*.

Karthik Raghunathan, Heeyoung Lee, Sudarshan Rangarajan, Nathanael Chambers, Mihai Surdeanu, Dan Jurafsky, and Christopher Manning. 2010. A multipass sieve for coreference resolution. In *Proceedings of the Conference on Empirical Methods in Natural Language Processing (EMNLP)*.

Altaf Rahman and Vincent Ng. 2012. Translation-based projection for multilingual coreference resolution. In *Proceedings of the Conference of the North American Chapter of the Association for Computational Linguistics: Human Language Technologies (NAACL-HLT)*.

Ananya Subburathinam, Di Lu, Heng Ji, Jonathan May, Shih-Fu Chang, Avirup Sil, and Clare Voss. 2019a. Cross-lingual structure transfer for relation and event extraction. In *Proceedings of the Conference on Empirical Methods in Natural Language Processing (EMNLP)*.

Ananya Subburathinam, Di Lu, Heng Ji, Jonathan May, Shih-Fu Chang, Avirup Sil, and Clare Voss. 2019b. Cross-lingual structure transfer for relation and event extraction. In *Proceedings of the Conference on Empirical Methods in Natural Language Processing (EMNLP)*.

Hieu Minh Tran, Duy Phung, and Thien Huu Nguyen. 2021. Exploiting document structures and cluster consistencies for event coreference resolution. In *Proceedings of the 59th Annual Meeting of the Association for Computational Linguistics and the 11th International Joint Conference on Natural Language Processing (ACL)*.

Gorka Urbizu, Ander Soraluze, and Olatz Arregi. 2019. Deep cross-lingual coreference resolution for less-resourced languages: The case of Basque. In *Proceedings of the Second Workshop on Computational Models of Reference, Anaphora and Coreference*.

Marc Vilain, John Burger, John Aberdeen, Dennis Connolly, and Lynette Hirschman. 1995. A model-theoretic coreference scoring scheme. In *Sixth Message Understanding Conference (MUC-6)*.

Xiaozhi Wang, Xu Han, Yankai Lin, Zhiyuan Liu, and Maosong Sun. 2018. Adversarial multi-lingual neural relation extraction. In *Proceedings of the International Conference on Computational Linguistics (COLING)*.

Shijie Wu and Mark Dredze. 2019. Beto, bentz, becas: The surprising cross-lingual effectiveness of BERT. In *Proceedings of the Conference on Empirical Methods in Natural Language Processing (EMNLP)*.

Shijie Wu and Mark Dredze. 2020. Are all languages created equal in multilingual BERT? In *Proceedings of the 5th Workshop on Representation Learning for NLP*.

Bishan Yang, Claire Cardie, and Peter Frazier. 2015. A hierarchical distance-dependent Bayesian model for event coreference resolution. In *Transactions of the Association for Computational Linguistics (TACL)*.

Bowei Zou, Zengzhuang Xu, Yu Hong, and Guodong Zhou. 2018. Adversarial feature adaptation for cross-lingual relation classification. In *Proceedings of the International Conference on Computational Linguistics (COLING)*.

# Multilingual and Multilabel Emotion Recognition using Virtual Adversarial Training

**Vikram Gupta**
ShareChat, India
vikramgupta@sharechat.co

## Abstract

Virtual Adversarial Training (VAT) has been effective in learning robust models under supervised and semi-supervised settings for both computer vision and NLP tasks. However, the efficacy of VAT for multilingual and multilabel text classification has not been explored before. In this work, we explore VAT for multilabel emotion recognition with a focus on leveraging unlabelled data from different languages to improve the model performance. We perform extensive semi-supervised experiments on SemEval2018 multilabel and multilingual emotion recognition dataset and show performance gains of **6.2%** (Arabic), **3.8%** (Spanish) and **1.8%** (English) over supervised learning with same amount of labelled data (10% of training data). We also improve the existing state-of-the-art by **7%**, **4.5%** and **1%** (Jaccard Index) for Spanish, Arabic and English respectively and perform probing experiments for understanding the impact of different layers of the contextual models.

## 1 Introduction

Emotion recognition is an active and crucial area of research, especially for social media platforms. Understanding the emotional state of the users from textual data forms an important problem as it helps in discovering signs of fear, anxiety, bullying, hatred etc. and maintaining the emotional health of the people and platform. With the advent of deep neural networks and contextual models, text understanding has advanced dramatically by leveraging huge amount of unlabelled data freely available on web. However, even with these advancements, annotating emotion categories is expensive and time consuming as emotion categories are highly correlated and subjective in nature and can co-occur in the same text. Psychological studies suggest that emotions like "anger" and "sadness" are correlated and co-occur more frequently than "anger" and "happiness" (Plutchik, 1980). In a multilingual setup, the annotation becomes even more challenging as annotator team are expected to be familiar with different languages and culture for understanding the emotions accurately. Imbalance in availability of the data across languages further creates problems, especially in case of resource impoverished languages. In this work, we investigate the following key points; *a) Can unlabelled data from other languages improve recognition performance of target language and help in reducing requirement of labelled data? b) Efficacy of VAT for multilingual and multilabel setup.*

To address the aforementioned questions, we focus our experiments towards *semi-supervised* learning in a *multilingual* and *multilabel* emotion classification framework. We formulate semi-supervised Virtual Adversarial Training (VAT) (Miyato et al., 2018) for multilabel emotion classification using contextual models and perform extensive experiments to demonstrate that unlabelled data from other languages $L_{ul} = \{L_1, L_2, \dots, L_n\}$ improves the classification on the target language $L_{tgt}$. We obtain competitive performance by reducing the amount of annotated data demonstrating cross-language learning. To effectively leverage the multilingual content, we use multilingual contextual models for representing the text across languages. We also evaluate monolingual contextual models to understand the performance differences between multilingual and monolingual models and explore the advantages of *domain-adaptive* and *task-adaptive* pretraining of models for our task and observe substantial gains.

We perform extensive experiments on the SemEval2018 (Affect in Tweets: Task E-c[1]) dataset (Mohammad et al., 2018) which contains tweets from Twitter annotated with 11 emotion categories across three languages - English, Spanish and Arabic and demonstrate the effectiveness of semi-supervised learning across languages. To the

[1] https://competitions.codalab.org/competitions/17751



*Proceedings of the 1st Workshop on Multilingual Representation Learning*, pages 74–85
November 11, 2021. 

best of our knowledge, our study is the first one to explore semi-supervised adversarial learning across different languages for multilabel classification. In summary, the main contributions of our work are the following:

- We explore Virtual Adversarial Training (VAT) for semi-supervised multilabel classification on multilingual corpus
- Experiments demonstrating **6.2%**, **3.8%** and **1.8%** improvements (Jaccard Index) on Arabic, Spanish and English by leveraging unlabelled data of other languages while using 10% of labelled samples.
- Improve state-of-the-art of multilabel emotion recognition by **7%**, **4.5%** and **1%** (Jaccard Index) for Spanish, Arabic and English respectively.
- Experiments showcasing the advantages of *domain-adaptive* and *task-adaptive* pretraining

## 2 Related Work

Semi-supervised learning is an important paradigm for tackling the scarcity of labelled data as it marries the advantages of supervised and unsupervised learning by leveraging the information hidden in large amount of unlabelled data along with small amount of labelled data (Yang et al., 2021), (Van Engelen and Hoos, 2020). Early approaches used self-training for leveraging the model's own predictions on unlabelled data to obtain additional information during training (Yarowsky, 1995) (McClosky et al., 2006). Clark et al. (2018) proposed cross-view training (CVT) for various tasks like chunking, dependency parsing, machine translation and reported state-of-the-art results. CVT forces the model to make consistent predictions when using the full input or partial input. Ladder networks (Laine and Aila, 2016), Mean Teacher networks (Tarvainen and Valpola, 2017) are another way for semi-supervised learning where temporal and model-weights are ensembled. Another popular direction towards semi-supervised learning is adversarial training where the data point is perturbed with random or carefully tuned perturbations to create an adversarial sample. The model is then encouraged to maintain consistent predictions for the original sample and the adversarial sample. Adversarial training was initially explored for developing secure and robust models (Goodfellow et al., 2014), (Xiao et al., 2018), (Saadatpanah et al., 2020) to prevent attacks. Miyato et al. (2016), Cheng et al. (2019), Zhu et al. (2019) showed that adversarial training can improve both robustness and generalization for classification tasks, machine translation and GLUE benchmark respectively. Miyato et al. (2016), Sachan et al. (2019), Miyato et al. (2018) then applied the adversarial training for semi-supervised image and text classification showing substantial improvements.

Emotion recognition is an important problem and has received lot of attention from the community (Yadollahi et al., 2017), (Sailunaz et al., 2018). The taxonomies of emotions suggested by Plutchik wheel of emotions (Plutchik, 1980) and (Ekman, 1984) have been used by the majority of the previous work in emotion recognition. Emotion recognition can be formulated as a *multiclass* problem (Scherer and Wallbott, 1994), (Mohammad, 2012) or a *multilabel* problem (Mohammad et al., 2018), (Demszky et al., 2020). In the *multiclass* formulation, the objective is to identify the presence of one of the emotion from the taxonomy whereas in a *multilabel* setting, more than one emotion can be present in the text instance. Binary relevance approach (Godbole and Sarawagi, 2004) is another way to break multilabel problem into multiple binary classification problems. However, this approach does not model the co-relation between emotions. Seq2Seq approaches (Yang et al., 2018), (Huang et al., 2021) solve this problem by modelling the relationship between emotions by inferring emotion in an incremental manner. An interesting direction for handling data scarcity in emotion recognition is to use distant supervision by exploiting emojis (Felbo et al., 2017), hashtags (Mohammad, 2012) or pretraining emotion specific embeddings and language models (Barbieri et al., 2021), (Ghosh et al., 2017).

With the emergence of contextual models like BERT (Devlin et al., 2018), Roberta (Liu et al., 2019) etc., the field of NLP and text classification has been revolutionized as these models are able to learn efficient representations from a huge corpus of unlabelled data across different languages and domains (Hassan et al., 2021), (Barbieri et al., 2021). Social media content contains linguistic errors, idiosyncratic styles, spelling mistakes, grammatical inconsistency, slangs, hashtags, emoticons etc. (Barbieri et al., 2018), (Derczynski et al., 2013) due to which off-the-shelf contextual models may not be optimum. We use *language-adaptive*, *domain-adaptive* and *task-adaptive* pre-training which has shown performance gains (Peters et al., 2019), (Gururangan et al., 2020), (Barbieri et al., 2021), (Howard and Ruder, 2018), (Lee et al., 2020) for different tasks and domains.

## 3 Methodology

We consider the task of multilabel emotion classification, where given a text $t \in T$ and $t = \{w_1, w_2, \ldots, w_l\}$, we predict the presence of $y$ emotion categories denoted by $\{1, 2, \ldots, y\}$. $T$ represents the corpus of all the sentences across the different languages and $w_i$ represent the tokens in the sentence. We leverage contextual models as feature extractors $\phi : t_i \rightarrow x_i$, where $x_i \in \mathbb{R}^d$ and $d$ is the dimension of the text representations and train a classifier over these representations.

### 3.1 Virtual Adversarial Training (VAT)

Virtual Adversarial Training (VAT) (Miyato et al., 2018) is a regularization method for learning robust representations by encouraging the models to produce similar outputs for the input data points and local perturbations. VAT creates the adversary by perturbing the input in the direction which maximizes the change in the output of the model. Since VAT does not require labels it is well suited for semi-supervised applications. Consider $x \in \mathbb{R}^d$ as the $d$ dimensional representation of the text and $y$ as the ground truth. Objective function of VAT ($L_{vadv}$) is represented as,

$$L_{vadv}(x, \theta) := D[p(y|x, \hat{\theta}), p(y|x + r_{vadv}, \theta)] \quad (1)$$

where,

$$r_{vadv} := arg\,max D[p(y|x, \hat{\theta}), p(y|x+r, \theta)] \quad (2)$$

and $||r||_2 < \epsilon$ and $r_{vadv} \in \mathbb{R}^d$. $D[p, p']$ measures the divergence between the two probability distributions and $r_{vadv}$ is the *virtual adversarial perturbation* that maximizes this divergence. In order to leverage the unlabelled data, the predictions from the current estimate of the model $\hat{\theta}$ are used as the target. However, it is not possible to exactly compute $r_{vadv}$ by a closed form solution or linear approximation as gradient $g$ (Equation 4) with respect to r is always zero at $r$ = 0. Miyato et al. (2018) propose fast approximation method to formulate $r_{adv}$ as:

$$r_{vadv} \approx \epsilon \frac{g}{||g||_2}, \quad (3)$$

where,

$$g = \nabla r D[p(y|x, \hat{\theta}), p(y|x + r, \hat{\theta})] \quad (4)$$

and $r = \epsilon * q$, where $q$ is a randomly sampled unit vector. With this approximation, we can use back-propagation to compute the gradients $g$ in Equation 4. The overall training objective, $L_{VAT}$ becomes:

$$L_{VAT} = L_{ce} + \alpha * L_{vadv} \quad (5)$$

where $L_{ce}$ is the multiclass classification loss and $L_{adv}$ is the adversarial loss. $\alpha$ is the balancing hyperparameter between the two losses.

### 3.2 Multilabel Virtual Adversarial Training (`mlVAT`)

We explore VAT for multilingual contextual models and multilabel classification. For computer vision tasks, perturbing the raw pixel values to generate adversarial examples is intuitive as the input space is continuous. However, contextual models use the indices of the words as input which are not present in the continuous domain and thus perturbing them is not optimal. Perturbing an index $k$ of a word $w_k$ to $k + r_{vadv}$ would not result in a word closer to $w_k$. To overcome this problem, instead of perturbing the input, we perturb the intermediate layer of the contextual models which form a continuous representation space and allows us to use VAT with contextual models. Similar strategy for text classification was also explored by Miyato et al. (2016). For modelling multilabel classification, we measure the divergence of multilabel outputs by Mean Square Error (MSE),

$$L_{vadv}(x, \theta) := MSE[p(y|x, \hat{\theta}), p(y|x+r_{vadv}, \theta)] \quad (6)$$

MSE is calculated over the logits normalized by sigmoid. This is important as the outputs in case of multilabel classification are not probability distributions across classes which renders the usage of KL-Divergence incompatible for this scenario. We also experiment by treating the probability for each emotion separately but our results demonstrate the effectiveness of Mean Square Error (MSE) for our task (Table 4). The overall training objective, $L_{\texttt{mlVAT}}$ is:

$$L_{\texttt{mlVAT}} = L_{bce} + \alpha * L_{vadv} \quad (7)$$

where, $L_{bce}$ is the multilabel binary cross entropy loss. We represent the text instances using monolingual/multilingual contextual representations.

### 3.3 Multilingual Semi-Supervised Setup

**mlVAT:** For each target language $L_{tgt}$, we randomly select a percentage of samples from the training set of this language and use them as labelled examples for training. We use the remaining data of the same language and the complete dataset of the other languages $L_{ul}$ as the unlabelled set. Each training batch is created by maintaining a ratio between labelled and unlabelled examples for stable training. For the labelled set, both multilabel classification loss $L_{bce}$ and adversarial loss $L_{vadv}$ is applied. For the unlabelled examples, only the adversarial loss $L_{vadv}$ is used.

**Sup**: We also train supervised classifiers (Sup) by using the same amount of labelled data for target language $L_{tgt}$. Supervised classifiers (Sup) act as baseline and help in measuring the gains obtained by semi-supervised learning. We vary the ratio of sampled labelled examples as 10%, 25%, 50% and 100% to study the progression of our framework across different amount of labelled data of the target language.

### 3.4 Multilingual Representation

For leveraging cross-learning between multiple languages in a semi-supervised setup, we experiment with different multilingual models. We experiment with off-the-shelf multilingual BERT, mBERT (Devlin et al., 2018) and XLM-R (Conneau et al., 2019) models which have been trained with corpus from multiple languages. Since we are performing emotion recognition on multilingual tweets, we evaluate the *domain-adaptive* multilingual model XLM-Tw (Barbieri et al., 2021) trained using a 198M tweet corpus across 30 languages over the XLM-R checkpoint. For exploring the effect of *task-adaptive* pretraining, we evaluate XLM-Tw-S, which is finetuned for sentiment analysis over tweets which is arguably a task related to emotion recognition.

### 3.5 Monolingual Representation

We also experiment with monolingual models trained over the corpus from the same language for comparison with multilingual models and setting up the baselines for each language: English BERT (E-BERT) (Devlin et al., 2018) for English, BetoBERT (Cañete et al., 2020) for Spanish and AraBERT (Antoun et al., 2020) for Arabic. We experiment with and without finetuning the representations to evaluate the performance of these representations out-of-the box and finetuning over our task.

| % | Method | JI | MiF1 | MaF1 |
|---|---|---|---|---|
| 10 | Sup | 44.05 | 57.86 | 40.91 |
| | mlVAT | **46.79** | **60.36** | **44.41** |
| 25 | Sup | 49.69 | 62.80 | 44.19 |
| | mlVAT | **51.08** | **63.96** | **47.31** |
| 50 | Sup | 53.95 | 66.26 | 48.57 |
| | mlVAT | **55.11** | **66.79** | **52.52** |
| 100 | Sup | 55.78 | 67.41 | 50.12 |
| | mlVAT | **57.31** | **68.18** | **52.15** |

Table 1: mlVAT and Supervised (Sup) experiments on **Arabic** across different ratios of labelled examples

| % | Method | JI | MiF1 | MaF1 |
|---|---|---|---|---|
| 10 | Sup | 54.15 | 66.33 | 48.94 |
| | mlVAT | **55.15** | **67.01** | **50.57** |
| 25 | Sup | 55.11 | 66.99 | 47.83 |
| | mlVAT | **56.54** | **68.52** | 51.18 |
| 50 | Sup | 57.20 | 69.14 | **54.14** |
| | mlVAT | **58.67** | **70.03** | 51.55 |
| 100 | Sup | 59.78 | 71.19 | 53.43 |
| | mlVAT | **60.70** | **71.90** | **56.10** |

Table 2: mlVAT and Supervised (Sup) experiments on **English** across different ratios of labelled examples

| % | Method | JI | MiF1 | MaF1 |
|---|---|---|---|---|
| 10 | Sup | 44.36 | 53.17 | 38.28 |
| | mlVAT | **46.05** | **54.83** | **42.49** |
| 25 | Sup | **52.89** | **61.30** | 48.99 |
| | mlVAT | 52.05 | 60.17 | **49.15** |
| 50 | Sup | 55.17 | 63.20 | 51.70 |
| | mlVAT | **55.70** | **63.39** | **54.19** |
| 100 | Sup | **57.04** | **65.31** | 51.53 |
| | mlVAT | 56.89 | 64.89 | **51.77** |

Table 3: mlVAT and Supervised (Sup) experiments on **Spanish** across different ratios of labelled examples

### 3.6 Dataset and Evaluation

We evaluate on the SemEval2018 dataset (Affect in Tweets: Task E-c) (Mohammad et al., 2018) dataset. The dataset consists of tweets scraped from twitter in English, Spanish and Arabic. Each tweet is annotated with the presence of 11 emotions *anger, anticipation, disgust, fear, joy, love, optimism, pessimism, sadness, surprise and trust.* Some tweets are neutral and do not have the presence of any emotion. The dataset has 3 splits - train, dev and test

(Table 15). Following Mohammad et al. (2018), we measure the multilabel accuracy using Jaccard Index (JI), Macro F1 (MaF1) and Micro F1 (MiF1) scores (Chinchor, 1992) over the test set of these languages.

## 4 Semi-Supervised Experiments

We select a percentage (10%, 25%, 50%, 100%) of the data from the target language as labelled data and use the remaining data from same language along with data of other languages as the unlabelled data. In Table 1 for Arabic, we see that by using 10%, 25%, 50% and 100% of the labelled data, mlVAT improves upon the results of training over the same amount of supervised data by **6.2%, 2.8%, 2.2% and 2.7%** (Jaccard Index;JI) respectively. Similar improvements are also observed on the micro F1 (MiF1) and macro F1 (MaF1). It is interesting to note that by using only 50% of the labelled data with unlabelled data, we are able to match the performance of supervised learning with 100% of the data for Spanish. This shows that mlVAT is able to leverage the unlabelled data of Spanish and English for improving the performance over Arabic language.

Similar observations on English can be made from Table 2 also where we notice an improvement of **1.8%, 2.6%, 2.6% and 2%** on the Jaccard Index and proportional improvements on other metrices also. For English also, we note that by using 10% of labelled data, mlVAT is able to improve on supervised results with 25% of the data. For Spanish, mlVAT helps for the 10% and 50% split as reported in Table 3 but is not able to improve all the metrics for the other splits. Overall, for majority of the languages and splits, we see that by adding unlabelled data, mlVAT improves upon the performance over supervised learning consistently and helps in decreasing the requirements for annotated data.

**Frozen backbone:** We perform semi-supervised experiments with frozen backbone to investigate the effect of mlVAT on the backbone and classification head. We repeat similar experiments as in previous sections for Spanish and English, but freeze the backbone and only train the classification head. From the Figure 1, we can observe that mlVAT consistently improves the performance for both languages over all the splits. This demonstrates that the performance gains are backbone-agnostic allowing for application of mlVAT on other backbones also.

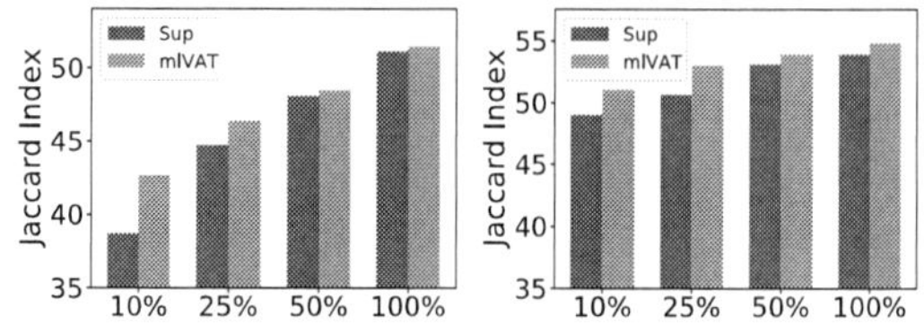


(a) Spanish (b) English

Figure 1: Comparison of Jaccard Index for English and Spanish across different ratio of labelled examples with *frozen backbone*. mlVAT (orange) improves upon supervised settings (Sup) (blue) for both languages.

| Loss | JI | MiF1 | MaF1 |
|---|---|---|---|
| mlVAT | 55.2 | 67.1 | 50.6 |
| mlVAT(w/o sig) | 50.7 | 63.5 | 41.6 |
| KLDivergence | 21.9 | 35.9 | 34.1 |

Table 4: Comparison of loss functions on English with 10% labelled data

**Loss Function:** We evaluate Mean Square Loss (mlVAT), MSE without sigmoid and KL-divergence (KLDivergence) loss in Table 4. MSE in presence of sigmoid shows superior performance than the other loss functions. The superior performance can be attributed to the normalization of the logits which encourages more stable activations and training. For experimenting with KL-divergence, we interpreted the normalized logits as probabilities but observed substantially poorer performance. We used English language with 10% of labelled examples and XLM-Tw model for these experiments.

| Ratio | 1 | 2 | 3 | 4 | 5 |
|---|---|---|---|---|---|
| JI | 55.1 | 54.4 | **55.2** | 53.6 | 52.9 |
| MiF1 | 66.9 | 66.4 | **67.0** | 65.8 | 65.3 |
| MaF1 | 50.0 | **50.9** | 50.8 | 50.5 | 47.0 |

Table 5: Comparison of batch ratios on English with 10% labelled data

**Unlabelled Batch Ratio:** In Table 5, we study the impact of ratio of the batch size of the unlabelled examples while keeping the batch size of the labelled data fixed. At higher ratios, the adversarial loss overpowers the supervised learning resulting in a performance drop. However, for the lower ratios, the we did not observe a consistent trend.

**Epsilon:** We study the impact of epsilon ($\epsilon$) on the performance in Table 6. Higher values create more aggressive adversarial samples with high pertur-

| $\epsilon$ | 0.1 | 0.25 | 0.5 | 0.75 | 1 |
|---|---|---|---|---|---|
| JI | 54.9 | 54.9 | **55.2** | 54.7 | 54.6 |
| MiF1 | 66.7 | 66.8 | **67.0** | 66.6 | 66.8 |
| MaF1 | 50.4 | 50.3 | **50.8** | 50.3 | 49.9 |

Table 6: Comparison of epsilon ($\epsilon$) values on English with 10% labelled data

bation while lower values may create insufficient perturbation. From our empirical experiments, we note that 0.5 works better than the other values and we use this for all our semi-supervised experiments.

## 5 Domain and Task Adaptive Pretraining

In this section, we perform supervised learning experiments with frozen and finetuned representations by using the labelled data of each language for evaluating the performance of *domain-adaptive*, *task-adaptive*, monolingual and multilingual contextual models. In Table 8, 9 and 7, we present the results for different monolingual and multilingual contextual models for the three languages with frozen backbones. We use English BERT (E-BERT), BetoBERT and AraBERT as monolingual models for English, Spanish and Arabic respectively. We note that for all the languages, mBERT performs substantially poorer than the monolingual contextual models of the respective languages. However, XLM-R which is another multilingual model performs competitive with the monolingual models which is not surprising as XLM-R has shown improvements over mBERT in other language tasks also (Conneau et al., 2019).

We further evaluate *Domain-adaptive* (XLM-Tw) and *Task-adaptive* (XLM-Tw-S) versions of the XLM-R multilingual model and observe substantial improvements. XLM-Tw-S improves the Jaccard Index (JI) by **5.5%, 6.5%** and **8.4%** for Arabic, English and Spanish respectively, highlighting the advantages of *task-specific* pretraining for contextual models. XLM-Tw also improves upon XLM-R for all the languages reiterating the importance of pretraining the contextual models with domain specific data.

We study the impact of finetuning the monolingual and best performing multilingual model on our task to compare the capabilities of multilingual models with monolingual after finetuning on the task. We notice that finetuning bridges the gap to some extent but still the domain adaptive multilingual XLM-Tw works better than the finetuned

| Model | JI | MiF1 | MaF1 |
|---|---|---|---|
| XLM-Tw-S | **52.0** | **64.4** | **47.9** |
| XLM-Tw | 49.3 | 62.2 | 47.1 |
| XLM-R | 45.2 | 58.4 | 42.9 |
| mBERT | 37.5 | 51.2 | 36.2 |
| AraBERT | 46.4 | 59.7 | 43.7 |

Table 7: Performance of pretrained models on Arabic

| Model | JI | MiF1 | MaF1 |
|---|---|---|---|
| XLM-Tw-S | **53.9** | **66.2** | **47.8** |
| XLM-Tw | 50.6 | 63.5 | 45.9 |
| XLM-R | 48.6 | 61.9 | 45.7 |
| mBERT | 44.7 | 57.6 | 39.2 |
| E-BERT | 48.2 | 61.4 | 42.9 |

Table 8: Performance of pretrained models on English

monolingual models for all the languages as shown in Table 10, 11 and 12. For English, the improvement is relatively moderate but for Spanish and Arabic, XLM-Tw demonstrates substantial gains.

### 5.1 Comparison with existing methods

**English**: Alhuzali and Ananiadou (2021) (SpanEmo) use sentences along with emotion categories as input to the contextual model and use label correlation aware loss (LCA) to model correlation among emotions classes. LVC-Seq2Emo (Huang et al., 2019) propose a latent variable chain transformation and use it with sequence to emotion for modelling correlation between emotions. BinC (Jabreel and Moreno, 2019) transform the multilabel classification problem into binary classification problems and train a recurrent neural network over this transformed setting. (Baziotis et al., 2018) (NTUA) used a Bi-LSTM architecture with self-attention models over word2vec trained on large collection of twitter tweets and were winner of the task. Huang et al. (2021) trained a sequence to emotion (Seq2Emo) encoder where the text is encoded using a bi-directional recurrent network and emotions are predicted by the decoder in an iterative fashion. Seq2Emo architecture allows for understanding the correlation between emotions. Yu et al. (2018) (DATN) use sentiments to improve emotion classification using bi-directional LSTM. Meisheri and Dey (2018) (TCS) uses SVM on manually engineered features.

**Spanish**: Mulki et al. (2018) (TW-StAR) used binary relevance transformation strategy over tweet

| Model | JI | MiF1 | MaF1 |
|---|---|---|---|
| XLM-Tw-S | **51.1** | **60.0** | **48.8** |
| XLM-Tw | 47.1 | 56.6 | 42.7 |
| XLM-R | 42.9 | 51.9 | 39.8 |
| mBERT | 37.0 | 44.8 | 31.2 |
| BetoBERT | 41.3 | 50.3 | 37.0 |

Table 9: Performance of pretrained models on Spanish

features while González et al. (2018) (ELiRF) explored preprocessing and adapted the tokeniser for Spanish tweets. MILAB was the wining entry in the SemEval2018 task. Hassan et al. (2021) (CER) finetuned the Spanish BERT representations (BetoBERT).

**Arabic**: For Arabic, Samy et al. (2018) (CA-GRU) extract contextual information from the tweets and uses them as context for emotion recognition using RNNs. Hassan et al. (2021) (CER) finetuned BERT representations. Alswaidan and Menai (2020) (HEF) proposed hybrid neural network using different embeddings. Badaro et al. (2018) (EMA) used preprocessing techniques like normalisation, stemming etc.

Overall, our results improve upon the existing approaches on Jaccard Index(JI) by **7%** for Spanish, **4.5%** for Arabic and around **1%** for English and setup a new state-of-the-art for all the three languages highlighting the efficacy of semi-supervised learning and *domain-adaptive* multilingual models.

### 5.2 Crosslingual Experiments

We combine data of all the three languages and train a combined model and test this model on the test set of each language. We notice that the combined model improves upon the performance of individual models for Arabic and Spanish (Table 13) while the performance of English is comparable.

In Table 14, we perform crosslingual experiments to evaluate the performance of a model trained on one language on another language. It is interesting to note that for Arabic and Spanish, the cross lingual performance is competitive with performance using some of the pretrained networks which is encouraging. We also observe that English demonstrates better crosslingual capability than Arabic and Spanish. A possible reason might be the large size of the English training dataset.

| Model | JI | MiF1 | MaF1 |
|---|---|---|---|
| mlVAT | **60.7** | **71.9** | 56.1 |
| XLM-Tw | 59.8 | 71.2 | 53.4 |
| E-BERT | 59.1 | 70.4 | 53.3 |
| SpanEmo | 60.1 | 71.3 | **57.8** |
| LVC-Seq2Emo | 59.2 | 70.9 | - |
| BinC | 59.0 | 69.2 | 56.4 |
| NTUA | 58.8 | 70.1 | 52.8 |
| Seq2Emo | 58.7 | 70.1 | 51.9 |
| DATN | 58.3 | - | 54.4 |
| TCS | 58.2 | 69.3 | 53.0 |

Table 10: Results on English

| Model | JI | MiF1 | MaF1 |
|---|---|---|---|
| mlVAT | 56.9 | 64.9 | 51.8 |
| XLM-Tw | **57.0** | **65.3** | 51.5 |
| BetoBERT | 52.7 | 60.8 | 48.7 |
| SpanEmo | 53.2 | 64.1 | 53.2 |
| CER | 52.4 | - | **53.7** |
| MILAB | 46.9 | 55.8 | 40.7 |
| ELiRF | 45.8 | 53.5 | 44.0 |
| TW-StAR | 43.8 | 52.0 | 39.2 |

Table 11: Results on Spanish

## 6 Probing Experiments

We perform experiments to evaluate the contribution of different layers of the XLM-Tw-S model. We extract representation of the tokens of a sentence from a particular layer of the contextual model and take an average across tokens for obtaining the representation of the sentence. We train a classifier over these sentence representations and report the results. From Figure 2, we note that higher layers provide better performance for all the three languages showing that the higher-order contextual information is useful for understanding the emotions in the text. Refer Appendix A for detailed results. Similar to Tenney et al. (2019), we also compute the improvement due to incrementally adding more layers to the previous layers and calculate the expected layer:

$$E_{\Delta}[l] = \frac{\sum_{l=1}^{L} l * \Delta^{(l)}}{\sum_{l=1}^{L} \Delta^{(l)}} \quad (8)$$

where, $\Delta^{(l)}$ is the change in the Jaccard Index metric when adding layer $l$ to the previous layers. We start from layer 0 and incrementally add higher layers for representing the tokens of the sentence

| Model | JI | MiF1 | MaF1 |
|---|---|---|---|
| mlVAT | **57.3** | **68.2** | **52.2** |
| XLM-Tw | 55.8 | 67.4 | 50.1 |
| AraBERT | 54.3 | 65.9 | 49.0 |
| SpanEmo | 54.8 | 66.6 | 52.1 |
| CA-GRU | 53.2 | 64.8 | 49.5 |
| CER | 52.9 | - | 48.9 |
| HEF | 51.2 | 63.1 | 50.2 |
| EMA | 48.9 | 61.8 | 46.1 |

Table 12: Results on Arabic

| Language | JI | MiF1 | MaF1 |
|---|---|---|---|
| EN | 59.4 | 70.6 | 55.7 |
| ES | 57.8 | 65.8 | 56.6 |
| AR | 57.8 | 68.6 | 55.5 |

Table 13: Experiments on the combination of languages

followed by averaging for representing the whole sentence. The expected layer for English, Spanish and Arabic computes to 6.9, 6.2 and 6.8 respectively showing that higher layers are useful for the task. This analysis is helpful to understand the improvement achieved by adding layers to the previous layers. For all the three languages, we obtain the best results on using the average of all the layers for representing the sentences which shows that different layers encapsulate complementary information about emotions.

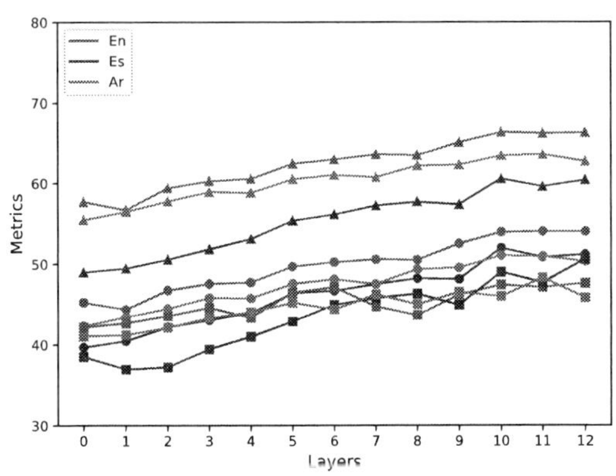


Figure 2: Performance metrices across different layers for XLM-Tw-S. Circle, Triangle and Square represent JI, MiF1 and MaF1 respectively.

| Train/Eval | JI | MiF1 | MaF1 |
|---|---|---|---|
| Es → En | 42.9 | 54.6 | 42.6 |
| Ar → En | 39.2 | 51.7 | 42.0 |
| En → Ar | 49.7 | 62.3 | 45.3 |
| Es → Ar | 46.4 | 57.2 | 44.9 |
| En → Es | 44.6 | 55.9 | 41.5 |
| Ar → Es | 40.0 | 51.1 | 41.9 |

Table 14: Crosslingual experiments between the languages

| Language | Train | Dev | Test |
|---|---|---|---|
| English | 6838 | 886 | 3259 |
| Arabic | 2278 | 585 | 1518 |
| Spanish | 3561 | 679 | 2854 |

Table 15: SemEval2018 dataset statistics

## 7 Training Details

We finetune the contextual models following huggingface[2] with a batch size of 8, learning rate of 2e-5 and weight decay of 0.01 using AdamW optimizer for 30 epochs. The classifier is a two layered neural network with 768 hidden dimensions and 11 output dimensions with 0.1 dropout. For mlVAT experiments, the number of examples sampled from the unlabelled set for each batch are 24, $\epsilon$ and $\alpha$ are set to 0.5 and 1 using cross validation. We apply sigmoid over the logits and train using binary cross entropy loss. We use validation set for finding optimal hyperparameters and evaluate on the test set using combination of training and validation set for training.

## 8 Conclusion

In this work, we explored semi-supervised learning using Virtual Adversarial Training (VAT) for multilabel emotion classification in a multilingual setup and showed performance improvement by leveraging unlabelled data from different languages. We used Mean Square Error (MSE) as the divergence measure for leveraging VAT for multilabel emotion classification. We also evaluated the performance of monolingual, multilingual and *domain-adaptive* and *task-adaptive* multilingual contextual models across three languages - English, Spanish and Arabic for multilabel and multilingual emotion recognition and obtained state-of-the-art results. We also performed probing experiments for understanding the impact of different layers of contextual models.

[2]https://huggingface.co/

## 9 Broader Impact and Discussion of Ethics

In recent years, deep learning approaches have played an important role in state-of-the-art natural language processing systems. However, obtaining labelled data for training these models is expensive and time consuming, especially for multilingual and multilabel scenarios. In such case, multilingual semi-supervised and unsupervised techniques can play a pivotal role. Our work introduces a semisupervised way for detecting and understanding textual data across multiple languages. Our methods could be used in sensitive contexts such as legal or healthcare settings, and it is essential that any work using our probe method undertake extensive quality assurance and robustness testing before using it in their setting. The datasets used in our work do not contain any sensitive information to the best of our knowledge.

## References


Hassan Alhuzali and Sophia Ananiadou. 2021. Spanemo: Casting multi-label emotion classification as span-prediction. *arXiv preprint arXiv:2101.10038.*

Nourah Alswaidan and Mohamed El Bachir Menai. 2020. Hybrid feature model for emotion recognition in arabic text. *IEEE Access*, 8:37843–37854.

Wissam Antoun, Fady Baly, and Hazem Hajj. 2020. Arabert: Transformer-based model for arabic language understanding. *arXiv preprint arXiv:2003.00104.*

Gilbert Badaro, Obeida El Jundi, Alaa Khaddaj, Alaa Maarouf, Raslan Kain, Hazem Hajj, and Wassim El-Hajj. 2018. EMA at SemEval-2018 task 1: Emotion mining for Arabic. In *Proceedings of The 12th International Workshop on Semantic Evaluation*, New Orleans, Louisiana. Association for Computational Linguistics.

Francesco Barbieri, Jose Camacho-Collados, Francesco Ronzano, Luis Espinosa Anke, Miguel Ballesteros, Valerio Basile, Viviana Patti, and Horacio Saggion. 2018. Semeval 2018 task 2: Multilingual emoji prediction. In *Proceedings of The 12th International Workshop on Semantic Evaluation*, pages 24–33.

Francesco Barbieri, Luis Espinosa-Anke, and Jose Camacho-Collados. 2021. A Multilingual Language Model Toolkit for Twitter. In *arXiv preprint arXiv:2104.12250.*

Christos Baziotis, Nikos Athanasiou, Alexandra Chronopoulou, Athanasia Kolovou, Georgios Paraskevopoulos, Nikolaos Ellinas, Shrikanth Narayanan, and Alexandros Potamianos. 2018. Ntua-slp at semeval-2018 task 1: Predicting affective content in tweets with deep attentive rnns and transfer learning. *arXiv preprint arXiv:1804.06658.*

José Cañete, Gabriel Chaperon, Rodrigo Fuentes, Jou-Hui Ho, Hojin Kang, and Jorge Pérez. 2020. Spanish pre-trained bert model and evaluation data. In *PML4DC at ICLR 2020.*

Yong Cheng, Lu Jiang, and Wolfgang Macherey. 2019. Robust neural machine translation with doubly adversarial inputs. *arXiv preprint arXiv:1906.02443.*

Nancy Chinchor. 1992. MUC-4 evaluation metrics. In *Fourth Message Uunderstanding Conference (MUC-4): Proceedings of a Conference Held in McLean, Virginia, June 16-18, 1992.*

Kevin Clark, Minh-Thang Luong, Christopher D Manning, and Quoc V Le. 2018. Semi-supervised sequence modeling with cross-view training. *arXiv preprint arXiv:1809.08370.*

Alexis Conneau, Kartikay Khandelwal, Naman Goyal, Vishrav Chaudhary, Guillaume Wenzek, Francisco Guzmán, Edouard Grave, Myle Ott, Luke Zettlemoyer, and Veselin Stoyanov. 2019. Unsupervised cross-lingual representation learning at scale. *arXiv preprint arXiv:1911.02116.*

Dorottya Demszky, Dana Movshovitz-Attias, Jeongwoo Ko, Alan Cowen, Gaurav Nemade, and Sujith Ravi. 2020. GoEmotions: A dataset of fine-grained emotions. In *Proceedings of the 58th Annual Meeting of the Association for Computational Linguistics*, pages 4040–4054, Online. Association for Computational Linguistics.

Leon Derczynski, Alan Ritter, Sam Clark, and Kalina Bontcheva. 2013. Twitter part-of-speech tagging for all: Overcoming sparse and noisy data. In *Proceedings of the international conference recent advances in natural language processing ranlp 2013*, pages 198–206.

Jacob Devlin, Ming-Wei Chang, Kenton Lee, and Kristina Toutanova. 2018. Bert: Pre-training of deep bidirectional transformers for language understanding. *arXiv preprint arXiv:1810.04805.*

Paul Ekman. 1984. Expression and the nature of emotion. *Approaches to emotion*, 3(19):344.

Bjarke Felbo, Alan Mislove, Anders Søgaard, Iyad Rahwan, and Sune Lehmann. 2017. Using millions of emoji occurrences to learn any-domain representations for detecting sentiment, emotion and sarcasm. In *Proceedings of the 2017 Conference on Empirical Methods in Natural Language Processing*, pages 1615–1625, Copenhagen, Denmark. Association for Computational Linguistics.

Sayan Ghosh, Mathieu Chollet, Eugene Laksana, Louis-Philippe Morency, and Stefan Scherer. 2017. Affect-LM: A neural language model for customizable affective text generation. Vancouver, Canada. Association for Computational Linguistics.

Shantanu Godbole and Sunita Sarawagi. 2004. Discriminative methods for multi-labeled classification. In *Pacific-Asia conference on knowledge discovery and data mining*, pages 22–30. Springer.

José-Ángel González, Lluís-F. Hurtado, and Ferran Pla. 2018. ELiRF-UPV at SemEval-2018 tasks 1 and 3: Affect and irony detection in tweets. In *Proceedings of The 12th International Workshop on Semantic Evaluation*, pages 565–569, New Orleans, Louisiana. Association for Computational Linguistics.

Ian J Goodfellow, Jonathon Shlens, and Christian Szegedy. 2014. Explaining and harnessing adversarial examples. *arXiv preprint arXiv:1412.6572*.

Suchin Gururangan, Ana Marasović, Swabha Swayamdipta, Kyle Lo, Iz Beltagy, Doug Downey, and Noah A Smith. 2020. Don't stop pretraining: adapt language models to domains and tasks. *arXiv preprint arXiv:2004.10964*.

Sabit Hassan, Shaden Shaar, and Kareem Darwish. 2021. Cross-lingual emotion detection. *arXiv preprint arXiv:2106.06017*.

Jeremy Howard and Sebastian Ruder. 2018. Universal language model fine-tuning for text classification. *arXiv preprint arXiv:1801.06146*.

Chenyang Huang, Amine Trabelsi, Xuebin Qin, Nawshad Farruque, Lili Mou, and Osmar R Zaiane. 2021. Seq2emo: A sequence to multi-label emotion classification model. In *Proceedings of the 2021 Conference of the North American Chapter of the Association for Computational Linguistics: Human Language Technologies*, pages 4717–4724.

Chenyang Huang, Amine Trabelsi, Xuebin Qin, Nawshad Farruque, and Osmar R Zaïane. 2019. Seq2emo for multi-label emotion classification based on latent variable chains transformation. *arXiv preprint arXiv:1911.02147*.

Mohammed Jabreel and Antonio Moreno. 2019. A deep learning-based approach for multi-label emotion classification in tweets. *Applied Sciences*, 9(6):1123.

Samuli Laine and Timo Aila. 2016. Temporal ensembling for semi-supervised learning. *arXiv preprint arXiv:1610.02242*.

Jinhyuk Lee, Wonjin Yoon, Sungdong Kim, Donghyeon Kim, Sunkyu Kim, Chan Ho So, and Jaewoo Kang. 2020. Biobert: a pre-trained biomedical language representation model for biomedical text mining. *Bioinformatics*, 36(4):1234–1240.

Yinhan Liu, Myle Ott, Naman Goyal, Jingfei Du, Mandar Joshi, Danqi Chen, Omer Levy, Mike Lewis, Luke Zettlemoyer, and Veselin Stoyanov. 2019. Roberta: A robustly optimized bert pretraining approach. *arXiv preprint arXiv:1907.11692*.

David McClosky, Eugene Charniak, and Mark Johnson. 2006. Effective self-training for parsing. In *Proceedings of the Human Language Technology Conference of the NAACL, Main Conference*, pages 152–159.

Hardik Meisheri and Lipika Dey. 2018. TCS research at SemEval-2018 task 1: Learning robust representations using multi-attention architecture. In *Proceedings of The 12th International Workshop on Semantic Evaluation*, pages 291–299, New Orleans, Louisiana. Association for Computational Linguistics.

Takeru Miyato, Andrew M Dai, and Ian Goodfellow. 2016. Adversarial training methods for semi-supervised text classification. *arXiv preprint arXiv:1605.07725*.

Takeru Miyato, Shin-ichi Maeda, Masanori Koyama, and Shin Ishii. 2018. Virtual adversarial training: a regularization method for supervised and semi-supervised learning. *IEEE transactions on pattern analysis and machine intelligence*, 41(8):1979–1993.

Saif Mohammad. 2012. #emotional tweets. In **SEM 2012: The First Joint Conference on Lexical and Computational Semantics – Volume 1: Proceedings of the main conference and the shared task, and Volume 2: Proceedings of the Sixth International Workshop on Semantic Evaluation (SemEval 2012)*, pages 246–255, Montréal, Canada. Association for Computational Linguistics.

Saif Mohammad, Felipe Bravo-Marquez, Mohammad Salameh, and Svetlana Kiritchenko. 2018. SemEval-2018 task 1: Affect in tweets. New Orleans, Louisiana. Association for Computational Linguistics.

Hala Mulki, Chedi Bechikh Ali, Hatem Haddad, and Ismail Babaoğlu. 2018. Tw-StAR at SemEval-2018 task 1: Preprocessing impact on multi-label emotion classification. In *Proceedings of The 12th International Workshop on Semantic Evaluation*, pages 167–171, New Orleans, Louisiana. Association for Computational Linguistics.

Matthew E Peters, Sebastian Ruder, and Noah A Smith. 2019. To tune or not to tune? adapting pretrained representations to diverse tasks. *arXiv preprint arXiv:1903.05987*.

Robert Plutchik. 1980. A general psychoevolutionary theory of emotion. In *Theories of emotion*, pages 3–33. Elsevier.

Parsa Saadatpanah, Ali Shafahi, and Tom Goldstein. 2020. Adversarial attacks on copyright detection systems. In *International Conference on Machine Learning*, pages 8307–8315. PMLR.

Devendra Singh Sachan, Manzil Zaheer, and Ruslan Salakhutdinov. 2019. Revisiting lstm networks for semi-supervised text classification via mixed objective function. In *Proceedings of the AAAI Conference on Artificial Intelligence*, volume 33, pages 6940–6948.

Kashfia Sailunaz, Manmeet Dhaliwal, Jon Rokne, and Reda Alhajj. 2018. Emotion detection from text and speech: a survey. *Social Network Analysis and Mining*, 8(1):1–26.

Ahmed E Samy, Samhaa R El-Beltagy, and Ehab Hassanien. 2018. A context integrated model for multi-label emotion detection. *Procedia computer science*, 142:61–71.

Klaus R Scherer and Harald G Wallbott. 1994. Evidence for universality and cultural variation of differential emotion response patterning. *Journal of personality and social psychology*, 66(2):310.

Antti Tarvainen and Harri Valpola. 2017. Mean teachers are better role models: Weight-averaged consistency targets improve semi-supervised deep learning results. *arXiv preprint arXiv:1703.01780*.

Ian Tenney, Dipanjan Das, and Ellie Pavlick. 2019. Bert rediscovers the classical nlp pipeline. *arXiv preprint arXiv:1905.05950*.

Jesper E Van Engelen and Holger H Hoos. 2020. A survey on semi-supervised learning. *Machine Learning*, 109(2):373–440.

Chaowei Xiao, Ruizhi Deng, Bo Li, Fisher Yu, Mingyan Liu, and Dawn Song. 2018. Characterizing adversarial examples based on spatial consistency information for semantic segmentation. In *Proceedings of the European Conference on Computer Vision (ECCV)*, pages 217–234.

Ali Yadollahi, Ameneh Gholipour Shahraki, and Osmar R Zaiane. 2017. Current state of text sentiment analysis from opinion to emotion mining. *ACM Computing Surveys (CSUR)*, 50(2):1–33.

Pengcheng Yang, Xu Sun, Wei Li, Shuming Ma, Wei Wu, and Houfeng Wang. 2018. SGM: Sequence generation model for multi-label classification. In *Proceedings of the 27th International Conference on Computational Linguistics*. Association for Computational Linguistics.

Xiangli Yang, Zixing Song, Irwin King, and Zenglin Xu. 2021. A survey on deep semi-supervised learning. *arXiv preprint arXiv:2103.00550*.

David Yarowsky. 1995. Unsupervised word sense disambiguation rivaling supervised methods. In *33rd annual meeting of the association for computational linguistics*, pages 189–196.

Jianfei Yu, Luis Marujo, Jing Jiang, Pradeep Karuturi, and William Brendel. 2018. Improving multi-label emotion classification via sentiment classification with dual attention transfer network. ACL.

Chen Zhu, Yu Cheng, Zhe Gan, Siqi Sun, Tom Goldstein, and Jingjing Liu. 2019. Freelb: Enhanced adversarial training for natural language understanding. *arXiv preprint arXiv:1909.11764*.

## A Probing Experiments

| Layers | JI | MiF1 | MaF1 |
|---|---|---|---|
| Layer 0 | 45.24 | 57.69 | 42.14 |
| Layer 1 | 44.37 | 56.68 | 42.67 |
| Layer 2 | 46.75 | 59.38 | 43.57 |
| Layer 3 | 47.57 | 60.27 | 44.59 |
| Layer 4 | 47.73 | 60.55 | 43.34 |
| Layer 5 | 49.70 | 62.43 | 46.46 |
| Layer 6 | 50.24 | 62.96 | 47.13 |
| Layer 7 | 50.58 | 63.56 | 44.73 |
| Layer 8 | 50.52 | 63.48 | 43.64 |
| Layer 9 | 52.51 | 65.11 | 46.20 |
| Layer 10 | 53.95 | 66.37 | 47.42 |
| Layer 11 | 54.02 | 66.23 | 47.10 |
| Layer 12 | 54.03 | 66.31 | 47.61 |

Table 16: Comparison of layer performance for English using XLM-Tw-S model

| Layers | JI | MiF1 | MaF1 |
|---|---|---|---|
| Layer 0 | 39.66 | 48.99 | 38.49 |
| Layer 1 | 40.43 | 49.45 | 36.94 |
| Layer 2 | 42.19 | 50.57 | 37.20 |
| Layer 3 | 43.03 | 51.83 | 39.42 |
| Layer 4 | 43.94 | 53.11 | 40.99 |
| Layer 5 | 46.38 | 55.37 | 42.88 |
| Layer 6 | 46.68 | 56.13 | 44.94 |
| Layer 7 | 47.51 | 57.24 | 45.78 |
| Layer 8 | 48.21 | 57.70 | 46.32 |
| Layer 9 | 48.13 | 57.35 | 44.92 |
| Layer 10 | 51.97 | 60.54 | 49.01 |
| Layer 11 | 50.86 | 59.59 | 47.70 |
| Layer 12 | 51.16 | 60.39 | 50.59 |

Table 17: Comparison of layer performance for Spanish using XLM-Tw-S model

| Layers | JI | MiF1 | MaF1 |
|---|---|---|---|
| Layer 0 | 42.30 | 55.45 | 41.04 |
| Layer 1 | 43.42 | 56.48 | 41.20 |
| Layer 2 | 44.47 | 57.77 | 42.11 |
| Layer 3 | 45.80 | 58.93 | 43.32 |
| Layer 4 | 45.76 | 58.81 | 44.03 |
| Layer 5 | 47.56 | 60.51 | 45.21 |
| Layer 6 | 48.13 | 61.02 | 44.36 |
| Layer 7 | 47.51 | 60.73 | 46.22 |
| Layer 8 | 49.36 | 62.18 | 45.01 |
| Layer 9 | 49.57 | 62.27 | 46.51 |
| Layer 10 | 51.05 | 63.42 | 46.01 |
| Layer 11 | 50.94 | 63.56 | 48.30 |
| Layer 12 | 50.32 | 62.71 | 45.82 |

Table 18: Comparison of layer performance for Arabic using XLM-Tw-S model

In Table 16, 17 and 18, we report the performance of each layer of frozen XLM-Tw-S model. We extract the layer representation of each token of the sentence and average them for representing the sentence. For all the languages, we note that the higher layers show superior performance.

# Analyzing the Effects of Reasoning Types on Cross-Lingual Transfer Performance

**Karthikeyan K***
Duke University
karthikeyan.k@duke.edu

**Aalok Sathe***
Massachusetts Institute of Technology
asathe@mit.edu

**Somak Aditya** and **Monojit Choudhury**
Microsoft Research India
{t-soadit,monojitc}@microsoft.com

## Abstract

Multilingual language models achieve impressive zero-shot accuracies in many languages in complex tasks such as Natural Language Inference (NLI). Examples in NLI (and equivalent complex tasks) often pertain to various types of sub-tasks, requiring different kinds of reasoning. Certain types of reasoning have proven to be more difficult to learn in a monolingual context, and in the crosslingual context, similar observations may shed light on zero-shot transfer efficiency and few-shot sample selection. Hence, to investigate the effects of types of reasoning on transfer performance, we propose a category-annotated multilingual NLI dataset and discuss the challenges to scale monolingual annotations to multiple languages. We statistically observe interesting effects that the confluence of reasoning types and language similarities have on transfer performance.

## 1 Introduction

Recent work has shown that masked language models such as XLM (Lample and Conneau, 2019), mBERT (Devlin et al., 2019) and XLM-RoBERTa (Conneau et al., 2019) can achieve efficient crosslingual transfer, in both zero-shot and few-shot settings. Such results have motivated researchers (K et al., 2020; Artetxe et al., 2020; Conneau et al., 2020) to investigate the underlying influencing factors behind transfer efficiency along different dimensions such as model capacity, language similarity and learning objective. However, such transfer efficiency is measured for natural language understanding (NLU) tasks which often cover a wide range of linguistic phenomena. Natural Language Inference is one such representative task which is known to require different types of reasoning and linguistic phenomena. In the monolingual context, recently, authors in Joshi et al. (2020a) extended previous work (Richardson et al., 2020; Salvatore et al., 2019) and listed a comprehensive list of types of reasoning capabilities required to solve the NLI examples in large public NLI datasets. Authors show that NLI requires a mix of 15 different types of reasoning capabilities (TaxiNLI), categorized broadly into Language, Logic and Knowledge. They observe that both BERT (Devlin et al., 2019) and RoBERTa (Liu et al., 2019) perform poorly in reasoning tasks such as *causal* and *coreference*, whereas they pick up *negation* easily; and observe that some categories are intrinsically harder for these models (both Transformers-based and pre-Transformers LSTM-based) to understand. Our central hypothesis of this work is, *crosslingual transfer gap* (Hu et al., 2020) and *few-shot performance* may depend on the type of reasoning required. To this end, we propose multilingual extension of the TaxiNLI dataset. Our zero-shot analysis strongly suggests that reasoning types play a critical role in transfer performance. In few-shot, some categories (such as Negation), show steady improvement in accuracy along-with increased cross-lingual alignment. For others (syntactic, logic) improvement varies across language. For causal, few-shot models fail to generalize well on a diagnostic gold set.

## 2 TaxiXNLI: Towards Multilingual Extension of TaxiNLI

In monolingual settings, various authors (Nie et al., 2019; Wang et al., 2018; Ribeiro et al., 2020) have proposed a shift from tracking end-to-end task accuracy to explicit categorizations of fundamental capabilities and to track such individual category-wise errors. While some of the proposed categories seem to capture relevant reasoning capabilities, they are often incomplete as they are tuned towards analyzing errors. Joshi et al. (2020a) recently proposed a categorization of the reasoning tasks involved in NLI. It takes inspiration from earlier literature in linguistics (Wittgenstein, 1922)

*Work done during internship at Microsoft Research India.



*Proceedings of the 1st Workshop on Multilingual Representation Learning*, pages 86–95
November 11, 2021. 

and logic (Sowa, 2010). According to Wittgenstein (1922), humans require a combination (or a sequence) of lexical, syntactic, semantic and pragmatic reasoning to gauge *meaning* from language (or *form*). The TaxiNLI categorization scheme, which defines three broad groups of reasoning Linguistic, Logical and Knowledge, aligns with our philosophy. Additionally, the proposed categorization is also useful because it retains the categories that are relevant for public NLI datasets, and the granularity is well-defined. Further, the availability of the annotated dataset makes it a perfect choice for the current study.

We introduce the categories briefly. For detailed definitions and examples, we refer the readers to Joshi et al. (2020a). Linguistic represents NLI examples where inference process is internal to the provided text; further divided into three categories `lexical`, `syntactic` and `factivity`. Logical denotes examples where inference may involve processes external to text, and grouped under *Connectives*, and *Deduction*. *Connectives* involve categories such as `Negation`, `boolean`, `quantifiers`, `conditionals` and `comparatives`. Lastly, *Deduction* involves different types of reasoning such as `relational`, `spatial`, `causal`, `temporal` and `coreference`. `Knowledge` indicates examples where external (`world`) or commonly assumed knowledge (`commonsense`) is required for inferencing.

| | Noise | | F1 | Acc | tr = 0, en = 1 |
|---|---|---|---|---|---|
| | Partial | Full | | | |
| **Hindi** | 18.4 | 8.9 | 0.22 | 0.81 | 0.44 |
| **Spanish** | 38.3 | - | 0.25 | 0.69 | 0.32 |
| **Swahili** | 39.8 | 36.8 | 0.21 | 0.84 | 0.34 |

Table 1: We show the percentage of full and partial noisy samples; F1, Accuracy scores with respect to the English TaxiNLI annotations for each language on the sampled set of examples. We also include percentage of category annotations where the annotated target category is zero, while the corresponding category in English is 1.

### 2.1 TaxiXNLI Dataset

**TaxiXNLI (translated)** The TaxiNLI dataset (Joshi et al., 2020a) consists of 10071 premise, hypothesis (P-H) pairs drawn from the MultiNLI (MNLI) dataset (Williams et al., 2018a). Each pair is annotated with the types of reasoning (among 15 categories) that are required to make the inference. To account for the asymmetric distribution of examples across taxonomic categories, we use the hierarchical taxonomy provided by Joshi et al. (2020a) to group some of the related categories together[1]. For our crosslingual analysis, we split the English examples equally[2] into train and test set (5k/5k) by balancing across taxonomic categories through iterative stratification (Sechidis et al., 2011). Inspired by prior work (Gerz et al., 2018; Joshi et al., 2020b), we choose Spanish, French, Russian, Hindi, Arabic, Vietnamese, Chinese, Swahili, and Urdu; which collectively cover a spectrum of varying resource (high - 4, medium - 3, low - 2) and typological diversity. We use the *Bing translator* to translate both train and test set into these nine languages.

Due to the noise inherent in automatic translation, first we perform a qualitative analysis of translated examples. Following Joshi et al. (2020a), we conduct manual annotations of TaxiNLI categories for a subset of translated pairs in three languages: Swahili, Hindi and Spanish, by native speakers. In addition to categories, we instruct them to indicate full, partial, and no noise translations. Among them, there were 8.95% (18.4) and 36.81% (39.8) were fully (and partially) noisy sentence-pairs in Hindi and Swahili, and Spanish had 38% partially noisy sentences. The percentage of examples where a category in English is 1, but the same in a translated language is zero are 44 (hi), 34 (sw) and 32% (es) respectively. Upon further analysis and interviews with the annotators, we discover changes (from 1 to 0) are due to 2 reasons: 1) partially noisy translations that make the premise and hypothesis somewhat unrelated; and, the TaxiNLI instructions instruct annotators not to proceed with category annotations for un-related neutral examples; 2) difference in reasoning adapted by individual annotators. Our analysis (detailed in next section), aligns with the intuition from the definitions that, translation to different languages does not change the reasoning categories in the Logical and Knowledge bucket.

**TaxiXNLI (diagnostic)** Motivated by the above study, we look towards the XNLI dataset (Conneau et al., 2018), that provides parallel P-H pairs in 15 languages. We sample 1.4k XNLI examples and annotate with a few selected interesting categories (Negation, Boolean, Spatial, Causal, Temporal, Knowledge). This is used as a diagnostic gold

[1]Logic: {Quantifier, Conditional, Comparative}; Deductions: {Relational, Spatial, Coreference, Temporal}; Knowledge: {World, Taxonomic}

[2]Category-wise splits are in Tab. 4.

| | Category | P (eng) | H (eng) | P (target) | H (target) |
|---|---|---|---|---|---|
| | Swahili | | | | |
| E1 | world (eng) | Middle Ages | The time period during which the Black Plague happened. | Zama za kati | Kipindi cha wakati ambapo pigo la Black lilitokea. |
| E2 | taxonomic (swa) | Carmel Man, a relation of the Neanderthal family, lived here 600,000 years ago. | Carmel Man isn't alive today. | Karmeli Man, uhusiano wa familia ya Neanderthal, aliishi hapa miaka 600,000 iliyopita. | Karmeli Man si hai leo. |
| E3 | spatial (swa) | I'm from New York. | I'm from Texas. | Mimi ni kutoka New York. | Mimi ni kutoka Texas. |
| E4 | temporal (eng) | They need individual support to attend conferences, present papers, publish their works, and keep in touch with others in their fields across the country. | They need a lot of funding to do their work effectively. | Wanahitaji msaada wa kibinafsi kuhudhuria mikutano, kuwasilisha makaratasi, kuchapisha kazi zao, na kuwasiliana na wengine katika nyanja zao nchini kote. | Wanahitaji fedha nyingi kufanya kazi zao kwa ufanisi. |
| E5 | temporal (swa) | So he says, No, from the school up, are all guerrillas. | He says everyone in this community is pacifistic. | Hivyo anasema, Hapana, kutoka shule, wote ni waasi. | Anasema kila mtu katika jamii hii ana mpango wa kutelezi. |
| E6 | negation (eng) | So it's almost like a second home. | Alas, I have never been to such a place. | Hivyo ni karibu kama nyumba ya pili. | Ole, sijawahi kuwa na sehemu hiyo. |
| E7 | negation (swa) | He argued that other extremists, who aimed at local rulers or Israel, did not go far enough. | He held the stance that the other extremists should have went further. | Alisema kwamba wengine wenye siasa kali, ambao walikusudia viongozi wa ndani au Israeli, hawakwenda mbali sana. | Yeye alishikilia msimamo kwamba wengine wenye siasa kali wanapaswa kwenda zaidi. |

Table 2: Interesting examples, where a category is marked in one language, but not in the other. The categories are mentioned in the second column, and in braces, we mention the language where the category is marked present. For example, in E1, category "world" is marked only in English. E1: a translation error, so marked neutral, E2: annotator needed to look up "Karmeli man", and understand relation with Neanderthal, E3: Swahili annotator used geographic reasoning, E4: English annotation is dubious, E5: wrong annotation in Swahili, E6: partial translation error, so neutral, E7: Swahili annotator misunderstood the sentence.

| | Category | P (eng) | H (eng) | P (target) | H (target) |
|---|---|---|---|---|---|
| | Hindi | | | | |
| E1 | world (eng) | As a result, their services may be more effective when conducted in the emergency department environment. | Their services might be more effective if they're done in the ED. | नतीजतन, आपातकालीन विभाग के माहौल में आयोजित होने पर उनकी सेवाएं अधिक प्रभावी हो सकती हैं। | यदि वे ईडी में किए जाते हैं तो उनकी सेवाएं अधिक प्रभावी हो सकती हैं। |
| E2 | world (hi) | Twenty islands have since been added, making the Cyclades the largest of the Greek island groups. | They have added just three more islands. | बीस द्वीपों के बाद से जोड़ा गया है, Cyclades ग्रीक द्वीप समूहों का सबसे बड़ा बना। | उन्होंने सिर्फ तीन और द्वीप जोड़े हैं। |
| E3 | taxonomic (eng) | Favored by the Ancient Egyptians as a source of turquoise, the Sinai was, until recently, famed for only one event but certainly an important one. | The Sinai was a source of gold for the Ancient Egyptians. | फ़िरोज़ा के एक स्रोत के रूप में प्राचीन मिस्र के इष्ट, सिनाई, हाल ही में जब तक, केवल एक घटना के लिए प्रसिद्ध है, लेकिन निश्चित रूप से एक महत्वपूर्ण एक था। | सिनाई प्राचीन मिस्रियों के लिए सोने का स्रोत था। |
| E4 | taxonomic( hi) | 'And I don't want to risk a fire fight with what appear to be horribly equal numbers.' | I don't want to get in a fight. | और मैं क्या बुरी तरह से बराबर संख्या में दिखाई देते है के साथ एक आग लड़ाई जोखिम नहीं करना चाहती। | मैं लड़ाई में नहीं पड़ना चाहता। |
| E5 | spatial (eng) | On the slopes of the hill you will find Edinburgh Zoo, located just behind Corstorphine Hospital. | Corstophine hospital is really far fromEdinburgh Zoo | पहाड़ी की ढलानों पर आपको एडिनबर्ग चिड़ियाघर मिलेगा, जो कॉर्स्टॉर्फिन अस्पताल के ठीक पीछे स्थित है। | Corstophine अस्पताल वास्तव में एडिनबर्ग चिड़ियाघर से दूर है |
| E6 | temporal (eng) | Both individuals agreed that the teleconference played no role in coordinating a response to the attacks of 9/11. | Neither party claimed that the phone meeting of the prior morning had been responsible for the actions taken in relation to the attacks on 9/11. | दोनों व्यक्तियों ने इस बात पर सहमति व्यक्त की कि टेलीकांफ्रेंस ने 9/11 के हमलों के प्रत्युत्तर के समन्वय में कोई भूमिका नहीं निभाई। | न तो पार्टी ने दावा किया कि पूर्व सुबह की फोन बैठक 9/11 पर हमलों के संबंध में की गई कार्रवाइयों के लिए जिम्मेदार रही थी। |
| E7 | temporal (hi) | By 1993, Penney was using EDI for processing 97 percent of purchase orders and 85 percent of invoices with 3,400 of its 4,000 suppliers. | Penney was using EDI in 1993 for processing much of its supply information. | 1993 तक, पेनी खरीद आदेशों के 97 प्रतिशत और 85 प्रतिशत चालानों को अपने 4,000 आपूर्तिकर्ताओं के 3,400 के साथ संसाधित करने के लिए ईडीआई का उपयोग कर रहा था। | पेनी अपनी आपूर्ति की अधिकांश जानकारी के प्रसंस्करण के लिए 1993 में ईदी का उपयोग कर रहा था। |
| E8 | negation (eng) | The handling and processing of the reagent, commonly limestone, is often done onsite, as is the treatment of the effluent as waste or processing into a saleable product (e.g. | The reagent is more often than not limestone, and is handled and processed onsite. | अभिकर् प, आमतौर पर चूना पत्थर की हैंडलिंग और प्रसंस्करण अक्सर ऑनसाइट किया जाता है, जैसा कि अपशिष्ट या प्रसंस्करण के रूप में बहिस्त्राव का उपचार एक बिक्री योग्य उत्पाद उदाहरण के लिए) में किया जाता है। | अभिवाक् त चूना पत्थर की तुलना में अधिक बार होता है, और इसे ऑनसाइट संभाला और संसाधित किया जाता ह। |
| E9 | negation (hi) | CHAPTER 6: HUMAN CAPITAL | Capital is money, not people. | अध्याय 6: मानव पूंजी | पैसा है, लोगों को नहीं। |

Table 3: Similar examples in Hindi. The categories are mentioned in the second column, and in braces, we mention the language where the category is marked present.

test set for our zero-shot and few-shot experiments. We will share the dataset publicly in `github.com/microsoft/TaxiXNLI`.

## 2.2 Automated Translation Error Analysis

To gauge the errors due to automated translation of English to different languages and inheriting the reasoning types from TAXINLI annotations, we hire native speakers in Hindi, Spanish and Swahili to re-annotate 200 carefully balanced samples. The annotators were trained similarly as described in Joshi et al. (2020a); and were additionally instructed to label noisy (partial or full) example pairs. We share the results in Table 1.

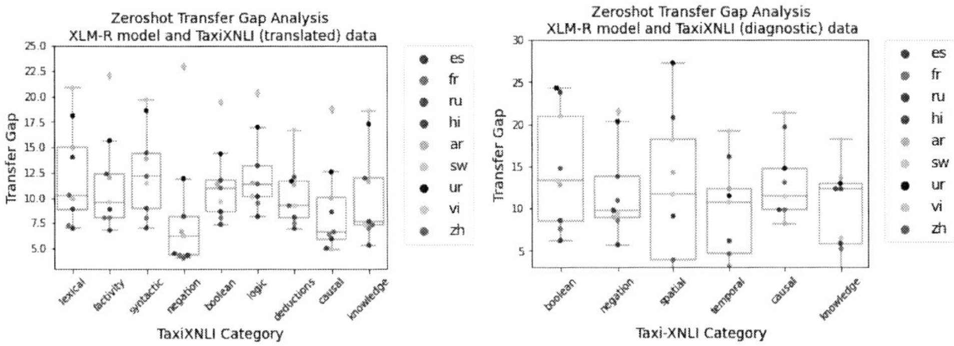


Figure 1: For each TAXINLI category and language, we plot the transfer gap on XLM-R, for both datasets.

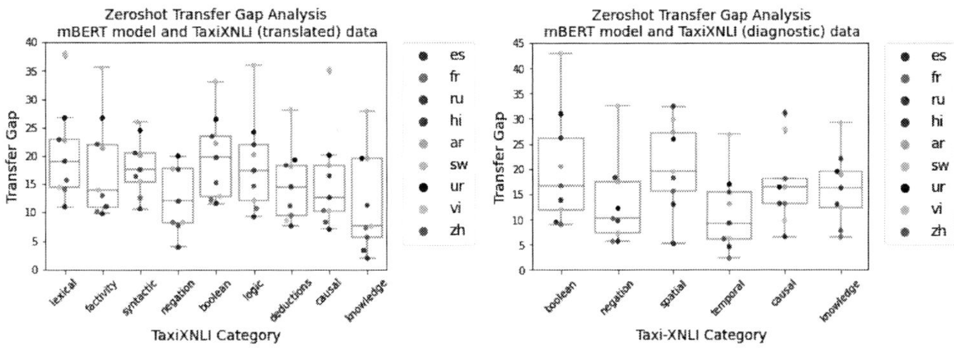


Figure 2: For each TAXINLI category and language, we plot the transfer gap on mBERT, for both datasets.

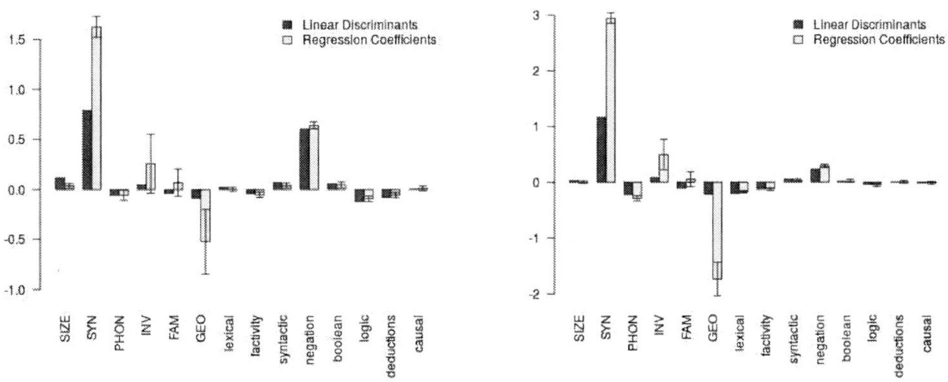


Figure 3: LDA and Regression coefficients obtained to model the NLI prediction correctness on TaxiXNLI (translated) by XLM-R (left) and M-BERT (Right), given language features and reasoning categories. (SYN/negation: ***, Logic: *, $p$-value $\leq 0$***, 0.001**, 0.01*)

**Interviews and Further Analysis** Our goal was to investigate two questions: 1) how noisy are the translations, 2) for non-noisy translations, do a reasoning category stay the same across languages.

While the noise level in both Hindi and Spanish is lower, translation accuracy for low-resource languages are still pretty poor. This prompted us to create the TaxiXNLI (diagnostic). We wanted to further investigate the second question, as the percentage of #tr=0,en=1 (indicating the categories which was present in English, but was not when translated to the corresponding target language) is lower than expected. After conducting an interview with the Swahili and the Hindi annotators about mismatching annotations, we found the following: 1) partially noisy translations often made the premise and hypothesis somewhat unrelated; and, based on TaxiNLI instructions annotators did not further annotate any categories; 2) TaxiNLI reasoning category annotations are subjective, as different annotators can follow different reasoning process. For example, for a *P: I am from New York. H: I am from Texas*; the Swahili translation was perfect *P: Mimi ni kutoka New York., H: Mimi ni kutoka Texas.*. But the Swahili annotator reasoned geographically, i.e., N.Y is far from Texas, so annotated it as *spatial* and the English annotator reasoned using world knowledge; 3) sometimes translation also slightly changed the word sense. For example, for the hypothesis *H: He held the stance that the other extremists should have went further.*, the translation was *Yeye alishikilia msimamo kwamba wengine wenye siasa kali wanapaswa kwenda zaidi.*, which loosely translates to "extremists should have went further in distance". More examples are in Table 2 and 3.

### 2.3 Dataset Statistics

| Category | Translation | | Diagnostic |
|---|---|---|---|
| | Train | Test | Test |
| lexical | 1362 | 1362 | - |
| factivity | 824 | 824 | - |
| syntactic | 1439 | 1438 | - |
| negation | 688 | 688 | 246 |
| boolean | 801 | 800 | 210 |
| logic | 895 | 896 | 207* |
| deductions | 1019 | 1019 | - |
| causal | 1176 | 1177 | 61 |
| knowledge | 301 | 301 | 154 |

Table 4: **Number of examples:** For each TaxiNLI categories, we report number of train and test examples in TaxiXNLI (translated) and TaxiXNLI (Diagnostic) respectively. * within logic, we only annotate spatial and temporal examples.

For both TaxiXNLI (translated) and TaxiXNLI (diagnostic), we report the number of training and test examples for each TaxiNLI categories in Table 4. In the diagnostic set, we annotate a total 1435 examples, among which there were 650 examples, where no selected category was marked.

| | lex | fact | synt | neg | bool | log | ded | caus | know |
|---|---|---|---|---|---|---|---|---|---|
| **mBERT** | 20.52 | 18.19 | 18.21 | 18.38 | 19.68 | 18.52 | 15.06 | 15.41 | 11.59 |
| **XLM-R** | 12.37 | 11.49 | 12.69 | 8.14 | 11.29 | 12.38 | 10.29 | 8.76 | 10.45 |
| $\Delta$ | 8.15 | 6.7 | 5.52 | 10.24 | 8.39 | 6.14 | 4.77 | 6.65 | 1.14 |

Table 5: **Transfer Gap and TaxiNLI categories:** For each category, we report the transfer gap averaged across languages and the reduction in the gap when we move from M-BERT to XLM-R.

## 3 Experimental Setup

For our experiments, we fine-tune Multilingual BERT and XLM-R (base)[3] on MultiNLI training (Williams et al., 2018b) data and select the best model using the MultiNLI validation set. We repeat the fine-tuning with 5 different seed values and for learning-rate in {2e-5, 3e-5}. For zero-shot experiments, we evaluate the best model on TaxiXNLI datasets for each language and taxonomic category. We measure the crosslingual transferability using transfer gap (Hu et al., 2020) which is defined as the difference between the performance on English and target language.

Whereas, for few-shot learning, for each of the target language and inference type pair, we continue to fine-tune the best MultiNLI fine-tuned XLM-R and M-BERT model using a random few TaxiXNLI (translated) training examples in that particular pair and then test the model on the same language and inference type pair. We repeat all our experiments with 5 different seeds (different examples each time) and report the average. For our analysis, we measure relative error reduction ($\text{RER} = \frac{(\text{accuracy}_N - \text{accuracy}_0)}{100 - \text{accuracy}_0}$) which provides measure of the error reduction from the initial step (zero-shot), relative to the initial step.

## 4 CrossLingual Cross-capability Insights

In this section, we discuss some important insights that we observe through the zero-shot and few-shot experiments. We highlight phenomena which are repeated across TaxiXNLI (translated) and TaxiXNLI (diagnostic) datasets.

[3]github.com/huggingface/transformers

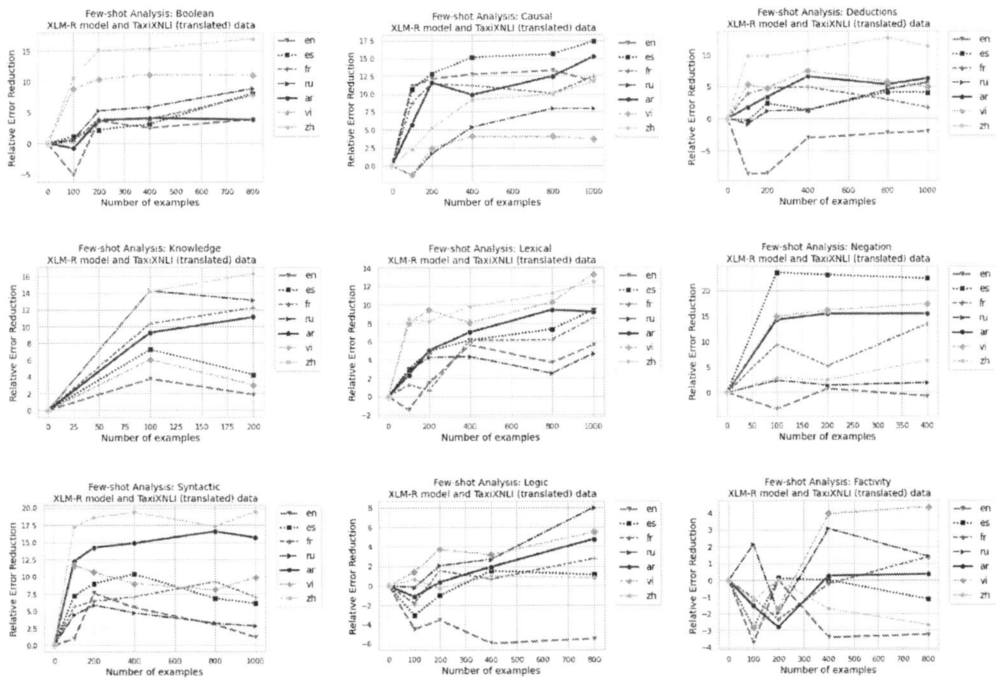


Figure 4: **Few Shot Accuracy (TaxiXNLI (translated), XLM-R):** For each TaxiNLI category and language, we plot Accuracy on TaxiXNLI (translated) test, when XLM-R MultiNLI model is fine-tuned on $N$ examples in that language and category

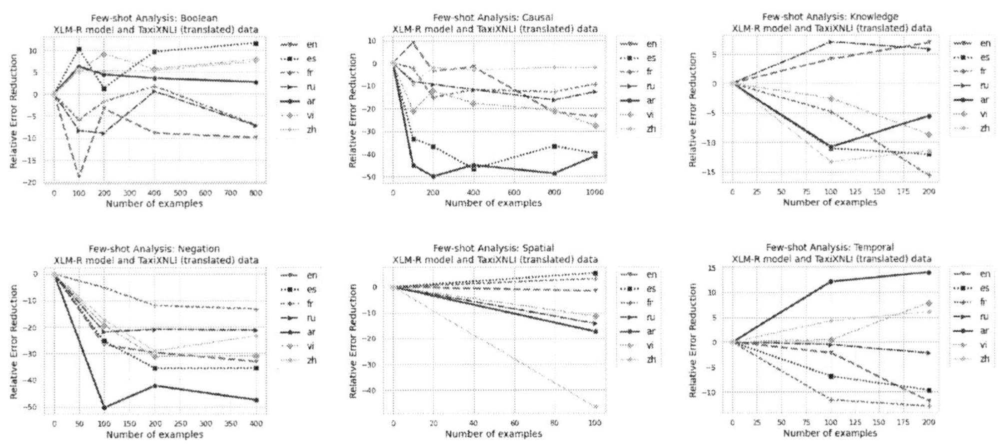


Figure 5: **Few Shot Accuracy (TaxiXNLI (diagnostic), XLM-R):** For each TaxiNLI category and language, we plot Accuracy on TaxiXNLI (diagnostic) test, when XLM-R MultiNLI model is fine-tuned on $N$ examples in that language and category

**Is Transferability uniform across categories? Does more pre-training help?** From Figure 1 and 2, we observe that the transferability of different inference types are non-uniform, especially in the case of XLM-R. In particular, transferability of `negation` (except for Swahili) is a lot better than `lexical`, `syntactic`, `boolean`, or `knowledge` inference types. The results on the TaxiXNLI (diagnostic) test confirms these observations. Further, from the results on TaxiXNLI (translated), in Table 5, we observe that the transfer gap for some categories such as `negation`, `boolean` can be reduced significantly by increasing the monolingual pre-training data (from M-BERT to XLM-

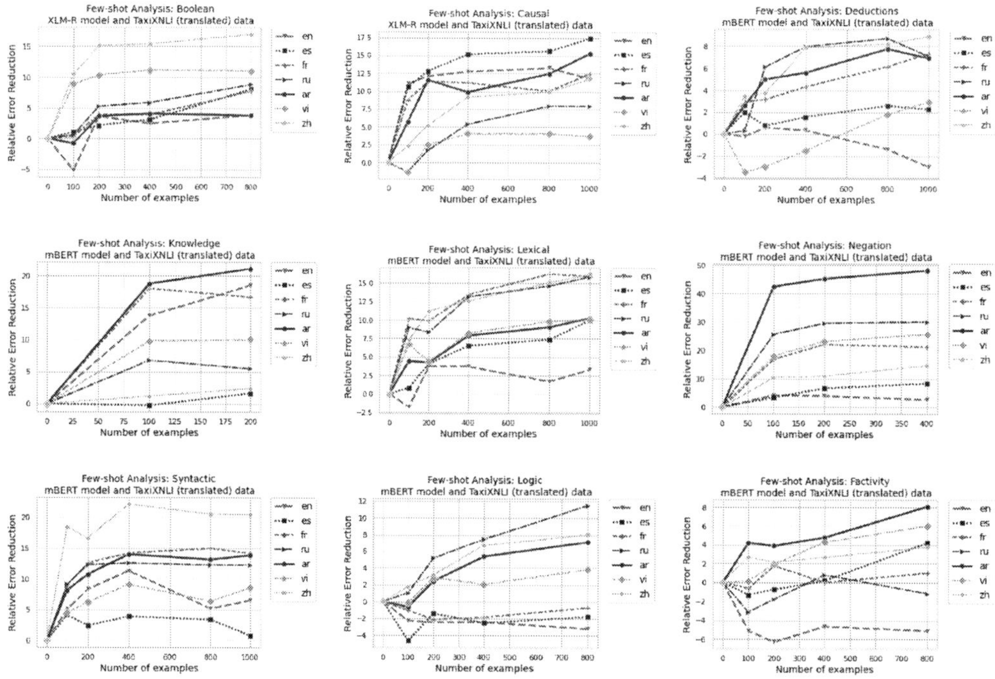


Figure 6: **Few Shot Accuracy (TaxiXNLI (translated), mBERT):** For each TaxiNLI category and language, we plot Accuracy on TaxiXNLI (translated) test, when mBERT MultiNLI model is fine-tuned on $N$ examples in that language and category

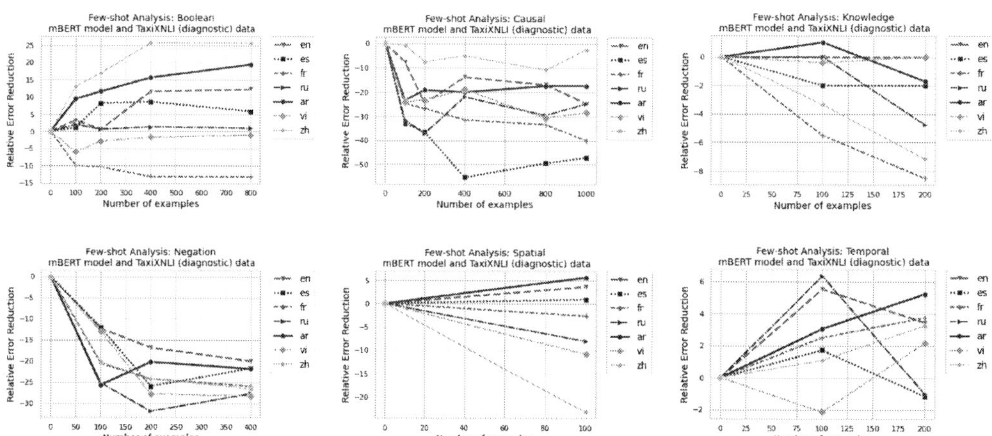


Figure 7: **Few Shot Accuracy (TaxiXNLI (diagnostic), mBERT):** For each TaxiNLI category and language, we plot Accuracy on TaxiXNLI (diagnostic) test, when mBERT MultiNLI model is fine-tuned on $N$ examples in that language and category

R), whereas for categories such as knowledge and deductions the transfer gap is not reduced much.

**Why does zero-shot transfer of Negation seem easy? And, why is Swahili the odd-one-out?** Negation seems easiest to transfer. A possible cause is in most languages, there are standard negation keywords. In English (among 1376 examples, TaxiXNLI-translated), most frequently occurring words are: not (543), never (172), no (260), didn't (73), No (42), nothing (45). It's possible that pretrained LMs learn correspondence between English and target language negation keywords. However, in Swahili, zero-shot transfer for Negation is bad. We observe that Swahili uses fused morphemes to indicate negation; for example, negation marker "Si" used for the pronoun "Mimi" (I), "Hatu" for "Sisi" (we). Sentence " I am not singing" becomes "Siimbi"; "We are not singing" becomes "Hatuiimbi". It's possible that with the comparatively limited pre-training data, XLM-R does not learn the correspondence between separate negative particles and fused morphemes.

**Language features or Reasoning categories – which affects transfer more?** Inspired by Lauscher et al. (2020), we extend their regression analysis to include category features. Since, multiple categories can exist per example, we create a feature-set for each example in TaxiXNLI (translated) test set. We include Lang2Vec features of its corresponding language (syntax, phonology, inventory, family, and GEO), and one-hot category vector (1 if it belongs to the category otherwise zero). We then use logistic regression (LR) and linear discriminant analysis (LDA) to predict which factors influence XLM-R's correct prediction (0/1) on TaxiXNLI (translated) dataset. As shown in Figure 3, with high $p$-values, negation, logic and deductions affect XLM-R's zero-shot performance. Interestingly, for mBERT, the language features correlate more highly with correct prediction.

**Do all categories improve under few-shot?** We plot the relative error reduction in the few-shot scenario (refer Fig. 4, and Fig. 5) for XLM-R. We only retain the high-resource languages for both, as translations for high-resource languages are quite accurate. In the TaxiXNLI (translated) set, for boolean, causal, deduction and knowledge, all languages improve uniformly with small variations. However, on TaxiXNLI (diagnostic) test, there is a large decrease in RER for causal and other categories. To investigate deeper, we analyze if few-shot improves crosslingual alignment. For each category, we take ([CLS]) embeddings of the English (pivot) sentence and its translated counterpart in target language from TaxiXNLI (translated) — and compute their pair-wise distances. In Table 6, We report the difference between average distance after few-shot (highest N) and at zero-shot. Both $L^2$ distance (and cosine) measure shows that for negation, the crosslingual alignment is increasing after few-shot. Though, results on the diagnostic set calls for careful experiments to test generalization.

| | ar | es | fr | hi | ru | sw | ur | vi | zh |
|---|---|---|---|---|---|---|---|---|---|
| **Negation** | -0.73 | -0.23 | 0.06 | -0.02 | 0.005 | -1.3 | -0.64 | -0.46 | -0.55 |
| **Min** | -0.912 | -0.55 | -0.797 | -0.75 | -0.54 | -1.3 | -1.009 | -0.74 | -0.88 |
| **Max** | 0.162 | 0.96 | 0.39 | 0.56 | 0.16 | -0.03 | -0.01 | 0.27 | 0.35 |

Table 6: Difference between L2 distances of sentence-pairs for each categories before and after few-shot. For *negation*, there is large decrease in distances, indicating higher crosslingual alignment.

## 5 Findings and Future Work

We proposed a multilingual extension of a reasoning type-annotated NLI dataset (TaxiNLI) in English – TaxiXNLI (translated) and a gold test set TaxiXNLI (diagnostic) to analyze transfer efficiency of multilingual language models. Our analysis strongly indicates that reasoning types play an important role in transfer capability. Our few-shot results demonstrate that for types such as Negation, improvement in transfer accuracy co-occurs with improved cross-lingual alignment. For causal, few-shot models fail to generalize well on the diagnostic set; and some categories hardly improve. In summary, NLI being central to NLU and NLP, this dataset and our ensuing analysis provides a way to broadly quantify the gaps in zero-shot transfer across various linguistic and logical dimensions.

## References

Mikel Artetxe, Sebastian Ruder, and Dani Yogatama. 2020. On the cross-lingual transferability of monolingual representations. In *Proceedings of the 58th Annual Meeting of the Association for Computational Linguistics*, pages 4623–4637, Online. Association for Computational Linguistics.

Alexis Conneau, Kartikay Khandelwal, Naman Goyal, Vishrav Chaudhary, Guillaume Wenzek, Francisco

Guzmán, Edouard Grave, Myle Ott, Luke Zettlemoyer, and Veselin Stoyanov. 2019. Unsupervised cross-lingual representation learning at scale. *arXiv preprint arXiv:1911.02116*.

Alexis Conneau, Ruty Rinott, Guillaume Lample, Adina Williams, Samuel R. Bowman, Holger Schwenk, and Veselin Stoyanov. 2018. Xnli: Evaluating cross-lingual sentence representations. In *Proceedings of the 2018 Conference on Empirical Methods in Natural Language Processing*. Association for Computational Linguistics.

Alexis Conneau, Shijie Wu, Haoran Li, Luke Zettlemoyer, and Veselin Stoyanov. 2020. Emerging cross-lingual structure in pretrained language models. In *Proceedings of the 58th Annual Meeting of the Association for Computational Linguistics*, pages 6022–6034, Online. Association for Computational Linguistics.

Jacob Devlin, Ming-Wei Chang, Kenton Lee, and Kristina Toutanova. 2019. Bert: Pre-training of deep bidirectional transformers for language understanding. In *Proceedings of the 2019 Conference of the North American Chapter of the Association for Computational Linguistics: Human Language Technologies, Volume 1 (Long and Short Papers)*, pages 4171–4186.

Daniela Gerz, Ivan Vulić, Edoardo Maria Ponti, Roi Reichart, and Anna Korhonen. 2018. On the relation between linguistic typology and (limitations of) multilingual language modeling. In *Proceedings of the 2018 Conference on Empirical Methods in Natural Language Processing*, pages 316–327.

Junjie Hu, Sebastian Ruder, Aditya Siddhant, Graham Neubig, Orhan Firat, and Melvin Johnson. 2020. Xtreme: A massively multilingual multi-task benchmark for evaluating cross-lingual generalization. *CoRR*, abs/2003.11080.

Pratik Joshi, Somak Aditya, Aalok Sathe, and Monojit Choudhury. 2020a. Taxinli: Taking a ride up the nlu hill. In *CoNLL*.

Pratik Joshi, Sebastin Santy, Amar Budhiraja, Kalika Bali, and Monojit Choudhury. 2020b. The state and fate of linguistic diversity and inclusion in the NLP world. In *Proceedings of the 58th Annual Meeting of the Association for Computational Linguistics*, pages 6282–6293, Online. Association for Computational Linguistics.

Karthikeyan K, Zihan Wang, Stephen Mayhew, and Dan Roth. 2020. Cross-lingual ability of multilingual BERT: an empirical study. In *8th International Conference on Learning Representations, ICLR 2020, Addis Ababa, Ethiopia, April 26-30, 2020*. OpenReview.net.

Guillaume Lample and Alexis Conneau. 2019. Cross-lingual language model pretraining. *Advances in Neural Information Processing Systems (NeurIPS)*.

Anne Lauscher, Vinit Ravishankar, Ivan Vulić, and Goran Glavaš. 2020. From zero to hero: On the limitations of zero-shot language transfer with multilingual transformers. In *Proceedings of the 2020 Conference on Empirical Methods in Natural Language Processing (EMNLP)*, pages 4483–4499.

Yinhan Liu, Myle Ott, Naman Goyal, Jingfei Du, Mandar Joshi, Danqi Chen, Omer Levy, Mike Lewis, Luke Zettlemoyer, and Veselin Stoyanov. 2019. Roberta: A robustly optimized bert pretraining approach. *arXiv preprint arXiv:1907.11692*.

Yixin Nie, Adina Williams, Emily Dinan, Mohit Bansal, Jason Weston, and Douwe Kiela. 2019. Adversarial nli: A new benchmark for natural language understanding. *arXiv preprint arXiv:1910.14599*.

Marco Tulio Ribeiro, Tongshuang Wu, Carlos Guestrin, and Sameer Singh. 2020. Beyond accuracy: Behavioral testing of NLP models with CheckList. In *Proceedings of the 58th Annual Meeting of the Association for Computational Linguistics*, pages 4902–4912, Online. Association for Computational Linguistics.

Kyle Richardson, Hai Hu, Lawrence Moss, and Ashish Sabharwal. 2020. Probing natural language inference models through semantic fragments. *Proceedings of the AAAI Conference on Artificial Intelligence*, 34:8713–8721.

Felipe Salvatore, Marcelo Finger, and Roberto Hirata Jr. 2019. A logical-based corpus for cross-lingual evaluation. In *Proceedings of the 2nd Workshop on Deep Learning Approaches for Low-Resource NLP (DeepLo 2019)*, pages 22–30.

Konstantinos Sechidis, Grigorios Tsoumakas, and Ioannis Vlahavas. 2011. On the stratification of multilabel data. *Machine Learning and Knowledge Discovery in Databases*, pages 145–158.

John F Sowa. 2010. The role of logic and ontology in language and reasoning. In *Theory and applications of ontology: philosophical perspectives*, pages 231–263. Springer.

Alex Wang, Amanpreet Singh, Julian Michael, Felix Hill, Omer Levy, and Samuel R Bowman. 2018. Glue: A multi-task benchmark and analysis platform for natural language understanding. *EMNLP 2018*, page 353.

Adina Williams, Nikita Nangia, and Samuel Bowman. 2018a. A broad-coverage challenge corpus for sentence understanding through inference. In *Proceedings of the 2018 Conference of the North American Chapter of the Association for Computational Linguistics: Human Language Technologies, Volume 1 (Long Papers)*, pages 1112–1122. Association for Computational Linguistics.

Adina Williams, Nikita Nangia, and Samuel Bowman. 2018b. A broad-coverage challenge corpus for sentence understanding through inference. In *Proceedings of the 2018 Conference of the North American*

*Chapter of the Association for Computational Linguistics: Human Language Technologies, Volume 1 (Long Papers)*, pages 1112–1122, New Orleans, Louisiana. Association for Computational Linguistics.

L. Wittgenstein. 1922. Tractatus logico-philosophicus. *London: Routledge, 1981.*

# Identifying the Importance of Content Overlap for Better Cross-lingual Embedding Mappings

**Réka Cserháti** and **Gábor Berend**
Department of Computer Science
University of Szeged
{cserhatir,berendg}@inf.u-szeged.hu

## Abstract

In this work, we analyze the performance and properties of cross-lingual word embedding models created by mapping-based alignment methods. We use several measures of corpus and embedding similarity to predict BLI scores of cross-lingual embedding mappings over three types of corpora, three embedding methods and 55 language pairs. Our experimental results corroborate that instead of mere size, the amount of common content in the training corpora is essential. This phenomenon manifests in that i) despite of the smaller corpus sizes, using only the comparable parts of Wikipedia for training the monolingual embedding spaces to be mapped is often more efficient than relying on all the contents of Wikipedia, ii) the smaller, in return less diversified Spanish Wikipedia works almost always much better as a training corpus for bilingual mappings than the ubiquitously used English Wikipedia.

## 1 Introduction

Word embedding methods (e.g. Mikolov et al., 2013b, Pennington et al., 2014, Bojanowski et al., 2017) have become an essential tool for representing words in most NLP tasks. These algorithms assign a low-dimensional vector to words based on the patterns of their contexts in a training corpus, and this way they locate the words in the vector space in a consistent way, so that words with similar meaning are assigned to similar vectors. Therefore, it can be assumed that the layout of the word vectors are near equivalent in independently trained models, so word embedding models in different languages can be aligned into a common space. Such alignments are a standard way of creating bi- or multilingual word embedding spaces, which are very useful for machine translation and a wide range of cross-lingual NLP tasks.

Although large pre-trained language models are superior to traditional word embeddings in many NLP tasks, one strength of these mapping-based methods is their extensive applicability, e.g. for low-resource languages or special domain (e.g. medical) data. Additionally, probably due to significantly lower resource requirements (Strubell et al., 2019) and often competitive results (Litschko et al., 2021), a large proportion of industrial NLP applications is still based on static word embeddings (Arora et al., 2020).

On the other hand, the results of the mappings and the performance of the multilingual models was still shown to be extremely dependent on the mapping scenario (Søgaard et al., 2018; Vulić et al., 2019, 2020). Previous work attributes low performance and non-isomorphism of monolingual embedding models to typological differences between languages, domain differences in the training corpora, insufficient resources, and under-training (Doval et al., 2020; Søgaard et al., 2018; Vulić et al., 2020).

We rely on popular bilingual alignment methods, and conduct a thorough analysis of the connection between the evaluation scores of the mappings and language relatedness, isomorphism of the source embeddings measured by several metrics, and some newly identified, easy to calculate corpus properties that are highly predictive of the bilingual mapping performance: the token overlap ratio in the vocabularies, and the distance between word distributions of the corpora. These combined with corpus size surpass existing isomorphism measures as predictors of bilingual mapping score.

Our goal is to help researchers and developers use resources more efficiently, and find the most appropriate setting for creating bilingual word embedding models. [1]

[1] Our codes, mapping dictionaries, and more mapping results are available at https://github.com/xerevity/mappability



*Proceedings of the 1st Workshop on Multilingual Representation Learning*, pages 96–106
November 11, 2021. 

## 2 Related Work

### 2.1 Mapping Algorithms

The success of the pioneering neural word embedding models (Mikolov et al., 2013b) almost immediately led to the idea of creating bilingual models using linear transformations (Mikolov et al., 2013a). The original problem is finding a mapping that transforms an embedding matrix close to another in a different language. Mikolov et al. (2013a) solve this with stochastic gradient descent, minimizing the squared euclidean distance of word pairs from a seed dictionary.

Subsequently, several works improved this mapping method: for example, Xing et al. (2015) normalize the source and target embeddings, and constrain the mapping to be orthogonal; Artetxe et al. (2016) center the mean, and find the transformation in closed form, solving a least squares problem. Later Artetxe et al. (2018a) proposed a multi-step framework consisting of mean-centering, normalization, whitening, and an orthogonal transformation. In contrast, *RCSLS* (Joulin et al., 2018) is based on relaxing the orthogonal restriction and returning to stochastic gradient descent with a different loss function, aiming to be consistent with the *CSLS* (Cross-domain Similarity Local Scaling; Conneau et al., 2018) retrieval method.

Additionally, aligning word embeddings in an unsupervised way, without any cross-lingual signal has also become an exciting topic, giving rise to diverse approaches of unsupervised embedding mappings. The first really successful solution by Conneau et al. (2018) is based on adversarial learning; Artetxe et al. (2018b) proposed an iterative self-learning method initialized by sorting embedding values; and Non-adversarial Translation by Hoshen and Wolf (2018) also uses self-learning, but a different method, initialized using PCA.

### 2.2 Analysis of Cross-Lingual Word Embeddings

Several works have already analyzed performance of cross-lingual embedding mappings (e.g. Kementchedjhieva et al., 2019; Glavaš et al., 2019; Vulić et al., 2019). More related to this paper, reasons why some settings do not work well were also investigated. For instance, Søgaard et al. (2018) use eigenvector similarity of nearest neighbor graphs to show that the isomorphic assumption does not hold in many cases, and report the negative effect of language and domain dissimilarity on the unsupervised embedding alignment method of Conneau et al. (2018).

In addition, Vulić et al. (2020) states that small corpora and under-training also play a significant role in non-isomorphism of word embeddings. Dubossarsky et al. (2020) also examine isomorphism, and suggest some new measures to quantify transferability of embedding spaces based on their spectral statistics: how similar their singular values are on the one hand, and their individual robustness measured by condition numbers, on the other hand.

In the rest of this paper, we supplement isomorphism measures with corpus similarity measures, and show that corpus similarity is one of the key factors influencing mapping scores in both supervised and unsupervised cases. We show that two corpora of sufficient size, coming from the same domain (Wikipedia in this case) can still be too different for good mapping scores, while good mappings are possible on relatively small corpora if other important conditions are met.

## 3 Experimental Setup

### 3.1 Corpora

In our experiments, we compare BLI (Bilingual Lexicon Induction) scores of embeddings trained on three types of corpora, all of them extracted from Wikipedia:

1. We use the full Wikipedia texts[2] of our 11 languages studied: Czech, Danish, German, Greek, English, Spanish, Finnish, Hungarian, Norwegian, Romanian and Turkish. These all come from the same domain (encyclopedia articles), which condition was reported to be necessary for sufficient unsupervised mappings by Søgaard et al. (2018). Nevertheless, this type is the least restricted in our experiments, and the sizes may be very dissimilar for different languages, but these are the largest among our experiments. We call this type of corpora loosely-comparable Wikipedia, or **L-Wiki** for short.

2. Even within the same domain, the content of the corpora may be very different, which might (and, according to our hypothesis, does) have a negative influence on the mappings. Therefore, we create a mildly-comparable (**M-Wiki**) corpus, separately for all of our 55 lan-

[2] As available at: https://linguatools.org/tools/corpora/wikipedia-monolingual-corpora/

guage pairs, by filtering articles with bidirectional cross-language links between the two Wikipedias. This is also expected to make sizes comparable within a language pair, but the different length of the articles may still cause dissimilarity in size. Additionally, the amount of filtered parts between different language pairs is especially variable.

3. In terms of both size and content, a parallel corpus between two languages is as similar as possible. As such, we use the WikiMatrix (Schwenk et al., 2021) parallel corpus (hereafter strictly-comparable Wiki or **S-Wiki**), which is also extracted from Wikipedia. The sizes here are substantially smaller than in the previous types, but also vary by language pairs.

This way, we have various levels of corpus size, language relatedness, and proportion of overlapping information among our experimental language pairs. To the best of our knowledge, our experiments are the first to analyze different corpus types, and to dissect the effects of corpus similarity on the quality of bilingual embedding mapping.

### 3.2 Training and Test Dictionaries

Since there is no available gold standard dictionary for most of our language pairs, we create silver dictionaries from the WikiMatrix parallel corpora using the word2word (Choe et al., 2020) tool, which generates translations for words based on parallel sentences. To ensure the quality of these, we generate two translations for each word above the mean frequency in the corpus, and only keep pairs that are mutual translations of each other. Then we randomly select (disjoint) training and test dictionaries with 3000 and 1000 source words, respectively.

### 3.3 Word Embedding Models

We train FastText (Bojanowski et al., 2017) word vectors on all of the above corpora using Gensim (Řehůřek and Sojka, 2010), with the following hyperparameters: dimensions: 300, negative samples: 5, context window: 5, minimum word count: 5, maximum vocabulary size: 200 000.

To create the cross-lingual models we use three mapping methods: supervised VecMap (Artetxe et al., 2018a), RCSLS (Joulin et al., 2018), and Non-adversarial Translation (NAT; Hoshen and Wolf, 2018) on the embeddings trained on three

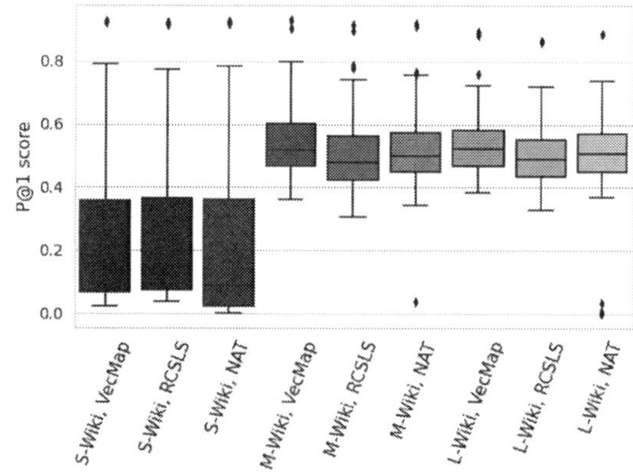


Figure 1: Distributions of BLI scores of embedding mappings using different methods and corpus types.

types of corpora and 110 language pairs, performing a total of 990 mappings as we separate different source–target directions of the same language pair.

We evaluate the models with P@1 scores, i.e. by finding the nearest neighbor of a source word among the target language embeddings, and see whether it is a correct translation according to our dictionary. We experimented with other, more sophisticated evaluation methods as well, but the scores did not change relative to each other.

## 4 Results and Analysis

### 4.1 Mapping Methods

We show the distributions of the used mapping algorithms on separate corpus types in Figure 1. Our first important observation is that the results are much more dependent on the corpus type than on the mapping algorithm. While mappings of mildly and loosely comparable corpora reach similar median scores and extremes, the strictly-comparable (hence a lot smaller) corpus mapping scores range much wider. The median of the S-Wiki scores is very low, but the highest scores and quantiles are in line with the other corpus types. Later we will also investigate in which cases do these mappings perform well, and why.

Another information visible in Figure 1 is that in our settings, VecMap performs the best among these three algorithms. However, except some cases where it completely fails, Non-adversarial Translation reaches competitive results to the other methods, despite the lack of supervision.

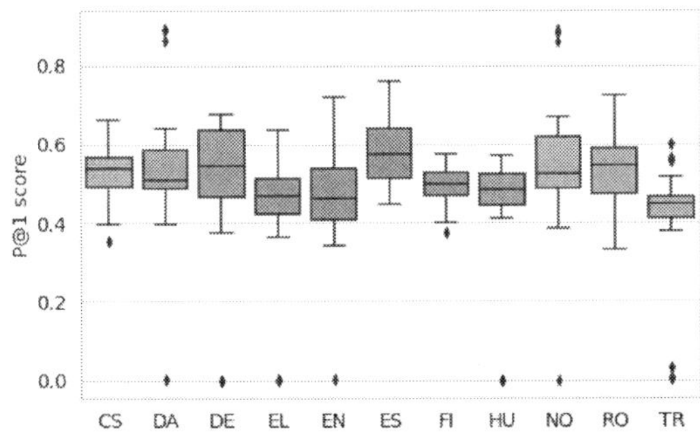


(a) Score distributions of languages involved in mapping embeddings trained on loosely-comparable full Wikipedia.

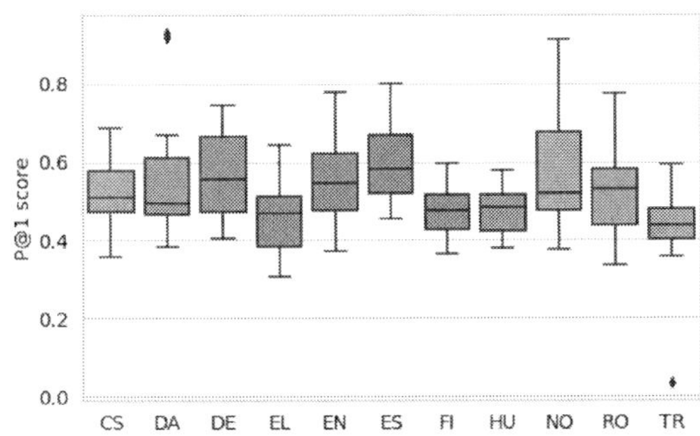


(b) Mapping scores of languages, with embeddings trained on mildly-comparable Wiki corpus.

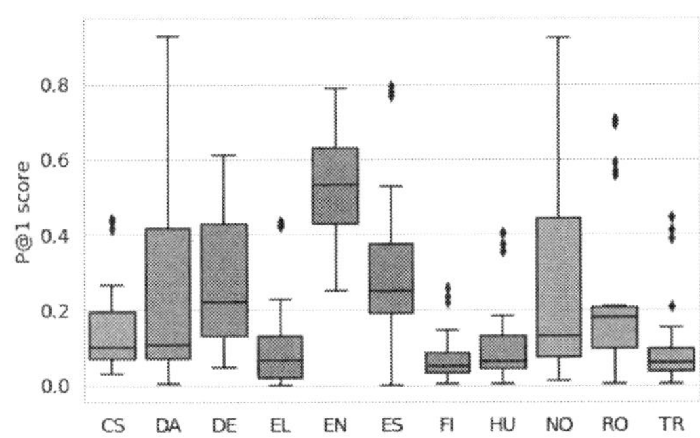


(c) Mapping scores of languages, with embeddings trained on a strictly-comparable (parallel) corpus.

Figure 2: Score distributions of embedding mappings involving a language (either as source or as target language).

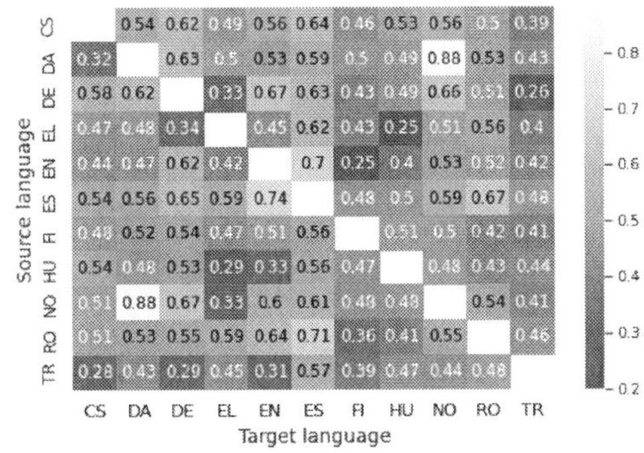


Figure 3: Average P@1 scores of loosely-comparable Wikipedia embedding mappings in all examined source–target pairs of languages.

## 4.2 Languages

The effect of the languages used on the performance of the cross-lingual embeddings has been widely studied (Vulić et al., 2019; Dubossarsky et al., 2020; Doval et al., 2020), but our evaluation on 110 pairs of 11 languages still shows interesting and instructive patterns. It is conspicuous in Figure 2a that, despite the widespread use of English as a transfer language, mappings of loosely-comparable Wikipedia embeddings involving Spanish perform substantially better. In this case, English Wikipedia probably covers too diverse and deep articles that none of the other Wikipedias do, which makes Spanish Wikipedia a better corpus for embedding mappings. However, using mildly-comparable Wikipedia weakens this phenomenon (see Figure 2b), which might suggest that instead of the corpus size, the real indicator of performance is the amount of overlapping information between the two corpora. We will deal with this hypothesis a lot more in the rest of this article.

Figure 3 shows the average performance of loosely-comparable Wikipedia mappings broken down by both source and target language. Beside some other interesting details, an outstanding result of the Danish–Norwegian mapping is clear. In this case, language relatedness, geographical and cultural similarity are all given, therefore we can assume that the two Wikipedias are also very similar in topics, style, editing, etc. This can be considered a case where all the necessary factors are met for obtaining a high-performing mapping.

From this figure it seems that only very close language relatedness is really beneficial, e.g. between Germanic and Romance languages, but Germanic

|  | L-Wiki | M-Wiki | S-Wiki |
|---|---|---|---|
| **Token overlap** | 0.458 | **0.747** | **0.942** |
| **Word distributions** | **–0.603** | –0.708 | –0.616 |
| **Size (log)** | 0.306 | 0.552 | 0.877 |

Table 1: Pearson correlation coefficients between P@1 scores and corpus properties.

languages, for example, can be mapped to linguistically very distant Finno-Ugrian languages just as well as to non-Germanic Indo-European languages, which might also be a useful observation for future work.

### 4.3 Corpus Size and Similarity

Our key observation is that one of the most required condition for good embedding mappings is corpus similarity, more precisely the amount of common contexts the words appear in, as a complement to previous claims pointing to language similarity and corpus size (Dubossarsky et al., 2020; Vulić et al., 2020).

We introduce two measures to quantify corpus similarity:

- *Token Overlap* is the ratio of token forms used in both corpora to the number of tokens used in one or both of them.

$$TO(V_1, V_2) = \frac{|V_1 \cap V_2|}{|V_1 \cup V_2|}$$

  Most of these shared tokens are probably words of foreign origin, having the same meaning, therefore their presence in large proportions indicates similar content in the texts. However, this measure is affected by language similarity as well, and is unusable with languages written in different scripts.

- As *Word Distribution Distance* between two corpora we take the normalized frequency distribution of words from our silver dictionary between the languages of the two corpora, and compute Jensen–Shannon divergence between them. This way, we use the words of the dictionary as keywords, and the divergence will be small only if the respective topics appear in a similar proportion in the corpora.

As Vulić et al. (2020) showed, mapping scores are greatly influenced by the size of the training corpora, therefore we include this information to

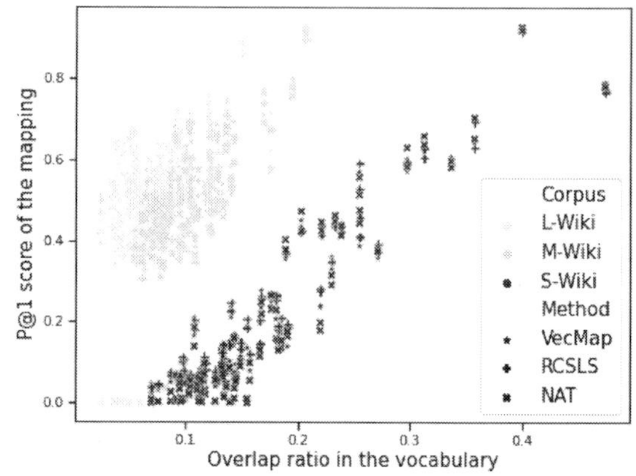


(a) Connection of mapping score to the proportion of overlapping tokens

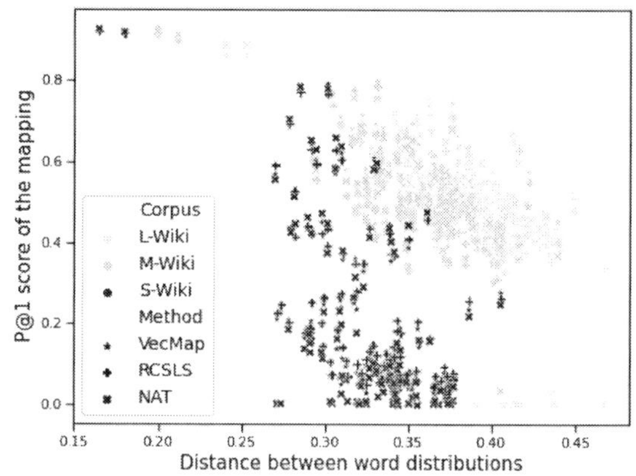


(b) Connection of mapping score to word distribution distance

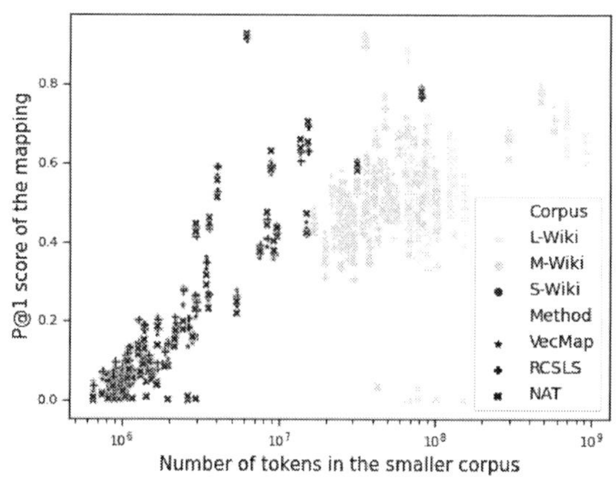


(c) Connection of mapping score to corpus size (on a logarithmic scale)

Figure 4: Relationship between performance of bilingual mappings and corpus properties.

our corpus data as well. We examined correlations using the token numbers of the source and the target corpus, the arithmetic and harmonic mean of them, and the minimum of them. The latter of these proved to be the most powerful indicator of mapping scores, so we use the minimum of token numbers of the two training corpora involved in the mapping to represent corpus size.

Figure 4 shows the connection of the mapping scores to the above defined corpus similarity measures and corpus size. All of these corpus properties seem to indicate performance well, as models with more overlap in their vocabularies, with more similar word distributions, or trained on a larger corpora perform generally better.

However, the parameters of the regression lines for corpus types differ clearly, implying that when we make the corpora mildly and strictly comparable, so overlap ratio and word distribution similarity increase, the results are not improving as much as we could have expected by extrapolating the scores of the full Wikipedia corpus. But similarly, the smaller size of comparable and parallel corpora does not directly lead to a decrease in performance either.

It can be clearly seen from Figure 4c, that although there is a connection between corpus size and cross-lingual mapping score as well, big corpora are neither necessary nor sufficient for good results: some of the best scores are reached by mapping embeddings trained on the Danish–Norwegian parallel corpus, having less than 10 million tokens, while the biggest corpora consist of approximately 1 billion tokens.

Also, correlations in Table 1 show that the relationship between corpus size and performance gets stronger as the corpus is filtered for overlapping articles (M-Wiki), and even stronger for parallel sentences (S-Wiki), again supporting our hypothesis that the amount of common information is an important factor for mappings. We measured corpus similarity by the number of common tokens and the distribution of dictionary words successfully, but there are probably other, more widely usable measures to be found in future work.

### 4.4 Content Overlap

To further validate our statement that common content in corpora greatly influences mapping scores, we conduct controlled experiments, in which we align embeddings of the same language, and construct the training corpora from subsets of a single Wikipedia. For 3 languages (English, Spanish and Hungarian) we create corpora in different sizes, and for all of these we select subsets that are matching in size, but contain 0%, 33%, 66%, or 100% of the text in the first corpus.

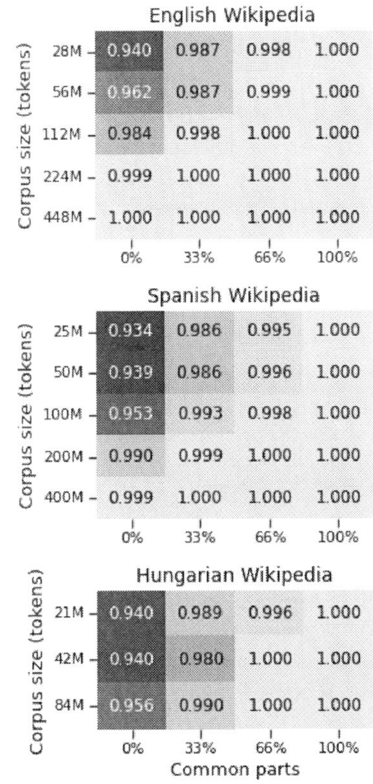


Figure 5: P@1 scores of RCSLS mappings of embeddings from Wikipedia parts of various overlap ratio and size.

This methodology allows us to examine the effects of size and content overlap explicitly (and exclude the effects of typological differences between languages). These parts, however, may contain very similar articles in the same field, which are not accounted as overlap. Probably this is why small size and zero overlap still yield very high P@1 scores, as shown in Figure 5. Still, the trends are convincing that content overlap is at least as important as corpus size. We show the scores of the RCSLS mapping, but the same patterns can be seen with other methods.

These results also imply that word embeddings represent word usage of a specific corpus, rather than a whole language, which is often forgotten in multilingual tasks. Therefore, it is possible that a corpus can even be too large compared to another if there are too many different contexts appearing in only one of them, which might explain why Spanish Wikipedia is superior to English as a training corpus. We can conclude that even among corpora of the same domain, corpus similarity is a major requirement for the success of word embedding alignment.

### 4.5 Embedding Isomorphism

Previous work has extensively studied the (non-) isomorphism of word embeddings, and its effect on bilingual alignments. This problem can be considered one of the core questions of bilingual mappings, since this method gains its inspiration and theoretical validity from the assumption that embeddings trained on different languages should be approximately isomorphic. However, our surprising results show that the degree of isomorphism is generally less correlated to BLI scores than corpus properties.

Measuring the degree of isomorphism between word embedding models is an interesting question in itself as well, and several solutions have already been proposed for it. We adopt five existing measures (for more details see the works cited below) and introduce a new one, based on the similarity of words.

| | L-Wiki | M-Wiki | S-Wiki |
|---|---|---|---|
| **Laplacian** | –0.557 | **–0.777** | **–0.396** |
| **SVG** | –0.174 | –0.275 | 0.157 |
| **Spectral** | –0.392 | –0.290 | 0.061 |
| **Effective Spectral** | –0.251 | –0.236 | –0.224 |
| **Relational** | **0.591** | 0.486 | 0.262 |
| **Neighbors** | 0.521 | 0.501 | –0.099 |

Table 2: Pearson correlation coefficients between P@1 scores and isomorphism.

| | L-Wiki | M-Wiki | S-Wiki |
|---|---|---|---|
| # | 62 | 72 | 27 |
| **Laplacian** | –0.851 | –0.681 | **–0.926** |
| **SVG** | –0.346 | –0.518 | –0.896 |
| **Spectral** | –0.383 | 0.170 | –0.548 |
| **Effective Spectral** | –0.174 | 0.118 | 0.265 |
| **Relational** | **0.895** | **0.879** | 0.921 |
| **Neighbors** | 0.839 | 0.704 | 0.898 |

Table 3: Pearson correlation coefficients between P@1 scores and isomorphism among mappings scoring 0.6 or higher. We indicate the number of mappings meeting this criterion below the corpus types.

- *Laplacian Isospectrality* (Søgaard et al., 2018) measures the difference between the Laplacian eigenvalues of word nearest neighbor graphs. We take the average isospectrality of 10 graphs, each constructed of 50 random words from our dictionary and their translations.

- *Singular Value Gap* (SVG; Dubossarsky et al., 2020) is the distance between the sorted singular values of the two word embedding matrices.

- *Spectral Condition* (Dubossarsky et al., 2020) is the harmonic mean of the condition numbers of the two embedding matrices, which measure their sensitivity to noise.

- *Effective Spectral Condition* (Dubossarsky et al., 2020) is the harmonic mean of the effective condition numbers of the two embedding matrices.

- *Relational Similarity* (Vulić et al., 2020) quantifies how similarly the two models rate the proximity of word pairs. We take 10,000 random word pairs and their translations from our dictionary, and compute the Pearson correlation coefficient between the two lists of cosine similarity scores between the pairs.

- *Neighbor Overlap* quantifies the overlap between the neighborhood of words in the embedding models. We take a word from the dictionary in one language, and find its 10 nearest neighbors among the dictionary entries. Then we count how many of the translations of these appear among the nearest neighbors of the translation of the original word. We repeat this 1000 times, and compute the average of the outcomes.

In Table 2 we show the correlations between the above isomorphism measures and mapping scores. It is interesting that while the connection between corpus properties and bilingual scores was the strongest in strictly-comparable corpora, the opposite seems to be true in this case: the performance of mapping embeddings trained on S-Wiki seems not to be very dependent on isomorphism. Often it even happens that the correlation to embedding similarity/dissimilarity turns into negative/positive in the strictly-comparable case.

This raises the question if it is possible that two models, in which the same word has different neighbors, are transformed so that the appropriate words still become nearest neighbors, or above a certain score isomorphism remains a requirement for bilingual performance. To answer this, we compute the correlations between isomorphism measures and mapping scores again, but only among mappings with P@1 score 0.6 or higher. Table 3 shows that in these cases performance does indeed depend on isomorphism, especially on Laplacian, relational, and neighbor similarities.

We can see that mapping scores are connected to the isomorphism of source embeddings, especially among the relatively well performing models. Therefore we can use both isomorphism and corpus similarity to predict bilingual performance, which we will do in the next section.

### 4.6 Predicting BLI Scores

In our final experiments, we try to predict the mapping scores from the above studied corpus and isomorphism measures. We make predictions based on our three corpus properties, six isomorphism measures, and all of these combined, using random forest regression with the default parameters in Scikit-learn (Pedregosa et al., 2011), evaluating the model with the Leave-One-Out method.

The results in Table 4 show that mapping scores are very well predictable in most cases, but this varies between corpus types and alignment methods. Properties of the corpus, however, are almost always better predictors than isomorphism; the only exception is Non-adversarial Translation of loosely-comparable Wikipedia embeddings.

Combining corpus and isomorphism measures usually does not lead to an improvement either, which could mean that isomorphism depends on corpus properties as well. To find this out, we make predictions of all isomorphism measures from our three corpus properties, and show the results in Table 5. From these we see that although isomorphism does not depend solely on corpus similarity, it is also greatly influenced by it.

It is important to note that we did not use language information at all, therefore these high scores mean that the above corpus measures are more important than language similarity, or at least they carry this information as well. These results again support our observation on the importance of corpus similarity for good performance of bilingual word embedding mappings.

| **L-Wiki:** | | | |
|---|---|---|---|
| | **VecMap** | **RCSLS** | **NAT** |
| **Corpus** | 0.770 | 0.709 | 0.366 |
| **Isomorphism** | 0.720 | 0.654 | 0.481 |
| **All** | 0.788 | 0.733 | 0.478 |
| **M-Wiki:** | | | |
| | **VecMap** | **RCSLS** | **NAT** |
| **Corpus** | 0.797 | 0.794 | 0.664 |
| **Isomorphism** | 0.672 | 0.670 | 0.581 |
| **All** | 0.799 | 0.780 | 0.658 |
| **S-Wiki:** | | | |
| | **VecMap** | **RCSLS** | **NAT** |
| **Corpus** | 0.975 | 0.981 | 0.971 |
| **Isomorphism** | 0.777 | 0.793 | 0.765 |
| **All** | 0.972 | 0.974 | 0.966 |

Table 4: R2 scores of the predictions of P@1 scores, using random forest regression based on our three corpus properties combined, six isomorphism measures combined, and all of these.

## 5 Conclusion

We examined the connection of embedding mapping scores to languages, corpus properties, and embedding isomorphism. We found that the Spanish Wikipedia is better for this purpose than the English Wikipedia, often used by default. This is explained by our other experiments on the relationship of corpus properties and mapping quality, where it turned out that corpus similarity is at least as important as corpus size, therefore the hugeness and wide diversity of the English Wikipedia can be harmful.

Moreover, we have seen that language similarity is really beneficial for very closely related languages only, e.g. between Germanic or Romance languages. Mapping scores are well predictable even without any information about the languages, based on three properties of the corpora: corpus size, proportion of common tokens, and distance of the word distributions. These data also surpass existing embedding isomorphism measures as predictors.

On the other hand, this paper focuses on BLI scores only, which were shown to not correlate perfectly with bilingual performance on downstream tasks (Glavaš et al., 2019). We suppose that to some extent our findings hold in downstream situations as well, since downstream performance cannot be independent of BLI scores, but this question

| L-Wiki: | | | |
|---|---|---|---|
| | **VecMap** | **RCSLS** | **NAT** |
| Laplacian | 0.737 | 0.740 | 0.754 |
| SVG | 0.617 | 0.595 | 0.601 |
| Spectral | 0.760 | 0.777 | 0.770 |
| Effective Spectral | 0.763 | 0.766 | 0.776 |
| Relational | 0.735 | 0.727 | 0.731 |
| Neighbors | 0.793 | 0.796 | 0.802 |
| **M-Wiki:** | | | |
| | **VecMap** | **RCSLS** | **NAT** |
| Laplacian | 0.524 | 0.517 | 0.537 |
| SVG | 0.746 | 0.731 | 0.737 |
| Spectral | 0.821 | 0.827 | 0.824 |
| Effective Spectral | 0.815 | 0.832 | 0.824 |
| Relational | 0.681 | 0.678 | 0.660 |
| Neighbors | 0.553 | 0.570 | 0.564 |
| **S-Wiki:** | | | |
| | **VecMap** | **RCSLS** | **NAT** |
| Laplacian | 0.443 | 0.453 | 0.437 |
| SVG | 0.621 | 0.655 | 0.649 |
| Spectral | 0.448 | 0.456 | 0.448 |
| Effective Spectral | 0.537 | 0.552 | 0.548 |
| Relational | 0.746 | 0.724 | 0.743 |
| Neighbors | 0.642 | 0.655 | 0.645 |

Table 5: R2 scores of the predictions of isomorphism, based on our three corpus properties combined, using random forest regression.

should be part of further research. The main difference between downstream and BLI evaluation scores is probably the importance of monolingual embedding quality: while two embedding matrices can be trained almost perfectly isomorphically on a relatively small parallel corpus, the monolingual performance of these embeddings probably lags behind embeddings trained on a big corpus, Wikipedia for example. But at the same time, this also shows that embeddings can be mapped very well even if they are not of the highest quality, but their corpora are similar enough.

## Acknowledgements

Réka Cserháti was supported by the ÚNKP-21-1 – New National Excellence Program of the Ministry for Innovation and Technology from the source of the National Research, Development and Innovation Fund.

The research presented in this paper was partly supported by the Ministry of Innovation and the National Research, Development and Innovation Office within the framework of the Artificial Intelligence National Laboratory Programme.

## References

Simran Arora, Avner May, Jian Zhang, and Christopher Ré. 2020. Contextual embeddings: When are they worth it? In *Proceedings of the 58th Annual Meeting of the Association for Computational Linguistics*, pages 2650–2663, Online. Association for Computational Linguistics.

Mikel Artetxe, Gorka Labaka, and Eneko Agirre. 2016. Learning principled bilingual mappings of word embeddings while preserving monolingual invariance. In *Proceedings of the 2016 Conference on Empirical Methods in Natural Language Processing*, pages 2289–2294, Austin, Texas. Association for Computational Linguistics.

Mikel Artetxe, Gorka Labaka, and Eneko Agirre. 2018a. Generalizing and improving bilingual word embedding mappings with a multi-step framework of linear transformations. In *Proceedings of the Thirty-Second AAAI Conference on Artificial Intelligence*, pages 5012–5019.

Mikel Artetxe, Gorka Labaka, and Eneko Agirre. 2018b. A robust self-learning method for fully unsupervised cross-lingual mappings of word embeddings. In *Proceedings of the 56th Annual Meeting of the Association for Computational Linguistics (Volume 1: Long Papers)*, pages 789–798.

Piotr Bojanowski, Edouard Grave, Armand Joulin, and Tomas Mikolov. 2017. Enriching word vectors with subword information. *Transactions of the Association for Computational Linguistics*, 5:135–146.

Yo Joong Choe, Kyubyong Park, and Dongwoo Kim. 2020. word2word: A collection of bilingual lexicons for 3,564 language pairs. In *Proceedings of the 12th Language Resources and Evaluation Conference*, pages 3036–3045, Marseille, France. European Language Resources Association.

Alexis Conneau, Guillaume Lample, Marc'Aurelio Ranzato, Ludovic Denoyer, and Herv'e J'egou. 2018. Word translation without parallel data. *ArXiv*, abs/1710.04087.

Yerai Doval, Jose Camacho-Collados, Luis Espinosa Anke, and Steven Schockaert. 2020. On the robustness of unsupervised and semi-supervised cross-lingual word embedding learning. In *Proceedings of the 12th Language Resources and Evaluation Conference*, pages 4013–4023, Marseille, France. European Language Resources Association.

Haim Dubossarsky, Ivan Vulić, Roi Reichart, and Anna Korhonen. 2020. The secret is in the spectra: Predicting cross-lingual task performance with spectral similarity measures. In *Proceedings of the 2020 Conference on Empirical Methods in Natural Language Processing (EMNLP)*, pages 2377–2390, Online. Association for Computational Linguistics.

Goran Glavaš, Robert Litschko, Sebastian Ruder, and Ivan Vulić. 2019. How to (properly) evaluate cross-lingual word embeddings: On strong baselines, comparative analyses, and some misconceptions. In *Proceedings of the 57th Annual Meeting of the Association for Computational Linguistics*, pages 710–721, Florence, Italy. Association for Computational Linguistics.

Yedid Hoshen and Lior Wolf. 2018. Non-adversarial unsupervised word translation. In *Proceedings of the 2018 Conference on Empirical Methods in Natural Language Processing*, pages 469–478, Brussels, Belgium. Association for Computational Linguistics.

Armand Joulin, Piotr Bojanowski, Tomas Mikolov, Hervé Jégou, and Edouard Grave. 2018. Loss in translation: Learning bilingual word mapping with a retrieval criterion. In *Proceedings of the 2018 Conference on Empirical Methods in Natural Language Processing*, pages 2979–2984, Brussels, Belgium. Association for Computational Linguistics.

Yova Kementchedjhieva, Mareike Hartmann, and Anders Søgaard. 2019. Lost in evaluation: Misleading benchmarks for bilingual dictionary induction. In *Proceedings of the 2019 Conference on Empirical Methods in Natural Language Processing and the 9th International Joint Conference on Natural Language Processing (EMNLP-IJCNLP)*, pages 3336–3341, Hong Kong, China. Association for Computational Linguistics.

Yu-Hsiang Lin, Chian-Yu Chen, Jean Lee, Zirui Li, Yuyan Zhang, Mengzhou Xia, Shruti Rijhwani, Junxian He, Zhisong Zhang, Xuezhe Ma, Antonios Anastasopoulos, Patrick Littell, and Graham Neubig. 2019. Choosing transfer languages for cross-lingual learning. In *Proceedings of the 57th Annual Meeting of the Association for Computational Linguistics*, pages 3125–3135, Florence, Italy. Association for Computational Linguistics.

Robert Litschko, Ivan Vulic, Simone Paolo Ponzetto, and Goran Glavas. 2021. Evaluating multilingual text encoders for unsupervised cross-lingual retrieval. In *Advances in Information Retrieval - 43rd European Conference on IR Research, ECIR 2021, Virtual Event, March 28 - April 1, 2021, Proceedings, Part I*, volume 12656 of *Lecture Notes in Computer Science*, pages 342–358. Springer.

Tomas Mikolov, Quoc V. Le, and Ilya Sutskever. 2013a. Exploiting similarities among languages for machine translation.

Tomas Mikolov, Ilya Sutskever, Kai Chen, Greg Corrado, and Jeffrey Dean. 2013b. Distributed representations of words and phrases and their compositionality. In *Neural and Information Processing System (NIPS)*.

Aitor Ormazabal, Mikel Artetxe, Gorka Labaka, Aitor Soroa, and Eneko Agirre. 2019. Analyzing the limitations of cross-lingual word embedding mappings. In *Proceedings of the 57th Annual Meeting of the Association for Computational Linguistics*, pages 4990–4995, Florence, Italy. Association for Computational Linguistics.

Barun Patra, Joel Ruben Antony Moniz, Sarthak Garg, Matthew R. Gormley, and Graham Neubig. 2019. Bilingual lexicon induction with semi-supervision in non-isometric embedding spaces. In *Proceedings of the 57th Annual Meeting of the Association for Computational Linguistics*, pages 184–193, Florence, Italy. Association for Computational Linguistics.

F. Pedregosa, G. Varoquaux, A. Gramfort, V. Michel, B. Thirion, O. Grisel, M. Blondel, P. Prettenhofer, R. Weiss, V. Dubourg, J. Vanderplas, A. Passos, D. Cournapeau, M. Brucher, M. Perrot, and E. Duchesnay. 2011. Scikit-learn: Machine learning in Python. *Journal of Machine Learning Research*, 12:2825–2830.

Jeffrey Pennington, Richard Socher, and Christopher Manning. 2014. GloVe: Global vectors for word representation. In *Proceedings of the 2014 Conference on Empirical Methods in Natural Language Processing (EMNLP)*, pages 1532–1543, Doha, Qatar. Association for Computational Linguistics.

Radim Řehůřek and Petr Sojka. 2010. Software Framework for Topic Modelling with Large Corpora. In *Proceedings of the LREC 2010 Workshop on New Challenges for NLP Frameworks*, pages 45–50, Valletta, Malta. ELRA. `http://is.muni.cz/publication/884893/en`.

Sebastian Ruder, Ivan Vulić, and Anders Søgaard. 2019. A survey of cross-lingual word embedding models. *Journal of Artificial Intelligence Research*, 65:569–631.

Holger Schwenk, Vishrav Chaudhary, Shuo Sun, Hongyu Gong, and Francisco Guzmán. 2021. WikiMatrix: Mining 135M parallel sentences in 1620 language pairs from Wikipedia. In *Proceedings of the 16th Conference of the European Chapter of the Association for Computational Linguistics: Main Volume*, pages 1351–1361, Online. Association for Computational Linguistics.

Anders Søgaard, Sebastian Ruder, and Ivan Vulić. 2018. On the limitations of unsupervised bilingual dictionary induction. In *Proceedings of the 56th Annual Meeting of the Association for Computational Linguistics (Volume 1: Long Papers)*, pages 778–788, Melbourne, Australia. Association for Computational Linguistics.

Emma Strubell, Ananya Ganesh, and Andrew McCallum. 2019. Energy and policy considerations for deep learning in nlp. *arXiv preprint arXiv:1906.02243*.

Ivan Vulić, Goran Glavaš, Roi Reichart, and Anna Korhonen. 2019. Do we really need fully unsupervised cross-lingual embeddings? In *Proceedings of the 2019 Conference on Empirical Methods in Natural Language Processing and the 9th International Joint Conference on Natural Language Processing (EMNLP-IJCNLP)*, pages 4407–4418, Hong Kong, China. Association for Computational Linguistics.

Ivan Vulić, Sebastian Ruder, and Anders Søgaard. 2020. Are all good word vector spaces isomorphic? In *Proceedings of the 2020 Conference on Empirical Methods in Natural Language Processing (EMNLP)*, pages 3178–3192, Online. Association for Computational Linguistics.

Chao Xing, Dong Wang, Chao Liu, and Yiye Lin. 2015. Normalized word embedding and orthogonal transform for bilingual word translation. In *Proceedings of the 2015 Conference of the North American Chapter of the Association for Computational Linguistics: Human Language Technologies*, pages 1006–1011, Denver, Colorado. Association for Computational Linguistics.

# On the Cross-lingual Transferability of Contextualized Sense Embeddings

**Kiamehr Rezaee**[1*], **Daniel Loureiro**[2*], **Jose Camacho-Collados**[3], **Mohammad Taher Pilehvar**[4]
[1] Department of Computer Engineering, Iran University of Science and Technology, Tehran, Iran
[2] LIAAD - INESC TEC, Department of Computer Science - FCUP, University of Porto, Portugal
[3] School of Computer Science and Informatics, Cardiff University, United Kingdom
[4] Tehran Institute for Advanced Studies, Khatam University, Tehran, Iran
k_rezaee@comp.iust.ac.ir, daniel.b.loureiro@inesctec.pt,
camachocolladosj@cardiff.ac.uk, mp792@cam.ac.uk

## Abstract

In this paper we analyze the extent to which *contextualized sense embeddings*, i.e., sense embeddings that are computed based on contextualized word embeddings, are transferable across languages. To this end, we compiled a unified cross-lingual benchmark for Word Sense Disambiguation. We then propose two simple strategies to transfer sense-specific knowledge across languages and test them on the benchmark. Experimental results show that this contextualized knowledge can be effectively transferred to similar languages through pre-trained multilingual language models, to the extent that they can outperform monolingual representations learned from existing language-specific data.

## 1 Introduction

Word Sense Disambiguation (WSD) is an indispensable component of language understanding (Navigli, 2009); hence, it has been one of the most studied long-standing problems in lexical semantics. Currently, the dominant WSD paradigm is the supervised approach (Raganato et al., 2017), which highly relies on sense-annotated data. Similarly to many other supervised tasks, the amount of labeled (sense-annotated) data for WSD highly determines downstream performance. One of the factors that make WSD a challenging problem is that creating sense-annotated data is an expensive and arduous process, i.e., the so-called knowledge-acquisition bottleneck (Gale et al., 1992). Moreover, WSD research often focuses on the English language. While datasets for other languages exist (Petrolito and Bond, 2014a; Pasini and Camacho-Collados, 2020), these are generally automatically generated (Delli Bovi et al., 2017; Pasini et al., 2018; Scarlini et al., 2020a; Barba et al., 2020) or not large enough for training supervised WSD models (Navigli et al., 2013a; Moro and Navigli, 2015).[1]

However, recent contextualized embeddings have proven highly effective in English WSD (Peters et al., 2018; Loureiro and Jorge, 2019; Vial et al., 2019; Loureiro et al., 2021), as well as in capturing high-level linguistic knowledge that can be shared or transferred across different languages (Conneau et al., 2020; Cao et al., 2020). Therefore, cross-lingual transfer has opened new opportunities to circumvent the knowledge acquisition bottleneck for less-resourced languages. In this paper, we aim at investigating this opportunity. To this end, we build upon recent research on cross-lingual transfer to compute contextualized sense embeddings and verify if semantic distinctions in the English language are transferable to other languages.

The contributions are threefold: (1) We adapt existing datasets to build a unified benchmark for cross-lingual WSD based on WordNet; (2) we test the effectiveness of contextualized embeddings for cross-lingual transfer in the context of WSD; and (3) we establish relevant and simple baselines for future work in cross-lingual WSD.[2]

## 2 Related Work

This works lies at the intersection of two areas of NLP research: Word Sense Disambiguation and cross-lingual semantic representation. Hence, we cover the recent relevant work in the corresponding literature.

### 2.1 Word Sense Disambiguation

WSD techniques can be broadly put into two categories: knowledge-based and supervised. The main difference lies in that the latter makes use of sense-annotated data for its training phase, whereas the former exploits the encoded knowledge in sense in-

Authors marked with a star (*) contributed equally.

[1] An exception to this pattern is the recent XL-WSD benchmark (Pasini et al., 2021), contemporary to this paper.

[2] Data and code are available at https://github.com/danlou/Zero-MWSD



*Proceedings of the 1st Workshop on Multilingual Representation Learning*, pages 107–115
November 11, 2021. ©2021 Association for Computational Linguistics

| | Train - SemCor | | Test - SemEval-15 | | | Test - SemEval-13 | | | | | Test - FN |
|---|---|---|---|---|---|---|---|---|---|---|---|
| | EN | IT | EN | IT | ES | EN | FR | DE | ES | IT | FA |
| Nouns | 87,002 | 43,058 | 512 | 515 | 512 | 1,637 | 1,438 | 958 | 1,176 | 1,448 | 3,063 |
| Verbs | 88,334 | 25,164 | 252 | 233 | 260 | – | – | – | – | – | 29 |
| Adj. | 31,753 | 16,029 | 136 | 159 | 119 | – | – | – | – | – | 366 |
| Adv. | 18,947 | 7,951 | 82 | 25 | 53 | – | – | – | – | – | 40 |
| ALL | 226,036 | 92,202 | 982 | 932 | 944 | 1,637 | 1,438 | 958 | 1,176 | 1,448 | 3,498 |
| RAW | 226,036 | 92,202 | 1,175 | 1,151 | 1,155 | 1,931 | 1,656 | 1,467 | 1,481 | 1,706 | 4,272 |

Table 1: Number of sense-annotated instances in the benchmark datasets after cleaning and unification. RAW counts correspond to number of instances in the original datasets before cleaning and unification.

ventories such as WordNet (e.g. semantic relations, sense glosses, distributions, etc.) for inference.

For the last decade, the supervised approach has been the dominant paradigm for WSD (Raganato et al., 2017), either the conventional feature-based systems (Zhong and Ng, 2010; Iacobacci et al., 2016), LSTM-driven techniques (Melamud et al., 2016; Yuan et al., 2016), or the more recent trend empowered by pre-trained language models (Loureiro and Jorge, 2019; Scarlini et al., 2020b). In the latter approaches, feature extraction strategies where sense embeddings are determined by averaging a word's contextualised representations have proven surprisingly effective (Loureiro et al., 2021), even in multilingual settings (Bevilacqua and Navigli, 2020; Raganato et al., 2020). We extend this simple idea to the cross-lingual setting, showing that the vanilla contextualized sense embeddings achieving outstanding results in the monolingual setting can also be effective for transferring knowledge across languages.

### 2.2 Cross-lingual representation

WSD performance is largely dependent on the availability of large amounts of manually-curated sense annotations. However, as usual in NLP, most of the sense-annotated corpora are dedicated to the English language only. Nonetheless, recent work on cross-lingual word embeddings has shown that it is possible to reliably align monolingual semantic spaces with minimal or no supervision (Artetxe et al., 2017; Zhang et al., 2017; Conneau et al., 2018). Moreover, pre-trained language models, like BERT (Devlin et al., 2019), have been shown to be effective in transferring knowledge across languages (Lample and Conneau, 2019; Pires et al., 2019; Artetxe et al., 2020). In this paper we build on these ideas to take the best of both worlds. Instead of transferring static word embeddings, the main idea is to learn sense embeddings (learned using multilingual language models) that can be shared across languages.

## 3 Cross-lingual WSD Benchmark

In order to develop a unified benchmark for cross-lingual Word Sense Disambiguation, we opted for Princeton **WordNet** (Fellbaum, 1998, PWN) as our reference sense inventory. Thanks to its completeness (covering different parts of speech) and open nature, PWN is regarded as the de facto sense inventory for WSD in English. Moreover, the multilingual efforts from Open Multilingual WordNet (Bond and Foster, 2013), linked to the English PWN, make this resource prompt to extensions for sense-annotated corpora in other languages. We use PWN v3.0 for all our experiments, including the unified cross-lingual benchmark, converting all datasets to both the same XML schema of Raganato et al. (2017) and a practical *json* format. In the following we describe the datasets used to build the cross-lingual WSD benchmark, with Table 1 summarizing their main statistics.

### 3.1 SemCor training sets

As training corpora we used SemCor (Miller et al., 1993), which consists of a collection of English documents annotated with PWN senses. Despite its age, SemCor remains the standard training corpus for WSD due to its large number of manual sense annotations. There have been several efforts towards providing sense annotations for translated versions of SemCor (Petrolito and Bond, 2014a). Consequently, we also considered the Italian version of SemCor included in MultiSemCor (Bentivogli and Pianta, 2005), which is the language with most PWN annotations available. MultiSemCor includes sense annotations from PWN v1.6; hence, we used the mappings from Daudé et al. (2000) to convert these into PWN v3.0 annotations.

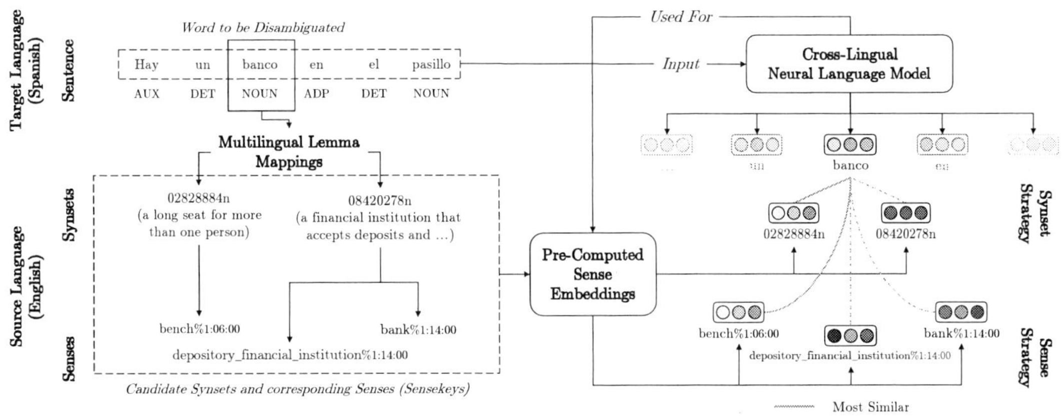


Figure 1: Overview of the proposed method for multilingual zero-shot word sense disambiguation. The example sentence presented ('There is a bench in the hall', in English) is using a different language (target) than our sense inventory (source), but using multilingual language models and lemma mappings, we demonstrate how it's still possible to perform disambiguation, using either variations of our method (sense and synset strategies).

### 3.2 Multilingual SemEval test sets

We considered two multilingual datasets: SemEval 2013 (Navigli et al., 2013a) available for English, French and Italian, and SemEval 2015 (Moro and Navigli, 2015), available for English, French, Italian, Spanish and German. These datasets were annotated with BabelNet (Navigli and Ponzetto, 2012), a resource that contains WordNet, among other linked sense inventories. Therefore, from each dataset we simply considered those disambiguated instances that could be mapped to PWN 3.0, while the rest of instances were removed. We also rely on BabelNet to gather a representative set of candidate senses for any given target word.

### 3.3 FarsNet

To extend the evaluation set beyond European languages, we first performed an exhaustive search for available WSD datasets that could be integrated into our benchmark, unsuccessfully.[3] To fill this gap, we constructed an evaluation set for a distant low-resource language: Farsi. This dataset was constructed based on example sentences provided with the FarsNet project (Shamsfard et al., 2010). As the largest Farsi WordNet available, FarsNet is constructed in a semi-automatic manner. In its latest version (v3.0), the lexical resource covers more than 100K lexical entries in around 40K synsets. FarsNet synsets are aligned with those in PWN 3.0, whenever a link could be established. This allows utilizing the resource in cross-lingual applications.

Many of the synsets in FarsNet are provided with a usage example sentence for one of the terms in the corresponding Farsi synset. We take this as the basis for the construction of the Farsi dataset. Specifically, there are more than 30K Farsi usage examples that are linked to the corresponding synsets in PWN. From these, we extract a set of 4,272 sentences for 3,498 unique target words, after discarding monosemous words and filtering. The distribution of instances over the four parts of speech can be found in Table 1.

## 4 Methodology

We describe two WSD strategies based on contextualized embeddings (§4.1) and propose adaptations to the cross-lingual setting (§4.2). Figure 1 provides an overview of the overarching methodology.

### 4.1 Contextualized Embeddings for WSD

One of the most effective, yet simple, solutions for WSD is matching contextualized embeddings against precomputed sense embeddings learned using the same Neural Language Model (NLM). This approach has been used by earlier works (Melamud et al., 2016; Peters et al., 2018; Loureiro and Jorge, 2019), achieving state-of-the-art results. In these works, sense embeddings (or what we refer to as *contextualized sense embeddings*) are computed from the average of all corresponding contextual embeddings in sense-annotated corpora. One limi-

[3]Our active search efforts are described in the appendix. In general, existing WSD datasets were either under a restrictive license, not available anymore, or not linkable to English PWN.

tation of contextualized sense embeddings is that they only cover those senses that are present in the underlying training corpus. This issue can be alleviated by exploiting the structure of the semantic network. For this, we leverage the simple graph-based propagation method described in Loureiro and Jorge (2019), which allows for a coverage of the entire sense inventory of PWN.

With this strategy we can easily test whether contextualized sense embeddings can be transferred across languages with a solution purely based on matching nearest neighbors only, without any other artifacts. Below we describe the sense-based strategy generally used in the literature for monolingual WSD (sense strategy), and propose a new strategy that can be directly used in a cross-lingual setting (synset strategy).

**Sense strategy.** This strategy is the standard approach used in most WSD methods. After computing our sense embeddings from sense-annotated corpora, we disambiguate target words during testing based on a nearest neighbour strategy using their contextualized embeddings.

**Synset strategy.** In this alternative strategy, we learn synset embeddings by converting the annotated sense labels to synset labels, thus learning representations from multiple word senses that refer to the same concept, and becoming less reliant on lexical features.

### 4.2 Cross-lingual Adaptations

In cross-lingual experiments we are given sense-annotated corpora in a source language but not in the target language. Therefore, a multilingual NLM such as mBERT (Devlin et al., 2019) or XLM-R (Lample and Conneau, 2019) is required.

We adapt the sense strategy to the cross-lingual setting as follows. Given the lemma and part-of-speech of a word in the target language, we first gather all the candidate synsets in the source language from Babelnet. Then each candidate synset is associated with one or more senses. For example, we can find two candidate PWN senses for the word *presente* (*present* in Spanish). The first sense corresponds to the PWN synset "intermediate between past and future" and the second to "being or existing in a specified place". Finally, we compute the cosine distance from the contextualized embeddings of target word (*presente*) to all the candidate contextualized sense embeddings from the source language (*present%3:00:01::* and *present%3:00:02::*, respectively), and select the closest candidate sense. Note that the synset strategy does not require adaptation because synsets are language-independent.

## 5 Evaluation

We evaluate the proposed strategies in two different settings, using WSD as our test bed: monolingual (Section 5.1) and cross-lingual (Section 5.2).

**Experimental setting.** We use **RoBERTa** (Liu et al., 2019) for monolingual experiments, and **XLM-R** (Conneau et al., 2020) for cross-lingual experiments.[4] These two models are state-of-the-art for English and multilingual tasks while sharing a very similar architecture. The most important difference between these models is that while RoBERTa is pre-trained only on English texts, XLM-R is pre-trained on 100 languages (unevenly distributed). We use the large variants of these models (355M parameters for each).[5] All results are measured according to the F-measure.

### 5.1 Experiment 1: Monolingual WSD

Before delving into the cross-lingual experiments, we present monolingual results in English and Italian (languages with training data) in Table 2. The aim of this experiment is twofold: (1) compare the effectiveness of the disambiguation strategies, and (2) compare the performance of monolingual (RoBERTa) and multilingual models (XLM-R).

**Baselines.** As additional baselines, we add the results of the original BERT-based **LMMS** model (Loureiro and Jorge, 2019) and Context2Vec (**C2V**) (Melamud et al., 2016), which is also based on a simple nearest neighbors strategy, in this case with an LSTM instead of a transformer model.

**Results.** Table 2 shows the results of this English monolingual experiment.[6] We report results in all datasets from the unified WSD evaluation framework of Raganato et al. (2017).[7] As expected, the

[4]Following Loureiro and Jorge (2019), we consider token-level embeddings as the average of sub-token embeddings, which is computed as the sum of embeddings from the last 4 layers of the corresponding NLM.

[5]Our code is based on the Fairseq toolkit (Ott et al., 2019). We run our experiments on a single RTX 2070, with a runtime under 2 hours for generating all embeddings used in this work.

[6]We experimented with NLMs trained exclusively on Italian (i.e. UmBERTo-CC and dbmdz-IT-XXL), but found that the senses learned using those models do not consistently outperform the MFS baseline on both test sets.

[7]Datasets of the unified WSD framework: Senseval-2 (Edmonds and Cotton, 2001), Senseval-3 (Mihalcea et al., 2004),

| Model | Strategy | SensEval-2 | SensEval-3 | SemEval-2007 | SemEval-2013 | SemEval-2015 | ALL |
|---|---|---|---|---|---|---|---|
| RoBERTa | Sense | **75.5** | 73.5 | **69.2** | 72.2 | 75.9 | **73.9** |
| | Synset | 74.4 | **74.1** | 68.4 | 72.1 | **76.0** | 73.6 |
| XLM-R | Sense | 71.0 | 67.8 | 61.5 | 70.1 | 72.1 | 69.5 |
| | Synset | 70.0 | 67.2 | 60.9 | 69.7 | 72.3 | 69.0 |
| LMMS | Sense | *75.4* | *74.0* | *66.4* | **72.7** | *75.3* | *73.8* |
| C2V | Sense | *71.8* | *69.1* | *61.3* | *65.6* | *71.9* | *69.0* |
| *MFS* | – | *65.6* | *66.0* | *54.5* | *63.8* | *67.1* | *64.8* |

Table 2: English monolingual F1 results on the evaluation framework of Raganato et al. (2017) for the two strategies: Sense (Se) and Synset (Sy).

purely monolingual model performs better than the multilingual one. As for the strategies, the usual sense strategy shows better performance. Nonetheless, the language-independent synset strategy attains competitive results, clearly outperforming a strong baseline such as Context2Vec, for example.

### 5.2 Experiment 2: Cross-lingual Transfer

We experimented with a pure zero-shot cross-lingual setting where senses are learned in one language (in our case English or Italian) and directly evaluated on another language. We employ the two strategies explained in Section 4.

**Baselines.** As baselines we include a random baseline (i.e., randomly picking a sense/synset from the target language's inventory), and a system that relies on the **static** word embeddings from XLM-R (i.e., input layer embeddings of XLM-R without making use of the context), instead of the **contextualized** sense embeddings obtained as described in Section 4.1.[8] The reason behind the possibility of using static word embeddings in this WSD setting lies in the fact that different senses of a word may be translated into different words in another language. This baseline makes use of the same sense and synset strategies.

**Results.** Table 3 shows the results for the zero-shot cross-lingual WSD experiment.[9] XLM-R outperforms the baselines by a large margin and proves to be robust in the cross-lingual setting (with performance in the same ballpark as in the monolingual setting). In particular, the fact that XLM-R outperforms the static embedding baseline by a large margin reinforces the idea that contextualized sense embedding are indeed transferable across languages (at least similar ones) to a large extent, which in turn opens up interesting avenues for future work on cross-lingual WSD. Nonetheless, as with English WSD, there are still many open questions as to what extent the fine granularity of PWN can be captured by automatic models.

Finally, as expected, learning representations using the larger English SemCor provides consistently better results than the smaller Italian counterpart, except for the distant language Farsi. More interestingly, XLM-R senses learned from English data can outperform the senses from the same model learned from language-specific data in the Italian test sets. Nonetheless, the simple synset strategy on Italian clearly surpasses the static baselines as well.

## 6 Conclusions

In this paper, we analyzed to what extent contextualized embeddings can be transferred across languages, using WSD as our test bed. To this end, we developed a unified framework that can be used for evaluating cross-lingual models. The first results are encouraging, as they show that multilingual language models can learn contextualized sense embeddings that can be effectively transferred from one language to another, attaining competitive results in WSD with no access to annotated data in the target language or external resources. One limitation of this work is in the nature of languages evaluated, which are all Indo-European for which test data was available. As future work it will be interesting to extend this benchmark to languages

SemEval-2007 (Agirre et al., 2007), SemEval-2013 (Navigli et al., 2013b), and SemEval-2015 (Moro and Navigli, 2015).

[8]We also tried to include Babelfy (Moro et al., 2014) as a multilingual knowledge-based baseline, without success. The latest public API of Babelfy misses over 50% of the instances in our benchmark and therefore the recall was suboptimal.

[9]English monolingual results slightly differ from those in Table 2, as in this case we focused on the BabelNet portion of the SemEval datasets (as explained in Section 3.2). For Italian we only report the synset strategy, as we could not have access to all the senses in MultiWordNet (Pianta et al., 2002).

| Language | Strategy | Type | SemEval-13 | | | | | SemEval-15 | | | FN |
|---|---|---|---|---|---|---|---|---|---|---|---|
| | | | EN | FR | DE | ES | IT | EN | IT | ES | FA |
| English | Se | Static | *38.1* | 28.0 | 50.1 | 38.7 | 41.0 | *41.5* | 45.2 | 40.6 | 48.7 |
| | | Contextualized | ***67.4*** | **60.7** | 57.5 | **69.7** | **66.1** | ***71.7*** | 69.1 | **68.0** | 55.4 |
| | Sy | Static | *41.0* | 30.6 | 48.2 | 39.4 | 43.2 | *39.8* | 46.2 | 43.6 | 48.2 |
| | | Contextualized | *66.3* | 59.0 | **58.3** | 66.8 | 64.9 | *71.4* | **69.5** | 67.2 | **56.4** |
| Italian | Sy | Static | 51.3 | 41.0 | 55.1 | 54.4 | 48.3 | 54.7 | 54.6 | 56.8 | 46.7 |
| | | Contextualized | 63.2 | 55.9 | 55.4 | 65.9 | *62.9* | 67.1 | *67.2* | 65.4 | **56.4** |
| *Random baseline* | | | 37.8 | 25.8 | 47.9 | 38.7 | 38.6 | 41.7 | 44.5 | 38.0 | 49.5 |

Table 3: F1 results using zero-shot cross-lingual transfer (XLM-R) with English or Italian annotations. Two different types of sense embedding: static (S) and contextualized (C). Monolingual setting (i.e., learn and test in the same language) is also included for completeness.

from different families, for which cross-lingual embedding transfer has been shown to be more challenging (Glavaš et al., 2019; Doval et al., 2020).

## References


Eneko Agirre, Lluís Màrquez, and Richard Wicentowski, editors. 2007. *Proceedings of SemEval-2007*.

Ali Alkhatlan, Jugal Kalita, and Ahmed Alhaddad. 2018. Word sense disambiguation for arabic exploiting arabic wordnet and word embedding. *Procedia Computer Science*, 142:50 – 60. Arabic Computational Linguistics.

Mikel Artetxe, Gorka Labaka, and Eneko Agirre. 2017. Learning bilingual word embeddings with (almost) no bilingual data. In *Proceedings of the 55th Annual Meeting of the Association for Computational Linguistics (Volume 1: Long Papers)*, pages 451–462, Vancouver, Canada. Association for Computational Linguistics.

Mikel Artetxe, Sebastian Ruder, and Dani Yogatama. 2020. On the cross-lingual transferability of monolingual representations.

Edoardo Barba, Luigi Procopio, Niccolo Campolungo, Tommaso Pasini, and Roberto Navigli. 2020. Mulan: Multilingual label propagation for word sense disambiguation. In *Proc. of IJCAI*, pages 3837–3844.

Luisa Bentivogli and Emanuele Pianta. 2005. Exploiting parallel texts in the creation of multilingual semantically annotated resources: the multisemcor corpus. *Natural Language Engineering*, 11(3):247–261.

Michele Bevilacqua and Roberto Navigli. 2020. Breaking through the 80% glass ceiling: Raising the state of the art in word sense disambiguation by incorporating knowledge graph information. In *Proceedings of the 58th Annual Meeting of the Association for Computational Linguistics*, pages 2854–2864.

Francis Bond and Ryan Foster. 2013. Linking and extending an open multilingual Wordnet. In *Proceedings of the 51st Annual Meeting of the Association for Computational Linguistics (Volume 1: Long Papers)*, pages 1352–1362, Sofia, Bulgaria. Association for Computational Linguistics.

Steven Cao, Nikita Kitaev, and Dan Klein. 2020. Multilingual alignment of contextual word representations. In *Proceedings of ICLR*.

Alexis Conneau, Kartikay Khandelwal, Naman Goyal, Vishrav Chaudhary, Guillaume Wenzek, Francisco Guzmán, Edouard Grave, Myle Ott, Luke Zettlemoyer, and Veselin Stoyanov. 2020. Unsupervised cross-lingual representation learning at scale. In *Proceedings of ACL*.

Alexis Conneau, Guillaume Lample, Marc'Aurelio Ranzato, Ludovic Denoyer, and Hervé Jégou. 2018. Word translation without parallel data. In *Proceedings of ICLR*.

J. Daudé, L. Padró, and G. Rigau. 2000. Mapping WordNets using structural information. In *Proceedings of the 38th Annual Meeting of the Association for Computational Linguistics*, pages 504–511, Hong Kong. Association for Computational Linguistics.

Claudio Delli Bovi, Jose Camacho-Collados, Alessandro Raganato, and Roberto Navigli. 2017. EuroSense: Automatic harvesting of multilingual sense annotations from parallel text. In *Proceedings of the 55th Annual Meeting of the Association for Computational Linguistics (Volume 2: Short Papers)*, pages 594–600, Vancouver, Canada. Association for Computational Linguistics.

Jacob Devlin, Ming-Wei Chang, Kenton Lee, and Kristina Toutanova. 2019. Bert: Pre-training of deep bidirectional transformers for language understanding. In *Proceedings of the 2019 Conference of the North American Chapter of the Association for*

Computational Linguistics: Human Language Technologies, Volume 1 (Long and Short Papers)*, pages 4171–4186.

Mona Diab, Musa Alkhalifa, Sabry ElKateb, Christiane Fellbaum, Aous Mansouri, and Martha Palmer. 2007. SemEval-2007 task 18: Arabic semantic labeling. In *Proceedings of the Fourth International Workshop on Semantic Evaluations (SemEval-2007)*, pages 93–98, Prague, Czech Republic. Association for Computational Linguistics.

Yerai Doval, Jose Camacho-Collados, Luis Espinosa Anke, and Steven Schockaert. 2020. On the robustness of unsupervised and semi-supervised cross-lingual word embedding learning. In *Proceedings of The 12th Language Resources and Evaluation Conference*, pages 4013–4023, Marseille, France. European Language Resources Association.

Philip Edmonds and Scott Cotton. 2001. SENSEVAL-2: Overview. In *Proceedings of SENSEVAL-2 Second International Workshop on Evaluating Word Sense Disambiguation Systems*, pages 1–5, Toulouse, France. Association for Computational Linguistics.

Christiane Fellbaum, editor. 1998. *WordNet: An Electronic Database*. MIT Press, Cambridge, MA.

William A. Gale, Kenneth Church, and David Yarowsky. 1992. A method for disambiguating word senses in a corpus. *Computers and the Humanities*, 26:415–439.

Goran Glavaš, Robert Litschko, Sebastian Ruder, and Ivan Vulić. 2019. How to (properly) evaluate cross-lingual word embeddings: On strong baselines, comparative analyses, and some misconceptions. In *Proceedings of the 57th Annual Meeting of the Association for Computational Linguistics*, pages 710–721, Florence, Italy. Association for Computational Linguistics.

Ignacio Iacobacci, Mohammad Taher Pilehvar, and Roberto Navigli. 2016. Embeddings for word sense disambiguation: An evaluation study. In *Proceedings of the 54th Annual Meeting of the Association for Computational Linguistics (Volume 1: Long Papers)*, pages 897–907, Berlin, Germany. Association for Computational Linguistics.

Peng Jin, Yunfang Wu, and Shiwen Yu. 2007. SemEval-2007 task 05: Multilingual Chinese-English lexical sample. In *Proceedings of the Fourth International Workshop on Semantic Evaluations (SemEval-2007)*, pages 19–23, Prague, Czech Republic. Association for Computational Linguistics.

Guillaume Lample and Alexis Conneau. 2019. Cross-lingual language model pretraining. *CoRR*, abs/1901.07291.

Yinhan Liu, Myle Ott, Naman Goyal, Jingfei Du, Mandar Joshi, Danqi Chen, Omer Levy, Mike Lewis, Luke Zettlemoyer, and Veselin Stoyanov. 2019. Roberta: A robustly optimized BERT pretraining approach. *CoRR*, abs/1907.11692.

Daniel Loureiro and Alípio Jorge. 2019. Language modelling makes sense: Propagating representations through WordNet for full-coverage word sense disambiguation. In *Proceedings of the 57th Annual Meeting of the Association for Computational Linguistics*, pages 5682–5691, Florence, Italy. Association for Computational Linguistics.

Daniel Loureiro, Kiamehr Rezaee, Mohammad Taher Pilehvar, and Jose Camacho-Collados. 2021. Analysis and evaluation of language models for word sense disambiguation. *Computational Linguistics*, pages 1–55.

Oren Melamud, Jacob Goldberger, and Ido Dagan. 2016. context2vec: Learning generic context embedding with bidirectional LSTM. In *Proceedings of The 20th SIGNLL Conference on Computational Natural Language Learning*, pages 51–61, Berlin, Germany. Association for Computational Linguistics.

Rada Mihalcea, Timothy Chklovski, and Adam Kilgarriff. 2004. The Senseval-3 English lexical sample task. In *Proceedings of Senseval-3: The Third International Workshop on the Evaluation of Systems for the Semantic Analysis of Text*, pages 25–28.

Rada Mihalcea and Phil Edmonds. 2004. Senseval-3: Third international workshop on the evaluation of systems for the semantic analysis of text. In *Association for Computational Linguistics*, volume 4.

George A. Miller, Claudia Leacock, Randee Tengi, and Ross Bunker. 1993. A semantic concordance. In *Proceedings of the 3rd DARPA Workshop on Human Language Technology*, pages 303–308, Plainsboro, N.J.

Andrea Moro and Roberto Navigli. 2015. Semeval-2015 task 13: Multilingual all-words sense disambiguation and entity linking. *Proceedings of SemEval-2015*.

Andrea Moro, Alessandro Raganato, and Roberto Navigli. 2014. Entity Linking meets Word Sense Disambiguation: a Unified Approach. *Transactions of the Association for Computational Linguistics (TACL)*, 2:231–244.

Roberto Navigli. 2009. Word Sense Disambiguation: A survey. *ACM Computing Surveys*, 41(2):1–69.

Roberto Navigli, David Jurgens, and Daniele Vannella. 2013a. SemEval-2013 task 12: Multilingual word sense disambiguation. In *Second Joint Conference on Lexical and Computational Semantics (*SEM), Volume 2: Proceedings of the Seventh International Workshop on Semantic Evaluation (SemEval 2013)*, pages 222–231, Atlanta, Georgia, USA. Association for Computational Linguistics.

Roberto Navigli, David Jurgens, and Daniele Vannella. 2013b. SemEval-2013 Task 12: Multilingual Word Sense Disambiguation. In *Proceedings of SemEval 2013*, pages 222–231.

Roberto Navigli and Simone Paolo Ponzetto. 2012. BabelNet: The automatic construction, evaluation and application of a wide-coverage multilingual semantic network. *Artificial Intelligence*, 193:217–250.

Manabu Okumura, Kiyoaki Shirai, Kanako Komiya, and Hikaru Yokono. 2010. SemEval-2010 task: Japanese WSD. In *Proceedings of the 5th International Workshop on Semantic Evaluation*, pages 69–74, Uppsala, Sweden. Association for Computational Linguistics.

Zeynep Orhan, Emine Çelik, and Demirgüç Neslihan. 2007. SemEval-2007 task 12: Turkish lexical sample task. In *Proceedings of the Fourth International Workshop on Semantic Evaluations (SemEval-2007)*, pages 59–63, Prague, Czech Republic. Association for Computational Linguistics.

Myle Ott, Sergey Edunov, Alexei Baevski, Angela Fan, Sam Gross, Nathan Ng, David Grangier, and Michael Auli. 2019. fairseq: A fast, extensible toolkit for sequence modeling. In *Proceedings of the 2019 Conference of the North American Chapter of the Association for Computational Linguistics (Demonstrations)*, pages 48–53, Minneapolis, Minnesota. Association for Computational Linguistics.

Tommaso Pasini and Jose Camacho-Collados. 2020. A short survey on sense-annotated corpora. In *Proceedings of The 12th Language Resources and Evaluation Conference*, pages 5759–5765, Marseille, France. European Language Resources Association.

Tommaso Pasini, Francesco Elia, and Roberto Navigli. 2018. Huge automatically extracted trainingsets for multilingual word SenseDisambiguation. In *Proceedings of the Eleventh International Conference on Language Resources and Evaluation (LREC 2018)*, Miyazaki, Japan. European Language Resources Association (ELRA).

Tommaso Pasini, Alessandro Raganato, Roberto Navigli, et al. 2021. Xl-wsd: An extra-large and crosslingual evaluation framework for word sense disambiguation. In *Proceedings of the AAAI Conference on Artificial Intelligence*. AAAI Press.

Matthew Peters, Mark Neumann, Mohit Iyyer, Matt Gardner, Christopher Clark, Kenton Lee, and Luke Zettlemoyer. 2018. Deep contextualized word representations. In *Proceedings of the 2018 Conference of the North American Chapter of the Association for Computational Linguistics: Human Language Technologies, Volume 1 (Long Papers)*, pages 2227–2237, New Orleans, Louisiana. Association for Computational Linguistics.

Tommaso Petrolito and Francis Bond. 2014a. A survey of WordNet annotated corpora. In *Proceedings of the Seventh Global Wordnet Conference*, pages 236–245, Tartu, Estonia. University of Tartu Press.

Tommaso Petrolito and Francis Bond. 2014b. A survey of wordnet annotated corpora. In *Proceedings Global WordNet Conference, GWC-2014*, pages 236–245.

Emanuele Pianta, Luisa Bentivogli, and Christian Girardi. 2002. Multiwordnet: developing an aligned multilingual database. In *First international conference on global WordNet*, pages 293–302.

Telmo Pires, Eva Schlinger, and Dan Garrette. 2019. How multilingual is multilingual BERT? In *Proceedings of the 57th Annual Meeting of the Association for Computational Linguistics*, pages 4996–5001, Florence, Italy. Association for Computational Linguistics.

Alessandro Raganato, Jose Camacho-Collados, and Roberto Navigli. 2017. Word sense disambiguation: A unified evaluation framework and empirical comparison. In *Proceedings of EACL*, pages 99–110, Valencia, Spain.

Alessandro Raganato, Tommaso Pasini, Jose Camacho-Collados, and Mohammad Taher Pilehvar. 2020. XL-WiC: A multilingual benchmark for evaluating semantic contextualization. In *Proceedings of the 2020 Conference on Empirical Methods in Natural Language Processing (EMNLP)*, pages 7193–7206, Online. Association for Computational Linguistics.

Bianca Scarlini, Tommaso Pasini, and Roberto Navigli. 2020a. Sense-annotated corpora for word sense disambiguation in multiple languages and domains. In *Proceedings of The 12th Language Resources and Evaluation Conference*, pages 5905–5911.

Bianca Scarlini, Tommaso Pasini, and Roberto Navigli. 2020b. SensEmBERT: Context-Enhanced Sense Embeddings for Multilingual Word Sense Disambiguation. In *Proceedings of the Thirty-Fourth Conference on Artificial Intelligence*. Association for the Advancement of Artificial Intelligence.

Mehrnoush Shamsfard, Akbar Hesabi, Hakimeh Fadaei, Niloofar Mansoory, Payam Noor, Ali Reza Gholi Famian, Somayeh Bagherbeigi, Elham Fekri, and Maliheh Monshizadeh. 2010. Semi automatic development of FarsNet; the Persian WordNet. In *Proceedings of 5th global WordNet conference*.

Kiyoaki Shirai. 2002. Construction of a word sense tagged corpus for SENSEVAL-2 Japanese dictionary task. In *Proceedings of the Third International Conference on Language Resources and Evaluation (LREC'02)*, Las Palmas, Canary Islands - Spain. European Language Resources Association (ELRA).

Loïc Vial, Benjamin Lecouteux, and Didier Schwab. 2019. Sense vocabulary compression through the semantic knowledge of wordnet for neural word sense disambiguation. In *Proceedings of the 10th Global WordNet Conference*.

Ralph Weischedel, Sameer Pradhan, Lance Ramshaw, Martha Palmer, Nianwen Xue, Mitchell Marcus, Ann Taylor, Craig Greenberg, Eduard Hovy, Robert Belvin, et al. 2011. Ontonotes release 4.0. *LDC2011T03, Philadelphia, Penn.: Linguistic Data Consortium.*

Dayu Yuan, Julian Richardson, Ryan Doherty, Colin Evans, and Eric Altendorf. 2016. Semi-supervised word sense disambiguation with neural models. In *Proceedings of COLING*, pages 1374–1385.

Meng Zhang, Yang Liu, Huanbo Luan, and Maosong Sun. 2017. Earth mover's distance minimization for unsupervised bilingual lexicon induction. In *Proceedings of the 2017 Conference on Empirical Methods in Natural Language Processing*, pages 1934–1945, Copenhagen, Denmark. Association for Computational Linguistics.

Zhi Zhong and Hwee Tou Ng. 2010. It makes sense: A wide-coverage word sense disambiguation system for free text. In *Proceedings of the ACL 2010 System Demonstrations*, pages 78–83, Uppsala, Sweden. Association for Computational Linguistics.

## A Appendix: Compilation of WordNet-based WSD Datasets

In addition to the datasets included in our benchmark, mostly composed of European languages, we made an effort to retrieve and compile datasets for other languages. In Table 4 we provide details about our unsuccessful attempts and issues to integrate existing WSD datasets in the literature, mainly taken from DKPro[10] and the survey of Petrolito and Bond (2014b). Not only are most of these datasets unavailable, we also learn from their respective publications that the sense inventories used often aren't based on WordNet, and thus would require manual remapping of annotations for integration into our benchmark.

[10] https://dkpro.github.io/dkpro-wsd/corpora/

| Resource | Language | # Instances | Inventory | Availability | License |
|---|---|---|---|---|---|
| Senseval-2 (Shirai, 2002) | Japanese | 10,000 | IKJ | N/A | N/A |
| Senseval-2 (Edmonds and Cotton, 2001) | Korean | N/A | N/A | N/A | N/A |
| Senseval-3 (Mihalcea and Edmonds, 2004) | Chinese | 1,204 | HowNet | Publicly Avail. | Public Domain |
| SemEval-2007 Task 5 (Jin et al., 2007) | Chinese | 3,621 | CSD | N/A | N/A |
| SemEval-2007 Task 11 (Orhan et al., 2007) | Turkish | 5,385 | TKD | N/A | N/A |
| SemEval-2007 Task 18 (Diab et al., 2007) | Arabic | 888 | AWN | N/A | N/A |
| SemEval-2010 Task 16 (Okumura et al., 2010) | Japanese | 2,500 | IKJ | On Request | Restrictive |
| OntoNotes (Weischedel et al., 2011) | Arabic | 200K | Coarse WN | For Members | Restrictive |
| OntoNotes (Weischedel et al., 2011) | Chinese | 800K | Coarse WN | For Members | Restrictive |
| Alkhatlan et al. (2018) | Arabic | 240 | AWN | N/A | N/A |

Table 4: Details about the various WSD datasets covering non-European languages surveyed in our work (N/A: Not Available; WN: WordNet; AWN: Arabic WordNet; we refer to respective papers for remaining acronyms).

# Small Data? No Problem! Exploring the Viability of Pretrained Multilingual Language Models for Low-Resource Languages

**Kelechi Ogueji, Yuxin Zhu, and Jimmy Lin**
David R. Cheriton School of Computer Science
University of Waterloo
{kelechi.ogueji, yuxin.zhu, jimmylin}@uwaterloo.ca

## Abstract

Pretrained multilingual language models have been shown to work well on many languages for a variety of downstream NLP tasks. However, these models are known to require a lot of training data. This consequently leaves out a huge percentage of the world's languages as they are under-resourced. Furthermore, a major motivation behind these models is that lower-resource languages benefit from joint training with higher-resource languages. In this work, we challenge this assumption and present the first attempt at training a multilingual language model on only low-resource languages. We show that it is possible to train competitive multilingual language models on less than 1 GB of text. Our model, named AfriBERTa, covers 11 African languages, including the first language model for 4 of these languages. Evaluations on named entity recognition and text classification spanning 10 languages show that our model outperforms mBERT and XLM-R in several languages and is very competitive overall. Results suggest that our "small data" approach based on similar languages may sometimes work better than joint training on large datasets with high-resource languages. Code, data and models are released at https://github.com/keleog/afriberta.

## 1 Introduction

Pretrained language models have risen to the fore of natural language processing (NLP), achieving impressive performance on a variety of NLP tasks. The multilingual version of these models such as XLM-R (Conneau et al., 2020) and mBERT (Devlin et al., 2019) have also been shown to generalize well to many languages. However, these models are known to require a lot of training data, which is often absent for low-resource languages. Also, high-resource languages usually make up a significant part of the training data, as it is hypothesized that they help boost transfer to lower-resource languages. Hence, there has been no known attempt to investigate if it is possible to pretrain multilingual language models solely on low-resource languages without any transfer from higher-resource languages, despite the numerous benefits that this could provide. Motivated by this gap in the literature, the goal of our work is to explore the viability of multilingual language models pretrained from scratch on low-resource languages and to understand how to pretrain such models in this setting.

We introduce AfriBERTa, a transformer-based multilingual language models trained on 11 African languages, all of which are low-resource.[1] We evaluate this model on named entity recognition (NER) and text classification downstream tasks on 10 low-resource languages. Our models outperform larger models like mBERT and XLM-R by up to 10 F1 points on text classification, and also outperform these models on several languages in the NER task. Across all languages, we obtain very competitive performance to these larger models. In summary, our contributions are as follows:

1. We show that competitive multilingual language models can be pretrained from scratch solely on low-resource languages without any high-resource transfer.

2. We show that it is possible to pretrain these models on less than 1 GB of text data and highlight the many practical benefits of this.

3. Our extensive experiments highlight important factors to consider when pretraining multilingual language models in low-resource settings.

4. We introduce language models for 4 languages, improving the representation of low-resource languages in modern NLP tools.

[1] One of the languages (Gahuza) is counted twice because it is a code-mixed language consisting of Kinyarwanda and Kirundi.



*Proceedings of the 1st Workshop on Multilingual Representation Learning*, pages 116–126
November 11, 2021. ©2021 Association for Computational Linguistics

Our results show that, for the first time, it is possible to pretrain a multilingual language model from scratch on only low-resource languages and obtain good performance on downstream tasks.

## 2 Related Work

In recent years, unsupervised learning of text representations has significantly advanced natural language processing tasks. Static representations from pretrained word embeddings (Mikolov et al., 2013; Pennington et al., 2014) were improved upon by learning contextualized representations (Peters et al., 2018). This has been noticeably improved further by pretraining language models (Radford et al., 2018; Devlin et al., 2019) based on transformers (Vaswani et al., 2017). These models have also been extended to the multilingual setting where a single language model is pretrained on several languages without any explicit cross-lingual supervision (Conneau et al., 2020; Devlin et al., 2019).

However, much of this progress has been focused on languages with relatively large amounts of data, commonly referred to as *high-resource languages*. There has especially been very little focus on African languages, despite the over 2000 languages spoken on the continent making up 30.1% of all living languages (Eberhard et al., 2019). This is further visible in NLP publications on these languages. In all the Association for Computational Linguistics (ACL) conferences hosted in 2019, only 0.19% author affiliations were located in Africa (Caines, 2019). Other works (Joshi et al., 2020) have also noted the great disparity in the coverage of languages by NLP technologies. They note that over 90% of the world's 7000+ languages are under-studied by the NLP community.

There have been a few works on learning pretrained embeddings for African languages, although many of them have been static and trained on a specific language (Ezeani et al., 2018; Ogueji and Ahia, 2019; Alabi et al., 2019; Dossou and Sabry, 2021). More recently, Azunre et al. (2021) trained a BERT model on the Twi language. However, they note that their model is biased to the religious domain because much of their data comes from that domain.

While some African languages have been included in multilingual language models, this coverage only scratches the surface of the number of spoken African languages. Furthermore, the languages always make up a minuscule percentage of the training set. For instance, amongst the 104 languages that mBERT was pretrained on, only 3 are African.[2] In XLM-R, there are only 8 African languages out of the 100 languages. In terms of dataset size, the story is the same. African languages make up 4.80 GB out of about 2395 GB that XLM-R was pretrained on, representing just 0.2% of the entire dataset (Conneau et al., 2020). In mBERT, African languages make up just 0.24 GB out of the approximately 100 GB that the model was pretrained on. All of this call for an obvious need for increased representation of African languages in modern NLP tools for the over 1.3 billion speakers on the continent.[3]

Pretrained language models have been shown to perform well when there is a lot of data (Liu et al., 2019; Conneau et al., 2020), but some works have focused on using relatively smaller amounts of data. Martin et al. (2020) showed that it is possible to obtain state-of-the-art result with a French BERT model pretrained on small-scale diverse data. In another work, Micheli et al. (2020) showed that training a French BERT language model on 100 MB of data yields similar performance on question answering as models pretrained on larger datasets. Furthermore, Ortiz Suárez et al. (2020) obtained state-of-the-art performance with ELMo (Peters et al., 2018) language models pretrained on less than 1 GB of Wikipedia text, and Zhang et al. (2020) show that RoBERTa language models (Liu et al., 2019) trained on 10 to 100 million tokens can encode most syntactic and semantic features in its learned text representations.

A common theme among these works is their focus on monolingual language models. While it is possible to learn monolingual language models on smaller amounts of data, it remains to be seen if it is possible in the multilingual case. Our work is the first, to the best of our knowledge, that focuses on pretraining a multilingual language model solely on low-resource languages without any transfer from higher-resource languages.

## 3 Methodology

### 3.1 Data

**Languages:** We focus on 11 African languages, namely Afaan Oromoo (also called Oromo),

[2] https://github.com/google-research/bert/blob/master/multilingual.md

[3] https://www.worldometers.info/world-population/africa-population/ (accessed on February 19, 2021)

| Language | Family | Speakers | Region |
|---|---|---|---|
| Afaan Oromoo | Afro-Asiatic | 50M | East |
| Amharic | Afro-Asiatic | 26M | East |
| Gahuza | Niger-Congo | 21M | East |
| Hausa | Afro-Asiatic | 63M | West |
| Igbo | Niger-Congo | 27M | West |
| Nigerian Pidgin | English Creole | 75M | West |
| Somali | Afro-Asiatic | 19M | East |
| Swahili | Niger-Congo | 98M | Central/East |
| Tigrinya | Afro-Asiatic | 7M | East |
| Yorùbá | Niger-Congo | 42M | West |

Table 1: **Language Information:** For each language, its family, number of speakers (Eberhard et al., 2019), and regions in Africa spoken.

| Language | # Sent. | # Tok. | Size (GB) |
|---|---|---|---|
| Afaan Oromoo | 410,840 | 6,870,959 | 0.051 |
| Amharic | 525,024 | 1,303,086 | 0.213 |
| Gahuza | 131,952 | 3,669,538 | 0.026 |
| Hausa | 1,282,996 | 27,889,299 | 0.150 |
| Igbo | 337,081 | 6,853,500 | 0.042 |
| Nigerian Pidgin | 161,842 | 8,709,498 | 0.048 |
| Somali | 995,043 | 27,332,348 | 0.170 |
| Swahili | 1,442,911 | 30,053,834 | 0.185 |
| Tigrinya | 12,075 | 280,397 | 0.027 |
| Yorùbá | 149,147 | 4,385,797 | 0.027 |
| Total | 5,448,911 | 108,800,600 | 0.939 |

Table 2: **Dataset Size:** Size of each language in the dataset covering numbers of sentences, tokens and uncompressed disk size.

Amharic, Gahuza (a code-mixed language containing Kinyarwanda and Kirundi), Hausa, Igbo, Nigerian Pidgin, Somali, Swahili, Tigrinya and Yorùbá. These languages all come from three language families: Niger-Congo, Afro Asiatic and English Creole. We select these languages because they are the languages supported by the British Broadcasting Corporation (BBC) News, which was our main source of data.[4] We also obtain additional data from the Common Crawl Corpus (Conneau et al., 2020; Wenzek et al., 2020) for languages available there, specifically Amharic, Afaan Oromoo, Amharic, Hausa, Igbo, Somali and Swahili. Table 1 provides details about the languages used in pretraining our models.

**Size:** The total size of our pretraining corpus is 0.94 GB (108.8 million tokens). In comparison, XLM-R was pretrained on about 2395 GB (164.0 billion tokens) (Conneau et al., 2020), and mBERT was trained on roughly 100 GB (12.8 billion tokens).[5] Following findings from Liu et al. (2019) and Conneau et al. (2020) that more data is always better for pretrained language modelling, our small corpus makes our task even more challenging, and one can already see that our model is at a disadvantage compared to XLM-R and mBERT.

| Language | XLM-R | mBERT | AfriBERTa |
|---|---|---|---|
| Afaan Oromoo | 0.10 | - | 0.05 |
| Amharic | 0.80 | - | 0.21 |
| Hausa | 0.30 | - | 0.15 |
| Somali | 0.40 | - | 0.17 |
| Swahili | 1.60 | 0.04 | 0.19 |
| Yorùbá | - | 0.06 | 0.03 |

Table 3: **Comparing Sizes Across Models:** Comparison of the dataset sizes (GB) of languages present in XLM-R, mBERT and AfriBERTa. "-" indicates language was not present in model's pretraining corpus.

Our corpus contains approximately 5.45 million sentences and 108.8 million tokens. Table 2 presents more details about the dataset size for each language. It can be observed that languages like Swahili, Hausa and Somali have the most amount of data, while languages like Tigrinya have very little data with just about 12,000 sentences.

For each language we pretrained on that is present in XLM-R or mBERT, we compare the size of that language in our dataset to its size in the pretraining corpora of mBERT and XLM-R. From the comparison details in Table 3, we can see that XLM-R always has more data for languages present in our pretraining corpus and theirs. In fact, on average, we can see that the size of the language is always at least two times more in XLM-R. For mBERT, we can see that AfriBERTa has more data for Hausa and Yorùbá, which are present in both corpora. However, one would expect that, given that both languages are in the Latin script, there should be enough high-resource transfer to help them outperform our model.

**Preprocessing:** We remove lines that are empty or only contain punctuation. Given that there is significant overlap between the African language corpora in Common Crawl and the BBC News data that we crawled, we perform extensive deduplication for each language by removing exact matched sentences. We also enforce a minimum length restriction by only retaining sentences with more than 5 tokens. We observe that the quality of the dataset

[4] `https://www.bbc.co.uk/ws/languages` (scraped up to January 17, 2021)

[5] `https://github.com/mayhewsw/multilingual-data-stats/tree/main/wiki`

from Common Crawl is very low, confirming recent findings from Caswell et al. (2021). Hence, we manually clean the data as much as we can by removing texts in the wrong language, while trying to throw out as little data as possible.

### 3.2 Model

We train a transformer (Vaswani et al., 2017) with the standard masked language modelling objective of Devlin et al. (2019) without next sentence prediction. This is also the same approach used in XLM-R (Conneau et al., 2020). We pretrain on text data containing all languages, sampling batches from different languages. We sample languages such that our model does not see the same language over several consecutive batches.

We utilize subword tokenization on the raw text data using SentencePiece (Kudo and Richardson, 2018) trained with a unigram language model (Kudo, 2018). We sample training sentences from different languages for the tokenizer following the sampling method described in Conneau and Lample (2019) with $\alpha = 0.3$.

### 3.3 Evaluation

**Pretraining:** We take out varying amounts of evaluation sentences from each language's original monolingual dataset, depending on the language's size. Our total evaluation set containing all languages consists of roughly 440,000 sentences. We evaluate the perplexity on this dataset to measure language model performance. However, following Conneau et al. (2020), we continue pretraining even after validation perplexity stops decreasing. Effectively, we pretrain on around 0.94 GB of data and evaluate on around 0.08 GB of data.

**NER:** We evaluate named entity recognition (NER) using the recently released MasakhaNER dataset (Adelani et al., 2021). The dataset covers the following ten languages: Amharic, Hausa, Igbo, Kinyarwanda, Luganda, Luo, Nigerian Pidgin, Swahili, Wolof and Yorùbá. The authors established strong baselines on the dataset ranging from simpler methods like CNN-BiLSTM-CRF to pretrained language models like mBERT and XLM-R.

**Text Classification:** We use the news topic classification dataset from Hedderich et al. (2020), which covers Hausa and Yoruba. The authors established strong transfer learning and distant supervision baselines. They find that both mBERT and XLM-R outperform simpler neural network baselines in few-shot and zero-shot settings.

### 3.4 Experimental Setup

All models are trained with the Huggingface Transformers library (Wolf et al., 2020) (v4.2.1). In the following initial experiments, we pretrain each model for 60,000 steps and use a maximum sequence length of 512. We pretrain using a batch size of 32 and accumulate the gradients for 4 steps. Optimization is done using AdamW (Loshchilov and Hutter, 2017) with a learning rate of 1e-4 and 6000 linear warm-up steps. We report F1 scores on the NER dataset averaged over 3 runs with different random seeds. Following initial explorations, we found a vocabulary size of 40k, excluding special tokens, to yield good results across different model sizes, so we use this for initial experiments.

NER models are trained by adding a linear classification layer to the pretrained transformer model and fine-tuning all parameters. Following Adelani et al. (2021), we train for 50 epochs with a batch size of 16, a learning rate of 5e-5 and also optimize with AdamW.

Text classification models are trained by adding a linear classification layer to the pretrained transformer model and fine-tuning all parameters. We train for 25 epochs with a batch size of 32, warm-up steps of 100, learning rate of 5e-5 and optimize with AdamW as well.

## 4 Results

### 4.1 Design Space Exploration

In this section, we compare variants of AfriBERTa models to each other in a bid to understand how to pretrain multilingual language models in small data regimes. We pretrain variants from the point of view of model architecture, taking three factors into consideration: (i) model depth, (ii) number of attention heads and (iii) vocabulary size. We define performance as "good transfer to downstream task". Because the NER dataset covers more languages, we fine-tune and evaluate our models on it.

**Model Depth:** We compare models with 4, 6, 8 and 10 layers. For each model, we use 4 attention heads and adjust the size of the hidden units and feed-forward layers so that all models have approximately the same number of parameters. From preliminary experiments, models with more than 10 layers did not yield substantially better performance. This is expected, given the small size of the

| # Layers | # Params | amh | hau | ibo | kin | lug | luo | pcm | swa | wol | yor | avg |
|---|---|---|---|---|---|---|---|---|---|---|---|---|
| 4 | 74.8M | <u>62.18</u> | 89.66 | 87.03 | 69.29 | 67.23 | 59.00 | 83.57 | 83.89 | <u>77.04</u> | 67.02 | 75.97 |
| 6 | 74.7M | 61.59 | 90.34 | 85.81 | 72.76 | 66.39 | <u>61.43</u> | <u>86.27</u> | 84.02 | 76.61 | <u>68.54</u> | 76.91 |
| 8 | 74.6M | 62.04 | <u>90.96</u> | 86.33 | 74.00 | <u>68.66</u> | 60.96 | 84.43 | 84.16 | 76.11 | 67.38 | 77.00 |
| 10 | 74.3M | 62.14 | 90.69 | <u>87.36</u> | <u>75.74</u> | 67.87 | 60.59 | 84.79 | <u>84.70</u> | 76.17 | 67.51 | **77.27** |

Table 4: **Effect of Number of Layers:** NER dev F1 scores (averaged over three different random seeds) on each language for models with different layer depth, but same number of parameters. The sizes of the embedding and feed-foward layers are adjusted such that feed-foward is always approximately 4 times embedding size. The highest F1-score per language is <u>underlined</u>, while the highest overall average is in **bold**.

| # Layers | # Att. Heads | # Params | amh | hau | ibo | kin | lug | luo | pcm | swa | wol | yor | avg |
|---|---|---|---|---|---|---|---|---|---|---|---|---|---|
| 4 | 2 | 60.1M | 58.23 | 88.78 | 84.63 | 71.28 | 65.68 | 56.91 | 83.84 | 82.44 | 76.69 | 64.64 | 74.99 |
| 4 | 4 | 60.1M | 60.09 | 89.34 | 87.08 | 72.95 | 68.25 | 60.10 | 84.08 | 83.17 | 76.29 | 66.73 | 76.44 |
| 4 | 6 | 60.1M | 60.26 | 89.49 | 86.01 | 72.69 | 67.82 | 59.85 | 84.68 | 83.73 | 76.22 | 67.66 | <u>76.46</u> |
| 6 | 2 | 74.3M | 60.54 | 89.72 | 87.25 | 72.68 | 70.23 | 59.98 | 84.52 | 83.25 | 76.00 | 67.00 | 76.74 |
| 6 | 4 | 74.3M | 63.29 | 90.19 | 86.05 | 74.26 | 68.58 | 59.23 | 84.74 | 83.46 | 77.62 | 67.04 | 76.80 |
| 6 | 6 | 74.3M | 60.38 | 90.86 | 86.70 | 73.12 | 68.54 | 61.68 | 84.59 | 82.80 | 79.02 | 68.48 | <u>77.31</u> |
| 8 | 2 | 88.5M | 60.32 | 90.55 | 85.32 | 75.38 | 69.89 | 62.73 | 85.50 | 83.51 | 79.07 | 68.09 | 77.78 |
| 8 | 4 | 88.5M | 61.90 | 90.79 | 86.67 | 74.28 | 68.45 | 61.57 | 85.64 | 83.88 | 78.48 | 70.16 | 77.77 |
| 8 | 6 | 88.5M | 60.92 | 90.16 | 86.95 | 74.71 | 70.66 | 60.75 | 85.48 | 84.87 | 78.04 | 71.16 | <u>**78.09**</u> |
| 10 | 2 | 102.6M | 59.87 | 90.78 | 87.10 | 73.73 | 66.29 | 60.03 | 85.04 | 83.47 | 81.12 | 69.06 | 77.40 |
| 10 | 4 | 102.6M | 63.95 | 91.33 | 87.11 | 75.24 | 68.96 | 63.36 | 85.66 | 84.67 | 74.60 | 69.27 | 77.80 |
| 10 | 6 | 102.6M | 63.94 | 90.54 | 87.39 | 75.90 | 69.19 | 61.73 | 85.77 | 84.66 | 75.64 | 69.48 | <u>77.81</u> |

Table 5: **Effect of Number of Attention Heads:** NER dev F1 scores (averaged over three different random seeds) on each language for different models with the same number of layers, but different number of attention heads. The highest F1-score per layer size is <u>underlined</u>, while the highest overall average is in **bold**.

data. Because of this, coupled with computational constraints, we do not explore settings with more than 10 layers.

As we can see from the results in Table 4, deeper models always outperform shallower models. However, the performance gain diminishes with size. For example, the gain from increasing the model to 6 layers from 4 layers is roughly 1 F1 point. However, the gain from increasing from 6 layers to 10 layers is only ~0.4. This corroborates the recent *universality overfitting* findings from Kaplan et al. (2020), who showed that the performance of transformer language models improves predictably as long as data size and model depth are scaled in tandem, otherwise there is a diminishing return.

In general, our results suggests that deeper models also work well when pretraining multilingual language models on small datasets. This follows previous works on understanding the cross-lingual ability of multilingual language models (K et al., 2019), which have shown that deeper models have better cross-lingual performance. However, gains from increasing depth are relatively minimal because of the size of our corpus.

**Number of Attention Heads:** For each layer size (4, 6, 8 and 10), we train models with three different numbers of attention heads: 2, 4 and 6. Again, initial experiments with more than 6 attention heads did not yield any better results, so we do not explore more than 6 heads. Results are presented in Table 5.

The results suggest that there is a diminishing return to the number of attention heads when the model is deep. Shallower models need more attention heads to attain competitive performance. However, when the model is deep enough, it is very competitive with as few as two attention heads. This suggests that results from recent works (K et al., 2019; Michel et al., 2019), which suggest that transformers can do without a large number of attention heads, also hold true for multilingual language models on small datasets.

**Vocabulary Size:** Previous works have suggested that on small datasets, one should employ a small vocabulary size (Sennrich and Zhang, 2019; Araabi and Monz, 2020). However, it remains to be seen if this holds in the multilingual setting since several languages will be competing for vocabulary

| # Layers | # Att. Heads | Vocab Size | # Params | amh | hau | ibo | kin | lug | luo | pcm | swa | wol | yor | avg |
|---|---|---|---|---|---|---|---|---|---|---|---|---|---|---|
| 8 | 6 | 25k | 76.9M | 60.56 | 89.96 | 85.84 | 73.23 | 69.67 | 61.86 | 85.11 | 84.34 | 75.40 | 68.35 | 77.09 |
| 8 | 6 | 40k | 88.5M | 60.92 | 90.16 | 86.95 | 74.71 | 70.66 | 60.75 | 85.48 | 84.87 | 78.04 | 71.16 | 78.09 |
| 8 | 6 | 55k | 99.9M | 63.65 | 90.17 | 87.28 | 72.47 | 67.47 | 61.49 | 85.59 | 85.09 | 77.56 | 69.06 | 77.35 |
| 8 | 6 | 70k | 111.5M | 66.17 | 91.25 | 87.74 | 77.44 | 68.29 | 59.91 | 87.00 | 87.05 | 77.49 | 68.82 | **78.33** |
| 8 | 6 | 85k | 123.1M | 62.35 | 90.42 | 87.44 | 77.01 | 68.20 | 61.98 | 86.46 | 85.87 | 72.84 | 70.14 | 77.82 |

Table 6: **Effect of Vocabulary Size:** NER dev F1 scores (averaged over three different random seeds) on the best model size with varying vocabulary sizes. The highest overall average F1-score is in **bold**.

| Language | In mBERT | In XLM-R? | In AfriBERTa? | CNN-BiLSTM CRF | mBERT (172M) | XLM-R base (270M) | AfriBERTa small (97M) | AfriBERTa base (111M) | AfriBERTa large (126M) |
|---|---|---|---|---|---|---|---|---|---|
| amh | no | yes | yes | 52.89 | 0.0 | 70.96 | 67.90 | 71.80 | **73.82** |
| hau | no | yes | yes | 83.70 | 87.34 | 89.44 | 89.01 | 90.10 | **90.17** |
| ibo | no | no | yes | 78.48 | 85.11 | 84.51 | 86.63 | 86.70 | **87.38** |
| kin | no | no | yes | 64.61 | 70.98 | **73.93** | 69.91 | 73.22 | 73.78 |
| lug | no | no | no | 74.31 | 80.56 | **80.71** | 76.44 | 79.30 | 78.85 |
| luo | no | no | no | 66.42 | 72.65 | **75.14** | 67.31 | 70.63 | 70.23 |
| pcm | no | no | yes | 66.43 | **87.78** | 87.39 | 82.92 | 84.87 | 85.70 |
| swa | yes | yes | yes | 79.26 | 86.37 | 87.55 | 85.68 | **88.00** | 87.96 |
| wol | no | no | no | 60.43 | **66.10** | 64.38 | 60.10 | 61.82 | 61.81 |
| yor | yes | no | yes | 67.07 | 78.64 | 77.58 | 76.08 | 79.36 | **81.32** |
| avg | – | – | – | 69.36 | 71.55 | **79.16** | 76.20 | 78.60 | 79.10 |
| avg (excl. amh) | – | – | – | 71.19 | 79.50 | **80.07** | 77.12 | 79.36 | 79.69 |

Table 7: **Comparison of NER Results:** F1-scores on the test sets of each language. XLM-R and mBERT results obtained from Adelani et al. (2021). The best score for each language and overall best scores are in **bold.** We also report the model parameter size in parentheses.

space and Conneau et al. (2020) have found that increasing the vocabulary size improves multilingual performance. We evaluate our best model size on varying vocabulary sizes and report results in Table 6. As we can see from the results, increasing the vocabulary size does not always yield good results on smaller datasets. While a small vocabulary size performs relatively poorly, medium sized vocabularies can sometimes outperform larger ones. Due to computation constraints, we selected vocabulary size of 70k for the final models below.

**Final Model Selection:** We release three AfriBERTa pretrained model sizes: small (4 layers), base (8 layers) and large (10 layers). Each model has 6 attention heads, 768 hidden units, 3072 feed-forward size and a maximum length of 512. Their respective parameter sizes are 97 million, 111 million and 126 million. We use float16 operations to speed up training and reduce memory usage. Pretraining is done for 460,000 steps with 40,000 linear warm-up steps and then the learning rate is decreased linearly. We pretrain with a batch size of 32 on 2 Nvidia V100 GPUs and accumulate the gradients for 8 steps.

### 4.2 NER Comparisons

As we can see in Table 7, even the AfriBERTa small model, which is almost three times smaller than XLM-R, obtains competitive NER results across all languages, trailing XLM-R by less than 3 F1 points. This represents a great opportunity for deployment in resource constrained scenarios, which is usually common for applications in low-resource languages. Our best performing model is AfriBERTa large, which outperforms mBERT and is very competitive with XLM-R across all languages. AfriBERTa large even outperforms both models on several languages that all three models were pretrained on, such as Hausa, Amharic and Swahili.

It should be noted that AfriBERTa large achieves all this with less than half of the number of parameters of XLM-R and about 45M fewer parameters than mBERT. Furthermore, we can see that our models performs very well on languages that were not part of our pretraining corpus, such as Luo, Wolof and Luganda. This demonstrates its strong cross-lingual capabilities, despite smaller parameter sizes and pretraining corpus size. A notable observation is that both mBERT and XLM-R out-

| Language | In mBERT | In XLM-R? | In AfriBERTa? | mBERT | XLM-R base | AfriBERTa large |
|---|---|---|---|---|---|---|
| hau | no | yes | yes | 83.03 | 85.62 | **90.86** |
| yor | yes | no | yes | 71.61 | 71.07 | **83.22** |

Table 8: **Comparison of Text Classification Results:** F1-scores on the test sets. The best score for each language is in **bold**.

perform AfriBERTa on Nigerian Pidgin, despite not being trained on the language. This is likely because of the language's high similarity with English. Nigerian Pidgin is an English Creole, meaning it borrows and shares a lot of its properties (including words) with English. Since both mBERT and XLM-R were pretrained on very large amounts of English data, it is no surprise that they perform so well on Nigerian Pidgin. In summary, our small, base and large models' performance are comparable to mBERT and XLM-R across all languages, despite being pretrained on a substantially smaller corpus and having fewer model parameters.

### 4.3 Text Classification Comparisons

We also compare our best model (AfriBERTa large) to XLM-R base and mBERT on text classification. As we can see from the results in Table 8, AfriBERTa large clearly outperforms both XLM-R and mBERT by over 10 F1 points on Yorùbá and up to 7 F1 points on Hausa. Results show that mBERT slightly outperforms XLM-R on Yorùbá, most likely because it was pretrained on it, while XLM-R was not. XLM-R also outperforms mBERT on Hausa, presumably for the same reason. It should be noted that our model was pretrained on around half as much Hausa data as XLM-R, but still outperforms it substantially.

An important observation is that AfriBERTa outperforms both XLM-R and mBERT on text classification, but not so much on the NER task. This suggests that, perhaps, some downstream tasks benefit from larger multilingual models with high-resource transfer than other tasks. However, we leave this interesting observation for future work.

## 5 Discussion

In this section, we discuss some other contributions of this work. At a high level, AfriBERTa presents the first evidence that multilingual language models are viable with very little training data. This offers numerous benefits for the NLP community, especially for low-resource languages.

**Opportunities for Smaller Curated Datasets:** Our empirical results suggest that state-of-the-art NLP methods like multilingual language models can be made more accessible for low-resource languages. Caswell et al. (2021) recently showed that web-crawled multilingual corpora available for many languages, especially low-resource ones, are usually of very low quality. They found issues such as wrong-language content, erroneous language codes and low-quality sentences. Our work opens the door to competitive multilingual language models on smaller curated datasets for low-resource languages.

Another possible benefit of these smaller curated datasets is that they would tend to contain local content as opposed to foreign content as is in the Wikipedia and other relatively larger datasets of these languages. Models trained on such datasets with local content could potentially be more useful to the speakers of the languages given that they would be trained on data with local context.

**Strength of Language Similarity:** Our work challenges the commonly held belief in the NLP community that lower-resource languages need higher-resource languages in multilingual language models. Instead, we empirically demonstrate that pretraining on similar low-resource languages in a multilingual setting may sometimes be better than pretraining using high-resource and low-resource languages together. This approach should be considered in future work, especially since there have been recent findings (Wang et al., 2020) that low-resource languages also experience negative interference in multilingual models.

**Potential Ethical Benefits:** Recent works have called for more considerations of ethics and related concerns in the development of pretrained language models (Bender et al., 2021). These concerns have ranged from environmental and financial (Strubell et al., 2019) to societal bias (Kurita et al., 2019; Basta et al., 2019)

We believe our work offers the potential to ad-

| Model | # Params | Data Size (GB) | # Tokens |
|---|---|---|---|
| XLM-R base | 270M | 2395 | 164.0B |
| mBERT | 172M | 100 | 12.8B |
| AfriBERTa base | 112M | 0.94 | 108.8M |

Table 9: **Comparing Sizes:** Comparison of datasets and model sizes between XLM-R, mBERT and AfriBERTa.

dress some of these concerns, while developing language technology for under-served languages. A comparison of model and data sizes of common multilingual models is presented in Table 9. Smaller dataset sizes, like ours, mean that these datasets can more easily be cleaned, filtered, analyzed and *possibly* de-biased in comparison to the humongous data sizes of larger language models. We have also shown that smaller-sized models can outperform larger models, despite using smaller training resources. This represents a potential for reduced environmental impact.

While "low-resource" is commonly used in the NLP community to describe a lack of data resources, Nekoto et al. (2020) have argued that "low-resource" also includes a wide range of societal problems, including computational constraints. Thus, our work embodies the broader spirit of "low-resource", as we develop more efficient models on smaller data sizes for under-served languages.

**Improving the Representation of African Languages in Modern NLP tools:** As discussed in section 2, there is very poor representation of African languages in modern NLP tools. Recently, there have been significant efforts towards closing this gap (Alabi et al., 2019; Ogueji and Ahia, 2019; Nekoto et al., 2020; Ahia and Ogueji, 2020; Fan et al., 2020; Azunre et al., 2021; Dossou and Sabry, 2021; Adelani et al., 2021). Our work follows along this path, as there is a need to build language technologies for the over 1.3 billion people on the continent. Besides showing that multilingual language models are viable on low-resource African languages with small training data, we also introduce the first language models for four of these languages: Kinyarwanda, Kirundi, Nigerian Pidgin and Tigrinya. These are four languages with over 50 million speakers (Eberhard et al., 2019) who are active users of digital tools. However, these languages have noticeably deficient support in NLP technologies. Our work represents an important step towards improving this.

## 6 Conclusion

In this work, we introduced AfriBERTa, a multilingual language model pretrained on less than 1 GB of data from 11 African languages. We show that this model is competitive with models pretrained on larger datasets and even outperforms them on some languages. Our comprehensive experiments also highlight important factors to consider when pretraining multilingual language models on smaller datasets. More importantly, we highlight some practical benefits of viable language models on smaller datasets. Finally, we release code, pretrained models and the dataset to stimulate further work on multilingual language models for low-resource languages.

## Acknowledgements

This research was supported in part by the Natural Sciences and Engineering Research Council (NSERC) of Canada and an AI for Social Good grant from the Waterloo AI Institute; computational resources were provided by Compute Ontario and Compute Canada.

## References

David Ifeoluwa Adelani, Jade Z. Abbott, Graham Neubig, Daniel D'souza, Julia Kreutzer, Constantine Lignos, Chester Palen-Michel, Happy Buzaaba, Shruti Rijhwani, Sebastian Ruder, Stephen Mayhew, Israel Abebe Azime, Shamsuddeen Hassan Muhammad, Chris Chinenye Emezue, Joyce Nakatumba-Nabende, Perez Ogayo, Aremu Anuoluwapo, Catherine Gitau, Derguene Mbaye, Jesujoba O. Alabi, Seid Muhie Yimam, Tajuddeen Gwadabe, Ignatius Ezeani, Rubungo Andre Niyongabo, Jonathan Mukiibi, Verrah Otiende, Iroro Orife, Davis David, Samba Ngom, Tosin P. Adewumi, Paul Rayson, Mofetoluwa Adeyemi, Gerald Muriuki, Emmanuel Anebi, Chiamaka Chukwuneke, Nkiruka Odu, Eric Peter Wairagala, Samuel Oyerinde, Clemencia Siro, Tobius Saul Bateesa, Temilola Oloyede, Yvonne Wambui, Victor Akinode, Deborah Nabagereka, Maurice Katusiime, Ayodele Awokoya, Mouhamadane Mboup, Dibora Gebreyohannes, Henok Tilaye, Kelechi Nwaike, Degaga Wolde, Abdoulaye Faye, Blessing Sibanda, Orevaoghene Ahia, Bonaventure F. P. Dossou, Kelechi Ogueji, Thierno Ibrahima Diop, Abdoulaye Diallo, Adewale Akinfaderin, Tendai Marengereke, and Salomey Osei. 2021. MasakhaNER: Named entity recognition for African languages. *CoRR*, abs/2103.11811.

Orevaoghene Ahia and Kelechi Ogueji. 2020. Towards supervised and unsupervised neural machine translation baselines for Nigerian Pidgin. *CoRR*, abs/2003.12660.

Jesujoba O. Alabi, Kwabena Amponsah-Kaakyire, David Ifeoluwa Adelani, and Cristina España-Bonet. 2019. Massive vs. curated word embeddings for low-resourced languages. the case of Yorùbá and Twi. *CoRR*, abs/1912.02481.

Ali Araabi and Christof Monz. 2020. Optimizing transformer for low-resource neural machine translation. In *Proceedings of the 28th International Conference on Computational Linguistics*, pages 3429–3435, Barcelona, Spain (Online). International Committee on Computational Linguistics.

Paul Azunre, Salomey Osei, Salomey Addo, Lawrence Asamoah Adu-Gyamfi, Stephen Moore, Bernard Adabankah, Bernard Opoku, Clara Asare-Nyarko, Samuel Nyarko, Cynthia Amoaba, Esther Dansoa Appiah, Felix Akwerh, Richard Nii Lante Lawson, Joel Budu, Emmanuel Debrah, Nana Boateng, Wisdom Ofori, Edwin Buabeng-Munkoh, Franklin Adjei, Isaac Kojo Essel Ampomah, Joseph Otoo, Reindorf Borkor, Standylove Birago Mensah, Lucien Mensah, Mark Amoako Marcel, Anokye Acheampong Amponsah, and James Ben Hayfron-Acquah. 2021. Contextual text embeddings for Twi. *CoRR*, abs/2103.15963.

Christine Basta, Marta R. Costa-jussà, and Noe Casas. 2019. Evaluating the underlying gender bias in contextualized word embeddings. In *Proceedings of the First Workshop on Gender Bias in Natural Language Processing*, pages 33–39, Florence, Italy. Association for Computational Linguistics.

Emily M. Bender, Timnit Gebru, Angelina McMillan-Major, and Shmargaret Shmitchell. 2021. On the dangers of stochastic parrots: Can language models be too big? In *Proceedings of the 2021 ACM Conference on Fairness, Accountability, and Transparency*, FAccT '21, page 610–623, New York, NY, USA. Association for Computing Machinery.

Andrew Caines. 2019. The geographic diversity of NLP conferences.

Isaac Caswell, Julia Kreutzer, Lisa Wang, Ahsan Wahab, Daan van Esch, Nasanbayar Ulzii-Orshikh, Allahsera Tapo, Nishant Subramani, Artem Sokolov, Claytone Sikasote, Monang Setyawan, Supheakmungkol Sarin, Sokhar Samb, Benoît Sagot, Clara Rivera, Annette Rios, Isabel Papadimitriou, Salomey Osei, Pedro Javier Ortiz Suárez, Iroro Orife, Kelechi Ogueji, Rubungo Andre Niyongabo, Toan Q. Nguyen, Mathias Müller, André Müller, Shamsuddeen Hassan Muhammad, Nanda Muhammad, Ayanda Mnyakeni, Jamshidbek Mirzakhalov, Tapiwanashe Matangira, Colin Leong, Nze Lawson, Sneha Kudugunta, Yacine Jernite, Mathias Jenny, Orhan Firat, Bonaventure F. P. Dossou, Sakhile Dlamini, Nisansa de Silva, Sakine Çabuk Balli, Stella Biderman, Alessia Battisti, Ahmed Baruwa, Ankur Bapna, Pallavi Baljekar, Israel Abebe Azime, Ayodele Awokoya, Duygu Ataman, Orevaoghene Ahia, Oghenefego Ahia, Sweta Agrawal, and Mofetoluwa Adeyemi. 2021. Quality at a glance: An audit of web-crawled multilingual datasets. *CoRR*, abs/2103.12028.

Alexis Conneau, Kartikay Khandelwal, Naman Goyal, Vishrav Chaudhary, Guillaume Wenzek, Francisco Guzmán, Edouard Grave, Myle Ott, Luke Zettlemoyer, and Veselin Stoyanov. 2020. Unsupervised cross-lingual representation learning at scale. In *Proceedings of the 58th Annual Meeting of the Association for Computational Linguistics*, pages 8440–8451, Online. Association for Computational Linguistics.

Alexis Conneau and Guillaume Lample. 2019. Cross-lingual language model pretraining. In *Advances in Neural Information Processing Systems*, volume 32. Curran Associates, Inc.

Jacob Devlin, Ming-Wei Chang, Kenton Lee, and Kristina Toutanova. 2019. BERT: Pre-training of deep bidirectional transformers for language understanding. In *Proceedings of the 2019 Conference of the North American Chapter of the Association for Computational Linguistics: Human Language Technologies, Volume 1 (Long and Short Papers)*, pages 4171–4186, Minneapolis, Minnesota. Association for Computational Linguistics.

Bonaventure F. P. Dossou and Mohammed Sabry. 2021. AfriVEC: Word embedding models for African languages. case study of Fon and Nobiin. *CoRR*, abs/2103.05132.

David M. Eberhard, Gary F. Simons, and Charles D. Fenning. 2019. Ethnologue: Languages of the worlds. (twenty second edition).

Ignatius Ezeani, Ikechukwu Onyenwe, and Mark Hepple. 2018. Transferred embeddings for Igbo similarity, analogy, and diacritic restoration tasks. In *Proceedings of the Third Workshop on Semantic Deep Learning*, pages 30–38, Santa Fe, New Mexico. Association for Computational Linguistics.

Angela Fan, Shruti Bhosale, Holger Schwenk, Zhiyi Ma, Ahmed El-Kishky, Siddharth Goyal, Mandeep Baines, Onur Celebi, Guillaume Wenzek, Vishrav Chaudhary, Naman Goyal, Tom Birch, Vitaliy Liptchinsky, Sergey Edunov, Edouard Grave, Michael Auli, and Armand Joulin. 2020. Beyond English-centric multilingual machine translation. *CoRR*, abs/2010.11125.

Michael A. Hedderich, David Adelani, Dawei Zhu, Jesujoba Alabi, Udia Markus, and Dietrich Klakow. 2020. Transfer learning and distant supervision for multilingual transformer models: A study on African languages. In *Proceedings of the 2020 Conference on Empirical Methods in Natural Language Processing (EMNLP)*, pages 2580–2591, Online. Association for Computational Linguistics.

Pratik Joshi, Sebastin Santy, Amar Budhiraja, Kalika Bali, and Monojit Choudhury. 2020. The state and fate of linguistic diversity and inclusion in the NLP world. In *Proceedings of the 58th Annual Meeting of the Association for Computational Linguistics*, pages 6282–6293, Online. Association for Computational Linguistics.

Karthikeyan K, Zihan Wang, Stephen Mayhew, and Dan Roth. 2019. Cross-lingual ability of multilingual BERT: an empirical study. *CoRR*, abs/1912.07840.

Jared Kaplan, Sam McCandlish, Tom Henighan, Tom B. Brown, Benjamin Chess, Rewon Child, Scott Gray, Alec Radford, Jeffrey Wu, and Dario Amodei. 2020. Scaling laws for neural language models. *CoRR*, abs/2001.08361.

Taku Kudo. 2018. Subword regularization: Improving neural network translation models with multiple subword candidates. In *Proceedings of the 56th Annual Meeting of the Association for Computational Linguistics (Volume 1: Long Papers)*, pages 66–75, Melbourne, Australia. Association for Computational Linguistics.

Taku Kudo and John Richardson. 2018. SentencePiece: A simple and language independent subword tokenizer and detokenizer for neural text processing. In *Proceedings of the 2018 Conference on Empirical Methods in Natural Language Processing: System Demonstrations*, pages 66–71, Brussels, Belgium. Association for Computational Linguistics.

Keita Kurita, Nidhi Vyas, Ayush Pareek, Alan W. Black, and Yulia Tsvetkov. 2019. Measuring bias in contextualized word representations. In *Proceedings of the First Workshop on Gender Bias in Natural Language Processing*, pages 166–172, Florence, Italy. Association for Computational Linguistics.

Yinhan Liu, Myle Ott, Naman Goyal, Jingfei Du, Mandar Joshi, Danqi Chen, Omer Levy, Mike Lewis, Luke Zettlemoyer, and Veselin Stoyanov. 2019. RoBERTa: A robustly optimized BERT pretraining approach. *CoRR*, abs/1907.11692.

Ilya Loshchilov and Frank Hutter. 2017. Fixing weight decay regularization in Adam. *CoRR*, abs/1711.05101.

Louis Martin, Benjamin Muller, Pedro Javier Ortiz Suárez, Yoann Dupont, Laurent Romary, Éric de la Clergerie, Djamé Seddah, and Benoît Sagot. 2020. CamemBERT: a tasty French language model. In *Proceedings of the 58th Annual Meeting of the Association for Computational Linguistics*, pages 7203–7219, Online. Association for Computational Linguistics.

Paul Michel, Omer Levy, and Graham Neubig. 2019. Are sixteen heads really better than one? In *Advances in Neural Information Processing Systems*, volume 32. Curran Associates, Inc.

Vincent Micheli, Martin d'Hoffschmidt, and François Fleuret. 2020. On the importance of pre-training data volume for compact language models. In *Proceedings of the 2020 Conference on Empirical Methods in Natural Language Processing (EMNLP)*, pages 7853–7858, Online. Association for Computational Linguistics.

Tomas Mikolov, Ilya Sutskever, Kai Chen, Greg S. Corrado, and Jeff Dean. 2013. Distributed representations of words and phrases and their compositionality. In *Advances in Neural Information Processing Systems*, volume 26. Curran Associates, Inc.

Wilhelmina Nekoto, Vukosi Marivate, Tshinondiwa Matsila, Timi Fasubaa, Taiwo Fagbohungbe, Solomon Oluwole Akinola, Shamsuddeen Muhammad, Salomon Kabongo Kabenamualu, Salomey Osei, Freshia Sackey, Rubungo Andre Niyongabo, Ricky Macharm, Perez Ogayo, Orevaoghene Ahia, Musie Meressa Berhe, Mofetoluwa Adeyemi, Masabata Mokgesi-Selinga, Lawrence Okegbemi, Laura Martinus, Kolawole Tajudeen, Kevin Degila, Kelechi Ogueji, Kathleen Siminyu, Julia Kreutzer, Jason Webster, Jamiil Toure Ali, Jade Abbott, Iroro Orife, Ignatius Ezeani, Idris Abdulkadir Dangana, Herman Kamper, Hady Elsahar, Goodness Duru, Ghollah Kioko, Murhabazi Espoir, Elan van Biljon, Daniel Whitenack, Christopher Onyefuluchi, Chris Chinenye Emezue, Bonaventure F. P. Dossou, Blessing Sibanda, Blessing Bassey, Ayodele Olabiyi, Arshath Ramkilowan, Alp Öktem, Adewale Akinfaderin, and Abdallah Bashir. 2020. Participatory research for low-resourced machine translation: A case study in African languages. In *Findings of the Association for Computational Linguistics: EMNLP 2020*, pages 2144–2160, Online. Association for Computational Linguistics.

Kelechi Ogueji and Orevaoghene Ahia. 2019. PidginUNMT: Unsupervised neural machine translation from West African Pidgin to English. *CoRR*, abs/1912.03444.

Pedro Javier Ortiz Suárez, Laurent Romary, and Benoît Sagot. 2020. A monolingual approach to contextualized word embeddings for mid-resource languages. In *Proceedings of the 58th Annual Meeting of the Association for Computational Linguistics*, pages 1703–1714, Online. Association for Computational Linguistics.

Jeffrey Pennington, Richard Socher, and Christopher Manning. 2014. GloVe: Global vectors for word representation. In *Proceedings of the 2014 Conference on Empirical Methods in Natural Language Processing (EMNLP)*, pages 1532–1543, Doha, Qatar. Association for Computational Linguistics.

Matthew Peters, Mark Neumann, Mohit Iyyer, Matt Gardner, Christopher Clark, Kenton Lee, and Luke Zettlemoyer. 2018. Deep contextualized word representations. In *Proceedings of the 2018 Conference of the North American Chapter of the Association for Computational Linguistics: Human Language Technologies, Volume 1 (Long Papers)*, pages

2227–2237, New Orleans, Louisiana. Association for Computational Linguistics.

Alec Radford, Karthik Narasimhan, Tim Salimans, and Ilya Sutskever. 2018. Improving language understanding by generative pre-training. Technical report, OpenAI.

Rico Sennrich and Biao Zhang. 2019. Revisiting low-resource neural machine translation: A case study. In *Proceedings of the 57th Annual Meeting of the Association for Computational Linguistics*, pages 211–221, Florence, Italy. Association for Computational Linguistics.

Emma Strubell, Ananya Ganesh, and Andrew McCallum. 2019. Energy and policy considerations for deep learning in NLP. In *Proceedings of the 57th Annual Meeting of the Association for Computational Linguistics*, pages 3645–3650, Florence, Italy. Association for Computational Linguistics.

Ashish Vaswani, Noam Shazeer, Niki Parmar, Jakob Uszkoreit, Llion Jones, Aidan N. Gomez, Łukasz Kaiser, and Illia Polosukhin. 2017. Attention is all you need. In *Advances in Neural Information Processing Systems*, volume 30. Curran Associates, Inc.

Zirui Wang, Zachary C. Lipton, and Yulia Tsvetkov. 2020. On negative interference in multilingual models: Findings and a meta-learning treatment. In *Proceedings of the 2020 Conference on Empirical Methods in Natural Language Processing (EMNLP)*, pages 4438–4450, Online. Association for Computational Linguistics.

Guillaume Wenzek, Marie-Anne Lachaux, Alexis Conneau, Vishrav Chaudhary, Francisco Guzmán, Armand Joulin, and Edouard Grave. 2020. CCNet: Extracting high quality monolingual datasets from web crawl data. In *Proceedings of the 12th Language Resources and Evaluation Conference*, pages 4003–4012, Marseille, France. European Language Resources Association.

Thomas Wolf, Lysandre Debut, Victor Sanh, Julien Chaumond, Clement Delangue, Anthony Moi, Pierric Cistac, Tim Rault, Remi Louf, Morgan Funtowicz, Joe Davison, Sam Shleifer, Patrick von Platen, Clara Ma, Yacine Jernite, Julien Plu, Canwen Xu, Teven Le Scao, Sylvain Gugger, Mariama Drame, Quentin Lhoest, and Alexander Rush. 2020. Transformers: State-of-the-art natural language processing. In *Proceedings of the 2020 Conference on Empirical Methods in Natural Language Processing: System Demonstrations*, pages 38–45, Online. Association for Computational Linguistics.

Yian Zhang, Alex Warstadt, Haau-Sing Li, and Samuel R. Bowman. 2020. When do you need billions of words of pretraining data? *CoRR*, abs/2011.04946.

# Mr. TyDi: A Multi-lingual Benchmark for Dense Retrieval

**Xinyu Zhang, Xueguang Ma, Peng Shi, and Jimmy Lin**
David R. Cheriton School of Computer Science
University of Waterloo

## Abstract

We present Mr. TYDI, a multi-lingual benchmark dataset for mono-lingual retrieval in eleven typologically diverse languages, designed to evaluate ranking with learned dense representations. The goal of this resource is to spur research in dense retrieval techniques in non-English languages, motivated by recent observations that existing techniques for representation learning perform poorly when applied to out-of-distribution data. As a starting point, we provide zero-shot baselines for this new dataset based on a multi-lingual adaptation of DPR that we call "mDPR". Experiments show that although the effectiveness of mDPR is much lower than BM25, dense representations nevertheless appear to provide valuable relevance signals, improving BM25 results in sparse–dense hybrids. In addition to analyses of our results, we also discuss future challenges and present a research agenda in multi-lingual dense retrieval. Mr. TYDI can be downloaded at `https://github.com/castorini/mr.tydi`.

## 1 Introduction

Retrieval approaches based on learned dense representations, typically derived from transformers, form an exciting new research direction that has received much attention of late. These dense retrieval techniques generally adopt a supervised approach to representation learning, where a labeled dataset is used to train two encoders—one for the queries and the other for texts from the corpus to be retrieved—whose output representation vectors are then compared with a simple comparison function such as inner product. Retrieval against a large text corpus is typically formulated as nearest neighbor search and efficiently executed using off-the-shelf libraries. In the literature, this is known as a "bi-encoder" design. Well-known examples include DPR (Karpukhin et al., 2020), ANCE (Xiong et al., 2021), and ColBERT (Khattab and Zaharia, 2020), but there is much recent work along these lines (Gao et al., 2020; Hofstätter et al., 2020; Hofstätter et al., 2021; Lin et al., 2021b), just to list a few papers.

Like all methods based on supervised machine learning, the effectiveness of the trained models on "out of distribution" (OOD) samples is an important issue since it concerns model robustness and generalizability. For dense retrieval, training data typically comprise (query, relevant passage) pairs, and in this context, OOD could mean that (1) the passage encoder is fed text from a different domain, genre, register, etc. than the training data, (2) the query encoder is fed queries that are different from the training queries, (3) the relationship between the inputs at inference time is different from the training samples (e.g., task variations), or (4) a combination of all of the above.

It is, in fact, already known that dense retrieval techniques generalize poorly across different corpora, queries, tasks, etc. Recently, Thakur et al. (2021) constructed a benchmark to specifically evaluate the zero-shot transfer capabilities of dense retrieval models by creating a framework that unifies over a dozen retrieval datasets spanning diverse domains. In a zero-shot setting, the authors found that BM25 remained the most effective overall. That is, dense retrieval techniques trained on one dataset can spectacularly fail on another dataset—exactly the out-of-distribution challenges we discussed above. In contrast, BM25, "just works" regardless of the corpus and queries, even though on "in distribution" samples, dense retrieval models are unequivocally more effective. Thus, learned dense representations are not as general and robust as BM25 representations.

This paper focuses on another aspect of the generalizability and robustness of learned representations for ranking: What if the encoders are applied to texts in languages different from the one they are trained in? Our focus is on *mono-*



*Proceedings of the 1st Workshop on Multilingual Representation Learning*, pages 127–137
November 11, 2021. 

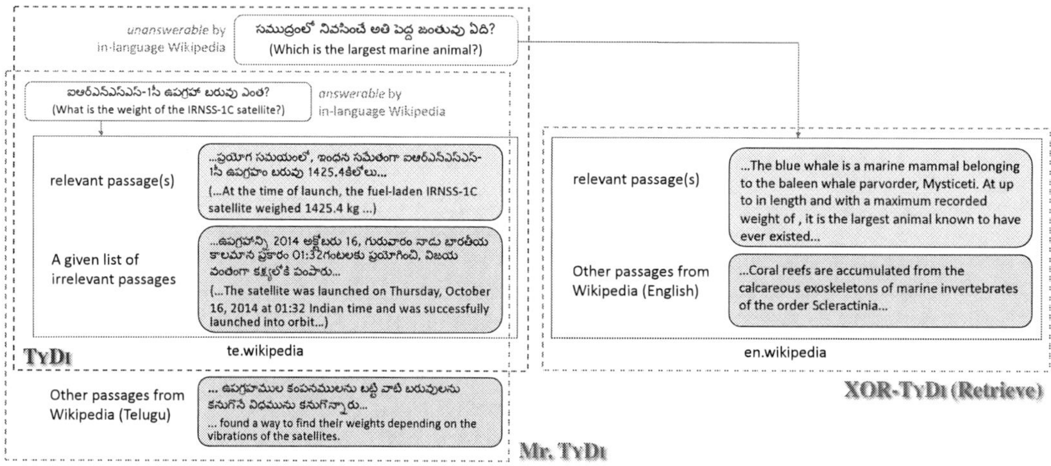


Figure 1: Comparison between TyDi, XOR-TyDi, and Mr. TyDi with an example in Telugu. The green blocks indicate relevant passages and the red blocks indicate non-relevant passages.

*lingual* retrieval in non-English languages (e.g., Bengali queries against Bengali documents) rather than *cross-lingual* retrieval, where documents and queries are in different languages (e.g., English queries against Arabic documents).

We view this work as having three main contributions: First, we construct and share Mr. TyDi, a multi-lingual benchmark dataset for mono-lingual retrieval in eleven diverse languages, designed to evaluate ranking with learned dense representations. This dataset can be viewed as the "open-retrieval" condition of the TyDi multi-lingual question answering (QA) dataset (Clark et al., 2020), and "Mr" in Mr. TyDi stands for "multi-lingual retrieval". We describe the construction of this dataset and how it is different from existing resources. Second, we report zero-shot baselines for Mr. TyDi, including a dense retrieval method based on a multi-lingual version of DPR (Karpukhin et al., 2020) that we call "mDPR". Third, we present a number of initial findings about baseline results that highlight future challenges and begin to define a research agenda in multi-lingual dense retrieval. Most interestingly, we find that although the zero-shot effectiveness of mDPR is much worse than BM25, dense representations appear to provide valuable relevance signals, improving BM25 results in sparse–dense hybrids.

## 2 Background and Related Work

In presenting a new benchmark dataset, one important question to answer is: Why is a new resource needed? We begin by addressing this question. The introduction already lays out the intellectual motivation for our work. Thus, we focus here on explaining why existing datasets are not sufficient. The answer is summarized in Figure 1.

Mr. TyDi is constructed from TyDi (Clark et al., 2020), a question answering dataset covering eleven typologically diverse languages. For each language, the creators provided annotators with a prompt (the first 100 characters of a Wikipedia article), who were asked to write a question that cannot answered by the snippet. Then, for each question, annotators were given the top Wikipedia article returned by Google search and asked to label the relevance of each passage in the article as well as to identify a minimal answer span (if possible). Given this procedure, the answer to the question may or may not be found in the passages from the selected article. The answer passages are always in the same language as the questions. Note that the questions in different languages are not comparable as they are created independently rather than through translation.

The weakness of TyDi from our perspective is that it is essentially a machine reading comprehension task like SQuAD (Rajpurkar et al., 2016) because candidate passages are all included as part of the dataset (i.e., the passages are from the top Wikipedia article returned by Google search). Instead, we need a resource akin to what QA researchers call the "open-domain" or "open-retrieval" task, where the problem involves retrieval from a much larger corpus (e.g., all of Wikipedia) (Chen et al., 2017). Thus, at a high level, Mr. TyDi can be viewed as an open-retrieval extension to TyDi.

Asai et al. (2021) created XOR-TyDi, a cross-lingual QA dataset built on TyDi by annotating answers in English Wikipedia for questions TyDi considered unanswerable in the original source (non-English) language. This was accomplished by randomly sampling 5,000 unanswerable (non-English) questions from TyDi, and then searching English Wikipedia articles for answers. Specifically, each non-English question was first translated into English; then, annotators were given the top-ranked English Wikipedia articles and asked to label passages containing the answer.

The XOR-TyDi dataset contains three overlapping tasks, but all of them are focused on the cross-lingual condition. Among the three tasks (XOR-EnglishSpan, XOR-Retrieve, and XOR-Full), XOR-Retrieve is most comparable to our work, but the retrieval target for the task is explicitly English Wikipedia articles rather than Wikipedia articles in the question's language. While the XOR-Full task requires systems to select answer spans from both English and target-language Wikipedia articles, the dataset does not provide ground truth for the intermediate retrieval step, thus it cannot be used for our evaluations.

The annotations of XOR-TyDi do not allow us to examine mono-lingual retrieval in non-English languages because the creators started with "unanswerable" non-English TyDi questions. Furthermore, since all answer passage annotations were performed on English Wikipedia, this doesn't help if we are interested in, for example, searching Finnish Wikipedia with Finnish questions.

Another point of comparison worth discussing is MKQA (Longpre et al., 2020), which comprises 10k question–answer pairs aligned across 26 typologically diverse languages. Questions are paired with exact answers in the different languages, and evaluation is conducted in the open-retrieval setting by matching those answers in retrieved text. There are two main differences between our work and MKQA: First, MKQA was created via translation in order to achieve cross-lingual alignment. In addition to the possible translation artifacts that such a process might introduce, which Clark et al. (2020) discussed at length, we argue that forced alignment creates non-natural questions, for the simple reason that speakers of different languages are likely to be interested in different topics. This is different from the "geographically dependent" questions that MKQA tries to avoid. Take the question "*who starred in the movie bridge over the river kwai*" as an example: While it does not involve any geographical preference, the question is probably less likely to be asked in, say, Swahili, compared to in English or Thai. Second, the builders of MKQA explicitly made the decision to create "retrieval-independent answer annotations" that are linked to Wikidata entities and a few other value types. This decision, we feel, restricts the range of natural language questions that are covered. The cross-lingual aspect of the dataset appears to be primarily limited to entity translations, which likely do not cover a wide range of linguistic phenomena (which is the reason that we are interested in typologically diverse languages to begin with). Thus, we believe that Mr. TyDi fills a gap in the evaluation space that is currently not occupied.

Many multi-lingual (both mono-lingual and cross-lingual) information retrieval and question answering datasets have been constructed over the past decades, via community-wide evaluations at TREC, FIRE, CLEF, and NCTIR. These test collections are typically built on newswire articles, although some evaluations use Wikipedia and scientific texts. While no doubt useful for evaluation, these test collections usually comprise only a small number of queries (at most a few dozen) with relevance judgments, which are insufficient to fine-tune dense retrieval models. Furthermore, whereas TyDi at least draws from comparable corpora (i.e., Wikipedia articles), these test collections are built on corpora from much more diverse sources. This makes it difficult to generalize across different languages. For these reasons, the above-mentioned IR and QA test collections are not suitable for tackling the research questions we are interested in.

## 3 Mr. TyDi

Having justified the need for a new benchmark dataset, this section describes the construction of Mr. TyDi, which can be best described as an open-retrieval extension to TyDi.

**Corpus** The formulation of any text ranking problem begins with a corpus $\mathcal{C} = \{d_i\}$ comprising the units of text to be retrieved. As the starting point, we used exactly the same raw Wikipedia dumps as TyDi.

| | | Train | | Dev | | Test | | Corpus Size |
|---|---|---|---|---|---|---|---|---|
| | | # Q | # J | # Q | # J | # Q | # J | |
| Arabic | (Ar) | 12,377 | 12,377 | 3,115 | 3,115 | 1,081 | 1,257 | 2,106,586 |
| Bengali | (Bn) | 1,713 | 1,719 | 440 | 443 | 111 | 130 | 304,059 |
| English | (En) | 3,547 | 3,547 | 878 | 878 | 744 | 935 | 32,907,100 |
| Finnish | (Fi) | 6,561 | 6,561 | 1,738 | 1,738 | 1,254 | 1,451 | 1,908,757 |
| Indonesian | (Id) | 4,902 | 4,902 | 1,224 | 1,224 | 829 | 961 | 1,469,399 |
| Japanese | (Ja) | 3,697 | 3,697 | 928 | 928 | 720 | 923 | 7,000,027 |
| Korean | (Ko) | 1,295 | 1,317 | 303 | 307 | 421 | 492 | 1,496,126 |
| Russian | (Ru) | 5,366 | 5,366 | 1,375 | 1,375 | 995 | 1,168 | 9,597,504 |
| Swahili | (Sw) | 2,072 | 2,401 | 526 | 623 | 670 | 743 | 136,689 |
| Telugu | (Te) | 3,880 | 3,880 | 983 | 983 | 646 | 664 | 548,224 |
| Thai | (Th) | 3,319 | 3,360 | 807 | 817 | 1,190 | 1,368 | 568,855 |
| Total | | 48,729 | 49,127 | 12,317 | 12,431 | 8,661 | 10,092 | 58,043,326 |

Table 1: Descriptive statistics for Mr. TYDI: the number of questions (# Q), judgments (# J), and the number of passages (Corpus Size) in each language.

Relevance annotations in TYDI are provided at the passage level (in the passage selection task), and thus we kept the same level of granularity in our corpus preparation. For articles covered by TYDI (identified by the article titles), we retained the original passages. For articles that are not covered by TYDI, we prepared passages using WikiExtractor[1] based on natural discourse units (e.g., two consecutive newlines in the wiki markup). Unfortunately, Clark et al. (2020) did not precisely document their passage segmentation method, but based on manual examination of our results, the generated passages appear qualitatively similar to the TYDI passages.

The result of the corpus preparation process is, for each language, a collection of passages from the Wikipedia articles in that language. To form the final passages that comprise the basic unit of retrieval, we prepend the title of the Wikipedia article to each passage. This creates retrieval units that can be more readily understood in isolation.[2]

**Task** While Mr. TYDI is adapted from a QA dataset, our task is mono-lingual *ad hoc* retrieval. That is, given a question in language $L$, the task is to retrieve a ranked list of passages from $\mathcal{C}_L$, the Wikipedia collection in the same language (prepared in the manner described above), where the retrieved passages are ranked according to their relevance to the given question.

Our assumption here is a standard "retriever–reader" framework (Chen et al., 2017) or a multi-stage ranking architecture (Lin et al., 2020), where we focus on the retriever (what IR researchers call candidate generation or first-stage retrieval). For end-to-end question answering, the output of the retriever would be fed to a reader for answer extraction. This focus on retrieval allows us to explore the research questions outlined in the introduction, and this formulation is consistent with previous work in dense retrieval, e.g., Karpukhin et al. (2020).

**Questions and Judgments** To prepare the questions, we started with all questions provided by TYDI and removed those without any answer passages or whose answer passages are all empty. We consider all non-empty annotated answer passages from TYDI as relevant to the corresponding question in Mr. TYDI. We adopt the development set of TYDI as our test set, since the original test data are not public. A new development set was created by randomly sampling 20% of questions from the original training set. We observed that some of the questions in TYDI are shared between the training and development set (but labeled with different answer passages). In these cases, we retained the duplicate questions only in the training set. Descriptive statistics for Mr. TYDI are shown in Table 1, where languages are identified by their two letter ISO-639 language codes.

In summary, relevant passages in Mr. TYDI are imputed from TYDI. Since Clark et al. (2020) only asked annotators to assess the top-ranked article for each question, there are likely relevant passages that have not been identified. Following standard assumptions in information retrieval, unjudged passages are considered non-relevant. Thus, it is likely

[1]`https://github.com/attardi/wikiextractor`

[2]Mr. TYDI v1.1 contains these article titles, whereas v1.0 did not. Results reported in this paper are with v1.1; for differences, please refer to the earlier version of our paper posted on arXiv.

that ranking models will retrieve false negatives, i.e., passages that are relevant, but would not be properly rewarded.

In other words, our judgments are far from exhaustive. This might be a cause for concern, but is a generally accepted practice in IR research due to the challenges of gathering complete judgments. The widely used MS MARCO datasets (Bajaj et al., 2018), for example, share this characteristic of having "sparse judgments". No claim is made about the exhaustiveness of the annotations, as both Mr. TYDI and MS MARCO provide only about one good answer per question. From a methodological perspective, findings based on MS MARCO "sparse judgments" are largely consistent with results from more expensive evaluation efforts (to gather more complete judgments), such as the TREC Deep Learning Tracks (Craswell et al., 2020, 2021). We expect a similar parallel here: more exhaustive judgments will change the absolute scores, but will likely not affect the findings qualitatively.

**Metrics** We evaluate results in terms of reciprocal rank and recall at a depth $k$ of 100 hits. The first metric quantifies the ability of a model to generate a good ranking, while the second metric provides an upper bound on end-to-end effectiveness (e.g., when retrieval results are fed to a reader for answer extraction). The setting of $k = 100$ is consistent with work in the QA literature.

## 4 Baselines

We provide a few "obvious" baselines for Mr. TYDI as a starting point for future research:

**BM25** We report results with bag-of-words BM25, a strong traditional IR baseline, with the implementation provided by Pyserini (Yang et al., 2017; Lin et al., 2021a), which is built on the open-source Lucene search library. Lucene provides language-specific analyzers for nine of the eleven languages in Mr. TYDI; for these languages, we used the Lucene implementations. For Telugu (Te) and Swahili (Sw), since Lucene does not provide any language-specific implementations, we simply used its whitespace analyzer. We report BM25 scores on two conditions, with default and tuned $k_1$ and $b$ parameters; the default settings are $k_1 = 0.9, b = 0.4$. Tuning was performed on the development set, on a per-language basis, via grid search on $k_1 \in [0.1, 1.6]$ and $b \in [0.1, 1.0]$, with step size 0.1, optimizing MRR@100.

**mDPR** Dense passage retriever (DPR) by Karpukhin et al. (2020) is a well-known bi-encoder model for open-domain QA that we adapt to mono-lingual retrieval in non-English languages by simply replacing BERT with multi-lingual BERT (mBERT),[3] but otherwise keeping all other aspects of the training procedure identical. This adaptation, which we call mDPR, was trained on the English QA dataset Natural Questions (Kwiatkowski et al., 2019) using Facebook's open-source codebase.

Our retrieval experiments with mDPR can be characterized as zero shot: We applied the same mBERT document encoder to convert passages from all eleven languages into dense vectors; similarly, we applied the same mBERT question encoder to all questions. Retrieval in each language was performed using Facebook's Faiss library for nearest neighbor search (Johnson et al., 2017); we used the FlatIP indexes. Experiments were conducted using the same codebase as the DPR replication experiments of Ma et al. (2021), with the Pyserini toolkit (Lin et al., 2021a) .

Our choice of zero-shot mDPR as a baseline deserves some discussion. At a high level, we are interested in the generalizability of dense retrieval techniques in out-of-distribution settings (in this case, primarily different languages). Operationally, our experimental setup captures the scenario where the model does not benefit from any exposure to the target task, even (question, relevant passage) pairs in the English portion of Mr. TYDI. This makes the comparison "fair" to BM25, which is similarly not provided any labeled data from the target task (in the case with default parameters).

**Sparse–Dense Hybrid** Our hybrid technique combines the scores of sparse (BM25) and dense (mDPR) retrieval results. The final fusion score of each document is calculated by $s_{\text{sparse}} + \alpha \cdot s_{\text{dense}}$, where $s_{\text{sparse}}$ and $s_{\text{dense}}$ represent the scores from sparse and dense retrieval, respectively. This strategy is similar to the one described by Ma et al. (2021). We take 1000 hits from mDPR and 1000 hits from BM25 and normalize the scores from each into $[0, 1]$ since the range of the two types of scores otherwise are quite different. If one hit isn't found in the other, the normalized score for that hit is set to zero. The weight $\alpha$ was tuned in $[0, 1]$ with a simple line search on the development set by optimizing MRR@100 with step size 0.01.

[3]Specifically, the `bert-base-multilingual-cased` model provided by HuggingFace (Wolf et al., 2020).

| | Ar | Bn | En | Fi | Id | Ja | Ko | Ru | Sw | Te | Th | Avg |
|---|---|---|---|---|---|---|---|---|---|---|---|---|
| BM25 (default) | 0.368 | 0.418 | 0.140 | 0.284 | 0.376 | 0.211 | 0.285 | 0.313 | 0.389 | 0.343 | 0.401 | 0.321 |
| BM25 (tuned) | 0.367 | 0.413 | 0.151 | 0.288 | 0.382 | 0.217 | 0.281 | 0.329 | 0.396 | 0.424 | 0.417 | 0.333 |
| mDPR | 0.260 | 0.258 | 0.162 | 0.113 | 0.146 | 0.181 | 0.219 | 0.185 | 0.073 | 0.106 | 0.135 | 0.167 |
| hybrid | $0.491^{\dagger}$ | $0.535^{\dagger}$ | $0.284^{\dagger}$ | $0.365^{\dagger}$ | $0.455^{\dagger}$ | $0.355^{\dagger}$ | $0.362^{\dagger}$ | $0.427^{\dagger}$ | 0.405 | 0.420 | $0.492^{\dagger}$ | 0.417 |

(a) MRR@100

| | Ar | Bn | En | Fi | Id | Ja | Ko | Ru | Sw | Te | Th | Avg |
|---|---|---|---|---|---|---|---|---|---|---|---|---|
| BM25 (default) | 0.793 | 0.869 | 0.537 | 0.719 | 0.843 | 0.645 | 0.619 | 0.648 | 0.764 | 0.758 | 0.853 | 0.732 |
| BM25 (tuned) | 0.800 | 0.874 | 0.551 | 0.725 | 0.846 | 0.656 | 0.797 | 0.660 | 0.764 | 0.813 | 0.853 | 0.758 |
| mDPR | 0.620 | 0.671 | 0.475 | 0.375 | 0.466 | 0.535 | 0.490 | 0.498 | 0.264 | 0.352 | 0.455 | 0.473 |
| hybrid | $0.863^{\dagger}$ | 0.937 | $0.696^{\dagger}$ | $0.788^{\dagger}$ | $0.887^{\dagger}$ | $0.778^{\dagger}$ | $0.706^{\dagger}$ | $0.760^{\dagger}$ | 0.786 | 0.827 | $0.875^{\dagger}$ | 0.809 |

(b) Recall@100

Table 2: Results of BM25 (with default and tuned parameters), mDPR, and the sparse–dense hybrid on the test set of Mr. TYDI. The symbol $^{\dagger}$ indicates significant improvements over BM25 (tuned) (paired $t$-test, $p < 0.01$).

## 5 Results and Analysis

We performed experiments on Mr. TYDI v1.1, where each passage contains the title of the Wikipedia article and the passage text. Table 2 reports results on the test set across all eleven languages; mean reciprocal rank (MRR) in the top table and recall in the bottom table, both at a cutoff of 100 hits; the final column reports the average across all languages. The rows report BM25 results (default and tuned), followed by results of mDPR and the sparse–dense hybrid. For the hybrid method, statistically significant improvements over tuned BM25 are denoted with the symbol $^{\dagger}$ based on paired $t$-tests ($p < 0.01$).

### 5.1 High-Level Findings

By comparing scores in each column, we observe that the absolute effectiveness of the techniques varies greatly across languages. Absolute scores are difficult to compare because both the questions and the underlying corpora are different. However, three high-level findings emerge:

First, we find that tuning BM25 parameters yields at most minor improvements for most languages, both in terms of MRR@100 and recall except for Telugu (cases where scores decrease slightly can be explained by noise in the training/test splits). This is a bit of a surprise, as parameter tuning usually yields larger overall gains, e.g., in the MS MARCO collections (Bajaj et al., 2018). Regardless, tuned BM25 serves as a competitive baseline for the remainder of our experiments.

Second, we notice that mDPR underperforms BM25 across all languages except for English. That is, in a zero-shot setting, retrieval using learned dense representations from mDPR (fine-tuned with NQ) is a lot worse than just retrieval using BM25-based representations. Clearly, mDPR is far less robust in cross-lingual generalizations. Even within the same language, mDPR seems to be sensitive to characteristics of the training data. Effectiveness on the English portion of Mr. TYDI is only slightly better than BM25, likely arising from the fact that we are applying an NQ-trained model on "out-of-distribution" questions.

Based on Karpukhin et al. (2020) and the experiments by Ma et al. (2021), we would have expected mDPR to beat BM25 for in-distribution training and inference. Since NQ is also based on Wikipedia, corpus differences are less likely an issue; these results suggest that questions in TYDI and NQ are qualitatively different.

Third, despite the fact that mDPR effectiveness is quite a bit worse than BM25, the MRR@100 of the sparse–dense hybrid is significantly higher than tuned BM25 for nine of the eleven languages (the exceptions are Swahili and Telugu). Rephrased differently, this means that although mDPR by itself is a poor dense retrieval model in a zero-shot setting, it nevertheless contributes valuable relevance signals that are able to improve over tuned BM25. On average, the hybrid results are around eight and five points absolute higher than tuned BM25 in terms of MRR@100 and recall, respectively.

Because absolute scores vary widely across languages, it is helpful to normalize the effectiveness of tuned BM25 to 1.0 and scale the effectiveness of mDPR and the hybrid approach appropriately; this is shown in Figure 2 (left) for MRR@100. As

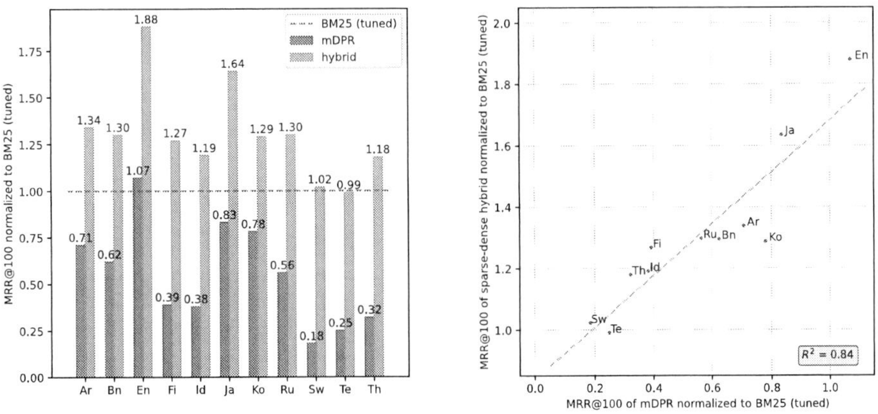


Figure 2: MRR@100 of mDPR and the sparse–dense hybrid normalized with respect to BM25 for each language (left); corresponding pairs for each language plotted as a scatter plot (right).

an example, from the leftmost bars, we see that the MRR@100 of mDPR in Arabic is 71% of BM25 but the sparse–dense hybrid improves over BM25 by 34% (stat. sig). We additionally plot the relation between the normalized effectiveness of mDPR and the hybrid approach in Figure 2 (right).

This plot shows a clear positive (linear) correlation, that is, better mDPR (relative) effectiveness translates into bigger improvements over BM25 in the sparse–dense hybrid. What is surprising, though, is that this relationship seems to hold even if the mDPR results are poor. For example, in Thai, the MRR@100 of mDPR is only 32% of BM25 (tuned), yet the hybrid yields a statistically significant 18% relative gain in the hybrid approach. However, there appear to be limits to our simple linear combination of relevance signals: for both Swahili and Telugu, the hybrid approach does not outperform tuned BM25, likely because mDPR effectiveness is too poor.

### 5.2 Components of Effectiveness

To provide a more in-depth analysis, we attempt to untangle effectiveness into two separate components: (1) retrieving a relevant passage and (2) placing the relevant passages into top ranks. The recall figures in Table 2 already quantify the first component, but MRR@100 alone does not tell the complete story for the second component, since the metric averages a bunch of zeros for questions where relevant passages do not appear in the top-100 hits. It could be the case, for example, that mDPR provides a good ranking for those queries where it retrieves a relevant result in the top 100.

The results of such an analysis, comparing BM25 (tuned) and mDPR, are shown in Figure 3 for all languages (ordered alphabetically). Each plot consists of a histogram and a line graph. The histogram captures the distribution of the ranks (binned by ten) where the relevant passage appears for each question.[4] Questions for which no relevant passage was found in the top-100 hits are tallied in the rightmost bar ("Not Found"). Thus, all questions are either in the rightmost bar (not found in the top-100 hits) or in one of the top-100 bins; these are exactly the components of recall, so the histograms are a more fine-grained way to visualize recall.

The superimposed line graphs in each plot show the ratio of the number of questions falling in each bin to the total number of questions in all top-100 bins (that is, we remove the "Not Found" bin and renormalize). These plots answer the following question: Given that the relevant passage appeared in the top-100 hits, how well did the model perform at ranking it? In other words, we have isolated the ranking ability of the model.

Looking only at the line graphs, these results tell us that for Arabic, Japanese, and Korean, BM25 and mDPR are comparable when we focus only on ranking—that is, given that the relevant passage appears in the top-100 hits. In other words, MRR@100 differences for these languages come mostly from the fact that mDPR misses many relevant passages that BM25 finds (i.e., exhibits lower

[4]If the question has multiple retrieved relevant passages, we only consider the smallest rank among them (i.e., the highest ranked relevant passage).

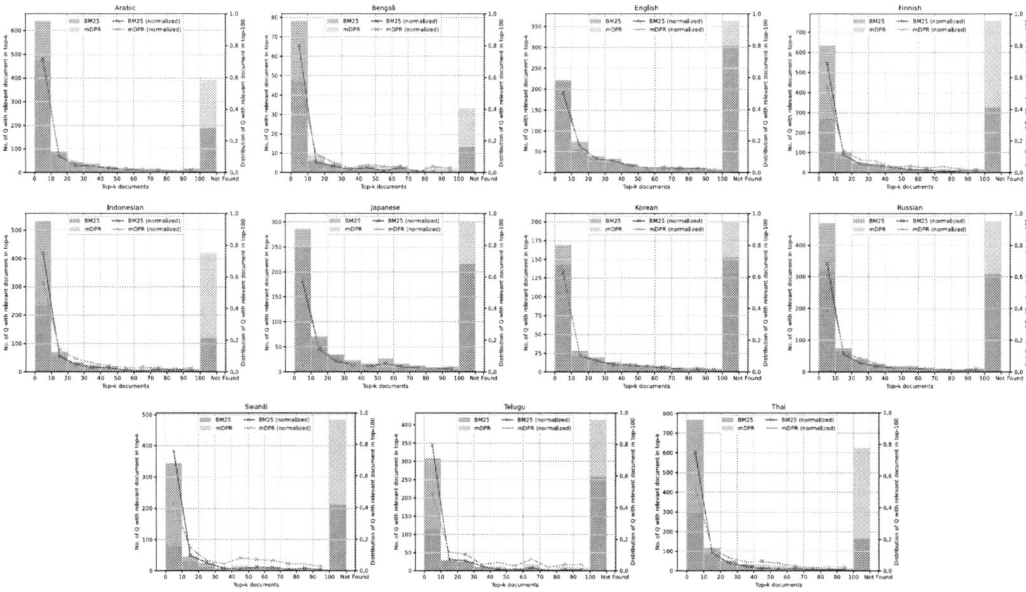


Figure 3: Analysis of recall and ranking effectiveness comparing BM25 (tuned) and mDPR. In each plot, the histogram shows the distribution of relevant passages; lines plot the distribution of relevant passages normalized to only questions where a relevant passage appears in the top-100 hits.

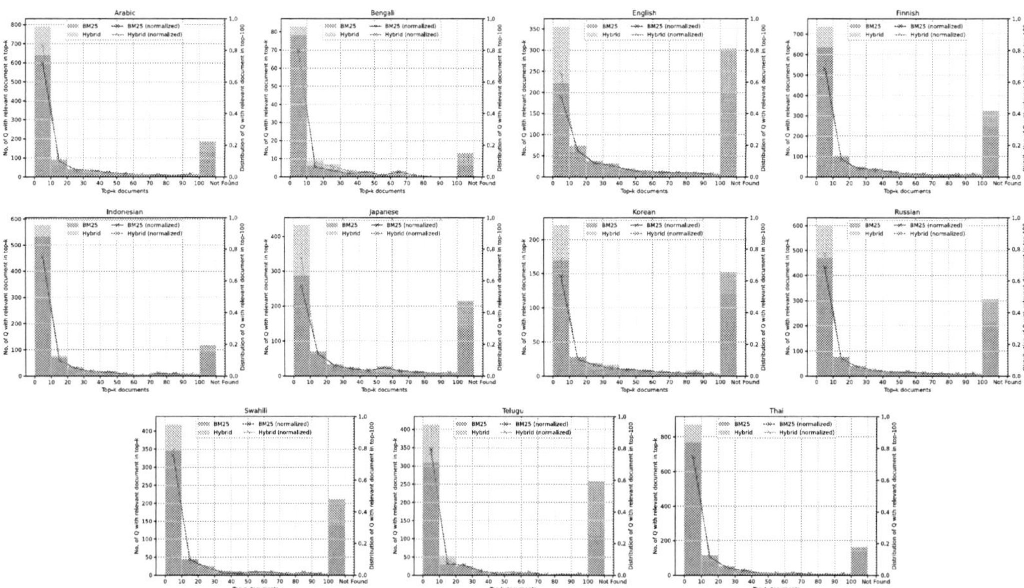


Figure 4: Analysis of recall and ranking effectiveness comparing BM25 (tuned) and the sparse–dense hybrid. Each plot is constructed in a similar manner as the plots in Figure 3.

recall). For the other languages, BM25 appears to exhibit *both* better recall and better ranking. Consider Swahili, for example, BM25 places many more relevant passages in the top 10 and also has far fewer questions where no correct answer appears in the top-100 hits. Thus, this analysis isolates the different failure modes of mDPR (dense retrieval) relative to BM25 (sparse retrieval).

The same analysis comparing BM25 (tuned) and the sparse–dense hybrid is shown in Figure 4. These plots reveal how the hybrid is improving the BM25 results. We see that gains in Bengali, Indonesian, Swahili, and Telugu come mostly from higher recall. That is, ranking capabilities are roughly comparable (the line plots largely overlap) but the hybrid approach has fewer queries where the relevant passage does not appear in the top-100 hits. For Thai, the gain comes from better ranking, while recall is just a small bit better (the "Not Found" bars are pretty close). For the other languages, hybrid improves both recall and ranking.

## 6 Future Work

Mr. TyDi provides a resource to begin exploring mono-lingual *ad hoc* retrieval with both dense and sparse retrieval techniques. In this paper, we have focused primarily on zero-shot baselines. Although zero-shot dense retrieval (mDPR) does not appear to be effective by itself, relevance signals from the model do appear to be complementary to sparse retrieval (bag-of-words BM25). We have identified *how* they are complementary (better recall vs. better ranking), but the behavior varies across languages, and we do not yet have an explanation for *why*; for example, do the typological characteristics of the language play a role?

For our experiments, we have decided to focus on zero-shot effectiveness because it serves as the natural baseline of any technique that tries more sophisticated approaches. Thus, the baselines here are foundational to any future work. We have explicitly decided not to report any language-specific fine-tuning results here, although preliminary experiments suggest that such techniques do bring about benefits. We have not yet systematically explored the broad design space of what Lin et al. (2020) calls "multi-step fine-tuning strategies", paralleling the explorations of Shi et al. (2020) in the context of transformer-based reranking models. There are many possible variations, for example, how many languages to use, what order to sequence data from different languages, possible data augmentation using machine translation, complementary data from other tasks, etc. There are a number of experiments that will allow us to tease apart the effects of language versus other aspects of training data distribution (e.g., NQ vs. TyDi). Exploration of this vast design space is the focus of our immediate future work.

In addition, we believe that our dataset can provide a probe to examine the nature of multi-lingual transformer models. Our experimental results show that absolute effectiveness varies quite a bit across languages. Some of these variations may be due to the nature of the queries, the size of the corpora, etc. However, we hypothesize that inherent properties of the transformer model play important roles as well, e.g., the size of the pretraining corpus in each language, typological and other innate characteristics of the languages, etc. We hope that Mr. TyDi can help us untangle some of these issues.

## 7 Conclusion

In this work, we introduce Mr. TyDi, a multi-lingual benchmark dataset for mono-lingual retrieval in eleven typologically diverse languages, built on TyDi. We describe zero-shot experiments using BM25, mDPR, and a sparse–dense hybrid. The experimental results are not surprising: as is already known from complementary experiments, dense retrieval techniques do not generalize well to out-of-distribution input. However, we find that even poor dense retrieval results provide valuable relevance signals in a sparse–dense hybrid.

Of course, this is only the starting point. With Mr. TyDi, we now have a resource to explore our motivating research questions regarding the behavior of dense retrieval models when fed "out of distribution" data, and from there, devise techniques to increase the robustness and generalizability of our techniques. The potential broader impact of this work is more equitable distribution of information access capabilities across diverse languages of the world—to help non-English speakers access relevant information in their own languages.

## Acknowledgements

This research was supported in part by the Canada First Research Excellence Fund and the Natural Sciences and Engineering Research Council (NSERC) of Canada; computational resources were provided by Compute Ontario and Compute Canada.

## References


Akari Asai, Jungo Kasai, Jonathan Clark, Kenton Lee, Eunsol Choi, and Hannaneh Hajishirzi. 2021. XOR QA: Cross-lingual open-retrieval question answering. In *Proceedings of the 2021 Conference of the North American Chapter of the Association for Computational Linguistics: Human Language Technologies*, pages 547–564.

Payal Bajaj, Daniel Campos, Nick Craswell, Li Deng, Jianfeng Gao, Xiaodong Liu, Rangan Majumder, Andrew McNamara, Bhaskar Mitra, Tri Nguyen, Mir Rosenberg, Xia Song, Alina Stoica, Saurabh Tiwary, and Tong Wang. 2018. MS MARCO: A Human Generated MAchine Reading COmprehension Dataset. *arXiv:1611.09268v3*.

Danqi Chen, Adam Fisch, Jason Weston, and Antoine Bordes. 2017. Reading Wikipedia to answer open-domain questions. In *Proceedings of the 55th Annual Meeting of the Association for Computational Linguistics (Volume 1: Long Papers)*, pages 1870–1879, Vancouver, Canada.

Jonathan H. Clark, Eunsol Choi, Michael Collins, Dan Garrette, Tom Kwiatkowski, Vitaly Nikolaev, and Jennimaria Palomaki. 2020. TyDi QA: A benchmark for information-seeking question answering in typologically diverse languages. *Transactions of the Association for Computational Linguistics*, 8:454–470.

Nick Craswell, Bhaskar Mitra, Emine Yilmaz, and Daniel Campos. 2021. Overview of the TREC 2020 deep learning track. *arXiv:2102.07662*.

Nick Craswell, Bhaskar Mitra, Emine Yilmaz, Daniel Campos, and Ellen M. Voorhees. 2020. Overview of the TREC 2019 deep learning track. *arXiv:2003.07820*.

Luyu Gao, Zhuyun Dai, Zhen Fan, and Jamie Callan. 2020. Complementing lexical retrieval with semantic residual embedding. *arXiv:2004.13969*.

Sebastian Hofstätter, Sophia Althammer, Michael Schröder, Mete Sertkan, and Allan Hanbury. 2020. Improving efficient neural ranking models with cross-architecture knowledge distillation. *arXiv:2010.02666*.

Sebastian Hofstätter, Sheng-Chieh Lin, Jheng-Hong Yang, Jimmy Lin, and Allan Hanbury. 2021. Efficiently teaching an effective dense retriever with balanced topic aware sampling. In *Proceedings of the 44th Annual International ACM SIGIR Conference on Research and Development in Information Retrieval (SIGIR 2021)*, pages 113–122.

Jeff Johnson, Matthijs Douze, and Hervé Jégou. 2017. Billion-scale similarity search with GPUs. *arXiv:1702.08734*.

Vladimir Karpukhin, Barlas Oguz, Sewon Min, Patrick Lewis, Ledell Wu, Sergey Edunov, Danqi Chen, and Wen-tau Yih. 2020. Dense passage retrieval for open-domain question answering. In *Proceedings of the 2020 Conference on Empirical Methods in Natural Language Processing (EMNLP)*, pages 6769–6781.

Omar Khattab and Matei Zaharia. 2020. ColBERT: Efficient and effective passage search via contextualized late interaction over BERT. In *Proceedings of the 43rd Annual International ACM SIGIR Conference on Research and Development in Information Retrieval (SIGIR 2020)*, pages 39–48.

Tom Kwiatkowski, Jennimaria Palomaki, Olivia Redfield, Michael Collins, Ankur Parikh, Chris Alberti, Danielle Epstein, Illia Polosukhin, Jacob Devlin, Kenton Lee, Kristina Toutanova, Llion Jones, Matthew Kelcey, Ming-Wei Chang, Andrew M. Dai, Jakob Uszkoreit, Quoc Le, and Slav Petrov. 2019. Natural Questions: A benchmark for question answering research. *Transactions of the Association for Computational Linguistics*, 7:452–466.

Jimmy Lin, Xueguang Ma, Sheng-Chieh Lin, Jheng-Hong Yang, Ronak Pradeep, and Rodrigo Nogueira. 2021a. Pyserini: A Python toolkit for reproducible information retrieval research with sparse and dense representations. In *Proceedings of the 44th Annual International ACM SIGIR Conference on Research and Development in Information Retrieval (SIGIR 2021)*, pages 2356–2362.

Jimmy Lin, Rodrigo Nogueira, and Andrew Yates. 2020. Pretrained transformers for text ranking: BERT and beyond. *arXiv:2010.06467*.

Sheng-Chieh Lin, Jheng-Hong Yang, and Jimmy Lin. 2021b. In-batch negatives for knowledge distillation with tightly-coupled teachers for dense retrieval. In *Proceedings of the 6th Workshop on Representation Learning for NLP (RepL4NLP-2021)*, pages 163–173.

Shayne Longpre, Yi Lu, and Joachim Daiber. 2020. MKQA: A linguistically diverse benchmark for multilingual open domain question answering. *arXiv:2007.15207*.

Xueguang Ma, Kai Sun, Ronak Pradeep, and Jimmy Lin. 2021. A replication study of dense passage retriever. *arXiv:2104.05740*.

Pranav Rajpurkar, Jian Zhang, Konstantin Lopyrev, and Percy Liang. 2016. SQuAD: 100,000+ questions for machine comprehension of text. In *Proceedings of the 2016 Conference on Empirical Methods in Natural Language Processing*, pages 2383–2392, Austin, Texas.

Peng Shi, He Bai, and Jimmy Lin. 2020. Cross-lingual training of neural models for document ranking. In *Findings of the Association for Computational Linguistics: EMNLP 2020*, pages 2768–2773.

Nandan Thakur, Nils Reimers, Andreas Rücklé, Abhishek Srivastava, and Iryna Gurevych. 2021. BEIR: A heterogenous benchmark for zero-shot evaluation of information retrieval models. *arXiv:2104.08663*.

Thomas Wolf, Lysandre Debut, Victor Sanh, Julien Chaumond, Clement Delangue, Anthony Moi, Pierric Cistac, Tim Rault, Remi Louf, Morgan Funtowicz, Joe Davison, Sam Shleifer, Patrick von Platen, Clara Ma, Yacine Jernite, Julien Plu, Canwen Xu, Teven Le Scao, Sylvain Gugger, Mariama Drame, Quentin Lhoest, and Alexander Rush. 2020. Transformers: State-of-the-art natural language processing. In *Proceedings of the 2020 Conference on Empirical Methods in Natural Language Processing: System Demonstrations*, pages 38–45.

Lee Xiong, Chenyan Xiong, Ye Li, Kwok-Fung Tang, Jialin Liu, Paul N. Bennett, Junaid Ahmed, and Arnold Overwijk. 2021. Approximate nearest neighbor negative contrastive learning for dense text retrieval. In *Proceedings of the 9th International Conference on Learning Representations (ICLR 2021)*.

Peilin Yang, Hui Fang, and Jimmy Lin. 2017. Anserini: Enabling the use of Lucene for information retrieval research. In *Proceedings of the 40th Annual International ACM SIGIR Conference on Research and Development in Information Retrieval (SIGIR 2017)*, pages 1253–1256, Tokyo, Japan.

# VisualSem: A High-quality Knowledge Graph for Vision & Language

**Houda Alberts**[1,*] **Ningyuan (Teresa) Huang**[5] **Yash R. Deshpande**[2] **Yibo Liu**[2]
**Kyunghyun Cho**[2] **Clara Vania**[4] **Iacer Calixto**[2,3]

[1]Rond Consulting, NL [2]New York University [3]ILLC, University of Amsterdam
[4]Amazon, UK [5]Johns Hopkins University, USA.
houda1996@hotmail.com, iacer.calixto@nyu.edu

## Abstract

An exciting frontier in natural language understanding (NLU) and generation (NLG) calls for (vision-and-) language models that can efficiently access external structured knowledge repositories. However, many existing knowledge bases only cover limited domains, or suffer from noisy data, and most of all are typically hard to integrate into neural language pipelines. To fill this gap, we release VisualSem: a high-quality knowledge graph (KG) which includes nodes with multilingual glosses, multiple illustrative images, and visually relevant relations. We also release a neural multi-modal retrieval model that can use images or sentences as inputs and retrieves entities in the KG. This multi-modal retrieval model can be integrated into any (neural network) model pipeline. We encourage the research community to use VisualSem for data augmentation and/or as a source of grounding, among other possible uses. VisualSem as well as the multi-modal retrieval models are publicly available and can be downloaded in this URL: `https://github.com/iacercalixto/visualsem`.

## 1 Introduction

Publicly-available multilingual resources such as Wikipedia are crucial when used as knowledge bases in recent neural language models (LMs) that retrieve documents in order to solve complex tasks such as open-ended question answering (Guu et al., 2020; Lewis et al., 2020b,a). However, Wikipedia's wealth of visual information is typically hard to use,[1] which prevents models from including rich *multi-modal data*. Although a small number of structured knowledge graphs (KGs) with images exist and are publicly available, they either cover limited domains (Xie et al., 2017; Mousselly Sergieh et al., 2018) or span multiple domains but with noisy images (Navigli and Ponzetto, 2012). To facilitate further progress in this direction, we introduce a new resource to enable research on LMs that efficiently retrieve *textual* and *visual contextual information* from KGs, where this information can be used for grounding, data augmentation, among other uses.

In this paper, we introduce VisualSem, a multilingual and multimodal KG with $\sim$ 90k nodes, $\sim$ 1.3M glosses and $\sim$ 938k images. VisualSem's nodes denote concepts and named entities, include multiple curated illustrative images, as well as glosses in up to 14 diverse languages. Typed semantic relations connect nodes in the graph, and nodes in VisualSem are linked to Wikipedia articles, WordNet synsets, and (when available) high-quality images from ImageNet (Deng et al., 2009). VisualSem integrates seamlessly with existing resources. Compared to existing multimodal KGs, VisualSem includes data from different sources and thus it is also more diverse in terms of the domains. We source the images in VisualSem using BabelNet (Navigli and Ponzetto, 2012), a large multilingual and multimodal resource that semi-automatically aggregates information from many different sources. We address the known issue of noisy images in BabelNet (Colla et al., 2018; Calabrese et al., 2020) by applying multiple filtering steps to ensure that we remove noise while maintaining breadth of coverage and image diversity.

We also release pre-trained models to retrieve entities from VisualSem using either images or sentences as queries in a $k$-nearest neighbor search. This effectively allows researchers to integrate entities and facts in VisualSem into their (neural) model pipelines. Code to generate and download VisualSem, as well as retrieval models, is publicly available.[2]

[*] Work initiated while in the University of Amsterdam during her MSc. research.

[1]See for instance `https://en.wikipedia.org/wiki/Wikipedia:Images` and `https://commons.wikimedia.org/wiki/Main_Page`.

[2]`https://github.com/iacercalixto/`



*Proceedings of the 1st Workshop on Multilingual Representation Learning*, pages 138–152
November 11, 2021. 

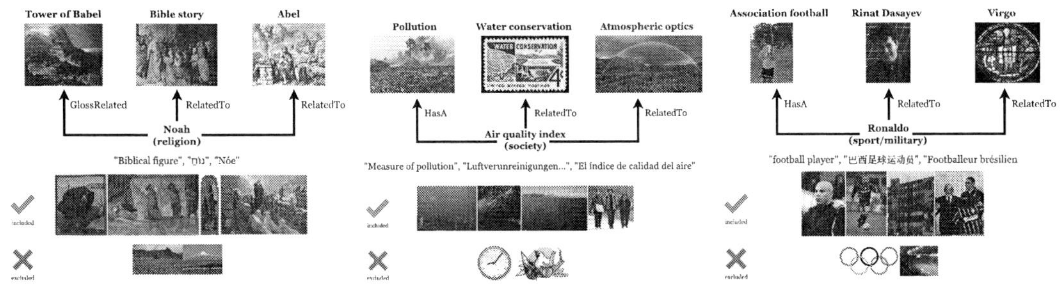


(a) Node "Noah". (b) Node "Air quality index". (c) Node "Ronaldo".

Figure 1: Example nodes in VisualSem, some of their glosses and images, and how they relate to other nodes. We also show examples of images we collected for the nodes that were filtered out and that were kept in following our data collection pipeline (Section 2.1).

Our main contributions are:

- We introduce VisualSem, a multi-modal knowledge graph designed to be used in vision and language research that integrates textual descriptions in up to 14 languages and images from curated sources.
- We build an image filtering pipeline to obtain a clean set of images associated to each concept in VisualSem.
- We provide an open source code base one can use to download and generate the KG, as well as multi-modal retrieval models that retrieve entities from the KG given images and sentences.

This paper is organised as follows. In Section 2 we explain how we build VisualSem and provide details on its data collection pipeline. In Section 3 we include dataset statistics and also analyse VisualSem's content and structure qualitatively. In Section 4, we describe the multi-modal retrieval models that use sentences and images to retrieve entities from the KG. In Section 5 we discuss relevant related work, including existing multi-modal knowledge bases and how they compare to our work. Finally, in Section 6 we discuss our main findings as well as provide avenues for future work.

## 2 Approach

VisualSem is a multilingual and multimodal knowledge graph consisting of $89,896$ unique nodes and $1,481,007$ facts, where each fact is a tuple <$n_i$, $r_j$, $n_k$> that denotes that node $n_i$ is connected to node $n_k$ via relation $r_j$. Each node $n$ denotes a *concept*, such as a WordNet synset or Wikipedia article (e.g., see example nodes in Figures 1a, 1b, and 1c). Relations $r_j$ can take one of 13 different semantic types. We select VisualSem's nodes and relations carefully: we include nodes that denote concepts and named entities with a strong visual component, and relations that encode relevant visual knowledge and/or knowledge relevant to solving tasks that require visual understanding (discussed next). We extract nodes, relations, and images in VisualSem using BabelNet v4.0 (Navigli and Ponzetto, 2012), a large multilingual KB that consolidates data from multiple knowledge graphs into one single graph.[3]

**Relation types** We follow previous work to choose relation types in VisualSem. Cui et al. (2018) propose to use 15 relation types with a strong visual component and that therefore are likely to help in vision and language tasks: *is-a*, *has-part*, *related-to*, *used-for*, *used-by*, *subject-of*, *depicts*, *receives-action*, *made-of*, *has-property*, *also-see*, *gloss-related*, *synonym*, *part-of*, and *located-at*. We use 13 out of the 15 proposed relation types, since we do not have examples with *depicts* and *also-see* in the nodes we select. We describe the data collection procedure next.

### 2.1 Data collection

We start by choosing a set of *seed* nodes we can guarantee is high-quality, well-curated, and visually relevant. We therefore use the BabelNet API[4] to get synsets corresponding to the $1,000$ ImageNet classes used in the ILSVRC image classification

visualsem.

[3]https://babelnet.org

[4]https://babelnet.org/guide

competition (Russakovsky et al., 2015) as our initial seed nodes.[5] We call these nodes our initial *node pool*. We choose this initial node pool since ImageNet already provides high-quality images associated to these nodes. We then follow an iterative procedure where in each step we add nodes to the node pool, until we reach the end of the algorithm. Specifically, in the first step, the node pool includes the $1,000$ seed nodes; in the second step, it will include the $1,000$ seed nodes plus the additional nodes gathered in the first step; and so on, until we reach $N$ nodes ($N = 90,000$). This procedure works by iterating over the following steps:

1. **Retrieve neighbors**: retrieve neighbor nodes for each node in the node pool using the BabelNet API;

2. **Validate images**: validate linked images and optionally remove those that do not meet certain quality criteria;

3. **Filter nodes**: filter out nodes that do not meet inclusion criteria;

4. **Update pool**: accept top-$k$ nodes among remaining nodes after sorting nodes according to their features.

**Retrieve neighbors** In this step we collect all first-degree neighbors for each node in the node pool, and remove any duplicate node retrieved if any exists. The neighbors are retrieved using the BabelNet v4.0 API (Navigli and Ponzetto, 2012) and can include nodes from multiple sources, such as multilingual Wikipedias, multilingual WordNets, among others. First-degree neighbors $n_k$ of node $n_i$ are those nodes directly connected via a relation which type $r_j$ is one of the 13 relation types, i.e., $<n_i, r_j, n_k = ?>$. In Table 1 we show a list of relation types in BabelNet, and how these were merged into the 13 types used in VisualSem.

**Validate images + Node filtering + Update pool** We collect images available for all first-degree neighbors retrieved in the previous step, and apply *four filters* to the available images: **i)** we check if images are valid files, **ii)** we remove duplicate or near-duplicate images, **iii)** we train a binary classifier to remove non-photographic images, and **iv)** we use OpenAI's CLIP (Radford et al., 2021) to remove images that do not minimally match *any*

[5] https://image-net.org/challenges/LSVRC/2014/browse-synsets

| BabelNet | VisualSem |
|---:|---:|
| is-a, is_a | is-a |
| has-part, has_part | has-part |
| related | related-to |
| use | used-for |
| used-by, used_by | used-by |
| subject-of, subject_of | subject-of |
| interaction | receives-action |
| oath-made-by | made-of |
| has_* | has-property |
| gloss-related | gloss-related |
| taxon-synonym | synonym |
| part-of, part_of | part-of |
| location, located_* | located-at |

Table 1: Relation types in BabelNet and their corresponding types in VisualSem. Asterisks (*) can match any number of characters.

of the node's glosses. At the end of each iteration, we require that each node has at least one image associated to it, and that it contains relations with other nodes with a minimum of two different relation types. If nodes do not satisfy these criteria, they are filtered out.

In more detail: **i)** From the total amount of image files we downloaded, an average of $\sim 6.3\%$ were invalid image files and thus removed, e.g., the downloaded file was in fact an audio file. **ii)** We find many images that are (near-)duplicates across different synsets, in which case we remove those duplicates using SHA1 hashing (Eastlake and Jones, 2001). **iii)** We use a binary classifier to validate images associated to each node in the pool of retrieved neighbors following the simple procedure described in Alberts and Calixto (2020). We use their ResNet-based coarse-grained binary classification model to further filter out undesirable images. In short, the image classification model is trained on a total of $6,000$ randomly sampled images (mostly sourced from Wikipedia and ImageNet) where 50% are good quality/photographic images, and the remaining are non-photographic/undesirable ones. We denote undesirable images as unclear/blurred/dark or low-quality images, and non-photographic images such as hand drawings, sketches, maps, icons, flags, graphs and other rendered images. Please refer to Alberts and Calixto (2020) for more details on the image classification model training and evaluation. We apply this step and remove images flagged with this binary classifier, since many images we obtain in practice are very noisy. **iv)** Finally, in our last filter in the image filtering process we use the

|  | # langs. | # nodes | # rel. types | # glosses | # images | # train | # valid | # test | sources |
|---|---|---|---|---|---|---|---|---|---|
| **WN9-IMG**[†] | 1 | 6,555 | 9 | N/A | 65,550 | 11,741 | 1,337 | 1,319 | WordNet |
| **FB15-IMG**[‡] | 1 | 11,757 | 1,231 | N/A | 107,570 | 285,850 | 29,580 | 34,863 | Freebase |
| **VisualSem** | 14 | 89,896 | 13 | 1,342,764 | 938,100 | 1,441,007 | 20,000 | 20,000 | Multiple[⋆] |

Table 2: VisualSem KG statistics. [⋆]Multiple sources include Wikipedia, WordNet, ImageNet, among others. [†]Xie et al. (2017). [‡]Mousselly Sergieh et al. (2018).

pre-trained CLIP model. CLIP has one text and one image encoder and is trained to maximize the dot-product of correct image-sentence pairs, and at the same time minimize that of random image-sentence pairs. We encode the $k$ English glosses $g_{i,k}$ and the $l$ images $a_{i,l}$ available for node $n_i$ with CLIP's text and image encoder, respectively. We then compute the dot-product between each image $a_{i,l}$ and each gloss $g_{i,k}$, keeping only the images that had at least one dot-product greater than $0.5$ with one of the English glosses. We choose the value of $0.5$ empirically by manually checking the quality of the image-gloss matches. We note that the motivation for keeping only images that match well with at least one gloss is the fact that the available glosses are by design descriptive of the node, and by making sure images align well with at least one of the available glosses we can make sure we filter out noisy and unrelated images (e.g., please refer to examples in Appendix A for more details).

Step (i) reduces the number of images from $\sim 5.6$ to $\sim 5.3$ million, step (ii) brings the number of images from $\sim 5.3$ to $\sim 2.1$ million, step (iii) further reduces images from $\sim 2.1$ to $\sim 1.5$ million, and finally step (iv) brings us to the final number of images in VisualSem, $938,100$.

After filtering out undesirable images in the retrieved neighbors, we discard any nodes in the neighborhood that do not have at least one associated image. Finally, for each node in the initial node pool we add the top-$k$ neighbour nodes ($k = 10$) to the pool and repeat. We prioritize visually relevant nodes with a larger number of images, nodes that include as many diverse relation types as possible, and especially nodes with less frequent relation types.

## 3 Data Statistics and Analysis

In this Section, we explore the structure and content of VisualSem. In Section 3.1, we report relevant statistics, as well as show some examples of nodes and relations in it. In Section 3.2, we provide a more qualitative analysis using unsupervised topic models to induce topic distributions for VisualSem.

### 3.1 Data Statistics

In Table 2, we show statistics comparing VisualSem and multimodal knowledge bases WN9-IMG and FB15-IMG.

**Glosses.** VisualSem has a total of $1,342,764$ glosses in $14$ different languages: Arabic, Chinese, Dutch, English, Farsi, French, German, Italian, Korean, Polish, Portuguese, Russian, Spanish, and Swedish. The languages were chosen to be representative of diverse linguistic families and to include many different scripts, while at the same time covering a high number of nodes. Nodes have on average $14.9$ glosses across all $14$ languages, and in Figure 2c we show the number of nodes that have at least one gloss in each language. Nodes with English (Korean) glosses have the highest (lowest) coverage: $89,896$ nodes have at least one English and $37,970$ at least one Korean gloss. **Example:** Node *Ronaldo (Brazilian footballer)* has four glosses in English, and one of these glosses is *Ronaldo Luís Nazário de Lima, commonly known as Ronaldo, is a retired Brazilian professional footballer who played as a striker*[6] (see Figure 1c).

**Images.** As shown in Table 2, VisualSem has a total of $938,100$ unique images. On average, there are $10.4$ images per node—similarly to WN9-IMG and FB15-IMG datasets—and in Figure 2a we show the distribution of images per node. The node with the greatest number of images is the concept *Russian culture* with $848$ images.[7]

**Relations.** VisualSem has 13 different relation types, and all its relations are typed. Relation types include: *is-a*, *has-part*, *related-to*, *used-for*, *used-by*, *subject-of*, *receives-action*, *made-of*,

[6]The same node also has glosses in French (3), German (2), Spanish (4), Italian (4), Russian (1), Dutch (3), Polish (1), Portuguese (3), Swedish (3), Mandarin (1), Arabic (1), Farsi (2), and Korean (1).

[7]It has BabelNet id `bn:01286889n` and is linked to Wikipedia article `https://en.wikipedia.org/wiki/Russian_culture`.

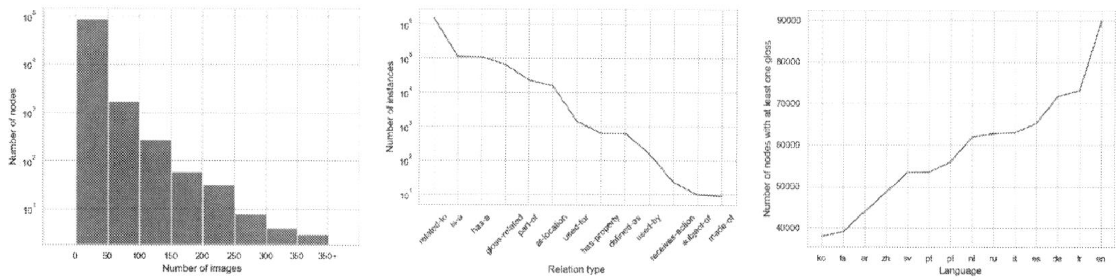


(a) Number of images per node. (b) Number of instances or facts (i.e., tuples <$n_i$, $r_j$, $n_k$>) per relation type. (c) Number of nodes with at least one gloss in each language.

Figure 2: VisualSem data statistics.

*has-property*, *gloss-related*, *synonym*, *part-of*, and *located-at*. In Table 1 we show the mapping from relations in BabelNet to the corresponding types in VisualSem. **Example:** In Figure 1 we show three example nodes and how they relate to other nodes in the KG. We note that most connections have the *related-to* relation type. In Figure 2b, we show the number of instances (i.e., tuples <$n_i$, $r_j$, $n_k$>) per relation type. There is a very large imbalance, with the type *related-to* accounting for about 82% of all existing relations in the KB. We note that had we not adopted measures to alleviate this issue in our data collection pipeline—e.g., prioritizing nodes that have less frequent relation types when adding to the node pool—this imbalance would have been much greater (see Section 2.1).

### 3.2 Topic Models

To further analyze the quality of our KG, we try to understand what topics are salient in VisualSem. We train a neural topic model with 20 latent topics using Embedded Topic Model (ETM; Dieng et al., 2020), which is an extension of Latent Dirichlet Allocation (LDA; Blei et al., 2003) that use pre-trained word embeddings. We let each node be a document, and each document's content be the combination of all its English glosses. In Table 3, we show the six most representative words per topic after stop-word removal. The topics covered are varied and can be clustered in broad domains such as 'sciences' (e.g., physics, chemistry, biology, space), 'society' (e.g., geography, politics, occupations), 'culture' (e.g., religion, history, food, fashion), among others (e.g., material, city). There is a trend towards representing factual knowledge, which is expected since glosses by definition describe facts about nodes. Concepts well covered in Wikipedia are also well covered in VisualSem.

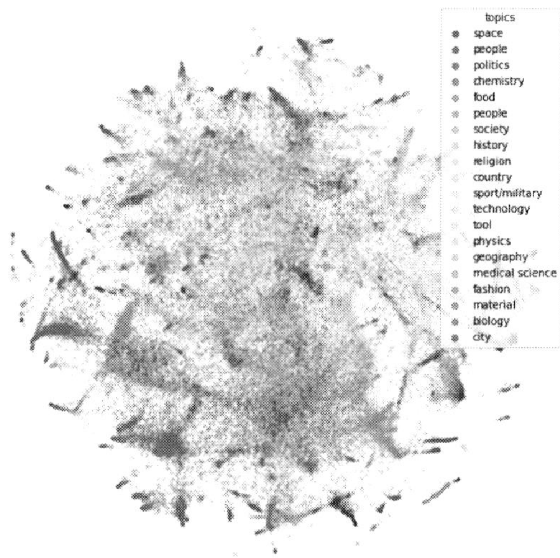


Figure 3: T-SNE plot for node embeddings where each node is represented as the average of its gloss embeddings. Topic assignments are used to colorise node embeddings, and topics are computed with the topic model described in Section 3.2 and Table 3.

### 3.3 Node visualisation via its glosses

We now visualise nodes with the t-SNE algorithm (van der Maaten and Hinton, 2008). We embed glosses as the average word embedding for each word in the gloss computed with multilingual fastText (Bojanowski et al., 2016). Similarly, we set each node $n_i$'s representation $\boldsymbol{n}_i$ as the average of all its gloss embeddings, across all languages. We use the ETM topic model trained in Section 3.2 to assign a topic for each node in VisualSem (i.e., the highest probability topic induced in the topic model), and colorise the node according to its predicted topic. We apply t-SNE to the node

| 1. space | 2. occupation | 3. politics | 4. chemistry | 5. food | 6. occupation | 7. society | 8. history | 9. religion | 10. country |
|---|---|---|---|---|---|---|---|---|---|
| planet | dance | party | gas | meat | actor | school | rome | religion | commune |
| constellation | physicist | rank | formula | bread | composer | institution | emperor | directed | autonomous |
| boat | painting | officer | atomic | cheese | band | economic | ireland | jesus | saxony |
| spacecraft | mathematician | politician | acid | sauce | painter | education | pope | jewish | philippine |
| moon | philosopher | minister | iron | vegetable | singer | agency | dynasty | bible | indonesia |
| mar | scientist | currency | solid | rice | musician | society | egypt | goddess | finland |
| **11. sports/military** | **12. technology** | **13. mixed** | **14. physics** | **15. geography** | **16. medicine** | **17. material** | **18. fashion** | **19. biology** | **20. city** |
| football | electrical | horse | image | bridge | blood | garment | hair | cat | museum |
| tank | data | ice | measure | switzerland | bone | clothing | fabric | shark | street |
| rifle | storage | wall | motion | wine | tissue | dress | soil | temperate | metro |
| team | electronic | blade | energy | valley | muscle | skirt | colour | subfamily | stockholm |
| carrier | signal | tool | wave | canton | organism | flag | cloth | beetle | tokyo |
| stadium | card | stone | radiation | archipelago | organ | garden | hat | grass | korea |

Table 3: Topics induced using the Embedded Topic Model on VisualSem English glosses (labels in bold are assigned manually).

embeddings $n_i$ and show the plot in Figure 3.[8] We highlight that nodes cluster well according to their predicted topic, and note that even though there clearly is some structure in the space induced by the KG glosses, finding hard boundaries across topics does not seem straightforward (at least for the majority of nodes closer to the center of the plot).

## 4 Entity Retrieval

In this section, we describe *retrieval models* that retrieve entities in the KB given a sentence or an image. Our use-case includes tasks with possibly multi-modal inputs—i.e., either a sentence, an image, or both—where we use these inputs to retrieve relevant entities from VisualSem. The idea is to ground the task inputs or to augment the available data to train the task model. This task could be text-only, such as named entity recognition or machine translation, or multi-modal, such as visual question answering or image captioning. We do not include experiments on specific tasks but instead leave that investigation for future work.

We use a standard *retrieval as ranking* framework where the model is trained to rank nodes in VisualSem given an input, and we use the top-$k$ ranked nodes as the results. These retrieval modules allow for an easy integration of VisualSem's entities, glosses, and images into neural pipelines.

We frame entity retrieval using sentences (henceforth *sentence retrieval*, Section 4.1) as a sentence-to-gloss ranking problem, and use glosses available in all languages in the model. Given an input sentence, we transform the resulting ranking over glosses into a ranking over nodes (i.e., by retrieving the nodes these glosses are linked to from their 1-to-1 mappings). We similarly frame retrieval using images (henceforth *image retrieval*, Section 4.2) as an image-to-gloss ranking problem, and use all English glosses available for retrieval.

[8]We use the following hyperparameters with t-SNE: perplexity is set to 70, and number of iterations to 5000.

| | # train | # valid | # test |
|---|---|---|---|
| Glosses | $1,286,764$ | $28,000$ | $28,000$ |
| Images | $898,100$ | $20,000$ | $20,000$ |

Table 4: VisualSem gloss and image splits. Gloss validation and test splits include $2,000$ entries for each of the 14 languages in VisualSem.

Experiments in this section use the gloss and image splits in Table 4. Training, validation and test splits for glosses and images are chosen randomly in order to facilitate their use by the research community in future experiments. Gloss validation and test splits are balanced regarding different languages, and each split includes $2,000$ examples for each of the 14 languages in VisualSem.

### 4.1 Sentence retrieval

VisualSem has $N = 89,896$ nodes with glosses in up to 14 languages. We encode glosses using Sentence BERT (SBERT; Reimers and Gurevych, 2019), which is a family of models based on bi-encoder architectures trained on the task of sentence similarity that have strong performance when used for retrieval/indexing. SBERT models are by default trained on English-only sentences to map semantically similar sentences to points close in the embedding space. We use a multilingual SBERT model trained using knowledge distillation to transfer knowledge from English to other languages, more specifically the `paraphrase-multilingual-mpnet-base v2` model (Reimers and Gurevych, 2020) trained on over 50 languages. We select the model from all publicly available models according to validation

| | Hits@k | | | Rank |
|---|---|---|---|---|
| | 1 ↑ | 3 ↑ | 10 ↑ | mean (std) ↓ |
| ar | 37.7 | 48.9 | 58.6 | 2,572 (18,369) |
| de | 48.9 | 58.3 | 66.7 | 1,590 (13,801) |
| en | 56.1 | 64.0 | 73.0 | 15,156 (133,161) |
| es | 60.5 | 69.3 | 76.4 | 693 (6,234) |
| fr | 53.4 | 62.3 | 70.1 | 1,967 (20,850) |
| it | 57.7 | 66.1 | 73.2 | 1,248 (16,216) |
| ko | 44.7 | 56.8 | 66.8 | 1,488 (19,586) |
| nl | 46.2 | 54.8 | 62.6 | 3,110 (31,413) |
| pt | **73.1** | **79.5** | **83.8** | 1,646 (34,586) |
| ru | 28.9 | 36.4 | 42.8 | 16,043 (55,115) |
| zh | 62.9 | 73.3 | 81.1 | 1,691 (26,218) |
| fa | 38.6 | 49.8 | 60.1 | 1,829 (9,089) |
| pl | 49.2 | 58.0 | 66.8 | 3,803 (25,605) |
| sv | 61.7 | 71.4 | 78.7 | **656 (6,865)** |
| **avg.** | 51.4 | 60.6 | 68.6 | 3,821 (43,430) |

Table 5: Sentence retrieval results on VisualSem test glosses. We report Hits@$k$, which is the percentage of time the correct node is retrieved in the top-$k$ results (higher is better) and the mean rank of the correct node (lower is better). According to Hits@$k$, Portuguese and Chinese have the best retrieval results, whereas worst results are obtained for Russian, Arabic, and Farsi. Best mean ranks are obtained with Spanish and Slovenian queries, and worst with Russian and English.

performance.[9]

Let $g_{i,j}$ be the $j$-th gloss in the set of glosses associated to node $i$, and $\boldsymbol{g}_{i,j}$ be gloss $g_{i,j}$'s 512-dimensional vector representation computed with SBERT. We implement the sentence retrieval using $k$-nearest neighbour ($k$-NN). We directly rank all glosses in the split given the query according to their cosine similarity, and use the node associated to the gloss with the highest cosine similarity as the retrieved node.

**Evaluation and Discussion** We use the SBERT model `paraphrase-multilingual-mpnet-base-v2` (Reimers and Gurevych, 2019, 2020), trained on over 50 languages using knowledge distillation on the task of sentence similarity. All languages covered in VisualSem are supported by the model. We directly use the 28,000 held-out test glosses (2k per language) for model evaluation and show the results in Table 5. We note that retrieval results are in general

| | Rank | Hits@k | | |
|---|---|---|---|---|
| | mean (std) ↓ | 1 ↑ | 3 ↑ | 10 ↑ |
| $k$-NN | 4,117 (16,705) | 10.0 | 16.5 | 25.6 |

Table 6: Image retrieval results on test images. We report Hits@$k$, which is the percentage of the time the correct node is retrieved in the top-$k$ results (higher is better) and the mean rank of the correct node (lower is better).

very good according to Hits@$k$. Portuguese and Chinese queries have the best sentence retrieval performance according to this metric, whereas querying the model using Russian, Arabic, and Farsi has the worse performance. We note that mean ranks show high variances, which indicate that retrieved nodes could be noisy despite the good Hits@$k$ scores. Surprisingly, mean ranks obtained with English and Russian queries are the highest (i.e., the lower the mean ranks, the better). We recommend that users use the sentence retrieval model with care when dealing with any of the low-quality languages.

### 4.2 Image retrieval

CLIP (Radford et al., 2021) is a discriminative model with a bi-encoder architecture trained on 400 million image-text pairs. It has one text and one image encoder and is trained to maximize the dot-product of correct image-sentence pairs, and at the same time to minimize the dot-product of random pairs. We use the pre-trained CLIP model `RN50x16` for image retrieval, which is the best released CLIP model at the time.[10]

We encode each image $v_k$ in the validation and test sets ($k = 20,000$) using CLIP image encoder, and denote each image $v_k$'s 768-dimensional vector representation generated with the image encoder by $\boldsymbol{v}_k$. We similarly encode all *training* English glosses $g_j$ for all nodes in VisualSem using CLIP text encoder, which similarly computes a 768-dimensional vector representation $\boldsymbol{g}_j$ for each English gloss.

**Evaluation and Discussion** We use the encoding of each of the 20k images in the validation and test sets, and frame node retrieval using images as queries as an image-to-gloss ranking problem. We rank *training* English glosses in VisualSem ac-

[9] Models available in `https://www.sbert.net/docs/pretrained_models.html#multi-lingual-models`.

[10] `https://github.com/openai/CLIP/blob/main/clip/clip.py`

cording to their cosine similarity with the input image, and use the node associated to the gloss with the highest cosine similarity as the retrieved node. When there are more than one English gloss associated to a node, we use the best ranking across all glosses as the ranking of the retrieved node. We report results in Table 6, and note that the quality of the image retrieval module is worse compared to the sentence retrieval. One of our plans for future work is to investigate how to improve VisualSem image retrieval module.

## 5 Related work

Knowledge bases (KBs) and KGs have a long and rich history, and many publicly available KBs exist and have been built for different purposes.[11] A seminal example is Cyc (Lenat et al., 1986), an early effort towards building a general-purpose knowledge base to store common sense facts and rules about how the world works. More recent examples of knowledge bases built with different purposes include WordNet (Miller, 1995; Bond and Paik, 2012), DBPedia (Auer et al., 2007), Wikidata (Vrandečić and Krötzsch, 2014), Freebase (Bollacker et al., 2008), YAGO (Rebele et al., 2016; Pellissier Tanon et al., 2020), ConceptNet (Speer and Havasi, 2012), ATOMIC (Sap et al., 2019), among many others (see Wang et al., 2017; Ji et al., 2020 for a detailed list of knowledge bases and algorithms). Our main goal is to design a KG to support research in vision & language, which none of the abovementioned KBs are designed to do.

**Multi-modal knowledge bases.** Two recently proposed multimodal knowledge bases are WN9-IMG (Xie et al., 2017) and FB15-IMG (Mousselly Sergieh et al., 2018): the former consists of a subset of entities and relations from WordNet and was built using the WN18 dataset proposed in Bordes et al. (2014), and additionally includes 10 images illustrating each entity; the latter is based on the FB15 dataset introduced by Bordes et al. (2013), which in turn consists of examples extracted from Freebase, and also includes 10 images per entity. Although these KBs include images, they are still restricted to a single data source and constrained in terms of the domains they encompass.

An exception is BabelNet (Navigli and Ponzetto, 2012), which is a very large KG that combines varied sources—such as Freebase, WordNet and Wikipedia in several languages, among many others—and includes over 54 million images mined mostly from Wikipedia and ImageNet. BabelNet can be seen as a high coverage KB, and in its version v4.0 has more than 15.7 million concepts in 284 languages. At times, images linked in BabelNet may have poor quality (Calabrese et al., 2020), e.g., blurred photos, images loosely related to the concept they illustrate, uninformative images such as icons, flags, or rendered graphs (see Figure 1 for examples). We build an *image filtering* pipeline that filters out noisy images linked in BabelNet, and we source the remaining high-quality images in VisualSem.

All the aforementioned KBs have in common the fact they are mostly *"entity-centric"*: nodes denote *concepts* and are associated with multimodal information. This is in contrast to "vision-centric" KBs such as Visual Genome (Krishna et al., 2017) and Visual KB (Zhu et al., 2015), where each instance in the dataset is an image with a *scene graph* representation to support visual query tasks. Besides visual queries, multimodal KBs have been designed for conversational reasoning (Moon et al., 2019) and node classification (Bloem et al., 2021). VisualSem is an entity-centric KG designed to support tasks at the intersection of vision and language.

## 6 Conclusions and Future work

We present the VisualSem knowledge graph with $\sim$ 90k nodes, over 1.3M glosses in up to 14 diverse languages, and around 938k curated and cleaned images illustrating nodes' concepts. VisualSem bridges a gap in the available resources to train grounded models of language, and is designed to be useful in vision and language research. We release neural entity retrieval models that accept text and image inputs. Sentences in any of the $\sim$ 50 languages supported by multilingual Sentence BERT can be used to retrieve entities from the KG, and we evaluate retrieval using all 14 languages in VisualSem in Table 5. Images can also be used to retrieve nodes using the state-of-the-art CLIP model, and visual entity retrieval is evaluated in Table 6. This allows researchers to easily integrate VisualSem into their (neural) model pipelines, and we encourage its use not just in tasks that involve vision and language, but across all sorts of language understanding and/or generation tasks, in *grounding* and/or in *data augmentation* settings.

[11]We do not differentiate between knowledge bases and knowledge graphs for the purposes of this work and use both terms interchangeably.

**Future Work** We will use VisualSem sentence/image retrieval mechanisms and gloss and image features for data augmentation in NLP tasks, e.g. word sense disambiguation and named entity recognition, and on vision and language tasks, e.g. image captioning and visual question answering. The reason for these tasks is that they all could intuitively benefit from the added knowledge, be it visual, textual, or multi-modal. We will also investigate how to improve the quality of the image and sentence retrieval modules, both central to the KG impact on current neural-based models. Finally, we plan to improve and grow the KG, which is under active development. We will particularly gauge whether there is interest from the research community in increasing its coverage to include other parts of, or the entirety of, Wikipedia, for example.

## Acknowledgements

IC has received funding from the European Union's Horizon 2020 research and innovation programme under the Marie Skłodowska-Curie grant agreement No 838188. KC is partly supported by Samsung Advanced Institute of Technology (Next Generation Deep Learning: from pattern recognition to AI) and Samsung Research (Improving Deep Learning using Latent Structure). KC also thanks Naver, eBay, NVIDIA, and NSF Award 1922658 for support. CV's work on this project at New York University was financially supported by Eric and Wendy Schmidt (made by recommendation of the Schmidt Futures program) and Samsung Research (under the project *Improving Deep Learning using Latent Structure*) and benefitted from in-kind support by the NYU High-Performance Computing Center. This material is based upon work supported by the National Science Foundation under Grant No. 1922658. Any opinions, findings, and conclusions or recommendations expressed in this material are those of the author(s) and do not necessarily reflect the views of the National Science Foundation.

## References

Houda Alberts and Iacer Calixto. 2020. Imagifilter: A resource to enable the semi-automatic mining of images at scale. *arXiv preprint*.

Sören Auer, Christian Bizer, Georgi Kobilarov, Jens Lehmann, Richard Cyganiak, and Zachary Ives. 2007. Dbpedia: A nucleus for a web of open data. In *The Semantic Web*, pages 722–735, Berlin, Heidelberg. Springer Berlin Heidelberg.

David M. Blei, Andrew Y. Ng, and Michael I. Jordan. 2003. Latent dirichlet allocation. *J. Mach. Learn. Res.*, 3(null):993–1022.

Peter Bloem, Xander Wilcke, Lucas van Berkel, and Victor de Boer. 2021. kgbench: A collection of knowledge graph datasets for evaluating relational and multimodal machine learning. In *Eighteenth Extended Semantic Web Conference - Resources Track*.

Piotr Bojanowski, Edouard Grave, Armand Joulin, and Tomas Mikolov. 2016. Enriching word vectors with subword information. *arXiv preprint arXiv:1607.04606*.

Kurt Bollacker, Colin Evans, Praveen Paritosh, Tim Sturge, and Jamie Taylor. 2008. Freebase: A collaboratively created graph database for structuring human knowledge. In *Proceedings of the 2008 ACM SIGMOD International Conference on Management of Data*, SIGMOD '08, page 1247–1250, New York, NY, USA. Association for Computing Machinery.

Francis Bond and Kyonghee Paik. 2012. A survey of wordnets and their licenses. In *Proceedings of the 6th Global WordNet Conference (GWC 2012)*, Matsue. 64–71.

Antoine Bordes, Xavier Glorot, Jason Weston, and Yoshua Bengio. 2014. A semantic matching energy function for learning with multi-relational data. *Mach. Learn.*, 94(2):233–259.

Antoine Bordes, Nicolas Usunier, Alberto Garcia-Durán, Jason Weston, and Oksana Yakhnenko. 2013. Translating embeddings for modeling multi-relational data. In *Proceedings of the 26th International Conference on Neural Information Processing Systems - Volume 2*, NIPS'13, page 2787–2795, Red Hook, NY, USA. Curran Associates Inc.

Agostina Calabrese, Michele Bevilacqua, and Roberto Navigli. 2020. Fatality killed the cat or: BabelPic, a multimodal dataset for non-concrete concepts. In *Proceedings of the 58th Annual Meeting of the Association for Computational Linguistics*, pages 4680–4686, Online. Association for Computational Linguistics.

Davide Colla, Enrico Mensa, Daniele P. Radicioni, and Antonio Lieto. 2018. Tell me why: Computational explanation of conceptual similarity judgments. In *Information Processing and Management of Uncertainty in Knowledge-Based Systems. Theory and Foundations*, pages 74–85, Cham. Springer International Publishing.

P. Cui, S. Liu, and W. Zhu. 2018. General knowledge embedded image representation learning. *IEEE Transactions on Multimedia*, 20(1):198–207.

J. Deng, W. Dong, R. Socher, L. Li, Kai Li, and Li Fei-Fei. 2009. Imagenet: A large-scale hierarchical image database. In *2009 IEEE Conference on Computer Vision and Pattern Recognition*, pages 248–255.

Adji B. Dieng, Francisco J. R. Ruiz, and David M. Blei. 2020. Topic modeling in embedding spaces. *Transactions of the Association for Computational Linguistics*, 8:439–453.

D. Eastlake and P. Jones. 2001. Rfc3174: Us secure hash algorithm 1 (sha1).

Kelvin Guu, Kenton Lee, Zora Tung, Panupong Pasupat, and Mingwei Chang. 2020. Realm: Retrieval-augmented language model pre-training. In *Proceedings of the 37th International Conference on Machine Learning*, volume 119 of *Proceedings of Machine Learning Research*, pages 3929–3938. PMLR.

Shaoxiong Ji, Shirui Pan, Erik Cambria, Pekka Marttinen, and Philip S Yu. 2020. A survey on knowledge graphs: Representation, acquisition and applications. *arXiv preprint arXiv:2002.00388*.

Ranjay Krishna, Yuke Zhu, Oliver Groth, Justin Johnson, Kenji Hata, Joshua Kravitz, Stephanie Chen, Yannis Kalantidis, Li-Jia Li, David A. Shamma, and et al. 2017. Visual genome: Connecting language and vision using crowdsourced dense image annotations. *International Journal of Computer Vision*, 123(1):32–73.

Doug Lenat, Mayank Prakash, and Mary Shepherd. 1986. Cyc: Using common sense knowledge to overcome brittleness and knowledge acquistion bottlenecks. *AI Mag.*, 6(4):65–85.

Mike Lewis, Marjan Ghazvininejad, Gargi Ghosh, Armen Aghajanyan, Sida Wang, and Luke Zettlemoyer. 2020a. Pre-training via paraphrasing. In *Advances in Neural Information Processing Systems*, volume 33, pages 18470–18481. Curran Associates, Inc.

Patrick Lewis, Ethan Perez, Aleksandra Piktus, Fabio Petroni, Vladimir Karpukhin, Naman Goyal, Heinrich Küttler, Mike Lewis, Wen-tau Yih, Tim Rocktäschel, Sebastian Riedel, and Douwe Kiela. 2020b. Retrieval-augmented generation for knowledge-intensive nlp tasks. In *Advances in Neural Information Processing Systems*, volume 33, pages 9459–9474. Curran Associates, Inc.

Laurens van der Maaten and Geoffrey Hinton. 2008. Visualizing data using t-SNE. *Journal of Machine Learning Research*, 9:2579–2605.

George A Miller. 1995. Wordnet: a lexical database for english. *Communications of the ACM*, 38(11):39–41.

Seungwhan Moon, Pararth Shah, Anuj Kumar, and Rajen Subba. 2019. Opendialkg: Explainable conversational reasoning with attention-based walks over knowledge graphs. In *Proceedings of the 57th Annual Meeting of the Association for Computational Linguistics*, pages 845–854.

Hatem Mousselly Sergieh, Teresa Botschen, Iryna Gurevych, and Stefan Roth. 2018. A Multimodal Translation-Based Approach for Knowledge Graph Representation Learning. In *Proceedings of the 7th Joint Conference on Lexical and Computational Semantics (*SEM 2018)*, page to appear. Association for Computational Linguistics.

Roberto Navigli and Simone Paolo Ponzetto. 2012. Babelnet: The automatic construction, evaluation and application of a wide-coverage multilingual semantic network. *Artificial Intelligence*, 193:217–250.

Thomas Pellissier Tanon, Gerhard Weikum, and Fabian Suchanek. 2020. Yago 4: A reason-able knowledge base. In *The Semantic Web*, pages 583–596, Cham. Springer International Publishing.

Alec Radford, Jong Wook Kim, Chris Hallacy, Aditya Ramesh, Gabriel Goh, Sandhini Agarwal, Girish Sastry, Amanda Askell, Pamela Mishkin, Jack Clark, et al. 2021. Learning transferable visual models from natural language supervision. *arXiv preprint arXiv:2103.00020*.

Thomas Rebele, Fabian M. Suchanek, Johannes Hoffart, Joanna Asia Biega, Erdal Kuzey, and Gerhard Weikum. 2016. Yago: A multilingual knowledge base from wikipedia, wordnet, and geonames. In *International Semantic Web Conference*.

Nils Reimers and Iryna Gurevych. 2019. Sentence-bert: Sentence embeddings using siamese bert-networks. In *Proceedings of the 2019 Conference on Empirical Methods in Natural Language Processing*. Association for Computational Linguistics.

Nils Reimers and Iryna Gurevych. 2020. Making monolingual sentence embeddings multilingual using knowledge distillation. *arXiv preprint arXiv:2004.09813*.

Olga Russakovsky, Jia Deng, Hao Su, Jonathan Krause, Sanjeev Satheesh, Sean Ma, Zhiheng Huang, Andrej Karpathy, Aditya Khosla, Michael Bernstein, Alexander C. Berg, and Li Fei-Fei. 2015. Imagenet large scale visual recognition challenge. *Int. J. Comput. Vision*, 115(3):211–252.

Maarten Sap, Ronan Le Bras, Emily Allaway, Chandra Bhagavatula, Nicholas Lourie, Hannah Rashkin, Brendan Roof, Noah A. Smith, and Yejin Choi. 2019. ATOMIC: an atlas of machine commonsense for if-then reasoning. In *The Thirty-Third AAAI Conference on Artificial Intelligence, AAAI 2019*, pages 3027–3035. AAAI Press.

Robyn Speer and Catherine Havasi. 2012. Representing general relational knowledge in ConceptNet 5. In *Proceedings of the Eighth International Conference on Language Resources and Evaluation (LREC-2012)*, pages 3679–3686, Istanbul, Turkey. European Languages Resources Association (ELRA).

Denny Vrandečić and Markus Krötzsch. 2014. Wikidata: A free collaborative knowledgebase. *Commun. ACM*, 57(10):78–85.

Q. Wang, Z. Mao, B. Wang, and L. Guo. 2017. Knowledge graph embedding: A survey of approaches and applications. *IEEE Transactions on Knowledge and Data Engineering*, 29(12):2724–2743.

Ruobing Xie, Zhiyuan Liu, Huanbo Luan, and Maosong Sun. 2017. Image-embodied knowledge representation learning. In *Proceedings of the 26th International Joint Conference on Artificial Intelligence*, IJCAI'17, page 3140–3146. AAAI Press.

Yuke Zhu, Ce Zhang, Christopher Ré, and Li Fei-Fei. 2015. Building a large-scale multimodal knowledge base system for answering visual queries. *arXiv preprint arXiv:1507.05670*.

## A Examples

We now show some example data in VisualSem to illustrate what kind of information is available in a node, including metadata, as well as what images are kept and what are filtered out. We select five topics (i.e., country, people, physics, biology, space) in the topic model discussed in Section 3.2 and show one example node in each, including: **multilingual glosses** in up 14 languages (we show a maximum of one gloss per language per node to avoid clutter); **images** linked to the node, including the ones filtered out by our procedure illustrated in Section 2; **relations** to other nodes in the KG (we show a maximum of three connected nodes to avoid clutter). We illustrate the five node examples in Figures 4–8, and we use these examples to support a discussion on the quality of the data.

First, we note that information described in a node's glosses can be repetitive across languages (e.g., in Figure 6 the glosses in English and Portuguese are translations of one another), but often can also be complementary (e.g., again in Figure 6 the gloss in French includes novel information such as the mention to leguminous crops, which does not appear neither in English nor Portuguese).

We also note that the removed images are most of the time non-photographic and/or noisy, in accord with our motivation. Images such as the map or the sketch in Figure 4, or the excluded images in Figures 7 or 8, are not *descriptive* of the node. However, a limited number of relevant images are sometimes excluded by our procedure (e.g., the field with animals in Figure 6), and conversely sometimes images that are tangentially related to a node are kept (e.g., the magnet in Figure 8).

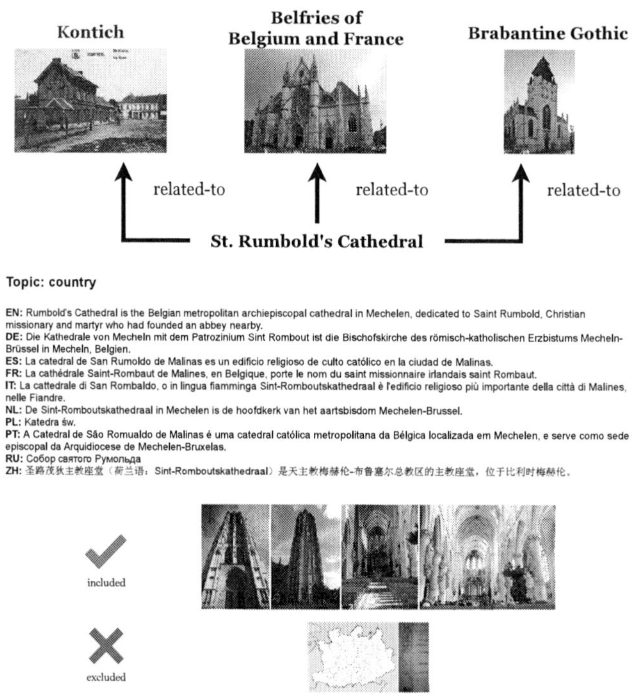


Figure 4: *St. Rumbold's Cathedral*. The node is connected to four other nodes (3 shown) with relation types `related-to` and `has-a` (not shown), and has a total of 23 images kept (4 shown).

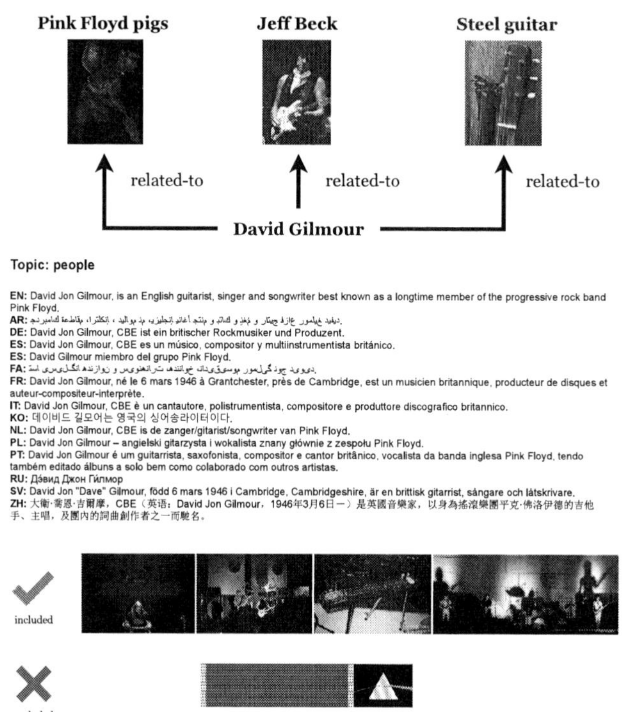


Figure 5: *David Gilmour*. The node is connected to 10 other nodes (3 shown) with 2 relation types `related-to` and `has-a` (not shown), and has a total of 10 images kept (4 shown).

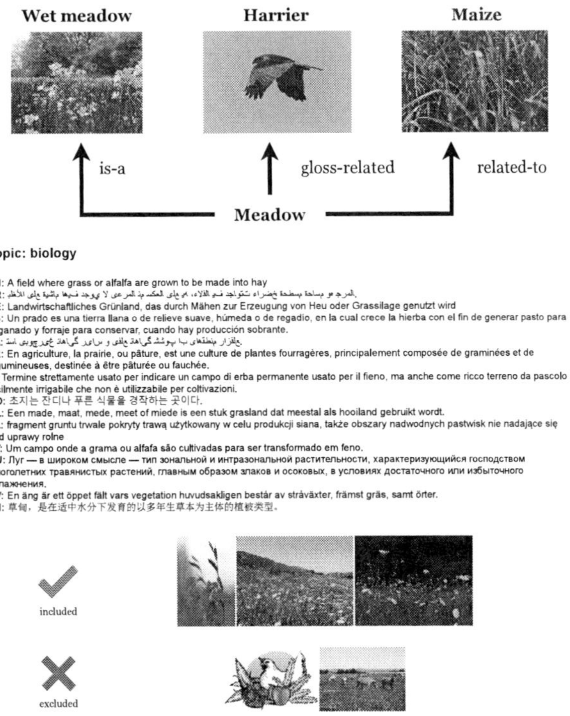


Figure 6: *Meadow*. The node is connected to 127 other nodes (3 shown) with relation types `related-to`, `gloss-related`, `is-a`, `has-a` (not shown), and has a total of 26 images kept (3 shown).

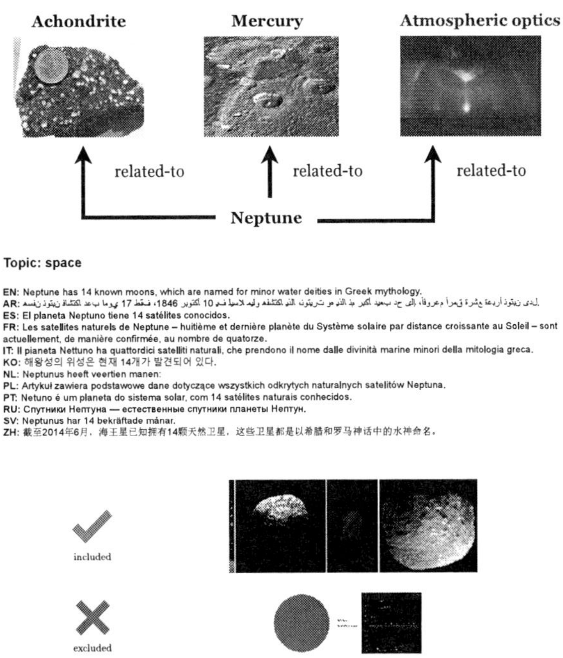


Figure 7: *Neptune*. The node is connected to 10 other nodes (3 shown) with relation types `related-to`, `is-a` (not shown), `has-a` (not shown), and has a total of 26 images kept (4 shown).

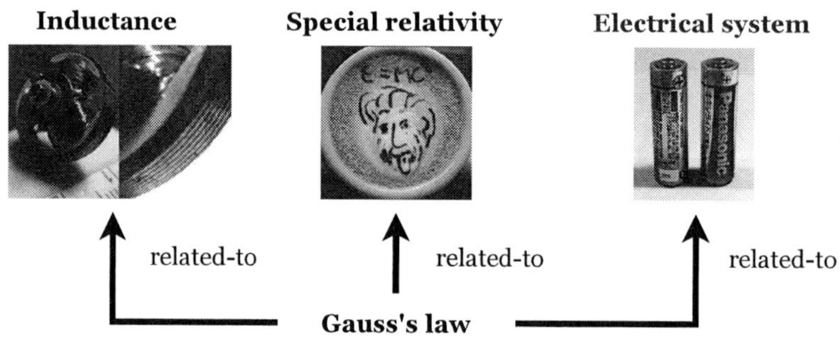


**Topic: physics**

**EN:** In physics, Gauss's law, also known as Gauss's flux theorem, is a law relating the distribution of electric charge to the resulting electric field.
**AR:** في الفيزياء، قانون جاوس الكهربي، المعروف أيضاً بإسم مبرهنة جاوس في التدفق الكهربي، والقانون يصف العلاقة بين توزيع الشحنة الكهربائية والمجال الكهربائي الناتج عنها.
**DE:** Das gaußsche Gesetz beschreibt in der Elektrostatik und Elektrodynamik den elektrischen Fluss durch eine geschlossene Fläche.
**ES:** En física la ley de Gauss, también conocida como teorema de Gauss, establece que el flujo de ciertos campos a través de una superficie cerrada es proporcional a la magnitud de las fuentes de dicho campo que hay en el interior de la misma superficie.
**FA:** قانون گاوس که با نام قضیه شار گاوس هم شناخته شده، قانونی در فیزیک است که ارتباط توزیع بار الکتریکی و میدان الکتریکی حاصل از آن را بیان میکند.
**FR:** En électromagnétisme, le théorème de Gauss permet de calculer le flux d'un champ électrique à travers une surface fermée contenant des charges électriques.
**IT:** Nella teoria dei campi vettoriali il teorema del flusso, noto anche come teorema di Gauss, afferma che i campi vettoriali radiali dipendenti dal reciproco del quadrato della distanza dall'origine hanno un flusso attraverso una qualunque superficie chiusa che dipende solo dalla carica in essa contenuta ed è indipendente dalla posizione interna delle cariche che lo generano.
**KO:** 가우스 법칙은 폐곡면을 통과하는 전기 선속이 폐곡면 속의 알짜 전하량에 비례한다는 법칙이다.
**NL:** De wet van Gauss geeft in de fysica de relatie weer tussen de elektrische flux door een gesloten oppervlak en de elektrische lading binnen het oppervlak.
**PL:** Prawo Gaussa dla elektryczności – prawo wiążące pole elektryczne z jego źródłem, czyli ładunkiem elektrycznym.
**PT:** A lei de Gauss é a lei que estabelece a relação entre o fluxo do campo elétrico através de uma superfície fechada com a carga elétrica que existe dentro do volume limitado por esta superfície.
**RU:** Теорема Гаусса — один из основных законов электродинамики, входит в систему уравнений Максвелла.
**SV:** I fysiken syftar Gauss lag på någon tillämpning av den generella matematiska satsen Gauss sats som ger sambandet mellan ytintegralen av något flöde, till exempel av vätska, som flödar ut ur en sluten yta och resultatet av källor som är inneslutna i den slutna ytan.
**ZH:** 高斯定律（Gauss' law）表明在闭合曲面内的电荷分佈與產生的電場之間的關係：

Figure 8: *Gauss' Law*. The node is connected to 6 other nodes (3 shown) with relation type `related-to`, and has a total of 5 images kept (3 shown).

# Vyākarana: A Colorless Green Benchmark for Syntactic Evaluation in Indic Languages

**Rajaswa Patil**
Cognitive Neuroscience Lab
BITS Pilani, Goa Campus
f20170334@goa.bits-pilani.ac.in

**Jasleen Dhillon**
Dept. of CS & IS
BITS Pilani, Goa Campus
f20170077@goa.bits-pilani.ac.in

**Siddhant Mahurkar**
Data Science Institute
Columbia University
sm5129@columbia.edu

**Saumitra Kulkarni**
Dept. of Computer Engineering
PICT, Maharashtra, India
kulkarnisaumitra98@gmail.com

**Manav Malhotra**
Dept. of Mathematics
BITS Pilani, Goa Campus
f20171016@goa.bits-pilani.ac.in

**Veeky Baths**
Cognitive Neuroscience Lab
BITS Pilani, Goa Campus
veeky@goa.bits-pilani.ac.in

## Abstract

While there has been significant progress towards developing NLU resources for Indic languages, syntactic evaluation has been relatively less explored. Unlike English, Indic languages have rich morphosyntax, grammatical genders, free linear word-order, and highly inflectional morphology. In this paper, we introduce *Vyākarana*: a benchmark of Colorless Green sentences in Indic languages for syntactic evaluation of multilingual language models. The benchmark comprises four syntax-related tasks: PoS Tagging, Syntax Tree-depth Prediction, Grammatical Case Marking, and Subject-Verb Agreement. We use the datasets from the evaluation tasks to probe five multilingual language models of varying architectures for syntax in Indic languages. Due to its prevalence, we also include a code-switching setting in our experiments. Our results show that the token-level and sentence-level representations from the Indic language models (IndicBERT and MuRIL) do not capture the syntax in Indic languages as efficiently as the other highly multilingual language models. Further, our layer-wise probing experiments reveal that while mBERT, DistilmBERT, and XLM-R localize the syntax in middle layers, the Indic language models do not show such syntactic localization.

## 1 Introduction

The Indian subcontinent is home to more than 450 languages spanning seven language families. Multilingualism and code-switching are common phenomenon across these languages. Traditionally, the region has been at the center of many linguistic studies due to its rich linguistic diversity (Emeneau, 1956). The Indo-Aryan and the Dravidian language families are the most prominent ones in the subcontinent, with more than a billion speakers combined. Recent work in computational linguistics has focused on clubbing together the major languages from these two language families into a single group called as *Indic Languages*.[1] Even with such a huge potential user base, the progress in building language technologies for the Indic languages has been limited. Most of the Indic languages fall under the category of low-resourced and mid-resourced languages. Some recent open-sourced efforts have tried to address this by developing various toolkits (Arora, 2020), frameworks (Kunchukuttan, 2020), language models, benchmarks, and datasets (Kakwani et al., 2020).

To perform well on natural language understanding tasks, a language model should have a good understanding of the various general aspects of the structure of language, like its grammar and syntax. The structure of Indic languages is quite rich in its morphosyntax, which is partially shared across the languages. Thus, performing language modeling and downstream tasks on a multilingual dataset of Indic languages helps capture typologically generalized stimuli across the languages and implicitly addresses the issue of data-scarcity. While there have been some efforts to analyze the role of multilingual training for Indic languages, it has been limited to downstream NLU tasks and large multilingual models which are not exclusively trained for Indic languages (Jain et al., 2020). In this work, we introduce a syntactic evaluation benchmark of *Colorless Green*[2] sentences in Indic languages: *Vyākarana*[3], which provides a challenging envi-

[1]From a linguistic perspective, the term *Indic* is used for the Indo-Aryan language family. However, in this work, we use the term to represent all the languages used in the subcontinent (following the recent work in "Indic NLP").

[2]*Colorless green* sentences are grammatically correct, but semantically nonsensical.

[3]Vyākarana is the Sanskrit term for grammar



*Proceedings of the 1st Workshop on Multilingual Representation Learning*, pages 153–165
November 11, 2021. 

ronment to evaluate multilingual language models for their syntactic abilities specifically. We use the dataset to conduct layer-wise probing of five multilingual language models to inspect their understanding of the syntax in Indic languages. We include the IndicBERT (Kakwani et al., 2020) and MuRIL (Khanuja et al., 2021)[4] models in our experiments, which are trained on Indic languages and English exclusively. We probe the models for four syntax-related tasks: PoS Tagging (POS), Syntax Tree-depth Prediction (STDP), Grammatical Case Marking (GCM), and Subject-Verb Agreement (SVA). In an attempt to capture the linguistic diversity in the Indian subcontinent, we include one language each from the Indo-Aryan (Hindi) and Dravidian (Tamil) language families in the dataset. In order to incorporate the prevalent phenomena of code-switching in these languages, we also include English-based script-mixed versions of these languages in our experiments. Our layer-wise probing experiments show that the Indic language models do not show syntactic localization and do not capture the syntax in Indic languages as efficiently as the other "highly multilingual language models".[5]

## 2 Background

Language models are usually evaluated with information theory-based perplexity measures. While these perplexity measures might show good agreement with a language model's natural language understanding (NLU) capabilities, they do not capture language models' syntactic abilities efficiently (Tran et al., 2018). Evaluating language models' syntactic abilities is quite important in furthering the research towards developing human-like robust language models (Linzen, 2020). Recent work has focused on the targeted syntactic evaluation of language models (Linzen et al., 2016; Lau et al., 2017; Gulordava et al., 2018; Marvin and Linzen, 2018; McCoy et al., 2019; Futrell et al., 2019), which takes inspiration from various psycholinguistic generalizations found in humans and assesses the role of syntax in the models' ability to perform various NLU tasks. While there has been significant progress towards building NLU evaluation benchmarks (Wang et al., 2018, 2019), the work in developing syntactic evaluation benchmarks has been quite recent and limited (Gauthier et al., 2020; Hu et al., 2020a; Mueller et al., 2020).

Probing is an alternative paradigm that can be used for syntactic evaluation of language models. Probing deals with quantifying the amount of linguistic information encoded in the pre-trained representations of language models (Adi et al., 2017; Conneau et al., 2018). While this does not provide a very detailed analysis of models' syntactic behavior, it can be used to compare the amount of syntactic information captured by the models, as well as the inner dynamics of how and where this information is encoded in the models (Hewitt and Manning, 2019; Jawahar et al., 2019; Lin et al., 2019; Liu et al., 2019; Tenney et al., 2019b; Rogers et al., 2020). Probing methods are also relatively compute-efficient, as they do not involve training or fine-tuning the language models.

With the recent development in multilingual language modeling, numerous evaluation studies have been performed to test the models' multilingual and cross-lingual abilities (Libovický et al., 2019; Rönnqvist et al., 2019; Pires et al., 2019; Wu and Dredze, 2019; Artetxe et al., 2020). Similar to monolingual language modeling paradigms, there has been significant work towards building multilingual evaluation benchmarks (Hu et al., 2020b; Kakwani et al., 2020; Liang et al., 2020). However, these benchmarks do not cover syntactic evaluation efficiently, with POS tagging being the sole syntax-related task. Some recent studies have tried to address this by building multilingual and cross-lingual syntactic evaluation suites with subject-verb agreement tasks (Gulordava et al., 2018; Mueller et al., 2020).

Alongside the developments in multilingual NLP, there has been some recent progress towards advancing Indic NLP (Arora, 2020; Jain et al., 2020; Kakwani et al., 2020; Kunchukuttan, 2020). While there are numerous datasets available to benchmark and compare multilingual language models on NLU tasks in Indic languages, there is no such resource available for syntactic evaluation in Indic languages.[6] Most recent works (Jain et al., 2020; Kakwani et al., 2020; Khanuja et al., 2021) rely on POS tagging with Universal Dependencies treebanks as the sole task to compare the syntactic abilities of Indic language models.

[4]Collectively called as "Indic language models" here on

[5]mBERT, DistilmBERT, and XLM-R

[6]To the best of our knowledge

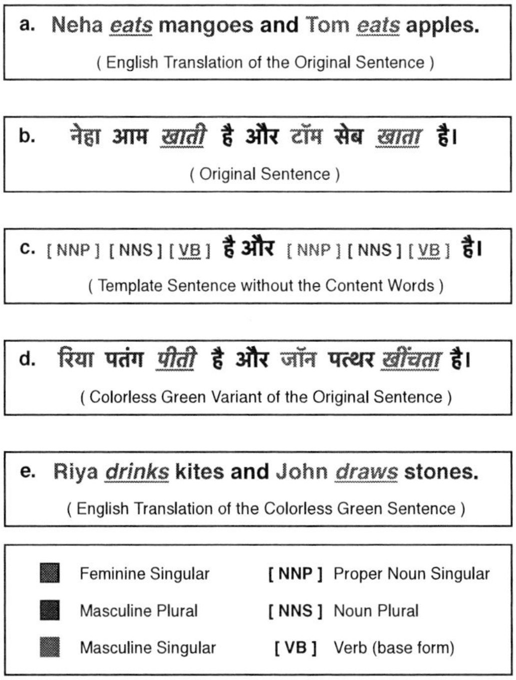


Figure 1: (a,b) - Comparing the linear word-order in English and Hindi; (b,c,d,e) - Constructing Colorless Green sentences in Hindi.

# 3 Vyākarana: A Colorless Green Benchmark[7]

Syntax in Indic languages has specific characteristics which make it more challenging to model. Unlike English, most of the Indic languages follow a free linear word-order, with the default order being SOV (subject-object-verb). Hence, the linear distance (in terms of the number of intervening words) between the verb and its subject is usually larger in Indic languages as compared to English (Figure 1a; Figure 1b). Indic languages like Hindi and Tamil also have grammatical genders and grammatical number, where the words are morphologically inflected in agreement with the gender and count of their corresponding head nouns (Figure 1b).

Usually, the syntactic evaluation of language models is conducted with syntax-related probing tasks (Jawahar et al., 2019), or with targeted syntactic evaluation through controlled psycholinguistic experiments (Gauthier et al., 2020). Performing such syntactic evaluations under a colorless green setting ensures that the models do not leverage any semantic or lexical cues and biases from the text to process its syntactic structure (Gulordava et al., 2018; Goldberg, 2019). Most of the evaluation tasks from both of these categories can be designed with a syntactic dependencies treebank. Hence, we construct a colorless green treebank for Indic languages, which can be used to perform various syntactic evaluation tasks under a colorless green setting.

[7]Example sentences from the benchmark dataset can be found in Appendix A

## 3.1 CG-HDTB: A Colorless Green Treebank for Hindi[8]

We use the Hindi Universal Dependency Treebank (HDTB) (Bhat et al., 2008; Palmer et al., 2009) to construct a new Colorless Green treebank for Hindi: *CG-HDTB*.[9] We follow the method proposed by Gulordava et al. (2018) to generate colorless green sentences. Given a sentence from the original HDTB treebank, we first convert it to a template colorless green sentence (Figure 1c) by removing all the content words (while retaining all the function words) from it. Each of the resulting gaps created by the removal of content words in the template sentence is then populated with a content word from another sentence in the treebank, where the grammatical information of the original and replacing content word is the same (Figure 1d). The resulting colorless green sentence still retains the same grammatical information and syntactic structure as the original sentence, whereas the random substitution of the content words ensures that it is rendered nonsensical (Figure 1a; Figure 1e).

| PoS Tag | Gen | Num | Case | Per |
|---|---|---|---|---|
| Noun | ✓ | ✓ | ✓ | |
| Verb | ✓ | ✓ | | ✓ |
| Adjective | ✓ | ✓ | ✓ | |
| Adverb | ✓ | ✓ | ✓ | |

Table 1: The grammatical information taken into account for various PoS categories of content words (Vikram, 2013).

The grammatical information taken into consideration while substituting the content words includes the Grammatical Gender **(Gen)** (masculine/feminine), Grammatical Number **(Num)** (singular/plural), Grammatical Case **(Case)** (Sec-

[8]In this section we use Hindi as a demonstrative language, where a similar approach is used for Tamil language.

[9]Similarly, we use the Tamil Universal Dependency Treebank (TTB) (Ramasamy and Žabokrtský, 2012) to construct a new Colorless Green treebank for Tamil: *CG-TTB*.

| Data Split | HDTB | | | CG-HDTB | | |
|---|---|---|---|---|---|---|
| | Sentences | Masculine | Feminine | Sentences | Masculine | Feminine |
| **Train** | 13304 | 104389 (70.37%) | 43951 (29.63%) | 6736 | 39178 (51.72%) | 36578 (48.28%) |
| **Dev** | 1659 | 13116 (70.47%) | 5496 (29.53%) | 6628 | 38638 (51.90%) | 35810 (48.10%) |
| **Test** | 1684 | 13253 (69.98%) | 5686 (30.02%) | 53124 | 308034 (51.91%) | 285322 (48.09%) |

Table 2: The number of sentences and the statistics for token-level grammatical gender feature in the HDTB and CG-HDTB treebank (the statistics are same for CG-HDTB and csCG-HDTB treebanks).

tion 3.2), and Person **(Per)** (first/second/third). This makes sure that the replacing content word is consistent with syntax and the morphological inflections of the original content word, keeping the morphosyntax of the sentence intact. The grammatical information required for every PoS category is different, as shown in Table 1. The HDTB treebank has an imbalanced count of Grammatical Gender features. Following an uncontrolled and random substitution of content words can result in a gender-imbalanced dataset of colorless green sentences. We eliminate this imbalance by controlling the grammatical gender information in the colorless green sentences. For every sentence in the HDTB treebank, we generate four colorless green sentences, where the gender encoding of the sentences is:

1. Exactly **same** as that of the original sentence.
2. Exactly **opposite** as that of the original sentence.
3. Entirely **masculine**.
4. Entirely **feminine**.

Apart from the PoS categories of content words mentioned in Table 1, we also adjust the gender-inflected Adposition tokens in the colorless green sentences in order to maintain the morphosyntax of the sentence. The statistics for the Grammatical Gender feature in the gender-imbalanced HDTB treebank and the gender-balanced CG-HDTB treebank are shown in Table 2. Further, we swap the train and test set of the HDTB treebank while generating colorless green sentences (Table 2). This allows the test set of CG-HDTB to be significantly bigger than the training set, providing a challenging test setting for the models' syntactic generalization capabilities.

Unlike Hindi, there is no publicly available treebank for Hindi-English code-switched setting with all the features that are required to obtain the colorless green sentences. Hence, we artificially create a code-switched treebank for Hindi-English: **csCG-HDTB**. The csCG-HDTB treebank is a parallel code-switched version of the CG-HDTB treebank. Following Khanuja et al. (2021)'s approach, we use the Indic-Trans library[10] to transliterate the tokens (Hindi-Devanagari script $\rightarrow$ English-Latin script) from each sentence in the CG-HDTB treebank.[11] While this only helps in incorporating the script-mixing aspect of code-switching, the approach can be scaled easily across different datasets and languages, eliminating the need of explicit annotations of morphosyntactic features on code-switched data.

### 3.2 Evaluation Tasks

The benchmark comprises four syntactic evaluation tasks. We borrow certain design principles for the benchmark from the XTREME benchmark Hu et al. (2020b):

1. **Task Difficulty:** The colorless-green setting, and a sufficiently large test-set ensure a certain level of difficulty across all the tasks. Further, some tasks require capturing long-range relationships and morphological inflections, which make them more challenging.
2. **Task Diversity:** We include both the token-level and the sentence-level evaluation tasks in the benchmark. This ensures that the benchmark evaluates representations from both the granularities.
3. **Data and Training Efficiency:** Under the colorless-green setting, each task has a large test-train ratio in terms of data samples (Table 3). Hence, the datasets for the evaluation tasks are quite challenging in terms of data and training efficiency.

We use the HDTB, CG-HDTB, and csCG-HDTB treebanks to construct datasets for all the evaluation tasks.[12] The statistics for the con-

[10] `https://github.com/libindic/indic-trans`

[11] Similarly, we create a code-switched treebank for Tamil-English: **csCG-TTB**.

[12] Similarly, we use the CG-TTB and csCG-TTB treebanks to conduct the experiments with the Tamil language (Appendix B).

| Data Split | HDTB | | | | CG-HDTB | | | |
|---|---|---|---|---|---|---|---|---|
| | POS | STDP | GCM | SVA | POS | STDP | GCM | SVA |
| **Train** | 281057 | 13304 | 151275 | 17034 | 141720 | 6736 | 76836 | 8536 |
| **Dev** | 35430 | 1659 | 19209 | 2127 | 140844 | 6628 | 76108 | 8508 |
| **Test** | 35217 | 1684 | 19027 | 2134 | 1123964 | 53124 | 605068 | 68136 |

Table 3: The number of tokens (for POS and GCM tasks) and the number of sentences (for STDP and SVA tasks) in the HDTB and CG-HDTB treebank (the statistics are same for CG-HDTB and csCG-HDTB treebanks).

structed datasets are given in Table 3.

**PoS Tagging (POS):** While PoS tagging is a very weak construct for a syntactic evaluation task, it is a preliminary step in syntactic processing. It is also the only existing syntax-related evaluation task used to compare currently available Indic language models. Hence, we include PoS tagging as the first evaluation task in the benchmark. The task is designed under a token-level multi-class single-label classification setting. We use the UPOS tags from the treebanks as the ground-truth labels for this task.

**Syntax Tree-depth Prediction (STDP):** Following the work done by Conneau et al. (2018) and Jawahar et al. (2019), we use the dependency trees from the treebanks to perform syntax tree-depth prediction task. Successful prediction of the depth of a dependency tree depicts the model's ability to get a surface-level estimate of a given sentence's syntactic structure. The task is designed under a sentence-level multi-class single-label classification setting.

**Grammatical Case Marking (GCM):** Given the nature of morphosyntax in Indic languages, case marking is an essential syntactic evaluation task. Unlike languages like English, a fixed linear word-order cannot be used to perform case marking in Indic languages. Instead, one must rely on morphological inflections and Adposition tokens in the sentence to assign appropriate grammatical cases. Moreover, a single token can be marked with a combination of multiple cases. In the HDTB treebank, the grammatical case feature has the following seven unique values: **accusative**, **nominative**, **accusative-inessive**, **dative-accusative**, **ergative-accusative**, **genitive-accusative**, and **instrumental-accusative**. Hence, this task is designed under a token-level multi-class single-label classification setting.

**Subject-Verb Agreement (SVA):** We include subject-verb agreement as an evaluation task to study the long-range syntactic dependencies in Indic languages. Unlike English, the subject-verb agreement in Indic languages is dependent on the grammatical number as well as the grammatical gender of the tokens. Following the work done by Linzen et al. (2016), we include all the tokens preceding (and excluding) the target verb in the sentence. Given such a sentence, the task is to predict the target verb's grammatical count and grammatical gender in agreement with its subject (head noun). Given that most of the Indic languages follow a free linear word-order and the default order is SOV (subject-object-verb), the number of intervening nouns is significantly higher than in English. Moreover, there is a high probability of the object acting as an attractor noun (Figure 1). Hence, the SVA task is significantly more challenging in Indic languages. The task is designed under a sentence-level multi-class single-label classification setting, given the four possible ground truth labels: **masculine-singular**, **masculine-plural**, **feminine-singular**, and **feminine-plural**.

## 4 Experiments[13]

### 4.1 Experimental Setup

We use the datasets constructed for the evaluation tasks to perform layer-wise probing[14] of token-level and sentence-level representations from the five transformer-based multilingual language models: mBERT (Devlin et al., 2019), XLM-R (Conneau et al., 2020), DistilmBERT (Sanh et al., 2019), IndicBERT (Kakwani et al., 2020), and MuRIL (Khanuja et al., 2021). We use a single linear-layer (initialized with the same weights across all the ex-

[13]In this section we discuss the experiments with the Hindi language data. Corresponding details about the experiments with the Tamil language data can be found in Appendix B.

[14]We do not fine-tune the models due to computational limitations. Instead, we report the probing metrics of the last layer and the best-performing layer of every model (Table 4).

| Treebank | Task | Last Layer | | | | | Best Layer | | | | |
|---|---|---|---|---|---|---|---|---|---|---|---|
| | | mBERT | XLM-R | DistilmBERT | IndicBERT | MuRIL | mBERT | XLM-R | DistilmBERT | IndicBERT | MuRIL |
| HDTB | POS | 0.9332 | **0.9567** | 0.8860 | 0.7827 | 0.7290 | 0.9409 (8) | **0.9615 (8)** | 0.8955 (5) | 0.8105 (2) | 0.7728 (1) |
| | STDP | **0.3886** | 0.1848 | 0.3815 | 0.3825 | 0.2588 | 0.4138 (3) | 0.3657 (1) | **0.4247 (3)** | 0.3995 (3) | 0.3969 (8) |
| | GCM | 0.7501 | **0.7733** | 0.7345 | 0.6509 | 0.6350 | 0.7775 (8) | **0.8006 (8)** | 0.7495 (4) | 0.6847 (3) | 0.6522 (1) |
| | SVA | **0.7083** | 0.6208 | 0.7015 | 0.5122 | 0.5178 | **0.7083 (12)** | 0.6208 (12) | 0.7015 (6) | 0.5125 (3) | 0.5718 (12) |
| | Average | **0.6951** | 0.6339 | 0.6759 | 0.5821 | 0.5352 | **0.7101** | 0.6872 | 0.6928 | 0.6018 | 0.5984 |
| CG-HDTB | POS | 0.8894 | **0.9143** | 0.8448 | 0.7418 | 0.6807 | 0.8932 (11) | **0.9232 (8)** | 0.8543 (5) | 0.7642 (6) | 0.7030 (2) |
| | STDP | 0.3455 | 0.2138 | 0.3254 | **0.3566** | 0.2318 | 0.3730 (6) | 0.3232 (3) | **0.3881 (5)** | 0.3756 (4) | 0.3570 (10) |
| | GCM | 0.6886 | **0.6967** | 0.6733 | 0.6216 | 0.5463 | 0.7050 (7) | **0.7234 (8)** | 0.6968 (4) | 0.6479 (2) | 0.5878 (3) |
| | SVA | 0.6003 | 0.5935 | **0.6040** | 0.3990 | 0.5568 | **0.6140 (8)** | 0.5935 (12) | 0.6040 (6) | 0.4451 (2) | 0.5568 (12) |
| | Average | **0.6310** | 0.6046 | 0.6119 | 0.5298 | 0.5039 | **0.6463** | 0.6408 | 0.6358 | 0.5582 | 0.5511 |
| csCG-HDTB | POS | 0.7543 | **0.7881** | 0.7422 | 0.7303 | 0.6752 | 0.7744 (7) | **0.8079 (10)** | 0.7596 (5) | 0.7608 (2) | 0.7011 (1) |
| | STDP | 0.3104 | 0.3429 | 0.3531 | **0.3805** | 0.2457 | 0.3879 (7) | 0.3584 (3) | 0.3843 (5) | **0.3909 (3)** | 0.3676 (7) |
| | GCM | 0.6415 | 0.6456 | **0.6533** | 0.6306 | 0.5653 | 0.6604 (8) | **0.6683 (8)** | 0.6549 (5) | 0.6535 (8) | 0.5859 (3) |
| | SVA | 0.5334 | **0.5629** | 0.5255 | 0.5389 | 0.5262 | 0.5650 (1) | 0.5629 (12) | **0.5752 (3)** | 0.5389 (12) | 0.5647 (11) |
| | Average | 0.5599 | **0.5849** | 0.5685 | 0.5701 | 0.5031 | 0.5969 | **0.5994** | 0.5935 | 0.5860 | 0.5548 |

Table 4: The weighted-F1 scores for the last layer and the best layer (layer-number mentioned in parenthesis) for the layer-wise probing experiments with the Hindi language data. (Corresponding results for the Tamil language data can be found in Appendix B.1)

periments) as the probing classifier for all the tasks and models. Since POS and GCM are token-level tasks, we use the first-subword token-embeddings as the input to the probing classifier. Whereas we use the special sentence-token embeddings for the sentence-level STDP and SVA tasks. We use Hugging Face's *transformers* library (Wolf et al., 2020) to access the pre-trained instances of these language models. The probing classifier is trained using the PyTorch library (Paszke et al., 2019). Given that all the evaluation tasks are designed under a multi-class single-label classification setting, we monitor the weighted-F1 scores to evaluate the models (Table 4).

## 4.2 Probing Results

Overall, due to the lack of semantic and lexical cues, and a larger test-set, all the models find the CG-HDTB data more challenging than the HDTB data (Table 4). The performance across all the models and tasks further deteriorates with the code-switched csCG-HDTB data. Given the considerably larger scale (model and pre-training data) of the XLM-R model, for the token-level tasks (POS and GCM), it significantly outperforms the other models for all the three treebanks. Whereas, for the sentence-level tasks (STDP and SVA), mBERT and DistilmBERT perform better than the rest of the models for HDTB and CG-HDTB data. This might be explained by the sentence-level pre-training tasks (Next Sentence Prediction) used by mBERT and DistilmBERT. Overall, for Hindi data, mBERT shows the best average weighted-F1 scores across the four tasks, and the Indic models perform the worst. On the other hand, XLM-R significantly outperforms the rest of the models under a code-switched Hindi-English setting (Table 4).

Even though the IndicBERT and MuRIL models outperform mBERT and XLM-R on many downstream NLU tasks (Kakwani et al., 2020; Khanuja et al., 2021), they consistently fail to catch-up in syntactic evaluation. Even DistilmBERT, a relatively smaller model, outperforms IndicBERT and MuRIL across all the tasks. There might be multiple plausible reasons behind this finding. Both IndicBERT, and MuRIL perform masked word/token language modeling and do not have a sentence-level pre-training task. Hence, while they are outperformed by mBERT and DistilmBERT, they outperform XLM-R on most of the sentence-level tasks with Hindi data. Moreover, they are significantly smaller in architecture size (IndicBERT) and dataset size as compared to the other models. mBERT, XLM-R, and DistilmBERT are highly multilingual language models, pre-trained on more than 100 languages. This might provide them with the linguistic and typological generalization required for modeling morphosyntax more efficiently than Indic models, which are only trained on a handful of Indic languages and English. Even though the MuRIL model is pre-trained with artificially generated parallel translated and transliterated sentences in Indic languages and their English counterparts, it is outperformed by XLM-R on the csCG-HDTB Hindi-English code-switched data. The XLM-R model has a small amount of natural code-switched data in its pre-training corpus, which might be the reason behind its dominance under the code-switching setting.

### 4.3 Localization of Syntactic Knowledge

It has been previously shown that linguistic knowledge is localized in the monolingual BERT (Rogers et al., 2020). While surface-level linguistic information like linear-word order and sentence-length is captured in the lower layers of the model (Jawahar et al., 2019; Lin et al., 2019), the syntactic knowledge is found in the middle-layers of the model (Hewitt and Manning, 2019; Jawahar et al., 2019). While basic syntactic operations are encoded in relatively lower-layers (Jawahar et al., 2019; Tenney et al., 2019a), more complex tasks with long-range syntactic dependencies are performed best by relatively higher layers (Goldberg, 2019). Rogers et al. (2020) explain this localization of syntactic knowledge using Liu et al. (2019)'s finding that the middle layers of BERT are most generalizing across tasks and the deeper layers are more task-specific. We investigate the localization of syntactic knowledge in multilingual language models by plotting the layer-wise performance across the various evaluation tasks with CG-HDTB data (Figure 2).

For token-level tasks (POS and GCM) (Figure 2a 2c), we find a pattern similar to that of monolingual BERT in mBERT, DistilmBERT, and XLM-R, where the weighted-F1 scores peak at the middle layers. The same, however, is not true for IndicBERT and MuRIL, which show declining weighted-F1 scores with increasing depth in the model. This suggests that with increasing depth, the layers become more task-specific. This is an unusual behavior for the Indic models, where investigating the cause for this should be an interesting research direction. The XLM-R model consistently outperforms the rest of the models across all the layers. Whereas the Indic language models consistently fall behind the other highly multilingual models. Between the Indic models, IndicBERT significantly outperforms MuRIL across all the layers.

For sentence-level tasks (STDP and SVA) (Figure 2b 2d), XLM-R, IndicBERT and MuRIL show no clear localization pattern[15]. mBERT and DistilmBERT show a consistent performance across all the layers, outperforming the rest of the models for both tasks. Similar to Jawahar et al. (2019)'s findings of the STDP task with monolingual BERT, they peak at the middle layers. However, the difference between the layers' performance is not very significant (Figure 2b). IndicBERT performs particularly well on the STDP task, showing comparable metrics with mBERT and DistilmBERT. While MuRIL starts lowest for STDP task, it eventually manages to outperform XLM-R, but still consistently lags behind IndicBERT (Figure 2b). Whereas, for SVA task, MuRIL performs better than IndicBERT for most of the layers (Figure 2d). XLM-R model shows a dip in performance in the middle layers for both the tasks, which is exactly opposite to that of the token-level tasks and previous findings with monolingual BERT.

## 5 Conclusion

This work presents a gender-balanced benchmark evaluation of Colorless Green sentences in Indic languages for syntactic testing of multilingual language models. By doing so, we aim to address the existing research gap in syntactic testing in Indic NLP. We introduce four new treebanks: CG-HDTB, csCG-HDTB, CG-TTB, and csCG-TTB for this purpose. We use the datasets from the treebanks to perform four syntax-related benchmarking evaluation tasks. In our experiments, we perform layer-wise probing of token-level and sentence-level representations from five different multilingual language models. Our experiments reveal that performing syntactic evaluation under a colorless green setting ensures that the semantic and lexical cues do not add evaluation artifacts in the form of higher-than-actual performance metrics. Further, the experiments also reveal that the multilingual language models suffer significantly under a code-switched setting, which is an important aspect in Indic languages. Overall, our experiments show that the currently available Indic language models do not capture syntax as efficiently as the other highly multilingual language models. Indic models seem to outperform other multilingual language models on various NLU tasks in Indic languages even with a certain lack of syntactic knowledge. This might suggest that the Indic language models do not rely significantly on syntax while making inferences on such NLU tasks. We also observe that training on large artificial corpora of transliterated texts do not help Indic language models in capturing syntax under a code-switched setting.

Further, we find that unlike the other highly multilingual language models, the currently available Indic language models do not show any syntactic localization in the middle layers. This is a unique

[15](with the exception of IndicBERT on task STDP)

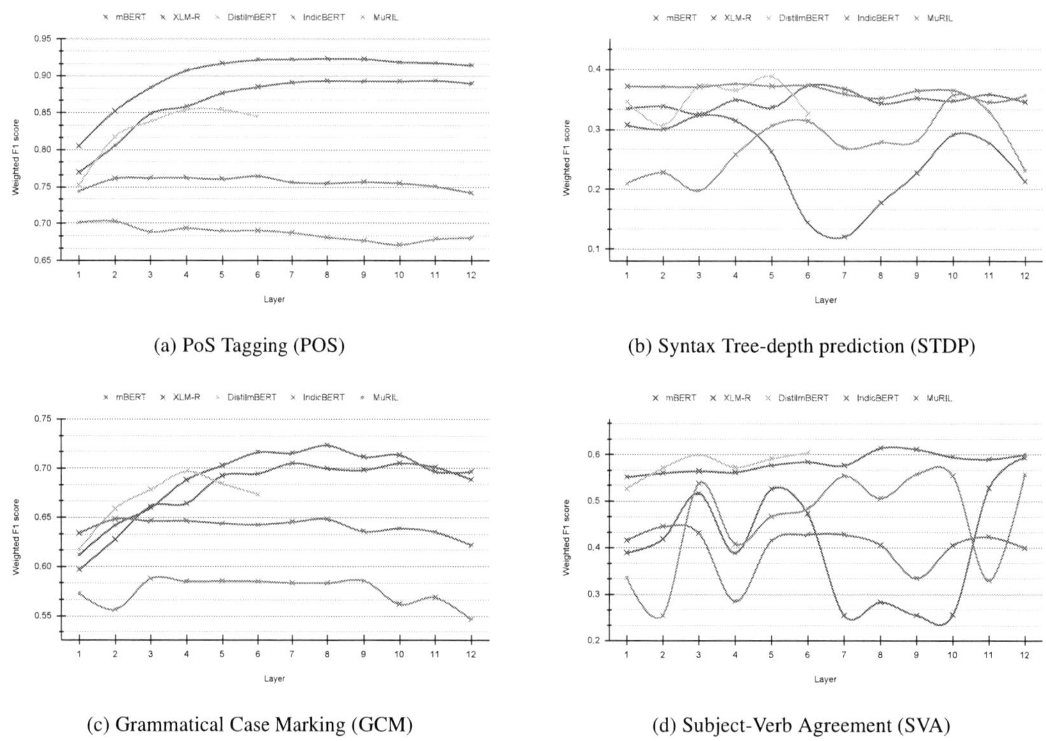


(a) PoS Tagging (POS)

(b) Syntax Tree-depth prediction (STDP)

(c) Grammatical Case Marking (GCM)

(d) Subject-Verb Agreement (SVA)

Figure 2: Weighted F1 scores for the layer-wise probing experiments with the CG-HDTB test set for the mBERT, DistilmBERT, XLM-R, IndicBERT, and MuRIL models.

behavior to the multilingual Indic language models, the cause and effects for which can be investigated in another independent study. While the current work only covers the Hindi and Tamil languages, it lays down the framework for performing syntactic evaluation in other Indic languages.

## 6 Development and Accessibility

As a continuation of the current work, we aim to cover more Indic languages and their code-switched counterparts in the benchmark. We aim to cover typologically different languages from both the Indo-Aryan, and the Dravidian language families, with a special focus on low-resourced Indic languages. This can be an extremely challenging task. Developing datasets for syntactic evaluation requires a certain level of linguistic expertise, which is usually found in the trained and native speakers of that particular language. While the methods used in this work relax these requirements upto some extent, they are dependent on existing syntactic dependency annotations. Such fine-grained annotations are not readily available for a majority of the Indic languages. Hence, we plan to open-source the benchmark datasets. We aim to continue developing the benchmark with open-source contributions from the trained and native speakers of various Indic languages.

The treebank datasets used for this benchmark are publicly available for benchmarking and development purposes on GitHub and the Hugging Face Datasets platform (Lhoest et al., 2021).[16]

## Acknowledgments

We would like to thank Greg Durrett for his feedback on an early draft of this work. We would also like to thank K. A. Geetha for contributing to our discussions around the work for the Tamil language.

## References

Yossi Adi, Einat Kermany, Yonatan Belinkov, Ofer Lavi, and Yoav Goldberg. 2017. Fine-grained analysis of sentence embeddings using auxiliary prediction tasks. In *5th International Conference on Learning Representations, ICLR 2017, Toulon, France, April 24-26, 2017, Conference Track Proceedings*. OpenReview.net.

[16]`https://github.com/rajaswa/indic-syntax-evaluation`

Gaurav Arora. 2020. iNLTK: Natural language toolkit for indic languages. In *Proceedings of Second Workshop for NLP Open Source Software (NLP-OSS)*, pages 66–71, Online. Association for Computational Linguistics.

Mikel Artetxe, Sebastian Ruder, and Dani Yogatama. 2020. On the cross-lingual transferability of monolingual representations. In *Proceedings of the 58th Annual Meeting of the Association for Computational Linguistics*, pages 4623–4637, Online. Association for Computational Linguistics.

Riyaz Ahmad Bhat, Rajesh Bhatt, Annahita Farudi, Prescott Klassen, Bhuvana Narasimhan, Martha Palmer, Owen Rambow, Dipti Misra Sharma, Ashwini Vaidya, Sri Ramagurumurthy Vishnu, et al. 2008. The hindi/urdu treebank project. In *Handbook of Linguistic Annotation*. Springer Press.

Alexis Conneau, Kartikay Khandelwal, Naman Goyal, Vishrav Chaudhary, Guillaume Wenzek, Francisco Guzmán, Edouard Grave, Myle Ott, Luke Zettlemoyer, and Veselin Stoyanov. 2020. Unsupervised cross-lingual representation learning at scale. In *Proceedings of the 58th Annual Meeting of the Association for Computational Linguistics*, pages 8440–8451, Online. Association for Computational Linguistics.

Alexis Conneau, German Kruszewski, Guillaume Lample, Loïc Barrault, and Marco Baroni. 2018. What you can cram into a single $&!#* vector: Probing sentence embeddings for linguistic properties. In *Proceedings of the 56th Annual Meeting of the Association for Computational Linguistics (Volume 1: Long Papers)*, pages 2126–2136, Melbourne, Australia. Association for Computational Linguistics.

Jacob Devlin, Ming-Wei Chang, Kenton Lee, and Kristina Toutanova. 2019. BERT: Pre-training of deep bidirectional transformers for language understanding. In *Proceedings of the 2019 Conference of the North American Chapter of the Association for Computational Linguistics: Human Language Technologies, Volume 1 (Long and Short Papers)*, pages 4171–4186, Minneapolis, Minnesota. Association for Computational Linguistics.

M. B. Emeneau. 1956. India as a lingustic area. *Language*, 32(1):3–16.

Richard Futrell, Ethan Wilcox, Takashi Morita, Peng Qian, Miguel Ballesteros, and Roger Levy. 2019. Neural language models as psycholinguistic subjects: Representations of syntactic state. In *Proceedings of the 2019 Conference of the North American Chapter of the Association for Computational Linguistics: Human Language Technologies, Volume 1 (Long and Short Papers)*, pages 32–42, Minneapolis, Minnesota. Association for Computational Linguistics.

Jon Gauthier, Jennifer Hu, Ethan Wilcox, Peng Qian, and Roger Levy. 2020. SyntaxGym: An online platform for targeted evaluation of language models. In *Proceedings of the 58th Annual Meeting of the Association for Computational Linguistics: System Demonstrations*, pages 70–76, Online. Association for Computational Linguistics.

Yoav Goldberg. 2019. Assessing bert's syntactic abilities. *CoRR*, abs/1901.05287.

Kristina Gulordava, Piotr Bojanowski, Edouard Grave, Tal Linzen, and Marco Baroni. 2018. Colorless green recurrent networks dream hierarchically. In *Proceedings of the 2018 Conference of the North American Chapter of the Association for Computational Linguistics: Human Language Technologies, Volume 1 (Long Papers)*, pages 1195–1205, New Orleans, Louisiana. Association for Computational Linguistics.

John Hewitt and Christopher D. Manning. 2019. A structural probe for finding syntax in word representations. In *Proceedings of the 2019 Conference of the North American Chapter of the Association for Computational Linguistics: Human Language Technologies, Volume 1 (Long and Short Papers)*, pages 4129–4138, Minneapolis, Minnesota. Association for Computational Linguistics.

Jennifer Hu, Jon Gauthier, Peng Qian, Ethan Wilcox, and Roger Levy. 2020a. A systematic assessment of syntactic generalization in neural language models. In *Proceedings of the 58th Annual Meeting of the Association for Computational Linguistics*, pages 1725–1744, Online. Association for Computational Linguistics.

Junjie Hu, Sebastian Ruder, Aditya Siddhant, Graham Neubig, Orhan Firat, and Melvin Johnson. 2020b. XTREME: A massively multilingual multi-task benchmark for evaluating cross-lingual generalisation. In *Proceedings of the 37th International Conference on Machine Learning*, volume 119 of *Proceedings of Machine Learning Research*, pages 4411–4421. PMLR.

Kushal Jain, Adwait Deshpande, Kumar Shridhar, Felix Laumann, and Ayushman Dash. 2020. Indic-transformers: An analysis of transformer language models for indian languages.

Ganesh Jawahar, Benoît Sagot, and Djamé Seddah. 2019. What does BERT learn about the structure of language? In *Proceedings of the 57th Annual Meeting of the Association for Computational Linguistics*, pages 3651–3657, Florence, Italy. Association for Computational Linguistics.

Divyanshu Kakwani, Anoop Kunchukuttan, Satish Golla, Gokul N.C., Avik Bhattacharyya, Mitesh M. Khapra, and Pratyush Kumar. 2020. IndicNLPSuite: Monolingual corpora, evaluation benchmarks and pre-trained multilingual language models for Indian languages. In *Findings of the Association for Computational Linguistics: EMNLP 2020*, pages 4948–4961, Online. Association for Computational Linguistics.

Simran Khanuja, Diksha Bansal, Sarvesh Mehtani, Savya Khosla, Atreyee Dey, Balaji Gopalan, Dilip Kumar Margam, Pooja Aggarwal, Rajiv Teja Nagipogu, Shachi Dave, Shruti Gupta, Subhash Chandra Bose Gali, Vish Subramanian, and Partha Talukdar. 2021. Muril: Multilingual representations for indian languages.

Anoop Kunchukuttan. 2020. The IndicNLP Library. `https://github.com/anoopkunchukuttan/indic_nlp_library/blob/master/docs/indicnlp.pdf`.

Jey Han Lau, Alexander Clark, and Shalom Lappin. 2017. Grammaticality, acceptability, and probability: A probabilistic view of linguistic knowledge. *Cognitive Science*, 41(5):1202–1241.

Quentin Lhoest, Albert Villanova del Moral, Yacine Jernite, Abhishek Thakur, Patrick von Platen, Suraj Patil, Julien Chaumond, Mariama Drame, Julien Plu, Lewis Tunstall, Joe Davison, Mario Šaško, Gunjan Chhablani, Bhavitvya Malik, Simon Brandeis, Teven Le Scao, Victor Sanh, Canwen Xu, Nicolas Patry, Angelina McMillan-Major, Philipp Schmid, Sylvain Gugger, Clément Delangue, Théo Matussière, Lysandre Debut, Stas Bekman, Pierric Cistac, Thibault Goehringer, Victor Mustar, François Lagunas, Alexander M. Rush, and Thomas Wolf. 2021. Datasets: A community library for natural language processing.

Yaobo Liang, Nan Duan, Yeyun Gong, Ning Wu, Fenfei Guo, Weizhen Qi, Ming Gong, Linjun Shou, Daxin Jiang, Guihong Cao, Xiaodong Fan, Ruofei Zhang, Rahul Agrawal, Edward Cui, Sining Wei, Taroon Bharti, Ying Qiao, Jiun-Hung Chen, Winnie Wu, Shuguang Liu, Fan Yang, Daniel Campos, Rangan Majumder, and Ming Zhou. 2020. XGLUE: A new benchmark datasetfor cross-lingual pre-training, understanding and generation. In *Proceedings of the 2020 Conference on Empirical Methods in Natural Language Processing (EMNLP)*, pages 6008–6018, Online. Association for Computational Linguistics.

Jindrich Libovický, Rudolf Rosa, and Alexander Fraser. 2019. How language-neutral is multilingual bert? *CoRR*, abs/1911.03310.

Yongjie Lin, Yi Chern Tan, and Robert Frank. 2019. Open sesame: Getting inside BERT's linguistic knowledge. In *Proceedings of the 2019 ACL Workshop BlackboxNLP: Analyzing and Interpreting Neural Networks for NLP*, pages 241–253, Florence, Italy. Association for Computational Linguistics.

Tal Linzen. 2020. How can we accelerate progress towards human-like linguistic generalization? In *Proceedings of the 58th Annual Meeting of the Association for Computational Linguistics*, pages 5210–5217, Online. Association for Computational Linguistics.

Tal Linzen, Emmanuel Dupoux, and Yoav Goldberg. 2016. Assessing the ability of LSTMs to learn syntax-sensitive dependencies. *Transactions of the Association for Computational Linguistics*, 4:521–535.

Nelson F. Liu, Matt Gardner, Yonatan Belinkov, Matthew E. Peters, and Noah A. Smith. 2019. Linguistic knowledge and transferability of contextual representations. In *Proceedings of the 2019 Conference of the North American Chapter of the Association for Computational Linguistics: Human Language Technologies, Volume 1 (Long and Short Papers)*, pages 1073–1094, Minneapolis, Minnesota. Association for Computational Linguistics.

Rebecca Marvin and Tal Linzen. 2018. Targeted syntactic evaluation of language models. In *Proceedings of the 2018 Conference on Empirical Methods in Natural Language Processing*, pages 1192–1202, Brussels, Belgium. Association for Computational Linguistics.

Tom McCoy, Ellie Pavlick, and Tal Linzen. 2019. Right for the wrong reasons: Diagnosing syntactic heuristics in natural language inference. In *Proceedings of the 57th Annual Meeting of the Association for Computational Linguistics*, pages 3428–3448, Florence, Italy. Association for Computational Linguistics.

Aaron Mueller, Garrett Nicolai, Panayiota Petrou-Zeniou, Natalia Talmina, and Tal Linzen. 2020. Cross-linguistic syntactic evaluation of word prediction models. In *Proceedings of the 58th Annual Meeting of the Association for Computational Linguistics*, pages 5523–5539, Online. Association for Computational Linguistics.

Martha Palmer, Rajesh Bhatt, Bhuvana Narasimhan, Owen Rambow, Dipti Misra Sharma, and Fei Xia. 2009. Hindi syntax: Annotating dependency, lexical predicate-argument structure, and phrase structure. In *The 7th International Conference on Natural Language Processing*, pages 14–17.

Adam Paszke, Sam Gross, Francisco Massa, Adam Lerer, James Bradbury, Gregory Chanan, Trevor Killeen, Zeming Lin, Natalia Gimelshein, Luca Antiga, Alban Desmaison, Andreas Kopf, Edward Yang, Zachary DeVito, Martin Raison, Alykhan Tejani, Sasank Chilamkurthy, Benoit Steiner, Lu Fang, Junjie Bai, and Soumith Chintala. 2019. Pytorch: An imperative style, high-performance deep learning library. In *Advances in Neural Information Processing Systems*, volume 32. Curran Associates, Inc.

Telmo Pires, Eva Schlinger, and Dan Garrette. 2019. How multilingual is multilingual BERT? In *Proceedings of the 57th Annual Meeting of the Association for Computational Linguistics*, pages 4996–5001, Florence, Italy. Association for Computational Linguistics.

Loganathan Ramasamy and Zdeněk Žabokrtský. 2012. Prague dependency style treebank for Tamil. In *Proceedings of the Eighth International Conference on Language Resources and Evaluation (LREC'12)*, pages 1888–1894, Istanbul, Turkey. European Language Resources Association (ELRA).

Anna Rogers, Olga Kovaleva, and Anna Rumshisky. 2020. A primer in bertology: What we know about how bert works. *Transactions of the Association for Computational Linguistics*, 8:842–866.

Samuel Rönnqvist, Jenna Kanerva, Tapio Salakoski, and Filip Ginter. 2019. Is multilingual BERT fluent in language generation? In *Proceedings of the First NLPL Workshop on Deep Learning for Natural Language Processing*, pages 29–36, Turku, Finland. Linköping University Electronic Press.

Victor Sanh, Lysandre Debut, Julien Chaumond, and Thomas Wolf. 2019. Distilbert, a distilled version of BERT: smaller, faster, cheaper and lighter. *CoRR*, abs/1910.01108.

Ian Tenney, Dipanjan Das, and Ellie Pavlick. 2019a. BERT rediscovers the classical NLP pipeline. In *Proceedings of the 57th Annual Meeting of the Association for Computational Linguistics*, pages 4593–4601, Florence, Italy. Association for Computational Linguistics.

Ian Tenney, Patrick Xia, Berlin Chen, Alex Wang, Adam Poliak, R Thomas McCoy, Najoung Kim, Benjamin Van Durme, Sam Bowman, Dipanjan Das, and Ellie Pavlick. 2019b. What do you learn from context? probing for sentence structure in contextualized word representations. In *International Conference on Learning Representations*.

Ke Tran, Arianna Bisazza, and Christof Monz. 2018. The importance of being recurrent for modeling hierarchical structure. In *Proceedings of the 2018 Conference on Empirical Methods in Natural Language Processing*, pages 4731–4736, Brussels, Belgium. Association for Computational Linguistics.

Shweta Vikram. 2013. Morphology: Indian languages and european languages. *International Journal of Scientific and Research Publications*, 3(6):1–5.

Alex Wang, Yada Pruksachatkun, Nikita Nangia, Amanpreet Singh, Julian Michael, Felix Hill, Omer Levy, and Samuel R. Bowman. 2019. Superglue: A stickier benchmark for general-purpose language understanding systems. *CoRR*, abs/1905.00537.

Alex Wang, Amanpreet Singh, Julian Michael, Felix Hill, Omer Levy, and Samuel Bowman. 2018. GLUE: A multi-task benchmark and analysis platform for natural language understanding. In *Proceedings of the 2018 EMNLP Workshop BlackboxNLP: Analyzing and Interpreting Neural Networks for NLP*, pages 353–355, Brussels, Belgium. Association for Computational Linguistics.

Thomas Wolf, Lysandre Debut, Victor Sanh, Julien Chaumond, Clement Delangue, Anthony Moi, Pierric Cistac, Tim Rault, Remi Louf, Morgan Funtowicz, Joe Davison, Sam Shleifer, Patrick von Platen, Clara Ma, Yacine Jernite, Julien Plu, Canwen Xu, Teven Le Scao, Sylvain Gugger, Mariama Drame, Quentin Lhoest, and Alexander Rush. 2020. Transformers: State-of-the-art natural language processing. In *Proceedings of the 2020 Conference on Empirical Methods in Natural Language Processing: System Demonstrations*, pages 38–45, Online. Association for Computational Linguistics.

Shijie Wu and Mark Dredze. 2019. Beto, bentz, becas: The surprising cross-lingual effectiveness of BERT. In *Proceedings of the 2019 Conference on Empirical Methods in Natural Language Processing and the 9th International Joint Conference on Natural Language Processing (EMNLP-IJCNLP)*, pages 833–844, Hong Kong, China. Association for Computational Linguistics.

## A Dataset Examples

| | | | Transliteration: |
|---|---|---|---|
| Original: | भैरव का स्थान उत्तराखंड में क्षेत्रपाल अथवा भूमिदेव के रूप में महत्वपूर्ण है । | | |
| CGI-A: | जम्मू के ग्राहक कांड में अफगानिस्तान अथवा नोएडा के रूप में महत्वपूर्ण है । | → | jammu ke graahak cond main afghanistan athwa noida ke rup main mahatvapurn he . |
| CGI-B: | भारती की ड्यूटी पुलिस में अंजलि अथवा प्रदर्शनी के रूप में महत्वपूर्ण है । | → | bharti kii duty police main anjali athwa pradarshnee ke rup main mahatvapurn he . |
| CGI-C: | बदरीनाथ के दृष्टया अक्तूबर में प्लान अथवा सीआरपीसी के रूप में महत्वपूर्ण है । | → | badrinath ke drushtya aktubar main plan athwa siarpisi ke rup main mahatvapurn he . |
| CGI-D: | क्रांति की क़दर पार्वती में सोसाइटी अथवा अंग्रेजी के रूप में महत्वपूर्ण है । | → | kranti kii qadar parvati main socity athwa angreji ke rup main mahatvapurn he . |

Figure 3: Example sentences from the CG-HDTB (left) and csCG-HDTB (right) treebank corresponding to an original sentence from the HDTB (top-left) treebank.

| | | | Transliteration: |
|---|---|---|---|
| Original: | பிகாரிலிருந்து ஏராளமான இளைஞர்கள் வேலை தேடி வெளி மாநிலங்களுக்கு குடிபெயர்ந்து வருகின்றனர். | | |
| CGI-A: | பிகாரிலிருந்து ஏராளமான ஆகியோர் காலம் தேடி வெளி முயற்சிகளுக்கு குடிபெயர்ந்து வருகின்றனர் . | → | bigarilrundhu bihar ilrundhu erauman akhiyor kalam theti weli mushcigaluku gudipeyarndhu varukinsener . |
| CGI-B: | பிகாரிலிருந்து ஏராளமான போலீஸார் வழக்கு தேடி வெளி முயற்சிகளுக்கு குடிபெயர்ந்து வருகின்றனர் . | → | bigarilrundhu bihar ilrundhu erauman polisar vanku theti weli mushcigaluku gudipeyarndhu varukinsener . |
| CGI-C: | பிகாரிலிருந்து ஏராளமான மனைவியர் வெளியுறவுத்துறை தேடி வெளி ஆண்டுகளுக்குப் குடிபெயர்ந்து வருகின்றனர் . | → | bigarilrundhu bihar ilrundhu erauman manavier veleuuddurai theti weli andugalukqup gudipeyarndhu varukinsener . |
| CGI-D: | பிகாரிலிருந்து ஏராளமான உறுப்பினர்கள் ரத்து தேடி வெளி முயற்சிகளுக்கு குடிபெயர்ந்து வருகின்றனர் . | → | bigarilrundhu bihar ilrundhu erauman ushupinars rattu theti weli mushcigaluku gudipeyarndhu varukinsener . |

Figure 4: Example sentences from the CG-TTB (left) and csCG-TTB (right) treebank corresponding to an original sentence from the TTB (top-left) treebank.

| Treebank | Task | Last Layer | | | | | Best Layer | | | | |
|---|---|---|---|---|---|---|---|---|---|---|---|
| | | mBERT | XLM-R | DistilmBERT | IndicBERT | MuRIL | mBERT | XLM-R | DistilmBERT | IndicBERT | MuRIL |
| CG-TTB | POS | **0.7444** | 0.7336 | 0.6431 | 0.5874 | 0.4539 | 0.7719 (9) | **0.7946 (7)** | 0.6809 (4) | 0.6327 (6) | 0.4741 (5) |
| | STDP | 0.0947 | 0.0716 | **0.2315** | 0.0716 | 0.0898 | 0.2209 (10) | 0.0898 (6) | **0.2819 (3)** | 0.0716 (1) | 0.2051 (11) |
| | GCM | **0.7319** | 0.6800 | 0.6336 | 0.5864 | 0.5878 | 0.7966 (7) | **0.8187 (6)** | 0.6765 (4) | 0.5864 (12) | 0.6040 (1) |
| | Average | **0.5237** | 0.4951 | 0.5027 | 0.4151 | 0.3772 | **0.5965** | 0.5677 | 0.5464 | 0.4302 | 0.4277 |
| csCG-TTB | POS | **0.5740** | 0.5416 | 0.5531 | 0.5024 | 0.4526 | **0.6012 (6)** | 0.5947 (6) | 0.5759 (5) | 0.5516 (8) | 0.4817 (4) |
| | STDP | 0.1029 | 0.1184 | **0.1476** | 0.0716 | 0.0716 | 0.2431 (11) | 0.1085 (1) | **0.2556** (4) | 0.0716 (12) | 0.1467 (7) |
| | GCM | 0.5931 | 0.5832 | 0.5627 | 0.5605 | 0.5717 | 0.6300 (11) | 0.6065 (8) | 0.5811 (2) | 0.5852 (4) | 0.5875 (7) |
| | Average | **0.4233** | 0.4144 | 0.4211 | 0.3782 | 0.3653 | **0.4914** | 0.4366 | 0.4709 | 0.4028 | 0.4053 |

Table 5: The weighted-F1 scores for the last layer and the best layer (layer-number mentioned in parenthesis) for the layer-wise probing experiments with the Tamil language data.

## B Experiments with Tamil Language

Due to limitations from the original TTB Tamil Universal Dependencies treebank, we do not cover certain grammatical-gender-based methods and experiments with Tamil language in the current work.[17] Here, we report all the other results for the CG-TTB and csCG-TTB treebank datasets.

### B.1 Probing Results

While comparing the performance between the models, all the observations and inferences discussed in Section 4.2 also hold true for the Tamil language data as seen in Table 5. Overall, we observe a relatively lower performance in the CG-TTB and csCG-TTB datasets (Table 5) as compared to CG-HDTB and csCG-HDTB datasets respectively (Table 4).

### B.2 Localization of Syntactic Knowledge

All the observations and inferences discussed in Section 4.3 also hold true for the Tamil language data as seen in Figure 5, Figure 6, and Figure 7. Due to a relatively lower performance on Tamil language data, all the figures are shifted downwards with almost similar trends and structures.

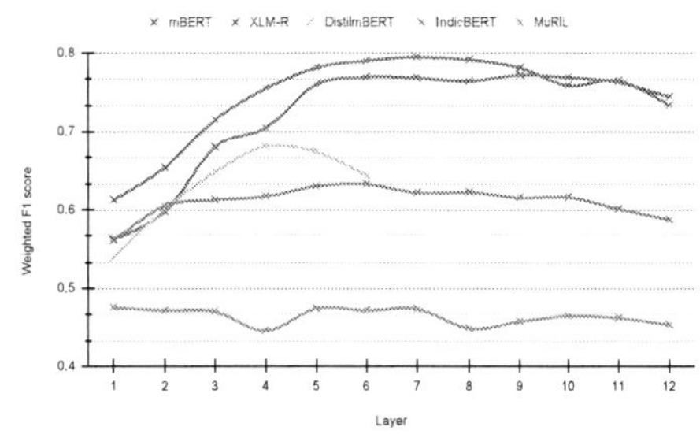


Figure 5: Weighted F1 scores for the layer-wise probing experiments with the CG-TTB test set for the POS task.

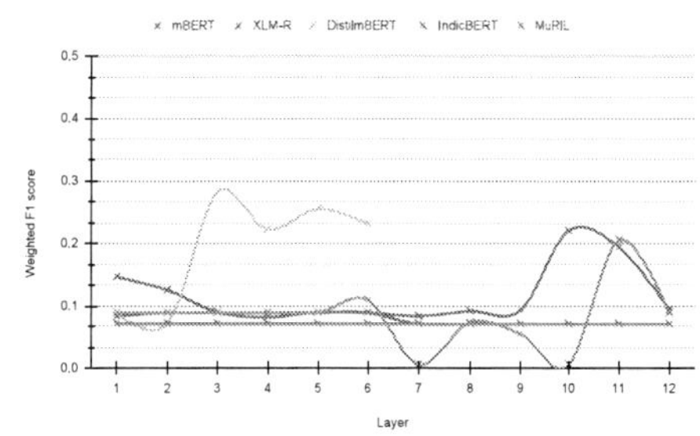


Figure 6: Weighted F1 scores for the layer-wise probing experiments with the CG-TTB test set for the STDP task.

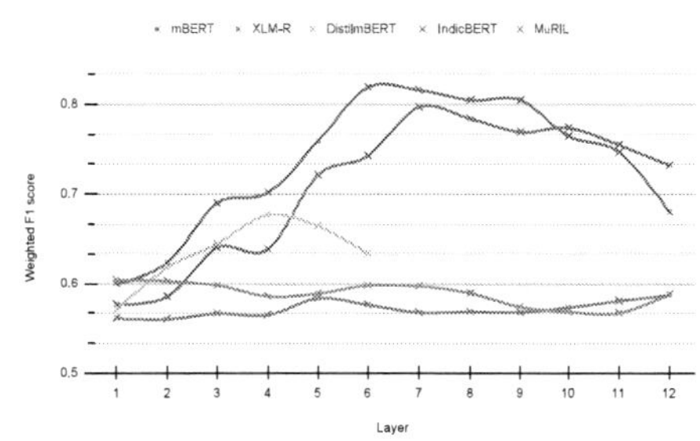


Figure 7: Weighted F1 scores for the layer-wise probing experiments with the CG-TTB test set for the GCM task.

[17]This includes the controlled generation of colorless green sentences with gender-balancing, and the Subject-Verb Agreement (SVA) task.

# Improving the Diversity of Unsupervised Paraphrasing with Embedding Outputs

**Monisha Jegadeesan***
Indian Institute of Technology Madras
monishaj.65@gmail

**Sachin Kumar**
Carnegie Mellon University
sachink@cs.cmu.edu

**John Wieting***
Carnegie Mellon University
jwieting@cs.cmu.edu

**Yulia Tsvetkov**
University of Washington
yuliats@cs.washington.edu

## Abstract

We present a novel technique for zero-shot paraphrase generation. The key contribution is an end-to-end multilingual paraphrasing model that is trained using translated parallel corpora to generate paraphrases into "meaning spaces" – replacing the final softmax layer with word embeddings. This architectural modification, plus a training procedure that incorporates an autoencoding objective, enables effective parameter sharing across languages for more fluent monolingual rewriting, and facilitates fluency and diversity in generation. Our continuous-output paraphrase generation models outperform zero-shot paraphrasing baselines, when evaluated on two languages using a battery of computational metrics as well as in human assessment.[1]

## 1 Introduction

Paraphrasing aims to rewrite text while preserving its meaning and achieving a different surface realization. It is an eminently practical task, useful in educational applications (Inui et al., 2003; Petersen and Ostendorf, 2007; Pavlick and Callison-Burch, 2016; Xu et al., 2016), information retrieval (Duboue and Chu-Carroll, 2006; Harabagiu and Hickl, 2006; Fader et al., 2014), in dialogue systems (Yan et al., 2016), as well as for data augmentation in a plethora of other tasks (Berant and Liang, 2014; Romano et al., 2006; Fadaee et al., 2017; Jin et al., 2018; Hou et al., 2018).

Generating diverse and coherent paraphrases is a difficult task. Unlike in machine translation, where naturally occurring parallel data in the form of translated news, books and talks are available in abundance on the web, naturally occurring paraphrase corpora are scarce. Most common approaches to paraphrasing are based on translation, in the form of bilingual pivoting (Mallinson et al., 2017a,b) or back-translation (Wieting and Gimpel, 2018; Hu et al., 2019a,b). This stems from the hypothesis that if two sentences in a language (e.g. English) have the same translation in another, (e.g. French) they must be paraphrases of each other. While these pipeline approaches bypass the problem of missing data, they propagate errors. Further, all neural paraphrasing models (e.g., Prakash et al., 2016; Gupta et al., 2018; Wang et al., 2019) predict discrete tokens through a final softmax layer. We hypothesize that softmax-based architectures restrict the diversity of outputs, biasing the models to copy words and phrases from the input, which has an effect opposite to the intended one in paraphrasing.

In this work, we introduce ParaVMF – a simple and effective method of training paraphrasing models by generating into embedding spaces (§2). Since parallel paraphrasing data is not available even in otherwise high-resource languages like French, we focus on an unsupervised approach. Using bilingual parallel corpora, we adapt multilingual machine translation (Johnson et al., 2017) to monolingual translation. We propose to train this model with translation and autoencoding objectives. The latter helps simplify the training setup by using only one language pair, whereas prior work required multiple language pairs and more data to stabilize training (Tiedemann and Scherrer, 2019; Buck et al., 2018; Guo et al., 2019; Thompson and Post, 2020). To encourage diversity, we propose to replace the final softmax layer in the decoder with a layer that learns to predict word vectors (Kumar and Tsvetkov, 2019). We show that predicting into word meaning representations increases diversity in paraphrasing by generating semantically similar words and phrases which are often neighbors in the embedding space.

We evaluate our proposed model on paraphras-

*Currently at Google LLC

[1]The code is available at https://github.com/monisha-jega/paraphrasing_embedding_outputs



*Proceedings of the 1st Workshop on Multilingual Representation Learning*, pages 166–175
November 11, 2021. ©2021 Association for Computational Linguistics

ing English and French sentences (§3). In several setups, standard automatic metrics and human judgment experiments show that our zero-shot paraphrasing model with embedding outputs generates more diverse and fluent paraphrases, compared to state-of-the-art methods (§4).

## 2 The ParavMF Model

Let the language to paraphrase in be $L_1$. Our goal is to learn a mapping $f(\mathbf{x}; \theta)$ parameterized by $\theta$. $f$ takes a text $\mathbf{x} = (x_1, x_2, \cdots, x_m)$ containing $m$ words as input, which can be a sentence or a segment in $L_1$. It then generates $\mathbf{y} = (y_1, y_2, \ldots, y_n)$ of length $n$ in the same language such that $\mathbf{x}$ and $\mathbf{y}$ are paraphrases. That is, $\mathbf{y}$ represents the same meaning as $\mathbf{x}$ using different phrasing. We assume that no direct supervision data is available, but there exists a bilingual parallel corpus between $L_1$ and another language $L_2$. We are also given pre-trained embeddings (Bojanowski et al., 2017) for words in both $L_1$ and $L_2$. The dimension of both the embedding spaces is $d$.

We use a standard transformer-based encoder-decoder model (Vaswani et al., 2017) as the underlying architecture for $f$. As visualized in the system diagram presented in the Appendix, $f$ is jointly trained to perform three tasks with a shared encoder and decoder: (1) translation from $L_1$ to $L_2$, (2) translation from $L_2$ to $L_1$ and (3) reconstructing the input text in $L_1$ (autoencoding).[2]

Towards our primary goal of meaning preservation, the translation objectives help the encoder map the inputs in both the languages to a common semantic space, whereas the decoder learns to generate language-specific outputs. On the other hand, with the autoencoding objective, we expose the model to examples where the input and output are in the same language, biasing the model to adhere to the start token supplied to it and decode monolingually. Using this training algorithm, we find in our experiments (§4), that the resulting paraphrases albeit meaning-preserving still lack in diversity. We identify two reasons for this issue. First, the model overfits to the autoencoding objective and just learns to copy the input sentences. We address this issue by using only a small random sample of the total training sentences for training with this objective.[3]

Second, we find that cross-entropy loss used to train the model results in peaky distributions at each decoding step where the target words get most of the probability mass. This distribution being another signal of overfitting also reduces diversity (Meister et al., 2020). We find in our preliminary experiments, that prior work to address this issue by augmenting diversity inducing objectives to the training loss (Vijayakumar et al., 2018) often comes at a cost of reducing meaning preservation. In this work, we propose using a different training loss which naturally promotes output diversity. We follow Kumar and Tsvetkov (2019), and instead of treating each word $w$ in the vocabulary as a discrete unit, we represent it using a unit-normalized pre-trained vector $\mathbf{e}$ learned using monolingual corpora (Bojanowski et al., 2017). At each decoding step, instead of predicting a probability distribution over the vocabulary using a softmax layer, we predict a $d$-dimensional continuous-valued vector $\hat{\mathbf{e}}$. We train our proposed model by minimizing von Mises-Fisher (vMF) loss—a probabilitistic variant of cosine distance—between the predicted vector and the pre-trained vector. At each step of decoding, the output word is generated by finding the closest neighbor (using cosine similarity) of the predicted output vector $\hat{\mathbf{e}}$ in the pre-trained embedding table. Since this loss does not directly optimize for a specific token but for a vector subspace which contains many similar meaning words, we observe that it has a higher tendency to generate diverse outputs than softmax-based models, both at the lexical and syntactic level as we show in our experiments.

Overall, the contribution of this work is twofold: (1) a translation and autoencoding based training objective to enable paraphrasing while preserving meaning without any parallel paraphrasing data, and (2) optimizing for vector subspaces instead of token probabilities to induce diversity of outputs.

## 3 Experiments

**Datasets** We evaluate paraphrasing in two languages: English and French. IWSLT'16 En↔Fr corpus (Cettolo et al., 2016) with ∼220K sentence pairs is used for training with translation objective, and 4450 sentences, randomly sampled ∼1% of the training data in $L_1$ (either En or Fr), for au-

[2]To bias the model against always decoding in the other language, unlike in Johnson et al. (2017); Tiedemann and Scherrer (2019), we provide a language-specific start token in the encoder input, in addition to the decoder input.

[3]We empirically determine this sample size to be ∼1% of the total number of training examples.

toencoding. We use the $L_1$ side of the IWSLT'16 dev set for early stopping with the autoencoding objective. We use IWSLT'16 test set for automatic evaluation consisting of 2331 samples in En and Fr each. For human evaluation we subsample 200 sentences from this set. We tokenize and truecase all the data using Moses preprocessing scripts (Koehn et al., 2007). We conduct additional experiments with a larger En–Fr corpus constructed using a 2M sentence-pair subset of the combination of the WMT'10 Gigaword (Tiedemann, 2012) and the OpenSubtitles corpora (Lison and Tiedemann, 2016).

**Implementation** We modify the standard seq2seq transformer model in OpenNMT (Klein et al., 2017) to generate word embeddings (Kumar and Tsvetkov, 2019), and train it with the vMF loss with respect to target vectors. We initialize and fix the input embeddings of the encoder and decoder with off-the-shelf (sub-word based) fasttext embeddings (Bojanowski et al., 2017) for both En and Fr and align the embeddings to encourage cross-lingual sharing (Artetxe et al., 2018). With a vocabulary size of 50K for each language, the combined vocabulary size of the encoder and the decoder is 100K. Both encoder and decoder consist of 6 layers with 4 attention heads. The model is optimized using Adam (Kingma and Ba, 2015), with batch size 4K, and 0.3 dropout. The hidden dimension size is 1024, the dimension of the embedding layers is 512. We add a linear layer to transform 300-dimensional pre-trained embeddings to 512-dimensional input vectors to the model. After decoding, we postprocess the generated output to replace words from $L_2$ by a look-up in the dictionary induced from the aligned embedding spaces.

**Baselines** Although unsupervised methods of paraphrasing with only monolingual data have been explored in recent works (Gupta et al., 2018; Yang et al., 2019; Roy and Grangier, 2019; Patro et al., 2018; Park et al., 2019) they have not been shown to outperform translation based baselines (West et al., 2020). Hence we compare our proposed approach with translation-based baselines only. First, we compare with bilingual pivoting baselines (Mallinson et al., 2017a,b) which pipeline two separate translation models, $L_1 \to L_2$, and $L_2 \to L_1$. We use two bilingual pivoting baselines, one based on continuous-output model (**BP-vMF**; the output vectors of the first model are first converted to discrete tokens before being fed to the next) and another based on softmax-based model (**BP-CE**).

To evaluate the impact of embedding outputs, we also compare our proposed model **PARAVMF** to softmax-based baseline **PARACE**, leaving other model components unchanged. **PARACE** is a modified bilingual version of the multilingual method proposed in Guo et al. (2019), the current state-of-the-art in zero-shot paraphrasing.

**Evaluation setup** There are many ways to paraphrase a sentence, but no manually crafted multi-reference paraphrase datasets exist, that could be used as test sets (and there are no datasets in languages other than English). We thus evaluate the generated paraphrases on semantic similarity and lexical diversity compared to the *input text*. Following prior work, we use the $n$-gram based metric **METEOR** (Banerjee and Lavie, 2005). Despite accounting for synonyms, it is not well-suited to evaluate paraphrases, since it typically assigns lower scores to novel phrasings, due to incomplete synonym dictionaries. We thus also include **BERTScore** (Zhang et al., 2020), computing cosine similarity between the contextual embeddings of two sentences. Naturally, just copying the inputs can also lead to high scores in these metrics. To evaluate lexical diversity, we follow Hu et al. (2019b) and include **IoU** – Intersection over Union (also called Jaccard Index) and Word Error Rate (**WER**). To measure structural diversity we use (constituency) Parse Tree Edit distance (**PTED**).[4] Note that model outputs that do not preserve meaning in paraphrasing (and generate totally different sentences) will also obtain high diversity scores, but these are not indicative of quality paraphrasing but will falsely contribute to high diversity scores if averaged across the entire test set. We thus measure the diversity only on subsets of the test set for which the strongest baseline (PARACE) and our model generate meaning-preserving paraphrases measured using BERTScore thresholds. We report the diversity scores for three such thresholds: 0.95, 0.9, 0.85, selected empirically such that the sample size is sufficiently large.

## 4 Results

**Automatic evaluation** We observe in table 1 that PARAVMF outperforms all baselines in meaning-

[4]Before computing the PTED, we prune the tree to a max height of 3, and discard all the terminal nodes. We employ Stanford CoreNLP (Manning et al., 2014) for parsing and APTED algorithm for edit distance (Pawlik and Augsten, 2015).

| Model | English | | French | |
|---|---|---|---|---|
| | BS↑ | MET.↑ | BS↑ | MET.↑ |
| BP-CE | 75.0 | 75.0 | 69.4 | 67.5 |
| BP-vMF | 72.1 | 72.2 | 65.5 | 64.2 |
| ParaCE | 83.5 | 87.4 | 82.3 | 81.6 |
| ParavMF | **88.6** | **91.6** | **87.2** | **86.4** |

Table 1: Meaning-preservation in generated paraphrases. BS: BertScore, MET: METEOR

preservation. Both pivoting based baselines perform poorly on average. This is a consequence of error propagation exacerbated in BP-vMF[5]. As a result, a very small fraction of generated sentences show meaning preservation (as measured by achieving a BERTScore greater than 0.85). Hence, we only compare the diversity in the two best meaning-preserving models, **ParaCE** and **ParavMF**. As shown in table 2, across all thresholds the latter model achieves higher lexical and syntactic diversity in the outputs. Ablation results in the Appendix show that both the autoencoding objective and the final embedding layer contribute to the improved quality of paraphrases. An additional benefit of our proposed model is that by replacing the softmax layer with word embeddings, ParavMF is trained 3x faster than the ParaCE baseline.

We further conduct a **manual evaluation** which quantifies the rate at which annotators find paraphrases fluent, consistent with input meaning, and novel in phrasing. In an A/B testing setup, we compare our proposed approach with the strongest baseline ParaCE.[6] 200 sentences sampled from the IWSLT English test were scored by two annotators independently, which yielded the inter-annotator agreement of 0.37 (fair agreement). Out of the sentences on which both annotators agree (142 out of 200), we find that ParavMF model outperforms the ParaCE model in 73% of votes. We show more details and some examples of ParavMF and ParaCE system outputs in the Appendix.

Finally, we also evaluate that our results hold on a **larger dataset in different domain**. We retrain ParavMF and ParaCE on $2M$ En–Fr corpus described in §3. [7] The results of automatic evaluation are presented in the Appendix. We conduct human evaluation on a sample of 200 sentences from this test set following the same A/B testing procedure as described above, with each sample rated by three annotators, resulting in a pairwise-average kappa agreement index of 0.21.[8] 42.9% ParavMF outputs were selected as better paraphrases, compared to 24.5% outputs from ParaCE, supporting our main results on the IWSLT dataset.

## 5 Related Work

Bilingual pivoting is a common technique used with bilingual data (Barzilay and McKeown, 2001; Ganitkevitch et al., 2013; Pavlick et al., 2015; Mallinson et al., 2017a). ParaNMT (Wieting and Gimpel, 2018) is a large psuedo-parallel paraphrase corpus constructed through back-translation (Wieting et al., 2017). Iyyer et al. (2018) augment it with syntactic constraints for controlled paraphrasing; ParaBank (Hu et al., 2019a) improves upon ParaNMT via lexical constraining of decoding; and ParaBank 2 (Hu et al., 2019b) improves the diversity of paraphrases in ParaBank through a clustering-based approach. Note that these works are focused on English. Here, we propose a language-independent approach relying only on abundant bilingual data. Our approach is most similar to Guo et al. (2019) who use bilingual and multilingual translation for zero-shot paraphrasing. They, however, observe that bilingual models are insufficient for paraphrasing and are often unable to produce the output in the correct language. We incorporate an autoencoding objective which simplifies and stabilizes training, and embedding-based outputs improving the diversity in paraphrasing.

## 6 Conclusion

We present ParavMF, an end-to-end model for generating paraphrases, trained solely with bilingual data, without any paraphrase supervision. We propose to generate paraphrases into meaning

[5]This is expected as vMF has been shown to slightly underperform CE for translation in prior work (Kumar and Tsvetkov, 2019). Our training procedure with an autoencoding objective alleviates this issue in ParavMF.

[6]Each judge is presented with a set of questions, each consisting of an input sentence and paraphrases generated by the two models as options, and is asked to choose the sentence that is fluent, meaning-preserving and offers a novel phrasing of the input. They are asked to choose neither if both sentences are dis-fluent and/or not able to preserve content. The options are shuffled.

[7]We use 4K English sentences subsampled (∼0.1% of the training data) from the same corpus for autoencoding. To further discourage copying, we use denoised autoencoding (Lample et al., 2018).

[8]We discarded around 53 samples with no clear majority among the annotator ratings and report the results on the remaining samples, further ignoring cases where the paraphrases from both the models were rated to be of similar quality.

| BERTScore threshold | Model | # (out of 2K) | ENGLISH IoU↓ | WER↑ | PTED↑ | # (out of 2K) | FRENCH IoU↓ | WER↑ | PTED↑ |
|---|---|---|---|---|---|---|---|---|---|
| 0.85 | PARACE | 710 | 94.3 | 4 | **0.5** | 710 | 94.3 | 3.9 | **0.55** |
| | PARAvMF | | **92.4** | **4.1** | 0.42 | | **92.7** | **4.1** | 0.42 |
| 0.9 | PARACE | 539 | 96.2 | 2.6 | **0.34** | 580 | 96.1 | 2.6 | **0.34** |
| | PARAvMF | | **94.5** | **2.9** | 0.29 | | **94.5** | **2.9** | 0.29 |
| 0.95 | PARACE | 300 | 98.8 | 0.8 | 0.15 | 380 | 98.7 | 0.8 | 0.15 |
| | PARAvMF | | **97.7** | **1.2** | **0.16** | | **97.7** | **1.2** | **0.16** |

Table 2: Diversity of meaning-preserving paraphrases compared to the test set. PARAvMF outperforms a strong baseline PARACE for both English and French, across all metrics for thresholds 0.85 and 0.9, and in IoU and WER for threshold of 0.95.

spaces as opposed to discrete tokens. This leads to significant improvements in quality and diversity of paraphrasing over strong baselines.

## Acknowledgments

This material is based upon work supported by the National Science Foundation (NSF) under Grants No. IIS2040926 and IIS2007960. The views and opinions of authors expressed herein do not necessarily state or reflect those of the NSF.

## References

Mikel Artetxe, Gorka Labaka, and Eneko Agirre. 2018. A robust self-learning method for fully unsupervised cross-lingual mappings of word embeddings. In *Proceedings of the 56th Annual Meeting of the Association for Computational Linguistics (Volume 1: Long Papers)*, pages 789–798, Melbourne, Australia.

Satanjeev Banerjee and Alon Lavie. 2005. METEOR: An automatic metric for mt evaluation with improved correlation with human judgments. In *Proceedings of the acl workshop on intrinsic and extrinsic evaluation measures for machine translation and/or summarization*, pages 65–72.

Regina Barzilay and Kathleen R. McKeown. 2001. Extracting paraphrases from a parallel corpus. In *Proceedings of the 39th Annual Meeting of the Association for Computational Linguistics*, pages 50–57.

Jonathan Berant and Percy Liang. 2014. Semantic parsing via paraphrasing. In *Proceedings of the 52nd Annual Meeting of the Association for Computational Linguistics (Volume 1: Long Papers)*, pages 1415–1425.

Piotr Bojanowski, Edouard Grave, Armand Joulin, and Tomas Mikolov. 2017. Enriching word vectors with subword information. *Transactions of the Association for Computational Linguistics*, 5:135–146.

Christian Buck, Jannis Bulian, Massimiliano Ciaramita, Wojciech Gajewski, Andrea Gesmundo, Neil Houlsby, and Wei Wang. 2018. Ask the right questions: Active question reformulation with reinforcement learning. In *International Conference on Learning Representations*.

Mauro Cettolo, Niehues Jan, Stüker Sebastian, Luisa Bentivogli, Roldano Cattoni, and Marcello Federico. 2016. The iwslt 2016 evaluation campaign. In *International Workshop on Spoken Language Translation*.

Pablo Duboue and Jennifer Chu-Carroll. 2006. Answering the question you wish they had asked: The impact of paraphrasing for question answering. In *Proceedings of the Human Language Technology Conference of the NAACL, Companion Volume: Short Papers*, pages 33–36. Association for Computational Linguistics.

Marzieh Fadaee, Arianna Bisazza, and Christof Monz. 2017. Data augmentation for low-resource neural machine translation. In *Proceedings of the 55th Annual Meeting of the Association for Computational Linguistics (Volume 2: Short Papers)*, pages 567–573.

Anthony Fader, Luke Zettlemoyer, and Oren Etzioni. 2014. Open question answering over curated and extracted knowledge bases. In *Proceedings of the 20th ACM SIGKDD International Conference on Knowledge Discovery and Data Mining*, page 1156–1165. Association for Computing Machinery.

Juri Ganitkevitch, Benjamin Van Durme, and Chris Callison-Burch. 2013. PPDB: The paraphrase database. In *Proceedings of the 2013 Conference of the North American Chapter of the Association for Computational Linguistics: Human Language Technologies*, pages 758–764. Association for Computational Linguistics.

Yinpeng Guo, Yi Liao, Xin Jiang, Qing Zhang, Yibo Zhang, and Qun Liu. 2019. Zero-shot paraphrase generation with multilingual language models. *arXiv preprint arXiv:1911.03597*.

Ankush Gupta, Arvind Agarwal, Prawaan Singh, and Piyush Rai. 2018. A deep generative framework for paraphrase generation. In *The Thirty-Second AAAI Conference on Artificial Intelligence*.

Sanda Harabagiu and Andrew Hickl. 2006. Methods for using textual entailment in open-domain question answering. In *Proceedings of the 21st International Conference on Computational Linguistics and 44th Annual Meeting of the Association for Computational Linguistics*, pages 905–912. Association for Computational Linguistics.

Yutai Hou, Yijia Liu, Wanxiang Che, and Ting Liu. 2018. Sequence-to-sequence data augmentation for dialogue language understanding. In *Proceedings of the 27th International Conference on Computational Linguistics*, pages 1234–1245. Association for Computational Linguistics.

J Edward Hu, Rachel Rudinger, Matt Post, and Benjamin Van Durme. 2019a. PARABANK: Monolingual bitext generation and sentential paraphrasing via lexically-constrained neural machine translation. In *Proceedings of the AAAI Conference on Artificial Intelligence*, volume 33, pages 6521–6528.

J. Edward Hu, Abhinav Singh, Nils Holzenberger, Matt Post, and Benjamin Van Durme. 2019b. Large-scale, diverse, paraphrastic bitexts via sampling and clustering. In *Proceedings of the 23rd Conference on Computational Natural Language Learning (CoNLL)*, pages 44–54. Association for Computational Linguistics.

Kentaro Inui, Atsushi Fujita, Tetsuro Takahashi, Ryu Iida, and Tomoya Iwakura. 2003. Text simplification for reading assistance: A project note. In *Proceedings of the Second International Workshop on Paraphrasing - Volume 16*, page 9–16. Association for Computational Linguistics.

Mohit Iyyer, John Wieting, Kevin Gimpel, and Luke Zettlemoyer. 2018. Adversarial example generation with syntactically controlled paraphrase networks. In *Proceedings of the 2018 Conference of the North American Chapter of the Association for Computational Linguistics: Human Language Technologies, Volume 1 (Long Papers)*, pages 1875–1885.

Lifeng Jin, David King, Amad Hussein, Michael White, and Douglas Danforth. 2018. Using paraphrasing and memory-augmented models to combat data sparsity in question interpretation with a virtual patient dialogue system. In *Proceedings of the Thirteenth Workshop on Innovative Use of NLP for Building Educational Applications*, pages 13–23. Association for Computational Linguistics.

Melvin Johnson, Mike Schuster, Quoc V. Le, Maxim Krikun, Yonghui Wu, Zhifeng Chen, Nikhil Thorat, Fernanda Viégas, Martin Wattenberg, Greg Corrado, Macduff Hughes, and Jeffrey Dean. 2017. Google's multilingual neural machine translation system: Enabling zero-shot translation. volume 5, pages 339–351.

Diederik P Kingma and Jimmy Ba. 2015. Adam: A method for stochastic optimization. In *International Conference on Learning Representations*.

Guillaume Klein, Yoon Kim, Yuntian Deng, Jean Senellart, and Alexander Rush. 2017. OpenNMT: Open-source toolkit for neural machine translation. In *Proceedings of ACL 2017, System Demonstrations*, pages 67–72. Association for Computational Linguistics.

Philipp Koehn, Hieu Hoang, Alexandra Birch, Chris Callison-Burch, Marcello Federico, Nicola Bertoldi, Brooke Cowan, Wade Shen, Christine Moran, Richard Zens, Chris Dyer, Ondřej Bojar, Alexandra Constantin, and Evan Herbst. 2007. Moses: Open source toolkit for statistical machine translation. In *Proceedings of the 45th Annual Meeting of the ACL on Interactive Poster and Demonstration Sessions*, page 177–180. Association for Computational Linguistics.

Sachin Kumar and Yulia Tsvetkov. 2019. Von Mises-Fisher loss for training sequence to sequence models with continuous outputs. In *International Conference on Learning Representations*.

Guillaume Lample, Alexis Conneau, Ludovic Denoyer, and Marc'Aurelio Ranzato. 2018. Unsupervised machine translation using monolingual corpora only. In *International Conference on Learning Representations*.

Pierre Lison and Jörg Tiedemann. 2016. Opensubtitles2016: Extracting large parallel corpora from movie and tv subtitles.

Jonathan Mallinson, Rico Sennrich, and Mirella Lapata. 2017a. Paraphrasing revisited with neural machine translation. In *Proceedings of the 15th Conference of the European Chapter of the Association for Computational Linguistics: Volume 1, Long Papers*, pages 881–893.

Jonathan Mallinson, Rico Sennrich, and Mirella Lapata. 2017b. Paraphrasing revisited with neural machine translation. In *Proceedings of the 15th Conference of the European Chapter of the Association for Computational Linguistics: Volume 1, Long Papers*, pages 881–893. Association for Computational Linguistics.

Christopher Manning, Mihai Surdeanu, John Bauer, Jenny Finkel, Steven Bethard, and David McClosky. 2014. The Stanford CoreNLP natural language processing toolkit. In *Proceedings of 52nd Annual Meeting of the Association for Computational Linguistics: System Demonstrations*, pages 55–60.

Clara Meister, Elizabeth Salesky, and Ryan Cotterell. 2020. Generalized entropy regularization or: There's nothing special about label smoothing. In *Proceedings of the 58th Annual Meeting of the Association for Computational Linguistics*, pages 6870–6886, Online. Association for Computational Linguistics.

Sunghyun Park, Seung-won Hwang, Fuxiang Chen, Jaegul Choo, Jung-Woo Ha, Sunghun Kim, and

Jinyeong Yim. 2019. Paraphrase diversification using counterfactual debiasing. In *Proceedings of the AAAI Conference on Artificial Intelligence*, volume 33, pages 6883–6891.

Badri Narayana Patro, Vinod Kumar Kurmi, Sandeep Kumar, and Vinay Namboodiri. 2018. Learning semantic sentence embeddings using sequential pairwise discriminator. pages 2715–2729.

Ellie Pavlick and Chris Callison-Burch. 2016. Simple PPDB: A paraphrase database for simplification. In *Proceedings of the 54th Annual Meeting of the Association for Computational Linguistics (Volume 2: Short Papers)*, pages 143–148.

Ellie Pavlick, Pushpendre Rastogi, Juri Ganitkevitch, Benjamin Van Durme, and Chris Callison-Burch. 2015. PPDB 2.0: Better paraphrase ranking, fine-grained entailment relations, word embeddings, and style classification. In *Proceedings of the 53rd Annual Meeting of the Association for Computational Linguistics and the 7th International Joint Conference on Natural Language Processing (Volume 2: Short Papers)*, pages 425–430. Association for Computational Linguistics.

Mateusz Pawlik and Nikolaus Augsten. 2015. Efficient computation of the tree edit distance. *ACM Trans. Database Syst.*, 40(1).

Sarah E Petersen and Mari Ostendorf. 2007. Text simplification for language learners: A corpus analysis. In *Workshop on Speech and Language Technology in Education*.

Aaditya Prakash, Sadid A. Hasan, Kathy Lee, Vivek V. Datla, Ashequl Qadir, Joey Liu, and Oladimeji Farri. 2016. Neural paraphrase generation with stacked residual LSTM networks. *CoRR*, abs/1610.03098.

Lorenza Romano, Milen Kouylekov, Idan Szpektor, Ido Dagan, and Alberto Lavelli. 2006. Investigating a generic paraphrase-based approach for relation extraction. In *11th Conference of the European Chapter of the Association for Computational Linguistics*. Association for Computational Linguistics.

Aurko Roy and David Grangier. 2019. Unsupervised paraphrasing without translation. In *Proceedings of the 57th Annual Meeting of the Association for Computational Linguistics*.

Brian Thompson and Matt Post. 2020. Paraphrase generation as zero-shot multilingual translation: Disentangling semantic similarity from lexical and syntactic diversity. *arXiv preprint arXiv:2008.04935*.

Jörg Tiedemann. 2012. Parallel data, tools and interfaces in opus. In *Proceedings of the Eight International Conference on Language Resources and Evaluation (LREC'12)*, Istanbul, Turkey. European Language Resources Association (ELRA).

Jörg Tiedemann and Yves Scherrer. 2019. Measuring semantic abstraction of multilingual NMT with paraphrase recognition and generation tasks. In *Proceedings of the 3rd Workshop on Evaluating Vector Space Representations for NLP*, pages 35–42.

Ashish Vaswani, Noam Shazeer, Niki Parmar, Jakob Uszkoreit, Llion Jones, Aidan N. Gomez, undefinedukasz Kaiser, and Illia Polosukhin. 2017. Attention is all you need. In *Proceedings of the 31st International Conference on Neural Information Processing Systems*, page 6000–6010.

Ashwin K Vijayakumar, Michael Cogswell, Ramprasath R. Selvaraju, Qing Sun, Stefan Lee, David Crandall, and Dhruv Batra. 2018. Diverse beam search: Decoding diverse solutions from neural sequence models.

Su Wang, Rahul Gupta, Nancy Chang, and Jason Baldridge. 2019. A task in a suit and a tie: Paraphrase generation with semantic augmentation. In *Proceedings of the AAAI Conference on Artificial Intelligence*, volume 33, pages 7176–7183.

Peter West, Ximing Lu, Ari Holtzman, Chandra Bhagavatula, Jena Hwang, and Yejin Choi. 2020. Reflective decoding: Unsupervised paraphrasing and abductive reasoning. *arXiv preprint arXiv:2010.08566*.

John Wieting and Kevin Gimpel. 2018. PARANMT-50M: Pushing the limits of paraphrastic sentence embeddings with millions of machine translations. pages 451–462.

John Wieting, Jonathan Mallinson, and Kevin Gimpel. 2017. Learning paraphrastic sentence embeddings from back-translated bitext. In *Proceedings of the 2017 Conference on Empirical Methods in Natural Language Processing*, pages 274–285. Association for Computational Linguistics.

Wei Xu, Courtney Napoles, Ellie Pavlick, Quanze Chen, and Chris Callison-Burch. 2016. Optimizing statistical machine translation for text simplification. *Transactions of the Association for Computational Linguistics*, 4:401–415.

Zhao Yan, Nan Duan, Junwei Bao, Peng Chen, Ming Zhou, Zhoujun Li, and Jianshe Zhou. 2016. DocChat: An information retrieval approach for chatbot engines using unstructured documents. In *Proceedings of the 54th Annual Meeting of the Association for Computational Linguistics (Volume 1: Long Papers)*, pages 516–525.

Qian Yang, Zhouyuan Huo, Dinghan Shen, Yong Cheng, Wenlin Wang, Guoyin Wang, and Lawrence Carin. 2019. An end-to-end generative architecture for paraphrase generation. In *Proceedings of the 2019 Conference on Empirical Methods in Natural Language Processing and the 9th International Joint Conference on Natural Language Processing (EMNLP-IJCNLP)*, pages 3132–3142. Association for Computational Linguistics.

| Model | Semantic Similarity BERTScore | METEOR |
|---|---|---|
| PARANMT | 61.6 | 62.1 |
| BP (vMF) | 44.6 | 57.4 |
| BP (CE) | 45.0 | 60.4 |
| PARACE | 65.9 | 81.7 |
| **PARAvMF** | **68.9** | **83.9** |

Table 3: Evaluation of paraphrase generation on the PARANMT test set.

Tianyi Zhang, Varsha Kishore, Felix Wu, Kilian Q. Weinberger, and Yoav Artzi. 2020. BERTScore: Evaluating text generation with bert. In *International Conference on Learning Representations*.

## A System diagram

The PARAvMF system is represented diagrammatically in Figure 1.

## B Example outputs

Sample outputs of the PARAvMF and PARACE models are shown in table 5.

## C Training on a Larger Translation Dataset

To measure the impact of the size of parallel translation data used for training, we conduct an experiment with a larger French-English corpus constructed using a $2M$ sentence-pair subset of the combination of the WMT'10 Gigaword (Tiedemann, 2012) and the OpenSubtitles corpora (Lison and Tiedemann, 2016). The semantic similarity scores and the diversity results are presented in table 4. The results of human evaluation are presented in the main paper.

## D Evaluation on PARANMT-50M Test Set

We evaluate the PARAvMF model (trained on English-French two-way translation data and English autoencoding data from the IWSLT'16 dataset) on test data sampled from PARANMT-50M (Wieting and Gimpel, 2018), to demonstrate its paraphrasing ability on out-of-domain input, in addition to enabling direct comparison with back-translated data, as shown in table 3. However, it is to be noted that the comparison is not a fair one, since PARAvMF is trained on just 220K data samples, wherease PARANMT is back-translated using a translation model that was trained on a bilingual dataset with a size of around $70M$.

## E Ablation

We proposed three changes in a multilingual MT setup to use bilingual data for paraphrasing, (1) predicting continuous outputs and training with vMF loss, (2) language-specific start tokens in the encoder, and (3) an autoencoding objective. In the results section of the main paper, by comparing our method to PARACE, we already established the importance of using vMF compared to cross-entropy. As shown in table 7, ablating either of the other remaining two components leads to considerable performance drop. This is because the ablated models generate outputs in $L_2$ since they are never exposed to monolingual examples during training. Additional, in our preliminary experiments, we also observe that increasing the size of autoencoding data too much beyond $\sim 1\%$ of the size of parallel translation data leads to a performance drop because the model just starts to learn to copy the input as-is rather than rephrasing.

| Model | ENGLISH BERTScore↑ | ENGLISH METEOR↑ |
|---|---|---|
| PARACE | 62.2 | 73.6 |
| PARAvMF | **71.6** | **79.6** |

(a) Semantic similarity between the test set and generated paraphrases

| BERTScore threshold | Model | # (out of 2K) | ENGLISH IoU↓ | ENGLISH WER↑ | ENGLISH PTED↑ |
|---|---|---|---|---|---|
| 0.85 | PARACE | 559 | 85.5 | 11.9 | **1.43** |
| | PARAvMF | | **82.5** | **12.4** | 1.42 |
| 0.9 | PARACE | 327 | 91.2 | 7.0 | **0.81** |
| | PARAvMF | | **87.9** | **8.3** | 0.64 |
| 0.95 | PARACE | 196 | 95.9 | 3.3 | 0.28 |
| | PARAvMF | | **93.9** | **3.9** | **0.29** |

(b) Diversity of meaning-preserving paraphrases compared to the test set

Table 4: Evaluation of paraphrase generation with PARAvMF trained on $2M$ English-French sentence pairs. It outperforms a strong cross-entropy based baseline (PARACE) on semantic similarity and majority of diversity metrics.

| | |
|---|---|
| Input | It 's expensive , it takes a long time , and it 's very complicated . |
| PARACE | It 's expensive takes a time , and it 's very complicated . |
| PARAvMF | It 's costly , It takes a long time , and it 's very difficult . |
| Input | These are things to talk about and think about now , with your family and your loved ones . |
| PARACE | These are things to talk about and think about now , with your family and your loved ones . |
| PARAvMF | These are things to speak of and think of now , with your family and the ones you love. |
| Input | So what opened my eyes ? |
| PARACE | So what opened my eyes ? |
| PARAvMF | So what is it that opened my eyes up ? |
| Input | And this work has been wonderful . It 's been great . |
| PARACE | And this work has been wonderful . It 's been great . |
| PARAvMF | This work has been wonderful and great . |
| Input | I wasn 't doing anything that was out of the ordinary at all . |
| PARACE | I wasn 't doing anything that was out of the regular regular at all . |
| PARAvMF | I was doing nothing that was not ordinary . |
| Input | It will make tons of people watch , because people want this experience . |
| PARACE | It will make tons of people watch , because people want this . |
| PARAvMF | Tonnes of people will look because they want this experience . |

Table 5: Comparison of selected sample outputs for the IWSLT Test Set between PARAvMF model and the baselines. PARAvMF not only exhibits content preservation, but also demonstrates fluency as well as lexical and syntactic diversity.

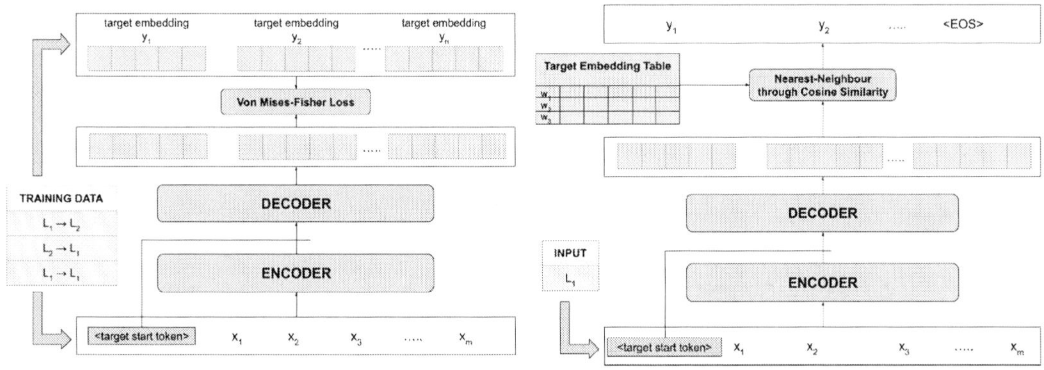


(a) Training Procedure

(b) Testing Procedure

Figure 1: The PARAvMF Model: The decoder generates continuous-valued vectors at each step. It is trained by minimizing von Mises-Fisher loss between the output vectors and the pre-trained embeddings of the target words. Start tokens signalling the target language are supplied to both the encoder and the decoder. The training data consists of translation samples, $L_1 \leftrightarrow L_2$ and autoencoding samples, $L_1 \rightarrow L_1$. During testing, the word in the target vocabulary whose embedding is closest to the generated output in terms of cosine similarity is output.

| Model | Votes (%) |
|---|---|
| PARACE | 39 (27.3%) |
| PARAvMF | **104 (72.7%)** |

Table 6: PARAvMF outperforms the baseline in manual A/B testing (English).

| Model | BLEU | BS | MET. |
|---|---|---|---|
| PARAvMF | 64.0 | 88.6 | 91.6 |
| - encoder start token | 0.86 | 46.0 | 12.0 |
| - autoencoding | 0.85 | 46.0 | 12.1 |

Table 7: Performance of PARAvMF without the proposed enhancements - removing either leads to a drastic performance drop

# The Effectiveness of Intermediate-Task Training for Code-Switched Natural Language Understanding

**Archiki Prasad**[*†1] **Mohammad Ali Rehan**[*2] **Shreya Pathak**[*2] **Preethi Jyothi**[2]
[1]UNC Chapel Hill [2]IIT Bombay
archiki@cs.unc.edu
{alirehan, shreyapathak, pjyothi}@cse.iitb.ac.in

## Abstract

While recent benchmarks have spurred a lot of new work on improving the generalization of pretrained multilingual language models on multilingual tasks, techniques to improve code-switched natural language understanding tasks have been far less explored. In this work, we propose the use of *bilingual intermediate pretraining* as a reliable technique to derive large and consistent performance gains using code-switched text on three different NLP tasks: Natural Language Inference (NLI), Question Answering (QA) and Sentiment Analysis (SA). We show consistent performance gains on four different code-switched language-pairs (Hindi-English, Spanish-English, Tamil-English and Malayalam-English) for SA and on Hindi-English for NLI and QA. We also present a code-switched masked language modeling (MLM) pretraining technique that consistently benefits SA compared to standard MLM pretraining using real code-switched text.

## 1 Introduction

Code-switching is a widely-occurring linguistic phenomenon in which multiple languages are used within the span of a single utterance or conversation. While large pretrained multilingual models like mBERT (Devlin et al., 2019) and XLM-R (Conneau et al., 2020) have been successfully used for low-resource languages and effective zero-shot cross-lingual transfer (Pires et al., 2019; Conneau et al., 2020; Wu and Dredze, 2019), techniques to help these models generalize to code-switched text have not been sufficiently explored.

Intermediate-task training (Phang et al., 2018, 2020) was recently proposed as an effective training strategy for transfer learning. This scheme involves fine-tuning a pretrained model on data from one or more *intermediate tasks*, followed by fine-tuning on the target task. The intermediate task could differ from the target task and it could also be in a different language. This technique was shown to help with both task-based and language-based transfer; it benefited target tasks in English (Vu et al., 2020) and helped improve zero-shot cross-lingual transfer (Phang et al., 2020).

In this work, we introduce *bilingual intermediate-task training* as a reliable training strategy to improve performance on three code-switched natural language understanding tasks: Natural Language Inference (NLI), factoid-based Question Answering (QA) and Sentiment Analysis (SA). Bilingual training for a language pair X-EN involves pretraining with an English intermediate task along with its translations in X. The NLI, QA and SA tasks require deeper linguistic reasoning (as opposed to sequence labeling tasks like part-of-speech tagging) and exhibit high potential for improvement via transfer learning. (The fact that NLI, QA and SA have more room for improvement compared to POS and NER tagging is evident from the leaderboard statistics in (Khanuja et al., 2020b).) We present SA results for four different language pairs: Hindi-English (HI-EN), Spanish-English (ES-EN), Tamil-English (TA-EN) and Malayalam-English (ML-EN), and NLI/QA results for HI-EN.[1]

Our main findings can be summarized as follows:

- Bilingual intermediate-task training consistently yields significant performance improvements on NLI, QA and SA using two different pretrained multilingual models, mBERT and XLM-R. We also show the impact of translation and transliteration quality on this training scheme.
- Pretraining using a masked language modeling (MLM) objective on real code-switched text can be used, in conjunction with bilingual

* Equal contribution
† Work done at IIT Bombay

[1]These tasks present an additional challenge with the Indian languages written using transliterated/Romanized text.



*Proceedings of the 1st Workshop on Multilingual Representation Learning*, pages 176–190
November 11, 2021. 

training, for additional performance improvements on code-switched target tasks. We also present a code-switched MLM variant that yields larger improvements on SA compared to standard MLM.

## 2 Methodology

**Intermediate-Task Training.** This scheme starts with a publicly-available multilingual model that has been pretrained on large volumes of multilingual text using MLM-based training objectives. This model is subsequently fine-tuned using data from one or more intermediate tasks before finally fine-tuning on code-switched data from the target tasks.

*Single Intermediate-Task Training* makes use of existing monolingual NLI, SA and QA datasets as intermediate-tasks before fine-tuning on the respective code-switched target tasks. For a language pair X-EN, where X $\in$ {ES, HI, TA, ML}, we explored the use of three different intermediate tasks:

1. Task-specific data in English (EN SING-TASK): In this setting, we carry out intermediate training using a (relatively) larger English corpus of the same task as our final downstream task.

2. Task-specific data in X (X SING-TASK): Here, we carry out intermediate training using a corpus of the same task in the matrix language (i.e., not English) present in our code switched corpus. This corpus can be constructed by translating a monolingual English corpus into the target language, and then further transliterating it to be consistent with the Romanized forms present in the target tasks[2].

3. Task-specific data in both English and X that we refer to as *bilingual intermediate-task training* (X-EN SING-TASK): This intermediate-task pretraining method involves creating training batches with an equal number of examples from both languages. We conjecture that interleaving training instances from both languages within a batch encourages the model to simultaneously perform well on both languages, and could subsequently translate to improved performance on code-switched text in these specific language pairs. This claim is borne out in our experimental results detailed in Section 4. (We also show the importance of mixing instances from both languages rather than adopting a sequential training strategy on instances from both languages in Section 4.2.)

[2]Code-switched data for some Indic languages in our target corpora were only available in the Romanized form. Therefore, we only work with Romanized text in all our experiments including intermediate tasks.

*Multi Intermediate-Task Training* involves two intermediate-tasks ($T_1$ and $T_2$) simultaneously. This training is done using two different task heads (one per task) with the pretrained models. Each batch is randomly populated with instances from tasks $T_1$ or $T_2$. We follow Raffel et al. (2020) to sample batches from task $T_1$ with probability $P_{T_1} = \frac{\min(e_{T_1},K)}{\min(e_{T_1},K)+\min(e_{T_2},K)}$ where $e_{T_1}$ and $e_{T_2}$ are the number of training examples in task $T_1$ and $T_2$, respectively; $P_{T_2}$ is similarly computed. The constant $K = 2^{16}$ is used to prevent over-sampling. We experiment with NLI and QA as the two intermediate-tasks $T_1$ or $T_2$ and refer to this system as HI-EN/NLI-QA MULTI-TASK. We use the merged EN and HI datasets from HI-EN SING-TASK for each task. We also explored MLM training on real code-switched text as one of the tasks, in addition to the merged X-EN task-specific intermediate-tasks (referred to as X-EN/MLM MULTI-TASK).

**Code-Switched MLM.** A common approach to training models for code-switched tasks is to perform additional MLM on real (or synthetic) code-switched text. However, randomly masking from the pool of all tokens in a sentence may not be the most effective use of real code-switched text and differentiating it from monolingual text, especially if one has access to word-level language tags. Given word-level language labels for each token in the code-switched sentences, we aim to emphasize switching via the MLM training objective by masking tokens from words that lie on the switching boundaries. We refer to this training strategy as *code-switched MLM*. For example, consider the following sentence where tokens that can be masked are enclosed within boxes for both the standard MLM and code-switched MLM strategies, respectively:

$\boxed{Yeh}_{\text{HI}}$ $\boxed{files}_{\text{EN}}$ $\boxed{ko}_{\text{HI}}$ $\boxed{desk}_{\text{EN}}$ $\boxed{pe}_{\text{HI}}$ $\boxed{rakh}_{\text{HI}}$ $\boxed{do}_{\text{HI}}$

$\boxed{Yeh}_{\text{HI}}$ $\boxed{files}_{\text{EN}}$ $\boxed{ko}_{\text{HI}}$ $\boxed{desk}_{\text{EN}}$ $\boxed{pe}_{\text{HI}}$ $rakh_{\text{HI}}$ $do_{\text{HI}}$

(EN Translation: Put these files on the desk.)

In the first sentence, tokens from all the words can be masked, as in standard MLM pretraining. In the second sentence that uses code-switched MLM pretraining, only tokens from words at the boundary of a language switch can be masked. To implement this, we need access to annotated language tags for each sentence or a highly accurate language identity detection system. (Neither of these were available for Tamil or Malayalam datasets; hence our results for code-switched MLM are restricted to Hindi and Spanish.) An analysis of the MLM data showed that 45% of all tokens belonged to words on a switching boundary, therefore, the MLM masking probability of these tokens was increased from 0.15 to 0.3 to roughly balance the number of tokens that are masked on average.

## 3 Experimental Setup

### 3.1 Code-switched Target Datasets

The HI-EN NLI dataset is from a recent code-switched benchmark GLUECoS (Khanuja et al., 2020a) comprising 1.8K/447 training/test examples, respectively. The HI-EN factoid-based QA dataset (Chandu et al., 2018a) is also from GLUECoS, consisting of 259/54 training/test question-answer pairs (along with corresponding context), respectively. While code-switched NLI and QA tasks were only available in HI-EN, we show SA results for four language pairs. The ES-EN SA dataset (Vilares et al., 2016) in GLUECoS consists of 2.1K/211/211 examples in train/dev/test sets, respectively. The HI-EN SA dataset (Patwa et al., 2020) comprises 15K/1.5K/3K code-switched tweets in train/dev/test sets, respectively. The train/dev/test sets in the TA-EN SA dataset (Chakravarthi et al., 2020b) and ML-EN SA dataset (Chakravarthi et al., 2020a) comprise 9.6K/1K/2.7K and 3.9K/436/1.1K code-switched YouTube comments, respectively. As the evaluation metric, we use accuracies for NLI and SA over two (entailment/contradiction) and three labels (positive/negative/neutral), respectively, and F1 scores for the QA task.

### 3.2 Intermediate Task Datasets

As intermediate tasks for NLI and QA, we used EN and HI versions of the MultiNLI dataset (Williams et al., 2018) with 250/10K examples in the train/dev sets and the SQuAD dataset (Rajpurkar et al., 2016) consisting of 82K/5K question-answer pairs in its train/dev sets, respectively. The HI translations for SQuAD (in Devanagari) are available in the XTREME (Hu et al., 2020) benchmark. We used *indic-trans* (Bhat et al., 2014) to transliterate the HI translations, since NLI and QA in GLUECoS use Romanized HI text. For sentiment analysis in ES-EN and HI-EN, we used the TweetEval (Barbieri et al., 2020) dataset (63K sentences in total) and its translations in ES and HI generated via MarianMT[3] (Junczys-Dowmunt et al., 2018) and IndicTrans MT (Ramesh et al., 2021), respectively, for intermediate-task training. For TA-EN and ML-EN, we used the positive, negative and neutral labelled sentences from the SST dataset (Socher et al., 2013) (100K instances) as the intermediate task. The TA and ML translations were also generated using the IndicTrans MT system. The translations were further transliterated using Bhat et al. (2014) for HI and the Bing Translator API[4] for TA and ML.

### 3.3 Masked Language Modelling Datasets

We use a corpus of 64K real code-switched sentences by pooling together data from prior work (Singh et al., 2018; Swami et al., 2018; Chandu et al., 2018b); we will call this corpus GEN-CS. We supplant this text corpus with an additional 28K code-switched sentences mined from movie scripts (referred to as MOVIE-CS in Tarunesh et al. (2021b)), which is more similar in domain to GLUECoS NLI. We further used code-switched text from Patwa et al. (2020), Bhat et al. (2017), and Patro et al. (2017) resulting in a total of 185K HI-EN sentences. For ES-EN, 66K real code-switched sentences were accumulated from prior work (Patwa et al., 2020; Solorio et al., 2014; AlGhamdi et al., 2016; Aguilar et al., 2018; Vilares et al., 2016). For TA-EN and ML-EN (Chakravarthi et al., 2020b, 2021; Banerjee et al., 2018; Mandl et al., 2020; Chakravarthi et al., 2020a), we used roughly 130K and 40K real code-switched sentences, respectively.

### 3.4 XTREME Translation-Transliteration

As mentioned previously, for intermediate-task training, we use the MultiNLI and SQuAD v1.1 data from the translate-train sets of the XTREME benchmark[5,6]. The Romanized version of

[3]Implementation used: http://bit.ly/MarianMT

[4]http://bit.ly/azureTranslate

[5]MultiNLI available at: https://storage.cloud.google.com/xtreme_translations/XNLI/translate-train/en-hi-translated.tsv

[6]SQuAD available at: https://storage.cloud.google.com/xtreme_translations/SQuAD/

| | Method | Es-En (X: Es) | | | Hi-En (X: Hi) | | | Ta-En (X: Ta) | | | Ml-En (X: Ml) | | |
|---|---|---|---|---|---|---|---|---|---|---|---|---|---|
| | | **F1** | **Prec.** | **Rec.** | **F1** | **Prec.** | **Rec.** | **F1** | **Prec.** | **Rec.** | **F1** | **Prec.** | **Rec.** |
| mBERT | Baseline | 60.95 | 61.93 | 60.43 | 68.17 | 68.75 | 68 | 76.07 | 75.33 | 77.66 | 75.46 | 75.72 | 75.64 |
| | +En Sing-Task | 65.11 | 66.00 | 65.00 | 69.14 | 69.72 | 68.96 | 76.41 | 75.69 | 78.11 | 76.49 | 76.78 | 76.44 |
| | +X Single-Task | 64.69 | 65.71 | 64.57 | 68.75 | 69.37 | 68.60 | 75.78 | 74.89 | 77.80 | 75.92 | 75.96 | 76.15 |
| | +X-En Single-Task | 66.64 | 67.61 | 66.21 | 69.20 | 69.63 | 69.06 | 76.75 | 76.11 | 78.63 | 77.00 | 77.16 | 77.04 |
| | +MLM | 62.02 | 62.93 | 61.29 | 69.89 | 70.58 | 69.76 | 76.73 | 76.14 | 78.53 | 76.13 | 76.23 | 76.24 |
| | +Code-Switched MLM | 63.88 | 64.81 | 63.13 | 70.33 | 71.17 | 70.10 | - | - | - | - | - | - |
| | +X-En/MLM Multi-Task | 67.01 | 68.11 | 66.72 | 69.99 | 70.29 | 69.91 | 77.23 | 76.6 | **79.16** | 77.49 | 77.56 | **77.58** |
| XLM-R | Baseline | 66.45 | 67.45 | 65.86 | 69.37 | 69.38 | 69.46 | 75.53 | 74.56 | 77.75 | 74.14 | 74.35 | 74.15 |
| | +En Sing-Task | 67.82 | 68.89 | 67.41 | 70.23 | 70.78 | 70.09 | 76.08 | 75.41 | 77.65 | 75.14 | 75.29 | 75.42 |
| | +X Single-Task | 66.68 | 68.40 | 66.29 | 69.96 | 70.38 | 69.83 | 76.36 | 75.52 | 77.88 | 76.12 | 76.10 | 76.24 |
| | +X-En Single-Task | 68.97 | 69.79 | 68.28 | 70.23 | 70.91 | 70.01 | 76.49 | 75.90 | 77.60 | 76.68 | 76.80 | 76.62 |
| | +MLM | 66.37 | 67.42 | 65.69 | 70.92 | 71.94 | 70.66 | 76.95 | 76.21 | 78.60 | 76.28 | 76.26 | 76.42 |
| | +Code-Switched MLM | 67.10 | 68.30 | 66.55 | **71.74** | **72.29** | **71.59** | - | - | - | - | - | - |
| | +X-En/MLM Multi-Task | **70.33** | **71.41** | **69.57** | 71.08 | 71.43 | 70.97 | **77.50** | **76.84** | 78.60 | **76.91** | **76.94** | 76.98 |
| | **Our Best Models** (Max) | 71.7 | 72.8 | 71.3 | 72.6 | 73.2 | 72.4 | 78 | 77 | 79 | 78 | 78 | 78 |

Table 1: Our main results for sentiment analysis. Best results for each model are underlined and the overall best results are in bold. All scores are weighted averages and are further averaged over five runs with random seeds. The last row gives the F1, precision and recall value for the method with the maximum F1 across all five seeds.

these datasets are generated using the *indic-trans* tool (Bhat et al., 2014) starting from their Devanagari counterparts. For NLI, we directly transliterated the premise and hypothesis. For QA, the context, question and answer were transliterated and the answer span was corrected. This was done by calculating the start and stop indices of the span, followed by a piece-wise transliteration. We finally checked if the context-span matched the answer text. All instances passed this check. To benefit future work in this direction, we provide these transliterated datasets[7].

### 3.5 Model Details

mBERT is a transformer model (Vaswani et al., 2017) pretrained using MLM on the Wikipedia corpus of 104 languages. XLM-R uses a similar training objective as mBERT but is trained on orders of magnitude more data from the CommonCrawl corpus spanning 100 languages and yields competitive results on low-resource languages (Conneau et al., 2020). We use the *bert-base-multilingual-cased* and *xlm-roberta-base* models[8] from the Transformers library (Wolf et al., 2019). We refer readers to Appendix A and Appendix B for more implementation details.

`translate-train/squad.translate.train.en-hi.json.`

[7] `https://www.cse.iitb.ac.in/~pjyothi/cs`

[8] We also explored a multilingual model IndicBERT (Kakwani et al., 2020) trained exclusively on Indian languages. However, preliminary experiments using this model did not yield satisfactory performance, so we did not pursue it further. In future work, we will aim to use other recently released pretrained models such as MuRIL (Khanuja et al., 2021).

## 4 Results and Analysis

### 4.1 Results on Sentiment Analysis

Table 1 shows our main results for SA on Es-En, Hi-En, Ta-En and Ml-En. We observe that bilingual intermediate-task training, X-En Sing-Task, outperforms En Sing-Task and X Sing-Task with both mBERT and XLM-R. The relative improvements of X-En Sing-Task over the baseline vary across language pairs reaching up to 9.33% for Es. For all language pairs except Hi-En, X-En/MLM Multi-Task is the best-performing system.[9] This demonstrates the benefits of MLM training in conjunction with intermediate-task training. A notable advantage of our bilingual training is that we outperform (or match) previous state-of-the-art with an order of magnitude less data. Our best Es-En system yields an F1 of 71.7 compared to Pratapa et al. (2018) with an F1 of 64.6. For Hi-En, our best F1 of 72.6 matches the 2[nd]-ranked system (Srinivasan, 2020) on SentiMix 2020 (Patwa et al., 2020). For Ta-En and Ml-En, our best systems match the score of the best TweetEval model in Gupta et al. (2021). While prior work required roughly 17M sentences in Es-En, 2.09M sentences in Hi-En and 60M tweets to train TweetEval for Ta and Ma, we use 192K, 180K, 330K and 240K sentences for the four respective language pairs. While MLM training (i.e., +MLM in Table 1) consistently improves over the baseline, we observe that code switched MLM (i.e., Code-Switched MLM

[9] We hypothesize the drop in performance for Hi-En could be attributed to domain differences between the SA and MLM corpora.

| | Method | GLUECoS NLI *(acc.)* | | GLUECoS QA *(F1)* | |
|---|---|---|---|---|---|
| | | Max | Mean | Max | Mean |
| mBERT | Baseline | 61.07 | 57.51 | 66.89 | 64.25 |
| | +MLM | 59.94 | 58.75 | 60.8 | 58.28 |
| | +EN SING-TASK | 62.40 | 60.73 | 77.62 | 75.77 |
| | +HI SING-TASK | 63.73 | 62.09 | 79.63 | 76.77 |
| | +HI-EN SING-TASK | 65.55 | 64.1 | 81.61 | 79.97 |
| | +HI-EN/NLI-QA MULTI-TASK | **66.74** | 65.3 | 83.03 | 80.25 |
| | +HI-EN/MLM MULTI-TASK | 66.66 | **65.61** | 81.05 | 79.11 |
| XLM-R | Baseline | - | - | 56.86 | 53.22 |
| | +MLM | - | - | 45.9 | 42.34 |
| | +EN SING-TASK | 66.22 | 63.91 | 82.04 | 80.92 |
| | +HI SING-TASK | 63.24 | 61.73 | 81.48 | 80.55 |
| | +HI-EN SING-TASK | 65.01 | 64.37 | 82.41 | 81.36 |
| | +HI-EN/NLI-QA MULTI-TASK | 64.49 | 64.35 | **83.95** | **82.38** |
| | +HI-EN/MLM MULTI-TASK | 66.66 | 65.01 | 82.1 | 80.44 |
| **Previous work on GLUECoS** | | | | | |
| mBERT (Khanuja et al., 2020b)[†] | | 59.28 | 57.74 | 63.58 | 62.23 |
| mod-mBERT (Chakravarthy et al., 2020) | | 62.41 | - | - | - |

Table 2: Our main results for NLI and QA from intermediate-task training. All scores are averaged over five runs with random seeds. Max and mean accuracies (for NLI) and F1-scores (for QA) over these runs are listed. Best results for each model are underlined and the overall best results are in bold. [†]Due to dataset changes, we cannot directly cite the results from the paper and report the numbers from the leaderboard after consulting the authors of GLUECoS.

in Table 1) provides additional performance gains for ES-EN and HI-EN. We do not report code-switched MLM results for TA-EN and ML-EN since we do not have access to language labels or a trained language identification system for either language. The ES-EN MLM dataset contains several sentences with no switching which are discarded for both standard and code-switched MLM. In Table 1, we compare +MLM and CODE-SWITCHED MLM only using sentences that contain code-switching.[10]

With access to translation and transliteration tools for a target language, we show superior results on four different language pairs for the sentiment analysis task. Even in resource-constrained settings like TA-EN and ML-EN, we obtain state-of-the-art performance using our proposed techniques. In Section 4.3, we will examine the influence of translation and transliteration quality on performance.

## 4.2 Results on NLI and QA

**NLI/QA SINGLE TASK Results.** Table 2 shows our main results for the NLI and QA tasks in HI-EN. (Code-switched benchmarks in other language pairs are not available for NLI and QA.) Among the SINGLE-TASK systems, HI-EN SING-TASK performs the best (based on mean scores) on both NLI[11] and QA. Another interesting observation is that XLM-R benefits more from EN SING-TASK while mBERT benefits more from HI SING-TASK, compared to the baseline. This could be attributed to XLM-R having encountered Romanized HI text during its pretraining unlike mBERT and the GLUECoS corpus contains only Romanized Hindi.

Using a merged HI-EN dataset for HI-EN SING-TASK training, with training batches consisting of both HI and EN instances, was critical for improved performance. Table 3 shows the difference in per-

| Intermediate-Task Paradigm | Max | Mean | Std. |
|---|---|---|---|
| | GLUECOS NLI *(acc.)* | | |
| EN SING-TASK | 62.40 | 60.73 | 1.78 |
| HI SING-TASK | 63.73 | 62.09 | 0.99 |
| HI-EN SING-TASK | 65.55 | 64.1 | 0.89 |
| Sequential Training: EN → HI | 62.02 | 59.94 | 1.83 |
| | GLUECOS QA *(F1)* | | |
| EN SING-TASK | 77.62 | 75.77 | 1.79 |
| HI SING-TASK | 79.63 | 76.77 | 1.86 |
| HI-EN SING-TASK | 81.61 | 79.97 | 1.29 |
| Sequential Training: EN → HI | 76.23 | 73.69 | 1.78 |

Table 3: Sequential bilingual training with mBERT yields poor performance on both NLI and QA. Scores correspond to five random runs with random seeds.

[10]On using the complete En-Es MLM corpus for +MLM, we obtained an F1 of 62.57 using mBERT and 67.6 using XLM-R on the SA test set of ES-EN.

[11]Like Chakravarthy et al. (2020), we also find that XLM-R baseline/+MLM on GLUECoS NLI does not converge and hence we do not report these scores in Table 2.

| Translate – Transliterate | Max | Mean | Std. |
|---|---|---|---|
| | GLUECOS NLI *(acc.)* | | |
| Manual – Google Translate API | 62.24 | 61.6 | 0.62 |
| Manual – *indic-trans* | 62.09 | 59.71 | 1.37 |
| Google Translate API (both) | 60.18 | 58.59 | 1.07 |
| | GLUECOS QA *(F1)* | | |
| Manual – Google Translate API | 79.32 | 77.33 | 2.22 |
| Manual – *indic-trans* | 78.09 | 76.35 | 1.36 |
| Google Translate API (both) | 78.44 | 76.72 | 1.22 |

Table 4: Effect of translation and transliteration quality on intermediate-task training, using HI-EN SING-TASK for NLI and QA. Scores correspond to five random runs with random seeds.

| Translate – Transliterate | Max | Mean | Std. |
|---|---|---|---|
| | GLUECOS NLI *(acc.)* | | |
| Manual – Google Translate API | 61.05 | 59.63 | 0.96 |
| Manual – *indic-trans* | 59.50 | 59.26 | 0.23 |
| Google Translate API (both) | 60.12 | 58.54 | 1.53 |
| | GLUECOS QA *(F1)* | | |
| Manual – Google Translate API | 73.50 | 71.36 | 1.46 |
| Manual – *indic-trans* | 70.19 | 68.26 | 1.26 |
| Google Translate API (both) | 72.73 | 69.63 | 2.2 |

Table 5: Effect of translation and transliteration quality on intermediate-task training, using HI SING-TASK for NLI and QA. Scores correspond to five random runs with random seeds.

formance between sequentially training on English followed by Hindi versus mixing instances from both languages as in HI-EN SING-TASK. We observe a clear deterioration in performance with sequential training, with the latter performing even worse than its monolingual counterparts (EN SING-TASK and HI SING-TASK). This confirms that bilingual training is essential to improved performance on code-switched tasks.

**NLI/QA MULTI TASK Results.** Table 2 shows that the MULTI-TASK systems yield additional gains over the SING-TASK systems. Using both NLI and QA as intermediate tasks benefits both NLI and QA for mBERT and QA for XLM-R, and corroborates observations in prior work (Tarunesh et al., 2021a; Phang et al., 2020). Although intermediate-task training is beneficial across tasks, the relative improvements in QA are higher than that for NLI (see Appendix C for some QA examples). We conjecture this is due to varying dataset similarity between intermediate-tasks and target tasks (Vu et al., 2020). In QA, this similarity is higher and in NLI the conversational nature and large premise lengths reduces this similarity. The effect of domain similarity is more pronounced with MLM training resulting in variations between absolute 1.5-2%. More experiments detailing when MLM training benefits the downstream tasks is described in Section 4.4.

### 4.3 Influence of Translation and Transliteration Quality

Transliteration and translation are the two key preprocessing steps employed for bilingual pretraining. Since we make use of existing translation and transliteration tools that are not error-free, it is useful to understand the impact of such translation and transliteration tools on final downstream task performance.

To assess the impact of both translation and transliteration quality on NLI and QA performance, we use two small datasets XNLI (Conneau et al., 2018) and XQuAD (Artetxe et al., 2020) for which we have manual HI (Devanagari) translations. We combined the test and dev sets of XNLI to get the data for intermediate-task training. We discarded all examples labelled *neutral* and instances where the crowdsourced annotations did not match the designated labels[12]. After this, we were left with roughly 4.2K/0.5K instances in the train/dev sets, respectively (the dev set is used for early stopping during intermediate-task training). For XNLI, the premises and hypotheses were directly translated and for XQuAD we adopted the same translation procedure listed in Hu et al. (2020).

In Table 4, we compare the performance of HI-EN SING-TASK using manual translations with translations from the Google Translate API[13], and also transliterations from this API with those from *indic-trans*. As expected, using manual translations is most beneficial to the downstream task. The use of Google Translate, however, does not significantly hamper performance. Similar to the results in Table 4 for bilingual intermediate-task training, we present a similar analysis in Table 5 when using task-specific data in HI SING-TASK with mBERT and observe the same trends. Keeping the translation method fixed as manual, we tried using *indic-trans* for transliteration instead of the Google API. We see this led to a decrease in performance in all the 4 cases (i.e., across two models and two tasks in Tables 4 and 5), thus indicating transliterations from the Google translate API would be a better choice as compared to *indic-trans*.[14]

[12] This was achieved via the *match* Boolean attribute (Conneau et al., 2018)

[13] https://cloud.google.com/translate

[14] We did not switch to Google Translate for all our main experiments due to the overhead of obtaining Google Translate-

| Task | Model | Translit Tool | F1 | Prec. | Rec. |
|---|---|---|---|---|---|
| TA SINGLE-TASK | mBERT | *indic-trans* | 75.42 | 74.72 | 76.62 |
| | | Bing API | 75.78 | 74.89 | 77.8 |
| | XLM-R | *indic-trans* | 75.51 | 74.87 | 76.66 |
| | | Bing API | 76.36 | 75.52 | 77.88 |
| ML SINGLE-TASK | mBERT | *indic-trans* | 74.7 | 74.82 | 74.71 |
| | | Bing API | 75.92 | 75.96 | 76.15 |
| | XLM-R | *indic-trans* | 74.68 | 74.82 | 74.66 |
| | | Bing API | 76.12 | 76.1 | 76.24 |

Table 6: Effect of transliteration quality of intermediate-tasks on SA results. Scores are weighted averages further averaged over 5 random runs.

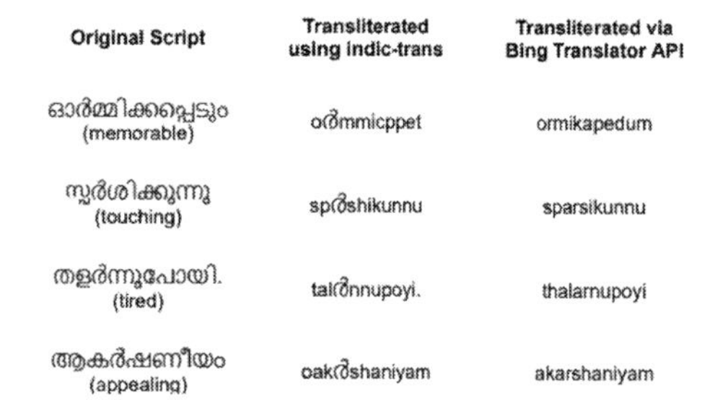


Figure 1: Different transliterations for some descriptive words in MA. *indic-trans* leaves some residual characters in the native script.

Table 6 shows the impact of transliteration on sentiment analysis of TA-EN and ML-EN. Again, we see that using an improved transliteration tool led to improved performance across both Tamil and Malayalam.

Figure 1 illustrates different MA transliterations. From the figure, we notice that *indic-trans* tends to retain some Malayalam characters in its native script (possibly due to incomplete Unicode support) and also does not produce very accurate transliterations. Transliterations from the Bing API are more phonetically accurate. Table 7 shows an example from the HI-EN NLI dataset, that is translated and transliterated using Google Translate and indic-trans. The color-coded transliterations indicate that *indic-trans* often uses existing English words as transliterations. While this is helpful for some specific (uncommon) words, in most cases it leads to ambiguity in sentence meaning (shown in blue). Further, these ambiguous words are far more common in the HI language, and thus have a greater impact on model performance.

In summary, developing more accurate tools for translation and transliteration would be very beneficial for downstream code-switched tasks.

### 4.4 MLM and Intermediate-Task Training

How does MLM pretraining in conjunction with intermediate-task training impact performance? What is the influence of changing the MLM corpus (and hence its domain) on final task performance? We address these questions in this section by focusing on NLI and QA for HI-EN using mBERT.

Table 8 provides a summary of our experiments on intermediate-task training of mBERT using only English (EN) and both English and Hindi (HI-EN) in conjunction with MLM in the MULTI-TASK setting described in Section 2.

From Table 8, we observe that intermediate training using MLM on code-switched data alone (i.e., the first row for each task) is not as effective as using both MLM and intermediate-task pretraining. NLI benefits from MLM in a multi-task setup in both monolingual and bilingual settings. Further, we note that adding in-domain MOVIE-CS data yields additional improvements for NLI. This shows that sufficient amount of in-domain data is needed for performance gains, and augmenting out-of-domain with in-domain code-switched text can be effective.

In the case of QA, MLM does not improve performance in the monolingual setting, although the mean scores are statistically close. In the bilingual setting, we see a clear improvement using GEN-CS for MLM training. However, using both GEN-CS and MOVIE-CS for MLM results in significant degradation of performance. We believe that this is due to the domain of the passages in GLUECoS QA being similar to the HI-EN blog data present in GEN-CS. However, the MOVIE-CS dataset comes from a significantly different domain and thus hurts performance. This indicates that in addition to the amount of unlabelled real code-switched text, when using MLM training, the domain of the text is very influential in determining the performance on downstream tasks (Gururangan et al., 2020).

For both NLI and QA, we observe the following common trend: Adding code-switched data from the training set of GLUECoS tasks (referred to as GLUECoS NLI CS and GLUECoS QA CS) degrades performance. This could be due to the quality of training data in the GLUECoS tasks. Each dialogue in the NLI data does not have a lot of content and is highly conversational in nature. In addition to this, the dataset is also very noisy. For example, a word *'humko'* is split into its characters *'h u m k o'*. Thus,

based transliterations for the large intermediate task datasets.

| Language | Premise/ Hypothesis | Label | Dataset |
|---|---|---|---|
| EN | **PREMISE:** Split Ends a Cosmetology Shop is a nice example of appositional elegance combined with euphemism in the appositive and the low key or off-beat opening.<br>**HYPOTHESIS:** Split Ends is an ice cream shop. | entailment | MultiNLI/ XNLI |
| HI (Google$^\diamond$) | **PREMISE:** split ends ek *kosmetolojee* shop epositiv *aur* kam kunjee ya oph-beet *opaning* mein vyanjana ke saath sanyukt eplaid laality ka ek achchha udaaharan hai.<br>**HYPOTHESIS:** split *ends* ek *aaisakreem* shop *hai*. | entailment | Translation$^\dagger$ |
| HI (Google$^\diamond$) | **PREMISE:** split inds ek *kosmetolojee* shop samaanaadhikaran shishtata *aur* kam kunjee ya of-beet *opaning* mein preyokti ke mishran ka ek achchha udaaharan *hai*.<br>**HYPOTHESIS:** split *ends* ek *aaisakreem* kee dukaan *hai*. | entailment | XNLI |
| HI (indic$^\star$) | **PREMISE:** split inds ek *cosmetology* shop samaanaadhikaran shishtataa *or* kam kunjee yaa of-beet opening main preyokti ke mishran kaa ek acha udhaaharan *he*.<br>**HYPOTHESIS:** split *ands* ek *icecream* kii dukaan *he*. | entailment | XNLI |

Table 7: NLI examples from some of our datasets. $\dagger$: obtained by translation of the second row using Google Translate API. $\diamond$: transliterated using Google Translate API, $\star$: transliterated using *indic-trans* (Bhat et al., 2014). In *blue*, we show some of the words with ambiguous transliterations by *indic-trans*. In *purple*, we show some words that are better transliterated by *indic-trans*. Best viewed in color.

| Language | MLM Data | Max | Mean | Std. |
|---|---|---|---|---|
| | | GLUECOS NLI *(acc.)* | | |
| - | GEN-CS | 59.94 | 58.75 | 0.93 |
| EN | - | 62.40 | 60.73 | 1.78 |
| | GEN-CS | <u>65.07</u> | <u>62.84</u> | 1.93 |
| HI-EN | - | 65.55 | 64.1 | 0.89 |
| | GEN-CS | 65.22 | 64.19 | 1.22 |
| | GENERAL + MOVIE CS | <u>**66.67**</u> | <u>**65.61**</u> | 0.86 |
| | GENERAL + MOVIE CS + GLUECOS NLI CS | 66.17 | 65.21 | 0.96 |
| | | GLUECOS QA *(F1)* | | |
| - | GEN-CS | 59.26 | 57.84 | 1.29 |
| EN | - | <u>77.62</u> | <u>75.77</u> | 1.79 |
| | GEN-CS | 76.23 | 75.49 | 1.03 |
| HI-EN | - | 81.61 | 79.97 | 1.29 |
| | GEN-CS | <u>**83.03**</u> | <u>**80.38**</u> | 1.68 |
| | GENERAL + MOVIE CS | 81.05 | 79.11 | 1.40 |
| | GENERAL + MOVIE CS + GLUECOS QA CS | 79.63 | 78.27 | 1.46 |

Table 8: Performance on different variations of MLM + intermediate-task training of mBERT. We underline the relatively best model and bold-face the model with the highest performance for each task.

MLM on such data may not be very effective and could hurt performance. For QA, passages in significant portions of the train set are obtained using *DrQA - Document Retriever module*[15] (Chen et al., 2017). These passages are monolingual in nature and thus potentially not useful for MLM training with code-switched text.

## 5 Related Work

While pretrained multilingual models are being increasingly used for cross-lingual natural language understanding tasks, their effectiveness for code-switched tasks has not been thoroughly explored. Winata et al. (2021) show that embeddings from pretrained multilingual models are not very effective for code-switched tasks and more work is needed to effectively adapt them.

Intermediate task-training has proven to be effective for many NLP target tasks (Pruksachatkun et al., 2020; Vu et al., 2020), as well as cross-lingual zero-shot transfer from English tasks on multilingual models such as XLM-R (Phang et al., 2020) and mBERT (Tarunesh et al., 2021a). Ours is the first work to show improved intermediate task-training strategies for code-switched target tasks.

Pires et al. (2019) and Hsu et al. (2019) showed that mBERT is effective for HI-EN part-of-speech tagging and a reading comprehension task on synthetic code-switched data, respectively. This was extended for a variety of code-switched tasks by Khanuja et al. (2020b), where they showed improvements on several tasks using MLM pretraining on real and synthetic code-switched text. Chakravarthy et al. (2020) further improved the NLI performance of mBERT by including large amounts of in-domain code-switched text during MLM pretraining.

Gururangan et al. (2020) empirically demonstrate that pretraining is most beneficial when the domains of the intermediate and target tasks are similar, which we observe as well. Differing from their recommendation of domain adaptive pretraining using MLM on large quantities of real code-switched data, we find intermediate-task training using significantly smaller amounts of labeled data to be more consistently beneficial across tasks and languages. In contrast to very recent work (Gupta et al., 2021) that reports results using a Roberta-based model trained exclusively for sentiment analysis and pretrained on 60M English tweets, we present a bilingual training technique that is consistently effective across tasks and languages while

[15] `https://github.com/facebookresearch/DrQA`

requiring significantly smaller amounts of data.
Instead of using mBERT and XLM-R that are very broad in their coverage of languages, it would be interesting to examine whether our observed trends hold when using pretrained models specifically trained for the chosen target languages. We could consider using very recent models like IndicBERT (Kakwani et al., 2020) and MuRIL (Khanuja et al., 2021) that are trained exclusively on Indian languages and have been shown to outperform mBERT on cross-lingual tasks (e.g., XTREME) and tasks like IndicGLUE, respectively. We leave this investigation for future work.

## 6 Conclusion

This is the first work to demonstrate the effectiveness of intermediate-task training for code-switched NLI, QA and SA on different language pairs, and present code-switched MLM that consistently benefits SA more than standard MLM. We also carry out ablations of transliteration systems and compare their performance across the same corpora translated using different techniques. We observe that high-quality translations and transliterations are important to derive performance improvements on downstream tasks.
For future work, we plan to continue exploring pretraining strategies, based on more informed masking objectives and task-adaptive techniques. One key limitation of the newly introduced code-switched MLM approach is the requirement of LID systems for the languages under consideration. Future work can focus on mitigating this requirement.

## 7 Acknowledgements

The authors would like to thank the anonymous reviewers for their useful and constructive comments that helped improve the draft.

## References


Gustavo Aguilar, Fahad AlGhamdi, Victor Soto, Thamar Solorio, Mona Diab, and Julia Hirschberg, editors. 2018. *Proceedings of the Third Workshop on Computational Approaches to Linguistic Code-Switching*. Association for Computational Linguistics, Melbourne, Australia.

Fahad AlGhamdi, Giovanni Molina, Mona Diab, Thamar Solorio, Abdelati Hawwari, Victor Soto, and Julia Hirschberg. 2016. Part of speech tagging for code switched data. In *Proceedings of the Second Workshop on Computational Approaches to Code Switching*, pages 98–107, Austin, Texas. Association for Computational Linguistics.

Mikel Artetxe, Sebastian Ruder, and Dani Yogatama. 2020. On the cross-lingual transferability of monolingual representations. In *Proceedings of the 58th Annual Meeting of the Association for Computational Linguistics*, pages 4623–4637, Online. Association for Computational Linguistics.

Suman Banerjee, Nikita Moghe, Siddhartha Arora, and Mitesh M. Khapra. 2018. A dataset for building code-mixed goal oriented conversation systems. In *Proceedings of the 27th International Conference on Computational Linguistics*, pages 3766–3780, Santa Fe, New Mexico, USA. Association for Computational Linguistics.

Francesco Barbieri, Jose Camacho-Collados, Luis Espinosa Anke, and Leonardo Neves. 2020. TweetEval: Unified benchmark and comparative evaluation for tweet classification. In *Findings of the Association for Computational Linguistics: EMNLP 2020*, pages 1644–1650, Online. Association for Computational Linguistics.

Irshad Bhat, Riyaz A. Bhat, Manish Shrivastava, and Dipti Sharma. 2017. Joining hands: Exploiting monolingual treebanks for parsing of code-mixing data. In *Proceedings of the 15th Conference of the European Chapter of the Association for Computational Linguistics: Volume 2, Short Papers*, pages 324–330, Valencia, Spain. Association for Computational Linguistics.

Irshad Ahmad Bhat, Vandan Mujadia, Aniruddha Tammewar, Riyaz Ahmad Bhat, and Manish Shrivastava. 2014. IIIT-H System Submission for FIRE2014 Shared Task on Transliterated Search. In *Proceedings of the Forum for Information Retrieval Evaluation*, pages 48–53. ACM.

Bharathi Raja Chakravarthi, Navya Jose, Shardul Suryawanshi, Elizabeth Sherly, and John Philip McCrae. 2020a. A sentiment analysis dataset for code-mixed Malayalam-English. In *Proceedings of the 1st Joint Workshop on Spoken Language Technologies for Under-resourced languages (SLTU) and Collaboration and Computing for Under-Resourced Languages (CCURL)*, pages 177–184, Marseille, France. European Language Resources association.

Bharathi Raja Chakravarthi, Vigneshwaran Muralidaran, Ruba Priyadharshini, and John Philip McCrae. 2020b. Corpus creation for sentiment analysis in code-mixed Tamil-English text. In *Proceedings of the 1st Joint Workshop on Spoken Language Technologies for Under-resourced languages (SLTU) and Collaboration and Computing for Under-Resourced Languages (CCURL)*, pages 202–210, Marseille, France. European Language Resources association.

Bharathi Raja Chakravarthi, Ruba Priyadharshini, Navya Jose, Anand Kumar M, Thomas Mandl, Prasanna Kumar Kumaresan, Rahul Ponnusamy, Hariharan R L, John P. McCrae, and Elizabeth Sherly. 2021. Findings of the shared task on offensive language identification in Tamil, Malayalam, and Kannada. In *Proceedings of the First Workshop on Speech and Language Technologies for Dravidian Languages*, pages 133–145, Kyiv. Association for Computational Linguistics.

Sharanya Chakravarthy, Anjana Umapathy, and Alan W Black. 2020. Detecting entailment in code-mixed Hindi-English conversations. In *Proceedings of the Sixth Workshop on Noisy User-generated Text (W-NUT 2020)*, pages 165–170, Online. Association for Computational Linguistics.

Khyathi Chandu, Ekaterina Loginova, Vishal Gupta, Josef van Genabith, Günter Neumann, Manoj Chinnakotla, Eric Nyberg, and Alan W. Black. 2018a. Code-mixed question answering challenge: Crowd-sourcing data and techniques. In *Proceedings of the Third Workshop on Computational Approaches to Linguistic Code-Switching*, pages 29–38, Melbourne, Australia. Association for Computational Linguistics.

Khyathi Chandu, Thomas Manzini, Sumeet Singh, and Alan W. Black. 2018b. Language informed modeling of code-switched text. In *Proceedings of the Third Workshop on Computational Approaches to Linguistic Code-Switching*, pages 92–97, Melbourne, Australia. Association for Computational Linguistics.

Danqi Chen, Adam Fisch, Jason Weston, and Antoine Bordes. 2017. Reading Wikipedia to answer open-domain questions. In *Proceedings of the 55th Annual Meeting of the Association for Computational Linguistics (Volume 1: Long Papers)*, pages 1870–1879, Vancouver, Canada. Association for Computational Linguistics.

Alexis Conneau, Kartikay Khandelwal, Naman Goyal, Vishrav Chaudhary, Guillaume Wenzek, Francisco Guzmán, Edouard Grave, Myle Ott, Luke Zettlemoyer, and Veselin Stoyanov. 2020. Unsupervised cross-lingual representation learning at scale. In *Proceedings of the 58th Annual Meeting of the Association for Computational Linguistics*, pages 8440–8451, Online. Association for Computational Linguistics.

Alexis Conneau, Ruty Rinott, Guillaume Lample, Adina Williams, Samuel Bowman, Holger Schwenk, and Veselin Stoyanov. 2018. XNLI: Evaluating cross-lingual sentence representations. In *Proceedings of the 2018 Conference on Empirical Methods in Natural Language Processing*, pages 2475–2485, Brussels, Belgium. Association for Computational Linguistics.

Jacob Devlin, Ming-Wei Chang, Kenton Lee, and Kristina Toutanova. 2019. BERT: Pre-training of deep bidirectional transformers for language understanding. In *Proceedings of the 2019 Conference of the North American Chapter of the Association for Computational Linguistics: Human Language Technologies, Volume 1 (Long and Short Papers)*, pages 4171–4186, Minneapolis, Minnesota. Association for Computational Linguistics.

Akshat Gupta, Sai Krishna Rallabandi, and Alan W Black. 2021. Task-specific pre-training and cross lingual transfer for sentiment analysis in Dravidian code-switched languages. In *Proceedings of the First Workshop on Speech and Language Technologies for Dravidian Languages*, pages 73–79, Kyiv. Association for Computational Linguistics.

Suchin Gururangan, Ana Marasović, Swabha Swayamdipta, Kyle Lo, Iz Beltagy, Doug Downey, and Noah A. Smith. 2020. Don't stop pretraining: Adapt language models to domains and tasks. In *Proceedings of the 58th Annual Meeting of the Association for Computational Linguistics*, pages 8342–8360, Online. Association for Computational Linguistics.

Tsung-Yuan Hsu, Chi-Liang Liu, and Hung-yi Lee. 2019. Zero-shot reading comprehension by cross-lingual transfer learning with multi-lingual language representation model. In *Proceedings of the 2019 Conference on Empirical Methods in Natural Language Processing and the 9th International Joint Conference on Natural Language Processing (EMNLP-IJCNLP)*, pages 5933–5940, Hong Kong, China. Association for Computational Linguistics.

Junjie Hu, Sebastian Ruder, Aditya Siddhant, Graham Neubig, Orhan Firat, and Melvin Johnson. 2020. XTREME: A massively multilingual multi-task benchmark for evaluating cross-lingual generalisation. In *Proceedings of the 37th International Conference on Machine Learning*, pages 4411–4421, Virtual. PMLR.

Marcin Junczys-Dowmunt, Roman Grundkiewicz, Tomasz Dwojak, Hieu Hoang, Kenneth Heafield, Tom Neckermann, Frank Seide, Ulrich Germann, Alham Fikri Aji, Nikolay Bogoychev, André F. T. Martins, and Alexandra Birch. 2018. Marian: Fast neural machine translation in C++. In *Proceedings of ACL 2018, System Demonstrations*, pages 116–121, Melbourne, Australia. Association for Computational Linguistics.

Divyanshu Kakwani, Anoop Kunchukuttan, Satish Golla, Gokul N.C., Avik Bhattacharyya, Mitesh M. Khapra, and Pratyush Kumar. 2020. IndicNLPSuite: Monolingual corpora, evaluation benchmarks and pre-trained multilingual language models for Indian languages. In *Findings of the Association for Computational Linguistics: EMNLP 2020*, pages 4948–4961, Online. Association for Computational Linguistics.

Simran Khanuja, Diksha Bansal, Sarvesh Mehtani, Savya Khosla, Atreyee Dey, Balaji Gopalan, Dilip Kumar Margam, Pooja Aggarwal, Rajiv Teja Nagipogu, Shachi Dave, Shruti Gupta, Subhash Chandra Bose Gali, Vish Subramanian, and Partha P. Talukdar. 2021. Muril: Multilingual representations for indian languages. *CoRR*, abs/2103.10730.

Simran Khanuja, Sandipan Dandapat, Sunayana Sitaram, and Monojit Choudhury. 2020a. A new dataset for natural language inference from code-mixed conversations. In *Proceedings of the The 4th Workshop on Computational Approaches to Code Switching*, pages 9–16, Marseille, France. European Language Resources Association.

Simran Khanuja, Sandipan Dandapat, Anirudh Srinivasan, Sunayana Sitaram, and Monojit Choudhury. 2020b. GLUECoS: An evaluation benchmark for code-switched NLP. In *Proceedings of the 58th Annual Meeting of the Association for Computational Linguistics*, pages 3575–3585, Online. Association for Computational Linguistics.

Ilya Loshchilov and Frank Hutter. 2019. Decoupled weight decay regularization. In *7th International Conference on Learning Representations, ICLR 2019, New Orleans, LA, USA, May 6-9, 2019*.

Thomas Mandl, Sandip Modha, Anand Kumar M, and Bharathi Raja Chakravarthi. 2020. Overview of the hasoc track at fire 2020: Hate speech and offensive language identification in tamil, malayalam, hindi, english and german. In *Forum for Information Retrieval Evaluation*, page 29–32.

Jasabanta Patro, Bidisha Samanta, Saurabh Singh, Abhipsa Basu, Prithwish Mukherjee, Monojit Choudhury, and Animesh Mukherjee. 2017. All that is English may be Hindi: Enhancing language identification through automatic ranking of the likeliness of word borrowing in social media. In *Proceedings of the 2017 Conference on Empirical Methods in Natural Language Processing*, pages 2264–2274, Copenhagen, Denmark. Association for Computational Linguistics.

Parth Patwa, Gustavo Aguilar, Sudipta Kar, Suraj Pandey, Srinivas PYKL, Björn Gambäck, Tanmoy Chakraborty, Thamar Solorio, and Amitava Das. 2020. SemEval-2020 task 9: Overview of sentiment analysis of code-mixed tweets. In *Proceedings of the Fourteenth Workshop on Semantic Evaluation*, pages 774–790, Barcelona (online). International Committee for Computational Linguistics.

Jason Phang, Iacer Calixto, Phu Mon Htut, Yada Pruksachatkun, Haokun Liu, Clara Vania, Katharina Kann, and Samuel R. Bowman. 2020. English intermediate-task training improves zero-shot cross-lingual transfer too. In *Proceedings of the 1st Conference of the Asia-Pacific Chapter of the Association for Computational Linguistics and the 10th International Joint Conference on Natural Language Processing*, pages 557–575, Suzhou, China. Association for Computational Linguistics.

Jason Phang, Thibault Févry, and Samuel R Bowman. 2018. Sentence encoders on stilts: Supplementary training on intermediate labeled-data tasks. *arXiv preprint arXiv:1811.01088*.

Telmo Pires, Eva Schlinger, and Dan Garrette. 2019. How multilingual is multilingual BERT? In *Proceedings of the 57th Annual Meeting of the Association for Computational Linguistics*, pages 4996–5001, Florence, Italy. Association for Computational Linguistics.

Adithya Pratapa, Monojit Choudhury, and Sunayana Sitaram. 2018. Word embeddings for code-mixed language processing. In *Proceedings of the 2018 Conference on Empirical Methods in Natural Language Processing*, pages 3067–3072, Brussels, Belgium. Association for Computational Linguistics.

Yada Pruksachatkun, Jason Phang, Haokun Liu, Phu Mon Htut, Xiaoyi Zhang, Richard Yuanzhe Pang, Clara Vania, Katharina Kann, and Samuel R. Bowman. 2020. Intermediate-task transfer learning with pre-trained language models: When and why does it work? In *Proceedings of the 58th Annual Meeting of the Association for Computational Linguistics*, pages 5231–5247, Online. Association for Computational Linguistics.

Colin Raffel, Noam Shazeer, Adam Roberts, Katherine Lee, Sharan Narang, Michael Matena, Yanqi Zhou, Wei Li, and Peter J. Liu. 2020. Exploring the limits of transfer learning with a unified text-to-text transformer. *Journal of Machine Learning Research*, 21(140):1–67.

Pranav Rajpurkar, Jian Zhang, Konstantin Lopyrev, and Percy Liang. 2016. SQuAD: 100,000+ questions for machine comprehension of text. In *Proceedings of the 2016 Conference on Empirical Methods in Natural Language Processing*, pages 2383–2392, Austin, Texas. Association for Computational Linguistics.

Gowtham Ramesh, Sumanth Doddapaneni, Aravinth Bheemaraj, Mayank Jobanputra, Raghavan AK, Ajitesh Sharma, Sujit Sahoo, Harshita Diddee, Mahalakshmi J, Divyanshu Kakwani, Navneet Kumar, Aswin Pradeep, Kumar Deepak, Vivek Raghavan, Anoop Kunchukuttan, Pratyush Kumar, and Mitesh Shantadevi Khapra. 2021. Samanantar: The largest publicly available parallel corpora collection for 11 indic languages.

Kushagra Singh, Indira Sen, and Ponnurangam Kumaraguru. 2018. A Twitter corpus for Hindi-English code mixed POS tagging. In *Proceedings of the Sixth International Workshop on Natural Language Processing for Social Media*, pages 12–17, Melbourne, Australia. Association for Computational Linguistics.

Richard Socher, Alex Perelygin, Jean Wu, Jason Chuang, Christopher D. Manning, Andrew Ng, and Christopher Potts. 2013. Recursive deep models for semantic compositionality over a sentiment treebank. In *Proceedings of the 2013 Conference on Empirical Methods in Natural Language Processing*, pages 1631–1642, Seattle, Washington, USA. Association for Computational Linguistics.

Thamar Solorio, Elizabeth Blair, Suraj Maharjan, Steven Bethard, Mona Diab, Mahmoud Ghoneim, Abdelati Hawwari, Fahad AlGhamdi, Julia Hirschberg, Alison Chang, and Pascale Fung. 2014. Overview for the first shared task on language identification in code-switched data. In *Proceedings of the First Workshop on Computational Approaches to Code Switching*, pages 62–72, Doha, Qatar. Association for Computational Linguistics.

Anirudh Srinivasan. 2020. MSR India at SemEval-2020 task 9: Multilingual models can do code-mixing too. In *Proceedings of the Fourteenth Workshop on Semantic Evaluation*, pages 951–956, Barcelona (online). International Committee for Computational Linguistics.

Sahil Swami, Ankush Khandelwal, Vinay Singh, Syed Sarfaraz Akhtar, and Manish Shrivastava. 2018. A corpus of english-hindi code-mixed tweets for sarcasm detection. *arXiv preprint arXiv:1805.11869*.

Ishan Tarunesh, Sushil Khyalia, Vishwajeet Kumar, Ganesh Ramakrishnan, and Preethi Jyothi. 2021a. Meta-learning for effective multi-task and multilingual modelling. *arXiv preprint arXiv:2101.10368*.

Ishan Tarunesh, Syamantak Kumar, and Preethi Jyothi. 2021b. From machine translation to code-switching: Generating high-quality code-switched text. In *Proceedings of the 58th Annual Meeting of the Association for Computational Linguistics*.

Ashish Vaswani, Noam Shazeer, Niki Parmar, Jakob Uszkoreit, Llion Jones, Aidan N Gomez, Ł ukasz Kaiser, and Illia Polosukhin. 2017. Attention is all you need. In *Advances in Neural Information Processing Systems*, pages 5998–6008.

David Vilares, Miguel A. Alonso, and Carlos Gómez-Rodríguez. 2016. EN-ES-CS: An English-Spanish code-switching Twitter corpus for multilingual sentiment analysis. In *Proceedings of the Tenth International Conference on Language Resources and Evaluation (LREC'16)*, pages 4149–4153, Portorož, Slovenia. European Language Resources Association (ELRA).

Tu Vu, Tong Wang, Tsendsuren Munkhdalai, Alessandro Sordoni, Adam Trischler, Andrew Mattarella-Micke, Subhransu Maji, and Mohit Iyyer. 2020. Exploring and predicting transferability across NLP tasks. In *Proceedings of the 2020 Conference on Empirical Methods in Natural Language Processing (EMNLP)*, pages 7882–7926, Online. Association for Computational Linguistics.

Adina Williams, Nikita Nangia, and Samuel Bowman. 2018. A broad-coverage challenge corpus for sentence understanding through inference. In *Proceedings of the 2018 Conference of the North American Chapter of the Association for Computational Linguistics: Human Language Technologies, Volume 1 (Long Papers)*, pages 1112–1122, New Orleans, Louisiana. Association for Computational Linguistics.

Genta Indra Winata, Samuel Cahyawijaya, Zihan Liu, Zhaojiang Lin, Andrea Madotto, and Pascale Fung. 2021. Are multilingual models effective in code-switching? In *Proceedings of the Fifth Workshop on Computational Approaches to Linguistic Code-Switching*, pages 142–153, Online. Association for Computational Linguistics.

Thomas Wolf, Lysandre Debut, Victor Sanh, Julien Chaumond, Clement Delangue, Anthony Moi, Pierric Cistac, Tim Rault, Rémi Louf, Morgan Funtowicz, et al. 2019. Huggingface's transformers: State-of-the-art natural language processing. *ArXiv*, pages arXiv–1910.

Shijie Wu and Mark Dredze. 2019. Beto, bentz, becas: The surprising cross-lingual effectiveness of BERT. In *Proceedings of the 2019 Conference on Empirical Methods in Natural Language Processing and the 9th International Joint Conference on Natural Language Processing (EMNLP-IJCNLP)*, pages 833–844, Hong Kong, China. Association for Computational Linguistics.

## Appendix

## A Implementation Details

The mBERT model comprises 179M parameters with the MLM head comprising 712K parameters. The XLM-R model comprises 270M parameters with an MLM head with 842k parameters. For both models, the NLI (sequence classification) and QA heads comprise 1536 parameters each. For SA (sequence classification) the head comprises of 2304 parameters.

## B Hyperparameter Tuning

In all experiments, we have used the AdamW algorithm (Loshchilov and Hutter, 2019) and a linear scheduler with warm up for the learning rate. These experiments were run on a single NVIDIA GeForce GTX 1080 Ti GPU. Some crucial fixed hyperparameters are: `learning_rate = 5e-5`, `adam_epsilon = 1e-8`, `max_gradient_norm = 1`, and `gradient_accumulation_steps = 10`.

### B.1 Intermediate-Task Training

The training for all the main intermediate-task experiments was carried out for 4 epochs and the model with the highest performance metric on the task dev set was considered (all the metrics stagnated after a certain point in training). For NLI + QA tasks, two separate models were stored depending on the performance metric on the respective dev set. No hyperparameter search was conducted at this stage. During bilingual training, the batches were interspersed—equal number of examples from English and Romanized HI within each batch. In the single-task systems, we used `batch_size = 8` and `max_sequence_length = 128` for NLI, `batch_size = 8` and `max_sequence_length = 256` for SA, `batch_size = 4` and `max_sequence_length = 512` for QA. During multi-task training, the `max_sequence_length` was set to the maximum of the aforementioned numbers and the respective batch-sizes. Any multi-task training technique requires at least 14-15 hours for validation accuracy to stagnate. Single task intermediate training requires 4-5 hours for monolingual versions and 8-9 hours for the bilingual version. SA data being smaller in size requires 8-9 hours for multitask, 4-5 hours for bilingual intermediate task and 1-2 hours for monolingual intermediate task. The `logging_steps` are set to approximately 10% of the total steps in an epoch.

### B.2 Fine-tuning on GLUECoS NLI & QA Tasks

The base fine-tuning files have been taken from the GLUECoS repository[16]. Given that there no dev sets in GLUECoS, and that the tasks are low-resource, we use train accuracy in NLI and train loss in QA as an indication to stop fine-tuning. Manual search is performed over a range of epochs to obtain the best test performance. For NLI, we stopped fine-tuning when training accuracy is in the range of 70-80% (which meant fine-tuning for 1-4 epochs depending upon the model and technique used). For QA, we stopped when training loss reached $\sim$ 0.1. Thus, we explored 3-5 epochs for mBERT and 4-8 epochs for XLM-R. We present the statistics over the best results on 5 different seeds. We used `batch_size = 8` and `max_sequence_length = 256` for GLUECoS NLI[17] and `batch_size = 4` and `max_sequence_length = 512` for GLUECoS QA. All our fine-tuning runs on GLUECoS take an average of 1 minute per epoch.

### B.3 Fine-tuning on downstream SA tasks

The dev set, being available for all language pairs was used to find the checkpoint with best F1 score, and this model was used for evaluation on the test set. The mean values were presented after carrying out the above procedure for 6 different seeds. The `logging_steps` are set to approximately 10% of the total steps in an epoch. Each epoch takes around 1 minute for TA, MA and ES, 2 minutes for HI (SemEval).

## C Example Outputs

In Table 9, we show some instances from the HI-EN QA dataset. The color-coded transliterations indicate that *indic-trans* often uses existing English words as transliterations. While for some specific (uncommon) words that is helpful, in most cases it leads to ambiguity in the sentence meaning (shown in blue). Further, these ambiguous words (in blue) are far more common in the HI language, and thus, have a greater impact on model performance. We also note that transliterations of these common words in the GLUECoS dataset matches closely with the transliterations produced using the

[16] `https://github.com/microsoft/GLUECoS`

[17] The sequence length was doubled as compared to the intermediate-task training to incorporate the long premise length of GLUECoS NLI. This resulted in higher accuracy.

| Language | QA Context | Dataset |
|---|---|---|
| HI-EN | Mitashi ne ek Android Tv ko Launch kiya hain. Jise tahat yeh Tv Android Operating System par chalta hain. Iski Keemat Rs. 51,990 rakhi gayi hain. Ab aaya Android TV Mitashi Company ne Android KitKat OS par chalne wale Smart TV ko Launch kar diya hain. Company ne is T.V. ko 51,990 Rupees ke price par launch kiya hain. Agar features ki baat kare to is Android TV ki Screen 50 inch ki hain, Jo 1280 X 1080 p ka resolution deti hain. USB plug play function ke saath yeh T.V. 27 Vidoe formats ko support karta hain. Vidoe input ke liye HDMI Cable, PC, Wi-Fi aur Ethernet Connectivity di gyi hain. Behtar processing ke liye dual core processor ke saath 512 MB ki RAM lagayi gyi hain. Yeh Android TV banane wali company Mitashi isse pahle khilaune banane ka kaam karti thi. Iske alawa is company ne education se jude products banane shuru kiye. 1998 mein stapith huyi is company ne Android T.V. ke saath-saath India ki pahli Android Gaming Device ko bhi launch kiya hain. | GLUECOS QA |
| EN | Their local rivals, Polonia Warsaw, have significantly fewer supporters, yet they managed to win Ekstraklasa Championship in 2000. They also won the country's championship in 1946, and won the cup twice as well. Polonia's home venue is located at Konwiktorska Street, a ten-minute walk north from the Old Town. Polonia was relegated from the country's top flight in 2013 because of their disastrous financial situation. They are now playing in the 4th league (5th tier in Poland) -the bottom professional league in the National – Polish Football Association structure. | SQuAD/XQuAD |
| HI (Google$^{\diamond}$) | unake sthaaneey pratidvandviyon, *poloniya voraso* ke paas kaaphee kam samarthak hain, phir bhee ve 2000 *mein* ekastraklaasa *chaimpiyanaship* jeetane *mein* kaamayaab rahe. unhonne 1946 *mein* desh kee *chaimpiyanaship* bhee jeetee, *aur* do baar *kap* bhee jeeta. *poloniya* ka ghareloo sthal konaveektarsaka street par sthit *hai*, jo old taun se uttar *mein* das *minat* kee paidal dooree par *hai*. apanee vinaashakaaree vitteey sthiti ke kaaran *poloniya* ko 2013 *mein* desh kee sheersh udaan se hata diya gaya tha. ab ve neshanal (polish polish esosieshan) sanrachana *mein* 4 ven leeg (polaind *mein* 5 ven star) *mein* khel rahe hain. | Translation$^{\dagger}$ |
| HI (Google$^{\diamond}$) | unake sthaaneey pratidvandviyon, *poloniya vaaraso*, ke paas kaaphee kam samarthak hain, phir bhee ve 2000 *mein* ekalastralaasa *chaimpiyanaship* jeetane *mein* kaamayaab rahe. unhonne 1946 *mein* raashtriy *chaimpiyanaship* bhee jeetee, *aur* saath hee do baar *kap* jeete. *poloniya* ka ghar konaveektarsaka street par sthit *hai*, jo old taun se uttar *mein* das *minat* kee paidal dooree par *hai*. *poloniya* ko 2013 *mein* unakee kharaab vitteey sthiti kee vajah se desh kee sheersh udaan se hata diya gaya tha. ve ab botam profeshanal leeg ke 4th leeg (polaind *mein* 5 ven star) neshanal polish futabol esosieshan sanrachana *mein* khel rahe hain. | XQuAD |
| HI (indic$^{\star}$) | unke sthaneey pratidwandviyon, *polonia warsaw*, ke paas kaaphi kam samarthak hai, phir bhi ve 2000 *main* ecrestlasa *championships* jeetne *main* kaamyaab rahe. unhone 1946 *main* rashtri *championships* bhi jiti, *or* saath hi do baar *cap* jite. *polonia* kaa ghar konwictarska street par sthit *he*, jo old toun se uttar *main* das *minute* kii paidal duuri par *he*. *polonia* ko 2013 *main* unki karaab vittiya sthiti kii vajah se desh kii sheersh udaan se hataa diya gaya tha. ve ab bottm profeshnal lig ke 4th lig (poland *main* 5 wein str) neshnal polish footbaal association sanrachana *main* khel rahe hai. | XQuAD |

Table 9: QA examples from some of our datasets. $^{\dagger}$: obtained by translation of the second row using Google Translate API. $^{\diamond}$: transliterated using Google Translate API, $^{\star}$: transliterated using *indic-trans* (Bhat et al., 2014). In *blue*, we show some of the words words with ambiguous transliteration by *indic-trans* and their counterparts. In *purple*, we show some words that are better transliterated by *indic-trans*. Best viewed in color.

| Language | Sentence | Label | Dataset |
|---|---|---|---|
| EN | It's definitely Christmas season! My social media news feeds have been all about Hatchimals since midnight! Good luck parents! | positive | TweetEval |
| HI$^{\diamond}$ | yeah nishchit roop se christmas ka mausam hai! mera social media news feed adhi raat se hatchimal ke baare mein hai! mata-pita ko shubhkamnayen! | positive | Translation$^{\dagger}$ |
| ES | ¡Es definitivamente la temporada de Navidad! Mis noticias en las redes sociales han sido todo acerca de Hatchimals desde medianoche! ¡Buena suerte padres! | positive | Translation$^{\ddagger}$ |
| ML$^{\diamond}$ | ith theerchayayum chrismas seesonnan, ente social media news feads ardharathri muthal hachimalsine kurichan! | positive | Translation$^{\dagger}$ |
| TA$^{\diamond}$ | itu nichchayam christumus column! nalliravu muthal enathu samook utaka seithi oottngal anaithum hatchimals patriadhu! petrors nalvazthukal! | positive | Translation$^{\dagger}$ |
| EN | the story and the friendship proceeds in such a way that you 're watching a soap opera rather than a chronicle of the ups and downs that accompany lifelong friendships . | negative | SST |
| HI$^{\diamond}$ | kahani or dosti is tarah se aage badhati hai ki op jeevan bhar ki dosti ke saath aane vale utaar-chadhav k kram k bajay ek dharavahik dekh rahe hain | negative | Translation$^{\dagger}$ |
| ES | la historia y la amistad proceden de tal manera que estás viendo una telenovela en lugar de una crónica de los altibajos que acompañan a las amistades de toda la vida. | negative | Translation$^{\ddagger}$ |
| ML$^{\diamond}$ | ajeevanantha sauhradangalil undakunna uyarchayeyum thazhchayeyum kurichulla oru kathayalla, marich oru sopp opera kanunna reethiyilan kathayum souhrdavum munnot pokunnath. | negative | Translation$^{\dagger}$ |
| TA$^{\diamond}$ | kadhaiyum natpum vaazhnaal muzhuvathum natputan inaintha etra erakangalin kalavarisai cottlum neengal oru soap oberov paarkkum vagaiyil selgiradhu. | negative | Translation$^{\dagger}$ |

Table 10: Sentiment analysis examples from our datasets. $^{\dagger}$: obtained by translation of the corresponding EN sentence using IndicTrans MT (Ramesh et al., 2021). $^{\ddagger}$: obtained by translation of the corresponding EN sentence using MarianMT. $^{\diamond}$: transliterated using Bing Translator API.

Google Translate API. Further, there is not a lot of difference between the machine and human translations, which might be due to translation bias. Table 10 shows examples from the sentiment analysis datasets in HI-EN, ES-EN, TA-EN and ML-EN.

# Shaking Syntactic Trees on the Sesame Street: Multilingual Probing with Controllable Perturbations

**Ekaterina Taktasheva**[*]
HSE University
Moscow, Russia

**Vladislav Mikhailov**
SberDevices, Sberbank
Moscow, Russia

**Ekaterina Artemova**
HSE University
Huawei Noah's Ark lab
Moscow, Russia

## Abstract

Recent research has adopted a new experimental field centered around the concept of text perturbations which has revealed that shuffled word order has little to no impact on the downstream performance of Transformer-based language models across many NLP tasks. These findings contradict the common understanding of how the models encode hierarchical and structural information and even question if the word order is modeled with position embeddings. To this end, this paper proposes nine probing datasets organized by the type of *controllable* text perturbation for three Indo-European languages with a varying degree of word order flexibility: English, Swedish and Russian. Based on the probing analysis of the M-BERT and M-BART models, we report that the syntactic sensitivity depends on the language and model pre-training objectives. We also find that the sensitivity grows across layers together with the increase of the perturbation granularity. Last but not least, we show that the models barely use the positional information to induce syntactic trees from their intermediate self-attention and contextualized representations.

## 1 Introduction

An extensive body of works is devoted to analyzing syntactic knowledge of Transformer language models (LMs) (Vaswani et al., 2017; Clark et al., 2019; Goldberg, 2019; Belinkov and Glass, 2019). BERT-based LMs (Devlin et al., 2019) have demonstrated their abilities to encode various linguistic and hierarchical properties (Lin et al., 2019; Jawahar et al., 2019; Jo and Myaeng, 2020) which have a positive effect on the downstream performance (Liu et al., 2019a; Miaschi et al., 2020) and serve as an inspiration for syntax-oriented architecture improvements (Wang et al., 2019; Bai et al., 2021; Ahmad et al., 2021; Sachan et al., 2021). Besides, a variety of pre-training objectives has been introduced (Liu et al., 2020a), with some of them modeling reconstruction of the perturbed word order (Lewis et al., 2020; Tao et al., 2021; Panda et al., 2021).

Recent research has adopted a new experimental direction aimed at exploring the syntactic knowledge of LMs and their sensitivity to word order employing *text perturbations* (Futrell et al., 2018, 2019; Ettinger, 2020). Some studies show that shuffling word order causes significant performance drops on a wide range of QA tasks (Si et al., 2019; Sugawara et al., 2020). However, a number of works demonstrates that such permutation has little to no impact during the pre-training and fine-tuning stages (Pham et al., 2020; Sinha et al., 2020, 2021; O'Connor and Andreas, 2021; Hessel and Schofield, 2021; Gupta et al., 2021). The latter contradict the common understanding on how the hierarchical and structural information is encoded in LMs (Rogers et al., 2020), and even may question if the word order is modeled with the position embeddings (Wang et al., 2020; Dufter et al., 2021).

This has stimulated a targeted probing of the LMs internal representations generated from original texts and their permuted counterparts (Sinha et al., 2021; Hessel and Schofield, 2021). A new type of *controllable* probes has been proposed, designed to test the LMs sensitivity to granular character- and sub-word level manipulations (Clouatre et al., 2021), as well as structured syntactic perturbations (Alleman et al., 2021). Despite the emerging interest in the field, little is investigated for languages other than English, specifically those with flexible word order.

This paper extends the ongoing research on the syntactic sensitivity to three Indo-European languages with a varying degree of word order flexibility: English, Swedish, and Russian. The contributions of this work are summarized as follows. First, we propose nine probing datasets in the languages mentioned above, organized by the type of

[*] etaktasheva@hse.ru



*Proceedings of the 1st Workshop on Multilingual Representation Learning*, pages 191–210
November 11, 2021. 

controllable syntactic perturbation: N-gram perturbation (**NgramShift**), shuffling parts of the syntactic clauses (**ClauseShift**) and randomizing word order (**RandomShift**). Despite that randomizing word order has been studied from many perspectives (see Section 2), **NgramShift** differs from similar approaches (Conneau et al., 2018; Ravishankar et al., 2019; Eger et al., 2020; Alleman et al., 2021) in that the N-grams correspond to *only* syntactic phrases (e.g. prepositional or numerical phrases) rather than random word spans. **ClauseShift** is a previously unexplored type of syntactic perturbation adopted from the syntactic tree augmentation method (Şahin and Steedman, 2018). Second, we apply a combination of parameter-free interpretation methods to test the sensitivity of two multilingual Transformer LMs: M-BERT (Devlin et al., 2019), and M-BART (Liu et al., 2020b). We hypothesize that M-BART is more robust to the perturbations as opposed to M-BERT since it is learned to restore the shuffled input during pre-training. We evaluate the discrepancy in the syntactic trees induced by the models from perturbed sentences against the original ones, along with the ability to distinguish between them by judging their linguistic acceptability (Lau et al., 2020). Finally, we analyze the relationship between the models' probe performance and position embeddings (PEs). To the best of our knowledge, it is one of the first attempts to introspect PEs regarding structural probing, particularly in the light of syntactic perturbations. The code and datasets are publicly available[1].

## 2 Related Work

**Syntax Probing** Most of the previous studies on the syntactic knowledge of LMs are centered around the concept of probing tasks, where a simple classifier is trained to predict a particular linguistic property based on the model internal representations (Conneau et al., 2018). The scope of the properties ranges from dependency relations (Tenney et al., 2018) to the depth of a syntax tree, and top constituents (Conneau et al., 2018). A variety of probing datasets and benchmarks have been developed. To name a few, Liu et al. (2019a) create a probing suite focused on fine-grained linguistic phenomena, including hierarchical knowledge. SyntaxGym (Gauthier et al., 2020) and LINSPECTOR (Şahin et al., 2020) allow for targeted evaluation of the LMs linguistic knowledge in a standardized and reproducible environment.

These studies have proved that LMs are capable of encoding linguistic and hierarchical information (Belinkov and Glass, 2019; Rogers et al., 2020). However, the probing paradigm has been lately criticized for relying on *supervised* probes, which can learn linguistic properties given the supervision, and make it challenging to interpret the results because of the additional set of parameters (Hewitt and Liang, 2019; Belinkov, 2021). Towards that end, Hewitt and Manning (2019) introduce a *structural* probe to explore a linear transformation of the embedding space, which best approximates the distance between words and depth of the parse tree. The method has proved to infer the hierarchical structure without any linguistic annotation (Kim et al., 2020). Maudslay and Cotterell (2021) propose a *Jabberwocky* probing suite of semantically nonsensical but syntactically well-formed sentences. The results demonstrate that the BERT-based LMs do not isolate semantics from syntax, which motivates further development of the probing field.

**Acceptability Judgements** Another line of works relies on the concept of acceptability judgments. The CoLA benchmark (Warstadt et al., 2019) and its counterpart for Swedish (Volodina et al., 2021) test LMs ability to identify various linguistic violations. Although Transformer LMs have outperformed the CoLA human solvers on the GLUE leaderboard (Wang et al., 2018), a granular linguistic analysis (Warstadt and Bowman, 2019) shows that the models struggle with long-distance syntactic phenomena as opposed to more local ones. Similar in spirit, BLiMP (Warstadt et al., 2020), and CLiMP (Xiang et al., 2021) allow to evaluate the LMs with respect to the acceptability contrasts, framing the task as ranking sentences in minimal pairs.

**Text Perturbations** Recent research has adopted a scope of novel approaches to investigating the LMs sensitivity to syntax corruption and input data manipulations. Starting from studies on randomized word order in LSTMs (Hill et al., 2016; Khandelwal et al., 2018; Sankar et al., 2019; Nie et al., 2019), text perturbations have emerged as an audacious experimental direction under the "pre-train & fine-tune" paradigm along with the interpreta-

[1]https://github.com/evtaktasheva/dependency_extraction

tion methods of modern LMs. Si et al. (2019); Sugawara et al. (2020) show that N-gram permutations and shuffled word order in the fine-tuning data cause BERT's performance drops up to 22% on a wide range of QA tasks. In contrast, several works report that models fine-tuned on such perturbed data still produce high confidence predictions and perform close to their counterparts on many tasks, including the GLUE benchmark (Ahmad et al., 2019; Sinha et al., 2020; Liu et al., 2021; Hessel and Schofield, 2021; Gupta et al., 2021). Similar results are demonstrated by the RoBERTa model (Liu et al., 2019b) when the word order perturbations are incorporated into the pre-training objective (Panda et al., 2021) or tested as a part of full pre-training on the perturbed corpora (Sinha et al., 2021). Sinha et al. (2021) find that the randomized RoBERTa models are similar to their naturally pre-trained peer according to parametric probes but perform worse according to the non-parametric ones.

Recognizing the need to further explore the LMs sensitivity to word order, Clouatre et al. (2021) and Alleman et al. (2021) conduct the interpretation analysis of LMs by means of *controllable* text perturbations. Clouatre et al. (2021) propose two metrics that score local and global structure of sentences perturbed at the granularity of characters and sub-words. The metrics allow identifying that both conventional and Transformer LMs rely on the local order of tokens more than the global one. Alleman et al. (2021) find that BERT builds syntactic complexity towards the output layer and demonstrates a growing sensitivity to the hierarchical phrase structure across layers. In line with these studies, we analyze the syntactic sensitivity of Transformer-based LMs, extending the experimental setup to the multilingual setting.

## 3 Controllable Perturbations

This work proposes three types of *controllable* syntactic perturbations varying in the extent of sentence corruption. We construct nine probing tasks[2] for three Indo-European languages[3]: English (West Germanic, analytic), Swedish (North Germanic, analytic), and Russian (Balto-Slavic, fusional). Based on the dominant constituent order, all three languages are classified as the SVO (Subject-Verb-Object) languages. Nevertheless, there are some differences between them regarding word order flexibility. Russian is known to exhibit free word order as all of the possible constituent reorderings are acceptable: SOV, OSV, SVO, OVS, VSO, VOS (Bailyn, 2012). English allows for only two of them, namely SVO and OSV (Prince, 1988). Swedish belongs to the verb-second languages, which poses different restrictions on the possible constituent reorderings (Börjars et al., 2003). Each dataset[4] consists of 10k pairs of the corresponding perturbed sentence and its original.

**NgramShift** tests the LM sensitivity to *local* perturbations taking into account the syntactic structure. We used a set of carefully designed morphosyntactic patterns to perturb N-grams that correspond to *only* syntactic phrases such as numeral phrases, determiner phrases, compound noun phrases, prepositional phrases, etc. Towards this, we applied TF-IDF weighting from scikit-learn library (Pedregosa et al., 2011) to build a ranked N-gram feature matrix from the corpora and further used it for the N-gram inversion. We used the N-gram range $\in [2; 4]$ for each language. Note that the number of words that change their absolute positions is similar for different values of $N$. Figure 1 illustrates the shift of the head in the prepositional phrase *"to school"* for the sentence *"He did not go to school yesterday"*.

He did not go to school yesterday

**En:** He did not go school to yesterday

**Ru:** Vchera on ne poshel shkolu v

**Sv:** Han gick inte skolan till igår

Figure 1: Examples of the N-gram perturbations (**NgramShift**). Languages: **En**=English, **Ru**=Russian, **Sv**=Swedish. The English sentence is translated to the other languages for illustrational purposes.

**ClauseShift** probes the LM sensitivity to *distant* perturbations at the level of syntactic clauses. We use the syntactic tree augmentation method (Şahin and Steedman, 2019) to rotate sub-trees around the root of the dependency tree of each sentence to form a new synthetic sentence. We then apply a set of manually curated language-specific heuristics to filter out sentences uncorrupted by the rotation procedure. Figure 2 outlines an example of the

[2]We use sentences from the CoNLL 2017 Shared Task on Multilingual Parsing from Raw Texts to Universal Dependencies (Ginter et al., 2017).

[3]https://wals.info

[4]A brief statistics is outlined in Appendix 1.

clause rotation perturbation for the sentence *"He manages to tell her that she has been resurrected"*.

He manages to tell her that she has been resurrected

**En:** That she has been resurrected he manages to tell her

**Sv:** Att hon har uppstått han lyckas berätta för henne

**Ru:** Chto ona byla voskreshena on smog rasskazat' ej

Figure 2: Examples of the clause rotation perturbation (**ClauseShift**). Languages: **En**=English, **Ru**=Russian, **Sv**=Swedish. The English sentence is translated to the other languages for illustrational purposes.

**RandomShift** tests the LM sensitivity to *global* perturbations obtained by shuffling the word order. This type represents an extreme case of sentence permutation and is useful for comparing the behavior of the models at the scale of the perturbation complexity. An example of the randomized word order perturbation for the sentence *"She wanted to go to London"* is presented in Figure 3.

She wanted to go to London

**En:** Wanted London go she to to

**Sv:** Ville London åka hon till att

**Ru:** Hotela London poehat' ona v

Figure 3: Examples of the word order shuffling (**RandomShift**). Languages: **En**=English, **Ru**=Russian, **Sv**=Swedish. The English sentence is translated to the other languages for illustrational purposes.

## 4 Experimental Setup

### 4.1 Models

The experiments are run on two 12-layer multilingual Transformer models released by the HuggingFace library (Wolf et al., 2020):

**M-BERT**[5] is pre-trained using masked language modeling (MLM) and next sentence prediction objectives, over concatenated monolingual Wikipedia corpora in 104 languages.

**M-BART**[6] is a sequence-to-sequence model that comprises a BERT encoder and an autoregressive GPT-2 decoder (Radford et al., 2019). The model is pre-trained on the CC25 corpus in 25 languages using text infilling and sentence shuffling objectives, where it learns to predict masked word spans and reconstruct the permuted input. We use only the encoder in our experiments.

[5]Model name: `bert-base-multilingual-cased`.

[6]Model name: `facebook/mbart-large-cc25`.

### 4.2 Interpretation Methods

**Parameter-free Probing** We apply two unsupervised probing methods to reconstruct syntactic trees from self-attention (**Self-Attention Probing**) and so-called "impact" (**Token Perturbed Masking**) matrices computed by feeding the MLM models with each sentence $s$ and its perturbed version $s'$. The trees are induced by Chu-Liu-Edmonds algorithm (Chu, 1965; Edmonds, 1968) used to compute the Maximum Spanning Tree starting from the root of the corresponding gold dependency tree (Raganato and Tiedemann, 2018; Htut et al., 2019; Wu et al., 2020). The probing performance is evaluated by the Undirected Unlabeled Attachment Score (UUAS), which reflects the percentage of words that have been assigned the correct head without taking the direction of relations and dependency labels into account (Klein and Manning, 2004).

**Self-Attention Probing** (Htut et al., 2019) allows to explore if attention heads encode complete syntactic trees. To this end, each layer-head attention matrix is treated as a weighted directed graph where the vertices represent words in the input sentence and edges are the attention weights. Model-specific special tokens such as `[CLS]`, `[SEP]`, <s>, </s> are excluded at the pre-processing stage to eliminate their impact on other tokens.

**Token Perturbed Masking** (Wu et al., 2020) extracts global syntactic information by measuring the impact one word has on the prediction of another in an MLM. The impact matrix is similar to the self-attention matrix as it reflects the inter-word relationships in terms of Euclidean distance, except that it is derived from the outputs of the MLM head. For the sake of space, we refer the reader to Wu et al. (2020) for more details.

**Representation Analysis** Hessel and Schofield (2021) propose two metrics to compare contextualized representations and self-attention matrices produced by the model for each pair of sentences $s$ and $s'$. *Token Identifiability (TI)* evaluates the similarity of the LM's contextualized representations of a particular token in $s$ and $s'$. It is high if the token representations are similar to one another. *Self-Attention Distance (SAD)* measures if each token in $s$ relates to similar words in $s'$ by computing row-wise Jensen-Shannon Divergence between the two self-attention matrices. It is low if an LM attends to the same words despite the perturbations.

**Pseudo-perplexity** Pseudo-perplexity (PPPL) is an intrinsic measure that estimates the probability of a sentence with an MLM similar to that of conventional LMs (Salazar et al., 2020). PPPL-based measures have proved to correlate with human ratings (Lau et al., 2017), match or outperform autoregressive LMs (GPT-2) in ranking hypotheses for downstream tasks and the BLiMP benchmark (Salazar et al., 2020), and perform at the human level in acceptability judgments (Lau et al., 2020). We use two PPPL-based measures under implementation[7] by Lau et al. (2020) to infer probabilities of the sentences and their perturbed counterparts. The *MeanLP* and *PenLP* measures are computed as the sum of pseudo-log-likelihood scores for each token in the sentence normalized by the total number of tokens. *PenLP* additionally scales the denominator with the exponent $\alpha$ to penalize the effect of high scores.

### 4.3 Positional Encoding

Various PEs have been proposed to utilize the information about word order in the Transformer-based LMs (Wang et al., 2020; Dufter et al., 2021). Surprisingly, little is known about what PEs capture and how well they learn the meaning of positions. Wang and Chen (2020) among the first present an extensive study on the properties captured by PEs in different pre-trained Transformers and empirically evaluate their impact on the downstream performance for many NLP tasks. In the spirit of this work, we aim at analyzing the impact of the PEs on the syntactic probe performance. Towards this end, we consider the following three configurations of PEs of the M-BERT and M-BART models: (1) **absolute**=frozen PEs; (2) **random**=randomly initialized PEs; and (3) **zero**=zeroed PEs.

## 5 Results

### 5.1 Parameter-free Probing

The discrepancy in the syntactic trees induced from the original sentences and their perturbed analogs is measured as the difference between the corresponding UUAS scores ($\delta$ UUAS). The lower the $\delta$ UUAS, the better is the syntax tree reconstructed from $s'$ with respect to the UUAS score for $s$.

**Self-Attention Probing** Figures 4 and 1 in Appendix 2 outline the task-wise heatmaps with the $\delta$ UUAS scores achieved by the M-BERT and M-BART models with **absolute** PEs for each layer-head pair, respectively. The models exhibit similar behavior, demonstrating positive correlation between the $\delta$ UUAS scores and the granularity of the perturbation. The overall pattern for both models is that they display little to no sensitivity to *local* and *distant* perturbations (**NgramShift**, **ClauseShift**) in contrast to the *global* ones (**RandomShift**). We provide examples of the dependency trees extracted from the self-attention matrices of the M-BERT model for the Swedish **NgramShift** task on Figure 5. The trees from both original (see Figure 5a) and perturbed (see Figure 5b) sentence versions receive the UUAS score of 0.86, demonstrating little changes in the assigned dependency heads under the local perturbation. On the contrary, randomizing word order (**RandomShift**) corrupts the syntactic structure significantly with a $\delta$ UUAS score of 0.33 (see Figure 8, Appendix 2).

**Token Perturbed Masking** The models show similar results to that of in **Self-Attention Probing**, with regards to the perturbation granularity (see Figure 6). In spite of that, the model performance on the **NgramShift** and **ClauseShift** reveal some differences between the encoders. M-BART generally achieves lower and close to zero $\delta$ UUAS scores, meaning to better restore the hierarchical information from the perturbed sentences (e.g., **ClauseShift**: [**Sv, Ru**]). We relate this to the fact that M-BART is pre-trained with the sentence shuffling objective.

**Language-wise Comparison** Another observation is that there are more insensitive attention heads on the Russian tasks, possibly indicating that it is harder to distinguish from the perturbations as opposed to English and Swedish, particularly on the **ClauseShift** task with typically longer and syntactically more complex sentences (see Figures 4, 1, Appendix 2). As for Swedish, which has a similar to English but stricter syntactic structure, M-BART tends to induce correct syntactic trees from the permuted sentences more frequently. This is indicated by negative $\delta$ UUAS scores on most tasks.

[7] https://github.com/jhlau/acceptability-prediction-in-context

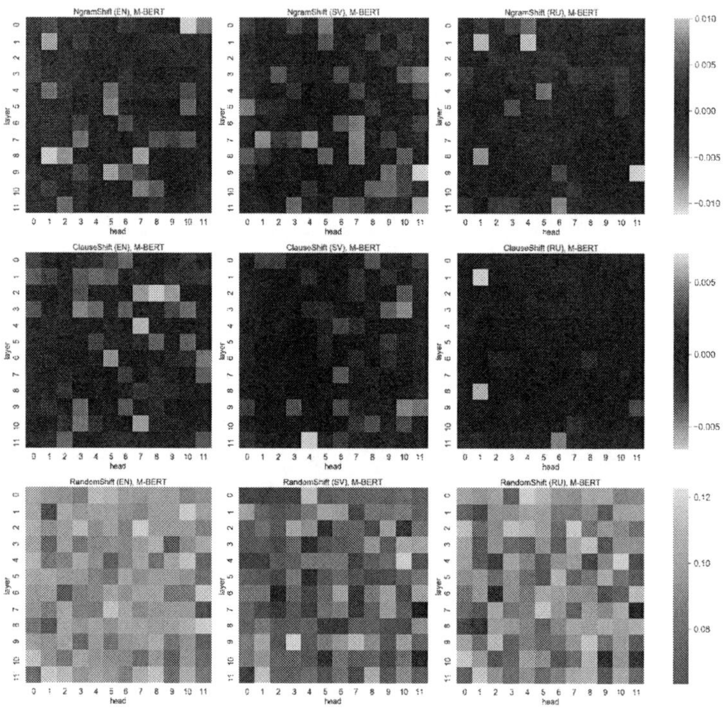


Figure 4: The task-wise heatmaps depicting the $\delta$ UUAS scores by M-BERT for each language. Method=**Self-Attention Probing**. PE=**absolute**. X-axis=Attention head index. Y-axis=Layer index. Tasks: **NgramShift** (top); **ClauseShift** (middle); **RandomShift** (bottom). Languages: **En**=English (left); **Sv**=Swedish (middle); **Ru**=Russian (right).

**Positional Encoding** Analysis of the positional encoding shows that despite the genuine belief that positional information contributes most to syntactic structure encoding, the models do not seem to rely on it as much as might be expected. Figure 2 (see Appendix 2) illustrates the distribution of $\delta$ UUAS scores for M-BERT with different PEs on English tasks. The heatmaps show that **zero** and **random** PEs only slightly affects the quality of the probe performance of the self-attention heads.

To analyze the impact of PEs from another perspective, for each pair of ($s$, $s'$) we compute the Euclidean distance (L2) between the corresponding impact (**Token Perturbed Probing**) and self-attention matrices (**Self-Attention Probing**) described in Section 4.2. The difference in the impact matrices produced by M-BERT model is generally observed only in the setting with **zero** PEs (see Figures 7; Figures 3-4, Appendix 2). In contrast, there is almost no difference between the representations generated by M-BART across all configurations of the PEs (see Figures 5-7, Appendix 2). This behavior is consistent with the head-wise results under **Self-Attention Probing** for all languages.

### 5.2 Representation Analysis

**Token Identifiability** The overall pattern for both models under the representation analysis is that for *local* and *distant* perturbations TI steadily decreases towards the output layer with rapid increases at layers $[1, 10]$ (see Figure 9, Appendix 3), and high for *global* perturbations (**RandomShift**). TI decreases when the perturbed inputs generate embeddings different from the intact ones. Despite that higher layers in both models are more sensitive, the perturbed representations remain similar to that of the original (Hessel and Schofield, 2021).

**Self-Attention Distance** The results by SAD show that both models score significantly lower with **random** and **zero** PEs (see Figure 10, Appendix 3), meaning lower sensitivity to the perturbations supported by the probing results (Section 5.1). This provides evidence that the encoders marginally rely on the positional information to induce the syntactic structure despite the distributions of the self-attention weights for the intact and perturbed sentences may differ according to the Jensen-Shannon divergence.

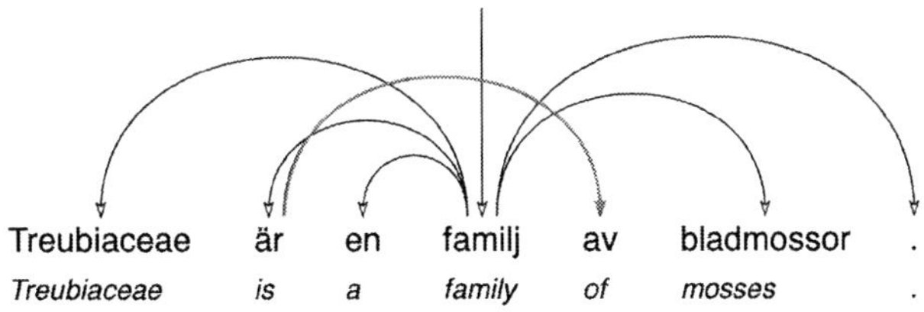


(a) `original`

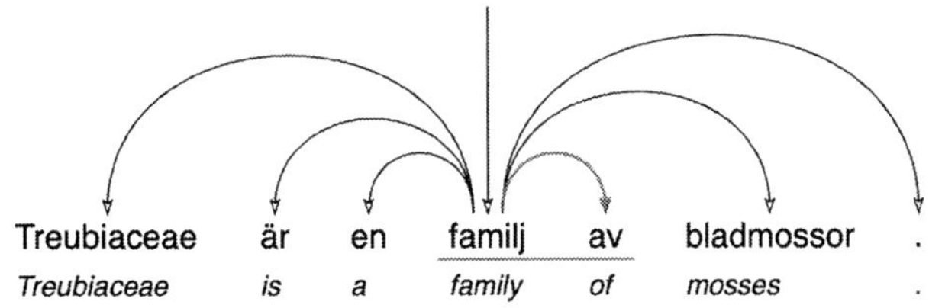


(b) `perturbed`

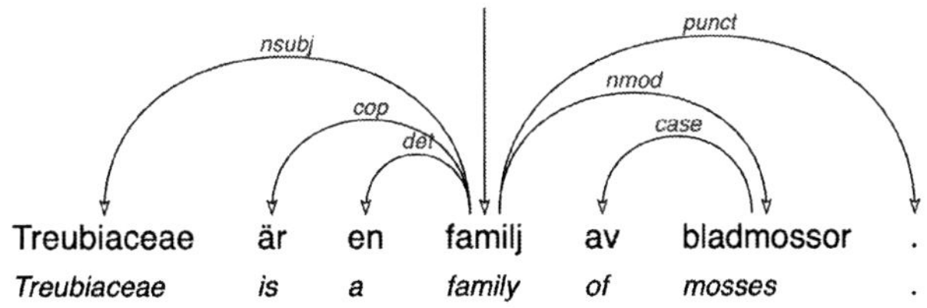


(c) `gold`

Figure 5: Graphical representations of the syntactic trees inferred for the Swedish sentence *Treubiaceae är en familj av bladmossor* 'Treubiaceae is a family of mosses' and its perturbed version. `original`=the original sentence; `perturbed`=the perturbed version; `gold`=gold standard. Task=**NgramShift**. Model=**M-BERT** (Layer: 11; Head: 2). Method=**Self-Attention Probing**. The perturbation is underlined with red, and incorrectly assigned dependency heads are marked with red arrows.

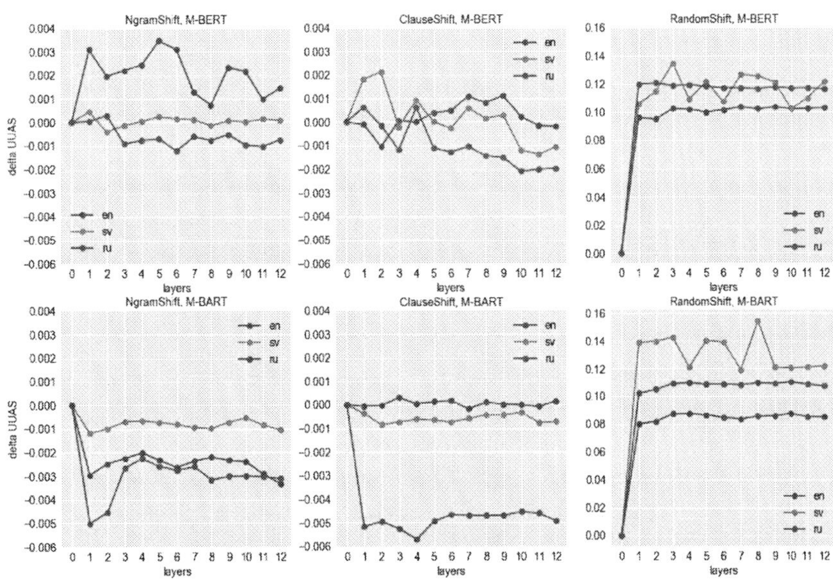


Figure 6: The probing performance in $\delta$ UUAS across layers under **Token Perturbed Probing**. PE=**absolute**. The scores are averaged over attention heads at each layer. X-axis=Attention head index. Y-axis=$\delta$ UUAS.

### 5.3 Pseudo-perplexity

Consistent with the results under parameter-free probing (Section 5.1) and representation analysis (Section 5.2), PPPL-based acceptability judgements[8] indicate that the encoders distinguish between the perturbations depending on their granularity. The overall trend is that for all languages the sentence pseudo-log-probability inferred from both LMs decreases with the increase of the perturbation complexity which is demonstrated by higher acceptability scores on **NgramShift**, but significantly lower scores on the **ClauseShift** and **RandomShift** (see Figures 11-12, Appendix 4). The statistical significance of the PPPL distributions is confirmed with Kolmogorov–Smirnov and Wilcoxon signed-rank tests (p-value $< 0.01$).

## 6 Discussion

**The syntactic sensitivity depends upon language** At present, English remains the focal point of prior research in the field of NLP, leaving other languages understudied. Our probing experiments on the less explored languages with different word order flexibility show that M-BERT and M-BART behave slightly differently in Swedish and Russian. While M-BART better restores the corrupted syntactic structure on most of the tasks for Swedish, there are fewer attention heads sensitive to the perturbations in Russian, which is revealed through the examination of head-wise attention patterns of both models. Besides, the encoders receive lower probing performance for Russian that can be contributed to the more complex syntax and flexible word order.

**Pre-training objectives can help to improve syntactic robustness** Analysis of the M-BERT and M-BART LMs that differ in the pre-training objectives shows that M-BERT achieves higher $\delta$ UUAS performance across all languages as opposed to M-BART pre-trained with the sentence shuffling objective. The lower $\delta$ UUAS probing performance indicates that M-BART better induces syntactic trees from both perturbed and intact sentences (see Section 5.1). Despite this, the representation and acceptability analysis demonstrate that M-BART is also capable of distinguishing between the perturbations (see Sections 5.2-5.3). A fruitful direction for future work is to analyze more LMs that differ in the architecture design and pre-training objectives.

**The LMs are less sensitive to more granular perturbations** The results of the parameter-free probing show that M-BERT and M-BART exhibit little to no sensitivity to *local* perturbations within syntactic groups (**NgramShift**) and *distant* perturbations at the level of syntactic clauses (**ClauseShift**). In contrast, the *global* perturbations (**RandomShift**) are best distinguished by the encoders. As the granularity of the syntactic corruption increases, we observe a worse probing performance under all considered interpretation methods. Namely, the results are supported by representation analysis metrics (see Section 5.2) that indicate higher susceptibility to major changes in the sentences structure (**RandomShift, ClauseShift**), and the PPPL-based measures (see Section 5.3) prescribing higher acceptability scores to sentences with more granular perturbations (**NgramShift**). We also find that the sensitivity to the hierarchical corruption grows across layers together with the increase of the perturbation complexity, which is in line with Alleman et al. (2021).

**M-BERT and M-BART barely use positional information to induce syntactic trees** Previous research has shown that the token embeddings capture enough semantic information to restore the syntactic structure (Vilares et al., 2020; Kim et al., 2020; Rosa and Mareček, 2019). Maudslay and Cotterell (2021) claim that syntactic abilities of BERT-based LMs are overestimated and raise the problem of isolating semantics from syntax. However, more recent studies show that Transformer encoders encode redundant information (Luo et al., 2021), may not sufficiently capture the meaning of positions and be unimportant for downstream tasks (Wang and Chen, 2020), including the setting with perturbed fine-tuning data (Clouatre et al., 2021). In spirit with the latter studies, our results under different PEs configurations reveal that M-BERT and M-BART do not need the precise position information to restore the syntactic tree from their internal representations. The overall behavior is that zeroed (except for M-BERT) or even randomly initialized PEs can result in the probing performance and one with absolute positions. We suppose that despite the absolute positions of words changes during the N-gram permutation and sub-tree rotation procedures, the word order within the clauses remains almost the same as in the intact sentence

[8]We present the results obtained by the *MeanLP* measure which are consistent with those of *PenLP*.

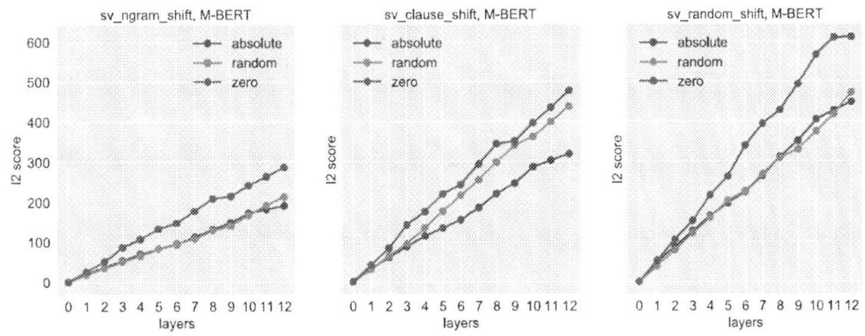


Figure 7: The Euclidean distances between the impact matrices computed by M-BERT with different PEs over each pair of sentences ($s$, $s'$) for Swedish. The distances are averaged over attention heads at each layer. Method: **Token Perturbed Masking**. Tasks: **NgramShift** (left); **ClauseShift** (middle); **RandomShift** (right)

(**NgramShift**, **ClauseShift**). That is, the more granular perturbations marginally confuse the LMs when: (i) predicting the masked word under **Token Perturbation Probing** which can be performed using *only* attention (Wang and Chen, 2020), or (ii) judging the acceptability of the sentence where the low token pseudo-log-probability can occur at the juxtaposition of the syntactic groups, and clauses (Alleman et al., 2021). We leave a more detailed exploration of the relationship between PEs and probing analysis for future work.

## 7 Conclusion

This paper presents an extension of the ongoing research on the controllable text perturbations to the multilingual setting and introspection of positional embeddings in pre-trained LMs. We introduce nine probing datasets for three Indo-European languages varying in their flexibility of the word order: English, Swedish, and Russian. The suite is constructed using language-specific heuristics carefully designed under linguistic expertise and organized by three types of syntactic perturbations: randomization of word order studied by previous research from many perspectives and less explored permutations within syntactic phrases and clauses. The method includes a combination of parameter-free probing methods based on the intermediate self-attention and contextualized representations, novel metrics for representation analysis, and acceptability judgments with pseudo-perplexity. We conduct a line of experiments to probe the syntactic sensitivity of two multilingual Transformers, M-BERT and M-BART, the latter of which is learned to reconstruct the word order during pre-training. The LMs are less sensitive to more granular perturbations and build hierarchical complexity towards the output layer. The analysis of the understudied relationship between the position embeddings and syntactic probe performance reveals that the position information is not necessary for inducing the hierarchical structure, which is a promising direction for a more detailed investigation. The results also show that the syntactic sensitivity may depend on the language and be enhanced by pre-training objectives. We believe there is still room for exploring the sensitivity to word order and syntactic abilities of modern LMs, specifically across a more diverse set of languages and models varying in the architecture design choices.

## Acknowledgements

Ekaterina Taktasheva and Ekaterina Artemova are partially supported by the framework of the HSE University Basic Research Program.

## References

Wasi Ahmad, Haoran Li, Kai-Wei Chang, and Yashar Mehdad. 2021. Syntax-augmented multilingual BERT for cross-lingual transfer. In *Proceedings of the 59th Annual Meeting of the Association for Computational Linguistics and the 11th International Joint Conference on Natural Language Processing (Volume 1: Long Papers)*, pages 4538–4554, Online. Association for Computational Linguistics.

Wasi Ahmad, Zhisong Zhang, Xuezhe Ma, Eduard Hovy, Kai-Wei Chang, and Nanyun Peng. 2019. On difficulties of cross-lingual transfer with order differences: A case study on dependency parsing. In *Proceedings of the 2019 Conference of the North American Chapter of the Association for Computational Linguistics: Human Language Technologies, Volume 1 (Long and Short Papers)*, pages 2440–2452,

Minneapolis, Minnesota. Association for Computational Linguistics.

Matteo Alleman, Jonathan Mamou, Miguel A Del Rio, Hanlin Tang, Yoon Kim, and SueYeon Chung. 2021. Syntactic perturbations reveal representational correlates of hierarchical phrase structure in pretrained language models. In *Proceedings of the 6th Workshop on Representation Learning for NLP (RepL4NLP-2021)*, pages 263–276, Online. Association for Computational Linguistics.

Jiangang Bai, Yujing Wang, Yiren Chen, Yaming Yang, Jing Bai, Jing Yu, and Yunhai Tong. 2021. Syntax-BERT: Improving pre-trained transformers with syntax trees. In *Proceedings of the 16th Conference of the European Chapter of the Association for Computational Linguistics: Main Volume*, pages 3011–3020, Online. Association for Computational Linguistics.

John F Bailyn. 2012. *The Syntax of Russian*. Cambridge University Press.

Yonatan Belinkov. 2021. Probing classifiers: Promises, shortcomings, and alternatives. *arXiv preprint arXiv:2102.12452*.

Yonatan Belinkov and James Glass. 2019. Analysis methods in neural language processing: A survey. *Transactions of the Association for Computational Linguistics*, 7:49–72.

Kersti Börjars, Elisabet Engdahl, Maia Andréasson, Miriam Butt, and Tracy Holloway King. 2003. Subject and Object Positions in Swedish. In *Proceedings of the LFG03 Conference*, pages 43–58. Citeseer.

Yoeng-Jin Chu. 1965. On the Shortest Arborescence of a Directed Graph. *Scientia Sinica*, 14:1396–1400.

Kevin Clark, Urvashi Khandelwal, Omer Levy, and Christopher D. Manning. 2019. What does BERT look at? an analysis of BERT's attention. In *Proceedings of the 2019 ACL Workshop BlackboxNLP: Analyzing and Interpreting Neural Networks for NLP*, pages 276–286, Florence, Italy. Association for Computational Linguistics.

Louis Clouatre, Prasanna Parthasarathi, Amal Zouaq, and Sarath Chandar. 2021. Demystifying Neural Language Models' Insensitivity to Word-Order. *arXiv preprint arXiv:2107.13955*.

Alexis Conneau, German Kruszewski, Guillaume Lample, Loïc Barrault, and Marco Baroni. 2018. What you can cram into a single $&!#* vector: Probing sentence embeddings for linguistic properties. In *Proceedings of the 56th Annual Meeting of the Association for Computational Linguistics (Volume 1: Long Papers)*, pages 2126–2136, Melbourne, Australia. Association for Computational Linguistics.

Jacob Devlin, Ming-Wei Chang, Kenton Lee, and Kristina Toutanova. 2019. BERT: Pre-training of deep bidirectional transformers for language understanding. In *Proceedings of the 2019 Conference of the North American Chapter of the Association for Computational Linguistics: Human Language Technologies, Volume 1 (Long and Short Papers)*, pages 4171–4186, Minneapolis, Minnesota. Association for Computational Linguistics.

Philipp Dufter, Martin Schmitt, and Hinrich Schütze. 2021. Position Information in Transformers: An Overview. *arXiv preprint arXiv:2102.11090*.

Jack Edmonds. 1968. Optimum branchings. *Mathematics and the Decision Sciences, Part*, 1(335-345):25.

Steffen Eger, Johannes Daxenberger, and Iryna Gurevych. 2020. How to probe sentence embeddings in low-resource languages: On structural design choices for probing task evaluation. In *Proceedings of the 24th Conference on Computational Natural Language Learning*, pages 108–118, Online. Association for Computational Linguistics.

Allyson Ettinger. 2020. What BERT is not: Lessons from a new suite of psycholinguistic diagnostics for language models. *Transactions of the Association for Computational Linguistics*, 8:34–48.

Richard Futrell, Ethan Wilcox, Takashi Morita, and Roger Levy. 2018. RNNs as Psycholinguistic Subjects: Syntactic State and Grammatical Dependency. *arXiv preprint arXiv:1809.01329*.

Richard Futrell, Ethan Wilcox, Takashi Morita, Peng Qian, Miguel Ballesteros, and Roger Levy. 2019. Neural language models as psycholinguistic subjects: Representations of syntactic state. In *Proceedings of the 2019 Conference of the North American Chapter of the Association for Computational Linguistics: Human Language Technologies, Volume 1 (Long and Short Papers)*, pages 32–42, Minneapolis, Minnesota. Association for Computational Linguistics.

Jon Gauthier, Jennifer Hu, Ethan Wilcox, Peng Qian, and Roger Levy. 2020. SyntaxGym: An Online Platform for Targeted Evaluation of Language Models. In *Proceedings of the 58th Annual Meeting of the Association for Computational Linguistics: System Demonstrations*, pages 70–76.

Filip Ginter, Jan Hajič, Juhani Luotolahti, Milan Straka, and Daniel Zeman. 2017. CoNLL 2017 shared task - automatically annotated raw texts and word embeddings. LINDAT/CLARIAH-CZ digital library at the Institute of Formal and Applied Linguistics (ÚFAL), Faculty of Mathematics and Physics, Charles University.

Yoav Goldberg. 2019. Assessing BERT's syntactic abilities. *arXiv preprint arXiv:1901.05287*.

Ashim Gupta, Giorgi Kvernadze, and Vivek Srikumar. 2021. BERT & Family Eat Word Salad: Experiments with Text Understanding. In *Proceedings of the AAAI Conference on Artificial Intelligence*, volume 35, pages 12946–12954.

Jack Hessel and Alexandra Schofield. 2021. How effective is BERT without word ordering? implications for language understanding and data privacy. In *Proceedings of the 59th Annual Meeting of the Association for Computational Linguistics and the 11th International Joint Conference on Natural Language Processing (Volume 2: Short Papers)*, pages 204–211, Online. Association for Computational Linguistics.

John Hewitt and Percy Liang. 2019. Designing and interpreting probes with control tasks. In *Proceedings of the 2019 Conference on Empirical Methods in Natural Language Processing and the 9th International Joint Conference on Natural Language Processing (EMNLP-IJCNLP)*, pages 2733–2743, Hong Kong, China. Association for Computational Linguistics.

John Hewitt and Christopher D. Manning. 2019. A structural probe for finding syntax in word representations. In *Proceedings of the 2019 Conference of the North American Chapter of the Association for Computational Linguistics: Human Language Technologies, Volume 1 (Long and Short Papers)*, pages 4129–4138, Minneapolis, Minnesota. Association for Computational Linguistics.

Felix Hill, Kyunghyun Cho, and Anna Korhonen. 2016. Learning distributed representations of sentences from unlabelled data. In *Proceedings of the 2016 Conference of the North American Chapter of the Association for Computational Linguistics: Human Language Technologies*, pages 1367–1377, San Diego, California. Association for Computational Linguistics.

Phu Mon Htut, Jason Phang, Shikha Bordia, and Samuel R Bowman. 2019. Do Attention heads in BERT track syntactic dependencies? *arXiv preprint arXiv:1911.12246*.

Ganesh Jawahar, Benoît Sagot, and Djamé Seddah. 2019. What Does BERT Learn about the Structure of Language? In *Proceedings of the 57th Annual Meeting of the Association for Computational Linguistics*, pages 3651–3657.

Jae-young Jo and Sung-Hyon Myaeng. 2020. Roles and Utilization of Attention Heads in Transformer-based Neural Language Models. In *Proceedings of the 58th Annual Meeting of the Association for Computational Linguistics*, pages 3404–3417.

Urvashi Khandelwal, He He, Peng Qi, and Dan Jurafsky. 2018. Sharp nearby, fuzzy far away: How neural language models use context. In *Proceedings of the 56th Annual Meeting of the Association for Computational Linguistics (Volume 1: Long Papers)*, pages 284–294, Melbourne, Australia. Association for Computational Linguistics.

Taeuk Kim, Jihun Choi, Daniel Edmiston, and Sang-goo Lee. 2020. Are pre-trained language models aware of phrases? simple but strong baselines for grammar induction. *arXiv preprint arXiv:2002.00737*.

Dan Klein and Christopher Manning. 2004. Corpus-based induction of syntactic structure: Models of dependency and constituency. In *Proceedings of the 42nd Annual Meeting of the Association for Computational Linguistics (ACL-04)*, pages 478–485, Barcelona, Spain.

Jey Han Lau, Carlos Armendariz, Shalom Lappin, Matthew Purver, and Chang Shu. 2020. How furiously can colorless green ideas sleep? sentence acceptability in context. *Transactions of the Association for Computational Linguistics*, 8:296–310.

Jey Han Lau, Alexander Clark, and Shalom Lappin. 2017. Grammaticality, Acceptability, and Probability: A Probabilistic View of Linguistic Lnowledge. *Cognitive science*, 41(5):1202–1241.

Mike Lewis, Yinhan Liu, Naman Goyal, Marjan Ghazvininejad, Abdelrahman Mohamed, Omer Levy, Veselin Stoyanov, and Luke Zettlemoyer. 2020. BART: Denoising sequence-to-sequence pre-training for natural language generation, translation, and comprehension. In *Proceedings of the 58th Annual Meeting of the Association for Computational Linguistics*, pages 7871–7880, Online. Association for Computational Linguistics.

Yongjie Lin, Yi Chern Tan, and RoBERT Frank. 2019. Open sesame: Getting inside BERT's linguistic knowledge. In *Proceedings of the 2019 ACL Workshop BlackboxNLP: Analyzing and Interpreting Neural Networks for NLP*, pages 241–253, Florence, Italy. Association for Computational Linguistics.

Nelson F. Liu, Matt Gardner, Yonatan Belinkov, Matthew E. Peters, and Noah A. Smith. 2019a. Linguistic knowledge and transferability of contextual representations. In *Proceedings of the 2019 Conference of the North American Chapter of the Association for Computational Linguistics: Human Language Technologies, Volume 1 (Long and Short Papers)*, pages 1073–1094, Minneapolis, Minnesota. Association for Computational Linguistics.

Qi Liu, Matt J Kusner, and Phil Blunsom. 2020a. A survey on contextual embeddings. *arXiv preprint arXiv:2003.07278*.

Yinhan Liu, Jiatao Gu, Naman Goyal, Xian Li, Sergey Edunov, Marjan Ghazvininejad, Mike Lewis, and Luke Zettlemoyer. 2020b. Multilingual denoising pre-training for neural machine translation. *Transactions of the Association for Computational Linguistics*, 8:726–742.

Yinhan Liu, Myle Ott, Naman Goyal, Jingfei Du, Mandar Joshi, Danqi Chen, Omer Levy, Mike Lewis, Luke Zettlemoyer, and Veselin Stoyanov. 2019b. RoBERTa: a Robustly Optimized BERT Pre-training Approach. *arXiv preprint arXiv:1907.11692*.

Zihan Liu, Genta I Winata, Samuel Cahyawijaya, Andrea Madotto, Zhaojiang Lin, and Pascale Fung. 2021. On the Importance of Word Order Information in Cross-lingual Sequence Labeling. In *Proceedings of the AAAI Conference on Artificial Intelligence*, volume 35, pages 13461–13469.

Ziyang Luo, Artur Kulmizev, and Xiaoxi Mao. 2021. Positional artefacts propagate through masked language model embeddings.

Rowan Hall Maudslay and Ryan Cotterell. 2021. Do Syntactic Probes Probe Syntax? Experiments with Jabberwocky Probing. In *Proceedings of the 2021 Conference of the North American Chapter of the Association for Computational Linguistics: Human Language Technologies*, pages 124–131.

Alessio Miaschi, Dominique Brunato, Felice Dell'Orletta, and Giulia Venturi. 2020. Linguistic profiling of a neural language model. In *Proceedings of the 28th International Conference on Computational Linguistics*, pages 745–756, Barcelona, Spain (Online). International Committee on Computational Linguistics.

Yixin Nie, Yicheng Wang, and Mohit Bansal. 2019. Analyzing Compositionality-Sensitivity of NLI Models. In *Proceedings of the AAAI Conference on Artificial Intelligence*, volume 33, pages 6867–6874.

Joe O'Connor and Jacob Andreas. 2021. What Context Features Can Transformer Language Models Use? *arXiv preprint arXiv:2106.08367*.

Subhadarshi Panda, Anjali Agrawal, Jeewon Ha, and Benjamin Bloch. 2021. Shuffled-token detection for refining pre-trained RoBERTa. In *Proceedings of the 2021 Conference of the North American Chapter of the Association for Computational Linguistics: Student Research Workshop*, pages 88–93, Online. Association for Computational Linguistics.

Fabian Pedregosa, Gaël Varoquaux, Alexandre Gramfort, Vincent Michel, BERTrand Thirion, Olivier Grisel, Mathieu Blondel, Peter Prettenhofer, Ron Weiss, Vincent Dubourg, et al. 2011. Scikit-learn: Machine learning in python. *the Journal of machine Learning research*, 12:2825–2830.

Thang M Pham, Trung Bui, Long Mai, and Anh Nguyen. 2020. Out of Order: How Important is the Sequential Order of Words in a Sentence in Natural Language Understanding Tasks? *arXiv preprint arXiv:2012.15180*.

Ellen F Prince. 1988. On Pragmatic Change: the Borrowing of Discourse Functions. *Journal of pragmatics*, 12(5-6):505–518.

Alec Radford, Jeff Wu, Rewon Child, David Luan, Dario Amodei, and Ilya Sutskever. 2019. Language Models are Unsupervised Multitask Learners.

Alessandro Raganato and Jörg Tiedemann. 2018. An analysis of encoder representations in transformer-based machine translation. In *Proceedings of the 2018 EMNLP Workshop BlackboxNLP: Analyzing and Interpreting Neural Networks for NLP*, pages 287–297, Brussels, Belgium. Association for Computational Linguistics.

Vinit Ravishankar, Lilja Øvrelid, and Erik Velldal. 2019. Probing multilingual sentence representations with X-probe. In *Proceedings of the 4th Workshop on Representation Learning for NLP (RepL4NLP-2019)*, pages 156–168, Florence, Italy. Association for Computational Linguistics.

Anna Rogers, Olga Kovaleva, and Anna Rumshisky. 2020. A primer in BERTology: What we know about how BERT works. *Transactions of the Association for Computational Linguistics*, 8:842–866.

Rudolf Rosa and David Mareček. 2019. Inducing Syntactic Trees from BERT Representations.

Devendra Sachan, Yuhao Zhang, Peng Qi, and William L. Hamilton. 2021. Do syntax trees help pre-trained transformers extract information? In *Proceedings of the 16th Conference of the European Chapter of the Association for Computational Linguistics: Main Volume*, pages 2647–2661, Online. Association for Computational Linguistics.

Gözde Gül Şahin and Mark Steedman. 2018. Data augmentation via dependency tree morphing for low-resource languages. In *Proceedings of the 2018 Conference on Empirical Methods in Natural Language Processing*, pages 5004–5009, Brussels, Belgium. Association for Computational Linguistics.

Gözde Gül Şahin and Mark Steedman. 2019. Data augmentation via dependency tree morphing for low-resource languages. *arXiv preprint arXiv:1903.09460*.

Gözde Gül Şahin, Clara Vania, Ilia Kuznetsov, and Iryna Gurevych. 2020. LINSPECTOR: Multilingual probing tasks for word representations. *Computational Linguistics*, 46(2):335–385.

Julian Salazar, Davis Liang, Toan Q. Nguyen, and Katrin Kirchhoff. 2020. Masked language model scoring. In *Proceedings of the 58th Annual Meeting of the Association for Computational Linguistics*, pages 2699–2712, Online. Association for Computational Linguistics.

Chinnadhurai Sankar, Sandeep Subramanian, Christopher Pal, Sarath Chandar, and Yoshua Bengio. 2019. Do neural dialog systems use the conversation history effectively? an empirical study. In *Proceedings of the 57th Annual Meeting of the Association for Computational Linguistics*, pages 32–37.

Chenglei Si, Shuohang Wang, Min-Yen Kan, and Jing Jiang. 2019. What does bert learn from multiple-choice reading comprehension datasets? *arXiv preprint arXiv:1910.12391*.

Koustuv Sinha, Robin Jia, Dieuwke Hupkes, Joelle Pineau, Adina Williams, and Douwe Kiela. 2021. Masked language modeling and the distributional hypothesis: Order word matters pre-training for little. *CoRR*, abs/2104.06644.

Koustuv Sinha, Prasanna Parthasarathi, Joelle Pineau, and Adina Williams. 2020. Unnatural language inference. *arXiv preprint arXiv:2101.00010*.

Saku Sugawara, Pontus Stenetorp, Kentaro Inui, and Akiko Aizawa. 2020. Assessing the Benchmarking Capacity of Machine Reading Comprehension Datasets. In *Proceedings of the AAAI Conference on Artificial Intelligence*, volume 34, pages 8918–8927.

Chongyang Tao, Shen Gao, Juntao Li, Yansong Feng, Dongyan Zhao, and Rui Yan. 2021. Learning to organize a bag of words into sentences with neural networks: An empirical study. In *Proceedings of the 2021 Conference of the North American Chapter of the Association for Computational Linguistics: Human Language Technologies*, pages 1682–1691, Online. Association for Computational Linguistics.

Ian Tenney, Patrick Xia, Berlin Chen, Alex Wang, Adam Poliak, R Thomas McCoy, Najoung Kim, Benjamin Van Durme, Samuel R Bowman, Dipanjan Das, et al. 2018. What do you learn from context? probing for sentence structure in contextualized word representations. In *International Conference on Learning Representations*.

Ashish Vaswani, Noam Shazeer, Niki Parmar, Jakob Uszkoreit, Llion Jones, Aidan N Gomez, Łukasz Kaiser, and Illia Polosukhin. 2017. Attention is all you need. In *Advances in neural information processing systems*, pages 5998–6008.

David Vilares, Michalina Strzyz, Anders Søgaard, and Carlos Gómez-Rodríguez. 2020. Parsing as Pretraining. 34:9114–9121.

Elena Volodina, Yousuf Ali Mohammed, and Julia Klezl. 2021. DaLAJ-a Dataset for Linguistic Acceptability Judgments for Swedish: Format, Baseline, Sharing. *arXiv preprint arXiv:2105.06681*.

Alex Wang, Amanpreet Singh, Julian Michael, Felix Hill, Omer Levy, and Samuel Bowman. 2018. GLUE: A multi-task benchmark and analysis platform for natural language understanding. In *Proceedings of the 2018 EMNLP Workshop BlackboxNLP: Analyzing and Interpreting Neural Networks for NLP*, pages 353–355, Brussels, Belgium. Association for Computational Linguistics.

Benyou Wang, Lifeng Shang, Christina Lioma, Xin Jiang, Hao Yang, Qun Liu, and Jakob Grue Simonsen. 2020. On Position Embeddings in BERT. In *International Conference on Learning Representations*.

Wei Wang, Bin Bi, Ming Yan, Chen Wu, Zuyi Bao, Jiangnan Xia, Liwei Peng, and Luo Si. 2019. Structbert: incorporating language structures into pre-training for deep language understanding. *arXiv preprint arXiv:1908.04577*.

Yu-An Wang and Yun-Nung Chen. 2020. What do position embeddings learn? an empirical study of pre-trained language model positional encoding. In *Proceedings of the 2020 Conference on Empirical Methods in Natural Language Processing (EMNLP)*, pages 6840–6849, Online. Association for Computational Linguistics.

Alex Warstadt and Samuel R. Bowman. 2019. Grammatical analysis of pretrained sentence encoders with acceptability judgments. *CoRR*, abs/1901.03438.

Alex Warstadt, Alicia Parrish, Haokun Liu, Anhad Mohananey, Wei Peng, Sheng-Fu Wang, and Samuel R. Bowman. 2020. BLiMP: The benchmark of linguistic minimal pairs for English. *Transactions of the Association for Computational Linguistics*, 8:377–392.

Alex Warstadt, Amanpreet Singh, and Samuel R. Bowman. 2019. Neural network acceptability judgments. *Transactions of the Association for Computational Linguistics*, 7:625–641.

Thomas Wolf, Lysandre Debut, Victor Sanh, Julien Chaumond, Clement Delangue, Anthony Moi, Pierric Cistac, Tim Rault, Remi Louf, Morgan Funtowicz, Joe Davison, Sam Shleifer, Patrick von Platen, Clara Ma, Yacine Jernite, Julien Plu, Canwen Xu, Teven Le Scao, Sylvain Gugger, Mariama Drame, Quentin Lhoest, and Alexander Rush. 2020. Transformers: State-of-the-art natural language processing. In *Proceedings of the 2020 Conference on Empirical Methods in Natural Language Processing: System Demonstrations*, pages 38–45, Online. Association for Computational Linguistics.

Zhiyong Wu, Yun Chen, Ben Kao, and Qun Liu. 2020. Perturbed masking: Parameter-free probing for analyzing and interpreting BERT. In *Proceedings of the 58th Annual Meeting of the Association for Computational Linguistics*, pages 4166–4176, Online. Association for Computational Linguistics.

Beilei Xiang, Changbing Yang, Yu Li, Alex Warstadt, and Katharina Kann. 2021. CLiMP: A benchmark for Chinese language model evaluation. In *Proceedings of the 16th Conference of the European Chapter of the Association for Computational Linguistics: Main Volume*, pages 2784–2790, Online. Association for Computational Linguistics.

# Appendix

## 1 Dataset Statistics

| | Language | NgramShift | ClauseShift | RandomShift |
|---|---|---|---|---|
| **num. tokens** | **Ru** | 105.8k | 199.7k | 95.6k |
| | **En** | 128.5k | 198.6k | 111.1k |
| | **Sv** | 134.1k | 192.9k | 100.7k |
| **unique tokens** | **Ru** | 25.2k | 46.1k | 27.8k |
| | **En** | 19.2k | 25.1k | 22.8k |
| | **Sv** | 23.2k | 25.7k | 17.8k |
| **tokens / sentence** | **Ru** | 10.9 | 19.9 | 10.5 |
| | **En** | 12.9 | 19.9 | 11.1 |
| | **Sv** | 13.4 | 19.3 | 10.1 |

Table 1: A brief statistics of the controlled perturbation datasets. Languages: **Ru**=Russian, **En**=English, **Sv**=Swedish.

## 2 Parameter-free Probing

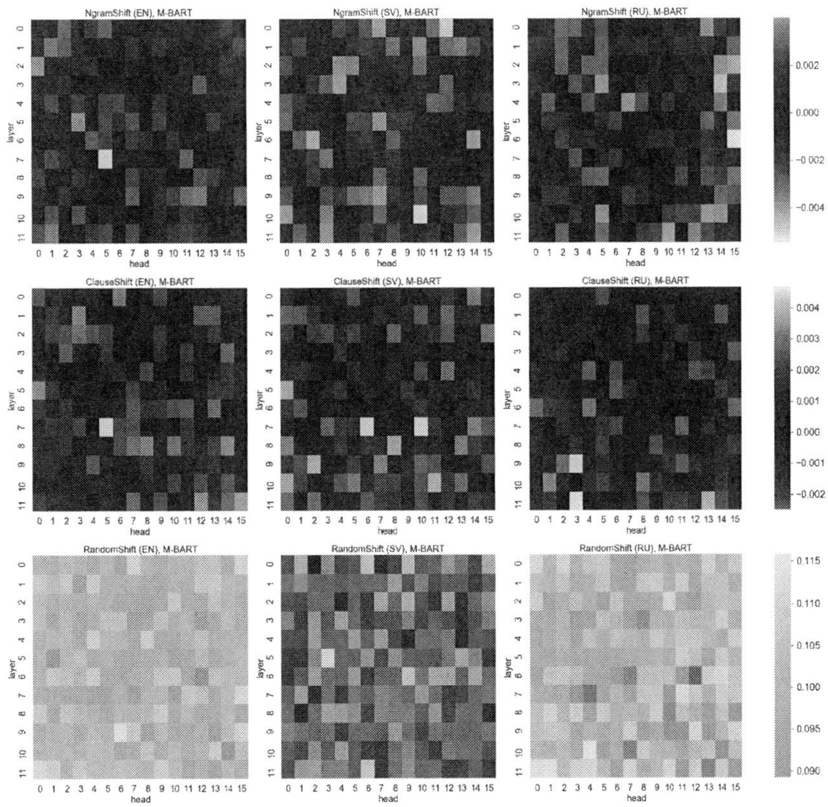

Figure 1: The task-wise heatmaps depicting the $\delta$ UUAS scores by M-BART for each language. Method=**Self-Attention Probing**. PE=**absolute**. X-axis=Attention head index. Y-axis=Layer index. Tasks: **NgramShift** (top); **ClauseShift** (middle); **RandomShift** (bottom). Languages: **En**=English (left); **Sv**=Swedish (middle); **Ru**=Russian (right).

| | **Language** | **M-BERT** | **M-BART** |
|---|---|---|---|
| **NgramShift** | **En** | 0.32; 0.33 | 0.31; 0.32 |
| | **Sv** | 0.30; 0.31 | 0.30; 0.31 |
| | **Ru** | 0.36; 0.38 | 0.37; 0.38 |
| **ClauseShift** | **En** | 0.20; 0.21 | 0.20; 0.21 |
| | **Sv** | 0.20; 0.21 | 0.20; 0.21 |
| | **Ru** | 0.20; 0.21 | 0.20; 0.21 |
| **RandomShift** | **En** | 0.37; 0.38 | 0.37; 0.37 |
| | **Sv** | 0.38; 0.41 | 0.37; 0.39 |
| | **Ru** | 0.39; 0.42 | 0.40; 0.41 |

Table 2: The UUAS scores by **Self-Attention Probing** method. The minimum and maximum values are given (min; max). Languages: **Ru**=Russian, **En**=English, **Sv**=Swedish.

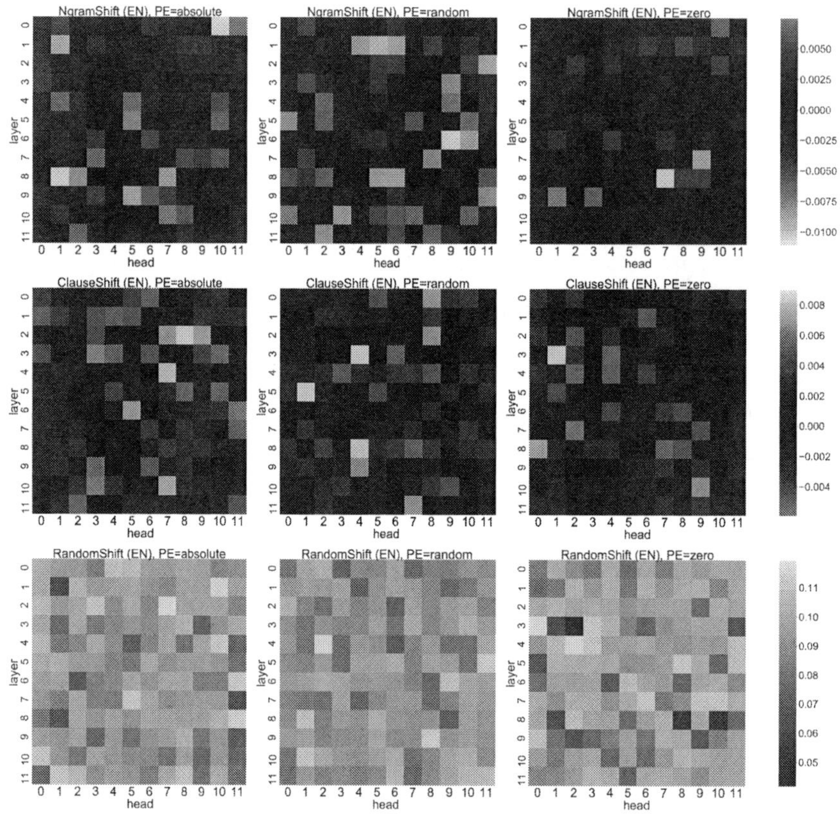


Figure 2: The task-wise heatmaps depicting the $\delta$ UUAS scores by M-BERT for each language. Method=**Self-Attention Probing**. PE: **absolute** (left); **random** (middle); **zero** (right). X-axis=Attention head index. Y-axis=Layer index. Tasks: **NgramShift** (top); **ClauseShift** (middle); **RandomShift** (bottom).

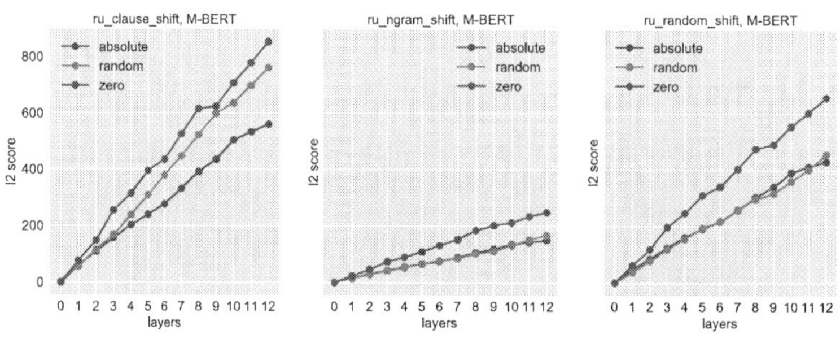


Figure 3: The Euclidean distance between the impact matrices computed by M-BERT with different PEs over each pair of sentences $(s, s')$ for Russian. The distances are averaged over attention heads at each layer. Method: **Token Perturbed Masking**. Tasks: **NgramShift** (left); **ClauseShift** (middle); **RandomShift** (right)

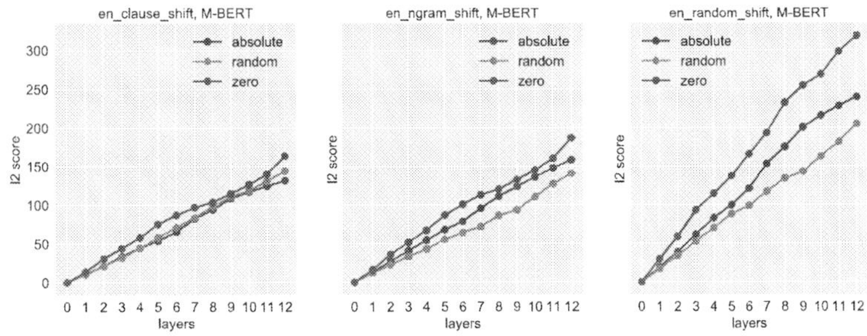


Figure 4: The Euclidean distance between the impact matrices computed by M-BERT with different PEs over each pair of sentences ($s$, $s'$) for English. The distances are averaged over attention heads at each layer. Method: **Token Perturbed Masking**. Tasks: **NgramShift** (left); **ClauseShift** (middle); **RandomShift** (right)

.

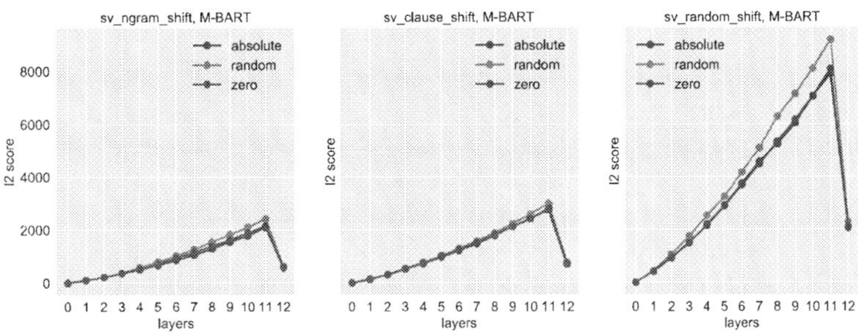


Figure 5: The Euclidean distance between the impact matrices computed by M-BART with different PEs over each pair of sentences ($s$, $s'$) for Swedish. The distances are averaged over attention heads at each layer. Method: **Token Perturbed Masking**. Tasks: **NgramShift** (left); **ClauseShift** (middle); **RandomShift** (right)

.

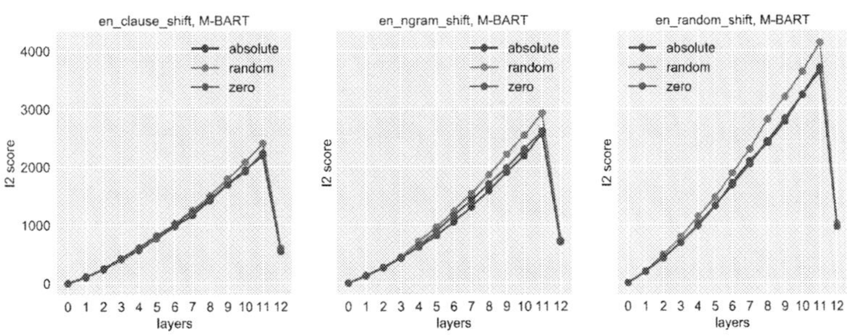


Figure 6: The Euclidean distance between the impact matrices computed by M-BART with different PEs over each pair of sentences ($s$, $s'$) for English. The distances are averaged over attention heads at each layer. Method: **Token Perturbed Masking**. Tasks: **NgramShift** (left); **ClauseShift** (middle); **RandomShift** (right)

.

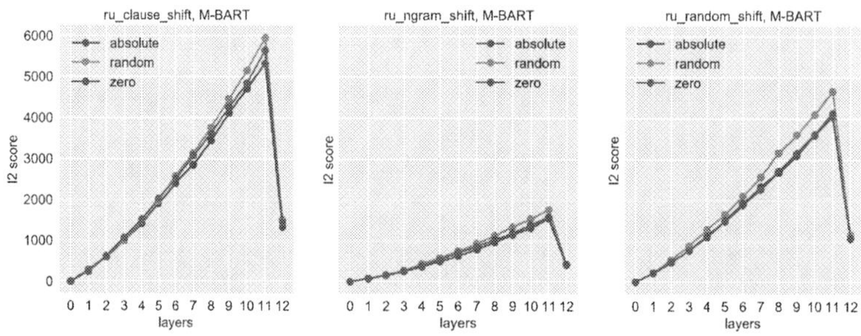


Figure 7: The Euclidean distance between the impact matrices computed by M-BART with different PEs over each pair of sentences $(s, s')$ for Russian. The distances are averaged over attention heads at each layer. Method: **Token Perturbed Masking**. Tasks: **NgramShift** (left); **ClauseShift** (middle); **RandomShift** (right)

| | Language | M-BERT | M-BART |
|---|---|---|---|
| NgramShift | En | 0.36; 0.44 | 0.31; 0.44 |
| | Sv | 0.37; 0.46 | 0.43; 0.53 |
| | Ru | 0.4244; 0.52 | 0.46; 0.54 |
| ClauseShift | En | 0.23; 0.29 | 0.23; 0.29 |
| | Sv | 0.25; 0.33 | 0.24; 0.33 |
| | Ru | 0.23; 0.28 | 0.22; 0.28 |
| RandomShift | En | 0.39; 0.47 | 0.39; 0.47 |
| | Sv | 0.46; 0.53 | 0.43; 0.53 |
| | Ru | 0.46; 0.54 | 0.43; 0.54 |

Table 3: The UUAS scores by **Token Perturbed Masking** probe. The minimum and maximum values are given (min; max). Languages: **Ru**=Russian, **En**=English, **Sv**=Swedish.

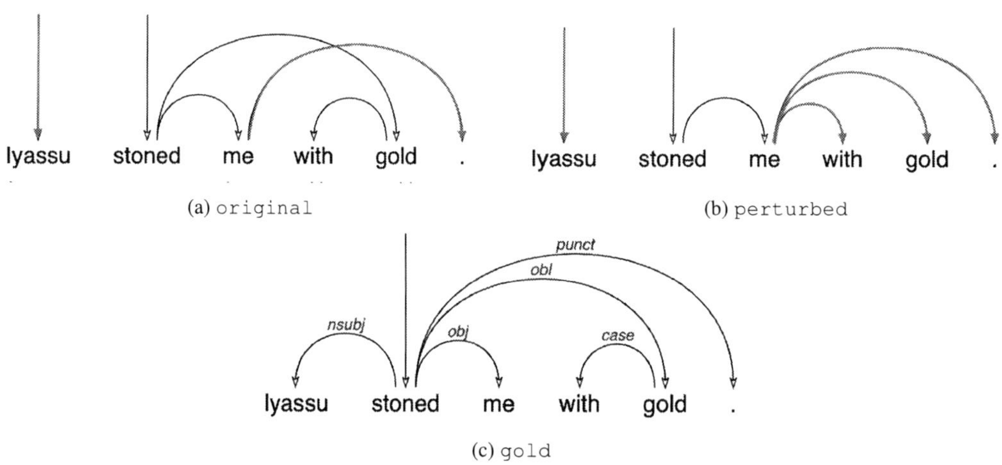


Figure 8: Graphical representations of the syntactic trees inferred for the English sentence *Iyassu stoned me with gold* and its perturbed version. `original`=the original sentence; `perturbed`=the perturbed version; `gold`=gold standard. Task=**RandomShift**. Model=**M-BERT** (Layer: 11; Head: 2). Method=**Self-Attention Probing**. The perturbation is underlined with red, and incorrectly assigned dependency heads are marked with red arrows.

# 3 Representation Analysis

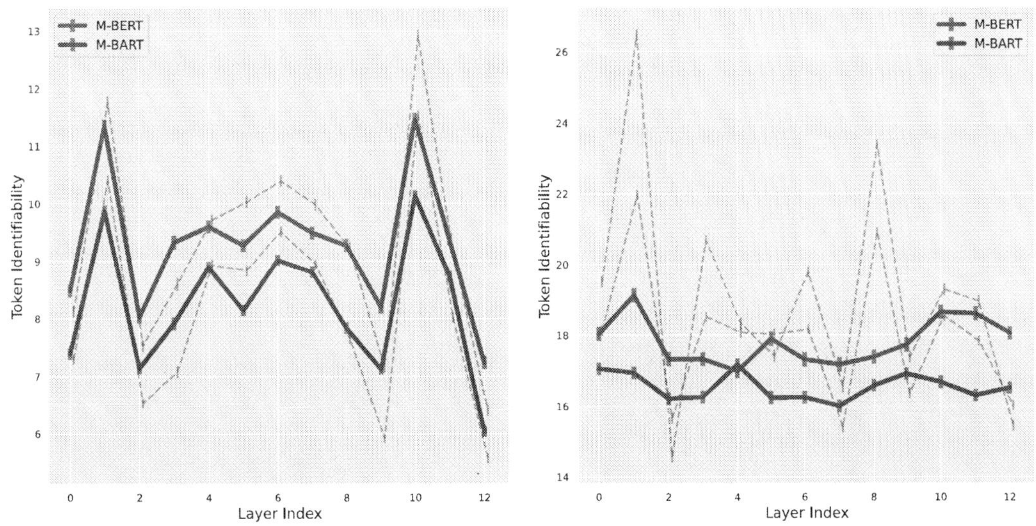


(a) **NgramShift** (b) **ClauseShift**

Figure 9: Token identifiability (TI) by layer for M-BERT and M-BART on the **NgramShift** (left) and **ClauseShift** (right) tasks for Russian. Dashed lines represent the scores computed over the intact sentences. X-axis=Layer index. Y-axis=TI.

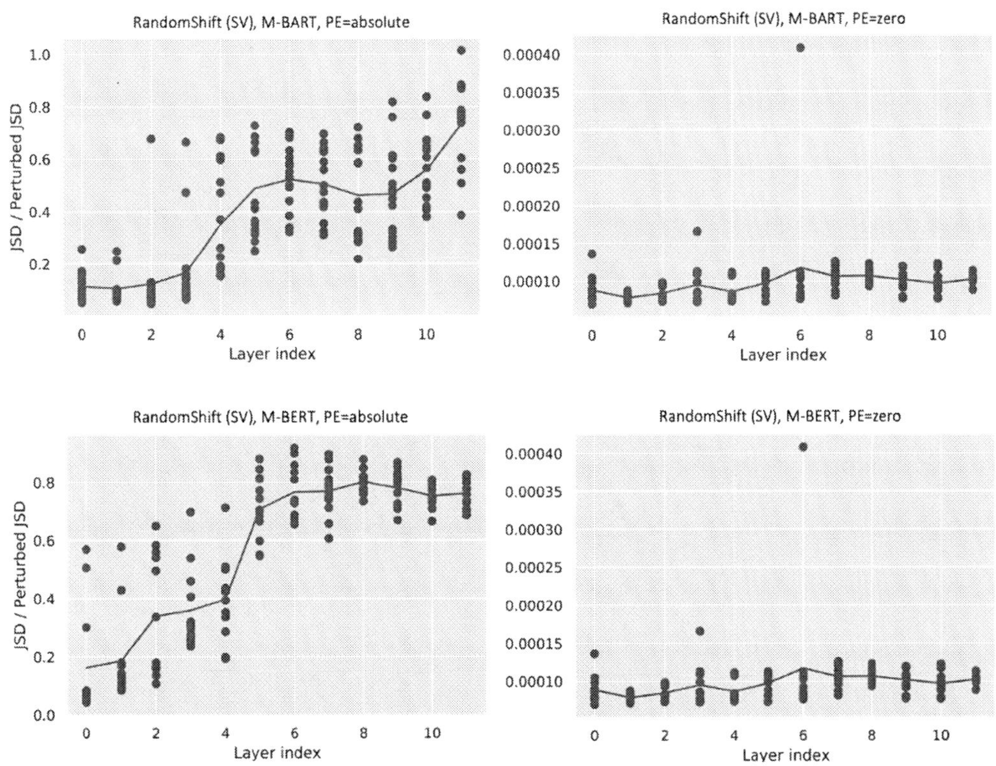


Figure 10: Self-Attention Distance (SAD) by layer for M-BART and M-BERT with absolute (left) and zeroed (right) positional embeddings on the **RandomShift** task for Swedish. X-axis=Layer index. Y-axis=SAD.

# 4 Acceptability Judgements

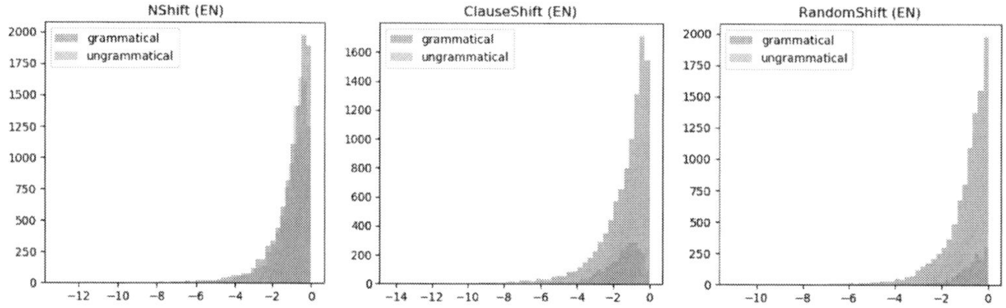


Figure 11: The *MeanLP* distributions for the perturbed (ungrammatical) and intact (grammatical) sentences by M-BART. Tasks: **NgramShift** (left); **ClauseShift** (middle); **RandomShift** (right).

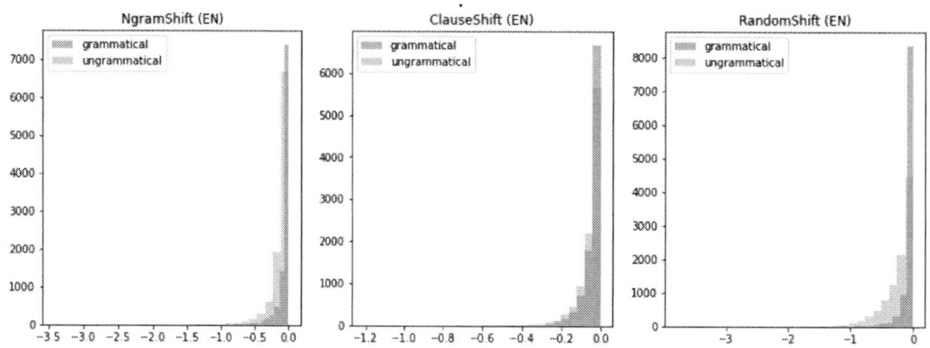


Figure 12: The *MeanLP* distributions for the perturbed (ungrammatical) and intact (grammatical) sentences by M-BERT. Tasks: **NgramShift** (left); **ClauseShift** (middle); **RandomShift** (right).

# Multilingual Code-Switching for Zero-Shot Cross-Lingual Intent Prediction and Slot Filling

**Jitin Krishnan Antonios Anastasopoulos Hemant Purohit Huzefa Rangwala**
George Mason University
Fairfax, VA, USA
{jkrishn2,antonis,hpurohit,rangwala}@gmu.edu

## Abstract

Predicting user intent and detecting the corresponding slots from text are two key problems in Natural Language Understanding (NLU). Since annotated datasets are only available for a handful of languages, our work focuses particularly on a zero-shot scenario where the target language is *unseen* during training. In the context of zero-shot learning, this task is typically approached using representations from pre-trained multilingual language models such as mBERT or by fine-tuning on data automatically translated into the target language. We propose a novel method which augments monolingual source data using multilingual code-switching via random translations, to enhance generalizability of large multilingual language models when *fine-tuning* them for downstream tasks. Experiments on the MultiATIS++ benchmark show that our method leads to an average improvement of $+4.2\%$ in accuracy for the intent task and $+1.8\%$ in F1 for the slot-filling task over the state-of-the-art across 8 typologically diverse languages. We also study the impact of code-switching into different families of languages on downstream performance. Furthermore, we present an application of our method for crisis informatics using a new human-annotated tweet dataset of slot filling in English and Haitian Creole, collected during the Haiti earthquake.[1]

## 1 Introduction

A cross-lingual setting is typically described as a scenario in which a model trained for a particular task in one *source* language (e.g. English) should be able to generalize well to a different *target* language (e.g. Japanese). While semi-supervised solutions (Muis et al., 2018; FitzGerald, 2020, *inter alia*) assume some target language data or translators are available, a zero-shot solution (Eriguchi et al., 2018; Srivastava et al., 2018; Xu et al., 2020) assumes none is available at training time. Having models that generalize well even to unseen languages is crucial for tackling real world problems such as extracting relevant information during a new disaster (Nguyen et al., 2017; Krishnan et al., 2020) or detecting hate speech (Pamungkas and Patti, 2019; Stappen et al., 2020), where the target language might be of low-resource or unknown.

Intent prediction and slot filling are two NLU tasks, usually solved jointly, which learn to model the intent (sentence-level) and slot (word-level) labels. Such models are currently used extensively for goal-oriented dialogue systems, such as Amazon's Alexa, Apple's Siri, Google Assistant, and Microsoft's Cortana. Finding the '*intent*' behind the user's query and identifying relevant '*slots*' in the sentence to engage in a dialogue are essential for effective conversational assistance. For example, users might want to '*play music*' given the slot labels '*year*' and '*artist*' (Coucke et al., 2018), or they may want to '*book a flight*' given the '*airport*' and '*locations*' slot labels (Price, 1990). A strong correlation between the two tasks has made jointly trained models successful (Goo et al., 2018; Haihong et al., 2019; Hardalov et al., 2020; Chen et al., 2019). In a cross-lingual setting, the model should be able to learn this joint task in one language and transfer knowledge to another (Upadhyay et al., 2018; Schuster et al., 2019; Xu et al., 2020). This is the premise of our work.

Highly effective transformer-based multilingual models such as mBERT (Devlin et al., 2019) and XLM-R (Conneau et al., 2020a) have found success across several multilingual tasks in recent years. In the zero-shot cross-lingual transfer setting with an unknown target language, a typical solution is to use pre-trained transformer models and fine-tune to the downstream task using the monolingual source data (Xu et al., 2020). However, Pires et al. (2019) showed that existing transformer-based represen-

[1]Implementation and dataset are available at https://github.com/jitinkrishnan/Multilingual-ZeroShot-SlotFilling.



*Proceedings of the 1st Workshop on Multilingual Representation Learning*, pages 211–223
November 11, 2021. 

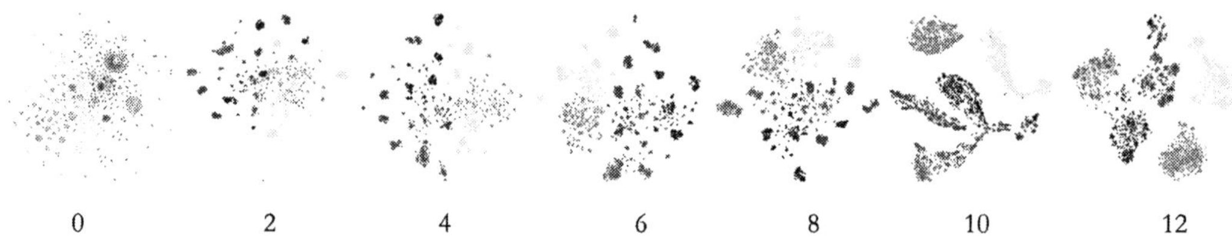


Figure 1: t-SNE plot of embeddings across the 12 multi-head attention layers of multilingual BERT. Parallelly translated sentences of MutiATIS++ dataset are still clustered according to the languages: English (black), Chinese (cyan), French (blue), German (green), and Japanese (red).

| **Intent** | atis_airfare | | | | | | | | |
|---|---|---|---|---|---|---|---|---|---|
| | | | | Original (English) | | | | | |
| **Words** | Show | me | round | trip | fares | from | Denver | to | Philadelphia |
| **Slots** | O | O | B-round_trip | I-round_trip | O | O | B-fromloc.city_name | O | B-fromloc.city_name |
| | | | | Chunk-level Code-Switched | | | | | |
| **Words** | 给 | 我 | 看 | 看 | ਸੈਰ | tarifas | desde | Denver | إلى | Филадельфия |
| **Slots** | O | O | O | O | B-round_trip | O | O | B-fromloc.city_name | O | B-fromloc.city_name |

Figure 2: An original example in English from MultiATIS++ dataset and its multilingually code-switched version. In the above code-switching example, the chunks are in Chinese, Punjabi, Spanish, English, Arabic, and Russian. '*atis_airfare*' represents an intent class where the user seeks price of a ticket.

tations may exhibit systematic deficiencies for certain language pairs. Figure 1 also verifies that the representations across the 12 multi-head attention layers of mBERT are still not shared across languages, instead forming clearly distinguishable clusters per language. This leads to a fundamental challenge that we address in this work: enhancing the language neutrality so that the fine-tuned model is generalizable across languages for the downstream task. To this goal, we introduce a data augmentation method via multilingual code-switching, where the original sentence in English is code-switched into randomly selected languages. For example, chunk-level code-switching creates sentences with phrases in multiple languages as shown in Figure 2. We show that mBERT can be fine-tuned for many languages starting only with monolingual source-language data, leading to better performance in zero-shot settings.

Further, we show how code-switching with languages from different language families impacts the model's performance on individual target languages, even finding some counter-intuitive results. For instance, training on data code-switched between English and Sino-Tibetan languages is as helpful for Hindi (an Indo-Aryan Indo-European language) as code-switching with other Indo-Aryan languages, and Turkic languages can be helpful for both Chinese and Japanese.

**Contributions:** **a)** We present a data augmentation method via multilingual code-switching to enhance the language neutrality of transformer-based language models such as mBERT for fine-tuning to a downstream NLU task of intent prediction and slot filling. **b)** By studying different language families, we show how code-switching can be used to aid zero-shot cross-lingual learning for low-resource languages. **c)** We release a new human-annotated tweet dataset, collected during Haiti earthquake disaster, for intent prediction and slot filling in English and Haitian Creole.

## 2 Methodology

This section describes our problem definition, code-switching algorithm, language families, and the training methodology.

### 2.1 Problem Definition

Given a source (S) and a set of target (T) languages, the goal is to train a classifier using data only in the source language and predict examples from the completely unseen target languages. We assume the target language is *unknown* during training (fine-tuning) time, which makes direct translation to target infeasible. In this context, we use code-switching ($cs$) to augment the monolingual source data. Thus, the input, augmented input, and output of our problem can be defined as:

**Algorithm 1:** Data Augmentation via Multilingual Code-Switching (Chunk-Level)

```
Input: X_ut^en, y^en, y_sl^en, l_T
Output: X_ut^cs, y^cs, y_sl^cs
X_ut^cs ← ∅, y^cs ← ∅, y_sl^cs ← ∅
lset = googletrans.languages − l_T
for i ∈ 1..k do
    for j ∈ 1..len(X_ut^en) do
        G^cs ← ∅, L^cs ← ∅
        chunks = slot_chunks(X_ut^en[j], y_sl^en[j])
        for c ∈ chunks do
            l ← random.choice(lset)
            t ← translate(c, l)
            G^cs ← G^cs ∪ t
            L^cs ← L^cs ∪ align_label(c, t)
        end
        X_ut^cs ← X_ut^cs ∪ G^cs
        y^cs ← y^cs ∪ y^cs[j]
        y_sl^cs ← y_sl^cs ∪ L^cs
    end
end
```

***Input:*** $X_{ut}^{S}$, $y^{S}$, $y_{sl}^{S}$, $l_T$
***Code-Switched Input:*** $X_{ut}^{cs}$, $y^{cs}$, $y_{sl}^{cs}$
***Output:*** $y^{T}$, $y_{sl}^{T} \leftarrow predict(X_{ut}^{T})$

where $X_{ut}$ represents sentences, $y$ their ground truth intent classes, $y_{sl}$ the slot labels for the words in those sentences, and $l_T$ the set of target languages. An example sentence, its intent class, and slot labels are shown in Figure 2.

## 2.2 Multilingual Code-Switching

Multilingual masked language models, such as mBERT (Devlin et al., 2019), are trained using large datasets of publicly available unlabeled corpora such as Wikipedia. Such corpora largely remain monolingual at the sentence level because the presence of intra-sentence code-switched data in written texts is likely scarce. The masked words that needed to be predicted usually are in the same language as their surrounding words. We study how code-switching can enhance the language neutrality of such language models by augmenting it with artificially code-switched data for fine-tuning it to a downstream task. Algorithm 1 explains this code-switching process at the chunk-level. When using slot filling datasets, slot labels that are grouped by BIO (Ramshaw and Marcus, 1999) tags constitute natural chunks, as shown in Figure 2. To summarize the algorithm, we take a sentence, take each chunk from that sentence, perform a translation into a random language using Google's NMT system (Wu et al., 2016), and align the slot labels to fit the translation, i.e., label propagation through alignment as the translated sentence do not preserve the number and order of words in the original sentence. At the chunk-level, we use a direct alignment. The BIO-tagged labels are recreated for the translated phrase based on the word tokens. More complex methods could be applied here to improve the alignment of the slot labels such as fast-align (Dyer et al., 2013) or soft-align (Xu et al., 2020), but we leave this for future work. Code-Switching at the word-level essentially translates every word randomly, while at the sentence-level translates the entire sentence. During the experimental evaluation process, to build a language-neutral model using monolingual source (English) data, **all eight target languages are excluded** from the code-switching procedure to avoid unfair model comparisons, i.e. removing target languages ($l_T$) from $lset$ in Algorithm 1.

| Group Name | Languages |
|---|---|
| Afro-Asiatic | Arabic (ar), Amharic (am), Hebrew (he), Somali (so) |
| Germanic | German (de), Dutch (nl), Danish (da), Swedish (sv), Norwegian (no) |
| Indo-Aryan | Hindi (hi), Bengali (bn), Marathi (mr), Nepali (ne), Gujarati (gu), Punjabi (pa) |
| Romance | Spanish (es), Portuguese (pt), French (fr), Italian (it), Romanian (ro) |
| Sino-Tibetan, Koreanic, & Japonic | Chinese (zh-cn), Japanese (ja), Korean (ko) |
| Turkic | Turkish (tr), Azerbaijani (az), Uyghur (ug), Kazakh (kk) |

Table 1: Selected language families to evaluate their impact on a target language.

**Complexity.** The augmentation process is repeated $k$ times per sentence producing a new augmented dataset of size $k \times n$, where $n$ is the size of the original dataset, i.e. space complexity of $\mathcal{O}(k \times n)$. For $T$ translations per sentence, Algorithm 1 has a runtime complexity of $\mathcal{O}(k \times n \times T)$ assuming constant time for alignment. Word-level requires as many translations as the number of words but sentence-level requires only one. An increase in the dataset size also increases the training time, but the advantage is one model appropriate for many languages.

## 2.3 Language Families

A language family is defined as a group of related languages that likely share a common ancestor. For example, Portuguese, Spanish, French, Italian, and Romanian are all derived from Latin (Rowe and Levine, 2017). We use language families to study their impact on the target languages. We augment the source language with code-switching to a particular language family. For instance, code-switching the English dataset with Turkic language family and testing on Japanese can reveal how closely the two are aligned in the vector space of a pre-trained multilingual model. We work with 6 language groups: Afro-Asiatic (Voegelin and Voegelin, 1976), Germanic (Harbert, 2006), Indo-Aryan (Masica, 1993), Romance (Elcock and Green, 1960), and Turkic (Johanson and Johanson, 2015), also grouping Sino-Tibetan, Koreanic and Japonic (Shafer, 1955; Miller, 1967).[2] Germanic, Romance, and Indo-Aryan are genera of the Indo-European family. Language groups and corresponding languages are shown in Table 1. Each group is selected based on a target language in the dataset, and the Afro-Asiatic family is added as an extra group. In experiments, $lset$ in Algorithm 1 will be assigned languages from a specific family.

### 2.4 Joint Training

Joint training is traditionally used for intent prediction and slot filling to exploit the correlation between the two tasks. This is done by feeding the feature vectors of one model to another or by sharing layers of a neural network followed by training the tasks together. So, a standard joint model loss can be defined as a combination of intent ($L_i$) and slot ($L_{sl}$) losses. i.e., $L = \alpha L_i + \beta L_{sl}$, where $\alpha$ and $\beta$ are corresponding task weights. Prior works (Goo et al., 2018; Schuster et al., 2019; Liu and Lane, 2016; Haihong et al., 2019) that use BiLSTM or RNN are now modified to BERT-based implementations explored in more recent works (Chen et al., 2019; Hardalov et al., 2020; Xu et al., 2020). A standard $Joint$ model consists of BERT outputs from the final hidden state (classification (CLS) token for intent and $m$ word tokens for slots) fed to linear layers to get intent and slot predictions. Assuming $h_{cls}$ represents the CLS token and $h_m$ represents a token from the remaining word-level tokens, the BERT model outputs are defined as (Chen et al., 2019; Xu et al., 2020):

$$\begin{aligned} p^i &= softmax(W^i h_{cls} + b^i) \\ p^{sl}_m &= softmax(W^{sl} h_m + b^{sl}) \ \forall m \end{aligned} \quad (1)$$

with a multi-class cross-entropy loss[3] for both intent ($L_i$) and slots ($L_{sl}$). We will use this model as our baseline for joint training. Our goal will be to show that code-switching on top of joint training improves the performance. The output of Algorithm 1 will be the input used for joint training on BERT for code-switched experiments.

## 3 Datasets

**Benchmark Dataset.** We use the latest multilingual benchmark dataset of MultiATIS++ (Xu et al., 2020), which was created by manually translating the original ATIS (Price, 1990) dataset from English (en) to 8 other languages: Spanish (es), Portuguese (pt), German (de), French (fr), Chinese (zh), Japanese (ja), Hindi (hi), and Turkish (tr). The dataset consists of utterances for each language with an *'intent'* label for *'flight intent'* and *'slot'* labels for the word tokens in BIO format. A sample datapoint in English is shown in Figure 2. Table 2 presents the dataset statistics for the benchmark dataset of MultiATIS++ as well as for the newly constructed dataset for disaster NLU.

**New Dataset for Disaster NLU.** We construct a new intent and slot filling dataset of tweets collected during natural disasters, in two languages: English (en) and Haitian Creole (ht). The tweets originally were released by Appen.[4] For English, a language expert labeled the tweets, and for Haitian Creole, we used Amazon Mechanical Turk with five annotators. Intent classes include: '*request*' and '*others*'. Slot filling consists of 5 labels: '*medical_help*', '*food*', '*water*', '*shelter*', and '*other_aid*'. Table 2 provides the dataset statistics.

## 4 Experimental Setup

We use the traditional cross-lingual task setting where each experiment consists of a source language and a target language. A model is trained on the source data (English) and evaluated on the target data (8 other languages). For code-switching experiments, the English dataset is augmented with multilingual code-switching before training. Our implementation is in PyTorch (Paszke et al., 2019) and we use the pre-trained *bert-base-multilingual-uncased* with *BertForSequenceClassification* (Wolf et al., 2020) model. Maximum epochs is set to 25 with an early stopping patience of 5, batch size of 32, and Adam optimizer (Kingma and Ba, 2014) with a learning rate of 5e−5. We select the best

[2]Each of the Sino-Tibetan, Koreanic, and Japonic families have a single high-resource member (Chinese, Korean, Japanese respectively). We only group them as an additional interesting data point, not because we ascribe to any theories that link them typologically.

[3]$L = -\frac{1}{n}\sum_{i=1}^{n}[y \log \hat{y}]$

[4]https://appen.com/datasets/combined-disaster-response-data/

| Language | Utterances | | | Tokens | | | Intents | Slots |
|---|---|---|---|---|---|---|---|---|
| | train | dev | test | train | dev | test | | |
| MultiATIS++ (Xu et al., 2020) | | | | | | | | |
| English | 4488 | 490 | 893 | 50755 | 5445 | 9164 | 18 | 84 |
| Spanish | 4488 | 490 | 893 | 55197 | 5927 | 10338 | 18 | 84 |
| Portuguese | 4488 | 490 | 893 | 55052 | 5909 | 10228 | 18 | 84 |
| German | 4488 | 490 | 893 | 51111 | 5517 | 9383 | 18 | 84 |
| French | 4488 | 490 | 893 | 55909 | 5769 | 10511 | 18 | 84 |
| Chinese | 4488 | 490 | 893 | 88194 | 9652 | 16710 | 18 | 84 |
| Japanese | 4488 | 490 | 893 | 133890 | 14416 | 25939 | 18 | 84 |
| Hindi | 1440 | 160 | 893 | 16422 | 1753 | 9755 | 17 | 75 |
| Turkish | 578 | 60 | 715 | 6132 | 686 | 7683 | 17 | 71 |
| Disaster Tweets (New Dataset) | | | | | | | | |
| English | 3518 | 490 | - | 16369 | 4242 | - | 2 | 5 |
| Haitian Creole | - | - | 520 | - | - | 2834 | 2 | 5 |

Table 2: Datasets & Statistics.

model on the validation set. Consistent with the metrics reported for intent prediction and slot filling evaluation in the past, we also accuracy for intent and micro F1[5] to measure slot performance.

### 4.1 Baselines & Upper Bound

Since we assume that target language is not known before hand, **Translate-Train (TT)** (Xu et al., 2020) method is not a suitable baseline. Rather, we set this to be an upper bound, i.e. translating to the target language and fine-tuning the model should intuitively outperform a generic model. Additionally, we add code-switching to this TT model to assess if augmentation negatively impacts its performance. The zero-shot baselines for the code-switching experiments use an **English-Only** (Xu et al., 2020) model, which is fine-tuned over the pre-trained mBERT separately for each task and an English-only **Joint** model (Chen et al., 2019).

## 5 Results & Discussion

**Effect of Multilingual Code-Switching.** Table 3 describes performance evaluation on the MultiATIS++ dataset. When compared to the state-of-the-art jointly trained English-only baseline, we see a $+4.2\%$ boost in intent accuracy and $+1.8\%$ boost in slot F1 scores on average by augmenting the dataset via multilingual code-switching **without requiring the target language**. From the significance tests, except for Spanish and German, all other languages were helped by code-switching for intent detection. For slot filling, improvement on Portuguese and French is insignificant. This suggests that code-switching primarily helped languages that are morphologically more different from the source language (English). For example, Hindi and Turkish have the highest intent performance improvement of $+16.1\%$ and $+9.8\%$ respectively. And for slots, Hindi and Chinese with $+6.0\%$ and $+4.3\%$ respectively. Japanese showed $+4\%$ improvement for intent and $+3.4\%$ for slots.

The runtime of the models in Table 5 (Appendix B) shows that code-switching is expensive, taking up to five hours for five augmentation rounds ($k = 5$). This is because there are $k$ times more data compared to the monolingual source data. Increasing the number of code-switchings ($k$) for a sentence from 5 to 50 improves the performance by $+1\%$, while increasing the run-time by a large margin. Hence, such tradeoffs should be considered when picking $k$ for real-world applications where time to deployment might be of the essense.

In the translate-train (upper bound) scenario, it is not immediately clear if augmentation helps, since data in the same language as the target are always preferable to other language or code-switched data. At a minimum, augmentation does not hinder upper-bound performance (Table 3).

For both intent and slot performance, the chunk-level model remained robust across the languages. For intent, the difference between word-level and sentence-level was insignificant. For slot, sentence-level was in par with chunk-level on average. Thus,

[5]To address class imbalance for slots, we use Micro F1 instead of Macro F1, which is why our F1 scores are inflated when compared to scores in (Xu et al., 2020).

| **Intent Acc.** | $m$ | es | de | zh | ja | pt | fr | hi | tr | **AVG** |
|---|---|---|---|---|---|---|---|---|---|---|
| English-Only Baseline* | 1 | 94.42 | 94.29 | 79.53 | 73.75 | 92.90 | 93.86 | 67.06 | 69.71 | 83.19 |
| $Joint_{en-only}$ Baseline* | 1 | 95.03 | 94.51 | 80.54 | 73.57 | 93.48 | 93.33 | 73.53 | 71.05 | 84.38 |
| Word-level CS† | 1 | 94.18 | 93.92 | 81.67 | 75.48 | 92.54 | 94.18 | 81.19 | 74.22 | 85.92 |
| Sentence-level CS | 1 | 94.60 | 93.53 | 81.21 | 75.01 | 93.10 | 93.24 | 82.37 | 75.11 | 86.02 |
| Chunk-level CS (CCS) | 1 | 95.12 | **95.27** | 83.88 | 74.27 | **94.20** | 93.48 | 82.73 | 77.51 | 87.06 |
| $Joint_{en-only}$* + CCS | 1 | **95.48** | 94.51 | **84.43**♠ | **76.48**♠ | 94.15♠ | **94.89**♠ | **85.37**♠ | **78.04**♠ | **87.92** |
| Upper Bound | | | | | | | | | | |
| Translate-Train (TT)* | 8 | 94.02 | 93.84 | 90.21 | 84.19 | 95.66 | 94.54 | 85.08 | 85.79 | 90.42 |
| $Joint_{TT}$* | 8 | 94.16 | 94.24 | 91.56 | 85.98 | 95.75 | 95.01 | 86.45 | 84.95 | 91.01 |
| $Joint_{TT}$* + CCS | 8 | 95.48 | 95.41 | 91.60 | 87.17 | 95.34 | 94.60 | 87.94 | 85.93 | 91.68 |
| **Slot F1** | $m$ | es | de | zh | ja | pt | fr | hi | tr | **AVG** |
| English-Only Baseline* | 1 | 96.16 | 96.73 | 83.12 | 78.81 | 95.63 | 95.40 | 77.05 | 88.09 | 88.87 |
| $Joint_{en-only}$ Baseline* | 1 | 96.12 | 96.76 | 84.95 | 79.60 | 95.76 | 95.76 | 77.63 | 88.92 | 89.44 |
| Word-level CS† | 1 | 95.81 | 96.33 | 85.46 | 79.33 | 96.27 | 95.08 | 79.10 | 86.86 | 89.28 |
| Sentence-level CS | 1 | 96.57 | **96.92** | 86.32 | 79.52 | **96.65** | 95.84 | 81.94 | 89.84 | 90.45 |
| Chunk-level CS (CCS) | 1 | **96.68** | 96.82 | 87.10 | 80.00 | 96.46 | **96.31** | 80.95 | **91.60** | 90.51 |
| $Joint_{en-only}$* + CCS | 1 | 96.09 | 96.56 | **88.61**♠ | **82.28**♠ | 96.01 | 95.94 | **82.28**♠ | 90.45♠ | **91.03** |
| Upper Bound | | | | | | | | | | |
| Translate-Train (TT)* | 8 | 96.89 | 96.04 | 93.48 | 85.29 | 96.35 | 96.02 | 82.03 | 91.21 | 92.16 |
| $Joint_{TT}$* | 8 | 96.92 | 95.66 | 93.64 | 87.84 | 96.11 | 95.95 | 82.98 | 91.15 | 92.53 |
| $Joint_{TT}$* + CCS | 8 | 96.98 | 96.27 | 93.37 | 85.87 | 95.88 | 95.44 | 82.00 | 91.31 | 92.14 |

Table 3: Performance evaluation of code-switching with setting $k = 5$. $CS$: Code-Switching. Reported scores are average of 5 independent runs (including a separate code-switched data for each run). $m$ = number of distinct models to be trained. *: modified BERT-based implementations (Chen et al., 2019; Xu et al., 2020). †: Similar to Qin et al., 2020 but modified for slot-filling task and also excluding target language from randomized switching. ♠: The difference is significant with $p < 0.05$ using Tukey HSD (conducted between $Joint_{en-only}$ + CCS versus $Joint_{en-only}$ Baseline for each language).

| **Intent Acc.** | ht |
|---|---|
| English-Only Baseline* | 56.12 |
| Translate-Train (TT) | 62.58 |
| Chunk-level CS (CCS) | 63.15 |
| $Joint_{en-only}$* + CCS | **63.73** |
| **Slot F1** | ht |
| English-Only Baseline* | 68.72 |
| Translate-Train (TT) | 69.96 |
| Chunk-level CS (CCS) | **70.27** |
| $Joint_{en-only}$* + CCS | 70.02 |

Table 4: Performance on disaster data in Haitian Creole (ht). $CS$ = Code-Switching. Reported scores are average of 5 independent runs (*: modified BERT-based).

we think that code-switching at chunk-level is safer for avoiding semantic discrepancies (which are a danger in the word-level) while also better encouraging intra-sentence language neutrality.

**Evaluation on Disaster Dataset.** We found that disaster data is more challenging than the ATIS dataset for transfer learning in NLU. The predictive performance is shown in Table 4. Code-Switching improved intent accuracy by $+12.5\%$ and slot F1 by $+2.3\%$, which is quite promising considering the domain mismatch (tweets vs airline guides). Joint training added $+0.9\%$ improvement to intent accuracy, however did not seem to help slot F1. This might imply a weaker correlation between the two tasks in real-world data, i.e. a mention of '*food*' or '*shelter*' in a tweet may not always mean that there is a '*request*' or vice-versa. The upper bound of translate-train method did not perform any better than the randomly code-switched model which seemed counter-intuitive. This might be due to the lack of strong representation for Haitian Creole in the pre-trained model, although it is similar to French, or due to the limitation of the machine translation system.

**Impact of Language Families.** Results of language family analysis are shown in Figure 3 for the 4 languages that showed significant improvements for both intent and slots in Table 3. The input in English is independently code-switched using 6 different language families. Note that the target language is always excluded from the group when evaluating on the same, i.e. Hindi is excluded from Indo-Aryan family when that family is being evaluated on it. Translate-train model is provided as a frame of reference and upper bound. Generally, as expected, we found that language families helped their corresponding languages, i.e. Romance helped Spanish, Germanic helped German, and so on. An exception is our loose group of Sino-Tibetan, Koreanic, and Japonic languages –for both Chinese and Japanese, languages from the Turkic language family helped more than others. On the other hand, the Sino-tibetan, Japonic, and Koreanic group helps Hindi more than other Indo-European languages. We believe this highlights the necessity

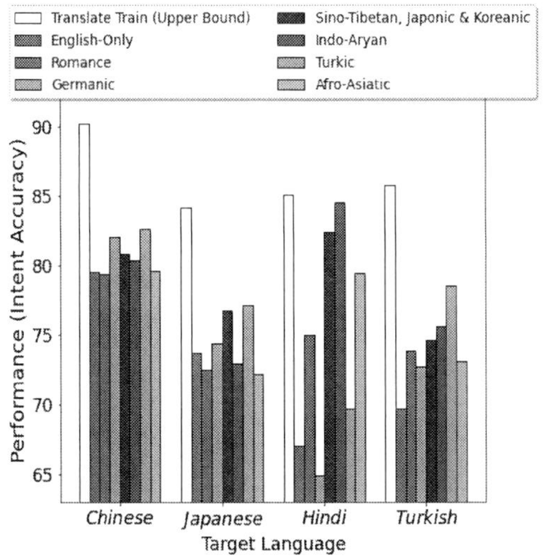


Figure 3: Impact of different language groups on the target languages.

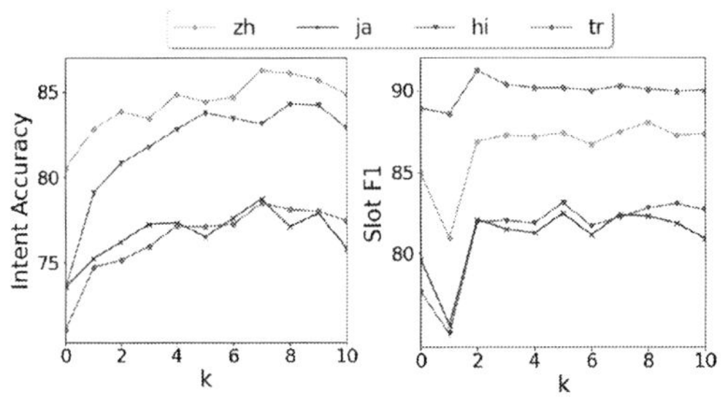


Figure 4: Performance as $k$ (augmentation rounds) increases (on mBERT).

for methods like the one of Xia et al. (2020) that can *a priori* identify the best helper language or group of languages that can benefit downstream tasks for low resource languages.

**Control Experiments on $k$.** Hyperparameter $k$ controls the amount of code-switched data. $k = 0$ represents original size with no code-switching, $k = 1$ represents original size with code-switching, and $k = 10$ means 10-times more code-switched data than the original. The main experiments in Table 3 use $k = 5$. Figure 4 shows how varying $k$ affects performance. For this analysis, we consider 4 target languages on which code-switching produced significant results in Table 3 on both Intent Accuracy and Slot F1: Chinese, Japanese, Hindi, and Turkish. Intuitively, we observe that as $k$ increases, too much code-switching becomes expensive in terms of runtime, while performance improvement slowly plateaus. For Slot F1 performance in all four cases, unlike Intent, we observe an interesting dip when $k = 1$, which represents the augmentation having just one copy of code-switching (without the original non-code-switched data), as compared to $k = 0$. Adding the original data to one round of code-switched data ($k = 2$) leads to big improvements. Overall, we see improvement for both tasks, with Slot F1 plateauing earlier. Table 5 and Figure 10 in Appendix B show the impact of code-switching on training runtime, which increases as $k$ increases. Thus, finding an optimal value of $k$ and specific language groups are essential for downstream applications.

**mBERT versus XLM-R.** Additional performance evaluations and benefits of code-switching on XLM-R (Conneau et al., 2020a), a stronger multilingual language model, are provided in Appendix A. Note that XLM-R is trained using Common-Crawl and is likely to be exposed to some code-switched data. Thus, we focus primarily on mBERT which largely remains monolingual at the sentence-level to identify the unbiased impact of code-switching during *fine-tuning*. Furthermore, runtime and hyperparameter tuning along with insights into layers to freeze before training are shown in Appendix B.

**Error Analysis.** Selecting intent classes with support $> 10$, Figure 5 shows how each class is positively or negatively impacted by code-switching. Improvement was primarily on '*airfare*', '*distance*' '*capacity*', '*airline*', and '*ground_service*' which had longer sentences such as '*Please tell me which airline has the most departures from Atlanta*' when compared to '*abbreviations*' and '*airport*' classes that included very short phrases like '*What does EA mean?*' However, note that Spanish and German did not improve much, aligning with our results in Table 3. For slot labels in Figure 6, we selected the ones with support $> 50$ and that have different characteristics, e.g. '*name*', '*code*', etc. The overall trend in slot performance shows improvements for labels such as '*day_name*', '*airport_code*', and '*city_name*' and slight variations in labels such as '*fight_number*' and '*period_of_day*', implying textual slots benefiting over numeric ones.

## 6 Related Work

**Cross-Lingual Transfer.** Researchers have studied cross lingual tasks in various settings such as sentiment/sequence classification (Wan, 2009; Eriguchi et al., 2018; Yu et al., 2018), named entity recognition (Zirikly and Hagiwara, 2015; Tsai

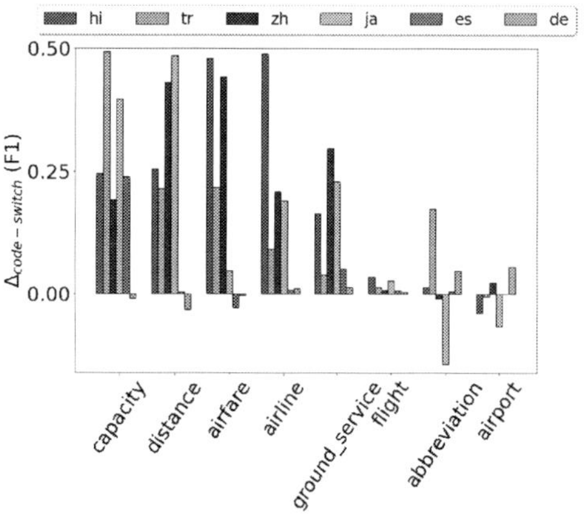


Figure 5: Impact of code-switching on intent classes.

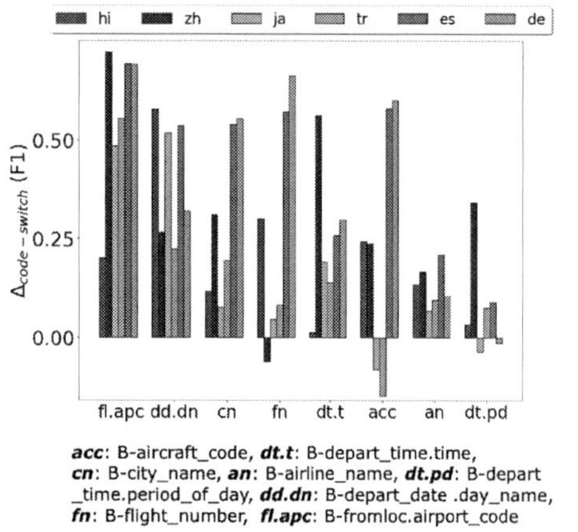


Figure 6: Impact of code-switching on slot labels.

et al., 2016; Xie et al., 2018), parts-of-speech tagging (Yarowsky et al., 2001; Täckström et al., 2013; Plank and Agić, 2018), and natural language understanding (He et al., 2013; Upadhyay et al., 2018; Xu et al., 2020). The methodology for most of the current approaches for cross-lingual tasks can be categorizes as: **a)** multilingual representations from pre-trained or fine-tuned models such as mBERT (Devlin et al., 2019) or XLM-R (Conneau et al., 2020a), **b)** machine translation followed by alignment (Shah et al., 2010; Yarowsky et al., 2001; Ni et al., 2017), or **c)** a combination of both (Xu et al., 2020). Before transformer models, effective approaches included domain adversarial training to extract language-agnostic features (Ganin et al., 2016; Chen et al., 2018) and word alignment methods such as MUSE (Conneau et al., 2017) to align fastText word vectors (Bojanowski et al., 2017). Recently, Conneau et al., 2020b show that having shared parameters in the top layers of the multilingual encoders can be used to align different languages quite effectively on tasks such as XNLI (Conneau et al., 2018).

Monolingual models for joint slot filling and intent prediction have used attention-based RNN (Liu and Lane, 2016) and attention-based BiLSTM with a slot gate (Goo et al., 2018) on benchmark datasets (Price, 1990; Coucke et al., 2018). These methods have shown that a joint method can enhance both tasks and slot filling can be conditioned on the learned intent. A related approach iteratively learns the relationship between the two tasks (Haihong et al., 2019) . Recently, BERT-based approaches (Hardalov et al., 2020; Chen et al., 2019) have improved results. On the other hand, cross-lingual versions of this joint task include a low-supervision based approach for Hindi and Turkish (Upadhyay et al., 2018), new datasets for Spanish and Thai (Schuster et al., 2019), and recently Xu et al. (2020) creating MultiATIS++, a comprehensive dataset in 9 languages. The joint task mentioned above in a pure zero-shot setting is one of the motivations for our work. A Zero-shot is the setting where the model sees a new distribution of examples only during test (prediction) time (Xian et al., 2017; Srivastava et al., 2018; Romera-Paredes and Torr, 2015). Thus, in our setting, we assume that target language is unknown during training, so that our model is generalizable across multiple languages.

**Code-Switching.** Linguistic code-switching is a phenomenon where multilingual speakers alternate between languages. Recently, monolingual models have been adapted to code-switched text in entity recognition (Aguilar and Solorio, 2019), part-of-speech tagging (Soto and Hirschberg, 2018; Ball and Garrette, 2018), sentiment analysis (Joshi et al., 2016) and language identification (Mave et al., 2018; Yirmibeşoğlu and Eryiğit, 2018; Mager et al., 2019). Recently, KhudaBukhsh et al., 2020 have proposed an approach to sample code-mixed documents using minimal supervision. Qin et al., 2020 allows randomized code-switching to include the target language, as shown in their Figure 3. In our context for example, if the target language is German, we ensure that there is no code-switching to German during training. We consider this distinction essential to evaluate a true zero-shot learning scenario and prevent any bias when comparing with translate-and-train. Yang et al. (2020) present a non-zero-shot approach that performs code-switching to target languages, and Jiang et al. (2020) present a code-switching based method to improve the ability of multilingual language models for factual knowledge retrieval. Contemporary work by Tan and Joty, 2021 makes use of both word and phrase-level code-mixing to switch to a set of languages to perform adversarial training for XNLI. Code-switching and other data augmentation techniques have been applied to the pre-training stage in recent works (Chaudhary et al., 2020; Kale and Siddhant, 2021; Dufter and Schütze, 2020). However, *pre-training* is outside the scope of this work. In addition to studying cross-lingual slot filling and language families, another key distinction of our method is that we completely ignore the target language during training to represent a fully zero-shot scenario. The main advantage is that with enhanced cross-lingual generalizability, it can be deployed out-of-the-box, as our training is conducted independently of the target language.

## 7 Conclusion & Future Work

Our study shows that augmenting the monolingual input data with multilingual code-switching via random translations at the chunk-level helps a zero-shot model to be language neutral when evaluated on unseen languages. This approach enhanced the generalizability of pre-trained language models such as mBERT when *fine-tuning* for downstream tasks of intent detection and slot filling. Additionally, we presented an application of this method using a new annotated dataset of disaster tweets. Further, we studied code-switching with language families and their impact on specific target languages. Addressing code-switching with language families during the pre-training phase and releasing a larger dataset of annotated disaster tweets in more languages are planned for future work.

## 8 Ethical Considerations

The tweet dataset that we constructed for disaster NLU was originally released by Appen[6], and we use it to construct slot labels in two languages: English (en) and Haitian Creole (ht). Data statement that includes annotator guidelines for the labeling jobs and other dataset information will be provided with the implementation. From a broader impact perspective, our code and developed models are open-source and allows NLP technology to be accessible to information systems for emergency services and social scientists in quickly deploying model during disaster events.

[6] https://appen.com/datasets/combined-disaster-response-data/


## Acknowledgements

This work was partially supported by U.S. National Science Foundation grants IIS-1815459, IIS-1657379, and 2040926. This work was also supported in part by the grant H-4Q21-009 from the Commonwealth Cyber Initiative, an investment in the advancement of cyber R&D, innovation, and workforce development (for more information about CCI, visit www.cyberinitiative.org). The authors are thankful to Ming Sun and Alexis Conneau for giving valuable insights on multilingual model training, as well as to the anonymous reviewers for their constructive feedback. We also acknowledge ARGO, a research computing cluster provided by the Office of Research Computing at George Mason University, were most experiments were conducted.


## References


Gustavo Aguilar and Thamar Solorio. 2019. From english to code-switching: Transfer learning with strong morphological clues. *arXiv preprint arXiv:1909.05158*.

Kelsey Ball and Dan Garrette. 2018. Part-of-speech tagging for code-switched, transliterated texts without explicit language identification. In *Proceedings of the 2018 Conference on Empirical Methods in Natural Language Processing*, pages 3084–3089.

Piotr Bojanowski, Edouard Grave, Armand Joulin, and Tomas Mikolov. 2017. Enriching word vectors with subword information. *Transactions of the Association for Computational Linguistics*, 5:135–146.

Aditi Chaudhary, Karthik Raman, Krishna Srinivasan, and Jiecao Chen. 2020. Dict-mlm: Improved multilingual pre-training using bilingual dictionaries. *arXiv preprint arXiv:2010.12566*.

Qian Chen, Zhu Zhuo, and Wen Wang. 2019. Bert for joint intent classification and slot filling. *arXiv preprint arXiv:1902.10909*.

Xilun Chen, Yu Sun, Ben Athiwaratkun, Claire Cardie, and Kilian Weinberger. 2018. Adversarial deep averaging networks for cross-lingual sentiment classification. *Transactions of the Association for Computational Linguistics*, 6:557–570.

Alexis Conneau, Kartikay Khandelwal, Naman Goyal, Vishrav Chaudhary, Guillaume Wenzek, Francisco Guzmán, Edouard Grave, Myle Ott, Luke Zettlemoyer, and Veselin Stoyanov. 2020a. Unsupervised cross lingual representation learning at scale. *arXiv preprint arXiv:1911.02116*.

Alexis Conneau, Guillaume Lample, Marc'Aurelio Ranzato, Ludovic Denoyer, and Hervé Jégou. 2017.

Word translation without parallel data. *arXiv preprint arXiv:1710.04087.*

Alexis Conneau, Guillaume Lample, Ruty Rinott, Adina Williams, Samuel R Bowman, Holger Schwenk, and Veselin Stoyanov. 2018. Xnli: Evaluating cross-lingual sentence representations. *arXiv preprint arXiv:1809.05053.*

Alexis Conneau, Shijie Wu, Haoran Li, Luke Zettlemoyer, and Veselin Stoyanov. 2020b. Emerging cross-lingual structure in pretrained language models. In *Proceedings of the 58th Annual Meeting of the Association for Computational Linguistics*, pages 6022–6034, Online. Association for Computational Linguistics.

Alice Coucke, Alaa Saade, Adrien Ball, Théodore Bluche, Alexandre Caulier, David Leroy, Clément Doumouro, Thibault Gisselbrecht, Francesco Caltagirone, Thibaut Lavril, et al. 2018. Snips voice platform: an embedded spoken language understanding system for private-by-design voice interfaces. *arXiv preprint arXiv:1805.10190.*

Jacob Devlin, Ming-Wei Chang, Kenton Lee, and Kristina Toutanova. 2019. Bert: Pre-training of deep bidirectional transformers for language understanding. In *Proceedings of the 2019 Conference of the North American Chapter of the Association for Computational Linguistics: Human Language Technologies, Volume 1 (Long and Short Papers)*, pages 4171–4186.

Philipp Dufter and Hinrich Schütze. 2020. Identifying elements essential for bert's multilinguality. In *Proceedings of the 2020 Conference on Empirical Methods in Natural Language Processing (EMNLP)*, pages 4423–4437.

Chris Dyer, Victor Chahuneau, and Noah A Smith. 2013. A simple, fast, and effective reparameterization of ibm model 2. In *Proceedings of the 2013 Conference of the North American Chapter of the Association for Computational Linguistics: Human Language Technologies*, pages 644–648.

William Denis Elcock and John N Green. 1960. *The romance languages*. Faber & Faber London.

Akiko Eriguchi, Melvin Johnson, Orhan Firat, Hideto Kazawa, and Wolfgang Macherey. 2018. Zero-shot cross-lingual classification using multilingual neural machine translation. *arXiv preprint arXiv:1809.04686.*

Jack GM FitzGerald. 2020. Stil–simultaneous slot filling, translation, intent classification, and language identification: Initial results using mbart on multi-atis++. *arXiv preprint arXiv:2010.00760.*

Yaroslav Ganin, Evgeniya Ustinova, Hana Ajakan, Pascal Germain, Hugo Larochelle, François Laviolette, Mario Marchand, and Victor Lempitsky. 2016. Domain-adversarial training of neural networks. *The Journal of Machine Learning Research*, 17(1):2096–2030.

Chih-Wen Goo, Guang Gao, Yun-Kai Hsu, Chih-Li Huo, Tsung-Chieh Chen, Keng-Wei Hsu, and Yun-Nung Chen. 2018. Slot-gated modeling for joint slot filling and intent prediction. In *Proceedings of the 2018 Conference of the North American Chapter of the Association for Computational Linguistics: Human Language Technologies, Volume 2 (Short Papers)*, pages 753–757.

E Haihong, Peiqing Niu, Zhongfu Chen, and Meina Song. 2019. A novel bi-directional interrelated model for joint intent detection and slot filling. In *Proceedings of the 57th Annual Meeting of the Association for Computational Linguistics*, pages 5467–5471.

Wayne Harbert. 2006. *The Germanic Languages*. Cambridge University Press.

Momchil Hardalov, Ivan Koychev, and Preslav Nakov. 2020. Enriched pre-trained transformers for joint slot filling and intent detection. *arXiv preprint arXiv:2004.14848.*

Xiaodong He, Li Deng, Dilek Hakkani-Tur, and Gokhan Tur. 2013. Multi-style adaptive training for robust cross-lingual spoken language understanding. In *2013 IEEE International Conference on Acoustics, Speech and Signal Processing*, pages 8342–8346. IEEE.

Zhengbao Jiang, Antonios Anastasopoulos, Jun Araki, Haibo Ding, and Graham Neubig. 2020. Multilingual factual knowledge retrieval from pretrained language models. *arXiv preprint arXiv:2010.06189.*

Lars Johanson and Éva Ágnes Csató Johanson. 2015. *The Turkic Languages*. Routledge.

Aditya Joshi, Ameya Prabhu, Manish Shrivastava, and Vasudeva Varma. 2016. Towards sub-word level compositions for sentiment analysis of hindi-english code mixed text. In *Proceedings of COLING 2016, the 26th International Conference on Computational Linguistics: Technical Papers*, pages 2482–2491.

Mihir Kale and Aditya Siddhant. 2021. Mixout: A simple yet effective data augmentation scheme for slot-filling. In *Conversational Dialogue Systems for the Next Decade*, pages 279–288. Springer.

Ashiqur R KhudaBukhsh, Shriphani Palakodety, and Jaime G Carbonell. 2020. Harnessing code switching to transcend the linguistic barrier. *arXiv preprint arXiv:2001.11258.*

Diederik P Kingma and Jimmy Ba. 2014. Adam: A method for stochastic optimization. *arXiv preprint arXiv:1412.6980.*

Jitin Krishnan, Hemant Purohit, and Huzefa Rangwala. 2020. Unsupervised and interpretable domain adaptation to rapidly filter social web data for emergency services. In *ASONAM.*

Bing Liu and Ian Lane. 2016. Attention-based recurrent neural network models for joint intent detection and slot filling. *arXiv preprint arXiv:1609.01454*.

Manuel Mager, Özlem Çetinoğlu, and Katharina Kann. 2019. Subword-level language identification for intra-word code-switching. In *Proceedings of the 2019 Conference of the North American Chapter of the Association for Computational Linguistics: Human Language Technologies, Volume 1 (Long and Short Papers)*, pages 2005–2011.

Colin P Masica. 1993. *The indo-aryan languages*. Cambridge University Press.

Deepthi Mave, Suraj Maharjan, and Thamar Solorio. 2018. Language identification and analysis of code-switched social media text. In *Proceedings of the Third Workshop on Computational Approaches to Linguistic Code-Switching*, pages 51–61.

Roy Andrew Miller. 1967. *The Japanese Language*. University of Chicago Press Chicago.

Aldrian Obaja Muis, Naoki Otani, Nidhi Vyas, Ruochen Xu, Yiming Yang, Teruko Mitamura, and Eduard Hovy. 2018. Low-resource cross-lingual event type detection via distant supervision with minimal effort. In *Proceedings of the 27th International Conference on Computational Linguistics*, pages 70–82.

Dat Tien Nguyen, Kamla Al-Mannai, Shafiq R Joty, Hassan Sajjad, Muhammad Imran, and Prasenjit Mitra. 2017. Robust classification of crisis-related data on social networks using convolutional neural networks. *ICWSM*, 31(3):632–635.

Jian Ni, Georgiana Dinu, and Radu Florian. 2017. Weakly supervised cross-lingual named entity recognition via effective annotation and representation projection. In *Proceedings of the 55th Annual Meeting of the Association for Computational Linguistics (Volume 1: Long Papers)*, pages 1470–1480.

Endang Wahyu Pamungkas and Viviana Patti. 2019. Cross-domain and cross-lingual abusive language detection: A hybrid approach with deep learning and a multilingual lexicon. In *Proceedings of the 57th Annual Meeting of the Association for Computational Linguistics: Student Research Workshop*, pages 363–370.

Adam Paszke, Sam Gross, Francisco Massa, Adam Lerer, James Bradbury, Gregory Chanan, Trevor Killeen, Zeming Lin, Natalia Gimelshein, Luca Antiga, Alban Desmaison, Andreas Kopf, Edward Yang, Zachary DeVito, Martin Raison, Alykhan Tejani, Sasank Chilamkurthy, Benoit Steiner, Lu Fang, Junjie Bai, and Soumith Chintala. 2019. Pytorch: An imperative style, high-performance deep learning library. In H. Wallach, H. Larochelle, A. Beygelzimer, F. d'Alché-Buc, E. Fox, and R. Garnett, editors, *Advances in Neural Information Processing Systems 32*, pages 8024–8035. Curran Associates, Inc.

Telmo Pires, Eva Schlinger, and Dan Garrette. 2019. How multilingual is multilingual bert? In *Proceedings of the 57th Annual Meeting of the Association for Computational Linguistics*, pages 4996–5001.

Barbara Plank and Željko Agić. 2018. Distant supervision from disparate sources for low-resource part-of-speech tagging. In *Proceedings of the 2018 Conference on Empirical Methods in Natural Language Processing*, pages 614–620.

Patti Price. 1990. Evaluation of spoken language systems: The atis domain. In *Speech and Natural Language: Proceedings of a Workshop Held at Hidden Valley, Pennsylvania, June 24-27, 1990*.

Libo Qin, Minheng Ni, Yue Zhang, and Wanxiang Che. 2020. Cosda-ml: Multi-lingual code-switching data augmentation for zero-shot cross-lingual nlp. *arXiv preprint arXiv:2006.06402*.

Lance A Ramshaw and Mitchell P Marcus. 1999. Text chunking using transformation-based learning. In *Natural language processing using very large corpora*, pages 157–176. Springer.

Bernardino Romera-Paredes and Philip Torr. 2015. An embarrassingly simple approach to zero-shot learning. In *International Conference on Machine Learning*, pages 2152–2161.

Bruce Rowe and Diane Levine. 2017. A concise introduction to linguistics. *Routledge. pp. 340–341*.

Sebastian Schuster, Sonal Gupta, Rushin Shah, and Mike Lewis. 2019. Cross-lingual transfer learning for multilingual task oriented dialog. In *Proceedings of the 2019 Conference of the North American Chapter of the Association for Computational Linguistics: Human Language Technologies, Volume 1 (Long and Short Papers)*, pages 3795–3805.

Robert Shafer. 1955. Classification of the sino-tibetan languages. *Word*, 11(1):94–111.

Rushin Shah, Bo Lin, Anatole Gershman, and Robert Frederking. 2010. Synergy: a named entity recognition system for resource-scarce languages such as swahili using online machine translation. In *Proceedings of the Second Workshop on African Language Technology (AfLaT 2010)*, pages 21–26.

Victor Soto and Julia Hirschberg. 2018. Joint part-of-speech and language id tagging for code-switched data. In *Proceedings of the Third Workshop on Computational Approaches to Linguistic Code-Switching*, pages 1–10.

Shashank Srivastava, Igor Labutov, and Tom Mitchell. 2018. Zero-shot learning of classifiers from natural language quantification. In *Proceedings of the 56th Annual Meeting of the Association for Computational Linguistics (Volume 1: Long Papers)*, pages 306–316.

Lukas Stappen, Fabian Brunn, and Björn Schuller. 2020. Cross-lingual zero-and few-shot hate speech detection utilising frozen transformer language models and axel. *arXiv preprint arXiv:2004.13850*.

Oscar Täckström, Dipanjan Das, Slav Petrov, Ryan McDonald, and Joakim Nivre. 2013. Token and type constraints for cross-lingual part-of-speech tagging. *Transactions of the Association for Computational Linguistics*, 1:1–12.

Samson Tan and Shafiq Joty. 2021. Code-mixing on sesame street: Dawn of the adversarial polyglots. *arXiv preprint arXiv:2103.09593*.

Chen-Tse Tsai, Stephen Mayhew, and Dan Roth. 2016. Cross-lingual named entity recognition via wikification. In *Proceedings of The 20th SIGNLL Conference on Computational Natural Language Learning*, pages 219–228.

Shyam Upadhyay, Manaal Faruqui, Gokhan Tür, Hakkani-Tür Dilek, and Larry Heck. 2018. (almost) zero-shot cross-lingual spoken language understanding. In *2018 IEEE International Conference on Acoustics, Speech and Signal Processing (ICASSP)*, pages 6034–6038. IEEE.

Charles Frederick Voegelin and Florence Marie Voegelin. 1976. Classification and index of the world's languages.

Xiaojun Wan. 2009. Co-training for cross-lingual sentiment classification. In *Proceedings of the Joint Conference of the 47th Annual Meeting of the ACL and the 4th International Joint Conference on Natural Language Processing of the AFNLP*, pages 235–243.

Thomas Wolf, Julien Chaumond, Lysandre Debut, Victor Sanh, Clement Delangue, Anthony Moi, Pierric Cistac, Morgan Funtowicz, Joe Davison, Sam Shleifer, et al. 2020. Transformers: State-of-the-art natural language processing. In *Proceedings of the 2020 Conference on Empirical Methods in Natural Language Processing: System Demonstrations*, pages 38–45.

Yonghui Wu, Mike Schuster, Zhifeng Chen, Quoc V Le, Mohammad Norouzi, Wolfgang Macherey, Maxim Krikun, Yuan Cao, Qin Gao, Klaus Macherey, et al. 2016. Google's neural machine translation system: Bridging the gap between human and machine translation. *arXiv preprint arXiv:1609.08144*.

Mengzhou Xia, Antonios Anastasopoulos, Ruochen Xu, Yiming Yang, and Graham Neubig. 2020. Predicting performance for natural language processing tasks. In *Proceedings of the 58th Annual Meeting of the Association for Computational Linguistics*, pages 8625–8646, Online. Association for Computational Linguistics.

Yongqin Xian, Bernt Schiele, and Zeynep Akata. 2017. Zero-shot learning-the good, the bad and the ugly. In *Proceedings of the IEEE Conference on Computer Vision and Pattern Recognition*, pages 4582–4591.

Jiateng Xie, Zhilin Yang, Graham Neubig, Noah A Smith, and Jaime G Carbonell. 2018. Neural cross-lingual named entity recognition with minimal resources. In *Proceedings of the 2018 Conference on Empirical Methods in Natural Language Processing*, pages 369–379.

Weijia Xu, Batool Haider, and Saab Mansour. 2020. End-to-end slot alignment and recognition for cross-lingual nlu. In *Proceedings of the 2020 Conference on Empirical Methods in Natural Language Processing (EMNLP)*, pages 5052–5063.

Jian Yang, Shuming Ma, Dongdong Zhang, ShuangZhi Wu, Zhoujun Li, and Ming Zhou. 2020. Alternating language modeling for cross-lingual pre-training. In *Proceedings of the AAAI Conference on Artificial Intelligence*, volume 34, pages 9386–9393.

David Yarowsky, Grace Ngai, and Richard Wicentowski. 2001. Inducing multilingual text analysis tools via robust projection across aligned corpora. Technical report, Johns Hopkins Univ Baltimore MD Dept of Computer Science.

Zeynep Yirmibeşoğlu and Gülşen Eryiğit. 2018. Detecting code-switching between turkish-english language pair. In *Proceedings of the 2018 EMNLP Workshop W-NUT: The 4th Workshop on Noisy User-generated Text*, pages 110–115.

Katherine Yu, Haoran Li, and Barlas Oguz. 2018. Multilingual seq2seq training with similarity loss for cross-lingual document classification. In *Proceedings of The Third Workshop on Representation Learning for NLP*, pages 175–179.

Ayah Zirikly and Masato Hagiwara. 2015. Cross-lingual transfer of named entity recognizers without parallel corpora. In *Proceedings of the 53rd Annual Meeting of the Association for Computational Linguistics and the 7th International Joint Conference on Natural Language Processing (Volume 2: Short Papers)*, pages 390–396.

## A mBERT versus XLM-R

We conduct an additional analysis on XLM-R (Conneau et al., 2020a) and compare it with mBERT (Devlin et al., 2019). The implementation is very similar in PyTorch (Paszke et al., 2019) but using the pre-trained *xlm-roberta-base* with *RobertaForSequenceClassification* (Wolf et al., 2020) as the XLM-R model. We observe that, setting $k = 5$, XLM-R outperforms mBERT on average (by 2% Intent Accuracy and 1.5% Slot F1). Individually, XLM-R improved Chinese, Japanese, Portuguese, and Turkish for Intent Prediction and German, Chinese, Japanese, Portuguese, and Hindi for Slot Filling as shown in Figure 7. We observe a trend similar to mBERT with $k$ on XLM-R shown in Figure 8. However, for XLM-R, we observe that randomized code-switching did not help Chinese for Intent Prediction and Hindi for Slot F1. If code-switched to a specific language family, instead of switching to random languages, it might improve their performance. A deeper dive into XLM-R and language families are left for future work.

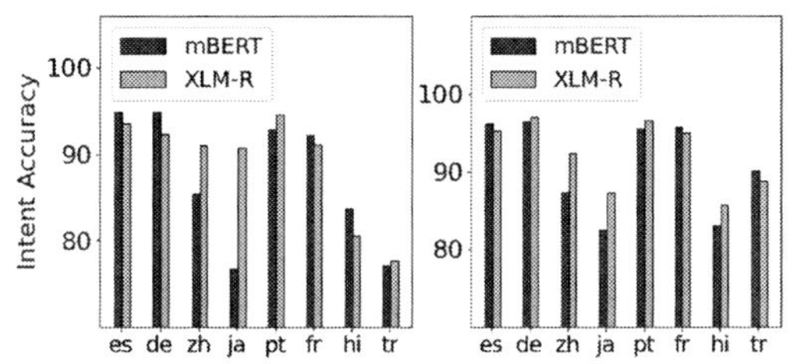


Figure 7: mBERT vs XLM-R: Performance

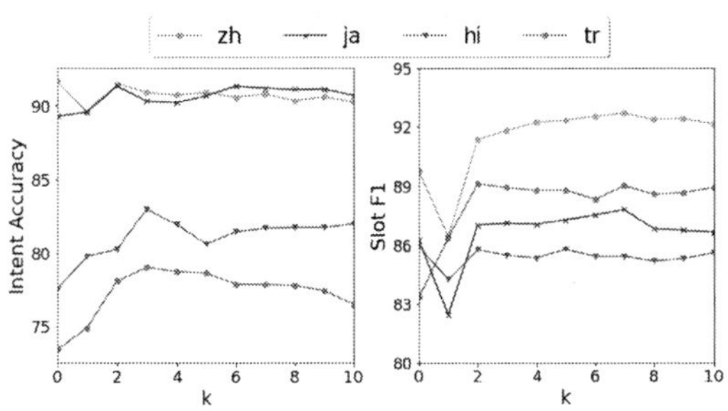


Figure 8: Performance as $k$ increases (on XLM-R).

## B Hyperparameter Tuning & Runtime

For joint training with same task weights, we tuned $\alpha$ and $\beta$ using grid search to see the strength of correlation between the tasks. For intent, the $(\alpha, \beta)$ combination of $(1.0, 0.6)$ performed well, while $(1.0, 1.0)$ for slots. This suggests that intent benefiting slot might be slightly more than slot benefiting intent. Additionally, during fine-tuning, freezing the layers of the transformer affected the model performance as shown in Figure 9. Keeping the first 8 layers frozen gave the best performance. By freezing the earlier layers, the transformer can retain its most fundamental feature information gained from the massive pre-training step, and by unfreezing some top layers, it can undergo fine-tuning. Additionally, latency for training a code-switched model is shown in Table 5 and how runtime varies with an increase in $k$ is shown in Figure 10.

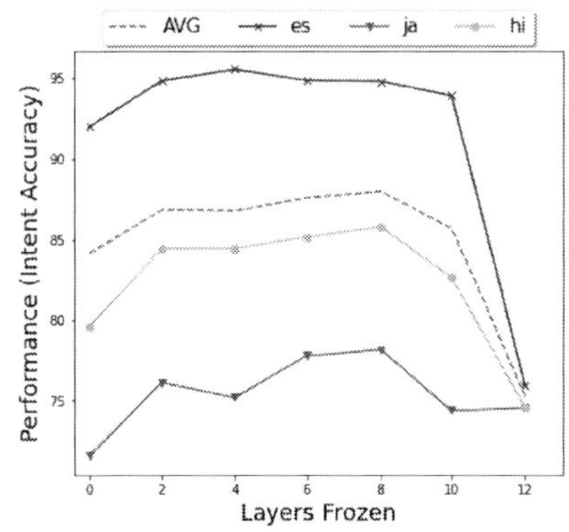


Figure 9: Freezing earlier layers and unfreezing a few at the top of the transformer appear to be most optimal.

| CS (k=5) | MTT | $\text{Joint}_{\text{en}}$ | $\text{Joint}_{\text{cs}}$ | $\text{Joint}_{\text{TT}}$ |
|---|---|---|---|---|
| 05:04:49 | 1:31:32 | 00:11:50 | 01:06:50 | 00:11:04 |

Table 5: Runtime on Google Colab (K80 GPU for training joint models). $MTT$: Machine Translation to Target. Note that $MTT$ and $J_{TT}$ are for one target language (averaged).

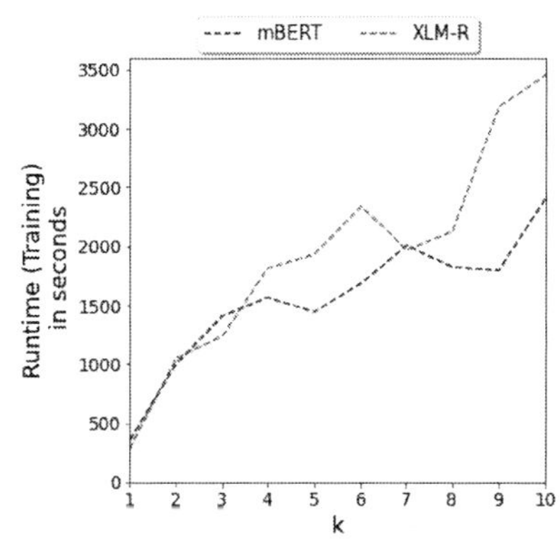


Figure 10: Training runtime as $k$ increases.

# Analysis of Zero-Shot Crosslingual Learning between English and Korean for Named Entity Recognition

♠Jongin Kim, ♠Nayoung Choi, ◇Seunghyun S. Lim, ♠Jungwhan Kim
♠Soojin Chung, ♠Hyunsoo Woo, ♣Min Song, ◇Jinho D. Choi
♠Department of Digital Analytics, Yonsei University, Seoul, South Korea
♣Department of Library and Information Science, Yonsei University, Seoul, South Korea
◇Department of Computer Science, Emory University, Atlanta, GA, USA
♠{jongin.kim, skdudenql11, jngwhnk, socheon, wkat}@yonsei.ac.kr
♣min.song@yonsei.ac.kr, ◇{slim72, jinho.choi}@emory.edu

## Abstract

This paper presents a English-Korean parallel dataset that collects 381K news articles where 1,400 of them, comprising 10K sentences, are manually labeled for crosslingual named entity recognition (NER). The annotation guidelines for the two languages are developed in parallel, that yield the inter-annotator agreement scores of 91 and 88% for English and Korean respectively, indicating sublime quality annotation in our dataset. Three types of crosslingual learning approaches, direct model transfer, embedding projection, and annotation projection, are used to develop zero-shot Korean NER models. Our best model gives the F1-score of *51%* that is very encouraging, considering the extremely distinct natures of these two languages. This is pioneering work that explores zero-shot crosslingual learning between English and Korean and provides rich parallel annotation for a core NLP task such as named entity recognition.

## 1 Introduction

Crosslingual representation learning aims to derive embeddings for words (or sentences) from multiple languages that can be projected into a shared vector space (Conneau et al., 2018; Schuster et al., 2019b; Conneau and Lample, 2019). One important application of crosslingual embeddings has been found for transferring models trained on a high-resource language to a low-resource one (Lin et al., 2019; Schuster et al., 2019a; Artetxe and Schwenk, 2019). The latest multilingual transformer encoders such as BERT (Devlin et al., 2019) and XLM (Conneau et al., 2020) have made it possible to develop robust crosslingual models through zero-shot learning that requires no labeled training data on the target side (Jebbara and Cimiano, 2019; Chidambaram et al., 2019; Chi et al., 2020). However, these approaches tend not to work as well for languages whose words cannot be easily aligned.

Our team is motivated to create a rich crosslingual resource between English and Korean, which are largely different in nature as English is known to be rigid-order, morphologically-poor, and head-initial whereas Korean is flexible-order, morphologically-rich, and head-final (Choi et al., 1994; Han et al., 2002; Hong, 2009). Creation of a high quality parallel dataset to facilitate crosslingual research can reduce the gap between these two languages, and advance NLP techniques in both languages.

This paper provides a comprehensive analysis of crosslingual zero-shot learning in English and Korean. We first create a new dataset comprising a large number of parallel sentences and annotate them for named entity recognition (NER; Sec. 3). We then adapt the crosslingual approaches and build NER models in Korean through zero-shot learning (Sec. 4). All models are experimented on our dataset and thoroughly compared to evaluate the feasibility of this work (Sec. 5). Our results are promising although depicting few challenges in zero-shot learning for English and Korean (Sec. 6). The contributions of this work can be summarized as follows:

- To create a crosslingual dataset that enables to develop robust zero-shot NER models in Korean.
- To present a new data selection scheme that can notably improve zero-shot model performance.
- To provide a comparative analysis among several crosslingual approaches and establish the initial foundation of this research.

## 2 Related Work

For crosslingual representation alignment, Artetxe et al. (2016) and Smith et al. (2017) suggested orthogonality constraints on the embedding transformation that led to better quality translation. Aldarmaki and Diab (2019) derived a context-aware crosslingual mapping from a parallel corpus using word alignment. Schuster et al. (2019b) aligned



*Proceedings of the 1st Workshop on Multilingual Representation Learning*, pages 224–237
November 11, 2021. ©2021 Association for Computational Linguistics

|  | Business | Lifestyle | Politics | Sci/Tech | Society | Sports | World | Regional | Others | Total |
|---|---|---|---|---|---|---|---|---|---|---|
| TRN | 109,464 | 132,606 | 92,877 | 55,420 | 164,414 | 52,214 | 70,487 | 57,490 | 12,881 | 747,853 |
| DEV | 666 | 733 | 728 | 718 | 711 | 715 | 763 | - | - | 5,034 |
| TST | 676 | 709 | 687 | 680 | 686 | 650 | 722 | - | - | 4,810 |
| Total | 110,806 | 134,048 | 94,292 | 56,818 | 165,811 | 53,579 | 71,972 | 57,490 | 12,881 | 757,697 |

(a) The number of parallel sentences by each category.

|  | Business | Lifestyle | Politics | Sci/Tech | Society | Sports | World | Regional | Others | Total |
|---|---|---|---|---|---|---|---|---|---|---|
| TRN | 65,901 | 63,131 | 41,233 | 27,924 | 76,450 | 34,662 | 29,765 | 34,510 | 6,197 | 379,773 |
| DEV | 100 | 100 | 100 | 100 | 100 | 100 | 100 | - | - | 700 |
| TST | 100 | 100 | 100 | 100 | 100 | 100 | 100 | - | - | 700 |
| Total | 66,101 | 63,331 | 41,433 | 28,124 | 76,650 | 34,862 | 29,965 | 34,510 | 6,197 | 381,173 |

(b) The number of parallel news articles by each category.

Table 1: The statistics of our English-Korean dataset. TRN/DEV/TST: the training/development/evaluation sets.

word embeddings from multilingual transformer encoders using context independent embedding anchors. Recent works based on multilingual pretrained language model aligns representations between languages in a unsupervised fashion. Devlin et al. (2019) proposed multilingual BERT that generates contextualized word embeddings for multiple languages in one vector space by simply sharing all languages' vocabulary. Conneau and Lample (2019) extends mBERT by introducing bilingual data and an extra pretraining task (Translation Language Modeling). Luo et al. (2021) adds a cross-attention module into the Transformer encoder to explicitly build the interdependence between languages.

For cross-lingual NER, Ni et al. (2017) presented weakly supervised crosslingual models using annotation and representation projection. Huang et al. (2019) made an empirical analysis of how sequential order and multilingual embeddings are used in crosslingual NER. Artetxe and Schwenk (2019) presented multilingual transfer models that used few-shot learning adapting supervising BEA, ranking and retraining for massive transfer. Wu and Dredze (2019) and Wu et al. (2020) directly transfers the NER model trained on the source language to the target language using crosslingual representations from multilingual encoders (Direct model transfer).

## 3 English-Korean Crosslingual Dataset

### 3.1 Data Collection

AI Open Innovation Hub (AI Hub) is an integration platform operated by the Korea National Information Society Agency that provides data, software, and computing resources for AI research. It has released the Korean-English AI Training Text Corpus (KEAT)[1] containing 1.6M English-Korean parallel sentences from various sources such as news media, government website/journal, law & administration, conversation and etc. For the present study, 800K parallel sentences from the news portion of this corpus are extracted.

### 3.2 Data Preprocessing

Since KEAT is not organized into documents, each sentence is composed independently although it comes with the URL of its original source. Thus, we group all sentences into news articles based on the URLs. Although there exist news articles with single sentence after the grouping process, we still include them in the train set in order to make full use of the parallel sentences provided, which will be used to train the word alignment model and the transformation matrix in Section 5. As a result, 757,697 sentences are selected, that are composed into 381,173 news articles, to create our English-Korean crosslingual dataset.

The news articles can be categorized into 9 sections: *Business*, *Lifestyle*, *Science/Technology*, *Society*, *Sports*, *World*, *Regional*, and *Others*. Among those, 200 articles are randomly sampled from each of the first 7 categories for our annotation in Section 3.4 and they are split into 50/50 to create the development and test sets for our experiments in Section 5. Table 1 describes the statistics of our dataset. All sections are uniformly distributed in DEV and TST, enabling to conduct comparative studies among these sections.

### 3.3 Pseudo Annotation

English sentences are tokenized and tagged with named entities by the open-source NLP tool called

[1] http://www.aihub.or.kr/aidata/87

| | $\texttt{CARDNIAL}_e$ | $\texttt{DATE}_e$ | $\texttt{EVENT}_e$ | $\texttt{FAC}_e$ | $\texttt{GPE}_e$ | $\texttt{LANGUAGE}_e$ | $\texttt{LAW}_e$ | $\texttt{LOC}_e$ | $\texttt{MONEY}_e$ |
|---|---|---|---|---|---|---|---|---|---|
| TRN | 207,618 (10.6) | 281,936 (14.5) | 29,548 (1.5) | 39,579 (2.0) | 315,014 (16.2) | 3,050 (0.2) | 11,821 (0.6) | 27,865 (1.4) | 26,751 (1.4) |
| DEV | 1,314 (11.6) | 1,534 (13.6) | 139 (1.2) | 146 (1.3) | 1,845 (16.3) | 21 (0.2) | 32 (0.3) | 151 (1.3) | 123 (1.1) |
| TST | 1,220 (11.1) | 1,552 (14.1) | 155 (1.4) | 151 (1.4) | 1,751 (15.9) | 29 (0.3) | 50 (0.5) | 154 (1.4) | 136 (1.2) |
| Total | 210,152 (10.7) | 285,022 (14.5) | 29,842 (1.5) | 39,876 (2.0) | 318,610 (16.2) | 3,100 (0.2) | 11,903 (0.6) | 28,170 (1.4) | 27,010 (1.4) |

| | $\texttt{NORP}_e$ | $\texttt{ORDINAL}_e$ | $\texttt{ORG}_e$ | $\texttt{PERCENT}_e$ | $\texttt{PERSON}_e$ | $\texttt{PRODUCT}_e$ | $\texttt{QUANTITY}_e$ | $\texttt{TIME}_e$ | $\texttt{WOA}_e$ |
|---|---|---|---|---|---|---|---|---|---|
| TRN | 68,700 (3.5) | 82,270 (4.2) | 394,226 (20.2) | 8,339 (0.4) | 352,918 (18.1) | 12,170 (0.6) | 16,736 (0.9) | 37,003 (1.9) | 35,193 (1.8) |
| DEV | 503 (4.4) | 517 (4.6) | 2,286 (20.2) | 61 (0.5) | 2,168 (19.2) | 70 (0.6) | 62 (0.6) | 148 (1.3) | 203 (1.8) |
| TST | 513 (4.7) | 443 (4.0) | 2,264 (20.6) | 52 (0.5) | 2,049 (18.6) | 91 (0.8) | 47 (0.4) | 156 (1.4) | 205 (1.9) |
| Total | 69,716 (3.5) | 83,230 (4.2) | 398,776 (20.2) | 8,452 (0.4) | 357,135 (18.1) | 12,331 (0.6) | 16,845 (0.9) | 37,307 (1.9) | 35,601 (1.8) |

(a) The number of pseudo-annotated named entities in the English sentences. WOA: WORK_OF_ART.

| | $\texttt{DAT}_k$ | $\texttt{DUR}_k$ | $\texttt{LOC}_k$ | $\texttt{MNY}_k$ | $\texttt{NOH}_k$ | $\texttt{ORG}_k$ | $\texttt{PER}_k$ | $\texttt{PNT}_k$ | $\texttt{POH}_k$ | $\texttt{TIM}_k$ |
|---|---|---|---|---|---|---|---|---|---|---|
| TRN | 156,013 (9.0) | 41,651 (2.4) | 235,179 (13.6) | 37,538 (2.2) | 285,898 (16.5) | 478,830 (27.6) | 312,578 (18.0) | 37,767 (2.2) | 136,731 (7.9) | 12,894 (0.7) |
| DEV | 752 (7.4) | 267 (2.6) | 959 (9.5) | 159 (1.6) | 1,807 (17.9) | 3,231 (32.0) | 1,909 (18.9) | 220 (2.2) | 748 (7.4) | 49 (0.5) |
| TST | 741 (7.5) | 257 (2.6) | 947 (9.6) | 174 (1.8) | 1,626 (16.5) | 3,142 (31.9) | 1,818 (18.5) | 249 (2.5) | 850 (8.6) | 40 (0.4) |
| Total | 157,506 (9.0) | 42,175 (2.4) | 237,085 (13.5) | 37,871 (2.2) | 289,331 (16.5) | 485,203 (27.6) | 316,305 (18.0) | 38,236 (2.2) | 138,329 (7.9) | 12,983 (0.7) |

(b) The number of pseudo-annotated named entities in the Korean sentences.

Table 2: The statistics of pseudo-annotated named entities by each tag in our English-Korean dataset. The numbers in the parentheses indicate the percentages of the corresponding tags for each set.

| | CARDNIAL | DATE | EVENT | FAC | GPE | LANGUAGE | LAW | LOC | MONEY |
|---|---|---|---|---|---|---|---|---|---|
| EN | 1,235 (10.9) | 1,496 (13.2) | 190 (1.7) | 160 (1.4) | 1,755 (15.5) | 25 (0.2) | 39 (0.3) | 150 (1.3) | 156 (1.4) |
| KR | 1,359 (12.3) | 1,381 (12.5) | 186 (1.7) | 158 (1.4) | 1,674 (15.1) | 21 (0.2) | 39 (0.4) | 141 (1.3) | 159 (1.4) |
| E ∩ K | 1,124 (10.9) | 1,324 (12.9) | 173 (1.7) | 154 (1.5) | 1,566 (15.2) | 21 (0.2) | 34 (0.3) | 135 (1.3) | 156 (1.5) |

| | NORP | ORDINAL | ORG | PERCENT | PERSON | PRODUCT | QUANTITY | TIME | WOA |
|---|---|---|---|---|---|---|---|---|---|
| EN | 625 (5.5) | 461 (4.1) | 2,217 (19.6) | 191 (1.7) | 2,118 (18.7) | 157 (1.4) | 65 (0.6) | 146 (1.3) | 147 (1.3) |
| KR | 540 (4.9) | 351 (3.2) | 2,249 (20.3) | 199 (1.8) | 2,129 (19.2) | 155 (1.4) | 67 (0.6) | 140 (1.3) | 142 (1.3) |
| E ∩ K | 529 (5.1) | 329 (3.2) | 2,042 (19.8) | 189 (1.8) | 2,048 (19.9) | 145 (1.4) | 65 (0.6) | 132 (1.3) | 131 (1.3) |

(a) Statistics of the development set (DEV).

| | CARDNIAL | DATE | EVENT | FAC | GPE | LANGUAGE | LAW | LOC | MONEY |
|---|---|---|---|---|---|---|---|---|---|
| EN | 1,117 (10.1) | 1,511 (13.7) | 207 (1.9) | 161 (1.5) | 1,701 (15.4) | 29 (0.3) | 57 (0.5) | 154 (1.4) | 165 (1.5) |
| KR | 1,253 (11.6) | 1,406 (13.0) | 205 (1.9) | 159 (1.5) | 1,635 (15.1) | 26 (0.2) | 52 (0.5) | 147 (1.4) | 172 (1.6) |
| E ∩ K | 1,018 (10.2) | 1,336 (13.4) | 196 (2.0) | 151 (1.5) | 1,517 (15.2) | 25 (0.3) | 51 (0.5) | 137 (1.4) | 164 (1.6) |

| | NORP | ORDINAL | ORG | PERCENT | PERSON | PRODUCT | QUANTITY | TIME | WOA |
|---|---|---|---|---|---|---|---|---|---|
| EN | 621 (5.6) | 397 (3.6) | 2,159 (19.6) | 215 (2.0) | 2,012 (18.2) | 172 (1.6) | 52 (0.5) | 148 (1.3) | 156 (1.4) |
| KR | 509 (4.7) | 287 (2.7) | 2,196 (20.3) | 223 (2.0) | 2,017 (18.7) | 176 (1.6) | 51 (0.5) | 133 (1.2) | 155 (1.4) |
| E ∩ K | 501 (5.0) | 274 (2.7) | 1,980 (19.8) | 214 (2.1) | 1,955 (19.5) | 161 (1.6) | 50 (0.5) | 132 (1.3) | 141 (1.4) |

(b) Statistics of the evaluation set (TST).

Table 3: The statistics of manually annotated named entities on the parallel sentences in the DEV and TST sets. The numbers in the parentheses indicate the percentages of the corresponding tags for each set. EN/KR: # of entities in the English/Korean sentences respectively, E ∩ K: # of entities existing in both English and Korean sentences.

ELIT[2] using the Flair model trained on OntoNotes (Pradhan et al., 2013). Korean sentences are tagged by a CRF-based model adapting KoBERT (Korean BERT)[3] trained on the corpus distributed by Cheon and Kim (2018). Note that the named entity types pseudo-annotated on the Korean sentences don't match with those of the English sentences for now, which will be matched in Section 3.4 in the case of DEV and TST. In addition, Korean sentences are processed by the Mecab morphological analyzer[4] that produces more linguistically sounding tokens than SentencePiece (Kudo and Richardson, 2018) in KoBERT. All named entities from the CRF tagger are then remapped to the tokens produced by the Mecab analyzer using heuristics so they can better reflect the previous morphology work in Korean (Hong, 2009). Words in every parallel sentence pair, tokenized by the ELIT and Mecab analyzers, are aligned by GIZA++, that has been adapted by many prior crosslingual studies (Och and Ney, 2003).

Table 2 shows the statistics of pseudo-annotated named entities in our dataset. The detailed descriptions of these tags are provided in Appendix A.1. The overall statistics are comparable between English and Korean, 2.5 and 2.3 entities per sentence, respectively. $\texttt{GPE}_e$, the 3rd most frequent tag in English, is not supported by the Korean tagger but

[2]https://github.com/emorynlp/elit
[3]https://github.com/eagle705/pytorch-bert-crf-ner
[4]https://bitbucket.org/eunjeon/mecab-ko/

rather tagged as $\texttt{ORG}_k$ or $\texttt{LOC}_k$, explaining why the numbers of these two tags in Korean are much greater than those of $\texttt{ORG}_e$ and $\texttt{LOC}_e$, respectively.

### 3.4 Parallel Annotation

We conduct a team of graduate students majoring in Data Science to manually tag named entities on all parallel sentences in the DEV and TST sets by taking the following 3 steps:[5]

1. For English, the pseudo-annotated entities are revised by the OntoNotes named entity guidelines (BBN, 2014; Maekawa, 2018), and missing entities are annotated as necessary.

2. For Korean, the pseudo-annotated entities are revised to match the English tagset, and missing entities are annotated as necessary.

3. Let $E = \{e_1, \ldots, e_n\}$ and $K = \{k_1, \ldots, k_m\}$ be the lists of entities from Steps 1 and 2 for a English and Korean sentence pair, respectively. Every entity pair $(e_i, k_j)$ is linked in our dataset if $e_i$ is the translation of $k_j$.

Note that every article in DEV and TST consists of at least 5 sentences with at least 2 named entities. Table 3 shows the statistics of the gold annotation. Out of 22,367 and 21,892 named entities annotated in English and Korean sentences, 20,300 of them are linked across the languages (above 90%).

| | English | Korean |
|---|---|---|
| Unlabeled | 92.7 | 90.4 |
| Labeled | 90.9 | 88.3 |

Table 4: Cohen's kappa scores measured for the English and Korean annotation. Unlabeled: matches only entity spans, Labeled: matches both the spans and the labels.

To estimate the inter-annotator agreement, 10 news articles from each of the first 7 sections in Table 1 are randomly picked and double annotated; the rest of DEV and TST are single annotated and sample checked. Table 4 shows the Cohen's kappa scores measured for the English and Korean annotation. The high labeled matching scores of 90.9 and 88.3 are achieved for those two languages respectively, implying that the single annotation in this dataset is expected to be of high quality as well.

### 3.5 Analytics by Languages

A couple of challenges are found during the parallel annotation. First, subjects are obligatory in English for most sentence forms whereas Korean is a pro-drop language so that entities in the subject position can be missing in Korean but not in English, which explains the greater number of entities in English. Second, certain inflectional morphemes in Korean can be dropped without violating the grammar, that often makes the labeling ambiguous. For instance, the literal translation of "*Korean Church*" would be "한국(Korea)+의('s) 교회(Church)", although it is the standard practice to drop "의('s)" in this case such that it becomes "한국(Korea) 교회(Church)". Given this translation, the annotator can be easily confused to annotate "한국(Korea)" as a geopolitical entity (GPE) instead of a nationality (NORP), which may lead to annotation disagreement.

Additional analytics by news sections and entity types are described in Appendix A.6

## 4 Zero-shot Crosslingual Learning

### 4.1 Overview of Approaches

Three crosslingual learning approaches are adapted to develop zero-shot Korean models. One is direct model transfer method following Wu and Dredze (2019). We reproduce the previous work which fine-tunes mBERT on English NER dataset and transfers the trained model to a target language, in our case, Korean. We fine-tune on OntoNotes, whereas the previous work fine-tuned on CoNLL 2003 NER dataset. The other two approaches that will be experimented are embedding preojection and annotation projection following Ni et al. (2017), although some modules in the implementation are updated or added: the encoders used to derive the embeddings from sentences, the word alignment tool, the training data selection scheme heuristics. Figure 1 illustrates an overview of two crosslingual learning approaches adapted to develop zero-shot Korean NER models. One is embedding projection (R1) that takes a labeled English sentence (R2) and generates English embeddings, (R3) which are fed into an orthogonal mapping (R4) then transformed into Korean embeddings (Section 4.2). The other is annotation projection (A1) that aligns words across the two languages and pseudo-annotates the Korean sentence, (A2) which are fed into an encoder (A3) to generate Korean embeddings (Section 4.3). The Korean embeddings generated by individual approaches are fed into a trainer to build the Korean NER models. No manual annotation is added to the Korean data; thus they both are zero-shot learning.

[5]The full annotation guidelines are available at https://github.com/emorynlp/MRL-2021

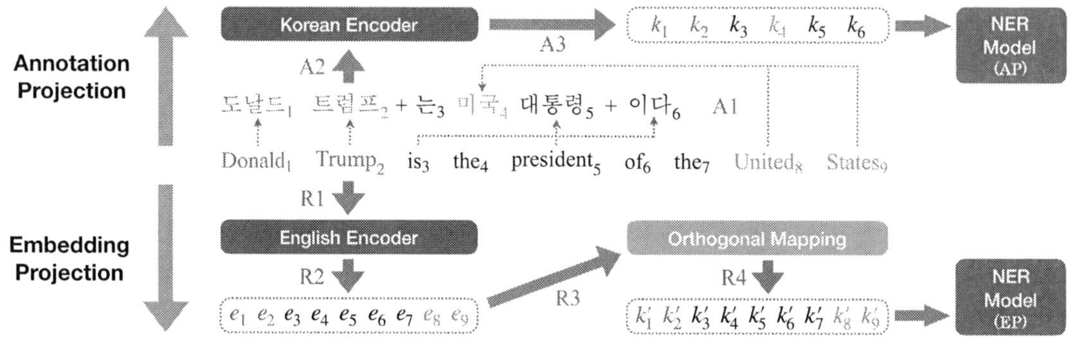


Figure 1: The overview of crosslingual methods, embedding projection (§4.2) and annotation projection (§4.3). The blue and red coded words and embeddings represent the PERSON and GPE entities, respectively. AP:Annotation Projection, EP:Embedding Projection

### 4.2 Embedding Projection

Let $X, Y \in \mathbb{R}^{n\times d}$ be parallel matrices between the source and target languages, where $n$ is the number of parallel terms (words or sentences) in those two languages. Let $x_i, y_i \in \mathbb{R}^{1\times d}$ be the $i$'th rows in $X$ and $Y$, which are the embeddings of the $i$'th terms in the source and target languages respectively, that refer to the same content. Then, the transformation matrix $W \in \mathbb{R}^{d\times d}$ can be found by minimizing the distance between $XW$ and $Y$ as follows:

$$\underset{W}{\text{argmin}} \|XW - Y\| \quad \text{s.t.} \quad W^T W = I$$

This optimization can be achieved by singular value decomposition as proposed by Artetxe et al. (2016), where $U, V \in \mathbb{R}^{d\times p}, \Sigma \in \mathbb{R}^{p\times p}$:

$$W = UV^T \quad \text{s.t.} \quad X^T Y = U\Sigma V^T$$

The transformation matrix $W$ is used to convert any English embedding $e_i$ into a Korean embedding $k'_i$ in Figure 1 such that $e_i \cdot W = k'_i \approx k_j$ where $k_j$ is the embedding from the Korean encoder that can be aligned with $e_i$. The NER model is trained on only English sentences represented by the transformed embeddings $k'_*$ and a pseudo-label annotated with an existing English NER model. During decoding, the model takes Korean sentences represented by the encoded embeddings $k_*$ and makes the predictions.

Given the latest contextualized encoders that generate different embeddings for the same word type by contexts (Peters et al., 2018; Devlin et al., 2019; Liu et al., 2019), the size of $X$ and $Y$ is as large as the number of all aligned words in the training data. It is worth saying that the transformed embedding space may be similar to the actual encoded space in the target language; however, the word order is still preserved as in the source language. Therefore, the model is limited to learn sequence information of the target language, which can be an issue for languages with very different word orderings.

### 4.3 Annotation Projection

Let $\mathbb{S} = \{S_1, \ldots, S_n\}$ and $\mathbb{T} = \{T_1, \ldots, T_n\}$ be lists of sentences in the source and target languages, and $(S_i, T_i)$ be the $i$'th pair of parallel sentences in those two languages. Let $S_i = \{s_{i1}, \ldots, s_{in}\}$ and $T_i = \{t_{i1}, \ldots, t_{im}\}$ where $s_i$ and $t_i$ are the $i$'th word in $S$ and $T$. Then, annotation projection can be performed as proposed by Ni et al. (2017):

1. Pseudo-label $S_{\forall i} \in \mathbb{S}$ using an existing model in the source language, in our case, ELIT (§3.2).

2. Pseudo-align words in every $(S_i, T_i)$ using an existing tool, in our case, GIZA++ (§3.2). If a consecutive word span $S_i^{j,k} = \{s_{ij}, .., s_{ik}\}$ is pseudo-labeled as the entity type $\ell$ as well as pseudo-aligned with a span $T_i^{a,b} = \{t_{ia}, .., t_{ib}\}$, $T_i^{a,b}$ is also pseudo-labeled with $\ell$.

The quality of pseudo annotation hugely depends on the performance of word alignment, which is generally not robust for the case of distant language pairs such as English and Korean. Thus, we propose a few constraints to filter out noisy annotation.

**Entity Matching** Let $\psi$ be a boolean. If $\psi = \texttt{F}$, all parallel sentences in $(\mathbb{S}, \mathbb{T})$ are used for training. If $\psi = \texttt{T}$, $(S_i, T_i)$ is selected for training only if all named entities in $S_i$ are properly labeled in $T_i$ by the above projection approach.

**Relative Frequency** Let $e$ be an entity term such as "도널드 트럼프 (Donald Trump)" in Figure 1. Let $L_e$ be a set of entity types pseudo-annotated for all occurrences of $e$ in the target language. Then, the relative frequency $P(\ell|e)$ for $\ell \in L_e$ and $e$ can be measured as follows, where $\text{COUNT}(\ell, e)$ is the number of occurrences for $e$ being labeled as $\ell$:

$$P(\ell|e) = \frac{\text{COUNT}(\ell, e)}{\sum_{\ell' \in L_e} \text{COUNT}(\ell', e)}$$

**Impurity** Let $F_e^\ell$ be a set of unique terms in the source language that are pseudo-aligned with the term $e$ labeled as $\ell$ in the target language such that $|F_e| \leq \text{COUNT}(l, e)$. Then, the impurity $M(\ell, e)$ is measured as follows where $\alpha$ is a smoothing factor:

$$M(\ell, e) = \frac{|F_e^\ell|}{\text{COUNT}(l, e) + \alpha}$$

The relative frequency $P(\ell|e)$ and the impurity $M(\ell, e)$ are used to assess pseudo-annotation reliability.

**Ann. Reliability** Let $E_i = \{(\ell_1, e_1), .., (\ell_q, e_q)\}$ be a list of all (entity term, label) pairs in the target sentence $T_i$. For each $T_i \in \mathbb{T}$, the following two scores, $f(T_i)$ and $g(T_i)$, are measured to estimate the reliability of the pseudo-annotation in $T_i$:

$$f(T_i) = \frac{\sum_{\forall(l,e) \in E_i} P(\ell|e)}{|E_i|}$$

$$g(T_i) = \frac{\sum_{\forall(l,e) \in E_i} M(\ell|e)}{|E_i|}$$

Given the annotation reliability metrics, our data selection scheme heuristic is as follows:

$$f(T_i) \geq \phi; \quad g(T_i) \leq \gamma; \quad |E_i| \geq \mu; \quad \psi = \mathtt{T}|\mathtt{F}$$

Only the target sentences satisfying all of the above constraints are used for training given the hyperparameters $\psi$, $\alpha$, $\phi$, $\gamma$, and $\mu$.

## 5 Experiments

### 5.1 Direct Model Transfer

The experimental settings of direct model transfer approach are identical with Wu and Dredze (2019). We freeze the bottom n layers (including n) of mBERT, where layer 0 is the embedding layer. The cases of n are {-1, 0, 3, 6, 9}, where -1 denotes fine-tuning all layers in mBERT. For word-level classification, a simple linear classification layer with softmax is added on mBERT. The hyperparameters we experiment on are the combitations of batch size {16, 32}, learning rate {2e-5, 3e-5, 5e-5}, and number of max epochs {3, 4}.

### 5.2 Multilingual Encoders

For embedding projection and annotation projection, two types of transformer encoders, mBERT (Devlin et al. 2019) and XLM-RoBERTa (Conneau et al. 2020) are considered. Both mBERT and XLM-R are further pretrained on the training data (TRN in Table 1) by individually feeding 1.5M sentences in both English and Korean.[6]

### 5.3 Embedding Projection

Two types of transformation matrices are derived by the embedding projection method (Section 4.2). One is a word-level matrix and the other is a sentence-level matrix. To evaluate the zero-shot Korean NER model performance (Table 6) when different size of parallel sentences are available, we use different subsets of sentences of increasing sizes(0, 1K, 10K, 100K, 200K, 400K, 747K; 0 to total # of sentences in TRN). Size 0 means the embeddings from source language are not transformed when fed into the NER model for training.

Word embeddings from the last hidden layer of each transformer encoder are extracted. For every parallel sentence pair, let $X_i$ and $Y_i$ be lists of word embeddings of the $i$'th sentence extracted from the last layer in the source and target encoders, respectively. Only embeddings for words that find alignments are included in $X_i$ and $Y_i$. If multiple words in the source language, $s_i$ and $s_j$, are aligned to one word, $t_k$, in the target language (e.g., United States $\rightarrow$ 미국 in Figure 1), the embeddings of $t_k$ are duplicated and added to $Y_i$ and vice versa s.t. $|X_*| = |Y_*|$. Let $x_{ij}$ and $y_{ij}$ be the $j$'th embeddings in $X_i$ and $Y_i$ that are guaranteed to be the embeddings of aligned words; thus, $X_i$ and $Y_i$ are completely in parallel. For the word-level transformation matrix $W^w$, $X_i$ and $Y_i$ from all parallel sentences are appended together to create $\mathbb{X}_i^w$ and $\mathbb{Y}_i^w$ respectively such that $\mathbb{X}_i^w \cdot W^w \approx \mathbb{Y}_i^w$.

Sentence embeddings are simply created by averaging the word embeddings of parallel source and target sentences. Let $X_i'$ and $Y_i'$ be lists of word embeddings of the $i$'th sentence extracted from the last layer in the source and target encoders. Note that words in $X_i'$ and $Y_i'$ are not aligned, thus no duplications of word embedding unlike $X_i$ and $Y_i$. For the sentence-level matrix $W^s$, the average em-

[6]There are 747.7K parallel sentence pairs in the training set (Table 1a); thus, the total number of individual sentences in both languages is 747.7K × 2 = 1.5M.

beddings of $X_i'$, $Y_i'$ are appended to create $\mathbb{X}_i^s$ and $\mathbb{Y}_i^s$ such that $\mathbb{X}_i^s \cdot W^s \approx \mathbb{Y}_i^s$.

For each sentence in the source language, embeddings from last hidden layer are transformed by $W^{w|s}$ and fed into the NER model for training (Section 5.5).

### 5.4 Annotation Projection

The annotation projection is performed to generate the pseudo-annotated Korean dataset (Section 4.3). The following 5 hyperparameters are tuned to filter out noisy annotation for training, where $\psi$, $\alpha$, and $\gamma$ are newly introduced by our work:

- $\psi$: if True, keep only sentences whose entities are completely matching between the two languages.
- $\alpha$: the smoothing factor to measure the impurity.
- $\phi$: retain sentences whose annotation reliability scores by relative frequency $\geq$ this threshold.
- $\gamma$: retain sentences whose annotation reliability scores by impurity $\leq$ this threshold.
- $\mu$: retain sentences that contain named entities whose quantities are $\geq$ this cutoff.

Once the pseudo-annotation is created, all Korean sentences are encoded by mBERT to generate Korean embeddings that are fed into the NER model.

### 5.5 NER Model

For embedding and annotation projections, a bidirectional LSTM-based NER tagger using a CRF decoder is adapted to build our NER models (Lample et al., 2016). Details of the hyperparameters are described in Appendix A.3

### 5.6 Results

Table 5 shows the best result of direct model transfer, mBERT fine-tuned on OntoNotes NER dataset and evaluated on our Korean TST set. All scores are reported in a form of mean (± standard deviation) after three developments. The best model is built under the setting when all layers including the embedding layer of mBERT are fine-tuned.

| Precision | Recall | F1 score |
|---|---|---|
| 46.92 (±0.85) | 46.28 (±1.49) | 46.59 (±1.02) |

Table 5: The best result of the baseline model on TST

Table 6 shows the zero-shot results from the embedding projection models in Section 5.3. Both mBERT and XLM-R models showed a performance improvement over 2% with embedding transformation. F1 score improves 2.47% (36.67% to 39.14%) and 2.32% (39.36% to 41.68%) for mBERT and XLM-R, respectively. Both models showed the best performance with embedding transformation matrix made of 200k$^w$. The number of parallel sentences used for training transformation matrix has a considerable impact on the Zero-shot learning.

| | Precision | Recall | F1 score |
|---|---|---|---|
| 0 | 41.63 (±0.2) | 32.78 (±1.2) | 36.67 (±0.0) |
| 1k$^w$ | 35.81 (±0.0) | 23.60 (±0.1) | 28.45 (±0.0) |
| 10k$^w$ | 40.73 (±0.2) | 36.43 (±0.6) | 38.46 (±0.4) |
| 100k$^w$ | 39.70 (±0.4) | 36.02 (±0.0) | 37.77 (±0.2) |
| 200k$^w$ | **42.17 (±0.0)** | 36.52 (±0.2) | **39.14 (±0.1)** |
| 400k$^w$ | 41.40 (±0.5) | **36.72 (±0.5)** | 38.91 (±0.1) |
| 747k$^w$ | 42.07 (±0.0) | 36.31 (±0.6) | 38.98 (±0.3) |
| 1k$^s$ | 27.76 (±2.6) | 06.32 (±0.9) | 10.29 (±1.4) |
| 10k$^s$ | 37.81 (±0.0) | 22.20 (±1.3) | 27.96 (±1.0) |
| 100k$^s$ | 39.19 (±1.0) | 29.54 (±0.6) | 33.69 (±0.8) |
| 200k$^s$ | 40.64 (±0.4) | 29.74 (±1.1) | 34.33 (±0.6) |
| 400k$^s$ | 41.04 (±0.1) | 30.20 (±0.6) | 34.79 (±0.4) |
| 747k$^s$ | 41.56 (±0.5) | 30.27 (±0.9) | 35.03 (±0.8) |

(a) mBERT

| | Precision | Recall | F1 score |
|---|---|---|---|
| 0 | 48.04 (±0.5) | 33.35 (±0.8) | 39.36 (±0.5) |
| 1k$^w$ | 42.20 (±0.7) | 26.68 (±0.1) | 32.69 (±0.2) |
| 10k$^w$ | 47.15 (±0.2) | 36.19 (±1.3) | 40.95 (±1.5) |
| 100k$^w$ | 47.87 (±0.1) | **36.57 (±0.5)** | 41.46 (±0.3) |
| 200k$^w$ | 48.58 (±0.2) | 36.50 (±0.7) | **41.68 (±0.4)** |
| 400k$^w$ | 47.55 (±0.6) | 36.47 (±0.2) | 41.28 (±0.1) |
| 747k$^w$ | 47.30 (±0.6) | 36.00 (±0.5) | 40.88 (±0.5) |
| 1k$^s$ | 41.02 (±1.9) | 15.84 (±1.6) | 22.76 (±1.3) |
| 10k$^s$ | 46.49 (±1.3) | 30.53 (±1.1) | 36.84 (±1.0) |
| 100k$^s$ | 47.64 (±0.3) | 34.29 (±0.4) | 39.88 (±0.3) |
| 200k$^s$ | 47.47 (±1.0) | 33.35 (±0.2) | 39.17 (±0.4) |
| 400k$^s$ | 48.19 (±0.4) | 33.37 (±1.0) | 39.43 (±0.8) |
| 747k$^s$ | **48.61 (±1.2)** | 33.63 (±1.0) | 39.75 (±1.0) |

(b) XLM-R

Table 6: Zero-shot NER results on TST using the embedding projection models in §5.3. mBERT/XLM-R$^{w|s}$: the English embeddings from mBERT/XLM-R are transformed by $W^{w|s}$. 0 means not transformed.

Table 7 shows the results from the annotation projection models with various configurations. About 9% gain is shown by the best model using only the entity matching constraint $\psi$ that effectively filters out 55% of the training data (row 3). A relative score of 50.25% is achieved by the model using only 21% of the training data, implying that a fair amount of noisy annotation is produced by the annotation projection approach.

The overall results show that the Annotation Projection approach achieves the best performance,

| $\psi$ | $\alpha$ | $\phi$ | $\gamma$ | $\mu$ | T | Precison | Recall | F1 score |
|---|---|---|---|---|---|---|---|---|
| F | 0 | 0 | 1 | 0 | 747K | **61.04 (±0.9)** | 32.02 (±0.5) | 42.00 (±0.5) |
| T | 0 | 0 | 1 | 0 | 329K | 57.04 (±0.6) | 46.15 (±0.4) | **51.02 (±0.4)** |
| T | 0 | 0.4 | 1 | 1 | 163K | 53.87 (±0.2) | 47.09 (±0.4) | 50.25 (±0.2) |
| T | 0 | 0.4 | 1 | 2 | 83K | 50.43 (±0.8) | **49.49 (±0.3)** | 49.95 (±0.4) |
| T | 0.5 | 0.4 | 0.5 | 2 | 44K | 49.92 (±0.8) | 48.23 (±0.6) | 49.05 (±0.3) |
| T | 0 | 0.4 | 0.5 | 1 | 91K | 49.88 (±1.0) | 46.89 (±1.5) | 48.31 (±0.4) |
| T | 0.5 | 0.4 | 0.5 | 1 | 91K | 50.95 (±0.4) | 46.73 (±0.4) | 48.74 (±0.1) |
| T | 0 | 0.4 | 0.5 | 2 | 44K | 47.52 (±0.8) | 48.70 (±0.7) | 48.10 (±0.2) |
| F | 0 | 0.4 | 1 | 2 | 435K | 57.78 (±1.8) | 33.11 (±1.9) | 42.06 (±0.5) |

Table 7: Zero-shot NER results on TST using the annotation projection models in §5.4. T: number of parallel sentence pairs used for training.

implying that considering the word order of the target language is critical in cross-lingual learning, especially in the case of distant language pairs. We expect further improvement of the annotation projection approach when adapting a more accurate word alignment tool or a data selection scheme, which we will further investigate.

## 6 Analysis

### 6.1 Error Distribution

Given the results of the best models for embedding and annotation projection approaches (Section 5.6), a total of 105 parallel sentences (15 pairs per news section) are randomly selected for error analysis.[7] Table 8 shows the distributions of the 5 error types.

| | NA | NE | WR | WL | WRL |
|---|---|---|---|---|---|
| EP | 7.64% | 35.03% | 28.02% | 14.01% | 15.28% |
| AP | 10.43% | 28.83% | 28.83% | 23.31% | 8.59% |

Table 8: Distributions of 5 error types from the samples. EP: embedding projection, AP: annotation projection, NA: no annotation, NE: no extraction, WR: wrong range, WL: wrong label, WRL: wrong range and label.

### 6.2 Error Analysis

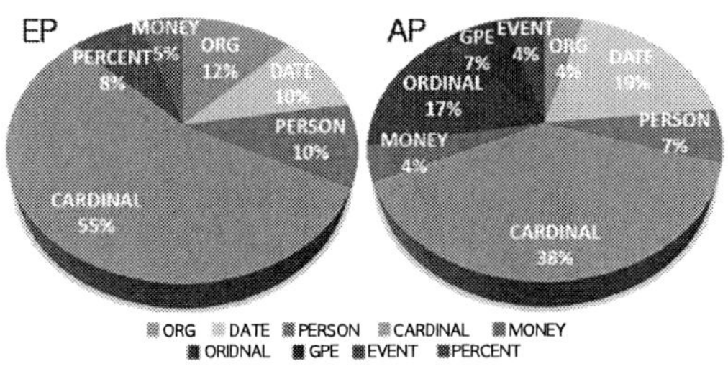


Figure 2: Comparison of entity type distribution of Wrong Range between EP and AP. Only entity types that have errors over 2 times are included in the chart.

Korean named entities describing cardinal are more prone to fall under Wrong Range than the other error types in both models. For example, the Korean entity "10개 (10 things)" comprises the quantity "10" and the metric "개 (things)" that is a generic measure word in Korean, whereas in English just write "10". The grammatical difference between English and Korean, where Korean uses measure words for quantifying the classes of objects while English does not in general, makes it difficult to accurately predict under the zero-shot learning setting.

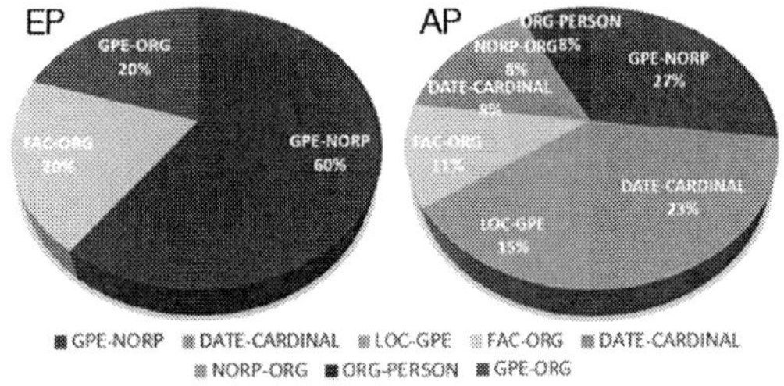


Figure 3: Comparison of entity type pair distribution of Wrong Label between EP and AP. Only entity type pairs that have errors over 2 times are included in the chart.

Wrong Label occurs frequently across all models when dealing with entities referring to nationality. As mentioned in Section 3.5, a single word in Korean can entail the meaning of both nationality and country. This overloaded word-sense characteristic makes entities that actually refer to nationality be mislabeled as GPE, which should have been labeled as NORP.

## 7 Conclusion

This paper presents a multilingual dataset that allows researchers to conduct crosslingual research between English and Korean. Our dataset contains high-quality annotation of named entities on parallel sentences from seven popular news sections. Given this dataset, Korean NER models are built by zero-shot learning using multilingual encoders. Our data selection scheme for annotation projection significantly improves the NER performance although it is still suboptimal. Our error analysis depicts unique characteristics in Korean that make it hard for zero-shot learning, challenges that we need to overcome in the future work.[8]

[7] Detailed descriptions of the five error types are provided in Appendix A.5.

[8] All our resources including dataset, source codes, and models are available at https://github.com/emorynlp/MRL-2021.

## Acknowledgments

This work was partly supported by the Institute of Information and Communications Technology Planning and Evaluation (IITP) grant funded by the Korean government (MSIT) (No. 2020-0-01361, Artificial Intelligence Graduate School Program (Yonsei University)).

## References

Hanan Aldarmaki and Mona Diab. 2019. Context-Aware Cross-Lingual Mapping. In *Proceedings of the 2019 Conference of the North American Chapter of the Association for Computational Linguistics: Human Language Technologies*, pages 3906–3911, Minneapolis, Minnesota.

Mikel Artetxe, Gorka Labaka, and Eneko Agirre. 2016. Learning principled bilingual mappings of word embeddings while preserving monolingual invariance. In *Proceedings of the 2016 Conference on Empirical Methods in Natural Language Processing*, pages 2289–2294, Austin, Texas.

Mikel Artetxe and Holger Schwenk. 2019. Massively Multilingual Sentence Embeddings for Zero-Shot Cross-Lingual Transfer and Beyond. In *Transactions of the Association for Computational Linguistics*, volume 7.

BBN. 2014. OntoNotes Named Entity Guidelines Version 14.0. Raytheon BBN Technologies.

Min-Ah Cheon and Jae-Hoon Kim. 2018. Definition of Korean Named-Entity Task. Technical report, Korea Maritime & Ocean University.

Ethan A. Chi, John Hewitt, and Christopher D. Manning. 2020. Finding Universal Grammatical Relations in Multilingual BERT. In *Proceedings of the 58rd Annual Meeting of the Association for Computational Linguistics*, ACL'20.

Muthu Chidambaram, Yinfei Yang, Daniel Cer, Steve Yuan, Yunhsuan Sung, Brian Strope, and Ray Kurzweil. 2019. Learning Cross-Lingual Sentence Representations via a Multi-task Dual-Encoder Model. In *Proceedings of the 4th Workshop on Representation Learning for NLP (RepL4NLP-2019)*, pages 250–259, Florence, Italy.

Key-Sun Choi, Young S. Han, Young G. Han, and Oh W. Kwon. 1994. KAIST Tree Bank Project for Korean: Present and Future Development. In *In Proceedings of the International Workshop on Sharable Natural Language Resources*, pages 7–14.

Alexis Conneau, Kartikay Khandelwal, Naman Goyal, Vishrav Chaudhary, Guillaume Wenzek, Francisco Guzmán, Edouard Grave, Myle Ott, Luke Zettlemoyer, and Veselin Stoyanov. 2020. Unsupervised Cross-lingual Representation Learning at Scale. In *Proceedings of the 58th Annual Meeting of the Association for Computational Linguistics*, ACL'20.

Alexis Conneau and Guillaume Lample. 2019. Cross-lingual Language Model Pretraining. In H. Wallach, H. Larochelle, A. Beygelzimer, F. d'Alché-Buc, E. Fox, and R. Garnett, editors, *Advances in Neural Information Processing Systems 32*, pages 7059–7069. Curran Associates, Inc.

Alexis Conneau, Ruty Rinott, Guillaume Lample, Adina Williams, Samuel Bowman, Holger Schwenk, and Veselin Stoyanov. 2018. XNLI: Evaluating Cross-lingual Sentence Representations. In *Proceedings of the 2018 Conference on Empirical Methods in Natural Language Processing*, pages 2475–2485, Brussels, Belgium.

Jacob Devlin, Ming-Wei Chang, Kenton Lee, and Kristina Toutanova. 2019. BERT: Pre-training of Deep Bidirectional Transformers for Language Understanding. In *Proceedings of the 2019 Conference of the North American Chapter of the Association for Computational Linguistics: Human Language Technologies, Volume 1 (Long and Short Papers)*, pages 4171–4186, Minneapolis, Minnesota.

Chung-Hye Han, Na-Rae Han, Eon-Suk Ko, Martha Palmer, and Heejong Yi. 2002. Penn Korean Treebank: Development and Evaluation. In *In Proceedings of the 16th Pacific Asia Conference on Language, Information and Computation*, PACLIC'02.

YoonPyo Hong. 2009. 21st Century Sejong Project Results and Tasks (21세기 세종 계획 사업 성과 및 과제). In *New Korean Life (새국어생활)*. National Institute of Korean Language.

Xiaolei Huang, Jonathan May, and Nanyun Peng. 2019. What Matters for Neural Cross-Lingual Named Entity Recognition: An Empirical Analysis. In *Proceedings of the 2019 Conference on Empirical Methods in Natural Language Processing and the 9th International Joint Conference on Natural Language Processing (EMNLP-IJCNLP)*, pages 6395–6401, Hong Kong, China.

Soufian Jebbara and Philipp Cimiano. 2019. Zero-Shot Cross-Lingual Opinion Target Extraction. In *Proceedings of the 2019 Conference of the North American Chapter of the Association for Computational Linguistics: Human Language Technologies, Volume 1 (Long and Short Papers)*, pages 2486–2495, Minneapolis, Minnesota.

Taku Kudo and John Richardson. 2018. SentencePiece: A simple and language independent subword tokenizer and detokenizer for Neural Text Processing. In *Proceedings of the 2018 Conference on Empirical Methods in Natural Language Processing: System Demonstrations*, pages 66–71, Brussels, Belgium.

Guillaume Lample, Miguel Ballesteros, Sandeep Subramanian, Kazuya Kawakami, and Chris Dyer. 2016. Neural Architectures for Named Entity Recognition.

In *Proceedings of the 2016 Conference of the North American Chapter of the Association for Computational Linguistics: Human Language Technologies*, pages 260–270, San Diego, California.

Yu-Hsiang Lin, Chian-Yu Chen, Jean Lee, Zirui Li, Yuyan Zhang, Mengzhou Xia, Shruti Rijhwani, Junxian He, Zhisong Zhang, Xuezhe Ma, Antonios Anastasopoulos, Patrick Littell, and Graham Neubig. 2019. Choosing Transfer Languages for Cross-Lingual Learning. In *Proceedings of the 57th Annual Meeting of the Association for Computational Linguistics*, pages 3125–3135, Florence, Italy.

Yinhan Liu, Myle Ott, Naman Goyal, Jingfei Du, Mandar Joshi, Danqi Chen, Omer Levy, Mike Lewis, Luke Zettlemoyer, and Veselin Stoyanov. 2019. RoBERTa: A Robustly Optimized BERT Pretraining Approach. *arXiv*, 1907.11692.

Fuli Luo, Wei Wang, Jiahao Liu, Yijia Liu, Bin Bi, Songfang Huang, Fei Huang, and Luo Si. 2021. VECO: Variable and flexible cross-lingual pretraining for language understanding and generation. In *Proceedings of the 59th Annual Meeting of the Association for Computational Linguistics and the 11th International Joint Conference on Natural Language Processing (Volume 1: Long Papers)*, pages 3980–3994, Online. Association for Computational Linguistics.

Emi Maekawa. 2018. Annotation guidelines for named entities version 1.1. Technical report, Search Results Web results National Institute of Information and Communications Technology.

Jian Ni, Georgiana Dinu, and Radu Florian. 2017. Weakly supervised cross-lingual named entity recognition via effective annotation and representation projection. In *Proceedings of the 55th Annual Meeting of the Association for Computational Linguistics (Volume 1: Long Papers)*, pages 1470–1480, Vancouver, Canada.

Franz Josef Och and Hermann Ney. 2003. A systematic comparison of various statistical alignment models. *Computational linguistics*, 29(1):19–51.

Matthew Peters, Mark Neumann, Mohit Iyyer, Matt Gardner, Christopher Clark, Kenton Lee, and Luke Zettlemoyer. 2018. Deep Contextualized Word Representations. In *Proceedings of the 2018 Conference of the North American Chapter of the Association for Computational Linguistics: Human Language Technologies, Volume 1 (Long Papers)*, pages 2227–2237, New Orleans, Louisiana.

Sameer Pradhan, Alessandro Moschitti, Nianwen Xue, Hwee Tou Ng, Anders Björkelund, Olga Uryupina, Yuchen Zhang, and Zhi Zhong. 2013. Towards Robust Linguistic Analysis using OntoNotes. In *Proceedings of the Seventeenth Conference on Computational Natural Language Learning*, pages 143–152, Sofia, Bulgaria.

Sebastian Schuster, Sonal Gupta, Rushin Shah, and Mike Lewis. 2019a. Cross-lingual Transfer Learning for Multilingual Task Oriented Dialog. In *Proceedings of the 2019 Conference of the North American Chapter of the Association for Computational Linguistics: Human Language Technologies, Volume 1 (Long and Short Papers)*, pages 3795–3805, Minneapolis, Minnesota.

Tal Schuster, Ori Ram, Regina Barzilay, and Amir Globerson. 2019b. Cross-Lingual Alignment of Contextual Word Embeddings, with Applications to Zero-shot Dependency Parsing. In *Proceedings of the 2019 Conference of the North American Chapter of the Association for Computational Linguistics: Human Language Technologies, Volume 1 (Long and Short Papers)*, pages 1599–1613, Minneapolis, Minnesota.

Samuel L. Smith, David H. P. Turban, Steven Hamblin, and Nils Y. Hammerla. 2017. Offline bilingual word vectors, orthogonal transformations and the inverted softmax. *CoRR*, abs/1702.03859.

Qianhui Wu, Zijia Lin, Guoxin Wang, Hui Chen, Börje F Karlsson, Biqing Huang, and Chin-Yew Lin. 2020. Enhanced meta-learning for cross-lingual named entity recognition with minimal resources. In *Proceedings of the AAAI Conference on Artificial Intelligence*, volume 34, pages 9274–9281.

Shijie Wu and Mark Dredze. 2019. Beto, bentz, becas: The surprising cross-lingual effectiveness of BERT. In *Proceedings of the 2019 Conference on Empirical Methods in Natural Language Processing and the 9th International Joint Conference on Natural Language Processing (EMNLP-IJCNLP)*, pages 833–844, Hong Kong, China. Association for Computational Linguistics.

# A Appendix

## A.1 Named Entity Tagsets

### A.1.1 English NER Tagset

There are 18 named entity tags annotated in the OntoNotes 5.0 as follows (Pradhan et al., 2013):[9]

- **CARDINAL**: Numerical terms not categorized in other categorizations. Numbers that indicate ages are included.
- **DATE**: Absolute or relative dates or periods. The period should last longer than 'TIME'. General expressions of dates are included too such as 'few months', 'that day', 'Next season' and 'First quarter'.
- **EVENT**: It means an official or widely known event, war, exhibition. Official events include ministerial meetings, general elections, presidential elections, exams (SAT), and prayers (U.S. national breakfast prayer). Social phenomena also include (Brexit) for widely known events.
- **FAC**: Objectives referring to facilities include buildings, airports, highways and bridge names.
- **GPE**: An object referring to a place or location, including the name of a country and the name of an administrative district, such as a city or state.
- **LANGUAGE**: Any named language.
- **LAW**: Named documents made into laws.
- **LOC**: Refers to the name of a place or location that does not belong to GPE. It also includes expressions covering the entire location of mountains, rivers, ocean names and Europe, Asia, etc.
- **MONEY**: Monetary values including units.
- **NORP**: It refers to nationality, religious groups and political groups (party).
- **ORDINAL**: All ordinal numbers such as first and second.
- **ORG**: It refers a community / group of people gathered together. For example, the name of the company, the name of the school, and the name of the sports team.
- **PERCENT**: Percentage expressions with % symbol or the word 'percent'.
- **PERSON**: Referring to a last name or full name of a particular person. It also includes nicknames for non-human creatures and characters in cartoons, dramas and movies.
- **PRODUCT**: Vehicles, Weapons, foods. IT services (including SNS) and medicine names are included.
- **QUANTITY**: Measurements as of weights or distances such as km, kg and etc.
- **TIME**: This tag indicates time expressions smaller than a day. This tag includes certain time indication, amount of time or any other expressions related to time. Even though an entity does not have numeral expressions but only words related to time (for instance, 'noon'), the words are tagged as 'Time'.
- **WORK_OF_ART**: Titles of books, songs, TV programs and art pieces. Title of games, awards, theories, records are included.

### A.1.2 Korean NER Tagset

There are 10 tags annotated in the copus distributed by the Korea Maritime and Ocean University:[10]

- **DAT**: Absolute dates. Public holidays and day of the week is included.
- **DUR**: Duration of incidents. Academically clarified periods such as Cretaceous period are also included.
- **LOC**: The name of a country and the name of an administrative district, such as a city or state. Words representing certain locations such as tour spot and stadium is also included. When location word becomes compound nouns with other words, it is not included.
- **MNY**: Monetary values including units. Bitcoin is not included.
- **NOH**: Any numerical expressions such as measurements of heights, temperatures, weights. Ordinal numbers are included.
- **ORG**: A group consisting of 2 or more people. The name of the company, the name of the school, and the name of the sports team.

[9] `https://catalog.ldc.upenn.edu/docs/LDC2013T19/OntoNotes-Release-5.0.pdf`

[10] `https://github.com/kmounlp/NER`

- **PER**: Personal name including first and last name. Any name referring to living things and nicknames for non-human creatures and characters in cartoons, dramas and movies are included.

- **PNT**: Percentage expressions with % symbol or the word 'percent'.

- **POH**: Product name, medicine, game, event, meeting, movies, songs, drama series, TV channels, daily and weekly magazines, emails, phone numbers are included.

- **TIM**: This tag indicates time expressions smaller than a day. This tag includes certain time indication, amount of time or any other expressions related to time. Even though an entity does not have numeral expressions but only words related to time (for instance, 'noon'), the words are tagged as 'Time'.

## A.2 English NER Performance

Table 9 shows the performance of the NER model in the ELIT toolkit on the English development and evaluation sets in our dataset.

| Category | Precision | Recall | F1-Score |
|---|---|---|---|
| Business | 81.01 | 80.39 | 80.70 |
| Lifestyle | 77.45 | 77.85 | 77.65 |
| Politics | 72.46 | 72.35 | 72.41 |
| Society | 74.19 | 73.52 | 73.86 |
| Sci/Tech | 80.76 | 81.20 | 80.98 |
| Sports | 80.07 | 79.76 | 79.92 |
| World | 81.90 | 82.02 | 81.96 |
| Total | 78.34 | 78.22 | 78.28 |

(a) Results on the development set.

| Category | Precision | Recall | F1-Score |
|---|---|---|---|
| Business | 77.44 | 77.72 | 77.58 |
| Lifestyle | 75.22 | 74.88 | 75.05 |
| Politics | 71.29 | 71.21 | 71.25 |
| Society | 71.24 | 70.48 | 70.86 |
| Sci/Tech | 77.48 | 77.42 | 77.45 |
| Sports | 80.86 | 79.91 | 80.38 |
| World | 82.25 | 82.73 | 82.49 |
| Total | 76.97 | 76.77 | 76.87 |

(b) Results on the evaluation set.

Table 9: Performance of the English NER model.

## A.3 Experimental Settings

### A.3.1 Task specific NER model for Embedding and Annotation Projections

The task specific NER model used : a 2-layer Bi-LSTM with a hidden size of 768 followed by a CRF layer. A dropout rate of 0.5 is applied on the input and the output of the Bi-LSTM. Adam with default parameters and a learning rate of 0.0001 are used for optimization. We trained the model for 10 epoch with a batch size of 32, and evaluate the model per a epoch.

## A.4 Comparison of NER performances (Zero-shot VS Existing)

We compare our best performing Zero-shot Korean NER model with the existing Korean NER model[11] on `TST`.

### A.4.1 Comparison Method

Since the number of named entity types that each model covers are different, named entity tags are mapped based on the definition of the tags. Our named entities are more fine-grained, which makes multiple tags (Zero-shot side) be mapped to one tag (Existing side). Named entity tags that cannot be mapped are discarded in both gold labels and predicted labels, thus not considered in the evaluation of the models.

### A.4.2 Comparison Result

Our zero-shot model yields a better performance than the existing model although it may be difficult to directly compare the two models. In the case of the existing Korean model, the low performance may be caused by the different annotation scheme between the datasets. In the case of our zero-shot model, the improvement of the performance are seen due to the coarse-grained named entities after the mapping.

| MODEL | Precision | Recall | F1-Score |
|---|---|---|---|
| Zero-shot | 0.61 | 0.55 | 0.58 |
| Existing | 0.46 | 0.53 | 0.49 |

Table 10: NER performances of Zero-shot Korean model and Existing Korean model on `TST`

## A.5 NER Error Types

Underlined words indicate entity boundaries, followed by their TAGs:

**`No Annotation`** occurs when the model extracts non-entity words as a named entity although they are not annotated in the gold data.

**Gold:** 신흥국 (Emerging Country)
**Auto::** <u>신흥국 (Emerging Country)</u>$_{\text{ORG}}$

[11] `https://github.com/monologg/KoBERT-NER`

`No Extraction` occurs when the model does not extract words as a named entity although they are annotated in the gold data.

**Gold:** 국회 (National Assembly)$_{\text{ORG}}$
**Auto:** 국회 (National Assembly)

`Wrong Range` occurs when the model extracts words as a named entity and only the range is wrong. This type of errors are words that are partially annotated with correct named entity tag.

**Gold:** 도널드 트럼프 (Donald Trump)$_{\text{PERSON}}$
**Auto:** 도널드 (Donald) 트럼프 (Trump)$_{\text{PERSON}}$

`Wrong Label` occurs when the model extracts words as a named entity with correct boundaries but only the tag type is wrong.

**Gold:** 하노이 (Hanoi)$_{\text{GPE}}$
**Auto:** 하노이 (Hanoi)$_{\text{PERSON}}$

`Wrong Range and Label` occurs when the model extract words as a named entity whose both range and tag type are wrong.

**Gold:** 60세 (60-years-old)$_{\text{CARDINAL}}$
**Auto:** 60$_{\text{DATE}}$ 세 (years-old)

### A.6 Analytics by News Sections and Entity Types

Table 11a describes the proportions of entity types per news section on DEV and TST combined. For *Lifestyle*, *Politics*, and *Sports*, PERSON is the most frequent entity type since many topics in these sections are centered around famous people (e.g., someone's biography, politicians, sports players). ORG on the other hand is the most frequent entity type for *Business*, *Society*, and *Sci/Tech* although those entities in *Society* refer to social groups while they generally refer to industrial companies in the other sections. GPE is the most and the 2nd-most frequent entity types for *World* and *Politics* where these entities refer to countries or regions in *World* but they are often related to geographical relationships between political figures in *Politics*.

Table 11b describes the proportions of news sections per entity type. CARDINAL, ORDINAL, and EVENT appear the most in *Sports* that involves many game events and statistics. DATE, ORG, and QUANTITY show fairly even proportions in every section as they are elemental to a variety of topics. GPE, LOC, and NORP give high proportions to both *Politics* and *World*. MONEY and PERCENT appear the most in *Business* that often deals with monetary issues. PERSON show high proportions in *Sports* and *Politics* as discussed above. FAC takes good portions in *Lifestyle*, *Business*, and *World*, which often mention facilities that people encounter daily (e.g., airports, bridges). TIME appears the most in *Sports* and *Society* that are full of dynamic events and issues. LANGUAGE is mostly found in *Society* although the sample size is too small to generalize. LAW, PRODUCT, and WORK_OF_ART appear the most in *Politics*, *Sci/Tech*, and *Lifestyle*, that focus on legal issues, tech products, and entertainment (e.g., music, movies, shows), respectively.

| | Business | Lifestyle | Politics | Society | Sci/Tech | Sports | World |
|---|---|---|---|---|---|---|---|
| CARDINAL | 284 (10.0) | 255 (11.3) | 245 (6.4) | 348 (13.2) | 309 (12.2) | 633 (15.4) | 278 (6.7) |
| DATE | 465 (16.4) | 335 (14.8) | 460 (12.0) | 455 (17.2) | 361 (14.3) | 464 (11.3) | 467 (11.2) |
| EVENT | 18 (0.6) | 51 (2.3) | 58 (1.5) | 18 (0.7) | 35 (1.4) | 142 (3.5) | 75 (1.8) |
| FAC | 61 (2.1) | 71 (3.1) | 28 (0.7) | 41 (1.6) | 26 (1.0) | 34 (0.8) | 60 (1.4) |
| GPE | 489 (17.2) | 230 (10.2) | 857 (22.3) | 239 (9.1) | 235 (9.3) | 305 (7.4) | 1,101 (26.5) |
| LANGUAGE | 4 (0.1) | 4 (0.2) | - | 43 (1.6) | - | 1 (0.0) | 2 (0.0) |
| LAW | 14 (0.5) | 2 (0.1) | 27 (0.7) | 19 (0.7) | 13 (0.5) | 8 (0.2) | 13 (0.3) |
| LOC | 26 (0.9) | 56 (2.5) | 81 (2.1) | 16 (0.6) | 28 (1.1) | 17 (0.4) | 80 (1.9) |
| MONEY | 106 (3.7) | 18 (0.8) | 12 (0.3) | 41 (1.6) | 59 (2.3) | 27 (0.7) | 58 (1.4) |
| NORP | 103 (3.6) | 111 (4.9) | 384 (10.0) | 41 (1.6) | 107 (4.2) | 104 (2.5) | 396 (9.5) |
| ORDINAL | 98 (3.5) | 81 (3.6) | 95 (2.5) | 110 (4.2) | 87 (3.4) | 300 (7.3) | 87 (2.1) |
| ORG | 728 (25.6) | 258 (11.4) | 609 (15.9) | 613 (23.2) | 736 (29.1) | 822 (20.0) | 610 (14.7) |
| PERCENT | 129 (4.5) | 8 (0.4) | 29 (0.8) | 79 (3.0) | 55 (2.2) | 21 (0.5) | 85 (2.0) |
| PERSON | 222 (7.8) | 552 (24.4) | 877 (22.8) | 456 (17.3) | 189 (7.5) | 1,127 (27.5) | 707 (17.0) |
| PRODUCT | 42 (1.5) | 28 (1.2) | 29 (0.8) | 29 (1.1) | 163 (6.5) | 3 (0.1) | 35 (0.8) |
| QUANTITY | 21 (0.7) | 16 (0.7) | 13 (0.3) | 19 (0.7) | 22 (0.9) | 6 (0.1) | 20 (0.5) |
| TIME | 20 (0.7) | 37 (1.6) | 24 (0.6) | 66 (2.5) | 39 (1.5) | 64 (1.6) | 44 (1.1) |
| WORK_OF_ART | 10 (0.4) | 151 (6.7) | 13 (0.3) | 7 (0.3) | 62 (2.5) | 24 (0.6) | 36 (0.9) |
| Total | 2,840 (100.0) | 2,264 (100.0) | 3,841(100.0) | 2,640 (100.0) | 2,526 (100.0) | 4,102 (100.0) | 4,154 (100.0) |

(a) Entities distribution by sections.

| | Business | Lifestyle | Politics | Society | Sci/Tech | Sports | World | Total |
|---|---|---|---|---|---|---|---|---|
| CARDINAL | 284 (12.1) | 255 (10.8) | 245 (10.4) | 348 (14.8) | 309 (13.1) | 633 (26.9) | 278 (11.8) | 2,352 (100.0) |
| DATE | 465 (15.5) | 335 (11.1) | 460 (15.3) | 455 (15.1) | 361 (12.0) | 464 (15.4) | 467 (15.5) | 3,007 (100.0) |
| EVENT | 18 (4.5) | 51 (12.8) | 58 (14.6) | 18 (4.5) | 35 (8.8) | 142 (35.8) | 75 (18.9) | 397 (100.0) |
| FAC | 61 (19.0) | 71 (22.1) | 28 (8.7) | 41 (12.8) | 26 (8.1) | 34 (10.6) | 60 (18.7) | 321 (100.0) |
| GPE | 489 (14.1) | 230 (6.7) | 857 (24.8) | 239 (6.9) | 235 (6.8) | 305 (8.8) | 1,101 (31.9) | 3,456 (100.0) |
| LANGUAGE | 4 (7.4) | 4 (7.4) | - | 43 (79.6) | - | 1 (1.9) | 2 (3.7) | 54 (100.0) |
| LAW | 14 (14.6) | 2 (2.1) | 27 (28.1) | 19 (19.8) | 13 (13.5) | 8 (8.3) | 13 (13.5) | 96 (100.0) |
| LOC | 26 (8.6) | 56 (18.4) | 81 (26.6) | 16 (5.3) | 28 (9.2) | 17 (5.6) | 80 (26.3) | 304 (100.0) |
| MONEY | 106 (33.0) | 18 (5.6) | 12 (3.7) | 41 (12.8) | 59 (18.4) | 27 (8.4) | 58 (18.1) | 321 (100.0) |
| NORP | 103 (8.3) | 111 (8.9) | 384 (30.8) | 41 (3.3) | 107 (8.6) | 104 (8.4) | 396 (31.8) | 1,246 (100.0) |
| ORDINAL | 98 (11.4) | 81 (9.4) | 95 (11.1) | 110 (12.8) | 87 (10.1) | 300 (35.0) | 87 (10.1) | 858 (100.0) |
| ORG | 728 (16.6) | 258 (5.9) | 609 (13.9) | 613 (14.0) | 736 (16.8) | 822 (18.8) | 610 (13.9) | 4,376 (100.0) |
| PERCENT | 129 (31.8) | 8 (2.0) | 29 (7.1) | 79 (19.5) | 55 (13.5) | 21 (5.2) | 85 (20.9) | 406 (100.0) |
| PERSON | 222 (5.4) | 552 (13.4) | 877 (21.2) | 456 (11.0) | 189 (4.6) | 1,127 (27.3) | 707 (17.1) | 4,130 (100.0) |
| PRODUCT | 42 (12.8) | 28 (8.5) | 29 (8.8) | 29 (8.8) | 163 (49.5) | 3 (0.9) | 35 (10.6) | 329 (100.0) |
| QUANTITY | 21 (17.9) | 16 (13.7) | 13 (11.1) | 19 (16.2) | 22 (18.8) | 6 (5.1) | 20 (17.1) | 117 (100.0) |
| TIME | 20 (6.8) | 37 (12.6) | 24 (8.2) | 66 (22.4) | 39 (13.3) | 64 (21.8) | 44 (15.0) | 294 (100.0) |
| WORK_OF_ART | 10 (3.3) | 151 (49.8) | 13 (4.3) | 7 (2.3) | 62 (20.5) | 24 (7.9) | 36 (11.9) | 303 (100.0) |

(b) Categories distribution by entities.

Table 11: Distribution comparisons between manually annotated entities and news sections in the English dataset (DEV and TST combined). Numbers in the parentheses indicate the percentages of the corresponding tags.

# Regularising Fisher Information Improves Cross-lingual Generalisation

**Asa Cooper Stickland**
University of Edinburgh
a.cooper.stickland@ed.ac.uk

**Iain Murray**
University of Edinburgh
i.murray@ed.ac.uk

## 1 Introduction

Multilingual pre-trained representations (Devlin et al., 2019; Huang et al., 2019; Conneau et al., 2020) are ubiquitous in state-of-the-art methods for cross-lingual transfer (Wu and Dredze, 2019; Pires et al., 2019). These methods learn from raw textual data in up to hundreds of languages. A typical pipeline transfers to another language by fine-tuning a downstream task in a high-resource language, often English.

Many recent works use 'consistency regularisation' to improve the generalisation of fine-tuned pre-trained models, both multilingual and English-only (Jiang et al., 2020; Aghajanyan et al., 2020; Wang et al., 2021; Zheng et al., 2021; Park et al., 2021; Liang et al., 2021). These works encourage model outputs to be similar between a perturbed and normal version of the input, usually via penalising the Kullback–Leibler (KL) divergence between the probability distribution of the perturbed and normal model. 'Generic' perturbations can be adversarial inputs (Jiang et al., 2020) or inputs with Gaussian or uniform noise (Aghajanyan et al., 2020). For cross-lingual generalisation in particular, probabilistic subword segmentations (Kudo, 2018) of the input or translations of the input generated by machine translation can be used (Wang et al., 2021; Zheng et al., 2021). Other work has found improvement by enforcing consistency for perturbations *within* models in addition to at the input (Hua et al., 2021; Liang et al., 2021).

While these works show improved generalisation compared to 'vanilla' fine-tuning, they present multiple explanations of the effectiveness of consistency regularisation. They also rarely compare to traditional regularisation methods like dropout or L2 regularisation. Finally such methods either require a complex adversarial training step (Jiang et al., 2020; Park et al., 2021), or tuning many hyper-parameters like type of noise, level of noise, and weight given to the consistency loss term.

We believe that consistency losses may be implicitly regularizing the loss landscape. In particular, we build on the work of Jastrzebski et al. (2021), who hypothesize that implicitly or explicitly regularizing trace of the Fisher Information Matrix (FIM), $\mathrm{Tr}(F)$, amplifies the implicit bias of SGD to avoid memorization. Briefly, the FIM is defined as $\mathbf{F}(\boldsymbol{\theta}) = E_{x\sim\mathcal{X},y\sim p_{\boldsymbol{\theta}}(y|x)}[g(x,y)g(x,y)^T]$, where $g(x,y)$ is the gradient w.r.t to $\boldsymbol{\theta}$ on the loss for label $y$ and input $x$. Jastrzebski et al. (2021) propose directly penalising a proxy of $\mathrm{Tr}(F)$, the **Fisher penalty** defined as $\|\frac{1}{B}\sum_{i=1}^{B} g(x_i,y_i)\|^2$.

In the multilingual setting we may wish to first fine-tune on a high-resource language like English, then further fine-tune on a smaller amount data in a lower-resource language, a 'two-stage' fine-tuning procedure. The FIM is a measure of the local curvature, and a small $\mathrm{Tr}(F)$ at the end of training implies a flatter minimum. Intuitively, such flat minima imply we can 'travel further' in parameter space before reaching a region of high loss, allowing for better performance in the two-stage fine-tuning setting.

Our (preliminary) key contributions are

- We show that the trace of the FIM is correlated with generalisation, confirming that the results of Jastrzebski et al. (2021) apply to cross-lingual transfer.
- Adding a direct Fisher penalty can achieve similar results to subword consistency regularization.
- We show for models fine-tuned on an English downstream task, improvements from fine-tuning on data from *another* language are correlated with low curvature (i.e. small trace of the FIM) in the English fine-tuned model.



*Proceedings of the 1st Workshop on Multilingual Representation Learning*, pages 238–241
November 11, 2021. ©2021 Association for Computational Linguistics

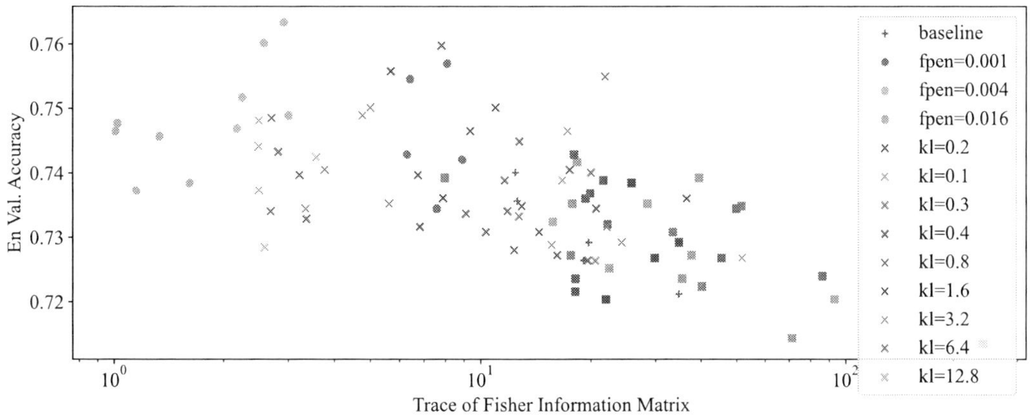


Figure 1: English validation set accuracy on a subset of the XNLI dataset vs. trace of the FIM at the end of training, for models with different weight given to consistency regularisation (crosses) and fisher penalty (circles) losses. For clarity we leave various models with different L2 penalties (squares) off the legend. kl=$k$ means a consistency loss was given weight $k$ during training. fpen=$k$ means the Fisher penalty was given weight $k$.

## 2 Initial Results

We first present a theoretical argument that in some simple situations, consistency losses penalize the trace of the FIM. We perturb model parameters $\boldsymbol{\theta}$ with small, zero-mean, i.i.d. noise $\boldsymbol{\epsilon}$. For small $\boldsymbol{\epsilon}$, we can Taylor expand the KL divergence between models with these parameters: $KL\left[p_{\boldsymbol{\theta}}(y \mid x) \mid\mid p_{\boldsymbol{\theta}+\boldsymbol{\epsilon}}(y \mid x)\right] \approx \frac{1}{2}\boldsymbol{\epsilon}^T F \boldsymbol{\epsilon}$, (see e.g., Dabak and Johnson, 2003). Taking expectations w.r.t. $\boldsymbol{\epsilon}$ and writing $\boldsymbol{\epsilon}^T F \boldsymbol{\epsilon}$ as a sum, we have,

$$\begin{aligned} \mathbb{E}_{\boldsymbol{\epsilon}\sim p(\boldsymbol{\epsilon})}[\boldsymbol{\epsilon}^T F \boldsymbol{\epsilon}] &= \textstyle\sum_{i,j} \mathbb{E}[\epsilon_i \epsilon_j F_{i,j}] \\ &= \textstyle\sum_{i\neq j} \mathbb{E}[\epsilon_i]\mathbb{E}[\epsilon_j] F_{i,j} + \sum_i \mathbb{E}[\epsilon_i^2] F_{i,i} \\ &= 0 + C \textstyle\sum_i F_{i,i} = C\,\mathrm{Tr}(F), \end{aligned} \quad (1)$$

where $C$ is the variance of the i.i.d. noise.

Consistency losses that use larger or more structured perturbations could potentially have a useful effect not captured by the Fisher Information Matrix alone. We empirically investigate the relationship between a subword segmentation consistency loss and penalizing the FIM. We use the same loss and hyper-parameters as Wang et al. (2021). All experiments use multilingual BERT.

Figure 1 presents results from an experiment on a subset (20k examples, with the small size chosen due to compute constraints) of the XNLI dataset (Conneau et al., 2018). It shows 1) a correlation between generalisation and small $\mathrm{Tr}(F)$, and 2) decreasing $\mathrm{Tr}(F)$ with increasing weight given to the consistency loss term. Additionally we see that directly penalising the FIM (models marked 'fpen=') has a similar effect to these consistency losses.

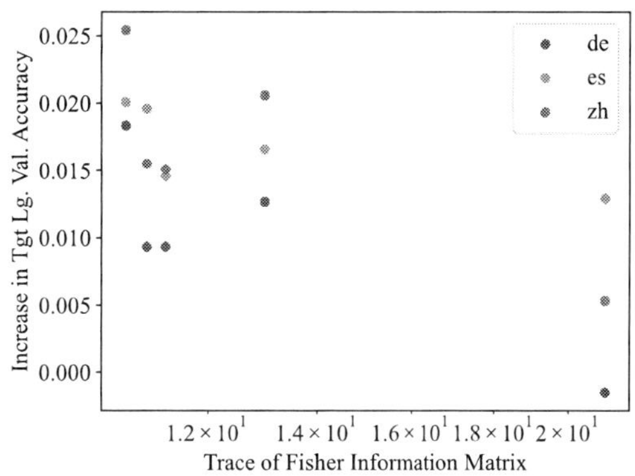


Figure 2: Increase in target language (either de, es or zh) validation set accuracy when fine-tuning on data in the target language vs. trace of the FIM after training on English, for the PAWS-X dataset (Yang et al., 2019).

Figure 2 shows the effect of small $\mathrm{Tr}(F)$, i.e. flat minima, on fine-tuning a model trained on English data on another language. To obtain non-English training data, we split the 2000 dev set examples in two, leaving 1000 training examples in each language and 1000 new dev examples. We see that improvements on the non-English language are correlated with flat minima.

We aim to confirm these initial results on more datasets, and use our insights to develop better multilingual fine-tuning techniques.

## References


Armen Aghajanyan, Akshat Shrivastava, Anchit Gupta, Naman Goyal, Luke Zettlemoyer, and Sonal Gupta. 2020. Better fine-tuning by reducing representational collapse. *arXiv preprint arXiv:2008.03156*.

Alexis Conneau, Kartikay Khandelwal, Naman Goyal, Vishrav Chaudhary, Guillaume Wenzek, Francisco Guzmán, Edouard Grave, Myle Ott, Luke Zettlemoyer, and Veselin Stoyanov. 2020. Unsupervised cross-lingual representation learning at scale. In *Proceedings of the 58th Annual Meeting of the Association for Computational Linguistics*, pages 8440–8451, Online. Association for Computational Linguistics.

Alexis Conneau, Ruty Rinott, Guillaume Lample, Adina Williams, Samuel Bowman, Holger Schwenk, and Veselin Stoyanov. 2018. XNLI: Evaluating cross-lingual sentence representations. In *Proceedings of the 2018 Conference on Empirical Methods in Natural Language Processing*, pages 2475–2485, Brussels, Belgium. Association for Computational Linguistics.

Anand Dabak and Don Johnson. 2003. Relations between Kullback-Leibler distance and Fisher information.

Jacob Devlin, Ming-Wei Chang, Kenton Lee, and Kristina Toutanova. 2019. BERT: Pre-training of deep bidirectional transformers for language understanding. In *Proceedings of the 2019 Conference of the North American Chapter of the Association for Computational Linguistics: Human Language Technologies, Volume 1 (Long and Short Papers)*, pages 4171–4186, Minneapolis, Minnesota. Association for Computational Linguistics.

Hang Hua, Xingjian Li, Dejing Dou, Chengzhong Xu, and Jiebo Luo. 2021. Noise stability regularization for improving BERT fine-tuning. In *Proceedings of the 2021 Conference of the North American Chapter of the Association for Computational Linguistics: Human Language Technologies*, pages 3229–3241, Online. Association for Computational Linguistics.

Haoyang Huang, Yaobo Liang, Nan Duan, Ming Gong, Linjun Shou, Daxin Jiang, and Ming Zhou. 2019. Unicoder: A universal language encoder by pre-training with multiple cross-lingual tasks. In *Proceedings of the 2019 Conference on Empirical Methods in Natural Language Processing and the 9th International Joint Conference on Natural Language Processing (EMNLP-IJCNLP)*, pages 2485–2494, Hong Kong, China. Association for Computational Linguistics.

Stanislaw Jastrzebski, Devansh Arpit, Oliver Åstrand, Giancarlo Kerg, Huan Wang, Caiming Xiong, Richard Socher, Kyunghyun Cho, and Krzysztof J. Geras. 2021. Catastrophic Fisher explosion: Early phase Fisher matrix impacts generalization. In *Proceedings of the 38th International Conference on Machine Learning, ICML 2021, 18-24 July 2021, Virtual Event*, volume 139 of *Proceedings of Machine Learning Research*, pages 4772–4784. PMLR.

Haoming Jiang, Pengcheng He, Weizhu Chen, Xiaodong Liu, Jianfeng Gao, and Tuo Zhao. 2020. SMART: Robust and efficient fine-tuning for pre-trained natural language models through principled regularized optimization. In *Proceedings of the 58th Annual Meeting of the Association for Computational Linguistics*, pages 2177–2190, Online. Association for Computational Linguistics.

Taku Kudo. 2018. Subword regularization: Improving neural network translation models with multiple subword candidates. In *Proceedings of the 56th Annual Meeting of the Association for Computational Linguistics (Volume 1: Long Papers)*, pages 66–75, Melbourne, Australia. Association for Computational Linguistics.

Xiaobo Liang, Lijun Wu, Juntao Li, Yue Wang, Qi Meng, Tao Qin, Wei Chen, Min Zhang, and Tie-Yan Liu. 2021. R-drop: Regularized dropout for neural networks. *CoRR*, abs/2106.14448.

Jungsoo Park, Gyuwan Kim, and Jaewoo Kang. 2021. Consistency training with virtual adversarial discrete perturbation. *CoRR*, abs/2104.07284.

Telmo Pires, Eva Schlinger, and Dan Garrette. 2019. How multilingual is multilingual BERT? In *Proceedings of the 57th Annual Meeting of the Association for Computational Linguistics*, pages 4996–5001, Florence, Italy. Association for Computational Linguistics.

Xinyi Wang, Sebastian Ruder, and Graham Neubig. 2021. Multi-view subword regularization. In *Proceedings of the 2021 Conference of the North American Chapter of the Association for Computational Linguistics: Human Language Technologies*, pages 473–482, Online. Association for Computational Linguistics.

Shijie Wu and Mark Dredze. 2019. Beto, bentz, becas: The surprising cross-lingual effectiveness of BERT. In *Proceedings of the 2019 Conference on Empirical Methods in Natural Language Processing and the 9th International Joint Conference on Natural Language Processing (EMNLP-IJCNLP)*, pages 833–844, Hong Kong, China. Association for Computational Linguistics.

Yinfei Yang, Yuan Zhang, Chris Tar, and Jason Baldridge. 2019. PAWS-X: A cross-lingual adversarial dataset for paraphrase identification. In *Proceedings of the 2019 Conference on Empirical Methods in Natural Language Processing and the 9th International Joint Conference on Natural Language Processing (EMNLP-IJCNLP)*, pages 3687–3692, Hong Kong, China. Association for Computational Linguistics.

Bo Zheng, Li Dong, Shaohan Huang, Wenhui Wang, Zewen Chi, Saksham Singhal, Wanxiang Che, Ting Liu, Xia Song, and Furu Wei. 2021. Consistency regularization for cross-lingual fine-tuning. *CoRR*, abs/2106.08226.

**Gap in pagination due to retracted papers.**

**Pages 242-247**

# Well-Defined Morphology is Sentence-Level Morphology

**Omer Goldman**
Bar Ilan University
omer.goldman@gmail.com

**Reut Tsarfaty**
Bar Ilan University
reut.tsarfaty@biu.ac.il

**Motivation and Background** Morphological tasks have gained decent popularity in NLP in recent years, with many shared tasks in various flavours (Cotterell et al., 2016; McCarthy et al., 2019; Kann et al., 2020; inter alia), supported mainly by UniMorph (McCarthy et al., 2020) a large multi-lingual dataset providing morphological analysis of standalone words in the form of inflection tables. The computational task in these settings relies heavily on the notion of a '*word*' as these are the elements analyzed and inflected, while the relation between words is left for semantic operations. However, a detailed examination of the data reveals that no pre-determined criterion exists for *what constitutes a word* for the purpose of morphological inflection, and it is set in a per-language fashion relying mostly on speaker intuition.

Specifically, the decision of what is a *word* is clearly *not* based on delimitation of white-spaces. For example, the Finnish phrase *olen ajatellut* is considered a word and is annotated as V;ACT;PRS;PRF;POS;IND;1;SG, and likewise the Albanian phrase *do të mendosh* as V;1;PL;IND;FUT. In contrast, the English equivalents *have thought* and *will think* respectively (corresponding to the exact same features-bundles and meanings) are absent, and their construction is considered syntactic.

Moreover, there is no cross-linguistically consistent set of features and phenomena covered by UniMorph. Thus, *negation* is included in Latvian inflection tables, but not in German ones, while *interrogativity* is included in the Turkish dataset but not in Arabic. In fact, some features of meaning clearly expressed at word-level are absent from UniMorph altogether, most notably for languages that express object concords on their verbs, as Georgian and Bantu languages.UniMorph is skewed, including only forms that *lack* these morphemes.

This poses a problem for the development of truly multi-lingual morphological models since the models are examined on different dimensions of meaning and different sets of features. The current method of data construction induces a bias related to typological and orthographic characteristics of the languages included, so English is considered an isolating language with tiny inflection tables of size 5, while Turkish is considered an agglutinative language with inflection tables of hundreds of forms, although both languages exhibit a complex system of tense and aspect pronounced using linearly separable morphemes with the main difference that the English morphemes are separated by white-spaces.

The quagmire surrounding words and their demarcation is far from being unique to morphological NLP. In fact, the linguistic literature points to no coherent definition of word whatsoever (Zwicky and Pullum, 1983; Lieber and Scalise, 2006, *inter alia*) and the stance that no such cross-lingual definition even exists is also heard (Haspelmath, 2011). We suggest to bypass this linguistic debate while providing true universality to modelling of morphological tasks.

**Proposal** In order to make morphological modelling truly universal and define morphological tasks with no unduly advantage provided to white-space intensive languages, we propose to shift the focus of annotation from *words* to *features*. I.e., we propose to fix the set of inflectional features in all inflectional morphology tasks. Models will be required to inflect lemmas or forms to any bundle legal in a language, regardless of that language's expression of the features – be it in one word, a periphrastic construction or even by syntactic means as word order. The features included will be all those that are expressed clearly as an inflectional morpheme in *some* language. This will set all languages on equal footing. The current version of our annotation scheme includes all the aforementioned features of meaning: tense-aspect-mood (TAM), negation, interrogativity and pronominal arguments. Thus, for example, models will be required



*Proceedings of the 1st Workshop on Multilingual Representation Learning*, pages 248–250
November 11, 2021. ©2021 Association for Computational Linguistics

| | ENG | | DEU | | HEB | | HEB$_{vocalized}$ | | TUR | |
|---|---|---|---|---|---|---|---|---|---|---|
| | word | sentence | word | sentence | word | sentence | word | sentence | word | sentence |
| LSTM | 0.56 | 0.20 | 0.14 | 0.00 | 0.33 | 0.14 | 0.53 | **0.33** | 0.47 | 0.26 |
| TRANSDUCE | 0.88 | **0.73** | 0.78 | 0.34 | 0.80 | **0.39** | 0.47 | 0.01 | 0.80 | **0.67** |
| MT5 | NA | 0.63 | NA | **0.42** | NA | 0.21 | NA | NA | NA | 0.32 |

Table 1: Word and sentence inflection results for all languages and systems. For every language the best performing system is marked in **bold**. Note that both word inflection models perform better in word inflection, confirming that sentence inflection is indeed a harder task.

| | ENG | DEU | HEB | TUR |
|---|---|---|---|---|
| UniMorph table size | 5 | 29 | 29 | 702 |
| intransitive table size | 450 | 512 | 132 | 702 |
| # inflection tables | 486 | 200 | 779 | 200 |

Table 2: Some statistics over the proposed MIGHTYMORPH data. The inclusion of periphrastic constructions expands the size of the inflection tables comparing to UniMorph even without additional arguments.

to inflect the lemma equivalent to LOVE into the features IND;PRS;NEG;INTR;SUBJ(2;SG);OBJ(1;SG) in all languages to resulting in Swahili *hunipendi?*, Turkish *beni sevmez misin?* and English *Don't you love me?*, regardless of the number of white-spaces.

**Task and Data** The specific morphological task in this paper is modelled after morphological reinflection (Cotterell et al., 2016) where given a word-form of a certain lemma and it's feature bundle models are asked to realize the form equivalent to another bundle of features. As mentioned, we consider simple sentences as forms, rather than words, to allow inflection for all included features in all languages. To keep sentences single-lemmaed verbs' arguments are filled in as pronouns.

We annotated a dataset for this task, MIGHTYMORPH, covering 4 languages: English, German, Turkish and Hebrew.[1] For each language we sampled verbal lemmas from UniMorph, giving priority to frequently used verbs, and for each lemma we exhaustively generated a full table of all simple sentences with their respective features. For every lemma, we manually determined all possible arguments using a monolingual dictionary, including both cased arguments and arguments licensed by an adposition, where arguments' features include person, number, gender and reflexivity. Some statistics of the generated data are provided in Table 2.

The data for our sentence reinflection task was sampled from MIGHTYMORPH. For each language, we sampled $10,000$ pairs of sentences with their morphological features from 200 inflection tables, such that each pair shares a lemma. We split the data $90\%$ for the train set and the rest are a test set. The lemmas in the train- and test-set are disjoint (Goldman et al., 2021).

[1]For Hebrew we have 2 versions: vocalized/unvocalized.

**Models** As an initial attempt at sentence inflection we apply SOTA models for word-inflection to both the word- and sentence-level inflection tasks:
- LSTM: by Silfverberg and Hulden (2018)
- TRANSDUCE: by Makarov and Clematide (2018)

Both models handle characters as input and output, treating white-space as yet another character rather than a special word-delimiter. In addition, moving to sentence inflection allows the use of contextualized pretrained language models. We used the MT5 (Xue et al., 2021) finetuned on each language separately. The morphological features were added to the input as new tokens with randomly initialized embeddings, and the rest of the input and output was tokenized using MT5's own tokenizer.

**Results** Table 1 compares the results for word- and sentence-inflection for the LSTM and TRANSDUCE models. It is clear that sentence inflection is a harder task. It is not surprising as it involves longer character sequences, and more sophisticated edits such as manipulating word order (e.g. S-V inversions English and German). On sentence inflection, the TRANSDUCE performs better on average, although variation across languages does occur.

**Conclusion** We suggest a paradigm shift for morphological NLP, from inflection table defined by the ill-defined concept of *word* to tables defined by a cross linguistically fixed set of *features*. We argue that this shift requires a mode from words to simple sentences. We believe our framework brings better universality to morphology-related NLP tasks and we formulated a sentence-reinflection task accompanied by suitable data. We showed that while this task is significantly harder, it also provides an opportunity to interface with contextualized LMs, thus it is a thread of research worth developing.

## References

Ryan Cotterell, Christo Kirov, John Sylak-Glassman, David Yarowsky, Jason Eisner, and Mans Hulden. 2016. The SIGMORPHON 2016 shared Task—Morphological reinflection. In *Proceedings of the 14th SIGMORPHON Workshop on Computational Research in Phonetics, Phonology, and Morphology*, pages 10–22, Berlin, Germany. Association for Computational Linguistics.

Omer Goldman, David Guriel, and Reut Tsarfaty. 2021. (un)solving morphological inflection: Lemma overlap artificially inflates models' performance.

Martin Haspelmath. 2011. The indeterminacy of word segmentation and the nature of morphology and syntax. *Folia Linguistica*, 45(1):31–80.

Katharina Kann, Arya D. McCarthy, Garrett Nicolai, and Mans Hulden. 2020. The SIGMORPHON 2020 shared task on unsupervised morphological paradigm completion. In *Proceedings of the 17th SIGMORPHON Workshop on Computational Research in Phonetics, Phonology, and Morphology*, pages 51–62, Online. Association for Computational Linguistics.

Rochelle Lieber and Sergio Scalise. 2006. The lexical integrity hypothesis in a new theoretical universe. *Lingue e linguaggio*, (1):7–32.

Peter Makarov and Simon Clematide. 2018. Neural transition-based string transduction for limited-resource setting in morphology. In *Proceedings of the 27th International Conference on Computational Linguistics*, pages 83–93, Santa Fe, New Mexico, USA. Association for Computational Linguistics.

Arya D. McCarthy, Christo Kirov, Matteo Grella, Amrit Nidhi, Patrick Xia, Kyle Gorman, Ekaterina Vylomova, Sabrina J. Mielke, Garrett Nicolai, Miikka Silfverberg, Timofey Arkhangelskiy, Nataly Krizhanovsky, Andrew Krizhanovsky, Elena Klyachko, Alexey Sorokin, John Mansfield, Valts Ernštreits, Yuval Pinter, Cassandra L. Jacobs, Ryan Cotterell, Mans Hulden, and David Yarowsky. 2020. UniMorph 3.0: Universal Morphology. In *Proceedings of the 12th Language Resources and Evaluation Conference*, pages 3922–3931, Marseille, France. European Language Resources Association.

Arya D. McCarthy, Ekaterina Vylomova, Shijie Wu, Chaitanya Malaviya, Lawrence Wolf-Sonkin, Garrett Nicolai, Christo Kirov, Miikka Silfverberg, Sabrina J. Mielke, Jeffrey Heinz, Ryan Cotterell, and Mans Hulden. 2019. The SIGMORPHON 2019 shared task: Morphological analysis in context and cross-lingual transfer for inflection. In *Proceedings of the 16th Workshop on Computational Research in Phonetics, Phonology, and Morphology*, pages 229–244, Florence, Italy. Association for Computational Linguistics.

Miikka Silfverberg and Mans Hulden. 2018. An encoder-decoder approach to the paradigm cell filling problem. In *Proceedings of the 2018 Conference on Empirical Methods in Natural Language Processing*, pages 2883–2889, Brussels, Belgium. Association for Computational Linguistics.

Linting Xue, Noah Constant, Adam Roberts, Mihir Kale, Rami Al-Rfou, Aditya Siddhant, Aditya Barua, and Colin Raffel. 2021. mT5: A massively multilingual pre-trained text-to-text transformer. In *Proceedings of the 2021 Conference of the North American Chapter of the Association for Computational Linguistics: Human Language Technologies*, pages 483–498, Online. Association for Computational Linguistics.

Arnold M Zwicky and Geoffrey K Pullum. 1983. Cliticization vs. inflection: English n't. *Language*, 59(3):502–513.

# Cross-Lingual Training of Dense Retrievers for Document Retrieval

**Peng Shi**[1], **Rui Zhang**[2], **He Bai**[1], **and Jimmy Lin**[1]

[1] David R. Cheriton School of Computer Science, University of Waterloo

[2] Department of Computer Science and Engineering, Penn State University

{peng.shi,he.bai,jimmylin}@uwaterloo.ca, rmz5227@psu.edu

## Abstract

Dense retrieval has shown great success for passage ranking in English. However, its effectiveness for non-English languages remains unexplored due to limitation in training resources. In this work, we explore different transfer techniques for document ranking from English annotations to non-English languages. Our experiments reveal that zero-shot model-based transfer using mBERT improves search quality. We find that weakly-supervised target language transfer is competitive compared to generation-based target language transfer, which requires translation models.

## 1 Introduction

Dense retrieval uses dense vector representations for semantic encoding and matching. However, most existing work focuses on high-resource languages such as English, where large-scale annotations are readily accessible. In this work, we focus on improving term-matching retrieval for low(er)-resource languages. We explore techniques for leveraging relevance judgments in English to train dense retrievers for document retrieval in non-English languages. Our experimental results show that combining dense retrieval and term-matching retrieval can obtain effectiveness improvements. Also, weakly-supervised target language transfer yields effectiveness competitive to generation-based target language transfer. This extended abstracted is an abridged version of Shi et al. (2021).

## 2 Cross-Lingual Relevance Transfer

We leverage the DPR model of Karpukhin et al. (2020), but using mBERT as the backbone model. During inference, we apply both bag-of-words exact term matching and dense retrieval. The relevance score of each document combines term matching scores with dense retrieval similarity via $S_{doc} = \alpha \cdot S_{term} + (1 - \alpha) \cdot S_{dense}$, where $\alpha$ is tuned via cross-validation.

**Model-Based Transfer.** By exploiting the zero-shot cross-lingual transfer ability of pretrained transformers such as mBERT (Devlin et al., 2019), we train the dense retriever in the source language and apply inference directly to the target languages.

**Target Language Transfer.** To bridge the language gap between training and inference, we explore two techniques for creating a target language transfer set. (1) *Generation-based query synthesis*, where the goal is to leverage powerful generation models to predict reasonable queries given documents in the target language. We choose mBART (Liu et al., 2020) as our query generation model. The input of the model is the passage and its learning target is the corresponding query. We use the translate–train technique to obtain the generation models. More specifically, we leverage Google Translate to translate English query–document pairs into the target languages. Then, we use passages in the target language collections as input and generate corresponding queries in the same language. (2) *Weakly-supervised query synthesis*. We can automatically build the target language transfer set without manual annotation effort by treating the titles of Wikipedia articles as queries and the corresponding documents as positive candidates. We also retrieve top 1000 documents with BM25 for each query; documents except for the positive candidate are labeled as negative.

**Two-Stage Training.** We apply two-stage training to learn the dense retrieval model. The encoders are first trained on source language (English) annotated data which are available in larger quantities; then the models are fine-tuned on the synthesized query–document pairs in the target language.

## 3 Experimental Setup

We conduct experiments on six test collections: NTCIR 8 in Chinese, TREC 2002 in Arabic, CLEF 2006 in French, FIRE 2012 in Hindi, FIRE 2012



*Proceedings of the 1st Workshop on Multilingual Representation Learning*, pages 251–253
November 11, 2021. 

| Model | AP | P@20 | nDCG | AP | P@20 | nDCG | AP | P@20 | nDCG |
|---|---|---|---|---|---|---|---|---|---|
| | NTCIR8-zh | | | TREC2002-ar | | | CLEF2006-fr | | |
| (0) BM25 | 0.4014 | 0.3849 | 0.4757 | 0.2932 | 0.3610 | 0.4056 | 0.3111 | 0.3184 | 0.4458 |
| (1) BM25+RM3 | 0.3384 | 0.3616 | 0.4490 | 0.2783 | 0.3490 | 0.3969 | 0.3421 | 0.3408 | 0.4658 |
| (2) NQ zero-shot | 0.4221$^\blacktriangle$ | 0.4164$^\blacktriangle$ | 0.5235$^\blacktriangle$ | 0.2943 | 0.3560 | 0.4012 | 0.3470 | 0.3469 | 0.4726 |
| (3) MS zero-shot | 0.4167$^\blacktriangle$ | 0.4164$^\blacktriangle$ | 0.5095$^\blacktriangle$ | 0.3024 | 0.3810$^\blacktriangle$ | 0.4285 | 0.3332 | 0.3418 | 0.4573 |
| (4) MS → QGen | 0.4258$^\blacktriangle$ | 0.4336$^\blacktriangle$ | 0.5308$^\blacktriangle$ | 0.2988 | 0.3800 | 0.4276 | 0.3331 | 0.3429 | 0.4564 |
| (5) MS → Wiki | 0.4135 | 0.4123$^\blacktriangle$ | 0.5055$^\blacktriangle$ | 0.3060$^\blacktriangle$ | 0.3750 | 0.4293 | 0.3456 | 0.3480 | 0.4743 |
| | FIRE2012-hi | | | FIRE2012-bn | | | TREC3-es | | |
| (0) BM25 | 0.3867 | 0.4470 | 0.5310 | 0.2881 | 0.3740 | 0.4261 | 0.4197 | 0.6660 | 0.6851 |
| (1) +RM3 | 0.3660 | 0.4430 | 0.5277 | 0.2833 | 0.3830 | 0.4351 | 0.4912 | 0.7040 | 0.7079 |
| (2) NQ zero-shot | 0.3939 | 0.4560 | 0.5408 | 0.2898 | 0.3980 | 0.4495$^\blacktriangle$ | 0.4910 | 0.6980 | 0.7007 |
| (3) MS zero-shot | 0.3944 | 0.4580 | 0.5461 | 0.2896$^\blacktriangle$ | 0.3900 | 0.4449 | 0.4950 | 0.7080 | 0.7171 |
| (4) MS → QGen | 0.3941 | 0.4660 | 0.5527 | 0.2887 | 0.3980 | 0.4486 | 0.4958$^\blacktriangle$ | 0.7180 | 0.7239 |
| (5) MS → Wiki | 0.3950 | 0.4630 | 0.5497 | 0.2898$^\blacktriangle$ | 0.4050 | 0.4549 | 0.4972$^\blacktriangle$ | 0.7180 | 0.7329 |

Table 1: Experimental results on baselines and our cross-lingual transfer methods. Model (0) and Model (1) show the effectiveness of BM25 and BM25 with RM3 query expansion. For each language, we select the higher P@20 of the two models as the term-based matching baseline. That is, for the French, Bengali, and Spanish collections, we use BM25+RM3 as the term-based matching baseline and for the others, we use BM25. Significant gains against the baselines are denoted with $\blacktriangle$.

in Bengali, TREC 3 in Spanish. For the evaluation metrics, we adopt AP, P@20, and nDCG@20. For model-based transfer, we explore Natural Question and MS MARCO as training datasets. For training the query generator in the target languages, we obtain training data by sampling 2000 query–passage pairs from MS MARCO and translate them into the target languages. Fisher's two-sided, paired randomization test (Smucker et al., 2007) at $p < 0.05$ was applied to test for statistical significance.

## 4 Results and Discussions

**Finding #1: Zero-shot model-based transfer improves term-based matching.** The results of zero-shot model-based transfer are shown in Model (2) and Model (3). Comparing with the corresponding baselines, we observe that model-based transfer, either NQ zero-shot or MS zero-shot, can improve retrieval effectiveness on P@20 for all collections, except NQ zero-shot on the TREC3-es dataset. We do not observe a clear winner between NQ and MS, though. These results indicate that mBERT-based DPR effectively transfers relevance matching across languages.

**Finding #2: Target language transfer benefits certain collections, and Wiki query synthesis is better than query generation.** Target language transfer results are shown in Model (4) and Model (5). MS → QGen and MS → Wiki denote the two-stage training strategy with different transfer sets, where QGen denotes generation-based query synthesis and Wiki denotes weakly-supervised query synthesis from Wikipedia. By comparing Model (4) with Model (3), we observe that second-stage training with generation-based query–document pairs can improve the effectiveness of P@20 over zero-shot model-based transfer on the Chinese, French, Hindi, Bengali, and Spanish collections. However, we see little improvement in terms of AP for all collections. By comparing Model (5) with Model (3), we find that second-stage training with weakly-supervised training data can improve P@20 over the zero-shot baselines on French, Hindi, Bengali, and Spanish.

Furthermore, by comparing these two transfer sets, we observe that, except for Chinese, Wiki obtains better retrieval effectiveness than QGen, which requires translation models for the target languages (which are expensive to build and not available for all languages).

## 5 Conclusion

We investigate the effectiveness of three transfer techniques for document ranking from English training data to non-English target languages. Our experiments in six languages demonstrate that zero-shot transfer using mBERT-based dense retrieval models improves term-based matching methods, and fine-tuning on augmented data in target languages can further benefit certain collections.

## References

Jacob Devlin, Ming-Wei Chang, Kenton Lee, and Kristina Toutanova. 2019. BERT: Pre-training of deep bidirectional transformers for language understanding. In *Proceedings of the 2019 Conference of the North American Chapter of the Association for Computational Linguistics: Human Language Technologies, Volume 1 (Long and Short Papers)*, pages 4171–4186, Minneapolis, Minnesota. Association for Computational Linguistics.

Vladimir Karpukhin, Barlas Oguz, Sewon Min, Patrick Lewis, Ledell Wu, Sergey Edunov, Danqi Chen, and Wen-tau Yih. 2020. Dense passage retrieval for open-domain question answering. In *Proceedings of the 2020 Conference on Empirical Methods in Natural Language Processing (EMNLP)*, pages 6769–6781, Online. Association for Computational Linguistics.

Yinhan Liu, Jiatao Gu, Naman Goyal, Xian Li, Sergey Edunov, Marjan Ghazvininejad, Mike Lewis, and Luke Zettlemoyer. 2020. Multilingual denoising pre-training for neural machine translation. *Transactions of the Association for Computational Linguistics*, 8:726–742.

Peng Shi, Rui Zhang, He Bai, and Jimmy Lin. 2021. Cross-lingual training with dense retrieval for document retrieval. *arXiv preprint arXiv:2109.01628*.

Mark D Smucker, James Allan, and Ben Carterette. 2007. A comparison of statistical significance tests for information retrieval evaluation. In *Proceedings of the sixteenth ACM conference on Conference on information and knowledge management*, pages 623–632.

**Association for Computational Linguistics**
209 N. Eighth Street
Stroudsburg, Pennsylvania 18360

CURRAN ASSOCIATES INC.
proceedings.com

ISBN 978-1-7138-9185-7